W9-DGE-119

VENEZUELA

COLOMBIA

GUYANA

SURINAM

FRENCH GUYANA

ECUADOR

Loreto

Amazonas

Pará

Amapá

Roraima

Maranhão

Ceará

Rio Grande do Norte

1 Piura

Amazonas

Cajamarca

San Martín

Acre

Rondônia

Piauí

Paraíba

Pernambuco

2

3

Huánaco

Pasco

Ancash

Junín

Lima

Madre de Dios

Pando

Beni

Mato Grosso

Goiás

Bahia

Alagoas

Sergipe

Cuzco

4

Ayacucho

5

Puno

Ica

Arequipa

6

7

La Paz

Oruro

Cocha-bamba

Santa Cruz

D.F.

Minas Gerais

Tarapacá

Chuqui-saca

Potosí

Tarija

Espírito Santo

Jujuy

PARAGUAY

São Paulo

Rio de Janeiro

1 Tumbes
2 Lambayeque
3 La Libertad
4 Huancavelica
5 Apurímac
6 Moquegua
7 Tacna

Anto-fagasta

Salta

Formosa

Paraná

Atacama

Catamarca

Tucu-mán

Santiago del Estero

Chaco

Corrientes

Misiones

Santa Catarina

La Rioja

Santa Fe

Rio Grande do Sul

Coquimbo

San Juan

Córdoba

Entre Ríos

San Luis

URUGUAY

Mendoza

Buenos Aires

La Pampa

CHILE

Neuquén

Río Negro

Chubut

Santa Cruz

South America

The Encyclopedia of
Cacti

Dr Willy Cullmann

Dr Erich Götz

Dr Gerhard Gröner

The Encyclopedia of
Cacti

Timber Press
Portland, Oregon

635.93347
C898e

PACKARD LIBRARY

JUN 28 1988

OF THE COLUMBUS COLLEGE OF ART AND DESIGN

© 1963, 1984 Eugen Ulmer GmbH & Co,
Wollgrasweg 41, 7000 Stuttgart 70

© English edition 1986 Alphabooks

First published as *Kakteen* by Eugen
Ulmer GmbH & Co

First published in North America 1987 by
Timber Press, 9999 S.W. Wilshire,
Portland, Oregon 97225.

ISBN 0-88192-100-9

Translation by Keith M. Thomas

Technical consultant: Jack Astley

All rights reserved. No part of this publication
may be reproduced, stored in a retrieval
system, or transmitted, in any form or by any
means, electronic, mechanical, photocopying,
recording or otherwise, without prior per-
mission in writing of the publishers.

Dust jacket photographs by G. Gröner

Printed and bound in the Federal Republic
of Germany

Preface

When we began revising the 'Cullman' for this new edition, we soon realized that the job would require more than just minor amendments and additions, as our scientific and practical knowledge relating to cacti had changed to such an extent since the last edition, revised by Willy Cullmann, was produced. For this reason we decided to rewrite the entire text, whilst remaining true to the aim of the original book: to provide the beginner and advanced cactus enthusiast alike with a manageable, practical book for study, reference, and pleasurable reading.

It proved necessary to expand both text and pictures to a considerable extent, and the book now covers about 750 species. Amongst the new features are identification keys for all genera, and the clear emphasis on those characteristics which are crucial to the identification of species. As a result the specific descriptions had to be kept very brief, otherwise the text would have grown unmanageably long. The nomenclature of cacti is still far from settled, and we have included all the important synonyms to aid the reader. We considered all new species with great care before deciding whether to include them. The number of species included for the first time is very large, but even so we have by no means been able to include all those now under cultivation, as virtually every globular cactus known is now being grown somewhere or other.

In this new edition Gerhard Gröner was chiefly responsible for the sections on cactus culture and the new photographs, while Erich Götz contributed the sections on cactus systematics and the information on the genera and species of cacti.

For their help and support we wish to thank Messrs. H. Brückner, J.D. Donald, W. Krahn, K. Rücker and H. Umgelter.

Stuttgart 1984   Dr Erich Götz
                    Dr Gerhard Gröner

Contents

Cacti in the Huntington desert garden (California). In the foreground a group of Mammillarias, in the background the large globes of Echinocactus grusonii.

The structure, mode of living and classification of cacti

External structure of cacti

Almost all of a plant's external characteristics have a definite role to play in its mode of living. Although we can only guess at the significance of many individual features, such conjecture is often the first step towards the acquisition of new knowledge. In any case bald descriptions and explanations of the appropriate specialized terminology make rather dry reading. For this reason we have attempted to show, as far as possible, the link between the external structural features of cacti and their possible effects.

The most striking feature of cacti is their exterior form. From the largest, tree-form cacti, growing up to 20 m. in height and more, the plants range through solitary columns with virtually no side shoots to globes and finally to flattened discs (see drawing). The most primitive species are probably shrubby plants, i.e. freely clustering species with side shoots sprouting from just above the ground. From these bushy species tree-like forms have developed, in which case the side shoots do not develop until some height above the ground, thus producing a distinct trunk. If, on the other hand, the plants do not develop beyond a fairly early stage, the resultant plant is columnar, with little or no branching, leading eventually to globular and disc-shaped species. These modifications undoubtedly occurred many times independently. Contiguous representatives of this long range of forms are sometimes found within a single genus. For example, the South American genera of *Lobivia* and

Echinopsis include elongated cylindrical cacti and round globular forms, and all the intermediate stages. The same applies to the genus *Echinocereus* in North America.

The external form is of great significance to the life of the plant. Tall, tree-like cacti need adequate precipitation, but if that requirement is met they are able to establish themselves supremely well. They form the most extensive root system and, once established, may reign over their site for centuries. It is virtually impossible for young cacti and other smaller species to survive within their domain. In their natural habitat cacti are usually generously spaced out. However, this does not mean that no seed falls on the ground between them. In fact, tests of the soil at any point show the presence of a quantity of seed. These seeds germinate immediately when there is enough moisture, but after a short time, when the ground dries out once more, almost all the seedlings disappear again. In fact the entire area is already interwoven by the roots of older plants, often standing a considerable distance away. The larger the plants are, the more and the longer roots they form, and the more water they can store. A further factor in their favour is that the surface area through which moisture is lost by evaporation is relatively smaller on the large cacti. Seedlings have a very poor prospect of surviving the first fairly severe dry period at sites which are already colonized. It is only when an old plant dies off or is removed that its smaller neighbours, now freed from competition, are able to grow strongly, and at that time several seedlings may manage to establish themselves.

Smaller plants may also receive less light, as they are likely to be in the shade of larger ones, although this is less significant for cacti growing in dry areas. Because of their very extensive root system plants with a similar external form hardly ever grow so close together that they can shade each other. On the other hand species with widely different natural forms, for example large, bushy Opuntias and small, green globular cacti underneath them are able to exploit water and light at the same site in different ways. Where the precipitation is even less, i.e. in true deserts, only the shrubby or smaller globular cacti are able to develop. They are often still of branching habit, but the side shoots branch immediately above the ground or even below the surface; these are termed sprouting or clustering species. Parts often break easily from these plants, then roll away over the ground, or get caught on animals. These 'pups' root readily and thus propagation occurs without the particularly vulnerable seedling stage. If the stems of bushy, densely branching cacti are broken off, they also root easily in nearly every case. It is even possible to cut off and root parts of completely solitary columnar cacti, to which asexual reproduction is foreign by nature. This whole range of natural means of propagation also represents a very convenient and straightforward method of propagation for the cacti enthusiast. It offers the additional advantage that the plants which result are absolutely identical genetically (see section on cuttings).

The primary series of forms shown in the horizontal sequence in the drawing on page 10 is complicated by other, rarer derivative forms. Opuntias and the jointed cacti, of which the

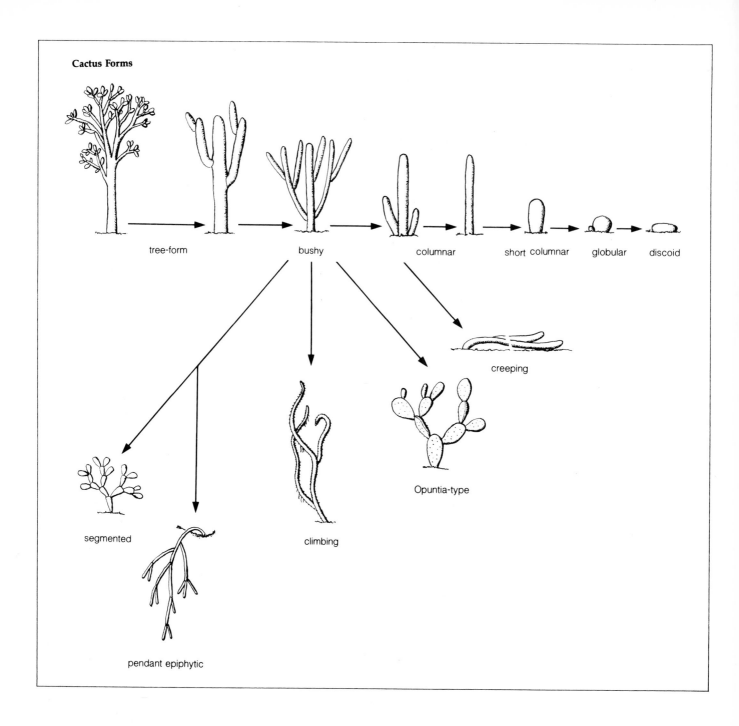

Cactus Forms

tree-form   bushy   columnar   short columnar   globular   discoid

creeping

segmented   climbing   Opuntia-type

pendant epiphytic

'Christmas cactus' is a well-known example, feature very short stem segments, or pads. These species are particularly easy to propagate by means of individual pads which are broken off or which fall off naturally.

Cacti of creeping habit are capable of spreading especially quickly. Where the stems rest on the earth new roots usually form rapidly. Such a plant can be divided into several pieces without harm, as each segment has its own roots. In this case even the initially rootless stage of the dismembered 'pup' or joint is avoided.

Cacti are succulents, i.e. they can store quite large quantities of water in their fleshy body. This characteristic has allowed them to colonize other inhospitable terrain in addition to the dry regions. Even in fairly moist areas there are isolated sites which are very dry, e.g. rock faces. Plants which are not able to store water rapidly become dehydrated in such conditions. For this reason we very often find cacti or other succulent plants (such as fleshy species of wall pepper or house leek) at these featureless rocky locations.

In terms of inhospitable habitats, it is but a short step from rocky terrain almost totally devoid of fine soil to the branches and trunks of trees. Plants which grow on other plants without being parasitic on them are termed epiphytes (epi = on, phyton = plant). Small plants find this mode of life advantageous. They nestle high up in trees and thus receive an adequate supply of light even in dense forest. On the dark, shaded forest floor they would not be able to flourish. For the epiphytic plant to survive it is essential that it absorbs water quickly and is able to store it. The small quantity of soil which collects in the forks of limbs or in the grooves of the bark dries out completely within a short period. For this reason epiphytes often have supplementary aerial roots, which are able to soak up rain water rapidly. Although most epiphytes are very effective storers of water, they only occur in large numbers in tropical regions with heavy precipitation. In Europe the only epiphytic plants are mosses and lichens, which are able to survive drying out after each fall of rain without suffering damage. Higher epiphytic plants are not able to tolerate dehydration, and most of them therefore store water. In contrast to parasites such as mistletoe, epiphytes do not grow on other plants only. Many species which are usually epiphytic are occasionally found growing on rocks. In culture epiphytes grow just as well or even better in a pot than on a piece of branch.

Epiphytes usually receive only a proportion of the light they require in their treetop habitat as the branches of the host tree generally grow more rapidly than they do. For this reason most epiphytic cacti have an enlarged surface area in order to catch more light. Either their stems are flattened, as in the leaf cacti and jointed species, or they are very thin and only a few millimetres thick, as in the case of *Rhipsalis* and *Hatiora*. The thick mantle of spines which protects ground-based cacti from grazing animals in the dry regions has in most cases been replaced by token bristles or hairs. In their evolutionary history cacti have

Lepismium plant on a tree trunk in Argentina.

lost their leaves, and they have not been developed anew, even though they would be useful in these conditions. Instead flat shoots have evolved. In fact the likelihood of genetic material combining in the same form, to produce the same characteristics, on two occasions within the genealogical history of one plant is very slight. Once forfeited, complex organs such as foliage leaves will never develop again. At best their place will be taken by entirely different organs such as flat shoots. This is an important biological rule (Dollo's rule). That these epiphytic cacti have developed from ordinary cacti is clear from the plants' form as seedlings. At that stage they often possess several ribs and spines or strong bristles. Cacti are well adapted to the rapid assimilation of water, storage of large quantities of moisture, and economy in its consumption, as befits plants of the dry regions. In consequence they also proved suitable for the epiphytic lifestyle, in which the water supply is also difficult. Most epiphytic cacti do not grow larger than small bushes, becoming woody at the base.

A further difficulty for epiphytic cacti

is dispersal. If the seeds were simply to be scattered, as in the case of most cacti, they would just fall on the shady forest floor instead of reaching new branches. For this reason epiphytic cacti usually have fleshy berries which are eaten by birds. The seed are then excreted unharmed. The seeds are generally very sticky, and stick to the branch when the bird wipes its beak or pecks at the berries on a branch.

Most climbing cacti are forest plants. Virtually none of their own tissues provide structural strength, and yet their thin stems quickly reach the upper, well-lit parts of the forest. The spines of limp, slender-stemmed cacti enable them to support themselves on other plants or rocks without slipping. Those cacti which coil or wind themselves round their host are able to anchor themselves even more securely. Very often these plants also develop aerial roots which serve as an aid to climbing, although their primary purpose is the provision of supplementary water. The thin stems are often many metres long, and the far distant ground roots find it difficult to supply the growing stem tips with water. Epiphytes can also develop from climbing plants if the ground-based roots are entirely abandoned, as in the case of *Epiphyllum*. This type of climbing plant is said to be the most elongated form of cactus. One *Hylocereus* species from Mexico is said to develop stems up to 100 m. long. The close relationship between climbing and epiphytic cacti is shown clearly in the genera which are related to *Epiphyllum*. Hybrids of the two exist.

Most of the forms of cacti in the main series shown on page 10 correspond to immature forms of shrubby cacti. Often newly developed species can be propagated at quite an early stage; they then retain their young form when mature. This process is termed neoteny or paedomorphosis, and it occurs very frequently in the genealogical history of plants and animals. For example, herbaceous plants in general can be construed as the descendants of ligneous or woody plants. The following basic rule applies to cacti: as the species becomes more and more derivative, so the degree of branching and lignification diminishes.

Formation of shoots

Cacti have few similarities with ordinary plants. They have no leaves, and their ribbed or warty bodies look quite different from the stems of normal plants. Nevertheless there are a few plants which bear the characteristic cactus flower, but have ordinary stems and leaves. This applies in particular to plants of the genus *Pereskia*, which usually form densely clustering bushes or small trees. The stems are round in section and only slightly succulent, and they produce entirely normal flat leaves. However, groups of spines grow on small, hairy cushions at the leaf axils, the spines being of uneven length. These structures are termed areoles, and are one of the fundamental characteristics of the cactus family. They occur in no other family of plants. Almost all the features of *Pereskia* indicate that it is the most primitive cactus genus.

On flowering plants side shoots grow from each leaf axil. Most of them do not develop fully, but stay as tiny buds. On many plants at least a proportion of the side buds develop into short shoots, in our apple and pear trees, for instance. On these short shoots the leaves grow from almost the same point. The areoles of the cactus are best equated with this type of short shoot, and this implies that the spines of the cactus are modified leaves. There are indeed thorns which have developed from leaves, for example, those of the Berberis, and this plant allows us to observe all the stages from thorny leaves to thorns. Botanists name such modified leaves or shoots thorns rather than spines. Spines are

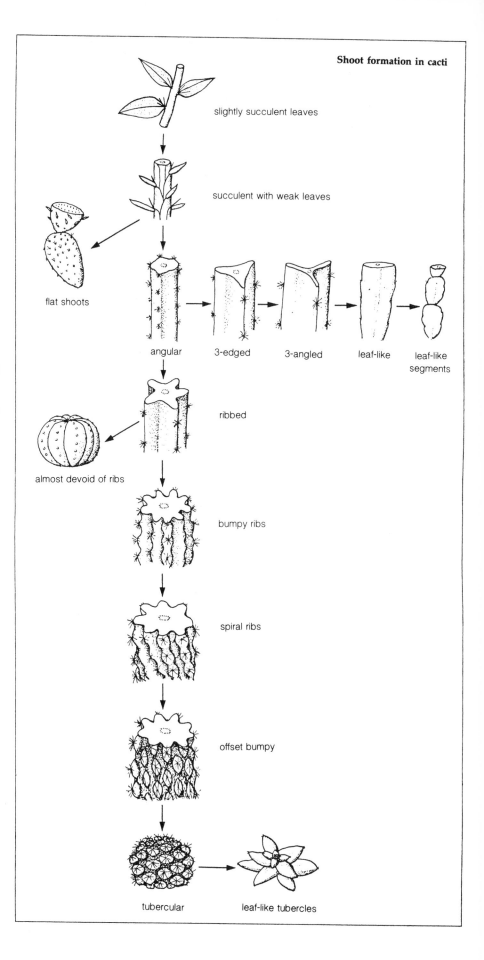

Shoot formation in cacti

slightly succulent leaves

succulent with weak leaves

flat shoots

angular   3-edged   3-angled   leaf-like   leaf-like segments

ribbed

almost devoid of ribs

bumpy ribs

spiral ribs

offset bumpy

tubercular   leaf-like tubercles

considered to be external growths on a shoot, as on the blackberry. The spines of the cactus are also modified leaves, and it is thus botanically correct to term them thorns. Nevertheless we have used the term spines throughout this book, simply because the term has become so universally accepted in relation to cacti. That the areoles contain buds is shown clearly when flowers or new shoots grow from them. Basically any areole is capable of producing shoots. If a plant is cut off just above any areole, a shoot appears to replace the lost end.

The leaves of many Pereskias are already very small and narrow. Leaves are also a feature of Opuntias, although they are circular in cross-section and soon fall off. The leaf-like pads of many Opuntias are, in contrast, readily recognized as flattened stems. When young they still bear token leaves, and new pads grow from the areoles of the leaf-like segments.

In contrast, secondary leaves never grow from true leaves.

In far more cases the round stems of the Pereskias have developed into angular or ribbed stems with humps or warts, properly termed tubercles. Here the areoles, which are arranged around the stem in a spiral formation like ordinary leaves, are disposed more and more distinctly in a definite number of vertical rows. Even so, the areoles of seedlings first appear in a spiral formation even on ribbed cacti.

A ribbed body is ideally suited to coping with sporadic water supplies. When water is scarce the folds sink in between the ribs, and when water is abundant the folds swell out. The overall form remains more or less the same at either extreme. A ribbed body can alter its volume while the area of the skin remains unchanged, in a similar fashion to a concertina. In contrast, the flat pads of *Opuntia* wrinkle up in a very uneven manner when they lose water. A further advantage of a ribbed body is that it offers a slightly enlarged surface area in relation to its volume, as is also the case with flat stems. Every green plant requires a certain amount of surface area in order to absorb sufficient light.

The number of ribs varies widely, reaching a large number in many species of *Trichocereus. Echinofossulocactus* is the extreme, with up to about 120 thin ribs, with an appearance similar to corrugated cardboard. The stems of the climbing cacti and many epiphytic cacti usually remain fairly slim, and are more or less rounded or only irregularly warty. As stems become thicker so they begin to feature ribs, which have evolved further to form thin wings or angles. In this form plants are able to flourish even when half-shaded. From three-winged stems we arrive eventually at the two-edged flat stems which look like leaves.

The ribs of many cacti are more or less deeply notched, thus forming humps. When light comes from overhead the humps tend to shade each other, and for this reason the ribs usually spiral upward at an angle if the humps are clearly defined. In species where the ribs are divided up into individual tubercles, as in the case of *Rebutia* or *Mammillaria*, the spiral rib pattern is often difficult to recognize. All that the eye sees is rows of tubercles intersecting at angles. As occurs with leaves, certain numbers occur particularly frequently — 5, 8, 13, 21, 34 . . . each number being the sum of its two predecessors. These numbers of rows produce the most compact and regular arrangement, with the least possible mutual shading.

The cacti which bear large tubercles are those which have developed farthest from the basic cactus forms. Such tubercles can bear a superficial similarity to leaves, as on *Ariocarpus* or *Leuchtenbergia*. However, the tubercles bear an areole from which flowers grow, and are therefore shoots rather than leaves.

In the case of many small globular or disc-shaped cacti, such as *Blossfeldia* or *Lophophora* only the rows of areoles remain to indicate ribs.

Spine formation

Almost every species of cactus features a slightly different spine formation. In many cases two sorts of spines can be clearly distinguished: central spines and radial spines (see drawing on page 15). The central spines are located in the middle of the areole and stand out stiffly, while the radial spines grow from the edge of the areole and spread out more or less radially. The radial and central spines may differ markedly: long, strong, rigid central spines coupled with thin, flexible, radial spines resting flat on the skin. This distinction indicates that they have different purposes: the central spines are defensive, and are often strikingly coloured so that they can be seen from a distance. The purpose of the slim radial spines is more to protect the plant from excessively strong solar radiation. They are often white and reflect the sunlight, thus shading virtually the entire body from the powerful sunshine.

There are several specialized spine forms in addition to the radial and central types. In most cases these are characteristic of individual species, very rarely of an entire genus. Spines which are curved into a hook at the tip, as found on many Mammillarias, are by no means a rarity. Such spines are particularly unpleasant to the cultivator, because it is easy to get caught up on them. If a powerful animal gets entangled, the entire plant may be torn out of the ground. Certain cacti are indeed dispersed by being carried about in the fur of fairly large animals in the same manner as burrs.

Maihuenia poeppigii, a cactus which forms distinct leaves

Comb-formation spines on Pelecyphora asseliformis

Many Ferocacti have giant spines resembling daggers, but these are by no means the most unpleasant form. Far worse, and probably the most effective spines of all, are those known as glochids. They only occur in the sub-family of the Opuntioideae and are a very important identifying feature of these plants. The glochids are no more than a few millimetres long and are very thin and brittle, and their many fine barbs can only be seen with the aid of a powerful magnifier or microscope. The glochids pierce the

skin very readily and then break off immediately. Because of their barbed form any movement only helps to push them deeper into the wound. They are painful for days on end, and may eventually cause an abscess. It is essential to take great care when handling Opuntias.

The only species of cacti which are generally spineless are the epiphytes. In dry, open conditions spineless cacti are exceptional, *Lophophora*, *Blossfeldia* and *Astrophytum asterias* being

examples. To replace the protection offered by spines it is known that *Lophophora* contains toxic substances, in this case the alkaloid mescalin. This is a powerful narcotic, used by North American Indian tribes. The almost spineless Selenicerei also contain a powerful drug, in this case the heart stimulant glycoside. *Selenicereus grandiflorus*, the 'Queen of the Night', is cultivated in greenhouses on a large scale for this reason, as the substance is a useful cardiac drug when administered in small doses. The milky sap of many Mammillarias, which is exuded instantly at the slightest injury, may also serve as a protection against insect damage.

Spines vary in number, length and colour from species to species, and even within a species the spines of individual plants vary within certain limits. In fact, the areoles on a single plant often bear spines which differ slightly. The differences in spine formation depend to a very great extent on the supply of nutrients, water and light.

The root system

Our knowledge of the structure of most plants' root systems is incomplete, and within the cactus realm we only differentiate between a small number of types. The vast majority of cacti have relatively thin, fibrous roots which extend over a wide

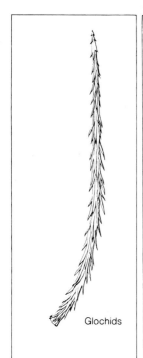

Glochids

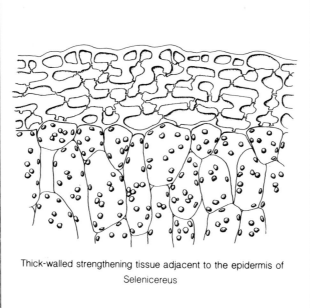

Thick-walled strengthening tissue adjacent to the epidermis of Selenicereus

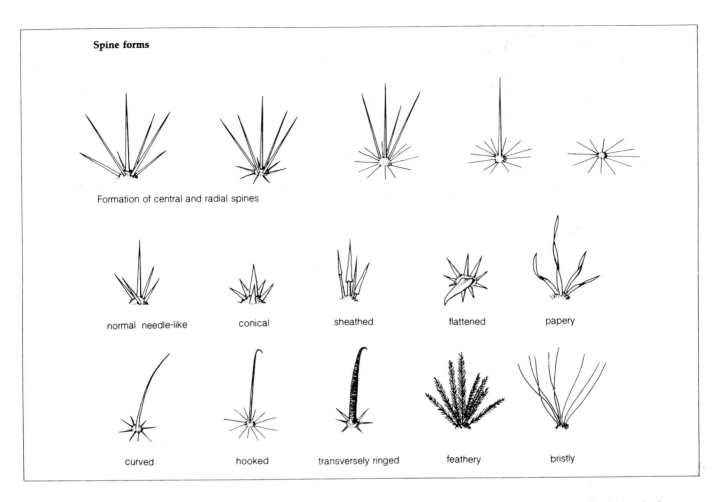

Spine forms

Formation of central and radial spines

normal needle-like   conical   sheathed   flattened   papery

curved   hooked   transversely ringed   feathery   bristly

area, and which allow them to exploit the superficial moisture of a large stretch of terrain. Where rainfall is slight, water does not penetrate far into the ground. Thus the only other form of root which is useful to a plant in a really dry location is one which extends very deep down, and can thus exploit underground water. Grown in pots, cacti have to form a quite different root system, but this appears to have little effect on most of them.

Cacti with beet-like taproots, such as *Sulcorebutia, Lophophora, Ariocarpus* and others, are the most resistant to drying out, as they use the root to store water as well as their stem. The root is better protected against high temperatures than the exposed part of the plant, as the temperature of the ground on a hot day drops markedly even a few millimetres below the surface.

Flower position

In the most primitive cacti, of the genus *Pereskia*, we find branching inflorescences, with each flower on its own stalk, but the flowers of all other cacti grow directly on the shoots. In some cases several flowers grow together from a single areole, as on *Myrtillocactus, Rhipsalis* and *Schlumbergera*.

Many cacti have large individual flowers, some of them among the largest in the plant kingdom. For example, the flowers of *Selenicereus grandiflorus*, the 'Queen of the Night', can be more than 20 cm. in diameter. In contrast the flowers of *Mammillaria* tend to be very small and inconspicuous individually, but form a close-packed garland around the crown of the plant, and look very striking. Both arrangements - large individual flowers or masses of small ones - ensure that pollinating creatures will notice them from a distance.

The flowers of most columnar cacti develop on the sides of the stem. Many small, globular species such as Lobivias and Rebutias are of similar habit. As a result the flowers are often close to the ground, although the flowers of most globular cacti develop from very young areoles close to or at the tip of the plant.

The flowers usually grow from normal areoles, with no prior indication. Certain columnar cacti and two genera of globular cacti, *Melocactus* and *Discocactus*, develop a formation termed the cephalium (cephale = head). This is a section of the plant with an entirely different spine formation, usually very hairy, from which the flowers grow. It was once considered that a cephalium was a very significant differentiating feature, but it has now become evident that cephalia are extremely variable. Werdermann makes the distinction between a true cephalium, which is formed before the flowers develop, and what he terms a pseudo-cephalium (pseudo = false), which grows at the same time as the flowers. Later a distinction was drawn between the grooved, recessed cephalium and the cowl-shaped type extending over the crown. There is

15

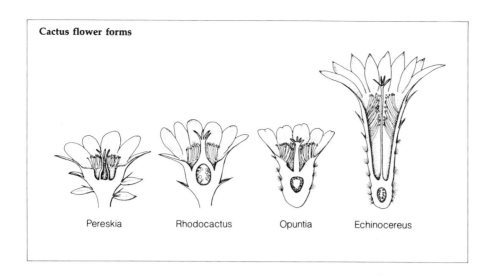

Cactus flower forms

Pereskia   Rhodocactus   Opuntia   Echinocereus

also a type of cephalium through which the stem grows when flowering is finished. The remains of the cephalium can then be seen as a conspicuously spiny or hairy ring round the stem. The dividing lines which were formerly drawn between the different types of cephalium have become blurred by more recently discovered transitional forms. In the case of the pseudo-cephalium, for example, species have been found in which the flowering areoles have slightly different hair or spine formations from the non-flowering examples. The cephalia of *Melocactus* and *Discocactus* stand out clearly from the rest of the body, and are thus the most clearly defined of all, and yet the two genera are not closely related. It is clear that the cephalium has developed independently in a number of different groups. For this reason the cephalium is no longer considered as a criterion by which to define the genera.

Even non-flowering cephalia, with their long white hair, are often clearly visible from a distance. The flowers themselves may well be insignificant in contrast, but are grouped closely together. The flower buds are very well protected under the dense hair, and are often almost impossible to find; in many cases even the young fruit are concealed as they ripen.

In some cases the flowers are not formed on the areoles, but in the recesses between them, a feature which may also represent a means of

protection. In one group of North American warty cacti we can observe an entire line of development of this feature. Some *Neolloydia* species feature elongated areoles, and the flowers develop at their upper edge. In *Thelocactus* the areole is extended in a furrow, while in *Coryphantha* the furrow runs right to the base, or axil, of the tubercle. The flower is then formed in the axil. The buds are thus very effectively protected between the tubercles. In many species the axils bear bristles or are densely covered in hair, so that the buds can develop in complete seclusion. Finally, no furrow is visible at all in *Mammillaria*.

The flowers

The drawing above shows the structure of the various types of cactus

flower. *Pereskia* retains a quite 'normal' flower, with all the parts at a common level at the base of the flower. In the closely related genus *Rhodocactus* the ovary, which contains the ovules, is inferior, i.e. it is located under the other parts of the flower. This may be seen as a means of protecting the delicate ovules from the creatures which visit the flower. In Opuntias the part of the flower in which the ovules are located bears areoles on the outside, with the usual spine formation. In this case we can describe the formation as an ovary enclosed in a small shoot. In fact young shoots often look very similar to flower buds when very small. In Pereskias and Opuntias further flowers may grow from the side of the young fruits. Even fruit which have fallen off may root and produce new joints from the areoles. Flower buds have also been

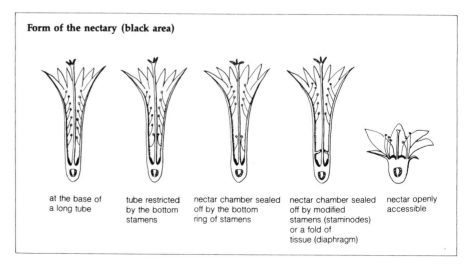

Form of the nectary (black area)

at the base of a long tube

tube restricted by the bottom stamens

nectar chamber sealed off by the bottom ring of stamens

nectar chamber sealed off by modified stamens (staminodes) or a fold of tissue (diaphragm)

nectar openly accessible

16

Top left: Ariocarpus kotschoubeyanus with clearly defined taproot

Centre left: On Myrtillocactus geometricans several flowers develop from one areole.

Bottom left: Pseudo-cephalium on Pilosocereus palmeri.

Top centre: Cephalium on Espostoa.

Top right. Lateral cephalium on Cleistocactus chrysocephalus

Centre right: Bi-laterally symmetrical flowers of Borzicactus cullmannianus.

Bottom right: The flowers of Carnegiea gigantea are visited by bats

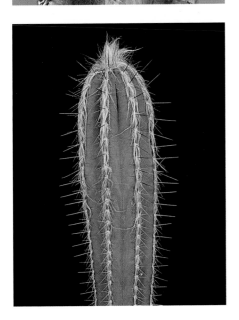

known to change into shoots, in *Notocactus* for example. The part of the cactus flower which holds the ovules does not equate exactly with the ovary of a typical flowering plant, but the term ovary is used throughout this text.

In most cacti the ovary is surmounted by a tubular structure) from which grow the stamens. At the base of the tube, or at the extreme bottom of the wall of the tube, is an area of glandular tissue which secretes nectar. This is a dilute sugar solution which is collected by visitors to the flower. In some cases the lowest stamens are located close to the style, with a resultant clearly defined nectar chamber. Where the stamens merge

Cactus flower types

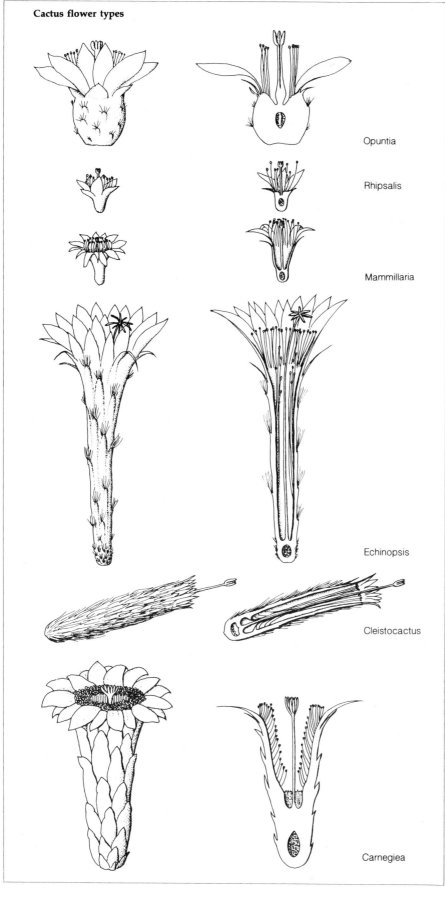

Opuntia

Rhipsalis

Mammillaria

Echinopsis

Cleistocactus

Carnegiea

together at the base, or a membrane reaches across to the style, the nectar chamber is almost totally enclosed. These arrangements protect the nectar, which can then only be obtained by insects with a correspondingly long proboscis.

The shape and colour of the flower are of great importance in terms of pollination. Cacti produce a variety of types of flower, as shown in the drawing. The most striking flowers are those which are visited mainly by nocturnal moths. These creatures have probosces several centimetres long, and those flowers which are exclusively pollinated by nocturnal moths possess a very long tube, and open towards evening, often only for a few hours. To ensure that they are clearly visible even at dusk, they are usually quite large, almost always white, cream or yellow, and generally have a powerful scent. Long-tubed flowers which remain open until the following noon or even longer are probably derived from these, although they are often a vivid red in colour, and have hardly any perfume. Such flowers are attractive to diurnal butterflies. The flowers may also be curved, and may be more or less bilaterally symmetrical (zygomorphic) e.g. *Borzicactus, Cleistocactus* and *Zygocactus*.

The most widespread types of flower are the medium-sized to small types with a tube which is not excessively long or narrow. Such flowers are visited chiefly by bees, which are able to collect quite large quantities of pollen thanks to the large number of stamens.

The flowers of *Pereskia* and the Opuntias - the most primitive species - are much less specialized. They spread out broadly, and their pollen and nectar are accessible to all visiting creatures. The flowers of a few epiphytic cacti, such as those of *Rhipsalis*, have also retrogressed to a very simple form. They are often only a few millimetres in size, have no tube and only a small number of petals and stamens. In consequence the nectar is openly on display, and all manner of insects, including flies with short probosces, can profitably visit them.

Finally there are cacti whose flowers are visited by bats, among them the flowers of *Cephalocereus* and *Stenocereus*. They open at night, but are broad, sturdy structures in comparison with the delicate flowers visited by moths, and usually radiate an unpleasant smell to attract their visitors, for whom they provide an ample supply of pollen and nectar.

The colouring of cactus flowers

Every imaginable colour is represented among cactus flowers with the exception of pure blue. This is only found on the tips of the petals of a single species, *Wittia amazonica*. A cultivated version of *Gymnocalycium* is also said to produce blue flowers. The colours of cactus flowers are produced by various substances which are dissolved in the cell fluid. These substances are not the blue or red anthocyanin or the chemically similar yellow flavone as in other flowering plants, but what are known as betacyanins. These nitrogenous dyes only occur in one other systematic group apart from cacti, viz. the family of the order of the Caryophyllales. This group includes the goosefoot (Chenopodiaceae) and beetroot, the pokeweed (Phytolaccaceae) and the ice plants (Mesembryanthemaceae or - the larger grouping - Aizoaceae), so popular with plant lovers, all of them leaf succulents. The dyestuffs which cacti have in common are one of the most important criteria by which they are categorized within the plant system.

As cacti differ so markedly from the Caryophyllales plant families in flower structure they are best defined within the plant system as their own order Cactales (with the single family Cactaceae) alongside the Caryophyllales. The anthocyanin and betacyanin dyes can be identified by a quite simple test. Anthocyanins change colour very strongly in the presence of acid or alkali. Blue anthocyanin, for example, turns red with acid (red cabbage and vinegar), while anthocyanins turn greenish with alkali. Betacyanins hardly change colour at all

in these tests. White flowers contain no dyes. The white colour comes simply from the fact that no green chlorophyll is formed in the cells, in contrast to ordinary foliage leaves. The many small air spaces between the cells reflect all the light, and the flower petal then appears to be white. If these air spaces are filled with fluid, the petals become translucent, as when they wither and die, or if the petal is left in water for a period.

The external covering of the flower tube and the ovary

The tube and the ovary are usually more or less densely covered with scales, although in some cases they are entirely absent. In the axils of the

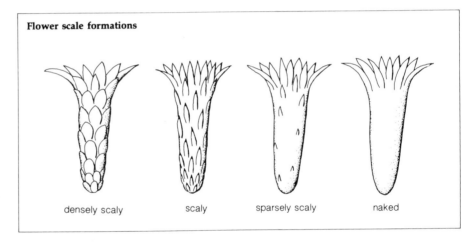

Flower scale formations

densely scaly   scaly   sparsely scaly   naked

scales are spines, bristles, hair, wool or short felt. Finally, the flower may be quite naked. The outside covering of the tube and the ovary is one of the most important factors in the classification of cacti. Wherever possible Backeberg defined all the genera so narrowly that only one type of flower covering occurred in each genus. In Buxbaum's system the external flower covering represented one of the two most important developmental series; the other was the structure of the seed. The usual sequence of development, from scaly, spiny flowers to those with neither scales nor spines clearly occurred in several different groups independently, in part if not in toto. The whole

matter is complicated by the fact that all possible combinations of covering occur. In some cases the spines are reduced in size, in others they are separated into central thorny spines and radial spines which are bristly or hairy - in similar fashion to ordinary areoles. Thus there are secondary sequences as well as the simple main development series. This is shown schematically in the drawing. Moreover, the shrinking of the scales is not necessarily related to the absence of spines or hairs. The genera *Gymnocalycium* and *Hylocereus*, for example, have characteristically large scales on their flowers, but the axils of the scales are completely bald.

In consequence it is possible to distinguish a very wide range of types of external flower covering, and thus the characteristic is a very good criterion by which to classify. Even so, it would not be advisable to define the genera by this feature alone, as the result would be to separate certain species which are closely related in other respects. The quality of the flower covering is an indispensable aid to defining cacti. It is always one of the first characteristics which is examined when an unknown cactus is encountered. In flowers which are recessed amongst tubercles or hairs this is not always easy, and where possible an entire flower has to be carefully twisted out.

The main purpose of the external flower covering is probably to protect the delicate flower bud, as otherwise it would be an obvious target for grazing

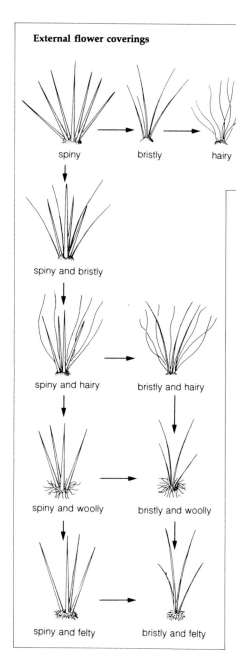

External flower coverings

spiny → bristly → hairy → woolly → felty → slightly woolly → bare

spiny and bristly

spiny and hairy → bristly and hairy

spiny and woolly → bristly and woolly

spiny and felty → bristly and felty

animals and a wide variety of rodents.

It is undoubtedly no coincidence that protective flower coverings are much less evident on the flowers of epiphytic cacti and the very tall columnar cacti, and also in species whose flower buds are protected in the tubercle axils, as in the case of Mammillarias and cacti with a cephalium.

Pollen grains and pollination

The usually numerous stamens produce large quantities of pollen grains. In a single *Carnegiea* flower, the 'Saguaro' of Arizona, a total of 3482 stamens was counted. The individual, microscopically small pollen grains stick together, forming small clumps, and because of this a visit by a single creature results in a very large number of pollen grains being transferred to the next flower. The pollen grains can

Scanning electron microscope photographs of the pollen grains of Cleistocactus (left, x 900 magnification) and Opuntia (right, x 550 magnification)

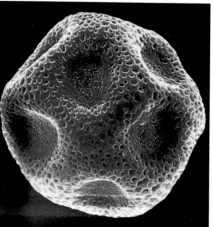

then fertilize all the many ovules of that flower. Recently the pollen grains of cacti have been the subject of further study. Using the scanning electron microscope pictures of exceptional resolution have been obtained, showing that the pollen grains vary very widely in their surface pattern (see illustrations). This characteristic is also an important factor in the establishment of a systematic classification of cacti.

The pollen grains first reach the stigma branches at the end of a long style. To ensure that pollen from the same flower does not reach the stigma branches the latter are either taller than the stamens, or they ripen later, when the pollen of the same flower has already been dispersed. This avoids self-fertilization, which would result in much more uniform descendants than with outside pollination. In the long term self-pollination would reduce the ability of the species to adapt to new conditions. Self-fertilization can also be prevented by the stigma lobes producing substances which prevent the pollen grains of the same plant germinating. There are certain cacti whose flowers are cleistogamous, that is, they remain more or less closed, and fertilize themselves. All this is of particular importance if the grower wishes to harvest seeds himself, or wishes to pollinate flowers artificially. For this reason the process is described in detail in the section dealing with cactus cultivation.

When the flowers are pollinated, it is usual for the upper part of the flower above the ovary to fall off, but in many genera the flowers simply dry out, and their remains are left on the fruit.

The fruit

The pollen grains germinate on the stigma and send long pollen tubes into the inside of the style. Eventually the tubes reach the ovules and are able to fertilize them. It is only after fertilization that the microscopically small ovules develop into seed. At the same time the ovary grows larger. Often the spines and bristles become stronger at this stage, to provide better protection for the young fruit.

Dry fruit of flowering plants nearly always dehisce, or burst when ripe, scattering the seeds individually. These fruit are usually not strongly coloured. Capsule fruit split at clearly defined weak points on the side or at the tip. Many cactus fruit, on the other hand, simply break open irregularly when ripe, scattering their seed. In other species the seed can escape only through an opening which is formed at the bottom of the fruit when it falls

bearing the glochids has to be removed with the greatest care before the flesh is eaten. For many species of cactus we either have no knowledge of the fruit or we only know that its characteristics are slightly variable, perhaps in how they split. For this reason the fruit are only rarely used in cactus systematics.

Berry fruit of an Opuntia

Fruit of a Trichocereus sp.

Oreocereus fossulatus with fruit

off. Many fruit decay only slowly and are eventually washed away by rain.

Fleshy fruit, on the other hand, are usually vividly coloured: red, yellow or white. These fruit are similar to berries, and contain very hard-shelled seed which are not damaged if the berries are eaten by birds. The seeds are later excreted unharmed, and are in this way scattered far and wide. Those genera which produce berry fruits, including the epiphytic cacti, the trailing cacti, *Cereus, Opuntia* and *Mammillaria*, are usually distributed over much larger areas than those with dry fruit.

These fleshy cactus fruit are often harvested and eaten by man, especially those of *Opuntia*, certain *Cereus* species and *Myrtillocactus*. The well-known fig cactus or Indian fig (*Opuntia ficus-indica*) is cultivated quite widely on account of its fruit, although the outside skin

The seed

In contrast, cactus seed is used increasingly for the purposes of classification. Sixty years ago Britton and Rose frequently used the external, easily identifiable seed characteristics as distinguishing features. The seed's colour is the first obvious characteristic. Opuntioideae have white to yellowish seeds, the other cacti black to brown. Black and brown seeds only differ in the quantity of dyestuff contained in the seed shell; black seeds are brown when young. The brown seeds are a derivative of the black ones, but they ripen at an earlier stage of development. The surface of the seeds may be glossy or matt. The finer surface patterning can only be seen with the aid of a very powerful magnifier, a dissecting microscope, or a scanning electron microscope, when an extremely wide variety of formations becomes evident. The outer skin cells of the seed shell may form a completely smooth, glossy surface. If the cells are arched in shape, the seeds appear warty and matt. If the warts are close together, tiny grooves are visible between them. Where the centre of the cells, making up the seed shell is depressed the seed surface appears to be dimpled. If the cells are very elongated the seed surface may show fine folds or bulges. Many seeds are also surrounded by a seed coat (aril), which may form a bone-hard shell, as in the Opuntias. Finally, the seeds may possess attachment formations, such as a strophiole. In some cases this can swell up and make the seed sticky. The colour and surface quality of the seed are undoubtedly significant factors in their germination. They decide the seed's adhesive power, how much they warm up in the sun, how well they absorb water, and how rapidly they swell. Usually a certain level of moisture has to be reached before the seeds of a particular species will germinate. This prevents seed germinating as a result of short, superficial rainfall.

Inside the seed shell is the embryo. This is a complete, small plant, with a short root (radicle), two leaves (cotyledons) and a short shoot (hypocotyl) linking them. Many cactus seeds contain a nutritive tissue as well as the embryo, but in most cases it is used up by the embryo as the seed ripens. As cactus seeds are so small they are not easy to dissect. Important features of the embryo can nevertheless be seen in the very small embryo plants (see drawing).

In many cacti, for example the Pereskias and epiphytes, the embryo plants look very similar to other flowering plants. They have large, flat cotyledons and a thin shoot. The embryo plants of more typical cacti are already distinctly succulent. The cotyledons become shorter and shorter and eventually disappear almost completely, leaving only tiny points.

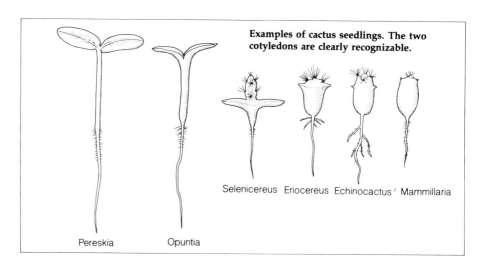

Examples of cactus seedlings. The two cotyledons are clearly recognizable.

Selenicereus Eriocereus Echinocactus Mammillaria

Pereskia

Opuntia

Scanning electron microscope photographs of the surface of various cactus seed

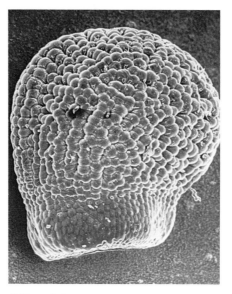

Echinopsis hamatacantha, x 45

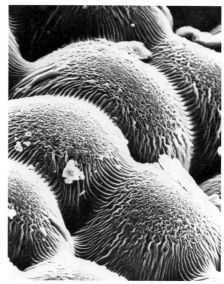

Echinopsis hamatacantha, x 550

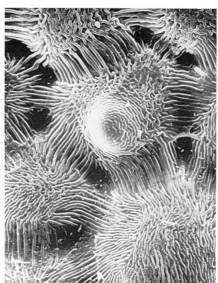

Echinopsis hamatacantha, x 1200

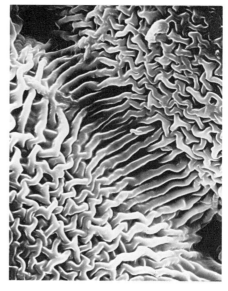

Echinopsis hamatacantha, x 2000

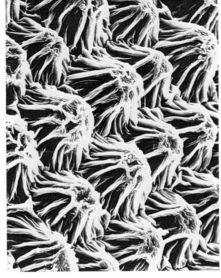

Notocactus mammulosus var. gracilis, x 40

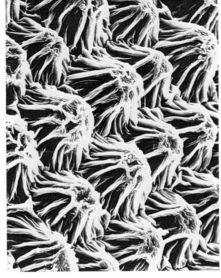

Notocactus mammulosus var. gracilis, x 300

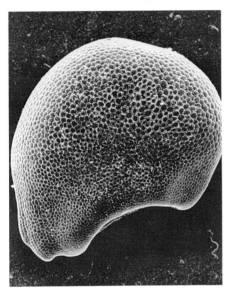

Neolloydia laui, x 30

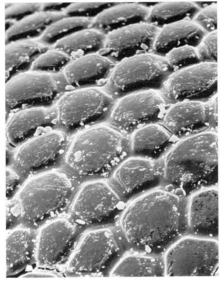

Neolloydia laui, x 300

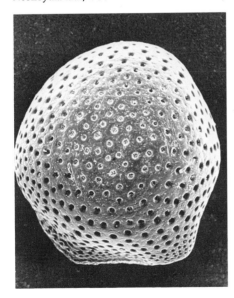

Neobesseya missouriensis, x 30

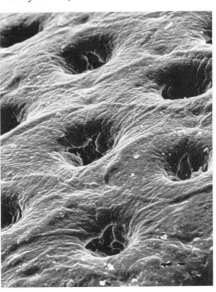

Neobesseya missouriensis, x 2500

The internal structure and physiology of cacti

Water economy

When a cactus is dissected, the major part of the plant appears to be a watery, translucent mass. This is the water storage tissue. Under the microscope this tissue appears to consist entirely of large, thin-walled, extremely densely packed cells, almost completely filled with cell fluid. The fluid does not usually consist of pure water, but of a thin, watery mucus. The living part of the cell is just a thin, colourless film of protoplasm, which nestles closely against the cell wall. This part contains the cell nucleus with the genetic material. Weighing scales can be used to measure the proportion of water in these tissues. To do this it is only necessary to weigh fresh pieces before and after drying. In cacti the water usually accounts for 90 per cent of the plant tissue by weight. This is an extremely high proportion, even for the fleshy parts of plants, and is approximately the same as very juicy fruit. For comparison, ordinary leaves contain about 85 per cent water. The tall, tree-shaped columnar cacti, e.g. *Carnegiea gigantea* or *Pachycereus pringlei*, are capable of storing enormous quantities of water in their stems. From their size and girth we can calculate that the volume is up to 3000 litres or more. A barrel-shaped *Echinocactus*, only about 2.5 m. in height, can still store about 800 litres of water.

Cacti are extremely economical in their use of this stored water. Every cactus enthusiast knows this well. Even the smaller cacti can usually survive the winter without watering, and at the end are only slightly shrunken. If individual stems of reasonable thickness are cut off, they lose water to the air at an extremely slow rate, and will remain alive for many months. Even in their hot native habitats we can assume that cacti can exist for a full year or two on their own water supplies. Indeed this ability is sometimes put to the test; for

Cactus seedlings with clearly visible succulent cotyledons

example, in the dry Brazilian bush known as the 'caatinga', which is rich in cacti, there are regions where rain sometimes does not fall for two years.

If the water storage tissue loses water, the cells first become slightly smaller, as they have elastic walls and are normally fully expanded with water. Soon the walls become slack, and collapse like a concertina. The cell walls are drawn inward, and the entire water tissue shrinks en masse, without

air entering. The more important vital tissues of the plant, in particular its outer skin and the green tissue beneath it, remain saturated with water all the while. These parts have higher osmotic pressures than the water storage tissue, and can gradually draw water from this tissue when they need it.

How do cacti lose water at all? As in all plants the outer surface of cacti cannot be completely airtight, as the

plant must be able to absorb carbon dioxide from the air. Carbon dioxide is one of the fundamental requirements, along with water, for the generation of the plant's organic materials, e.g. the cellulose of the cell walls and the albumin of the protoplasm. The outer skin of green plants therefore has many small pores, known as stomata (see drawing). When there is a water shortage, the edges of the pores can be drawn together and the opening sealed. Even then a little water evaporates through the entire surface of the plant, although the amount is only one tenth as much as when the stomata are open. This low rate of evaporation is due mainly to a very fine membrane called the cuticle, which is no more than a few thousandths of a millimetre thick, and is secreted outward by the cells of the epidermis or outer skin. The cuticle of cacti is no thicker than that of ordinary plants, but is clearly of very special quality, as the rate of water loss through it is extremely slight. Admittedly an additional factor in favour of cacti is that their surface area is very small in relation to the plants' volume, but evaporation through the plant, termed transpiration, is a function of surface area rather than of the plant's volume. The centimetre-thick flat pad of an *Opuntia* has a surface area:volume ratio around 200 times more favourable than a beech leaf, whose thickness is only ¹⁄₂₀ mm.

How then are these lost water supplies

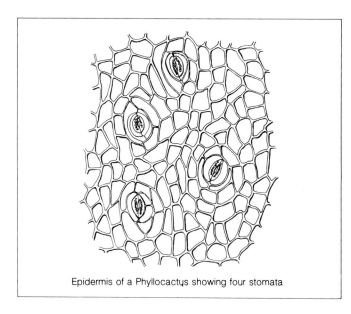

Epidermis of a Phyllocactus showing four stomata

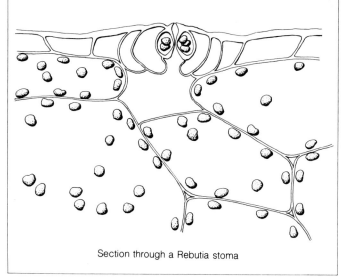

Section through a Rebutia stoma

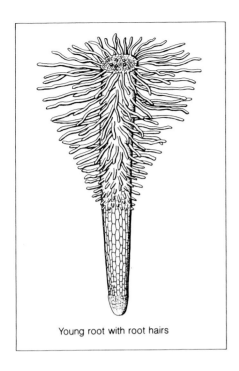

Young root with root hairs

when water losses are great, osmotic values hardly rise at all. This is the means by which ordinary plants are to some extent able to adapt to drier ground. In cacti severe water losses occur so slowly that during the period of shortage so much carbohydrate is used up that the osmotic value may in fact fall slightly.

The absorption of rain or dew through the surface of the stems is hardly significant, as the cuticle is practically impervious to water, but it is possible that many cacti are able to absorb some dew via their dense mantle of dead hair, or by means of specialized spines.

The rate of water transport inside the body of a cactus does not need to be very rapid, as the rate of transpiration is generally low. The actual water transport tissues are therefore very small. They can be recognized by the naked eye as fine, lighter-coloured threads (see drawing) in a transverse or longitudinal section, and are termed

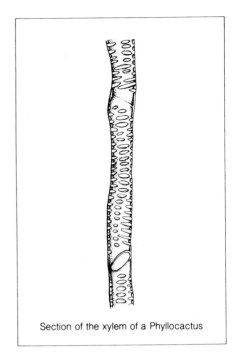

Section of the xylem of a Phyllocactus

replaced from time to time? In this respect cacti differ little from other plants. They absorb water through their roots when the ground is moist. At such times cacti are able to replenish their water supplies in a very short time, thanks to their wide ranging system of fine roots. The roots have fine hairs (see drawing) which are only visible under a microscope, and whose sole purpose is to absorb water; these hairs are developed anew within a few hours to a few days when they are needed. If water is scarce in the ground, cacti very quickly cease absorbing water. Other plants native to the dry regions, especially small bushes with sturdy, small leaves, are much more efficient in this respect. They develop far higher suction forces than cacti, and absorb the last traces of water from a greater depth with their long, straight roots. Cacti, on the other hand, absorb water only when conditions are favourable, otherwise they exist on their own supplies. With osmotic values between 4 and 20 atmospheres in their shoots they are unable to develop suction pressures higher than ordinary forest plants in Europe, according to Walter. Osmotic values above 12 atmospheres are only found in the Opuntias, which are particularly undemanding. Even

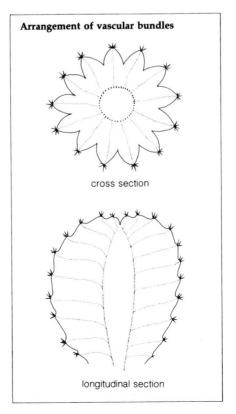

Arrangement of vascular bundles

cross section

longitudinal section

the xylem (Greek xylon = wood) as they are slightly woody. They consist of elongated cells with thick walls which have many thinner areas, which are the points through which moisture is transmitted to adjacent cells. Most of the water simply diffuses slowly from the water storage tissues to the green outer tissue regions as a result of differences in osmotic pressure. In a *Ferocactus wislizenii*, for example, the osmotic pressure was 5.11 atmospheres internally, while it had risen to 8.84 atmospheres at the plant's surface. In general, the vegetative areas at the tips of the stems have osmotic values which are higher than the rest of the body by a few atmospheres. As a result these zones draw water from the rest of the body. Even Opuntias which are kept completely dry produce new pads, the water for which is drawn from old pads until the latter finally die off completely.

Photosynthesis and light

In our examination of transverse sections through cactus bodies the relatively thin layer of green tissue below the epidermis was very obvious.

25

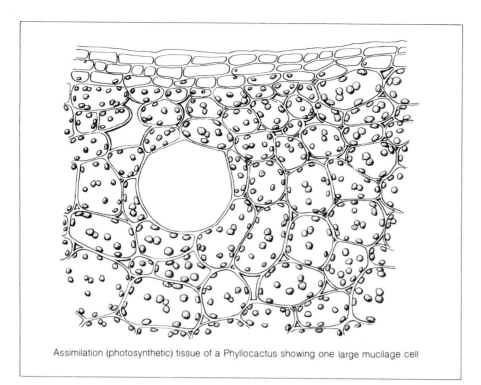

Assimilation (photosynthetic) tissue of a Phyllocactus showing one large mucilage cell

proportion, and because of the small surface area which is available for the absorption of carbon dioxide, cacti grow relatively slowly even under favourable conditions. In fact, if cacti grow in a location with a more plentiful supply of water they are rapidly outstripped and supplanted by the much faster growing thin-leaved plants. The vast majority of cacti need a copious supply of light, and cannot tolerate shade for any length of time. Only amongst the epiphytic cacti are there species which continue growing when the light is poor.

The sugar which is the direct product of photosynthesis is usually converted by cacti into starch and stored in this form. The starch grains are often located in particular regions of the stem. During a period of growth new cell walls and entire roots can be formed very quickly from the stored starch. The starch is converted back

As in all plants this green tissue is the actual nutritional or assimilation tissue (see drawing). In cacti this part only accounts for a small proportion of the total mass. Air, with its small proportion (up to 0.03 per cent) of carbon dioxide, passes through the opened stomata to the assimilation tissue. The cells absorb this gas and combine it with water to form organic substances such as sugar and starch. The energy required for this process is provided by light, and in consequence the process is termed photosynthesis.

As cacti usually live in very hot, dry locations, they would lose too much water if they were to open their stomata in daytime like other plants. Cacti and other succulent plants therefore keep their stomata closed in daytime, but open them at night. During the night temperatures are lower, air humidity is higher and solar radiation is absent, and hence even with the stomata open very little water evaporates. Other plants which have adapted to dry conditions have to exploit to the full the few days when water is plentiful, and therefore have a high number of stomata per unit of surface area to allow maximum photosynthesis when conditions permit, but succulents manage with a relatively small number. The carbon

dioxide absorbed at night cannot be utilized immediately in the absence of light energy, and it therefore has to be stored until the following day. To this end it is dissolved in an organic acid, pyruvic acid, and stored in the form of malic acid. It can be separated again from this acid on the following day and processed quite normally by photosynthesis. The carbon dioxide which is produced in succulents by respiration of organic substances does not escape outwards, but is again combined in the form of malic acid. It has long been observed that the pH value of cactus body tissues alters rhythmically over the course of a day. For example, a very high pH value was measured in an *Opuntia* in the late afternoon, and on the following early morning the cell fluid was very acid. Evidently most of the carbon dioxide stored in the malic acid up to late afternoon had been used up in the process of photosynthesis; during the night further carbon dioxide was stored in malic acid until the early morning, which resulted in the high level of acidity.

Thus cacti are as economical in their use of carbon dioxide as they are with water. Nevertheless, because of their structure, of which the assimilation tissue comprises only a relatively small

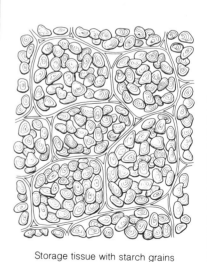

Storage tissue with starch grains

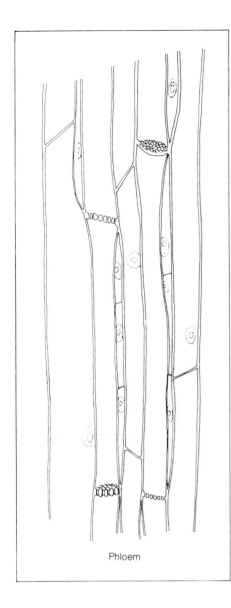

Phloem

into water-soluble sugar which is then transported to the growth zone via the phloem, or sieve tubes (see drawing). Each vascular bundle consists of phloem and xylem (the water-transport tissue).

Temperature

In the hot regions where cacti usually grow one might expect that the plants would be damaged by heat, but cacti scarcely ever exhibit such injury. They do warm up to a very marked extent: temperatures of 52°C have been recorded inside cacti, without the plants suffering damage. Nor can cacti cool themselves by transpiration. Temperatures higher than this are hardly ever reached in natural conditions. During the night the cactus cools down again, and the stored water slows down the rate at which the plant heats up in the daytime. Experiments have shown that stems die after a period at 55°C.

The same does not apply to the temperature on the outside surface of the cactus body. Here the temperature may well rise above a tolerable level. Scorch marks can even occur in Europe if a plant is subjected to a sudden change of location, or if drops of water are allowed to stay on the skin, and although only the outer skin is damaged and the plant itself is not harmed such marks are very disfiguring. Young, growing stems are particularly vulnerable. Many cacti are well protected against solar radiation. Either they mature with a bloom formed by a white to blue-green coating of wax which reflects most of the radiation, or they are protected with dense white areole wool consisting of dead hairs. For a long time it was thought that the ribs of cacti were one means by which the plants had adapted to heat. The ribs do effectively raise the area available for radiating heat, just like a ribbed radiator. Nevertheless, according to recent investigations ribs or tubercles have the opposite effect: they raise the temperature.

Succulents are much less adept at tolerating cold than heat. Some cacti are able to survive slight frosts. The cell fluid does not freeze in such conditions, as the substance in the cactus cells is not pure water, but water in which substances such as sugar and organic acids are dissolved, the effect of which is to lower the fluid's freezing point by a few degrees Celsius. It is likely that no cactus could survive a complete freeze followed by thawing out. The ice formation and subsequent thawing would damage the fine membrane systems too severely. On the other hand many cacti suffer permanent damage even when temperatures remain far above freezing point. It has not been established how such temperatures can damage cactus tissues. The plants' sensitivity to cold does not remain constant throughout the year. As winter approaches they slowly become more resistant to cold, but in the summer they are particularly vulnerable to sudden cold snaps.

The extremes of temperature which can just be tolerated are certainly important, but the temperature range within which the plants are able to make new growth is equally significant. Above and below this range the plant loses by respiration more than it gains by photosynthesis, and the net result is a loss of substance. The same occurs when the cactus receives too little light. If it is left in such unfavourable conditions for a long period it will gradually starve to death. In fact cacti are extremely resistant to such conditions; they can survive on their own stored supplies for months on end. Different species have widely different compensation points (the point at which they can just continue to make growth) in terms of temperature and light intensity, which vary according to the natural conditions under which the species grows.

Soil

Along with water, light and warmth, the other vital factor to cacti is the soil. When the cactus absorbs the water in the ground it also takes in the nutritive salts dissolved in it. Cacti require no great quantities of these salts. The dry substance of the cactus body is a small proportion of its weight, and most of that consists of organic materials (principally cellulose), which are formed by photosynthesis. The absorbed nutritive salts correspond to ash. Even in a globular cactus weighing about 100 grams this only amounts to about 0.5 gram. It follows that heavy doses of fertilizer containing mineral salts are not necessary, except for the very fast growing species. As cacti have relatively low osmotic values, and therefore do not develop great suction forces, they are only capable of absorbing very weak solutions of fertilizer. If a higher concentration is given their roots even tend to lose water. Terrain whose surface is continually enriched with easily soluble salts, as occurs quite frequently in hot, dry areas, is not usually colonized by cacti. On the other hand, land with a hard superficial crust of gypsum crystals, which are not highly soluble, is often found colonized by cacti.

Most cacti prefer a slightly acid soil and do not like any substantial proportion of lime which pushes the pH value of the soil into the alkaline sector. In general terms cacti require a loose, well-drained soil, as their roots require access to the oxygen of the air, which is only available in sufficient quantities if the soil is not densely packed.

Usually it is not the specific type of soil - clay, loam, sand, leaf mould, etc. - which is crucial to success with cacti, but rather particular characteristics of that soil, such as its pH value and its porosity. This is evident from the fact that in culture these soil constituents can be replaced by quite different materials whose only similarity is in the physical or chemical characteristics mentioned. Even artificial soils such as styromull, Perlite etc., can possess these qualities. Most cacti have even been successfully cultivated by the hydroculture technique. Nevertheless the fact remains that many species of cactus require specific types of soil. Where this is the case the section of the book dealing with that species or genus mentions the fact.

Protection

Plants with such a long period of growth as cacti need good protection. Their spines, and the milky sap of many Mammillarias, account for a considerable proportion of the organic substances they produce. As long as the spines are still young, their cell structure can be observed quite clearly under the microscope. Later the cell walls become thicker as the spines grow stronger, and eventually hardly anything is left to be seen of the original cell pattern.

Older cacti gradually become brown in colour at the base. This colouring indicates the formation of many layers of tough cork, which provides very

effective protection. As its cells are as intimately grouped as the original outer skin, and as the cell walls consist mainly of cork, which is completely impervious to water, this tissue is an excellent means of preventing water evaporating. Small cacti very often possess a brown corky zone where the shoot leaves the ground; when the earth heats up the highest temperature is reached right at the surface, especially if it is dark in colour, but as the individual, fully formed cork cells are filled with air the material is a very effective heat insulator, and thus provides the plant with effective protection from overheating in this highly vulnerable area.

Reproduction

We have to differentiate clearly between asexual reproduction by means of cuttings and grafting, and sexual reproduction by means of seed. In asexual reproduction the new plants are genetically identical to their parent; they are simply parts of the mother plant separated off. When a cutting is first removed from a plant it has a moist cut surface, as very many cells are inevitably cut through and their fluid content lost. To avoid the evaporation of too much water by this or any other kind of damage, the cut surface of a cactus very quickly seals itself. As soon as the cut surface and the adjacent cell layers have dried out, evaporation virtually ceases. After a few days the underlying living cells form a corky layer (see drawing), with the result that the cut area is now completely sealed off. Cork tissue can be formed by any living cactus cells when required. This is not true of root formation. Only certain cells in the cut surface are capable of forming roots; they are grouped in small regions in the vascular bundles, and constitute the cambium. The cambium is located between the xylem and the phloem, both of which were also formed by the cambium. As the vascular bundles are disposed in a ring in the centre of the stem the cutting's roots are often produced in an annular formation.

The process of grafting is an entirely different matter. In this case the cut surfaces must not be allowed to dry

out; the living cells of both cut surfaces must come into intimate contact. This is not difficult, but once again success depends on the meeting of cells of the cambium of the two parts. At least some of them have to unite for the graft to grow together properly.

In sexual reproduction by seed the genetic material of the two parent plants is combined in a new pattern. In this case the plant which produces the seed is termed the mother plant, and that which supplies the pollen the father plant. The seedlings produced are not exactly identical to either of the two parents. To some extent a spread of characteristics occurs, the range depending on how genetically pure the parent plants were.

The structure of cactus flowers and their pollination, i.e. the transfer of pollen grains from one flower to the other, has already been described. Actual fertilization, on the other hand, is a process which can only be observed with the help of a microscope. Flower pollen consists of a very large number of microscopically small pollen grains. These have a strong outer membrane, the extine, which consists of sporopollenin, a material which is extremely resistant chemically. The extine is pushed outward by the cell, in a similar manner to the cuticle of an epidermis cell. The extine of many

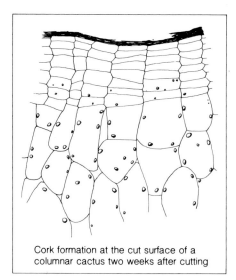

Cork formation at the cut surface of a columnar cactus two weeks after cutting

types of cactus pollen grain features a fine surface pattern. The pollen grains usually remain viable for no more than a few days, although they can be kept alive longer if stored in cool and dry conditions, as is described later in the section dealing with cactus cultivation.

If a pollen grain comes into contact with the surface of a suitable stigma the extine bursts at one of its preformed weak points. The cellulose wall beneath the extine then expands, and gradually a tube grows from the

fertilization the ovule develops at a rapid rate, growing many times larger in the process. The fertilized egg cell turns into the embryo - the small new plant - while the fertilized secondary embryo sac nucleus forms the nutritive tissue. The integuments eventually form the hard seed shell. These elements constitute the essential parts of the ripe seed. In many cacti the nutritive tissue is used up by the embryo while the seed is ripening.

The point at which the seed was joined is termed the hilum. The

seed to germinate are described in greater detail in the section dealing with propagating from seed.

It may be many years before the taller columnar cacti flower for the first time. When they are older the larger tree-form or bushy cacti develop a considerable quantity of woody tissue in their stems to reinforce their structure. This wood is also produced by the cambium, and eventually forms a cylindrical layer. The wood of cacti does not have obvious annual rings, thus it is not possible to establish the age of the plants in this way. Nevertheless, it is thought that some of the very large tree-shaped cacti such as *Carnegiea* may be 250 years old. Cactus wood consists mainly of elongated fibrous cells with thick, ligneous walls. In contrast to most other tyes of wood these cells remain alive, and are used to store starch. Water conduction is carried out mainly by long, tube-like cells - the xylem - whose inter-connecting walls have been dissolved (see page 25).

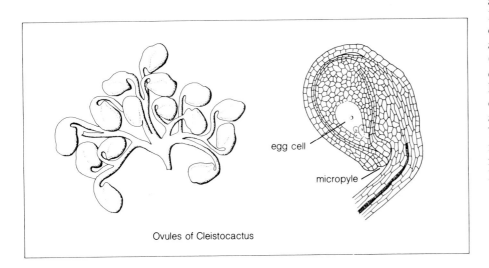

egg cell

micropyle

Ovules of Cleistocactus

pollen grain. The pollen grains only require a sugar solution in order to germinate, and this they find on the surface of the stigma. If the parts of the pollen grain and tube are dyed it is possible to see what is termed the vegetative nucleus, which controls the growth of the pollen tube, at the tip of the tube extending from the germinated pollen grain. Behind it is the generative nucleus. The pollen tube now attaches itself to an ovule inside the ovary. The ovule has two coats (integuments), which leave only a small orifice (micropyle) open for the entry of the pollen tube. The generative nucleus divides into two sperm nuclei, one of which eventually fuses with the egg cell, which is located just behind the micropyle. This process is known as fertilization, and produces a new combination of genetic material from the mother and father plant. The second sperm nucleus fuses with the secondary embryo sac nucleus. After this double

former micropyle is also often recognizable on the ripe seed as a minute orifice. The seed shell is often finely patterned, and pictures taken with a scanning electron microscope show this in beautiful detail (see pages 22-3). Many cactus seeds also feature other specialized structures, such as a seed coat (aril) or a strophiole. The aril forms a bulge around the ripening seed, and is formed from the minute stalk of the ovule. A strophiole is a more or less spongy or corky appendage close to the micropyle.

When the seed germinates, it first swells up. The seed shell then bursts open, releasing the radicle. Initially the most important task for the seed is to absorb water, as the nutritive substances in the seed are sufficient for a short period only. As cactus seeds usually germinate directly on the ground the small green embryos are able to begin photosynthesis very quickly. The conditions required for

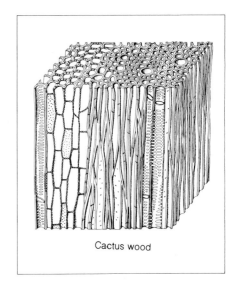

Cactus wood

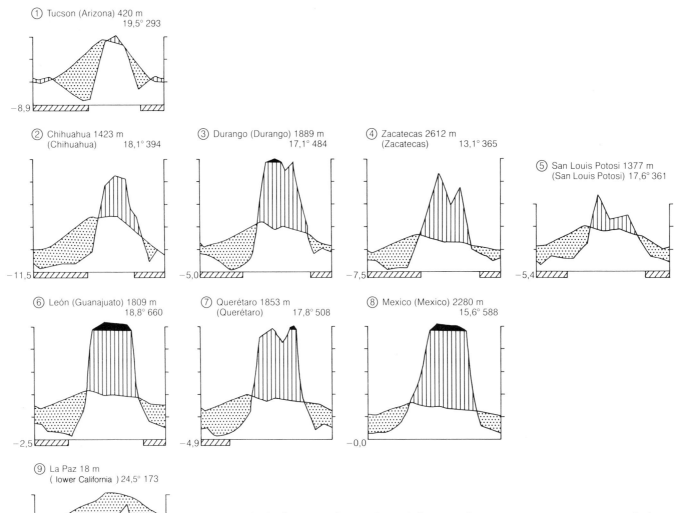

① Tucson (Arizona) 420 m
19,5° 293
−8,9

② Chihuahua 1423 m
(Chihuahua) 18,1° 394
−11,5

③ Durango (Durango) 1889 m
17,1° 484
−5,0

④ Zacatecas 2612 m
(Zacatecas) 13,1° 365
−7,5

⑤ San Louis Potosi 1377 m
(San Louis Potosi) 17,6° 361
−5,4

⑥ León (Guanajuato) 1809 m
18,8° 660
−2,5

⑦ Querétaro 1853 m
(Querétaro) 17,8° 508
−4,9

⑧ Mexico (Mexico) 2280 m
15,6° 588
−0,0

⑨ La Paz 18 m
(lower California) 24,5° 173

Climate of important cactus-growing regions

Cacti occur in North and South America in a very wide variety of climates. The most easily understood representations of climate are the climatic diagrams developed by Walter. To allow comparison we have included a number of diagrams of this type drawn from the *Klimadiagramm-Weltatlas* by H. Walter and L. Lieth (1967). Those selected refer to some of the most important cactus growing regions.

In this type of climatic diagram the temperature variation and the level of precipitation for each month are represented as graphs on a suitable scale. From the way in which the two curves overlap we can see the dry periods (dotted areas) and the moist periods (hatched areas) at a glance. The general data for annual average temperature and annual precipitation (top right on each diagram) are less informative, as it is the distribution and variation which are the important factors. On the other hand, the period in which frosts might occur (diagonal hatched bars under some diagrams) is very important, as it indicates the hardness of the winter, as does the absolute minimum temperature (the lowest temperature ever recorded) which is stated at bottom left on some of the diagrams.

The first of the four climatic diagrams for North America is of Tucson in Arizona, the region where the giant columnar cacti *Carnegiea gigantea* grow. Some rain falls in winter and in summer, but there are arid periods in between. Slight frosts are possible over a large part of the year. Chihuahua in the Northern highlands of Mexico has a similar climate, except that the precipitation falls almost exclusively in the Summer. The remaining places on the Mexican highlands - Durango, Zacatecas, León in the state of Guanajuato, Querétaro and Mexico in the far South - all have a very similar type of climate. In general terms precipitation increases towards the south, and the possible frost period becomes slightly shorter.

Climatic diagrams of South America

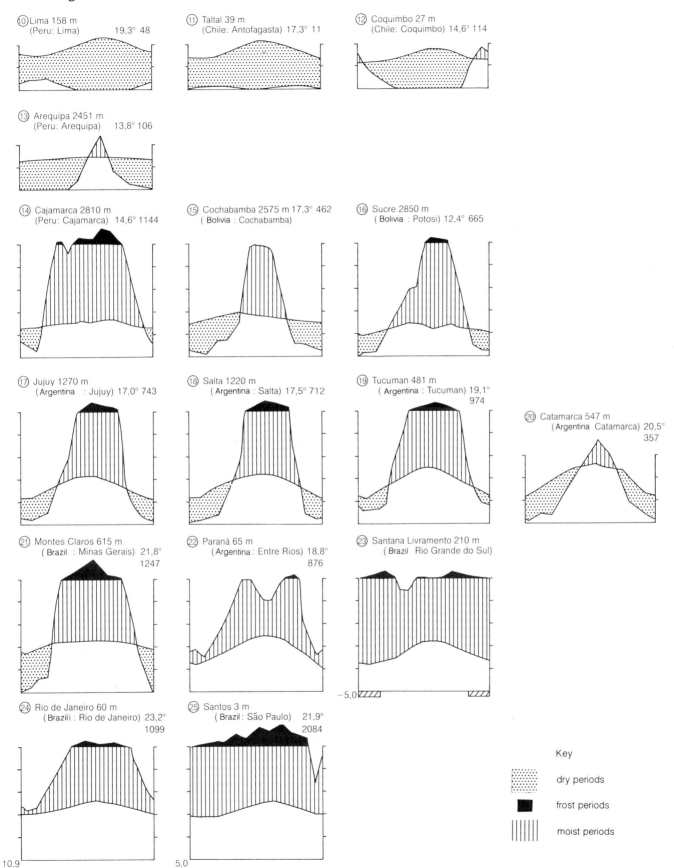

⑩ Lima 158 m
(Peru: Lima)   19,3° 48

⑪ Taltal 39 m
(Chile: Antofagasta) 17,3° 11

⑫ Coquimbo 27 m
(Chile: Coquimbo) 14,6° 114

⑬ Arequipa 2451 m
(Peru: Arequipa)   13,8° 106

⑭ Cajamarca 2810 m
(Peru: Cajamarca) 14,6° 1144

⑮ Cochabamba 2575 m 17,3° 462
(Bolivia : Cochabamba)

⑯ Sucre 2850 m
(Bolivia : Potosi) 12,4° 665

⑰ Jujuy 1270 m
(Argentina   : Jujuy) 17,0° 743

⑱ Salta 1220 m
(Argentina : Salta) 17,5° 712

⑲ Tucuman 481 m
(Argentina : Tucuman) 19,1°
                                    974

⑳ Catamarca 547 m
(Argentina Catamarca) 20,5°
                                        357

㉑ Montes Claros 615 m
(Brazil : Minas Gerais) 21,8°
                                       1247

㉒ Paraná 65 m
(Argentina : Entre Rios) 18,8°
                                       876

㉓ Santana Livramento 210 m
(Brazil Rio Grande do Sul)

−5,0

㉔ Rio de Janeiro 60 m
(Brazili : Rio de Janeiro) 23,2°
                                         1099

㉕ Santos 3 m
(Brazil: São Paulo)   21,9°
                                    2084

10,9

5,0

Key

dry periods

frost periods

moist periods

31

La Paz on the lower Californian peninsula offers a different climatic type. Here every month is arid, i.e. the rate of evaporation is greater than that of precipitation. Water is available to plants for only a very short time after each rainfall, and usually in the summer only. The climatic diagrams are based on average values taking account of measurements over many years.

In the drier climates the variations from year to year are usually very substantial, thus it is not rare for conditions to be much more extreme than those shown in the average climatic diagrams shown here. The more important cactus regions in South America are even more variable in terms of climate than those of North America. In order to allow easier comparison between the climatic diagrams of the Northern and Southern hemispheres, the months of the latter regions are arranged so that the warmest months fall in the centre of the diagram, i.e. they begin with the month of July, rather than January.

The western side of the Andean slope facing the Pacific Ocean consists of a region of desert and semi-desert stretching from Northern Peru to central Chile, which is rich in cacti. As examples of conditions here we have included the climatic diagrams for Lima in Peru and Taltal in Northern Chile. Both show extremely low precipitation. Rainfall increases rapidly at quite a small distance from the coast towards the Andean declivity. Coquimbo in central Chile has a rainy period in winter, and represents a transitional area between the desert and the Mediterranean climate found further south. In the more elevated sites in the Andes, which are home to a great many popular species of cacti such as Lobivias, Rebutias, Sulcorebutias, Parodias, many species of *Echinopsis* etc., precipitation occurs mainly in the summer, with the winter being the dry season. At a still greater altitude average temperatures decrease steadily, and frost may occur in more or less long periods of the year. Arequipa in Peru, on the western slope of the Andes, is reminiscent of the Peruvian coastal desert with its long dry season, but its main precipitation occurs in summer. The

remaining climatic diagrams from the Andes are fairly similar, from Cajamarca in Northern Peru via Cochabamba and Sucre in Bolivia as far as Jujuy, Salta and Tucuman in Northern Argentina. Catamarca at the Eastern foot of the Andes is very low in precipitation. On the Eastern side of South America the open scrubby region known as the 'Caatinga' of the Brazilian states of Bahia and Minas Gerais is very rich in cacti. As an example of this type of climate we have included Montes Claros from Minas Gerais. It features very high average levels of temperature and annual precipitation, but the rain falls predominantly in summer, with a marked dry season in the winter.

Further south the precipitation is more evenly distributed. Paraná in Argentina is still fairly dry in the cooler season, while the climatic diagram for Santana Livramento in the Brazilian state of Rio Grande do Sul shows no arid season. Nevertheless a number of cacti, in particular species of *Notocactus, Gymnocalycium* and *Frailea*, come from the Rio Grande do Sul and neighbouring Uruguay. They grow on very well-drained, sandy soil, or on screes or rocks; at such sites there are relatively dry places in spite of the high precipitation.

The epiphytic cacti, which come mainly from the coastal rain forests of the states of Rio de Janeiro and Sao Paulo, experience virtually no dry period in their native habitat and very even, high temperatures the whole year round, as shown in the climatic diagrams for Rio de Janeiro and Santos.

It is clear that the many and varied species of popular cacti originate in very different climatic regions. Nevertheless the vast majority of species thrive quite satisfactorily if their native climatic type is simply imitated in a general manner. Most species can be fitted into one of the climatic types shown in the following table. Some species, for example those from the Rocky Mountains in North America, do not fit into any of the six, and they are especially difficult to cultivate. In the table the numbers of the climatic diagrams which fit the categories are stated in brackets.

Top left: Columnar cacti and Opuntias in Arizona

Top right: Stenocereus hystrix in Cuba

Bottom left: The giant cactus Carnegiea gigantea in the Arizona desert

Bottom right: Teddy bear cacti (Opuntia bigelovii) in the evening sunshine in the Mojave desert.

Mammillaria halei in lower California.

Matucana weberbaueri in its native habitat in Peru

Climatic type	Important cactus locations
1. Dry upland and mountain climate (2-8, 13-20); with summer rain and dry, cool winter, often with slight frosts.	Mexican highlands, Andean uplands of Peru, Bolivia and N. Argentina
2. Warm coastal climate (9-11); with low, irregular precipitation, hot, no frosts.	Lower California, coastal desert from Peru to N. Chile
3. Tropical dry climate (21); even warmth with a rainy period in summer and a dry period in winter.	E. Brazil (Bahia, Minas Gerais)
4. Moist sub-tropical climate (22, 23); frost-free, warm climate with more or less evenly distributed precipitation, no distinct dry period.	S.E. Brazil (Rio Grande do Sul), Uruguay, Paraguay
5. Desert and semi-desert with winter rain (12); with long summer dry period, no frosts.	Central Chile, S. California
6. Rain forest climate (24,25); even warmth and high precipitation distributed over the entire year.	Atlantic coast of Mexico and Central America, coastal mountains of Brazilian E. coast, especially the states of Rio de Janeiro and Sao Paulo.

The development of the cactus system

When Europeans first came face to face with cacti, after the discovery of America, they were undoubtedly amazed at such curious plant forms. Nevertheless not many species of cactus were brought back to Europe at first. A few which did arrive, such as Opuntias, very quickly escaped and established themselves wild in the Mediterranean area, and today have all the appearance of indigenous species. Linnaeus, the great Swedish natural history researcher who introduced the present method of scientific plant and animal nomenclature, knew only 25 species of cactus in 1753. These he included in the single genus of *Cactus*.

The voyage of Alexander von Humboldt to Mexico and South America, and the voyages of discovery of others, eventually brought cacti to the attention of more and more people. The Geneva botanist P. de Candolle was able to distinguish 164 species in 1828. Cacti now became increasingly popular as house plants, and for cultivation in greenhouses. Karl Spitzweg's painting of 'the cactus lover' is well known. Gradually large private collections were assembled. The largest of the last century was probably that of the Prince of Salm-Dyck, who himself described many new species. The German doctor Georg Engelmann, who emigrated to America, was the first botanist to travel through the south-west of the United States, where he discovered and described a very large number of new species, especially Opuntias and Echinocerei. In 1898 the Professor of Botany at Berlin, Karl Schumann, wrote his *Gesamtbeschreibung der Kakteen*, which was the first extensive work dealing with cacti. His division of the plants into three main groups, the sub-families Pereskioideae, Opuntioideae and Cactoideae (Cereoideae), has not been questioned since that time (see page 36). Schumann was acquainted with 670 species and defined 21 genera. Almost all columnar cacti were included in the genus *Cereus*, and only

Browningia altissima in Peru

a small number of genera were distinguished among the globular cacti. The bulk of the species was encompassed by just two genera: *Echinocactus* and *Mammillaria*.

The second major work on cacti was produced in America. The botanists Nathaniel L. Britton, director of the Botanical Gardens of New York, and Joseph N. Rose travelled through Mexico, the United States and several South American countries. They observed many species in their natural habitat, and were able to collect them. This was the richest collection of

material ever assembled, and resulted in their four-volume work *The Cactaceae*. Britton and Rose sub-divided many of the earlier, more or less artificial genera into smaller more natural ones. These new genera were based principally on the flower formation rather than on the external form of the plants. The work of Britton and Rose became the springboard for all later cactus systems, although the 124 genera they established were considered to be too narrowly defined by many people. In general terms their closely defined genera only gained general acceptance

after the Second World War. The earlier names coined by Schumann remained in use for a long time, especially within the European cactus trade. Clearly the earlier divisions according to external form had been of greater practical value, because it was easier to classify non-flowering plants. Now it was only possible to establish the genus of plants when they produced flowers.

Britton and Rose also sub-divided the Cactoideae into eight simple and clear sub-groups (see page 38). The German succulents researcher Alwin Berger was then the first to attempt to classify cacti more phylogenetically, i.e. according to their development over time. In America the work of Britton and Rose has remained the standard reference work on cacti. In 1941 Marshall improved the genus key slightly, and included all the species which had been newly described in the meantime. The number of genera had now risen to 139 by dint of further sub-divisions. About 1700 species were known at that time.

In Europe however, Backeberg split up the genera of Britton and Rose, eventually creating 233 genera which he described in his *Cactus Lexicon*. Unfortunately his work includes no species key and even his genera are not always clearly defined. Apart from Backeberg's *Cactus Lexicon* and his earlier six-volume work *Die Cactaceae*, no more recent works have been produced which describe all species of cactus. Thus the works of Backeberg are usually still considered as being part of the basic reference library.

In addition to Backeberg, Professor Franz Buxbaum made an intensely detailed study of the family of cacti. Taking the work of Berger as his starting point, his main effort was aimed at reforming the cactus system on a more phylogenetic basis. He replaced the groups of Britton and Rose with quite differently defined groupings, based more closely on genetic history. In contrast to Backeberg he did not sub-divide the genera established by Britton & Rose and Marshall substantially, confining himself to the obviously non-uniform ones. In 1967 Hunt made an attempt to draw up unambiguous characteristics for all genera. He reunited many of the genera established by Britton and Rose, especially among the Phyllocacti, and ended up by naming 84 genera. However his genera, which are by no means excessively closely defined in comparison with other plant families, have not found wide acceptance. At least some of the minor genera established by Backeberg have since been reunited, and this is shown in the definitive list of cactus names drawn up by Donald in 1974 and published in the magazine *Ashingtonia*.

This work is probably the best basis for generic and species names which has been produced to date.

As well as the extensive works on cacti by the authors mentioned above, substantial contributions to our knowledge of cacti have been made by many cactus collectors in North and South America, including Haage, Cardenas, Rauh, Ritter, Rausch, Lau, Hutchison, Buining, Horst, Lembcke, Krahn, Knize and many others. Further details of at least some of the significant cactus researchers is to be found in the index of authors.

Summary of the sub-families of cacti

Sub-family **Pereskioideae**

Includes the genera *Pereskia, Rhodocactus* and *Maihuenia*
Slightly succulent shrubs or trees.
Flat, ribbed leaves or persistent cylindrical leaves without glochids.
Flowers without tube, ovary superior or inferior.
Seed without seed coat, black, glossy.

Sub-family **Opuntioideae**

Includes the genera *Peireskiopsis, Quiabentia, Opuntia, Pterocactus* and *Tacinga*
Stem succulent, flat or round-section leaves with glochids, soon falling off.
Flowers without tube or with short tube.
Ovary always inferior.
Seed with rock-hard seed coat, white or yellowish.

Sub-family **Cactoideae** (Cereoideae)

Includes all remaining cactus genera.
Stem succulent, without leaves, areoles rarely scaly, without glochids.
Flowers generally with distinct tube (except *Rhipsalis*), ovary always inferior.
Seed with seed coat or thin aril membrane only, black or brown.

The difficulties of cactus systematics

The most important systematic groups (categories) are as follows:

Category	Example
Division	Seed plants
Class	Dicotyledon (two seed leaves)
Order	Cactales
Family	Cactaceae (cacti)
Sub-family	Cactoideae
Tribe	Notocacteae
Genus	*Gymnocalycium*
Species	*mihanovichii* (Fric & Gürke)Br. & R.
Sub-species	
Variety	var. *friedrichii* Werderm.
Cultivar (sort)	cv. Rubra'

This hierarchy appears to be very clear, but in practice there are many difficulties. Let us consider more closely the various categories from the family down to the smallest units, the cultivars and sorts.

Families are for the most part clearly defined large groups, and this holds true for cacti. In the section of the book which discussed the external structure of cacti we saw how cacti differ clearly from all other families of seed plant in a whole series of characteristics. The three sub-families of cactus are also very clear and therefore generally acknowledged. They differ from each other in spine formation and in the structure of the flowers and seed (see page 36). By far the majority of genera and species belong to the sub-family Cactoideae. Within this sub-family, however, the tribes, or sub-groups, are by no means conclusively defined and there are now several different co-existent systems. They in turn have been modified in detail by many different authors. How is this possible? The layman could be excused for imagining that only one natural system can possibly exist, but the fact of the matter is that different systems arise when different authors prefer different types of characteristic on which to base their system.

The original principal basis of subdivision was the external form of the plant, with distinctions drawn between columnar, globular, warty, leaf-bearing and so on. This book also uses this criterion in an artificial genus key, but it does not coincide with natural groups. Columnar, globular and warty cacti have evolved many times independently of each other. For example, similar tubercles are found in the genera *Mammillaria* and *Rebutia*, but the flowers are produced at quite different positions: in *Mammillaria* they appear in the axils of the tubercles, and in *Rebutia* on the tips of the tubercles. The flowers and seed are also different in structure. *Mammillaria* occurs almost exclusively in North America, *Rebutia* in South America. The one common feature - the tubercles - is of little significance when compared with the many features which are different, and which indicate that the two are not closely related. Some closely related species occur in columnar and globular forms at the same time, e.g. amongst Lobivias or Echinocerei. In fact the external forms do not fall into natural groups. If we then consider other characteristics of non-flowering plants, such as the rib count and the spine formation, it ceases to be possible to establish natural groups in this way. Nevertheless, the external form is the characteristic of a plant which is easiest to establish, and for this reason it remains a very important aid in identifying the genera and species of cacti.

Berger and later Britton and Rose in particular included simple flower and seed characteristics in the basis of their system, as was standard and long-established practice with other plant families. When these supplementary characteristics were taken into account, the earlier genera based on external form were sub-divided to a very great degree. The system became much more complex, but at the same time more features were drawn upon in order to define the genera, and the new groups were separated by more natural boundaries. Newly discovered non-flowering plants could not be brought into the system at first. Soon it became clear that individual flower characteristics such as bilateral symmetry, different forms of covering on the flower and the tube, sealed nectar chambers, etc., had also evolved several times, i.e. they were convergent. Considered on their own these features were inconclusive about relationships between species. It is also clear that other unusual features do not necessarily express a relationship. For example, the location of the flowers in *Mammillaria* in the axils of unfurrowed tubercles appears to be very unusual, but according to Buxbaum this feature also developed several times. In fact to date no individual characteristics have been found which are reasonably widespread and which have only evolved once, and which could be used to define natural groups within the sub-family of Cactoideae. All the more important characteristics are such simple modifications that they could easily have evolved many times within unrelated groups.

In his system Backeberg emphasized very strongly the geographical distribution of the plants in addition to the external covering of the flowers. Groups separated according to geographical distribution alone are not satisfactory, however, and a plant whose natural location is not known, which is a cultivated species, or which now grows wild in the Mediterranean region or in Australia, should not be allowed to evade the clutches of the system so easily.

A system should always be based on the genetic features of the plant itself. Today Buxbaum's classification of the

The classification of cactus genera according to different systems (contd.)

Britton and Rose 1919–1923	Marshall 1941	Buxbaum 1974	in this book	Backeberg 1966
sub-family Cactoideae **tribe Leptocereae**				
Leptocereus	Leptocereus	Leptocereus	Leptocereus	Leptocereus
—	—	Calymmanthium	Calymmanthium	Calymmanthium
(Lemaireocereus)	(Lemaireocereus)	Armatocereus	Armatocereus	Armatocereus
Neoraimondia	Neoraimondia	Neoraimondia	Neoraimondia	Neoraimondia Neocardenasia
Neoabbottia	Neoabbottia	Neoabbottia	Neoabbottia	Neoabbottia
—	—	Samaipaticereus	Samaipaticereus	Samaipaticereus Yungasocereus
tribe Hylocereae				
Nyctocereus	Nyctocereus	Nyctocereus	Nyctocereus	Nyctocereus
Brachycereus	Brachycereus	Brachycereus	Brachycereus	Brachycereus
Peniocereus	Peniocereus	Peniocereus	Peniocereus	Peniocereus
	Neoevansia			
Wilcoxia	Wilcoxia	Wilcoxia	Wilcoxia	Wilcoxia
Acanthocereus	Acanthocereus	Acanthocereus	Acanthocereus	Acanthocereus
Dendrocereus	Dendrocereus	Dendrocereus	Dendrocereus	Dendrocereus
Harrisia —	Harrisia Eriocereus	Harrisia Eriocereus	Harrisia Eriocereus	Harrisia Eriocereus Roseocereus
Heliocereus	Heliocereus	Heliocereus	Heliocereus	Heliocereus
Aporocactus	Aporocactus	Aporocactus	Aporocactus	Aporocactus
Selenicereus Deamia	Selenicereus Deamia	Selenicereus	Selenicereus Deamia	Selenicereus Deamia
—	—	Cryptocereus	Cryptocereus	Cryptocereus
Strophocactus	Strophocactus	Strophocactus	Strophocactus	Strophocactus
Hylocereus Wilmattea	Hylocereus Wilmattea	Hylocereus	Hylocereus Wilmattea	Hylocereus Wilmattea
Mediocactus	Mediocactus	Mediocactus	Mediocactus	Mediocactus
Werckleocereus	Werckleocereus	Werckleocereus	Werckleocereus	Werckleocereus
Weberocereus	Weberocereus	Weberocereus	Weberocereus	Weberocereus
Eccremocactus	Eccremocactus	Eccremocactus	Eccremocactus	Eccremocactus

The classification of cactus genera according to different systems (contd.)

BRITTON and ROSE 1919–1923	MARSHALL 1941	BUXBAUM 1974	in this book	BACKEBERG 1966
Epiphyllum	Epiphyllum	Epiphyllum	Epiphyllum	Epiphyllum Marniera
Nopalxochia —	Nopalxochia —	Nopalxochia	Nopalxochia	Nopalxochia Pseudonopalxochia Lobeira
Chiapasia	Chiapasia	Chiapasia	Chiapasia	Chiapasia
Disocactus	Disocactus	Disocactus	Disocactus	Disocactus
Pseudorhipsalis	Pseudorhipsalis	Pseudorhipsalis	Pseudorhipsalis	Pseudorhipsalis
Wittia	Wittia	Wittia	Wittia	Wittia
Pfeiffera	Pfeiffera	Pfeiffera	Pfeiffera	Pfeiffera
Acanthorhipsalis	Acanthorhipsalis	Acanthorhipsalis	Acanthorhipsalis	Acanthorhipsalis
Erythrorhipsalis	Erythrorhipsalis	Erythrorhipsalis	Erythrorhipsalis	Erythrorhipsalis
Hatiora —	Hatiora —	Hatiora	Hatiora Pseudozygocactus	Hatiora Pseudozygocactus
Rhipsalidopsis	Rhipsalidopsis	Rhipsalidopsis	Rhipsalidopsis	Rhipsalidopsis
Schlumbergera	Schlumbergera	Schlumbergera	Schlumbergera	Schlumbergera Epiphyllopsis
Zygocactus Epiphyllanthus	Zygocactus Epiphyllanthus	Zygocactus	Epiphyllanthus	Zygocactus Epiphyllanthus
Rhipsalis	Rhipsalis	Rhipsalis	Rhipsalis	Rhipsalis
Lepismium	Lepismium	Lepismium	Lepismium	Lepismium

tribe Pachycereae

BRITTON and ROSE 1919–1923	MARSHALL 1941	BUXBAUM 1974	in this book	BACKEBERG 1966
—	—	Pterocereus	Pterocereus	Pterocereus
Escontria (Pachycereus, Cephalocereus)	Escontria (Pachycereus, Pilocereus)	Escontria	Escontria (some Pterocereus)	Escontria Anisocereus
Lemaireocereus (Pachycereus)	Lemaireocereus	Heliabravoa Stenocereus	Heliabravoa Stenocereus	Heliabravoa Stenocereus Lemaireocereus Ritterocereus Isolatocereus Hertrichocereus Marshallocereus Marginatocereus
Pachycereus	Pachycereus, some Lemaireocereus	Pachycereus Mitrocereus Pseudomitrocereus (Mitrocereus)	Pachycereus Mitrocereus Backebergia	Pachycereus Mitrocereus Backebergia

41

The classification of cactus genera according to different systems (contd.)

BRITTON and ROSE 1919–1923	MARSHALL 1941	BUXBAUM 1974	in this book	BACKEBERG 1966
Machaerocereus	Machaerocereus	Machaerocereus	Machaerocereus	Machaerocereus
Rathbunia	Rathbunia	Rathbunia	Rathbunia	Rathbunia
Carnegiea	Carnegiea	Carnegiea	Carnegiea	Carnegiea
Lophocereus	Lophocereus	Lophocereus	Lophocereus	Lophocereus
Cephalocereus	(Pilocereus) Cephalocereus, Pilocereus Cephalocereus Pilocereus —	Neobuxbaumia Cephalocereus	Neobuxbaumia Cephalocereus Haseltonia Pilosocereus Neodawsonia	Neobuxbaumia Rooksbya Cephalocereus Haseltonia Pilosocereus Neodawsonia
(Lemaireocereus)	(Lemaireocereus)	Polaskia	Polaskia	Polaskia
Myrtillocactus	Myrtillocactus	Myrtillocactus	Myrtillocactus	Myrtillocactus
tribe Browningieae				
—	—	Rauhocereus	Rauhocereus	Rauhocereus
—	—	Castellanosia	Castellanosia	Castellanosia
Browningia — —	Browningia — —	Browningia	Browningia	Browningia Azureocereus Gymnocereus
tribe Cereae				
Jasminocereus	Jasminocereus	Jasminocereus	Jasminocereus	Jasminocereus
Stetsonia	Stetsonia	Stetsonia	Stetsonia	Stetsonia
Cereus	Cereus	Cereus	Cereus Subpilocereus	Cereus Subpilocereus
Monvillea	Monvillea	Monvillea Praecereus Brasilicereus	Monvillea Brasilicereus	Monvillea Brasilicereus
(Cephalocereus)	(Pilocereus)	Coleocephalocereus	Coleocephalocereus	Coleocephalocereus
— —	— —	Pseudopilocereus Buiningia	Pseudopilocereus Buiningia	Pseudopilocereus (Appendix) Buiningia (Appendix)
(Cephalocereus)	Stephanocereus	Stephanocereus	Stephanocereus	Stephanocereus
Arrojadoa	Arrojadoa	Arrojadoa	Arrojadoa	Arrojadoa
tribe Trichocereae				
—	—	—	Lasiocereus	Lasiocereus
Trichocereus (some Lobivia)	Trichocereus (some Lobivia)	Trichocereus	Trichocereus	Trichocereus Leucostele Helianthocereus

The classification of cactus genera according to different systems (contd.)

Britton and Rose 1919–1923	Marshall 1941	Buxbaum 1974	in this book	Backeberg 1966
Echinopsis (some Lobivia)	Echinopsis (some Lobivia)	Echinopsis	Echinopsis	Echinopsis Pseudolobivia
(Lobivia, Echinopsis)	Acanthocalycium	Acanthocalycium	Acanthocalycium	Acanthocalycium
(Lobivia)	(Lobivia, Eriosyce)	Soehrensia	(Trichocereus)	Soehrensia
Lobivia	Lobivia	Lobivia	Lobivia	Lobivia Acantholobivia
Chamaecereus	Chamaecereus	Chamaecereus		Chamaecereus
(Trichocereus)	(Trichocereus)	Weberbauerocereus	Weberbauerocereus	Weberbauerocereus
Binghamia	Binghamia	Haageocereus	Haageocereus	Haageocereus
Espostoa	Espostoa	Espostoa	Espostoa	Espostoa Pseudoespostoa
— Facheiroa — —	Facheiroa		Facheiroa Thrixanthocereus Vatricania	Facheiroa Thrixanthocereus Vatricania
(Cephalocereus)	(Cephalocereus)	Austrocephalocereus	Austrocephalocereus	Austrocephalocereus
Zehntnerella	Zehntnerella	Zehntnerella	Zehntnerella	Zehntnerella
Leocereus	Leocereus	Leocereus	Leocereus	Leocereus
(Echinopsis) —	Arthrocereus —	Arthrocereus Pygmaeocereus	Arthrocereus Pygmaeocereus	Arthrocereus Pygmaeocereus
(Echinopsis)	(Echinopsis)	Setiechinopsis	Setiechinopsis	Setiechinopsis
Rebutia	Rebutia	Rebutia	Rebutia	Rebutia Aylostera Mediolobivia
—	(Rebutia)	Sulcorebutia	Sulcorebutia	Sulcorebutia
Mila	Mila	Mila	Mila	Mila
Borzicactus — — —	Borzicactus — — —	Borzicactus (Matucana) Loxanthocereus	Borzicactus Hildewintera	Borzicactus Clistanthocereus Seticereus Bolivicereus Loxanthocereus Akersia Winterocereus
Oreocereus —	Oreocereus	Oreocereus Morawtzia	Oreocereus	Oreocereus Morawetzia
Arequipa	Arequipa	Arequipa	Arequipa	Arequipa
Matucana	Matucana	Matucana	Matucana	Matucana Submatucana
Denmoza	Denmoza	Denmoza	Denmoza	Denmoza
Oroya	Oroya	Oroya	Oroya	Oroya

The classification of cactus genera according to different systems (contd.)

Britton and Rose 1919–1923	Marshall 1941	Buxbaum 1974	in this book	Backeberg 1966
Cleistocactus — —	Cleistocactus — —	Cleistocactus	Cleistocactus	Cleistocactus Cephalocleistocactus Seticleistocactus
—	(Cephalocereus)	Micranthocereus	Micranthocereus	Micranthocereus
tribe Notocacteae				
Corryocactus Erdisia	Corryocactus Erdisia	Corryocactus	Corryocactus	Corryocactus Erdisia
Austrocactus	(Notocactus)	Austrocactus	Austrocactus	Austrocactus
Neoporteria — — (Malacocarpus) (Malacocarpus)	Neoporteria — — Pyrrhocactus (Parodia)	Neoporteria Pyrrhocactus Islaya	Neoporteria	Neoporteria Neochilenia Horridocactus Reicheocactus Delaetia Pyrrhocactus Islaya
Copiapoa —	Copiapoa —	Copiapoa Pilocopiapoa	Copiapoa	Copiapoa Pilocopiapoa
Malacocarpus	Notocactus Malacocarpus	Notocactus	Notocactus	Notocactus Brasilicactus Eriocactus Malacocarpus (Wigginsia)
Frailea	Frailea	Frailea	Frailea	Frailea
Astrophytum	Astrophytum	Astrophytum	Astrophytum	Astrophytum
—	—	Uebelmannia	Uebelmannia	Uebelmannia (**Appendix**)
Hickenia	Parodia	Parodia	Parodia	Parodia
—	Blossfeldia	Blossfeldia	Blossfeldia	Blossfeldia
Gymnocalycium —	Gymnocalycium —	Gymnocalycium	Gymnocalycium	Gymnocalycium Brachycalycium
(Lobivia)	Weingartia	Weingartia	Weingartia	Weingartia
—	Neowerdermannia	Neowerdermannia	Neowerdermannia	Neowerdermannia
Eriosyce —	Eriosyce —	Eriosyce	Eriosyce	Eriosyce Rhodentiophila
Eulychnia	Eulychnia	Eulychnia	Eulychnia	Eulychnia Philippicereus
Discocactus	Discocactus	Discocactus	Discocactus	Discocactus
Cactus	Melocactus	Melocactus	Melocactus	Melocactus

The classification of cactus genera according to different systems (contd.)

BRITTON and ROSE 1919–1923	MARSHALL 1941	BUXBAUM 1974	in this book	BACKEBERG 1966
tribe Echinocereae				
Bergerocactus	Bergerocactus	Bergerocactus	Bergerocactus	Bergerocactus
Echinocereus	Echinocereus	Echinocereus	Echinocereus Morangaya	Echinocereus
tribe Cacteae				
Echinocactus Homalocephala	Echinocactus Homalocephala	Echinocactus	Echinocactus	Echinocactus Homalocephala
Pediocactus — Utahia Sclerocactus — Toumeya —	Pediocactus — Utahia Sclerocactus Coloradoa Toumeya —	Pediocactus — Utahia Sclerocactus Coloradoa Toumeya	Pediocactus	Pediocactus Pilocanthus Utahia Sclerocactus Coloradoa Toumeya Navajoa
Ancistrocactus	Ancistrocactus	Ancistrocactus	Ancistrocactus	Ancistrocactus
Echinomastus	Echinomastus	Echinomastus	(Neolloydia)	Echinomastus
Thelocactus, (Ferocactus) (Ferocactus) Hamatocactus	Thelocactus Hamatocactus	Thelocactus Hamatocactus	Thelocactus (Ancistrocactus) (Ancistrocactus, Ferocactus)	Thelocactus Glandulicactus Hamatocactus
— —	(Strombocactus) —	(Toumeya) Normanbokea	Turbinicarpus	Turbinicarpus (Pelecyphora, Gymnocactus)
Neolloydia — —	Neolloydia (some Thelocactus) —	Neolloydia Rapicactus Cumarinia (Dolichothele)	Neolloydia	Neolloydia Gymnocactus
Lophophora	Lophophora	Lophophora	Lophophora	Lophophora
Strombocactus	Strombocactus	Strombocactus	Strombocactus	Strombocactus
—	Aztekium	Aztekium	Aztekium	Aztekium
Leuchtenbergia	Leuchtenbergia	Leuchtenbergia	Leuchtenbergia	Leuchtenbergia
—	Obregonia	Obregonia	Obregonia	Obregonia
Ariocarpus —	Ariocarpus Neogomesia	Ariocarpus	Ariocarpus	Ariocarpus Roseocactus Neogomesia
Epithelantha	Epithelantha	Epithelantha	Epithelantha	Epithelantha
Pelecyphora	Pelecyphora	Pelecyphora	Pelecyphora	Pelecyphora
—	Encephalocarpus	Encephalocarpus	Encephalocarpus	Encephalocarpus

The classification of cactus genera according to different systems (contd.)

BRITTON and ROSE 1919–1923	MARSHALL 1941	BUXBAUM 1974	in this book	BACKEBERG 1966
Ferocactus	Ferocactus	Ferocactus	Ferocactus	Ferocactus
Echinofossulocactus	Echinofossulocactus	Echinofossulocactus	Echinofossulocactus	Echinofossulocactus
Escobaria	Escobaria	Escobaria	Escobaria	Escobaria
Neobesseya	Neobesseya	Neobesseya	Neobesseya	Neobesseya
Ortegocactus	Ortegocactus	Ortegocactus	Ortegocactus	Ortegocactus
Neomammillaria	Mammillaria (and Porfiria)	Mammillaria (and Mammiloydia, Leptocladodia)	Mammillaria	Mammillaria (and Porfiria)
Bartschella Phellosperma Dolichothele (Neomammillaria) (Neomammillaria) Solisia Mamillopsis Cochemiea	Solisia Mamillopsis Cochemiea	Dolichothele Oehmea Pseudomammillaria (Mammillaria) Mamillopsis Cochemiea		Krainzia Bartschella Phellosperma Dolichothele Solisia Mamillopsis Cochemiea
Coryphantha	Coryphantha	Coryphantha	Coryphantha	Coryphantha Lepidocoryphantha

156, Backeberg 233) shows that their boundaries are very flexible. This situation has resulted in innumerable synonyms, as many species are listed in genera which have been defined more or less broadly by different authorities. A large proportion of cactus species is known by two or more commonly used names.

As the genera are such important systematic units, they at least should be very clear groups which are marked out from each other unambiguously by means of particular characteristics. Groups which do not satisfy this criterion should be classified as less significant units, e.g. as sub-genera, like several of Backeberg's minor genera. In this book we have attempted to check that all the genera are to some extent clearly defined by particular characteristics. The basic unit of the system is the species. The species is the natural community within which propagation takes place, and it too should be clearly defined from all other species within the genus. Checking that this is the case is a much more difficult task.

Defining a species, as with a genus, calls for standardized descriptions, i.e. descriptions based on a common pattern. In many cases the species descriptions are very incomplete. Even when a description seems to be highly detailed a gap may subsequently appear when characteristics which were previously not considered significant are raised in status. For this reason the 'type specimen', i.e. the plant from which the first description was prepared, should be preserved in a public collection. Living plants, if possible cuttings taken from the original type specimen, should also be cultivated in different public collections. This is relatively easy to accomplish in the case of small globular cacti. For larger columnar cacti or Opuntias only gardens enjoying a warm climate can be considered, where the cacti can be kept in the open air; Southern Europe, California and Florida are the obvious choices. The type specimen may, of course, supply a complete description, but such a description is by no means sufficient to define the species in absolute terms. For this the range of

variation at the native location has to be considered, so that minor variations are taken into account. A further point of particular importance in the definition of a species is detailed knowledge of its geographical distribution. In many cases this is very imperfectly known. Collectors frequently fail to state the exact location of their find. Many species are only known from one site, or from a few locations. Unfortunately it is precisely the geographical distribution of a species which gives the first indication that the plant represents a geographical race or sub-species, or even on occasion a naturally occurring hybrid.

The descriptions of most species of cactus are incomplete even in quite simple characteristics, and their breadth of variation and geographical distribution insufficiently known. Most cases of natural or artificial hybrids have only been observed as isolated examples. For this reason it is hardly surprising that cactus species continually have to be split up, re-united, or their definitions modified.

Geographical races are today mostly classified as sub-species. Such races, distinguished by certain characteristics, inhabit particular regions, but at the borders they blend into hybrid forms with others, as they readily hybridize between themselves. On the other hand genuine species only exceptionally form hybrids, even though they may be very similar in appearance and occur in the same area. Even though particular species are found to hybridize readily under experimental conditions, the same does not necessarily occur in nature, where distances are greater, or a natural obstacle, e.g. a range of mountains, keeps the two apart. In practice this means that two separate species have developed, even though the dividing line between them may not have been finally drawn. If the distribution regions overlap at any point, the two species may be found to blend completely into one another once more. In contrast to other plant familes, hardly any sub-species of cacti have been established to date, because the geographical distribution of the vast majority of species is still very imperfectly known. Many of today's species may well prove to be tomorrow's sub-species. A variety has one or a few distinct differences in its appearance, but it is not usually centred on a particular area within the distribution region of the species, but occurs sporadically in several regions. A form usually only differs in a single characteristic, e.g. by a slightly different flower colour. A sort or cultivar is somewhat similar, but has been cultivated or raised by man.

Natural or artificial hybrids do not fit into this sequence of systematic classification. If allowed to reproduce sexually, the characteristics of the new plants will show a very wide variation. If the parent species are not known, as is often the case with artificial hybrids, they can be considered to be sorts of the nearest species.

The only plants not covered by the system are those modified by their environment. Cacti, however, tend to be highly variable, especially in culture. The spines vary in number and length within certain limits, even the colour might be slightly different,

Many species are highly variable in flower colour, as in this example: Lobivia jajoiana

but these variations are not inherited. The result of this characteristic is that there is not a natural line of descent, as is usual in systematics. All these problems illustrate the difficulties involved in developing a clear, satisfactory cactus system. Moreover cacti as a group of plants are still developing vigorously, and in consequence the species and genera are still very closely related.

A system's first purpose is classification, i.e. it must define clear groups by means of certain characteristic features. An indispensable part of this process is the key, for it is the key which shows whether the stated descriptions really allow the genera and species to be distinguished. Good, clear descriptions which are simply listed in sequence do not immediately show the differences between species. As a means of classifying they are therefore far too complex. It is not possible to compare each species in turn with a large number of long descriptions. A good classification must also embrace all known species.

In practice this means that wherever possible a classification should only make use of simple characteristics, as

these are all that is known of the majority of species. A thorough classification which only covers a proportion of known species is no replacement for a previous, less thorough classification which does include all species. For this reason Backeberg's work is still often preferable as a classification, even though it has obvious deficiencies; no other comprehensive work has been produced to date. A good classification usually concurs more or less with a natural system, i.e. a system which acknowledges varying degrees of inter-relationship. In fact a good classification, like a good system, is not based on individual characteristics alone, but on the widest possible variety of characteristics (e.g. see sub-families of cacti, page 36). It is an unfortunate fact that clear descriptions of a large proportion of cactus genera, including at least the three dozen or so simplest and most significant features, are simply not available. Good species keys do exist for a very small number of genera, which include no more than a small number of species.

The second important task of systematics is to clarify the phylogeny

47

or evolutionary history, but this is even more difficult. To fulfil this aim we have to find series of characteristics and follow their line of development. However, it is seldom that the process throws up clearly definable groups; more often we find branches which are only interconnected by long sequences or progressions of modified characteristics. Defining these 'tendencies' in words presents the greatest difficulty. For this reason it is rare that a phylogenetic scheme can replace a classification. On the other hand it may prove to offer an extremely valuable means of deepening our understanding of a group, may provide the stimulus for new research, and may in so doing further the cause of classification.

Cactus names

Most cactus enthusiasts are keen to known the correct names of their plants, but this is not an easy matter.

As is the case with other indoor plants and orchids the number of English names which has been invented is very small, and enthusiasts have been obliged to come to terms with the scientific names, usually based on Latin or Greek. This form of nomenclature does have certain advantages: the names are used and acknowledged internationally, and they are unambiguous; as far as possible they are best left unaltered. Unfortunately cactus scientific names have suffered far more amendments than the names of other plant groups. Let us consider one scientific name as an example:

Echinocactus chrysacanthion K. Schum.

The first word, always written with a capital, is the generic name, and all species of that genus share it. This part of the name is of particular importance to the beginner as the species within a genus often require very similar cultural conditions, and it is usually sufficient to know the genus in order to provide the correct conditions for the plant. The second name, which is always written in lower case nowadays, is species-specific, and thus defines the species. Although the genus name may be used on its own

the species name may not, as the same term may recur in any of the vast variety of plant genera. Each genus name cannot be used more than once in the plant kingdom.

The final part of the designation is the name of the author, i.e. the first person to describe the species. The author is not necessarily the individual who discovered the plant. The longer authors' names are usually abbreviated, but they should not be shortened too drastically or in an arbitrary way (see abbreviations of authors' names at the end of this book). The author's name is hardly ever mentioned when people are discussing cacti, but scientific papers and the more painstaking written works always state it. In fact, in relation to cactus names the author's name is very important, as there are so many names in use which refer to the same species.

According to the Rule of Priority the first published name for a species is essentially the only valid one. If the same species is later ascribed another name erroneously then the later name is invalid. This does not occur very often and is easily corrected. A more frequent occurrence is the subsequent sub-division of an original cactus genus into smaller genera. If this should happen, the genus name is changed. In our example the name now runs as follows:

Parodia chrysacanthion (K. Schum.) Backeb.

The original species name is retained, the original author is placed in brackets, and the name of the author who allotted the species to the new genus is added. The original name is now termed the basionym. In many cases the sub-division of a genus into several small ones does not find universal acceptance, and in this instance the two names co-exist as synonyms, i.e. names with the same meaning. It can be confusing and annoying to find several names for one and the same species, but this does not necessarily imply a mistake. Greater difficulties arise when two authors use the same or an entirely different name for something which is only slightly different, and their descriptions do not entirely agree.

Quite often the original description is inaccurate or incomplete, and later has to be completed. If this second author notes fairly major variations, his name is also added in the following form:

Backeb. emend. Buxb. (emend = emendavit, i.e. 'amended by').

In many cases it has proved impossible to clarify a confused issue. For this reason there is now a mandatory procedure to be carried out when a new species is discovered: a specimen of the original plant has to be lodged in a public collection as a 'type specimen', as has already been mentioned. By this means it is possible to check or supplement the species description at a later date, should doubt arise. The description, i.e. the itemizing of those features which distinguish the new plant from the most closely related species, must be written in Latin. This procedure is laid down in a comprehensive book entitled the *International Code for Botanic Nomenclature*.

Very often a plant's systematic status is altered, e.g. a species may be downgraded to a variety, or - more rarely - a variety may be upgraded to a species. Here again the original varietal or species name is retained, the original author is placed in brackets, and the new author is added.

For example, the species *Rebutia violaciflora* Backeb. has now become the variety *Rebutia minuscula* K. Schum. var. *violaciflora* (Backeb.) Buin. & Donald.

Synonyms have flourished and multiplied more abundantly amongst cacti than in any other plant group. There are many reasons for this, as explained earlier in this book, but it is always advisable not to use provisional names, i.e. names which are not validated by the proper description (nomen nudum, abbreviated to n.n., plural: nomina nuda). Such names only foster confusion. It is far better to list such plants simply under the name of the collector and its collection number, e.g. A. Müller 627, or at least to make the provisional name clearly identifiable as such by setting it in quotation marks.

The species names of cacti are usually more permanent than the genus names, and the unchanging species names and bracketed author names are very helpful in recognizing synonyms. For example, the two names *Opuntia floccosa* Salm-Dyck and *Tephrocactus floccosus* (Salm-Dyck) Backeb. can be easily recognized as synonyms with the help of the common species name *floccosus* and author Salm-Dyck.

The genus name is not based on a description but simply refers to the first species of that genus to be described. Thus the extent and content of a genus often changes substantially when new species are discovered. Only the first species remains unchanged. Above the level of the species the names are only very loosely connected with the descriptions. A further complication is that many generic names are used in different ways; sometimes they refer to the original group, occasionally to a broader group, and sometimes to a narrower, sub-divided group. The plant's name hardly ever indicates this, the appendices s.l. (sensu lato - in the wider sense) and s.str. (sensu stricto - in the narrower sense) or sensu (in the sense of), e.g. sensu Backeb., being used rarely.

Geographical distribution of cacti

Cacti are almost exclusively confined to the New World. A few isolated species occur in Canada in the north, while to the south they extend to the southern tip of South America. In the Old World only a few *Rhipsalis* species are to be found. This hardly seems to be sufficient evidence for claiming that cacti had already developed before the continents drifted apart in the Cretaceous period. The *Rhipsalis* species of the Old World are virtually identical to those of the New World; an unlikely situation after such a long separation. Moreover, *Rhipsalis* does not belong to the most primitive genera. The original genera are those of the sub-families of Pereskioideae and Opuntioideae. In fact *Rhipsalis* is a representative of one of the most derivative genera of the highly developed Cereoideae. In view of this

we have to consider the possibility of dispersal by birds. *Rhipsalis* has mistletoe-like berries with sticky seed, which are the most likely type to be distributed by birds. Evidence of this is the large distribution area of *Rhipsalis* in the New World. Another possibility is that English sailors in the sailing ship epoch took *Rhipsalis* branches back to England instead of the mistletoe branches which are so popular at Christmas time, and that the plants spread from there.

In practice then, cacti are virtually confined to the New World. Other groups of succulents are also confined to either the New or the Old World. For example, the Agaves only occur in the New World. Aloes, Stapelianthus, Mesembryanthemaceae and succulent Euphorbiaceae, in contrast, are confined to the Old World, with South Africa boasting a very large number of species. The only succulents with virtually world-wide distribution are the thick-leaved Crassulaceae, although many other plant groups are represented in all continents. We can deduce from this that most succulent groups, with the exception of the Crassulaceae, are not very old in terms of the Earth's history. In many desert and dry regions, for example the Sahara and Australia, there are almost no succulents, which indicates that the succulent groups have not reached all the regions which would be suitable for them to colonize. Further evidence of this is the fact that Opuntias quickly became completely wild in Australia and South Africa once they had been introduced, and subsequently became a pest. In the Mediterranean region Opuntias and Agaves have also made themselves quite at home since the discovery of America. That cacti are a relatively young group, and are still in the process of evolution, is clear from the close relationships between the genera. Artificial hybridization is possible between very many of them, and even Pereskias, which look so different from other cacti, can be used as the rootstock onto which any other species can be grafted. In other plant families grafting is only possible in exceptional cases between closely-related genera, such as between quince and pear. As cacti in general, and the sub-family of Cereoideae in particular,

are such a young group, their geographical distribution still accurately reflects the lines of development and dispersal of the genera and species.

Backeberg as well as Buxbaum placed great emphasis on geographical distribution when establishing their systems. Backeberg's subgroups of the Cereoideae are defined solely in geographical terms, not by common genetic distinguishing features, as is standard practice in systematics (see page 38). The situation relating to Buxbaum's tribes is largely similar. Here too with a few exceptions they inhabit geographically coherent regions. The Mexican genus *Astrophytum* is one of the exceptions; it is included - probably erroneously - in the Notocacteae, which are otherwise of purely South American distribution.

The regions in which particular cactus species or genera are confined vary widely. Of particular interest are distribution regions which are very small, very large, or incoherent, i.e. scattered. Small communities often occur in mountainous areas; in Mexico in particular and in the Andes cactus populations frequently become isolated on a mountain side or an enclosed valley as a species spreads out. Initially these isolated communities simply remain in their tiny area, but eventually they may evolve into new species if allowed to develop for a long period without disturbance. In fact, many species of cactus are only known from a single location.

More rarely a very small distribution area represents all that is left of what was once a wider region. Examples of this might be the small distribution area of the genus *Maihuenia* and various *Pereskia* species, which are among the most primitive of cacti. Other species are inevitably confined to a small area because they have adapted to special conditions there.

The various species of *Pediocactus* in North America have become specialized to cold, dry mountainous situations, for example, and these regions are naturally very small and widely spaced.

Very large distribution regions can also

be explained in different ways, among them the method of dispersal. Most cactus seed have no special features to aid dispersal. The small, dry seeds fall from the fruit to the ground and are at best swept away over fairly short distances by rain. Slightly more efficient are the large, air-filled fruit of many *Neoporterias*. When the fruits break off, a small hole is left in the base. The fruit is rolled along by the wind, and the seed are scattered as they fall out of the hole. A much more efficient method of dispersal is provided by the fleshy fruit of some cacti, which are eaten by birds. It comes as no surprise, therefore, that species with berry-type fruit such as *Cereus* and *Rhipsalis* are particularly widely distributed. Many spiny or bristly cactus fruit may be dispersed like burrs, which get caught in the coat of animals and carried long distances in this way.

An exceptionally simple form of vegetative propagation can also be responsible for wide-ranging distribution, as in the case of *Opuntia*, whose pads break off.

Other species are particularly tolerant of unfavourable conditions, and this characteristic may favour a wide distribution. The few frost-hard cactus species which are not expressly mountain plants, e.g. many Opuntias, *Coryphantha vivipara* and *Neobesseya missouriensis*, are among the most widespread cactus types, extending far to the north of North America and in some cases to Canada. The other factor which could affect dispersal is a particularly effective means of protection. Opuntias have been able to spread exceptionally rapidly in Australia because their glochids effectively prevented animals eating them. It was only when a native caterpillar was introduced that they could be contained. An exception to this thesis appears to be the spineless Peyotl cactus (*Lophophora*), which is apparently unprotected, and yet is remarkably widespread: from southern Texas to central Mexico. However, the plant is almost completely camouflaged in the terrain and does have chemical protection in the form of the narcotic mescalin, and these characteristics may have helped it to spread.

**Distribution of cactus genera
(153 genera in total)**

10 Number of genera represented in the region

② Number of endemic genera

Regions with more than 50 genera

Regions with 30-50 genera

Regions with 15-30 genera

Regions with less than 15 genera

Cacti vary rarely inhabit incoherent or scattered distribution regions; very occasionally this applies to a genus, but almost never to a species.

Backeberg was probably justified in splitting up former broadly defined genera with incoherent distribution regions into smaller genera inhabiting coherent areas. For the same reasons Backeberg and Buxbaum advocated a strict separation of genera into North and South American groups, even though exceptionally close external similarities occur in many genera found in the two continents. Because of the geographical separation these similarities are now interpreted as the result of parallel development.

Cacti have been most successful in the dry regions, as their ability to store water gives them an advantage in such situations. Unfortunately it is not possible at present to quote the number of species indigenous to the different regions of the New World to any degree of accuracy. Even in generic terms (see map) some of the data is very approximate, especially for the regions of Brazil. The number of genera in each region also depends on how narrowly the genera are defined; for example, whether the *Mammillaria* are split up into several genera, or considered as a single overall group. The map is drawn according to the 153 genera which are recognized in this book. Brazil, the USA and Canada have been divided into smaller regions, mostly along the borders of the federal states, to facilitate comparison. In spite of its obvious deficiencies the map does show a few interesting facts.

It shows quite clearly that the cactus genera are grouped around two main centres. Mexico, with 60 of the 153 genera, boasts the largest number, while the second centre - Peru, Bolivia and Northern Argentina, i.e. the central part of the Andes - is also very rich in genera, each country having between 34 and 40. At the same time these two areas also have the largest number of endemic genera, i.e. those which are only found in a particular area. Mexico, with 23 endemic genera, is once more head and shoulders above the rest. In the Andean region only Peru with 8 endemic genera has a substantial number which are restricted to the country. The fact that an area is now inhabited by a particularly wide variety of cacti does not necessarily mean that they evolved there; they might well have developed somewhere quite different. However, these centres do at least indicate which regions have been of particular importance to the evolution of cacti for the last few million years. We cannot trace cacti back further than this, as no fossils have been found. It is also a fact that the areas with most cacti may not necessarily be those which provide the most suitable conditions for the plants. An ideal region for cacti, perhaps a dry, semi-desert plain, does not always contain very many different cactus species, even when cacti constitute the entire vegetation. Districts where mountains divide the terrain into small patches often contain a much greater number of different species, even though they are not obvious to the eye, as they have a much wider variety of locations to colonize.

In comparison with Mexico and the central Andes - the two major regions of the New World which are warm and dry - the other regions are much less rich in cacti. The map does show, however, that there is a third region with a substantial number of cactus genera. This is the south-east coast of Brazil, especially the region comprising the federal states of Rio de Janeiro, Minas Gerais and Sao Paulo, which are home to 26 genera, 9 of them endemic. In this region the forest cacti are particularly highly developed, especially epiphytic species.

Isolated regions such as islands are often found to host large numbers of endemic genera of the older plant families, including many isolated genera, but this does not apply to cacti. The only notable exception is the Galapagos islands. Two of the three cactus genera found in this group of islands do not occur elsewhere. Outside the three main cactus regions the number of genera gradually diminishes. In North America cacti are thinly represented outside the sub-tropical regions, while Argentina and Chile towards the south can only offer a small number. The tropical rain-forest region of the Amazon is also low in cacti. More notable is the fact that only a small number of cactus genera is listed for the broad, fairly dry Campos terrain of the Brazilian uplands, although they may well feature in the vegetation there.

Cactus culture

Cacti come from regions whose climate and range of vegetation differ markedly from those found in central and northern Europe. Here there is a moderate climate with precipitation distributed evenly throughout the year, but with a wide variation in day length, and considerable variations in temperature between summer and winter, with smaller variations between day and night. In the plants' natural habitat there are sometimes distinct rainy and dry periods, but the day length remains largely the same through the year; in some areas the temperature difference is greater between day and night than between summer and winter. It is up to the cactus cultivator to adopt measures to recreate the natural conditions required for his plants to ensure good, healthy growth and flower formation.

The different aspects of cultural conditions should not be viewed in isolation. For example, the frequency and quantity of water required depend on the levels of warmth and light, on the size of the pots or pans and the permeability of the soil mixture. Nevertheless we shall begin by discussing the fundamental essentials for successful cactus cultivation individually, to avoid confusion.

The following sections contain a mass of information and many recommendations concerning cactus soil, light, watering, feeding and other points. The comprehensiveness of the data may confuse the beginner at first, but we would like to reassure you right from the start by stating that cacti are extraordinarily rewarding, robust and forgiving plants. Once you understand the basic sequence of events in plants, and if you meet their basic needs, you will be amazed how little trouble and work they demand, and how abundantly they reward your care and understanding with their sturdy growth and beautiful appearance.

Plant containers

Plant containers are a very important factor in the successful growing of cacti. Most cacti are shipped to retail outlets in small pots which are economical in terms of space while they are being transported and sold, and which provide adequate protection to the plant. During the raising of the cacti these small pots are sunk in a large greenhouse bed and kept in a carefully regulated greenhouse climate. In these conditions cacti will make good growth even in small pots. However, the plants should not be kept in them for long as they do not offer an adequate, balanced environment in the long term. The small pot heats up very quickly in the sun, and cools down equally rapidly when the sunshine is over. Most important of all, the soil dries out very quickly, with the result that the plant is subjected to a constant alternation between wet and dry. Inevitably then, the enthusiast will want to transplant his new acquisitions from the small commercial pots into other plant containers. There are several possible options.

Clay pots

By tradition the standard container is the individual pot. Its obvious, indisputable advantage is that each plant can be removed from the collection using plant tongs or a large pair of tweezers. They can then be photographed, their state of health can be checked, they can be repotted or even discarded if they have become diseased or died. Plants standing in pots can also be regrouped at any time. If on the other hand the cacti are kept together in a pan, one or other of them may grow particularly strongly and tend to force out or literally overshadow smaller plants.

It is important to consider carefully the material of which pots and trays are made. The notion that the containers should be porous, i.e. should allow air to pass through the walls, is absolutely fallacious, but it is still believed in some quarters. In fact ordinary clay pots are definitely harmful, as they ensure that the water which is provided for the plants quickly evaporates. The soil becomes as dry as dust and the fine roots adjacent to the pot wall become parched and burnt as the clay heats up strongly in the sun. While the soil in the pot remains moist a considerable amount of heat is lost due to latent heat of evaporation. Moreover, all the salts dissolved in the water are precipitated in the clay wall as the water evaporates, forming increasingly thick white deposits. In areas with hard water the result is an increase in lime in the wall of the clay pot, and eventually the soil becomes alkaline (basic). As most cacti prefer slightly acid soil (pH 5 to 6) growth may then cease, the roots wither, and in the end the plant may die.

On the other hand clay pots can be recommended for cactus cultivation provided that several of them are embedded in a mixture of peat and sand in a greenhouse bed, a flat pan or a flower trough. With this arrangement a balance of moisture is maintained between the embedding material and the cactus soil through the porous clay wall of the pot. Many species do not like to be kept completely dry in the dormant period, and in this case the embedding material alone can be watered slightly to maintain a mild degree of humidity in the root ball. We recommend a mixture of peat and sand as embedding material; it is very difficult to persuade pure peat to absorb moisture again after it has dried out completely, as can happen during the dormant period.

Clay pots can also be recommended for the cultivation of succulents in more northerly latitudes, where sunshine is not so strong. The pots do not dry out so rapidly when sunshine is scarce and atmospheric humidity is very high, and the generally quite soft water does not usually cause lime deposits.

Plants in clay pots should be embedded in a pan or trough in a mixture of peat and sand.

Plastic pots

Many years ago growers in England and southern France realized that cacti which were cultivated in metal pans and trays looked much more healthy than plants in clay containers. Initially it was thought that the metal might be the reason, perhaps providing a trace element (i.e. an element which influences growth when present in the most minute quantities), but tests have shown that it is the impermeable pot wall which makes the difference. Nowadays plenty of suitable containers are available made of non-porous materials, especially plastic. The base of the container must have holes or slots to allow excess water to drain away easily. Plastic trays must have reasonably rigid walls, so that the weight of the soil and the plants does

not distort them too severely; this could damage the fine roots. The plastic pots which are now produced in many shapes, sizes and colours, have generally proved highly suitable for cactus culture. They are light in weight, the plant drops out of the pot easily when it has to be moved, and the pots can easily be cleaned and then reused. They are also cheap to buy. Naturally plastic pots should also be of a certain minimum size in order to ensure that the soil temperature and moisture content are maintained at a reasonably even level.

Square plastic pots are particularly popular, as they fit together snugly to save space. The overall impression is then of an integrated bed of cacti, or a

'cactus landscape', but retaining the advantages of cultivation in individual pots. These pots are available commercially in a range of sizes.

Many cactus growers consider the commercial square pots to be too shallow, especially for cacti with tap roots. Others prefer shallower pots, or like all pots to be the same depth, regardless of width, in order to emphasize the impression of a coherent cactus area, as mentioned above. It is important that any pots which are particularly tall or shallow should be suitable for the prevailing cultural conditions: the temperature range, the water storage capacity of the soil used, and the method of watering adopted.

Plastic pots can easily be cut using a fine-toothed saw or a heated knife, and easily and permanently glued to form pots of the desired depth and diameter. Uhu-Plast has proved an excellent adhesive for this purpose. Once glued, the plastic pots should be left to dry out for several days until the adhesive solvent has completely evaporated. In this way many cactus growers have assembled a collection of pots of uniform depth, with the exception of those intended for columnar cacti. The ratio of surface area to volume remains constant for all pots, and thus for all plants, if you adopt this procedure. If this is not the case, there is a risk that the small pots would be dry while the bottom layers of soil in the larger (and correspondingly deeper) pots were still moist. If the plants are then watered uniformly, as is necessary when a collection becomes extensive, then the plants in small pots might receive too little water and those in larger pots rather too much. The long roots of the species with taproots tend to be squashed up in shallow pots, but still seem to thrive.

More recently very deep square plastic pots have become available commercially, which are very good for species with a tap root. This type of pot has only only been produced in a few sizes to date.

Sometimes the cacti in a collection are cultivated in plastic pots and clay pots side by side. In this situation the plants in the plastic pots only require about one third of the quantity of water required for comparable plants in clay pots. This is the effect of the high rate of water evaporation through the porous wall of the clay pot, as already mentioned.

Ordinary plastic pots are only a practical proposition up to a certain size. For larger plants refrigerator trays can be used; they are easily obtained, but are much more expensive than the other alternative: clay pots again. The main disadvantage of the pots - their porosity - can be eliminated by painting them with a liquid, acid-resistant, plastic material, which can be bought in paint shops. New clay pots and clay pans must also be soaked thoroughly for several days before use,

as they are usually also strongly alkaline.

Seed pans

Small plants and seedlings should not be planted out individually in small pots. They thrive best in groups of several in trays or pans, in which the roots are able to develop without restriction. The plants should be spaced out with twice their body diameter between them. Experience suggests that the mutual 'competition' of the roots is a stimulus to growth, while the greater volume of soil provides a more even level of moisture and balanced conditions for growth. Multi-pots are particularly recommended, especially for cultivating young plants; these are plastic trays with a top plate in which the individual pots are moulded. Their advantage is that they can easily be watered from underneath, but it is difficult to remove individual plants from the top plate. Many cactus enthusiasts group several of their larger plants together in trays or troughs, which are then supplemented with decorative stones and similar materials to form attractive miniature cactus landscapes. If you wish to try this, it is important that the cacti planted together have a similar pattern of growth and vegetative rhythm, otherwise the small, slow-growing curiosities may be forced out by fast-growing columnar species or groups of plants, or a species requiring dry conditions by the autumn will receive too much water, because its neighbour is just producing a flower and still requires moisture.

Planting out in a bed

If you have a large projecting window box for succulents, or a heated greenhouse, you might also consider planting out cacti in a bed, perhaps in the central bed of a cactus greenhouse. Columnar species in particular really need to be planted out. Only then will their root system - often extending a distance of several metres - develop fully; they will then grow amazingly well and even produce flowers. In

exceptional cases the large Cerei will produce annual shoots up to almost a metre long. Many Opuntias, Echinocerei and Mammillarias will only produce good growth and their full beauty in such conditions.

Cactus soil

If you read a number of cactus books, or leaf through cactus magazines, you will be offered a large number of different recipes for cactus soils. That cactus enthusiasts recommend different mixtures indicates that its composition cannot be crucial on its own to the successful growth of cacti. Many cactus growers have commented on the bigotry and narrow-mindedness shown by people who defend a particular type of soil and attack another. Quite clearly there is a certain amount of leeway in the composition of the soil. The only basic requirements are that it should be adequately permeable and slightly acid.

Ingredients of cactus soil

If you are just transplanting one or two cacti, you can use the small bags of pre-packed, ready-mixed cactus soil available commercially. It is usually relatively rich in humus and is suitable for green Mammillarias, Notocacti or Rebutias with their fibrous roots. If you possess more cacti and would like to match the cactus soil more accurately to the different species, you will have to mix the soil yourself.

Older cactus books in particular generally list the constituents of a good cactus soil as old, dark humus-rich compost, plus friable, non-sticky loam, coarse sand and fine-fibred peat. Good compost consists of manure or leaf mould made of rotted autumn leaves, stored for three to five years and turned over many times. Such compost is dense black in colour, fine in texture and crumbly. Fresh compost or manure which still contain non-decomposed organic matter is a constant source of root disease and decay, and should not be used.

Loam is a very variable commodity. A loam suitable for cactus culture should contain little clay. It should not be possible to roll the material into thin worms between your hands. Loam suitable for plants must not harden after watering.

Peat can be a valuable constituent of cactus soil. It raises the capability of the substrate to store nutrients, and has the ability to act as a buffer, preventing too rapid and too extreme variations in the substrate. The humic acids contained in peat produce a slightly acid reaction in the soil, as cacti prefer. Peat which is insufficiently rotted, moist, or has been stored in an air-tight container, can be a breeding ground for harmful fungi.

Many cactus enthusiasts find it too onerous or uncertain a matter to seek out, mix and store compost, loam and peat, and consider the resultant soil's composition too variable. One proven solution is to replace these three constituents with a widely available standard soil, e.g. John Innes No. 2 compost. This material, if from a good manufacturer, is of constant quality and balanced composition, and it is also good value, especially in the larger packs. If you wish to be completely sure that no harmful fungi or pests are contained in the soil, you can sterilize it by steaming. For small quantities the material can be poured into a small fabric bag, placed in a domestic sterilizing pot and subjected to steam for about half an hour. The soil can also be disinfected by means of appropriate chemical preparations, but in this case it is absolutely essential to observe the instructions for use supplied with them, and not to cut short the period recommended before the soil is used. Preparations for chemical decontamination of soil are generally available only in quite large containers, which are designed for the needs of the professional nurseryman. Soil bought commercially is already free from harmful seeds.

An important constituent of cactus soil is sand. This should be rather coarse-grained, and must on no account contain fine, dust-like particles. Sharp quartz sand is especially good. We recommend that mined sand should be washed, as it often contains fine particles which tend to stick together like cement when it becomes dry. Limy, alkaline sand is unusable.

A suitable soil for many cacti - but not for epiphytes - is thoroughly weathered igneous rock, for example granite or gneiss waste. When properly weathered the stone can be crumbled in the hand. If it is similar in grain structure to coarse sand or fine gravel, this igneous rock can be used without additives, although it is better to add some humus in the form of fine, crumbly peat which will help to retain moisture in the soil. Recently this kind of weathered igneous rock has been made available by a number of commercial firms. Depending on its history, igneous rock waste may be so severely weathered that after two or three years of cactus culture it disintegrates into a fine dust. This dust gathers in the bottom of the cactus pot and can kill the roots. The best sort of material is that which includes a high proportion of durable quartz.

Many cactus growers add basalt chippings to their soil, especially for plants which prefer a very porous soil. These chippings are used as a road surfacing material and for scattering on roads in winter, and are widely available for this reason. The finer grades should be selected - between rice and pea in size, and of course it is vital to check that the chippings are completely free of road salt, and that they are not limestone. Limestone will produce bubbles of gas if a few drops of dilute hydrochloric acid (about 5 per cent) are applied to it, but basalt will not. A disadvantage of basalt chippings is that they are heavy. Please note also that chippings store neither water nor nutrients.

In recent years lava waste has become popular in some quarters as a constituent of cactus soil. Lava waste is available in a variety of grades from builders' merchants, and in smaller quantities in pet shops, although prices vary very widely. Lava waste is a porous volcanic material, relatively heavy and dark in colour. It is capable of absorbing and storing a considerable quantity of water. In the first wave of enthusiasm pure lava waste was declared to be the ideal soil for cacti, but since then the facts have been considered more soberly. Pure lava waste can probably only be recommended for cacti native to

Melocactus cultivated in lava waste

extreme habitats. Watering has to be carried out with great care; lava waste can be wet at the bottom of the pot when it seems to be quite dry at the surface. However, the addition of the correct proportion of lava waste to cactus soil can be recommended unconditionally. The grades between 3 and 7 mm. in size are especially useful; the dust particles, which tend to clump together, should be washed or sieved out. Larger fragments of lava, which are sometimes contained in the waste, can be very decorative if skilfully arranged between the plants. Brick chippings or rubble are similar, but before use it is important to check that they are not alkaline. Here again, be sure to wash or filter out the fine brick dust.

Many cactus enthusiasts use pumice gravel as an additive to their soil. Pumice is a material which occurs in areas which have experienced volcanic activity in the past, and is widely used in the building trade. It is usually slightly acid, is relatively light in weight and highly porous, and is therefore able to store water. Pumice gravel should also be washed or sieved, and only the coarse material

used - between sand and fine gravel in size.

The structure, i.e. the looseness and friability of the soil, can be improved by a number of materials which have come onto the market in the last few years and which are becoming more and more popular in gardening. Styromull is a white, lightweight, foam which is not harmful to plants and does not deteriorate. Each grain consists of a large number of small, closed air-filled cells. Styromull does not absorb water or nutrients, and therefore can be considered to 'dilute' the soil, but the soil stays warmer because of the trapped air. For this reason it is especially useful when large tubs or troughs or enclosed cactus beds are to be planted.

Vermiculite does not maintain its structure if kept moist for a long period. In time it disintegrates and forms a sludge in which cactus roots can suffocate, and for this reason it should only be added in small quantities to soils which are replaced annually.

Perlite has proved a very useful material. It is a natural mineral (a

silicate of aluminium), blown up at high temperature to form something similar to popcorn. This white, sterile, non-rotting material should be used in its 'coarse sand' grades, between millet and rice grains in size. With its numerous, extremely fine, open pores it absorbs roughly three times its own weight in moisture, and thus stores water and nutrients very effectively. Excess water simply drains away, thus avoiding stagnant moisture, which is harmful to cacti. Soil incorporating Perlite is also looser in structure and better aerated.

Many cactus enthusiasts use up to one third Perlite in their soil. Other growers complain that the material's light weight causes it to migrate slowly to the top of the soil. Taking a balanced view, we feel that an addition of 10-15 per cent Perlite to cactus soil can certainly be recommended.

Acidity and alkalinity of the soil

An important factor in the successful culture of cacti is the soil reaction, i.e.

whether our soil shows an alkaline, neutral or acid reaction. It is likely that all cacti prefer an acid soil, but although many of them will also thrive in neutral soil, almost all species stop growing and slowly die if the soil is alkaline. We would like to discuss the basic principles of soil reaction in a little more detail here. Soil reaction varies according to the number of hydrogen ions present in the soil; ions are electrically charged (positive or negative) atoms or molecules. If, for example, there are 0.0000001 g of hydrogen ions present in one litre of pure water, the number 1 is in seventh place after the point, and this corresponds to a pH value of 7; if 0.001 g of hydrogen ions are present then the pH value is 3. The pH value therefore expresses the concentration of hydrogen ions. The abbreviation pH is an abbreviation of the latin word pondus (weight) and the Greek word hydrogenium meaning hydrogen. Soil with a pH value around 7 is neutral, from 1 to 6.4 acid, and more than 7.3 alkaline. With certain exceptions, cacti thrive best when the reaction value is pH 4.5 to 6.5. Thus it is very important to establish the pH value of cactus soil,

and the best method is to test the individual constituents of the soil. This is done using a small device called a pH meter , available commercially. An indicator fluid is poured onto a small soil probe. After a short period the fluid changes colour, and the pH value can be directly read from a graduated colour scale supplied. Red means acid, green neutral, and bluish alkaline. We advise that you test the pH value of materials which normally react neutral or even acid, because some pumice gravel, for example, is slightly alkaline. This by no means renders it unusable, but before mixing it in it you must pour acidified water (pH around 3) through it several times.

Cacti are 'lime hating' plants. All plants, even those which require a very acid soil reaction, need the element calcium for proper growth, and calcium is contained in lime. However, for cacti it must not be provided in alkaline form, or in a form which subsequently has an alkaline effect. Thus burnt lime, slaked lime or carbonic acid lime must not be used, instead about one heaped teaspoon of manuring lime or raw gypsum from a plaster works should be added to a bucket of soil. Gypsum is a neutral calcium compound which is difficult to dissolve in water.

Proven soil mixtures

The following mixture makes a soil which can be used for most cacti:

- one third compost, loam and peat - or standard soil, e.g. John Innes No. 2;
- one third coarse sand, if necessary with chippings added;
- one third Perlite, and perhaps also brick rubble and igneous rock waste.

Compost, peat, loam, standard soil, Perlite, pumice gravel, lava and brick waste and to some extent igneous rock waste are all able to store water, thus they increase the power of the soil to retain moisture. Sand and chippings store no water. Plants which like more moisture thus require less sand and chippings while plants sensitive to moisture need rather more sand and chippings in the soil.

Cacti which appreciate a proportion of humus in the soil in their native habitat can be given a slightly higher proportion of standard soil, compost or peat. Cacti which live on weathered mineral terrain, on the other hand, should not be given any compost, and hardly any standard soil. For these plants a largely mineral soil should be made up, consisting of well weathered loam plus a high proportion of sand, chippings, pumice gravel, lava waste, brick rubble and igneous rock waste. Epiphytes, which root in the humus lodged in the forks of branches and the furrowed bark of their host plants, are best provided with a soil very rich in humus, with a high proportion of sphagnum peat. In the chapter dealing with propagation by sowing we will go into more detail in the use of sphagnum moss.

In general terms then, the composition of cactus soil is not crucial. The proportions mentioned are not fixed, and can safely be varied quite widely. The crucial aspect is the structure of the substrate: it must be thoroughly permeable, must not be too fine-grained and must not tend to compact or clump together. It should also be slightly acid.

Light and temperature

Light and warmth are indispensable to cacti. Using sunlight and chlorophyll the plants combine the carbon dioxide in the air and the water in the ground to produce carbohydrates; the process is termed photosynthesis. The carbohydrates are the raw materials for new growth and are also the plants' source of energy. However, plant metabolism does not start to function until a certain temperature is reached, which in the case of cacti is around 10-15°C.

Light requirements

In their native habitats cacti - with the exception of the epiphytic species - inhabit very brightly lit sites, and are only slightly shaded if at all by neighbouring plants. Cacti have evolved many methods of protecting themselves from the intense solar radiation. Many species which come to us from totally unshaded deserts or from steppe terrain like Northern Chile are not bright green in colour, but have a grey or whitish bloom. Other cacti are so densely enveloped in spines or hairs that they look white, yellow or brown instead of green. The light-coloured outer surface and the dense covering of spines or hair reflect the light. Many cacti are brown or black, and this colouring may provide protection to the chlorophyll which is essential for life. The surface of other cacti is folded into a large number of ridges, waves or leaf-like blades, so that parts of the plant shade each other.

The many forms of protection are essential features of a healthy cactus plant. In Europe it is essential to provide very bright light and a location which receives at least some sunshine during the vegetative period from April to October. In the long term cacti cannot flourish standing by a dark north-facing window or even by a bright window if they are not close to it. If a plant turns a light-green colour and grows elongated and lush - a condition termed etiolation - that is a sure sign that the lighting is inadequate and the plant is degenerating.

The cactus grower often has one particularly bright site and one rather more shady position available. There are a few genera which can be kept in a slightly shady position. Mostly these are plants which are green in overall appearance, and are not protected by dense spines or hairs. However, even these cacti, with their ability to tolerate some degree of shade, must on no account be kept in a dark situation. Ideally these plants would be provided with sunshine in the morning or evening and slight shade from the brilliance of the midday sun. Most cacti can be left in a darker situation during the dormant period (November to February), although it will be necessary to water less and keep temperatures lower to prevent the plants producing shoots at the wrong time. Cacti should not be left entirely in the dark even during the period of dormancy; a certain amount of light keeps the plant's metabolism ticking over, reduces the danger of fungus infection, and promotes the formation of flowers in plants which flower early in the spring.

Shading

Almost all cacti like to be cultivated in a bright, sunny position, but they must be acclimatized to the full sunlight gradually when they are first moved from a darker winter position to the summer location. Even cacti grown in a greenhouse all year round sometimes need to acclimatize to strong sunlight after the dark months of winter. In March and April days with brilliant warm sunshine can occur quite suddenly after a long period of dreary weather. This sudden increase in light and warmth can burn or scorch the cacti, with whole areas of the outer skin destroyed. If this should happen, the plant is not able to regenerate these unsightly patches, although they may grow over again in the course of several years. For this reason it is important for the cactus grower to pay particular attention to the weather in the early part of the year. The plants protect themselves from a sudden increase in light intensity by turning a gentle shade of red, produced by means of a red protective dye stored in their cells as a pigment. You can help the plants to get used to higher levels of light by providing slight shade on very bright and warm days in the early part of the year. Many cactus lovers paint the panes of the greenhouse or garden frame with greenhouse shading paint, but this has the disadvantage that the paint reduces the already scant light on dull days too. A better solution is use wooden shutters or fabric blinds (not too dense) which can be quickly rolled up at any time. This type of shading arrangement may be fitted in the greenhouse or cold frame at the outset. In an emergency the plants can be protected by laying sheets of thin tissue paper over them around the middle of the day if hot weather occurs without warning. However, shading of this sort should only be considered as a temporary aid to acclimatization. On no account shade the plants for too long, otherwise they become 'soft' and tend towards etiolation.

The composition of the light

For cacti to thrive the composition of the light they receive is as important as its intensity (radiation strength). In their native conditions cacti are subject to the full spectrum of light, but in the European and temperate North American environment and conditions of culture the spectrum is often much narrower. Because of the dust and haze which gathers over our urban areas the intensity of the light which reaches us is reduced, especially in the ultra-violet region. Moreover glass absorbs ultra-violet light almost completely. Cacti from elevated mountainous regions, such as the high Andes, receive strong ultra-violet radiation in their natural habitat, and these plants should occasionally be provided with unfiltered sunlight when cultivated. On fine days, especially in autumn, the cover of the garden frame should be opened wide, and as the days rapidly grow shorter in the

autumn it is very important to provide cacti with the maximum quantity of light on such days. If the plants are to harden off fully, produce fine spine formations and beautiful flowers, and are to be generally healthy, much depends on the light they receive in the autumn. For this reason the cactus enthusiast should eschew all shade at this time of the year, clean the glass planes in the garden frame and also the greenhouse if necessary. Dirty glass can absorb more than one third of the light which strikes it.

Artificial lighting

Many cactus lovers attempt to compensate for the lack of overall light intensity and the shortage of ultra-violet light in particular by providing supplementary lighting with fluorescent lamps. Sometimes special strip lights are recommended, offering enhanced radiation of the part of the spectrum which promotes assimilation. Examples of this type of lamp in strip light form are the 'Osram L Fluora' and the 'Sylvania GroLux'. Artificial or supplementary lighting of cacti should not consist exclusively of these tubes, as their spectrum is unbalanced. Their characteristic pinkish-bluish light, which falsifies colours, is often supplemented by other types of fluorescent tubes. The 'TrueLite' strip lights often used by aquarium and terrarium enthusiasts provide a spectrum similar to that of sunlight, according to their manufacturer, including the ultra-violet part of the spectrum. They are relatively expensive, but offer long life in compensation.

Fluorescent tubes can certainly supply the essential minimum quantity of light to allow cacti to overwinter in a cellar, and their use helps the cacti to survive the winter in good shape. However, they cannot replace the full sunshine which is required in the vegetative period by cacti native to the dry regions.

In the botanical gardens of Tübingen, Germany, successful experiments have been carried out using special fluorescent tubes to provide supplementary lighting for plants from the high Andean plains. These tubes

are used in photo-copying machines and produce a high proportion of ultra-violet light (e.g. Osram HNP 202). The plants exhibited natural growth, a compact form, and produced the silver-white hair formation typical of their native habitat. These experiments are now being extended to include cacti from the high mountain regions.

Temperature

An important factor in cactus culture is to maintain the temperatures to which the plants are accustomed. Bearing in mind the extremely wide range of conditions which occur in the natural habitat, it should be evident that it is not possible to keep together a collection of cacti whose native conditions are too disparate. Nevertheless the experience of cactus growers over many years of cultivation has shown that cacti are very well able to adapt, and that many different species can be kept under standardized conditions. The most favourable average temperatures have proved to be 25-35°C on sunny days in summer and 15-25°C on overcast days. The nocturnal temperature should drop to 10-17°C. In winter the daytime temperature should reach 8-15°C and sink to around 5°C at night.

If cacti have to be overwintered in the dark (by 'dark' we include a position in a room away from a window) then the daytime temperature must not exceed 10°C, so that they do not shoot and become etiolated too early. Once a plant has suffered in this way it takes years of careful culture to bring it back to its full beauty.

All the temperatures stated should be measured in the shade. Temperatures in full sunlight will be at least 10°C higher. In summer the recommended temperature is maintained by opening or closing greenhouse ventilators, closing the windows of the room or frame in use, and in winter by heating.

Within the recommended range of temperatures tropical lowland cacti, including those from the hot regions of the Caribbean, Brazil and Central America, prefer the higher temperatures. These plants can suffer

Cacti for selected light and temperature conditions

Light and temperature in the vegetative period	Light and temperature in dormant period	Suitable cacti	Suitable position for cacti
Full sun, hot	Cool (3-8°C); short night frosts are tolerated. Bright	From the genus *Echinocereus* the sub-group of the Pectinates and plants from the *E. triglochidiatus* group. Probably also some *Ariocarpus* and *Coryphantha*.	Suitable for greenhouse or garden frame in full sun, where winter temperatures may be very cool.
Full sun, hot	Moderate overwintering temperature (5-10°C)	White and densely spined Mammillarias, *Thelocactus, Coryphantha, Ariocarpus, Turbini-carpus*, very many Echinocerei, robust *Astrophytum* such as *A. capricorne*.	Suitable for greenhouse or frame in full sun.
Full sun, hot	Relatively warm over-wintering (c. 15°C)	*Melocactus, Discocactus, Ferocactus, Echinocactus, Espostoa, Haageocereus,* Mammillarias from lower California, hairy and glaucous Cerei, e.g. *Pilosocereus*. More sensitive *Astrophytum* such as *A. asterias*	Suitable for greenhouse in full sun, which must be kept relatively warm in winter.
Full sun, but not too hot (if possible not above 35°C). Good ventilation. Nocturnal cooling is important.	Cool (3-8°C), short night frosts are tolerated	*Lobivia* (incl. *Chamaecereus*); *Oreocereus* (incl. *Morawetzia*); *Sulcorebutia: Trichocereus* (incl. *Helianthocereus*); *Oroya; Neowerdermannia*; sub-group *Pseudolobivia* in the genus *Echinopsis*; sub-group *Digitorebutia* in the genus *Rebutia; Neobesseya missouriensis; Mammillaria (Mammillopsis) senilis*; sub-group *Tephrocactus* in the genus *Opuntia*.	Suitable for hard cold-frame cultivation or bright, well ventilated greenhouse. Some of them possibly on outside window ledge sheltered from rain in the vegetative period.
Subdued sun (protection from brilliant midday sun in spring and summer). Not too hot (if possible not above 35°C). Good ventilation. Nocturnal cooling is important.	Cool (3-8°C); short night frosts are tolerated	Sub-groups *Rebutia* and *Aylostera* in the genus *Rebutia*. Robust Mammillarias, e.g. *M. rhodantha*; robust Gymnocalyciums, e.g. *G. gibbosum* or *G. bruchii*.	Suitable for greenhouse or frame out of full sun, some of them suitable for indoor culture.
Subdued sun (protection from brilliant midday sun in spring and summer). Not too hot (if possible not above 35°C). Good ventilation.	Moderate overwintering temperature (5-10°C)	Green Mammillarias; *Notocactus, Gymno-calycium, Echinofossulocactus, Cleistocactus*, sub-group *Neochilenia* in the genus *Neoporteria, Parodia, Copiapoa*	Suitable for greenhouse or frame out of full sun, some of them suitable for indoor culture.
Half shade (in spring and summer morning and/or evening sun only, full sun in late autumn and winter), not too hot.	Moderate overwintering temperature (5-10°C)	'Phyllocacti' (*Nopalxochia* hybrids)	Suitable for half-shaded greenhouse, robust forms indoors by the east- or west-facing windows.
Bright, but out of the sun if possible, not above 25-30°C, high atmospheric humidity.	Relatively warm over-wintering (not below 15°C)	*Rhipsalis* and other epiphytic cacti	Shady greenhouse with relatively high atmospheric humidity (orchid climate), or purpose-built flower window or showcase with regulated climate.

damage in winter if temperatures drop below 15°C. In contrast, cacti from the Andes, or from elevated locations in Mexico, like to be cultivated in very bright but not necessarily very hot conditions. For this reason an adequate, effective system of ventilation is an absolute necessity for these plants, as stagnant heat is injurious to them. They also appreciate marked temperature differences between day and night. Many of these high-altitude species can even survive frosts during the overwintering period, provided that they are dry. Please refer to the section dealing with 'winter-hard cacti' for further details.

Watering (soil and atmospheric humidity)

The moisture in the air and in the ground are important aspects of cactus culture. The assumption that cacti hardly ever need to be watered because they are plants of the desert is incorrect. It is true that many of the more extreme succulent plants, including the majority of cacti, can withstand drought conditions for years, but they are not able to grow and flower during that period, and they will shrink considerably.

The basic rules of watering

This is the basic rule: when a plant is growing or producing buds, then it needs water; the faster it is growing, the more it requires. If a particular plant is kept in a bright, warm situation, the same rule applies in winter, as there are certain cacti which flower in that season, for example *Mammillaria plumosa*.

A second rule also applies: the higher the temperature in which the plants are kept the more water they require, as the rate of evaporation rises with temperature; as temperatures fall in autumn, so the quantity of water we give must be reduced.

At temperatures below 10-15°C cacti are no longer able to assimilate moisture. For this reason the vast majority of cacti should not be watered at all if the temperature is constantly below this level. The only exceptions here are those cacti which are reluctant to produce new shoots in the spring after a long dry period in the winter; a minimal level of moisture should be maintained in their pots. This can be achieved by providing very small quantities of water - by the teaspoon - or by moistening the embedding material if the plants are cultivated in clay pots. At the other extreme, if summer temperatures rise too high many cacti pass into a state of dry dormancy. If you find that some plants have ceased growing in the middle of the summer then you should stop watering, as many species (e.g. the Rebutias) have a regular summer dormant period by nature, i.e. it is an adaptation to their native conditions. If they start growing again in the autumn, then they can again be watered. It is much more dangerous to water too much than too little. Too little water reduces growth and flower formation; too much water can cause the plant body to burst along its length, the roots may rot, and at worst the whole plant may rot.

The fact is that individual cacti need to be watered individually; when you have worked with cacti for a fairly long period you will eventually gain an intuitive knowledge of when they require water. An overall strategy for watering, i.e. the number of ml. which should be given to each plant per day or per week, simply cannot be formulated, as the conditions under which the plants are maintained in individual collections differ too widely. For example, in areas with a high water table the atmospheric humidity in a greenhouse will be high, which prevents the soil drying out quickly. At the other extreme the very dry air in a sunny flower window guarantees that the water provided evaporates rapidly. In any case you should never water while a pot is still damp, but only when it has been dry for at least one and preferably several days, as the moisture is retained in the depth of the pot for quite a long period.

A fundamental error is to water cacti 'just a little bit' every day. It is much better to water more generously, but at fairly long intervals. If you are unsure whether to water, do not go by the appearance of the soil, as a dry surface does not necessarily indicate that the mass of the soil is also dry. It is better to feel the soil with your fingers.

As a general guideline it is evident that an even but low level of soil humidity deep in the pot is ideal for most cacti during the growth period. Epiphytes are a special case; their soil should never be allowed to dry out completely. Please note that Cerei usually require more water than the globular forms, as their surface area (through which evaporation takes place) is relatively much greater.

In summer watering should be carried out towards evening, while in spring and autumn the morning is the better time. On a warm day in the spring it is advisable to give the plants a thorough spraying, in order to wash off the dust which accumulates in winter, and to clean the plants' stomata. In the warm period of high summer the plants can also be sprayed with water occasionally. Cacti whose surface carries a chalky, whitish or bluish wax covering should never be sprayed, as unsightly blotches may result.

As a general rule water should be applied to the soil rather than to the cactus; in particular, avoid getting water on the crown of the plants. If you do the water may stay there for quite long periods, and may lead to rotting if weather conditions are unfavourable.

When watering, and especially when spraying, always use water which is at room temperature, i.e that has been allowed to stand for a while. If you water or spray with a hose connected directly to the water mains, the very cold water may be sufficient to

stimulate sensitive plants to produce corky tissue, and fungus attack is also likely. If possible, it is a good idea to water thoroughly and generously at the beginning of a period of fine weather. Cacti should not be too moist at the beginning of a period of cool, dull weather. In bad weather the plant requires less water as the rate of evaporation is much slower. The danger here is that the plants might be standing in wet soil for a relatively long time, and this is fundamentally harmful to cacti.

In terms of the seasons, a general plan for watering would be as follows: In March or April, at the end of the winter dormant period, cacti should first be misted with water then sprayed gently. The misting and spraying will promote the production of new root hairs, and the plants can then be watered more generously after about April - May. From mid-July to mid-August many cacti have a dry dormant period, during which they are watered less. From mid-August to mid-September watering can again be more generous, as many cacti grow quite strongly in this season. After mid-October only a very little water should be given, or even none at all.

The water used for watering

The water given to cacti should not be too hard, and should be slightly acid. The best water is of course rainwater, but this is only available in limited quantities in some areas. In large cities and industrial areas rainwater should not be collected except during constant, heavy rain. The water which falls first, especially after a long dry period, is too severely contaminated with dirt and industrial dust to be usable.

The hardness of mains water is usually a result of dissolved calcium and magnesium compounds. The prolonged use of hard water for watering will eventually cause a build-up of relatively insoluble calcium compounds in the soil, and thus render it alkaline. Alkaline soil may cause the roots to die off and the plant to perish. If your mains water is only

slightly to moderately hard, these consequences can be avoided by adding a little acid to the water before use.

A simple method of determining the acidity or otherwise of our mains water is by using 'indicator paper', which can be bought from any chemist's shop or drug store. A small strip of this paper is held 1 to 2 cm. deep in the water, after which its colour is compared with the colour scale supplied. If necessary, acid can then be added to the water until a pH value of 5 to 6 is obtained. Various acids can be used for this purpose, in particular dilute nitric acid, phosphoric acid, citric acid and oxalic acid. The cactus enthusiast should be fully aware of the dangers involved with using acids, and the high toxicity of oxalic acid in particular, and must store these substances where it is impossible for children to reach them. The first named acids can be obtained from the chemist or drug store in liquid form, and can be measured out using a dropper; the latter two are bought as powders and dissolved in water. In order to avoid increasing the proportion of a particular chemical in the soil, it is best to change the acid used fairly frequently. Hydrochloric acid is not recommended because the chlorine contained in it can damage the plants if the concentration is allowed to build up. If you use oxalic acid the water should be allowed to stand for a few hours after adding the acid. If you do this, most of the calcium will precipitate out in the form of insoluble calcium oxalate. Remove the deposit before using the water.

If the surface of the soil should become encrusted after a long period of watering with calcareous water, it should be loosened from time to time with a pointed wooden stick. When it becomes necessary, the topmost layer of soil should be removed entirely and replaced with fresh soil, unless it proves necessary to repot the plant altogether.

Watering from underneath, the flooding process, hydroculture

In their native conditions cacti draw moisture upward from the ground, and for this reason cultivated cacti should also be watered from the bottom rather than from the top. The standard provision for this is to stand the cactus pots in large, flat trays or pans made of metal, plastic, or wood lined with plastic film. These pans should be as close as possible to truly level, as even a slight inclination provides some plants with much more water than others. An alternative is to exploit an intentional slight slope. If you know that the cacti on the right will receive more water than those on the left when water is added, then the plants which like moisture should be accommodated towards the right and those from the extreme dry regions should be on the left. Pans made of metal should be coated with a suitable paint which plants can tolerate, otherwise there is a danger that the slightly acidified water might dissolve substances from the metal which are harmful to the plants.

The practice of watering from underneath involves adding that quantity of water to the pan which is completely soaked up by the substrate within 10 to 30 minutes. On no account should water remain in the pan for hours, let alone days. After a few hours you will notice that the water which has been absorbed has penetrated to the surface of the pots, and has turned the cactus soil a dark colour. Watering by this method is very thorough and effective. As a general rule you can reckon that the plants will now need no more water for two to four weeks - to the great relief of the cactus grower, who can now go on holiday with an easy conscience.

The flooding method of cactus culture is based even more strongly on watering from underneath. For this process we need galvanized metal boxes or wooden boxes lined with PVC film, about 30 cm. deep, standing on a slightly sloping surface. At their lowest point there must be a tap or other form of valve, so that water can be held in the boxes and then allowed to run out again. A short length of hose (through which the water or fertilizer solution is added) is placed in one corner of the empty box, which is then filled with pumice gravel of coarse-sandy to fine-gravel grade, with the inlet hose projecting a few centimetres above the surface. Cacti can then be planted in the box (or even seeds sown). Water or fertilizer solution is poured in via the hose until the fluid level is about 10 cm. above the bottom, after closing the outlet valve. The fluid is then allowed to stand for 5 to 10 minutes, after which the excess is allowed to run away by opening the tap. One flooding is sufficient for several weeks, depending on weather and atmospheric humidity. In spring and late autumn the amount of flooding should be much less, and in winter no flooding should be carried out at all. Seedlings in particular have been shown to grow amazingly well under these conditions.

Brick chippings may be used instead of pumice gravel. The same procedure has been successfully tried in individual pots; for example, cacti standing in individual pots in pure pumice gravel, and the pots grouped together in pans as already described. In cactus cultivation using the flooding method the soil absorbs the moisture very rapidly even after a protracted dry period, whereas a dried-out, felted-up root ball incorporating a high proportion of peat is often very difficult to dampen again. The soil quickly dries out superficially after the excess water has run away, but it does retain a mild level of moisture deep down for a long time.

Several cactus growers have reported that their plants have flourished and grown very well by this means of cultivation, but there is a potential danger. No ordinary soil is available to supplement the nutrients supplied, and for this reason it is essential to provide the plants with a balanced fertilizer containing all the necessary minerals. There is also a possibility that there will be an accumulation in the soil of metabolic residue products and certain chemical substances which cannot be neutralized.

To complete the picture we have to mention hydroculture. Experiments have established that cacti, inhabitants of extremely dry locations, are even capable of surviving in the conditions of hydroculture, i.e. in special containers with their roots permanently submerged in a dilute nutrient solution. This method is so unnatural for cacti that it is only mentioned here in passing. The roots produced by this method are very fragile, and when the cactus is planted in normal soil they easily become kinked and then tend to rot, which can cause the plant to die.

Atmospheric moisture

In the native habitat of many cacti, for example in the coastal deserts of South America and the high mountain regions, the temperature by night is substantially lower than by day. In such conditions atmospheric humidity can reach very high levels. The dew which precipitates from this high humidity can be absorbed by suitably adapted cacti through their outer skin - the spines may act as condensation points for the moisture in the air - and through a very wide-ranging but shallow root system. This adaptation explains how such cacti are able to survive in regions where hardly any rain falls for years on end. The nocturnal precipitation of dew is clearly important to many cacti. We can imitate dew precipitation by applying a mist of water, using a very fine spray, late in the evening or early in the morning, corresponding to the plants' natural conditions. Please note that watering in this way must involve producing a very fine veil of moisture which evaporates again during the first hours of the day. On no account should the surface of the plants be allowed to stay wet for days on end, as this promotes fungus infections. The water used for misting should be as far as possible lime-free - rainwater or softened water is ideal - otherwise deposits may form on the spines and the skin of the cacti in the course of time. Epiphytes are especially appreciative of misting, as they are accustomed to high levels of atmospheric humidity in their native locations.

Fertilizer

Some people still believe that cacti must not be fed, as this will cause them to grow flabby. This is incorrect. Many cacti grow in regions with a hot, tropical climate, others in areas with large temperature differences between summer and winter and even between day and night. In such conditions the soil is very often subject to severe weathering, which process rapidly releases a plentiful supply of nutritive substances for the plants. For example, there are areas where the evaporation of water drawn up from the ground carries dissolved mineral salts to the surface of the plants, resulting in efflorescence and salt crystallization. In view of this it must be correct to provide our plants with ample quantities of nutritive salts in their water supply, and indeed this approach has been successful. After all, the pots and pans in which we grow cacti only provide them with a small fraction of the soil into which they are able to send their roots in their home location. The important factor is how we feed them.

A supply of particular mineral substances is essential to any plant if it is to grow and flourish. The main nutrients are nitrogen (chemical symbol N), phosphorus (P), potassium (K), sulphur (S), calcium (Ca) and magnesium (Mg). Plants also require trace elements including boron, iron, cobalt, copper, manganese, molybdenum and zinc, and these minerals are equally indispensable to the plants, albeit in tiny quantities. Different plant species are not uniform in their requirement for nutrients and trace elements. Cacti have adapted to the conditions of their native environment by growing slowly and in a compact form, and their overall growth is much less and slower than that of other plants. The nutrient which is the chief stimulus and promoter of growth in plants is nitrogen. Fertilizers rich in nitrogen have the expected effect on cacti:

initial growth is luxuriant, but the plants do become flabby and extremely vulnerable to disease; the spines are thin and colourless, and the plants are less likely to flower. For this reason the nutritive salts used in cactus fertilizer must contain less nitrogen than the salts used for other plants. A good nutritive salt for cacti must contain less than 8 per cent of nitrogen, and for this reason standard general-purpose garden fertilizers are not suitable. The only fertilizers which should be used are what many companies term flowering fertilizers, in contrast to growth fertilizers, or - preferably - special cactus fertilizers. Cactus seedlings and plants recently transplanted into good soil require absolutely no nitrogen at first; the soil contains an adequate supply. We also introduce easily absorbed nitrogen into the soil in the form of nitrates when we acidify the water with nitric acid.

The only cacti which can be given a relatively high-nitrogen fertilizer are the very vigorous plants such as many species of columnar cactus, *Opuntia* and *Echinopsis*, but even then only at fairly long intervals.

Phosphorus and potassium are both of great significance to healthy plants. A good supply of these two nutrients promotes sturdy, compact growth, and increases the plants' ability to flower, and their resistance to fungal and pest attack and to cold conditions. A good cactus fertilizer should therefore contain an above-average proportion of phosphorus and potassium.

Calcium (Ca) also deserves a special mention; many cactus enthusiasts consider it to be an important factor in the formation of powerful and strongly-coloured spines. An adequate supply of calcium is often provided by calcareous water. If additional calcium is given, it must not be in a form which would make the soil alkaline. We recommend that a little manuring lime is added now and then to the water which is given to the plants. Occasionally a little superphosphate can also be dissolved in the water. This substance is acid in nature; it contains gypsum and also supplies the cacti with extra phosphorus and sulphur. Many recipes for cactus

fertilizer have been published, but we cannot advise the beginner to mix his own fertilizer from the raw materials. The reaction of the different mineral salts with the soil and with each other is often difficult to predict, even for experts. The raw materials are often difficult to obtain, and precise mixing really demands highly accurate scales, especially when we are dealing with the trace elements. It is much simpler either to use an established commercial cactus fertilizer, or any low-nitrogen fertilizer such as Phostrogen, or tomato fertilizer.

Many cactus growers add a certain amount of fertilizer to their soil. Ordinary standard compost already contains fertilizer, but if the soil is 'diluted' with large quantities of Perlite, sand, chippings, pumice gravel and other non-nutritive substances, then fertilizer as described above may be necessary. If you do this, be sure to mix the fertilizer in very thoroughly. Peru-Guano is a rather unbalanced fertilizer containing a relatively high proportion of phosphorus, but comparatively little potassium. Because of this an admixture of Peru-Guano should be supplemented with periodic doses of other fertilizers.

Recently greater attention has been given to the provision of the trace elements mentioned above. With the admixture of sand, chippings, Perlite and similar substances the soil is in one sense diluted, and thus relatively low in nutrients. In an attempt to resolve the problem, many cactus enthusiasts use pure potassium phosphate as fertilizer, while others use a mixture of an ordinary plant fertilizer with potassium phosphate. This process produces the desirable result of reducing the nitrogen content of the fertilizer, but has the undesirable side-effect of reducing its trace element content. We advise the cactus grower to pay particular attention to the provision of trace elements. A lack of these minerals is undoubtedly one cause of unsatisfactory growth and flowering in cacti, especially if the plants have not been transplanted for a long time. Peru-Guano is an example of a compound which contains an adequate proportion of trace elements.

Special fertilizers rich in trace elements have been produced recently; these can even be mixed in with the soil as a precautionary measure.

When to feed

As a general rule cacti should not be fed during the dormant period, nor shortly before nor shortly after. Before the dormant period the cacti must be allowed to finish their shooting and should not be stimulated to new growth. For the same reason nutrients must not be given during the dormant period. When the roots are completely dry it is important not to apply fertilizer, so the first, careful watering after the dormant period should contain no nutrients.

In the vegetative period, roughly from April/May to the beginning/middle of August in the Northern Hemisphere, fertilizer can be added whenever the plants are watered, i.e. every 10 to 20 days. Dissolve the nutritive salts in water, using the quantities recommended in the instructions supplied with the product. The amount suggested is usually about 1 gram of nutrient per litre of water. Liquid fertilizers are also available; these are measured out with the help of a measuring beaker which is often supplied in the form of the container's cap. When you are watering with a nutrient solution take care not to spray the liquid over the plants, as unsightly chemical residues may be left on the body and spines.

Epiphytes

Epiphytes are the exception to our rule concerning high-nitrogen fertilizers. These plants grow in nitrogen-rich rotten matter high up in trees, and can therefore tolerate fertilizers which are richer in nitrogen, i.e. ordinary garden fertilizers available from garden shops. This applies equally to the vigorous Selenicerei which usually also root in humus. Even these humus-rooting plants should only be given general-purpose fertilizer alternately with cactus fertilizer, rather than general-purpose fertilizer alone.

Repotting

As with other indoor plants cacti need to be transplanted from time to time, but as individually necessary rather than in accordance with a general stratagem, so as to avoid disturbing the plants unnecessarily. Cacti should be repotted if they have been standing in the same pot for a number of years and have finally reached a size which no longer bears a reasonable relationship to the pot, or if growth and flower formation are in decline. Transplanting is also advisable if a cactus looks unwell - whether as a result of an accumulation of harmful substances in the soil, or possibly through attack by pests such as mealy bug. Repotting should be carried out in late winter if possible, or in the early spring, when the plants are in their dormant period. The soil round the plants is dry, and the new soil should be equally so. This dryness reduces to a minimum the danger of rot resulting from the inevitable root damage caused by transplanting. At this time hardly any young root tips are present, and the plant's new growth is not disturbed. The first task when cacti are to be repotted is to set up a suitable work area, such as a table in the greenhouse or in a spare room, or perhaps the kitchen table can be commandeered and protected with a few old newspapers. The equipment you will need, the new soil substrate and new cactus pots should all be prepared beforehand. Cactus spines can inflict painful injuries if you do not take particular care when handling the plants, so your hands should be protected with thick leather work gloves for this process. They are available from garden shops and building merchants. During the dormant period, when the soil is dry, cacti are very easily removed from plastic pots. The surface layer of soil is loosened with a blunt wooden stick or a pencil, then the pot is carefully inverted - and the plant complete with root ball will slide out. Cacti can be

rather difficult to release from old clay pots. If this should occur, grip the neck of the root with your gloved hand and strike the top edge of the pot against the edge of the table to release the root ball. If there is a large crock over the drain hole, you can attempt to push the root ball out using a wooden stick or pencil. If a valuable plant is really firmly anchored, the old pot has to be broken up, otherwise the plant may be damaged by tugging too strongly. Root balls which are felted up can be loosened carefully using a blunt wooden stick. The old soil can be shaken out of the roots, and old, dead roots carefully shaken off or rubbed off. Sometimes roots are found at the bottom of the pot which have grown round and round in a circular pattern forming many layers, some of them up to 1 m. long. The longest roots should be cut down to a length of about 25 cm. using a sharp knife, to stimulate strong new root formation in the fresh, healthy soil.

The root system must be carefully checked for disease and infestation. Diseased roots are cut back to sound tissue using a sharp knife. If rot has already reached the neck of the root then this also must be cut off. The plant can then either be grafted or left for at least four weeks for the cut surfaces to dry off, after which time it will grow new roots like a cutting. This is also a good time to remove any undesired or redundant offsets or pups from the mother plant. Large cut surfaces on the roots and the damaged areas resulting from removing the pups should be dusted with charcoal powder to avoid possible rot.

The new plant container should not be too large; the plant should be able to send its roots throughout the soil available to it within a short period. Clay crocks should be placed over the drainage holes of the new pot, or alternatively a drainage layer of small pebbles, igneous rock waste or

Repotting cacti with powerful spines: hold the plant firmly with two flat wooden sticks and add soil from the sides using a small scoop.

Styromull can be placed in the pot first. The next stage is to hold the plant in the pot in a gloved hand, and check that it is located centrally and at a height which will give the same soil surface level as in the old pot. Cactus soil is then carefully added from all sides, with the help of a small toy spade or an old spoon. The pot should be banged lightly on the table several times, so that the loose soil runs into the spaces between the roots. Finally the soil should be pressed down lightly. Do not press down too hard, and on no account ram the soil down; on the one hand fine roots will be torn off, on the other the soil will be very densely compacted. Cacti should not be watered after repotting; leave them dry for about a week in a shady position. During this period any damage caused by the disruption will heal, and no rot will occur.

When repotting cacti which are particularly spiny, or Opuntias with their innumerable small spines, even stout leather gloves do not provide adequate protection. In such cases we recommend that the cacti should be held firm between two small, flat wooden sticks, roughly in the manner of chopsticks. Cacti which form clusters, with a shallow, fibrous root system, should not be planted in too deep a pot, as their roots will not penetrate the deeper soil layers. Shallow pans are more suitable. At the other extreme are cacti with taproots. Many of these species are denizens of extreme climatic zones, and are adapted to extreme economy in their use of water. These plants are often sensitive to stagnant moisture around the neck of the root and the taproot itself. Therefore it is better to bed the neck of the root and the taproot in a very permeable substrate containing a high proportion of small pebbles, coarse sharp sand and Styromull. Large columnar cacti, which are not very stable in the new pot after transplanting, can be supported with a stick until they are once more firmly anchored.

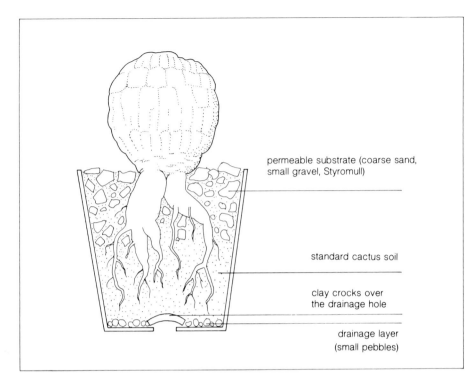

permeable substrate (coarse sand, small gravel, Styromull)

standard cactus soil

clay crocks over the drainage hole

drainage layer (small pebbles)

Species with a taproot are sensitive to moisture; they should be planted as shown here (please refer also to the text)

Cacti and their flowers

For many beginners to cactus culture success in persuading their plants to flower is of great importance. The first cacti which flower under their own care will often remain a cherished memory for many years. More experienced cactus growers judge their skill and their methods of cultivation by their success in producing flowers from species which are considered to be difficult in terms of flowering. Thus the formation of flowers in cacti and the factors which influence flowering are of interest to all cactus enthusiasts.

The production of cactus flowers is viewed in different ways by different cultivators. On the one hand we have the amateur enthusiast, whose aim is to obtain cactus flowers at all costs. His purpose is to produce flowers from plants which may well be temperamental, rare, or may only flower at an advanced age. The professional nurseryman, on the other hand, also wants flowers - because flowering plants are easier to sell - but he also wants the flowers at a

particular time of year: flowering Christmas cacti at Christmas, flowering Easter cacti at Easter, and flowering *Mammillaria zeilmanniana* on Mother's Day. Experiments have been made in controlling the time of flower development of a number of interesting plants. The main control mechanism is the supply of light - where necessary with artificial supplementary lighting or shading - and the temperature.

Let us return to the point of view of the enthusiastic amateur. What are the factors which influence the flowering of cacti? The research which has been carried out to date, and which only applies to a small number of species, leads us to conclude that there are several significant influences. If a cactus is to flower it must first reach a certain minimum size and a certain minimum age. The size and age may vary widely from genus to genus, and the following list gives a few examples. Calculated from the date of sowing, one might expect the first flowers to

appear after the following periods:

Rebutia minuscula	1 - 2 years
Mammillaria zeilmanniana, *M. prolifera*	2 - 3 years
Gymnocalycium baldianum, *G. andreae*	3 - 4 years
Mammillaria elegans, Notocactus ottonis, *Lobivia jajoiana, Mammillaria rhodantha,* *M. parkinsonii*	4 - 5 years
Echinocereus triglochidiatus	5 - 6 years
Notocactus leninghausii	7 - 9 years
Oreocereus trollii, *Trichocereus candicans*	10 - 15 years

Even in closely related genera there can be considerable differences in flowering characteristics. For example *Echinopsis* species are capable of flowering as much younger and smaller plants than many of the closely related Trichocerei, most of which only flower at an advanced age. In hybrids between Echinopses and Trichocerei the offspring often retain the beautiful flowers of the Trichocerei but unfortunately also their tendency not to flower until they have reached an advanced age. The cultivators of hybrids between *Echinopsis* and *Trichocereus* sometimes have to wait for a long time for the first flowers. Clearly the minimum flowering age is genetically based.

Most columnar cacti need to attain a considerable size before they are able to flower, but if the top of a flowering columnar cactus is cut off and rooted as a cutting, then it retains its flowering capability and will flower as a much smaller plant. The reason behind this is that the small cutting also contains flowering hormones and can therefore produce flowers. If the cutting grows, one would expect that the flowering hormone would gradually be diluted, and that flowering would eventually cease, but this is not the case. Perhaps the flowering hormone, once formed, stimulates the plant to form more of the same substance. In other instances it has proved possible to transfer the flowering hormone to non-flowering plants by the technique of grafting, and thereby persuade them also to produce flowers.

As well as the size and age of the

plant, feeding is a very important factor in the production of flowers. If a plant is fed too much nitrogen and becomes flabby, vegetative growth is promoted at the expense of the plant's willingness to flower. The enthusiast therefore should take considerable trouble to provide his cacti with a balanced, low-nitrogen fertilizer, rich in phosphorus and potassium.

One essential factor in the formation of flowers in cacti is the strict observance of a dormant period. It is during this period of dormancy that the pattern of flower formation is laid down. Research into this aspect has been carried out on a number of cacti (W. Runger: *Licht und Temperatur im Zierpflanzenbau* - Light and temperature in the raising of ornamental plants - 1976) and the results showed that the ideal dormant period in terms of flower formation was 40-70 days at a temperature of 10°C or slightly lower in the case of *Notocactus tabularis* and *N. scopa, Mammillaria zeilmanniana, M. bocasana* and *M. longicoma, Rebutia marsoneri, R. krainziana* and *R. minuscula* ssp. *violaciflora, Gymnocalycium baldianum* and *Echinopsis aurea*. As the length of the cool period is increased, the number of flowers formed also rises. High levels of light intensity during and especially after the cool period further reinforces the effect, and even more flowers are formed. The day length usually has no influence on flower formation in temperatures up to 10°C. If temperatures are kept higher, more flowers are formed when the period of daylight is kept short than when it is longer. In the case of *Rhipsalidopsis gaertneri*, the Easter cactus and one of the epiphytic cacti, the formation of flowers varies according to temperature and day length. The optimum values are a cool period of 50 days at 10-15°C and short day-time lighting.

Epiphytic cacti such as *Rhipsalis* when kept the whole year round in even warmth and humidity in a greenhouse, usually flower only when the days become shorter.

The experienced cactus grower will think the recommended temperature of 10°C rather high for ideal flower formation in Rebutias, for example. However, these are just the species which are subject to wide variations in temperature between day and night in their home conditions, rather than the even temperatures which were probably inevitable in the research mentioned above, in order to allow reasonable analysis of the investigations. This agrees with the experience of collectors in Germany, who have found that these cacti flower outstandingly well if they are left in temperatures which vary in the range -3 to +12°C during the dormant period.

In addition to light and temperature a further important factor in cactus flower formation is that the plants should be kept fairly dry or even completely dry during the dormant period. Many cactus growers are convinced that cacti which are reluctant to flower can be forced into forming flowers by keeping the plants consistently dry until well into the spring.

If too much water is given too early - thus stimulating vegetative growth - the points from which flowers would have grown may either regress or be modified into shoots. Our basic advice is not to water flowering cacti in the spring if the flower buds are clearly visible.

In fact there are many cacti whose genetic material causes them to flower readily and abundantly, and others which only produce flowers rarely and in small numbers. To mention a few examples, *Mammillaria dixanthocentron, M. geminispina, M. plumosa, M. viperina* or *M. yaquensis* rate as reluctant to flower. One factor here may well be that we have not yet established the correct conditions for the culture of many plants which grow under extreme conditions in their homeland. But even within individual species there are evident genetic differences in the willingness to flower of plants. In view of this variation, if you sow a large number of seed of one species you should not retain just those seedlings which grow particularly strongly, but should watch for those seedlings which also set flowers early on.

The yellow form of Lobivia silvestrii can only survive if grafted on a green stock.

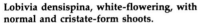
Lobivia densispina, white-flowering, with normal and cristate-form shoots.

Cristate form of Haageocereus multangularis var. turbidus

Grafting

The grafting of cacti is the subject of considerable controversy amongst cactus enthusiasts. Many decry grafted cacti as unnatural or aesthetically unacceptable, while advocates are equally passionate in their defence. Cacti are grafted for a variety of reasons. By grafting a slow growing cactus onto a vigorous stock the plant grows more rapidly, with the result that the nurseryman can obtain large saleable plants more quickly. Grafted on a tall rootstock, many cacti grow twice to ten times as quickly as on their own roots. Cacti can be brought to flowering maturity several years earlier by grafting. This aspect is of great importance to those who are raising cactus hybrids, in which case it is vital for them to see the colour and form of the flowers of a hybrid as soon as possible, so that further work with the hybrids can be carried out. The flowers of many newly discovered species are not yet known. By accelerating the production of mature plants the flowers are also produced earlier, thus enriching our knowledge. Some cacti mutations have occurred which lack chlorophyll (a freak genetic modification); these plants, including the red-coloured varieties of *Gymnocalycium mihanovichii* var. *friedrichii* or the yellow forms of *Lobivia*

(Chamaecereus) silvestrii are not viable because of their lack of chlorophyll, and therefore must be grafted to survive. Grafting can also be used as a means of propagating cacti.

Regrafting involves leaving a stump of the scion on its former rootstock; the scion then produces shoots which can in turn be grafted or rooted. This method of propagation is especially

Cristate form of Espostoa lanata.

important with rare species, or those which tend to hybridization, where the the object is to propagate from plants which are known to be genetically true. The fan-like and massed cristate forms of cacti, which are popular with many cactus enthusiasts because of their weird shapes and unusual spine formations, can usually only be kept alive in the long-term if grafted. Furthermore, rare cacti which develop a diseased root and for which there is scant likelihood of a cutting taking root, can be rescued by grafting. Many cactus growers try to adapt temperamental cacti from extreme habitats and climates to the conditions prevailing in their collection by grafting them onto a sturdy, strong growing stock. This technique perhaps represents the point at which cactus grafting should cease. Many cactus lovers would claim that the proper approach is to find out the conditions under which these plants grow in the wild, and then to try to keep them in similar conditions, growing on their own roots. In fact, it is precisely the slow-growing cacti from extreme regions which suffer most from the technique, looking greatly altered, puffed up and flabby when grafted. The overall impression is generally of inferior spine formation and a greener colour, and the plants are often more susceptible to fungus infection and infestation. Purely from the aesthetic

69

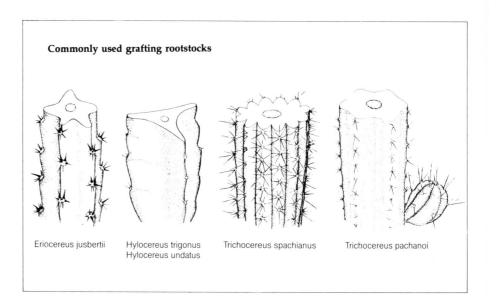

Commonly used grafting rootstocks

Eriocereus jusbertii   Hylocereus trigonus   Trichocereus spachianus   Trichocereus pachanoi
Hylocereus undatus

point of view, many cactus enthusiasts find the appearance of a globular species grafted on a tall rootstock unattractive. Overall the grafting of cacti can be considered as a valuable technique in the cultivation of cacti, provided that it is used for a genuine purpose. Grafting should not be carried out indiscriminately, and only when really necessary. Cacti which grow well and flower on their own root, should not be grafted as a matter of course; after all, even the plants used as rootstock are not totally devoid of problems in cultivation.

Standard rootstock species

Cactus species suitable for use as stocks for grafting include the sturdy, fast-growing types, typically Cerei, and especially the Trichocerei. *Eriocereus jusbertii* in particular was a very popular rootstock in the early decades of cactus breeding. The drawing shows the appearance of this fresh green to blue-green plant, with its subulate (awl-shaped) spines, red when young and turning black later, and light-coloured areoles. Its native habitat is not known; it may even be a hybrid. Once it has reached a height of about 30 cm. it produces large, white flowers. *Eriocereus jusbertii* likes a nutritious, humus-rich soil and constant humidity. It should not be completely dry even in winter, and should not be kept in temperatures lower than 10-12°C. In earlier times

cactus enthusiasts often cultivated their cacti in a hotbed, in which the mild bottom warmth and high level of nutrition resulted in *Eriocereus jusbertii* and the cacti grafted onto it growing magnificently. It was also claimed that the stock transmitted its willingness to flower to the scion, leading to early flowers. If you are able to offer conditions similar to those described, especially in winter, *Eriocereus jusbertii* is a good stock. It cannot be recommended for cool and dry winter conditions however, as it does not resume growth until late in the spring, and even then only with some reluctance.

Not quite so sensitive, but equally appreciative of reasonably high winter temperatures, is *Trichocereus spachianus*. This plant, a native of northern Argentina, is glossy green, has 10 to 15 low ribs, and about 10 needle-like, stiff, sharp spines per areole, 1 to 2 cm. long, and yellow to light brown in colour. The large number of piercing spines makes grafting difficult, and *Trichocereus spachianus* also has a tendency to produce unsightly corky tissue at the base. For these reasons it is not so widely used as a rootstock, although it does accept the scion well.

For a sturdy rootstock which grows rapidly we recommend *Trichocereus macrogonus* and - in particular - *Trichocereus pachanoi*, especially for those enthusiasts who keep their cacti cool and dry in the winter. These two species are very similar in appearance;

both have a green to blue-green body, often with 7 ribs. The spine formation of *Trichocereus macrogonus* is slightly more pronounced than that of *Trichocereus pachanoi*; the latter is sometimes almost spineless in culture. The spine formation is quite variable, and in some cases is not even uniform on one plant, as shown in the drawing.

Hylocerei of the *Hylocereus trigonus* and *Hylocereus undatus* group have gained increasing popularity as rootstocks amongst nurserymen in recent years, a trend which probably started in Japan. These cacti, easily recognized by their triangular cross-section, are climbing plants from the primeval forests of the Caribbean. Under conditions which the nurseryman can easily create in a well-equipped greenhouse, this stock produces very good growth in the scion. The soft flesh and spineless habit of the rootstock make the grafting process itself a simple matter. These species cannot be recommended as a rootstock to the ordinary enthusiast, however. They like a uniform, moist, warm climate, as might be expected from their native habitat. Excessively low temperatures, dryness and especially the use of cold water for watering result in the stock languishing and rotting, and hence often the loss of the scion.

Echinopsis offsets are often recommended, but our experience with them has been discouraging. They are not suit-

cacti are grafted onto a fast-growing stock there is a danger that they will degenerate and produce unnatural, flabby growth. Because of their robust nature these Trichocerei also form ideal stocks for cacti which are to be overwintered cool. As *Trichocereus pasacana* and especially *Trichocereus fulvilanus* have very powerful spine formations, grafting requires a degree of skill - and sometimes it seems a terrible insult to disfigure a plant with such splendid spines.

Techniques of grafting

The period of growth is the best time for grafting, i.e. from the end of May to the beginning of August in the Northern Hemisphere. The stock plant should be in good condition and growing strongly.

The height at which the graft is made varies according to purpose. If the graft is intended to produce a beautiful, permanent plant, then the cut is made as low as possible, perhaps 4-5 cm. above the soil surface, so that the rootstock is not conspicuous when the scion has grown. However, if maximum possible rate of growth is to be achieved, then the appearance of the plant can be ignored and the graft carried out as high as possible. Wherever possible the stock should have a greater diameter than the scion, so that the latter has a stable base.

able as a permanent rootstock because they are prone to sprouting, and do not grow well for long. Their only use is to produce strong growth in small plants, which are then grafted again the following year.

Strong-growing Opuntias also represent a sound, robust stock for a period of one year, but the scion usually has to be regrafted. Only *Opuntia bergeriana* can be considered as a permanent rootstock, for Cerei in particular, for which it produces a sturdy, rock-hard root. If you wish to graft Cerei then *Opuntia bergeriana* is recommended, although *Cereus* species usually grow well on their own roots. It has been shown that it is better for the health of the stock if any side shoots are left to grow out and removed in the autumn or the following spring, rather than being removed immediately.

Experienced growers also value the Trichocerei group based on *Trichocereus pasacana* and *Trichocereus fulvilanus* as rootstocks. These Trichocerei are very robust; they can be overwintered cool and dry, and will even survive short night frosts without problem. They hardly produce any shoots at all, which is in their favour, as the production of lateral shoots from the rootstock can be a real nuisance. The *Trichocereus* species named above do grow slowly, but they produce a good thick stem. For this reason they are especially suitable for grafting cacti which grow slowly by nature. If such

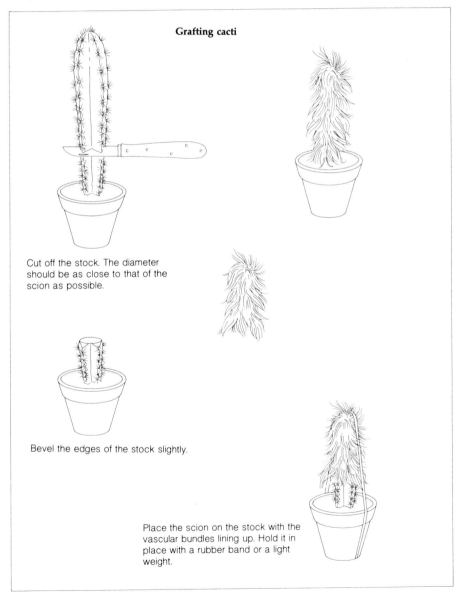

Grafting cacti

Cut off the stock. The diameter should be as close to that of the scion as possible.

Bevel the edges of the stock slightly.

Place the scion on the stock with the vascular bundles lining up. Hold it in place with a rubber band or a light weight.

The part of the rootstock through which the cut is made must be at least 3 to 4 months old. New-grown tissue tends to collapse, and in nearly all cases the scion is then rejected. The only situation in which a fairly young rootstock may be used is when very young seedlings are to be grafted. At the other extreme the tissue to be cut must not be many years old. If it has lignified (become woody) then the two plants will not unite in the majority of cases. There is a way of ensuring a successful bond in most cases of this type. If you cut into the rootstock and find it very woody, then make an intermediate graft using *Trichocereus schickendantzii*, which is very soft-fleshed and grows virtually anywhere. This intermediate piece on which we then graft our scion should be around 3 cm. high. The two grafts can be carried out simultaneously, i.e. you do not have to wait until *T. schickendantzii* has become established. *T. schickendantzii* produces shoots very profusely, and every collection should include at least one example to supply shoots for this form of intermediate grafting.

The principle of grafting is to bring the freshly cut surfaces of the two plants together, with their vascular bundles in contact, and to hold the stock and scion together under pressure until they have united. This may take a few days to a few weeks, depending on the age of the plants and the weather. On average the scion begins growing about 3 to 4 weeks after being grafted.

Various grafting procedures have been developed, some of which cannot be taken seriously. For this reason we shall only discuss the two proven methods: the horizontal graft and wedging. The most important grafting technique is that using the horizontal cut. It is used for all plants whose bodies are round (globular cacti, Cerei) or oval (Opuntias) in cross-section. The tool required is a knife with a thin, sharp, non-rusty blade. After each cut the blade should be cleaned and dried. If you are dealing with particularly precious plants the blade should be dipped in alcohol in order to disinfect it. Make sure it is dry before using it again.

The graft should be carried out on a warm, sunny day, as then the scion and stock will unite more quickly and without problem. Cut through the stock at the desired height using a single, smooth pull - not sawing to and fro, and not using great pressure. The tip of the stock which has been removed is placed on one side. The edges of the ribs of the stock have to be removed, along with any groups of spines which are in the way, in this case by cutting out the areoles. The plant to be grafted is now cut through, and again the edges of the ribs cut back slightly. Should the cut surface of the stock have sunken in irregularly in the meantime (usually because the stock is too young), or the cut surface has already dried out noticeably (because you have taken too long in preparing the scion), then a further thin slice should be cut from the stock. The scion is now slid sideways onto the stock, so that neither air nor injurious foreign bodies can get between the two surfaces, either of which could hinder growth. The grafting can only succeed if the vascular bundles of the stock and the scion are aligned as accurately as possible. They are clearly visible as rings, and at least a few of the bundles must be in line. For this reason if the scion is much smaller than the base it should not be positioned exactly central, but offset to one side, located over one section of the stock's ring of vascular bundles.

The scion should now be weighted down in this position and not allowed to shift. This can be achieved in a number of simple ways. For example, rubber bands can be stretched over the scion and under the pot, taking care to route them over the drainage hole to avoid them jumping off sideways. Two to four such bands can be fitted, crossing over each other. Alternatively we can take a triangular sheet of glass, one corner of which is placed on the scion, its opposite edge resting on one or more bricks. If the scion is large, the weight of the glass sheet can be supplemented by a stone or a piece of metal placed above the scion. The weight should be adjusted so that it presses the scion down firmly, but - obviously - without squashing it. If the scion is quite tall a

useful method is to tie two stones or pieces of metal of equal weight to a length of string perhaps 20 to 30 cm. long - or perhaps a strip of plastic cut from a plastic bag - which is then fitted over the plants with the band or cord running over the crown of the scion. However, the best method we have seen is the use of Aulbach grafting rings. This method was invented by the cactus enthusiast F. Aulbach, from Haibach near Aschaffenburg. A metal ring is fitted with rubber bands which cross over at its centre, and the ring is placed over the plants with the crossing point of the bands located centrally over the top of the scion. It makes no difference how tall the scion is. If the scion sinks as a result of shrinkage of the cut surface, the pressure still remains constant. There is no danger of the device slipping off, as in the case of rubber bands stretched round scion and pot. A variety of sizes and weights of metal ring is available, providing the ideal ring for any size of scion. Aulbach rings seem to be a reliable and at the same time simple aid to grafting. If the scion has fragile spines the pressure of the rubber bands or cords used to press it down onto the stock can be cushioned using a piece of foam rubber between the bands and the scion. In fact there is little need for concern; if the graft is successful the resultant vigorous growth will soon bring the compressed spines back into shape.

It is essential to work quickly when grafting, as growth will be retarded if the cut surfaces dry out. The freshly grafted plant should be placed in a light, warm, but not sunny position, and you should avoid the temptation to spray or mist the cut surfaces to keep them wet. The rubber bands can be removed after 10 to 14 days, but the grafted plant should still be handled carefully at first. After a further two weeks the crown of the scion should show new growth, and its healthy general condition and amply filled-out body will show that the graft has been successful. If the two plants do not unite the scion will show no fresh growth, and it will fall off the stock either by itself or at the slightest touch. If this should happen, make new cuts and repeat the attempt. The

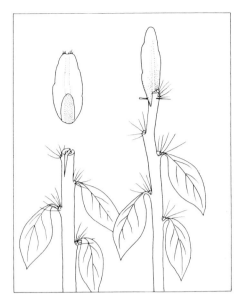

Wedging (here on Pereskia): the base of the leaf is trimmed at an angle on both sides. The scion and stock are then held together with a long cactus spine.

tip of the rootstock which was cut off can be rooted again after cutting back the edges of the ribs slightly to encourage the new roots to form at the centre rather than from the edges. It is then allowed to dry out for three to four weeks before rooting. One year later it will be ready to serve as a rootstock itself. If the plant from which the scion was taken has an intact root system, this also can be used. Once again the edges of the ribs should be cut back slightly so that water will run off the cut surface. In most cases the stump will produce small shoots which can be used for further grafts, and thus help to propagate a rare plant.

Special grafting techniques

If the stems you wish to graft are very thin, such as those of *Wilcoxia*, *Corryocactus* or similar species, then the following procedure should be adopted: cut a piece about 4 cm. long, and slice it in half along its length, cutting exactly down the centre. Lay the cut surface on the rootstock, i.e. with the stem of the scion horizontal. If the ring of vascular bundles on the stock is broad enough, both halves can be placed on the stock side by side. This type of graft usually produces shoots from several areoles, producing

a fine, bushy plant. Naturally some suitable means of pressing the scion down on the stock has to be devised.

Wedging is only recommended if really thin stems have to be grafted, such as the joints of the Christmas or Easter cactus, or seedlings of leaf cacti. They are best grafted on *Eriocereus jusbertii* or *Eriocereus bonplandii* at a height of about 30 cm. This technique can produce beautiful miniature tree-form cacti. The graft is carried out as follows: the stock should be relatively slender; remove the tip and cut vertically downward to a depth of 2 to 3 cm. The scion is then prepared, using a razor blade for preference, by cutting away the outer skin on both flat sides to form a wedge shape. The cut faces should be about 2 cm. long. The wedge-shaped end is then slipped into the slit in the stock. A fairly long cactus spine is pushed horizontally through the graft to hold the scion in place.

Finally we come to two specialized grafting techniques: seedling grafting and tall grafting. In general terms it takes a few years, and in some cases many years, for seedlings to become mature adult plants. Seedling grafting can shorten this growth or maturation period quite significantly. The best time to graft the seedlings is after the first small spines have developed. An

outstanding species as rootstock for this technique is *Peireskiopsis*, with its thin stems, vigorous growth and powerful spine formation. This species also starts flowering when very young. Grafting on *Peireskiopsis* should only be carried out in the first half of the year; grafts made later in the year have repeatedly turned out unsuccessful. To carry out the graft a clean razor blade must be used. If this is brand new, it must be degreased wth soapy water then dried well, leaving no traces of soap. Fast-growing *Cereus* seedlings about 3 to 10 cm. in height also make a suitable stock. The *Cereus* stock is cut off just below the crown, while the seedling is trimmed in such a way that it is as close to a globular form as possible. If the ring of vascular bundles of the stock is reasonably large, then it will be clear upon close examination that it is composed of individual points, each of which is a vascular bundle. You now have to place the tiny axis of the seedling accurately on one such point. The general rule that the youngest tissue is unsuitable for grafting does not hold true for seedling grafts. On the contrary, seedlings can only grow on young tissue. In favourable weather the stock and scion usually unite within 24 hours. Naturally the downward pressure which is exerted to hold the delicate seedlings on the

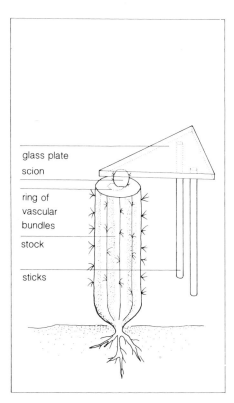

Seedling grafting

stock must be extremely gentle. We recommend a small triangular sheet of thin glass, its three points resting on the seedling and two sticks pushed into the soil next to the stock. In fact the seedlings will usually 'take' even if not weighted down. The seedling scions are best kept in slightly 'clammy' air. When the scions have reached a size when they appear to be fat balls surmounting a thin stalk, they can then be regrafted, or cut off, allowed to dry out for about 10 days, and then rooted.

Tall grafting is carried out using vigorous Cerei 1 to 3 m. tall as the stock, either at their crown or on their side shoots. The most successful grafts of this type can only be achieved using Cerei planted out in a greenhouse bed. Onto these plants are grafted scions about 2 to 5 cm. in diameter, as high up on the stock as possible. For example, the scions could be seedlings one or two years old, grown by the seedling graft technique just described, and thus already very large. The growth which they then produce on the large old Cerei is enormous, and only a year later the scions will exhibit a spine formation which is in no way

inferior to that of imported plants. After a few more years, however, these large, vigorous scions have to be removed and rooted separately. Their growth then slows down and eventually ceases altogether, a phenomenon which has not been fully explained, but which is presumably connected with the age of the stock. In their natural habitat branching Cerei also produce more and more side shoots, while the main stems cease growing.

Caring for cacti over the course of the year

This section is aimed mainly at the beginner, and presents a guide to the different aspects of cultivating cacti through the seasons. Basically the text covers the requirements of the commoner species, and where particular types call for special treatment - such as the winter-hard and epiphytic cacti - we refer you to the separate sections dealing with them.

This is a summary, and the problems are only covered briefly. A more detailed description can be found in the corresponding section of the book devoted to cactus culture. The time of year stated in the summary may well have to be varied slightly, according to whether the you live in a district with a relatively mild or harsh climate.

Early spring

In the case of cacti which flower in the early spring (mid-February to late March) the end of the winter dormant period is marked by the eruption of buds and the start of new growth at the crown. Among the earliest flowering species in the year are *Notocactus (Brasilicactus) haselbergii, Turbinicarpus valdezianus, Mammillaria pennispinosa, Mammillaria magallanii* and *Mammillaria moelleriana*.

Cacti which are not early flowering species can still be transplanted. Plants

should be repotted if they have grown too large for their containers, or if their soil is exhausted. When repotting in early spring the move should be from dry soil to dry soil. Cactus growers who have a heated sowing pan can sow seed in March. Depending on the immediate micro-climate, cactus enthusiasts who cultivate their plants on a window ledge, in an unheated greenhouse or in a garden frame will want to move the plants out of their winter quarters to the summer location in March - April. Precautions should be taken against isolated night frosts; temporary heating is one answer, or old woollen blankets kept close at hand for covering the coldframe.

At this time of year great care needs to be exercised to prevent scorching - including plants cultivated by a window. Cacti which have grown unaccustomed to sunshine during the dormant period can be damaged in March and April by the rapid increase in intensity and duration of solar radiation. For this reason it is wise to prepare some means of shading the plants for those unusually sunny days in early spring and the spring proper. The glass panes of the greenhouse can be painted with shading paint or covered with shading fabric; in an emergency the cacti can even be covered with sheets of tissue paper.

At this time of year the cacti also have to be accustomed to moisture again. Care is required here, particularly if the plants have been kept completely dry during the winter. On warm days in early spring they should be misted with warm water, and later sprayed over. This procedure washes off the dust and grime which accumulate in the winter, and stimulates the plants to form new root hairs. Only then are the cacti capable of absorbing the water which is given subsequently. The basic rule here is that the first water should be given slowly and sparingly in the early part of the year. With many cacti there is a danger that flower buds which have already formed will not actually develop flowers if they are stimulated into vegetative growth early on by watering too early and too generously. A clear example of this is the Echinocerei. For this reason it is important that the cactus enthusiast should not be hurried into giving generous doses of water in the early spring by one or two exceptionally fine days.

Spring (April to mid-June)

Cactus collections now present a splendid sight. Many cacti are in full bloom, including the majority of Mammillarias, Lobivias and Rebutias, while the Notocacti and *Echinopsis* species flower slightly later.

Non-flowering cacti should be given an adequate supply of moisture after about the end of May, while the flowering plants require it even earlier. After mid- May a low-nitrogen cactus feed can be added to the water, but do not apply the fertilizer solution to completely dry plants. In May and June the cacti are in full growth. Grafting can be carried out, and cuttings can be taken and rooted after an adequate period for drying out. Plants which show no growth in June are probably diseased. They should be carefully unpotted; diseased roots, or those under severe pest attack, have to be drastically cut back. After the cut surfaces have been dried the plant should be rerooted in the same manner as a cutting.

After April to May seed can be sown even without artificial soil heating. The seed pans should be kept in somewhat shady light, and must not be allowed to dry out completely at any time during the period of germination.

Summer (mid-June to mid-August)

The flowers of the summer-flowering species now add a dash of colour to cacti collections, including many Gymnocalyciums, Parodias, Coryphanthas and Astrophytums. Most cacti are in full growth. Much light and air are required, and any shading left over from the spring should be removed. The plants can now be watered and fed generously. Watering should be from underneath wherever possible. Excessive watering or spraying over the cacti can result in salt deposits on plants' bodies and spines, and the risk of fungus infection is also increased.

Many spring-flowering species, including many Mammillarias, Echinocerei and Rebutias, have a short summer rest in July to mid-August, and they should be watered less at this time. During this dormant period these spring-flowering plants may be repotted, but they must not be watered again until several days after transplanting.

Autumn (mid-August to mid-November)

A few Mammillarias, such as *Mammillaria rhodantha* and *Mammillaria hidalgensis* are still in flower, and to a lesser extent *Ariocarpus* and plants of the genus *Neoporteria* are also in bloom. For most cacti it is clear that the vegetative period is now over. The plants' new growth should be maturing, so that they will be able to survive the winter dormant period in good shape. The autumn is also a very important time in terms of strong spine formation, and for the initial stage of flower setting for the following spring.

After the end of August no more fertilizer should be given. After mid-September the amount of watering should be reduced, and after mid-October the quantity should be very small or even zero. Fresh air and large quantities of light - preferably unfiltered sunlight - are very important to the hardening-off process. The windows of the greenhouse and the garden frame should be opened wide, the panes cleaned, and the plants given no shade at all.

Cacti planted out should be left outside as long as possible to harden them off, but they must be protected from rainfall. Plants which do not produce their flowers until the autumn, and those which show a further burst of growth in autumn, should be found a particularly warm and sunny location, and kept slightly more moist.

Winter (mid-November to mid-February)

Only a few cacti are flowering now, including *Mammillaria schiedeana* and *Mammillaria plumosa,* the epiphytic Christmas cacti and many *Rhipsalis* species. These flowering plants should be kept warmer and moister than other cacti during this period.

Depending on the immediate climate and the state of the weather, cacti should be removed to their winter quarters in late October to mid-November. As the plants have been kept dry since mid-October and are by now slightly shrivelled, you do not need to be over-anxious when moving them; a brief, slight night frost will not harm the more robust species at this time. If you have a heated greenhouse the thermostat should be reset to the winter temperature, and the general level of weather-proofing should be improved by sealing all gaps, fitting plastic film underneath the glass, and similar measures.

When ensconced in their winter quarters the plants should again be checked carefully for disease and pests. Plants which show any trace of rot must be cut back to healthy tissue using a knife which is disinfected for each plant, and then newly rooted in the spring as a cutting, after a long period to dry off. Cacti affected by fungus infections and completely dehydrated plants should be discarded immediately complete with their soil, and the pots cleaned carefully before re-use. Fungal infections are best kept at bay by plenty of fresh air and a light position even in the winter quarters.

In the winter location the temperature should be around 5-10°C, and the plants should receive little or no water at all. After the end of January cacti which are not among the spring-flowering types can be repotted. The winter is also the time when the cactus enthusiast might care to extend his knowledge by studying specialist literature, and updating the notes, slides and information accumulated during the growth seasons.

The propagation of cacti

Cacti can be propagated from seed and by taking cuttings. If cuttings are rooted, the resultant plants are absolutely identical genetically to the mother plant. This is a crucial advantage if you wish to propagate a particularly fine example of a plant and obtain genetically identical offspring. The cactus enthusiast with an interest in botany might also be keen to have a genetically true offset of the very plant which was the subject of the original description. One unfortunate side-effect of mass propagation from cuttings is that any noteworthy plant which produces shoots readily is soon represented in all the cactus collections in the district. The danger then is that cactus enthusiasts might come to think of that particular plant as the only true representative of that species. The situation also results in a certain impoverishment in the genetic base of our collections.

Growing from seed, on the other hand, produces new individuals with a broad spread of variation. The cactus grower is then in a position to examine his multifarious seedlings and select the the most vigorous plants, those with the finest coloured spines, or those which flower early and profusely, and in this way build up an outstanding collection in the course of time.

Growing from seed is a relatively rapid means of acquiring new or rare species, which are often unavailable for years on end as adult plants. To every serious cactus enthusiast propagation from seed is a stimulating occupation. He will be fascinated to see how the seedling develops through the immature stage to the adult plant, sometimes changing shape and spine formation markedly in the process. Stocks of cacti in their native habitat are already greatly diminished, and the

Most cacti can be raised from seed without difficulty. Plants in controlled conditions are usually more vigorous than imported specimens. In just a few years seedlings can develop into handsome plants.

fact that raising cacti from seed makes further cactus imports largely superfluous is another important factor in its favour. Raising cacti from seed differs in several respects from the process with other plants. If you go about it correctly, your chances of success are 100 per cent.

Cactus seed

Sowing cactus seed and raising the young plants is a very pleasurable occupation, but does involve some work for the cultivator. Bearing in mind this investment in time, it is wise to consider carefully which cactus species you wish to raise at the outset.

Some species can only be raised from seed with great difficulty and much effort. For example, many Parodias produce very small seed, often as fine as dust particles; the minute seedlings which germinate from these tiny seeds do not reach the point where they can first be picked out for a very long time. Until that time they - and their guardian - are in a constant state of battle against the enemy forces of algae and fungi. The seeds of other cacti, including those of some Opuntias, are generally slow to germinate. Many of these seeds have special requirements: they have to swell up beforehand, or they require a fairly long dormant period - sometimes at low temperatures - or the hard seed shell needs to be filed away before sowing. Finally there are cacti such as certain *Ariocarpus* species whose seed do germinate well, but whose young plants grow extremely slowly. To the experienced cactus grower it is particularly satisfying if he succeeds in raising 'difficult' cacti from seed. The beginner, on the other hand, would be well advised to make his first experiments with seed with the easier species. Among these can be counted the majority of Cerei, Echinofossulocacti, Echinopses, Gymnocalyciums, Lobivias, Mammillarias, Notocacti and Rebutias.

The cactus cultivator has two options: he can buy cactus seed, or he can use his own or seed donated by friends. In either case they must be capable of germination. The seed of *Ariocarpus* and many Opuntias retain their power to germinate for up to a decade, but the germinating power of *Rebutia* seed is markedly diminished after as little as one year. Cactus seed should therefore come from the previous year's harvest wherever possible. In a few cases fresh seed does not, in fact, germinate well, and requires a certain period of dormancy before sowing. If you have plenty of seed available it is a good idea to sow half one year, and the remainder in the following year. Unfortunately the state of the seed is not evident from its appearance. The buoyancy test, which states that seed which sink are capable of germination, while those which float are not, is completely unreliable when applied to the seed of succulents and cacti. It is also important that the plants which grow from the seed should be as described on the label. It is very frustrating when seed purchased as *Gymnocalycium andreae* produces hybrid plants resulting from accidental insect pollination. And if a collector wishes to raise *Notocactus uebelmannianus* from

seed, because his collection lacks that species, he is likely to feel somewhat cheated if, because of a mix-up by the seed merchant, he obtains the common *Notocactus ottonis*. For these reasons it is best to stick to sound, well-established companies when buying cactus seed. Of special value is imported seed collected at the plants' native location. This applies in particular if the seed was collected by experts from precisely defined plants, and is then sold with the location printed on the packet. As there are often considerable distances between individual cactus sites in the wild, you run little risk of unwanted hybrids with this type of seed. In fact, cacti raised from such seed can be used as a basis for studying the differences between the plant communities at the native location.

If you wish to collect cactus seed for yourself or for friends, then that seed also should be capable of germination, and not include any accidental hybrids, with which few people will be pleased. Naturally it is important to select good-looking, vigorous parent plants which produce plenty of flowers. Generally two parent plants are required in order to obtain seed. A few cactus species, including those in the genera *Frailea* and *Rebutia*, set seed after self-pollination. Self-pollination means that the stigma of one flower is pollinated with the pollen from the same flower, or from another flower on the same plant. Cross pollination, i.e. fertilization with pollen from the flower of another plant, is nevertheless to be preferred because of the broader genetic base of the descendant plants. The two plants required for cross pollination must be genetically different. For example, it is not permissible to use one plant as parent which is an offset of the other parent plant, and equally the two plants must

not be offsets or shoots of the same mother plant.

To be sure of avoiding undesirable hybrids both the intended parent plants should be placed under bells or cages made of wire or nylon gauze shortly before the flowers break out. The bell can be home-made with a simple basic frame of wood or stiff wire and a covering of mosquito gauze. Pollination is carried out when the flowers are in full bloom, the stigma lobes have opened, the anthers are ripe and the flower pollen is powdery. A soft paintbrush is commonly used for the actual pollination, although it is also possible to physically transfer the anthers from one flower to the stigma of the other flower using fine tweezers. If you wish to pollinate a number of different flowers one after the other, you must use different paintbrushes; after use the brushes must be thoroughly cleaned, for instance by rinsing in clinical alcohol. They must be completely dry before being used for pollination again.

The pollinated flowers must be marked immediately, for example by fitting a label of a conspicuous colour. The label can be inscribed with the date of pollination and the plant number of its pollination partner. An alternative is to wrap a brightly coloured woollen thread round each pollinated flower. A list is then drawn up, noting the colour of the thread, and the date of pollination. The pollinated plants are kept under the gauze bell until the flower is completely withered.

Many cactus enthusiasts worry as to whether the cacti earmarked as parent plants will bloom simultaneously, but their fears are usually unfounded. It is simply amazing how often it happens that different cacti of one species open their flowers exactly on the same day. However, should the parent plants bloom at different times the pollen has to be stored (see section on raising hybrids, page 103). Cactus seeds are only fully viable if they are harvested when completely ripe. Many cacti develop a fleshy berry, and this should be removed when ripe. At this stage it is usually a deep red in colour. The ripe berry must be removed carefully and completely, otherwise it can lead to soiling or even - as occasionally occurs with Echinocerei - rotting of the mother plant. The cactus seed are washed out of the ripe berry. If the seeds are of sufficient size, this can be done in a tea strainer or a small linen bag and luke-warm water. Finally they are laid out on paper and dried. Other cactus species have dry fruits which burst when ripe, releasing their seed. Here the cultivator must be able to recognize the right moment for harvest, and carefully gather the seed when the seed capsules are already slightly open - the seeds could easily roll away and get lost otherwise. The harvested cactus seed should be labelled with the name and the year of harvest. In order to avoid mildew the cactus seed should be stored in such a way that air can get at them, i.e. not in plastic bags or airtight containers, but in open glass bottles or jars or in paper bags. Cactus seed should be kept dry and at room temperature until they are sown.

The seed tray

Seed is sown in an enclosed, but easily ventilated seed tray, or in a propagator in the greenhouse. A wide variety of sowing and seedling boxes and trays with clear, transparent plastic covers is available commercially. The plastic canopy is essential in order to mantain the humidity in the box. The seeds require relatively high atmospheric humidity in order to germinate, and they must never dry out during the germination period. Many types of propagator are fitted with some form of soil heating, while the better types can be fitted with a heater thermostat which allows the temperature to be set exactly to the level required.

The seedling box should stand in a well-lit location, but must not be placed in full sunshine without protection as brilliant sun would damage the delicate seedlings. For this reason the box must be lightly shaded when the sun is out, perhaps with a sheet of tissue paper laid over the top. The box can also be fitted with artificial lighting; for example, a warm-tone fluorescent strip light can be fitted above the seed pan. Its light output must be balanced for the requirements of the young seedlings, as strong infra-red light (dark red light) delays germination, while bright red light promotes it. An ordinary filament lamp is not recommended for lighting the seed pan, as its output includes too high a proportion of infra-red. The lighting above the seed pan should be switched on for about twelve hours in the daytime, but the lamp should not be fitted too close over the seed pan. A thermometer placed on the surface of the soil should not indicate more than 30°C even when the lighting has been on for a long period. A heated, thermostatically controlled propagator fitted with artificial lighting provides the indoor cultivator with virtually the same advantages as the gardener with a greenhouse. Nevertheless a quite simple version devoid of heating and artificial lighting can produce excellent results with cacti if used with skill.

Trays made of expanded polystyrene can be used as seed boxes. These trays are poor conductors of heat. No water evaporates through the base and walls, and thus there is no loss of latent heat of vaporization. Because of this characteristic the seedlings are guaranteed the essential 'warm feet'. If such a tray is to be used a second time for the same purpose it must be cleaned thoroughly beforehand and disinfected. The trays must have several base holes, so that excess water can flow away, thus permitting watering from underneath.

Many cactus enthusiasts prefer to sow seed in individual pots, and in this case shallow plastic pots are best. Taller pots may be cut down using a fine saw, a hot knife or a soldering iron. Only one sort of seed should be sown in each pot. If large seed trays are used the danger is that seed from one area are swished off to a different area when the tray is watered, and thus mixed up with another sort of seed. The result is invariably confusion. This problem is avoided if you use individual pots. Any fungus attack which occurs is also restricted to one container, whereas with a large seed pan there is always the danger that any a fungus attack will gradually infect the entire pan.

Small individual pots would be subject to rapid and severe changes in temperature and moisture if they were simply set up alone, and this would be a hopeless situation for the germination of seeds. For this reason the individual pots are grouped together in the propagator. This is the only successful method of raising seed in individual pots, as it is the only means of maintaining the temperatures and in particular the atmospheric humidity required for germination. If a heating cable is installed in the bottom of the box, a thin layer of moist sand should be laid over it, and the pots placed on this layer. The sand distributes the warmth from the heating cable.

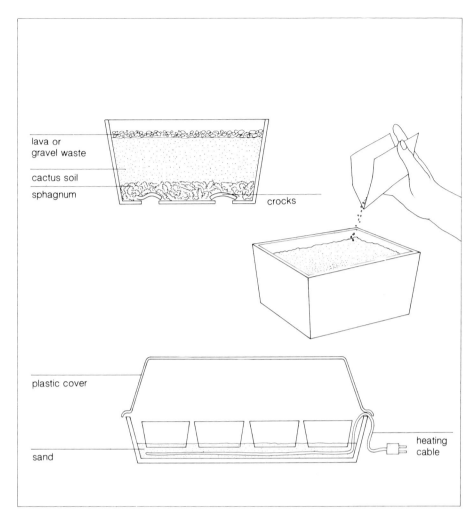

lava or gravel waste

cactus soil

sphagnum

crocks

plastic cover

sand

heating cable

The seed should be sown evenly and not too densely. The seed pots are placed in a heated propagator.

Seed composts

The bottom layer in the seed pan or the pots should be peat (sphagnum peat if possible), to a depth of 2 cm. This type of peat has a pH value of 3 to 3.2 with a minimal nutritional content (research by the Hesse research institute for vines, fruit and gardening in Geisenheim). The peat is able to absorb large quantities of water in its elongated dead cells, and slowly yield it again. It still contains moisture when it is apparently dry. Furthermore, experience shows that sphagnum does not contain mealy bug, provided that it is reasonably fresh, i.e. not several years old. Over the sphagnum peat is placed a light, sandy cactus soil, almost up to the rim of the pan or pots. A proportion of 10-20 per cent of Perlite in this compost promotes the seedlings' root

formation. The soil can be rendered free of other seed beforehand by steaming it. Finally, a 1-2 mm. thick layer of gravel or lava waste is added. This is purely mineral, and is not susceptible to fungus attack. It prevents the surface of the soil becoming encrusted, and stimulates the seedlings to form strong roots. Gravel or lava waste must be sieved down to a grain size of 1-1.5 mm. diameter, then washed to remove the dust particles, as they lead to the formation of mud and crusts. The coarse sandy grains of vermiculite or pumice gravel can also be used as a constituent of the soil, or as the superficial layer.

After the soil has been added, the seed pans or pots should be banged down a few times on the workbench to settle the soil slightly. If you are using a pan or tray, the soil surface can now be divided up for the individual species by pushing glass strips or labels into the soil. Don't forget to insert a label stating the names of the species in each zone. The origin of the seed and the date of sowing should also be noted. This concludes the preparations for sowing.

Sowing, germination and initial growth of the seedlings

The cactus seed must be evenly distributed over the surface if they are to develop well. A useful aid here is to fold a sheet of stiff paper roughly the size of a postcard along its length, and pour the cactus seed into the trough so formed. Now hold the paper pourer inclined slightly downward above the area to be sown, and tap it gently with the other hand. The seeds roll forward out of the paper trough and can be distributed over the soil surface.

The seed should now be pressed gently into the soil using a flat tool - for example a matchbox or the bottom of a medicine bottle. The seeds must be in intimate contact with the soil, otherwise they can easily dry out during germination. Cactus seed need light for germination, so it is best not to sieve soil over the seed.

If you are using a seed pan, the different species should be disposed in such a manner that globular plants are not located behind columnar ones. The latter are fast growing, and without an artificial light source they will shade the smaller plants. It is worth considering this aspect at the outset, and grouping the species according to the expected size of the seedlings.

The cactus seed may have the remains of fruit flesh and fungus spores adhering to them, and in this case it may be wise to treat them with a proprietary seed dressing in order to avoid an attack by fungus during germination.

Each species of seed is placed dry in a small glass bottle or test tube, and a small quantity of fungicide added. The seed and the chemical are then mixed up thoroughly by shaking the container. The excess dressing is then filtered off through a very fine sieve - check that the mesh size is smaller than the size of the cactus seed. The seeds are now protected from fungal infection by a very thin film of dressing chemical. As a further precaution a fine mist of Chinosol (0.05 per cent, or 0.1 per cent if fungus attack is already present) can be applied over the pans and pots after sowing. Benlate, which is also effective against fungal infections, should not be used until the seedlings have started to grow, i.e. not before or during germination. The pots or pans should now be soaked in luke-warm water until they are completely sodden with water, right up to the superficial layer of gravel. Chinosol can also be added to this water in the stated dilution. The pans or pots are now placed in the propagator and the transparent cover fitted, so that a moist, warm atmosphere is formed. If you do not have a propagator, a glass sheet can be placed over the seed pan. It should be angled in such a way that condensation runs off away from the pans; it should not drip onto the seedlings. Some growers simply tie their seed pots in a clear plastic bag. Some research has already been done into the ideal conditions for the germination of cactus seed. As already mentioned, cacti require light to germinate. This applies in particular to the upland species. The propagator must therefore be placed in a bright but not sunny position. If there is insufficient natural light, supplementary artificial lighting should be provided.

For the majority of cacti the ideal germinating temperature has proved to be 20-25° C. Upland cacti such as Oreocerei, Rebutias and Lobivias germinate very well in temperatures as low as 15-20°C. Warmth-loving cacti, including Coryphanthas, Echinocacti and many Mammillarias prefer slightly higher germinating temperatures (20-30°C). Temperatures below 10 and above 30-35°C inhibit germination.

If you have an electrically heated propagator set the thermostat to the appropriate value. If there is no supplementary heating, then a place must be found indoors or in the greenhouse where a suitable temperature can be reliably expected. The temperature should be monitored using a maximum/minimum thermometer. Nocturnal cooling down to 15-18°C promotes germination, and helps to ensure healthy seedlings, as they would cool off in the same way in their native habitats. Seed can be sown successfully as early as December or January if you have a greenhouse which provides good overhead light even in winter, or a propagator fitted with a heating system and supplementary lighting. Many cactus enthusiasts are of the opinion that seedlings begun this early show substantially advanced development even in their first year. If you have to rely on natural light and natural warmth you should wait until March - April for sowing. If the seed are sown too early, and if unfavourable weather delays germination, then the danger of failed germination and fungus infection is very high. In our experience cacti sown in March - April, with lengthening sunshine and increasing warmth, grow extremely vigorously. In fact they often catch up with the seedlings sown earlier, whose advantage was gained at the expense of so much extra effort.

Many species of cacti, including *Astrophytum* and *Coryphantha*, germinate within a week, while Mammillarias usually require two weeks; other species, amongst them a few Opuntias, take longer. During this period the seeds and seedlings must not be allowed to dry out. Once the majority of seedlings have formed their first spines, the glass panes over the sowing pans or the lid of the propagator can be raised slightly. Moist, warm air is essential for cactus seed to germinate. Unfortunately such humid air also promotes the development of harmful fungi, and too long an exposure to such conditions weakens the seedlings. For this reason the clammy atmosphere should be maintained for no longer than necessary. When the seedlings have grown a little stronger the glass sheet or cover of the propagator can be removed entirely. A further advantage of sowing in individual pots is evident here: those species which have grown more rapidly can be taken out of the propagator, whilst others which are still germinating can be left inside. It is important to note down the date of sowing, the recorded temperatures, the time taken to germinate and the rate of growth of the individual species, as this information can be valuable for subsequent sowings.

The seedlings are best left in the seed pan or propagator for several months. During the whole of this time care must be taken that the soil does not become alkaline and that no fungus growth occurs. For this reason it is best to water with clean rainwater or with acidified water. If the seedlings suddenly cease making progress in the pans in which they had previously been thriving, the reason is often that the surface of the soil in the seed pan has become alkaline. If there is no sphagnum peat in the pan then this can easily occur. Seedling pans have to be kept constantly moist, and as a result water constantly evaporates from its surface. As the water evaporates its alkaline constituents are continuously precipitated in the top layer. This often happens at a very rapid rate. The condition is not difficult to recognize; simply check the top layer with a pH meter or indicator paper. If the result is alkaline, the pots and pans should be carefully placed in water which has been acidified to pH 4, and left there for a few hours. After this treatment vigorous growth will soon resume. It is a wise precaution to mist with Chinosol solution every four weeks to guard against fungus infection for as long as the seedlings remain small.

Pots and seedlings are watered by placing them in water for about half an hour, or by running water into the tray through the short vertical pipe mentioned earlier. The water used should be slightly acid (please refer to the section on water used for watering). Fertilizer should be added to the water from around the time that spines begin to form on the seedlings. Potassium phosphate has proved to be a very suitable feed. In the first six months 3 grams are added per 10 litres of water, later 10 grams per 10 litres of water. The seedlings will make excellent progress with this fertilizer. An adequate supply of nitrogen and the essential trace elements is evidently present in the soil.

When the seedlings have grown to the extent that the cushion formed by the closely spaced plants starts to arch up in the centre, or when the seedlings have achieved a diameter of about 1 cm., it will soon be necessary to prick them out. Pricking out means separating the seedlings and setting them in fresh soil spaced further apart. Under favourable conditions this can be carried out in early summer, although it might be necessary to wait to the following spring if conditions are less favourable. Pricking out should cease by the autumn, as the seedlings would not grow on vigorously and would start the winter in a weakened state.

When pricking out it is essential to· avoid damaging the roots of the seedlings too severely. The soil in the seedling pot should be dry, as it will then disintegrate very easily, and will release the seedlings almost undamaged. For the pricking out process pointed wooden sticks varying from the diameter of a pencil to half that size are ideal for making holes for the plants, and for inserting the seedlings. When first pricked out, the young plants, now with a diameter of 0.5-1 cm., are planted in pans or fairly large pots in groups of several, rather than in individual pots. They should be spaced out with twice the plants'

diameter between them. If the spacing is greater, the plants' roots do not spread right through the soil, but if the spacing is smaller it soon becomes necessary to prick out again. The young plants should be kept in a light, but not sunny situation, especially after repotting. In their natural habitat the seedlings usually develop in the shade of older cacti or other plants.

The young plants should be growing strongly and have reached a diameter of 2-3 cm. before they are pricked out again, and this time they can be moved to individual pots. If young plants are raised en masse, multi-pot trays can also be used. If you opt for multi-pots it is best to use them only once wherever possible, as it can be difficult to insert and remove individual plants.

When pricking out for the second time sphagnum peat should again be added to the bottom of the individual pots or to the multi-pots. The plants should be watered with a nutrient solution, applied from the bottom if possible. When the young plants have rooted they are moved to a sunny location, for example on planks hung up close under the greenhouse roof. The cacti grow amazingly strongly in such a position, developing strong and colourful spine formations, and many globular species will flower at an age of only two or three years. This method of raising plants is now widely accepted as a very effective technique.

Cuttings

Taking cuttings is the simplest method of propagating cacti. It requires no special equipment, and is nearly always successful.

The best times of year for taking cuttings are the spring and early summer. In autumn many cacti do not form new roots so readily, and in any case roots which are newly formed in autumn will often not survive the winter. Cuttings are removed from the mother plant using a clean, sharp knife. If shoots (pups) are twisted or torn out of the mother plant, both the mother plant and the shoot may be severely damaged. When taking

cuttings from columnar cacti the edges of the cut surface should be cut back slightly to ensure that the new roots grow from the centre of the cut surface, pointing downward, instead of growing out sideways from the edges. Cuttings of epiphytic cacti such as 'Phyllocacti', must be cut prior to rooting. The thin, woody points at which the shoots are linked do not form good roots. The best roots are formed from the broadest sides of the 'leaves'.

The cut surfaces must be allowed to dry out before they will root. The small cut surface of a shoot from a clustering cactus dries out in one or two weeks, but the larger cut surface of a *Cereus* cutting takes one or two months to dry out and seal thoroughly. During this period the cuttings must stand vertically, as new roots always try to grow downwards. If, for example, a *Cereus* cutting is left on its side for a week, roots will form on the side rather than from the cut surface. For this reason cuttings from columnar cacti or from 'Phyllocacti' should be clumped together and set vertically in an empty flower pot. Larger *Cereus* cuttings can be hung up in a vertical position.

After the cuttings have dried off, they are placed vertically on a permeable and rot-resisting soil where they will form roots. The should include a high proportion of gravel, Perlite or lava waste. The rooting compost should be very slightly moist, but must not be wet. One way of providing the right level of humidity is to half-fill a clay pot with the rooting soil, and place the cuttings vertically in the pot. This clay pot is then set in a larger pot, packed round with a mixture of peat and sand. The bedding material can now be kept constantly slightly moist, and its moisture will diffuse through the clay pot to the rooting compost. This gentle moisture prevents the cuttings shrinking too drastically, and promotes the formation of roots.

Please be patient while the roots are forming. Fairly large cuttings from columnar cacti will sometimes not form roots for a year, although shoots from clustering species rarely present problems. Sometimes the shoots form small roots whilst still attached to the

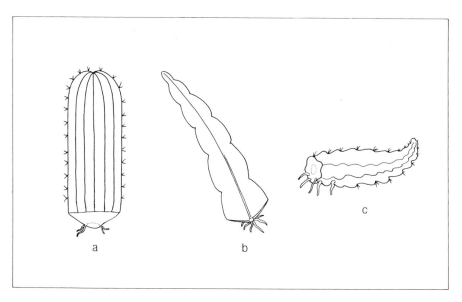

mother plant. This is often observed with plants of the genera *Echinopsis, Sulcorebutia* and *Lobivia*, for example.

A rooting hormone is available commercially which is designed to promote root formation, but opinions on its effectiveness vary widely. The experience of the authors is negative.

The cuttings must not be planted out finally until the roots are clearly visible. It is better to be sparing with water in the first weeks after planting, until the plant's roots have thoroughly penetrated the soil in the pot. During the whole period in which the cuttings are dried off and rooted they should be kept warm and light, but not in a sunny position.

If you take cuttings or shoots from a plant with a tap root you may well be disappointed to see no evidence of real growth many months after planting. If you suspect disease and remove the plant from the pot, the reason becomes obvious; initially the cutting concentrates its effort into forming the typical tap root. Even though no growth is evident above the soil, the plant may well have made considerable progress underground. Only when the tap root has formed, generally in the second year, will the exposed part of the shoot also grow.

If you wish to raise young plants more rapidly, you can attempt to graft them on a strong-growing rootstock instead of waiting for them to form roots. Please refer in this case to the section on grafting.

Rooting cuttings. The cuttings of columnar cacti should be cut back slightly around the cut surface, so that the roots develop from the centre and not from the sides (a). The cuttings of Phyllocacti also have to be trimmed. The broadest points of the 'leaves' produce particularly good roots (b). The cuttings must be left vertical whilst forming roots. A columnar cactus left on its side will form roots on the lower side and will grow in a curved shape (c).

The rooting of cuttings.
1 – cutting
2 – clay pot
3 – rooting substrate
4 – peat – sand mixture
5 – external pot

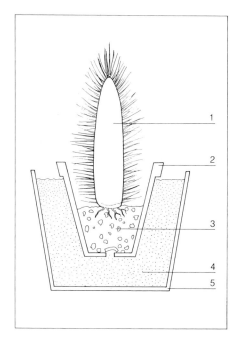

Building up and accommodating a cactus collection

The beginner to cactus culture is advised to think hard about how to build up and accommodate his cactus collection right from the outset. To a considerable extent these two factors are likely to decide whether he will gain countless hours of pleasure from thriving plants and beautiful flowers, or will suffer many disappointments and failures. Some cacti are robust and virtually indestructible, and can be cultivated successfully under a very wide variety of conditions. Others demand specific cultural conditions, and will not flourish if they cannot be provided. In view of these differences, it makes sense to start by considering the various possible methods of accommodating the plants, with their advantages and disadvantages, and then to decide rationally which plants can be cultivated successfully with the facilities available.

Window ledge culture

Nearly all cactus growers start with one or two cacti cultivated on a window ledge. Indeed for many cactus enthusiasts there is absolutely no alternative to the window ledge. Unfortunately it is a highly unbalanced and extreme location for any sort of plant, as the indoor climate is designed to suit humans first and foremost. Compared with a greenhouse or a garden frame a room suffers the following disadvantages: in the vegetative period average temperatures are lower, although the level of heating may be high for short, sporadic periods. In winter temperatures are relatively high. Atmospheric humidity is always relatively low and sunlight always comes from one side.

Cacti love light and sun, and cannot be cultivated in just any handy spot in the room, even if they might look particularly attractive there. What they need is a brightly lit window and a position close up to the glass with no intervening curtain. North-facing windows or those in the shade of other buildings are not suitable. Windows facing south-east or south to south-west are a better bet. Wherever possible the window should be one which is only rarely opened, otherwise you will find that clearing away the plants to open the window soon becomes an almighty nuisance. In any case cacti do not like to be moved frequently. It is important not to turn the plants round unnecessarily, so it is advisable to put a pencil mark on the pot to indicate the side on which the light normally falls. With the light coming from one side it is inevitable that the plants will grow slightly asymmetrically, and in so doing their most beautiful side, with the finest spine formation, will inevitably face outward, i.e. away from the eyes of the observer in the room.

From the point of view of light provision a south-facing window is the best for the cultivation of cacti, provided that the plants are not kept in excessively small clay pots. Such containers heat up too rapidly in the direct sun, and dry out quickly. It is very much better to keep the cacti either in plastic pots or to embed the clay pots in a fairly large pan or tray. The embedding compost should be a mixture of peat and sand. Embedding clay pots in a larger pan or tray protects the plants' roots from wide-ranging temperature variations and overheating, and evens out the water supply. The overall effect is to provide a more favourable set of conditions for growth. In the dormant period you only need to moisten the embedding compost slightly to maintain a regular level of mild moisture in the soil, without watering the plants directly. The larger surface of soil also tends to increase the atmospheric humidity in the immediate area of the plants, which is usually very low indoors.

A purpose-built flower window offers much better facilities for indoor cactus culture. This is a part of the room divided off from the living area by a glass partition. The climate of the plant area can therefore be different from the climate of the living area, to some extent at least. The flower window should be fitted with a tray in which the cacti can be planted out, or their pots embedded. An arrangement for providing gentle shade should be fitted to cater for the warm days which occur without warning in spring.

Examples of cacti suitable for growing on a window ledge

Position	Suitability for cacti	Suitable species
Ledge or shelf within a room	Generally speaking too dark for cacti	At best Christmas cacti or similar, if the location is relatively bright.
Indoor window sill, north-facing window	Bright, but out of the sun. Light from one side only. Relatively cool in summer, relatively warm in winter.	Christmas cacti (*Schlumbergera*). Easter cacti (*Rhipsalidopsis*). Other epiphytic cacti such as *Rhipsalis* in an extended flower window (because of the higher atmospheric humidity required).
Indoor window sill, east- or west-facing window	Light from one side only. Bright, but morning or evening sun only. Winter temperatures in the room rather high for ordinary cacti.	'Phyllocacti' (*Epiphyllum* hybrids). In a slightly more sunny position (south-east- or south-west-facing window): 'Green' Mammillarias such as *M. rhodantha, M. zeilmanniana, M. centricirrha, M. hidalgensis*. Notocacti such as *N. ottonis*. 'Green' Cleistocacti such as *C. smaragdiflorus*. Small 'green' Gymnocalyciums such as *G. bruchii, G. andreae, G. baldianum*. Columnar cacti such as *Cereus peruvianus*. Echinopses in the narrower sense. If a cool winter locatin can be provided also Rebutias such as *R. krainziana, R. deminuta*, etc.
Indoor window sill, south-facing window	Light from one side only. When the sun shines it becomes very warm on one side. Winter temperature relatively high. Not an easy location. Watering calls for particular skill. If possible embed pots in a pan.	Densely spined Mammillarias such as *M. bombycina, M. parkinsonii, M. elongata, M. microhelia*. Astrophytums such as *A. ornatum* or *A. myriostigma*. Ferocacti, perhaps *F. latispinus*. Densely spined, hairy or glaucous Cerei such as *Browningia hertlingiana, Stenocerus beneckei, Cephalocereus senilis*, Haageocerei. Opuntias which remain small, such as *O. microdasys*. Thelocacti, perhaps *T. bicolor*
Outdoor window sill, (especially with south-east- or south-west-facing window)	If protection from penetrating rainfall is provided this is a good location for robust cacti during the vegetative period. A bright, cool (5-10°C) location should be found for overwintering.	Robust Echinopses (including *Pseudolobivia*), Rebutias (inc. *Aylostera, Digitorebutia, Mediolobivia*), Lobivias (incl. *Chamaecereus*), Sulcorebutias, Mammillarias, Notocacti, Gymnocalyciums, small Trichocerei. Plant cacti out in pans or embed them. If rain reaches the plants now and then, select a very permeable soil substrate.

Access to the flower window on the side facing the room should be via sliding doors or windows, to allow the cultivator to work conveniently in the window area. The partition's task is to keep the living room air out, as it is always too dry and in winter is too warm. A dangerous build-up of heat in the summer and excessively low temperatures on cold winter nights can be avoided by opening these windows slightly. Some means of communication with the outside air should be fitted which keeps the rain out and is capable of being closed snugly. A south-facing flower window of this kind is often unsuitable for other plants because of the intensity of the sunshine, but highly ornamental settings of cacti and other succulents can be maintained in it for years.

Viewed over all, the indoor cultivation of cacti cannot hope to be a balanced form of culture, and for this reason not all species are suitable. If you intend using an ordinary room window which does not have the benefit of full sunshine we recommend sturdy species which are not too densely spined, and therefore are green in overall appearance, such as the more robust species of the following genera: *Mammillaria, Notocactus, Echinopsis, Rebutia, Echinofossulocactus, Gymnocalycia, Parodia, Cleistocactus* and the *Nopalxochia* hybrids 'Phyllocacti'. If the window is in full sun, a few of the white *Mammillaria* species, the smaller Opuntias and columnar cacti can be cultivated. If you have a flower window situated in full sun you might like to experiment with Ferocacti, Thelocacti or Astrophytums because of their highly decorative appearance, but these beautiful plants do require special care. A shady position by a window is only really suitable for a few epiphytic cacti in the long term, such as the well-known Christmas and Easter cacti. If you have a flower window situated in shade, this will guarantee a reasonably high level of atmospheric humidity, making it suitable for other epiphytic cacti, including some from the genus *Rhipsalis*.

The outside window ledge offers entirely different conditions, and can provide an interesting diversion. During the vegetative period many cacti such as *Echinopsis*, 'Phyllocacti', Lobivias, Gymnocalyciums, Rebutias and others are quite content outside the window, and the fresh air in the summer usually agrees with the plants very well. This is particularly true if the site offers protection from heavy

for the amateur, thanks to putty strips, permanently flexible putty and the putty-less fixing methods possible with profiled aluminium section frames. One drawback is the high level of heat conduction of glass, which leads to heat losses in winter. If you wish to minimize this disadvantage you can double- glaze the greenhouse in the manner of a double-glazed house window, although this brings with it the danger that algae or dirt will collect between the panes. Double-glazed panels are available commercially, but we cannot recommend them because of their great weight, and because small greenhouses rarely accept standard panel sizes.

Perspex is a very interesting material for the construction of small greenhouses, especially in the form of bridged double sheeting. The low weight of the sheets means that the greenhouse structure can be kept lighter. Heat insulation qualities are good because of the air chamber in the bridged double sheets. The many bridging strips also diffuse the light, and 85-90 per cent of the light is transmitted. Early on the manufacturers emphasized that the perspex used for garden purposes allowed ultra-violet light to pass through; more recent information from the companies does not include this note. Perspex does not alter or yellow with age, but it is relatively soft. It must therefore be cleaned with care to avoid scratches. Fixing the perspex sheets to the greenhouse is not a simple matter, as they expand strongly when heated. For this reason they cannot be screwed in place or fixed permanently with putty, but must be allowed to move. As many collections show, cacti flourish equally well under silica glass and perspex bridged double sheeting. There is no evident difference in the results of cultivation.

Other plastics are also used as cladding material for small greenhouses, but it is important to check beforehand whether these materials are sufficiently resistant to the rigours of hail, whether they age quickly and suffer a serious loss in light transmission after only a few years, and whether they provide adequate heat insulation.

Compared with plants growing in the open air, those in a greenhouse often receive no more than half of the energy radiated by the sun because of the angled fall of the light, and the obstruction of the frame components and the staging.

The ventilation of the greenhouse should be given careful attention at the stage of designing or selecting the structure. A greenhouse in which cacti are cultivated should be in as sunny a location as possible. Because of the 'greenhouse effect' solar radiation will cause it to heat up quickly, and for this reason large ventilation windows must be designed into the structure from the outset. We recommend that ventilators are fitted in the roof, through which hot air can escape, and also in the vertical walls, through which the cooler outside air can flow in. This is the only way to ensure an effective throughflow of air. It is important that you should consider the matter of ventilation carefully right at the start of the project. Almost all cacti like to stand in a well-lit position, but many plants suffer if they are kept in excessive heat. Only the real desert species are adapted to constant high temperature and the dry air which is usually associated with it. Automatic window openers make acclimatization of the greenhouse much easier. They are either operated electrically by a switching relay, or hydraulically if the windows are heavy.

A further point which should be given due consideration at the planning stage is whether and by what means the greenhouse is to be heated. Indisputably the best form of heating is by warm water, which offers even, easily controlled warmth provided that the heating pipes are of generous size. For example, it is a simple matter to install double the number of pipes on one side of the greenhouse, and thereby guarantee that the temperature will be 5°C higher on that side than the other. The high mountain species can then be kept cooler during the winter than the tropical types. The ideal system to achieve this is fully-automatic oil-fired heating, which can be connected to the domestic heating system where this is feasible. In this case a thermostat in the greenhouse is

indispensable, and a time switch is also desirable. The desired daytime temperature can then be set, along with a a lower nocturnal temperature, and the time of day at which the change-over takes place. We strongly recommend that a second thermostat should be connected to your front doorbell; the system is adjusted so that the bell rings when the temperature drops about 2-3°C below a set value. If the automatic heating system should fail, an electric or paraffin heater can be pressed into service, or even a second boiler fed by solid fuel and connected in parallel; damage to the plants is then avoided. We would advise against the long-term use of portable paraffin heaters which do not have an external chimney. These heaters produce exhaust gases, and it is not known precisely to what extent these gases can be toxic to the plants.

Expensive to run, but very clean and simple to install, is electrical heating. Because of the relatively high cost of electricity this method demands effective insulation in the greenhouse to counter heat losses: double glazing or perspex bridged double sheeting; in winter the side glazing should be lined with expanded polystyrene sheets (the sides are not so important for letting in light); plastic film or bubble film should be fitted on the underside of the roof panels, and all crevices and joints should be sealed, especially those round doors and windows. Electrical heating can be recommended if the collection comprises genera and species which prefer to be kept cool in winter, as a relatively low winter temperature can easily be maintained. In this case the heating is not required so frequently nor so intensely, and the system installed can be less powerful in the first place. Often an electric oil-filled radiator or a hot-air blower is enough. If you have to overwinter warmth-loving cacti in such a greenhouse a form of low-power electric soil heating can be fitted in a sheltered corner of the bed.

If you are toying with the idea of setting up a greenhouse do not restrict your research to the advertising material supplied by the manufacturers. Take the trouble to view other gardeners' greenhouses and those at garden centres, and make very careful comparisons of their construction, light transmission, heating facilities and interior fittings.

The interior fittings of the greenhouse

This is another area in which the enthusiast has a chance to develop his own ideas.

The interior fittings of the greenhouse should be considered and planned right at the start, when the type of greenhouse is being decided. If the greenhouse can be built large enough, it is very useful to divide off a small space which can be used for repotting, pricking out, grafting, storing spray equipment and other tools, as well as empty plant containers and soil. In many greenhouses this space does not exist, and its absence is sorely felt. If the main space is large enough, we suggest setting up a central bed about 1.60 m. wide for Cerei. A wall about 30 cm. high, and extending a further 20 cm. down into the earth, defines this central bed. As fresh brickwork is strongly alkaline and thus poisonous to cactus roots, plastic sheeting should be placed against the wall before filling the bed with earth, so that the soil does not come into contact with the wall. On the floor of the bed, which can be left as natural earth, a layer about 10 cm. thick of pure, coarse pumice gravel or old brick or tile rubble should be laid for drainage, and the bed then filled up with cactus soil. At this point the bed should be watered with a powerful pest control agent. Several weeks later, when the soil has settled down and dried out, planting can begin. We can then assume that the pests which might have been present in the soil have been destroyed. A better alternative is to buy steamed soil from a garden centre. Around the central bed a walkway about 90 cm. wide can be laid. From the walkway to the vertical side glazing is the space for the side staging, which should not be more than about 1 m. wide, otherwise it will be difficult to get to the plants closest to the window. On the north-facing

short side of the greenhouse a trellis can be set up for Queen of the Night and other climbing Cerei. The greenhouse staging must be of strong construction, as it has to bear a considerable load. Many cactus growers use plant trays as the staging surface, thus forming high-level beds.

The space in the greenhouse usually starts to become cramped after just a few years. Many enthusiasts then consider whether they can accommodate more plants high up under the glass on supplementary staging. If this is done, the staging should be positioned so that it blocks as little light as possible from the cacti standing on the greenhouse benches, or in the central bed. With cacti, which are so greedy for light, there is a considerable risk that the extra space gained with the intermediate staging is paid for by a reduction in the rate of growth of the plants underneath.

If the glazing reaches down to the ground plants may be cultivated under the benches, but only those which demand little light. At best a few epiphytic cacti or potential grafting stocks can be considered.

There are many other points to be considered, but we can only mention them here very briefly. If you have no permanent work area, then at least provide yourself with a work table. If you fix castors to its feet, the table can be rolled away under the plant staging when it is not needed. One absolute essential is a water container. It can be positioned to collect the water which flows off the greenhouse roof and down a gutter, or mains water can be left in it to stand and thus warm up. The container may be a fixed concrete trough or a tub made of impact-resistant plastic. It should hold at least as much water as is required to water all the plants at once. The greenhouse structure should also be fitted with hooks and eyes to which wires can be attached. These can be used to hold tillandsias, orchids or epiphytic cacti planted in wooden baskets. These wires can also be used to retain a system of lightweight interior shading, and in winter an interior layer of plastic film. It is extremely helpful if mains water and electric current are available inside the greenhouse. The

electrical installation, time switches, thermostats and relays should be installed neatly and in a workmanlike fashion, and they should be waterproof and easy to check. Finally, maximum/minimum thermometers and a good hygrometer give an accurate indication of the climate in the greenhouse, and are an important aid to successful cactus culture. An abundance of other small aids to gardening is also available, of which we have mentioned only a few, but they make a vast difference to the pleasure which is to be gained from a greenhouse.

Cacti for the greenhouse

A well-equipped greenhouse offers you the chance to establish and maintain a wide variety of special climates. For this reason cacti with very different cultural requirements can successfully be cared for in the greenhouse, and in a sense it is not necessary to recommend particular species.

On the other hand there are certain basic characteristics of the greenhouse climate which cannot be influenced by its owner. For instance, it may be situated in a harsh mountain climate, or in a warm plain; it might be in a large garden, where it is never shaded, or it might be jammed in between houses, so that it only receives full sun for a few hours per day. In the fullness of time the enthusiast will learn from his own experience which cacti thrive especially well in his greenhouse, and which do poorly, without having to consider the matter profoundly beforehand. Nevertheless it makes sense - and helps to prevent disappointment - if you consider from the start which cacti are likely to be well suited to the conditions obtaining in your greenhouse. To do this you first have to observe what temperatures occur in your greenhouse, and how long and in which parts it receives full sunshine. If it is situated in full sunshine in a warm region then it is naturally suited to the care of sun-loving, warmth-loving cacti. In this situation you might like to build up a collection of Melocacti, Discocacti, Astrophytums and white Mammillarias. On the other hand high mountain cacti such as Lobivias, Rebutias, Sulcorebutias and others will not be happy in these conditions, even with maximum ventilation and shading. These cacti might thrive in a well-ventilated greenhouse in a region with a harsher climate. Slight shading from a tree or a house in the hours around midday would be no drawback to the cultivation of Notocacti, green Mammillarias, Gymnocalyciums and many Parodias. If your greenhouse is strongly shaded by surrounding houses and trees you might prefer to concentrate on epiphytic cacti.

These examples will give you some idea of the broad scope which exists for experiment if you have a greenhouse.

Building up a cactus collection

The majority of cactus collections include representatives of all manner of genera. Such a collection usually evolves as a result of the enthusiastic beginner grabbing at everything which has a 'cactus' label, or perhaps he buys or raises all the cacti which he finds especially attractive. The alternative is to build up a collection in a considered fashion. The following sections are simply intended to indicate a few possible lines to follow. It is certainly a help to the the beginner if he formulates a clear idea of his aim in collecting cacti. The vast range of species available makes it easy to find something for every taste.

What cultural conditions can you provide?

Before deciding to specialize in a particular group of species, you must check which cacti are suitable for the conditions of culture you can offer.

Where will you grow the plants? Whether it is to be the window ledge, an outside bed, a garden frame or a greenhouse there are genera and species which are particular suitable. You can find out which they are by reading the experiences of other growers published in the specialist literature, by studying details of the plants' native habitat, and not least by your own experience. Don't be discouraged if you do not have a greenhouse; many cacti do better in a garden frame or by a window than they do in the greenhouse.

How much light will the plants receive? It can be interesting to keep a log of the hours of sunshine in each season. If your site only receives half the available sunlight, it would not be wise to concentrate on desert cacti, whereas many Rebutias, green Mammillarias, Gymnocalyciums and Notocacti will grow better in such a position than in brilliant sun.

If you have a maximum/minimum thermometer it is also instructive to establish the range of temperatures which actually occur. Temperature control by means of ventilation and shading are only effective within certain limits, and call for considerable effort on the part of the gardener. On cloudless days in a position in full sun it is hardly possible to avoid high temperatures. At such times atmospheric humidity may reach very low values. These conditions will be appreciated by many Echinocerei, Astrophytums, Coryphanthas, Thelocacti and others, whereas you will probably have little success with Parodias, Rebutias or Notocacti.

The winter location for the plants should also be considered. A cold, dry and dark situation, as often has to be accepted when cultivating cacti in a cold frame, will present problems with many cacti of the genera *Espostoa*, *Ferocactus, Melocactus, Discocactus* and others. On the other hand high mountain cacti, e.g. from the South American Andes, like cool, dry conditions for overwintering. With a cool, dry location you will have problems with rootstock bases such as *Eriocereus jusbertii* and the Hylocerei which have lately come into fashion. *Trichocereus* stocks are much less sensitive.

Not the least of your considerations should be the amount of space which is available for the cacti. Ideally you should be able to accommodate enough plants to satisfy your demands in your chosen specialization without having to cram the cacti too closely together. Please bear in mind the telltale signs of an overloaded collection, and its inevitable result: the cacti are so close together that it is

Part of a collection of Sulcorebutias (front three rows) and Rebutias (rear two rows).

92

Part of a fine collection of Astrophytums

A small collection of beautifully spined cacti

almost impossible to reach particular plants; it becomes difficult to recognize the first signs of a pest attack, or even that a rare plant is flowering for the first time. The cacti are set up on all sorts of temporary staging and shelves, and the plants are robbing each other of light. You can no longer keep track of the collection, and you water the one plant twice and its neighbour not at all. Once your collection gets out of hand in this way, you will soon lose all pleasure in it.

Cacti of one genus

Here are a few examples of specialization. A popular method is to collect cacti of a single genus. For example, all the Echinocerei or all the Notocacti which can be found. Those genera which are in the focus of current research are especially popular, as are those in which new, previously unknown species are currently being discovered and described. It is a great thrill for any cactus grower to raise plants from seed imported from its native habitat or from shoots, and to produce plants which have been unknown until then. Many cactus enthusiasts think along the same lines, with the result that certain areas of specialization fall into and out of favour. In the last few decades distinct waves of popularity

have been identifiable, including the Chilean genera, (*Copiapoa, Neoporteria* and others), the Parodias, the Brazilians (*Uebelmannia, Discocactus, Melocactus* and others) and the Sulcorebutias. If an entire genus cannot satisfactorily be collected in the space available, then it is better to restrict yourself at the outset to a sub-genus or a group. Examples might be the white Mammillarias, the

Echinocerei with pectinate (comb-formation) spines, or the large Lobivias of the jajoiana-chrysantha group with their beautiful flowers.

Collecting cacti of one genus makes it possible to carry out interesting studies about distribution areas, relationships, breadth of variation and lines of development within the genus. The more advanced grower might like to

A collection of 'white hairy' cacti: Cleistocactus strausii (left and back right), Espostoa melanostele (centre), Cephalocereus senilis (right).

93

make contact with other cactus enthusiasts and scientists who are interested in the same subjects. Sometimes the amateur can help to clarify disputed species, and may write articles on the appearance, flowers and culture of species which have previously not been described, or only inadequately.

Cacti from one geographical area

Another form of specialization involves collecting cacti from a particular region, regardless of genus. One advantage of this approach is that the plants collected are likely to require fairly uniform cultural conditions. It can also be rewarding and useful to make studies of the climate, vegetation and plant communities found in the chosen region, and even to study its culture and history. This form of specialization is especially recommended to cactus growers who are obliged to work with extreme or unbalanced conditions of culture. For example, if you live in the mountains you might concentrate on cacti from the Andean highlands, which are likely to grow better in your locality than anywhere in the lowlands. These might include the genera *Oroya*, *Oreocereus*, *Lobivia*, *Sulcorebutia*, *Neowerdermannia*, *Weingartia*, the sub-group Digitorebutia of the genus *Rebutia* and the sub-group Tephrocactus of the genus *Opuntia*.

Where a genus, sub-genus or group is restricted to a narrowly defined distribution area, then both approaches to collecting can be combined. As an example, if you can have suitable facilities you could build up a special collection of the Mammillarias from lower California. Success in caring for these large-flowered and beautifully spined plants depends to a considerable extent on the research which you are prepared to do into the conditions which these rather temperamental plants experience in their precisely defined natural habitat. The same applies to the *Islaya* species whose habitats are the Southern Peruvian coastal deserts.

Cacti with one type of colouring

It can be fascinating to collect cacti with similar colouring. Examples might be the globular and columnar cacti with gleaming white, brilliant yellow and red/brown to dark brown spines, mainly of the genera *Mammillaria*, *Parodia*, *Neoporteria*, *Haageocereus*, *Cleistocactus*, *Notocactus*, *Espostoa*, *Pilosocereus* and others. Other cacti have spines which are less conspicuously coloured than the plant body. Noteworthy examples of this type of colouring are the Chilean species of *Neoporteria* and *Copiapoa* with their dark brown to black/brown overall appearance, the chalky bloomed bodies of other *Copiapoa* species and *Stenocereus beneckei*, and the glaucous examples of *Browningia hertlingiana* and many Opuntias.

A collection of Mammillarias with their gloriously coloured spines, surrounded by colourful Haageocerei and other columnar cacti looks quite splendid. It can also be stimulating to show the breadth of variation in spine colouring of a particular species by grouping similarly coloured plants together. An interesting study would be to investigate the spine colouring of the descendants of parent plants with particularly strongly coloured spines. You might also care to study the extent to which plants alter their spine formation as they age, and under different lighting conditions.

Cacti for hybridizing

Many cactus lovers build up their collection with the aim of raising cactus hybrids. Large and interestingly coloured flowers are the usual attraction; the cultivator crosses several species in an attempt to combine different characteristics in a single plant. This type of hybridization is generally carried out within the genera *Epiphyllum*, *Heliocereus*, *Nopalxochia* and *Selenicereus* (Phyllocacti), and the genera *Lobivia*, *Echinopsis* and *Trichocereus*. The process of hybridizing is very interesting and leads to a deeper understanding of the problems inherent in the procedure, and of the

science of genetics in general. Nevertheless we feel obliged to issue a warning on this subject to every cactus grower: the practice will swallow up much of your time and space. Following the various combinations of characteristics over two or three generations takes a long time, as you have to wait three to five years for each generation to reach flowering maturity. Two seed capsules are small, and the seed can be sown in one small pot, but the young plants which develop may take up a square metre of soil before they are finally capable of flowering!

There are many other possible approaches to building up a collection in a systematic fashion. Many cactus growers collect the fan-like cristate forms. Other enthusiasts specialize in cacti whose appearance is unusual, such as those of the genera *Ariocarpus*, *Leuchtenbergia*, *Obregonia* and *Aztekium*. Other specialists prefer the 'problem' plants, i.e. plants which present particular difficulties in culture, propagation or flowering.

There is one last approach to building up a cactus collection which we wish to mention - an approach which is as valid as any other. In this case the cactus enthusiast acquires one plant or another simply because he finds it particularly attractive. Without the benefit of systematic planning, and with no scientific aspirations he gradually assembles a fine collection consisting of a few Opuntias, some columnar cacti and a number of globular species, from which he obtains a great deal of simple pleasure.

Labelling and the card index

Once a cactus collection reaches a respectable size it is no longer possible to remember the names and essential features of the plants. Almost all cactus growers equip each cactus pot with a label which notes at least the name of the plant. The plastic stick-in labels available commercially are ideal for this. They are usually white in colour, but there are also yellow and red versions which can be used to distinguish particular plant groups, e.g. plants which have to be kept in particularly bright or warm conditions in winter. The plastic labels can be inscribed using a hard pencil, a special label pen or waterproof labelling inks or Indian ink. The latter are much more legible and long-lasting. If you have a typewriter perforated tear-off labels are available on the roll, along with special typewriter ribbons. Clear transparent labels have also appeared in the shops recently. Weatherproof labelling inks or Indian inks are used to write on them, and they are very inconspicuous and unobtrusive. Earlier versions of transparent labels tended to become brittle after a few years.

Many cactus enthusiasts like to keep a note of where each plant came from, the year it was acquired, the flower colour and perhaps other interesting characteristics, as well as the genus and species name. If all this information is to be accommodated the labels themselves become rather large, which do nothing to improve the uniform image of the cactus collection, and may even obstruct the light to small plants.

For this reason many cactus growers use smaller labels which bear nothing but an abbreviation of the genus name, the species name and a number. The rest of the plant's characteristics are entered in a card index which is numbered sequentially in accordance with the numbering of the plants. Special card indexes are available commercially for use with plant collections, but any type of card index can be used and arranged according to your own ideas. The card index should be stored in the proper box, protected from dust and moisture, and close to the plants wherever possible. With the index close to hand, notes and observations on the plants can be entered in the card index without wasting time or forgetting things. A plant card index constantly kept up to date is an indispensable tool to the serious enthusiast.

We ought to mention briefly that the usual colour descriptions such as 'dark red', 'wine red', 'brick red', 'signal red' and so on are misleading, ambiguous, and do not differentiate clearly enough

between hues, especially if you are raising hybrid plants. A colour chart is produced by the Royal Horticultural Society, and many cactus enthusiasts use the colour charts produced by paint manufacturers, but unfortunately no one colour chart has become accepted as the norm.

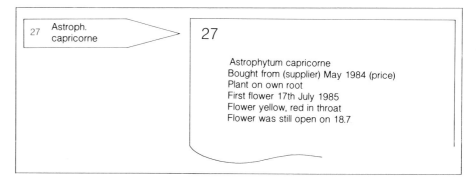

Example of a plant label and plant card index entry.

Special cultural problems

In this chapter we shall discuss a number of special questions relating to cactus culture, as well as matters which apply only to particular groups of cacti.

Epiphytic cacti

The cultivation of epiphytic cacti must be based on the conditions in the plants' native habitat. Growing these species is more closely akin to the cultivation of orchids and bromeliads, which grow in a similar environment, than to ordinary cacti. Epiphytic cacti do not like excessively powerful sunshine, and they should not be subjected to the brilliance of the midday sun; the gentle radiation of the early morning and evening is ideal for them. The plants' natural growth form is generally pendant, or hanging, especially species of the genera *Rhipsalis, Rhipsalidopsis, Schlumbergera* (with *Zygocactus*). For this reason many of these plants should not be grown in ordinary cactus pots, but in flat pans, hanging baskets or orchid baskets. The soil mixture should be light and permeable, and should be slightly acid. Orchid compost is suitable, or a loam with the addition of coarse sand, Perlite, peat or fragmented sphagnum peat. A layer of small crocks is useful at the bottom to aid water drainage. The soil for epiphytes should never hold stagnant moisture - make sure drainage is really effective - but on the other hand it should not be allowed to dry out completely. Ideally you should water somewhat more generously in the growth period, and with more restraint in the dormant period, but it is important that there should always be a mild level of humidity in the soil.

The roots of epiphytic cacti are sensitive and should be disturbed as little as possible, and for this reason they should only be repotted when it is absolutely essential. Normal flower fertilizer can be used, i.e. the special low-nitrogen cactus feeds are not essential, but you must avoid the build-up of salts in the soil. For this reason the fertilizer should be used at a weaker concentration than usual. Liquid fertilizers are recommended, of the type and concentration recommended for orchids and tillandsias.

True epiphytic cacti are generally not kept in a greenhouse with other cacti as the cultural conditions required are too different. On the other hand they flourish outstandingly well in greenhouses whose climate is set up for the cultivation of epiphytic orchids or bromeliads. For this reason epiphytic cacti are more often grown by orchid growers and tillandsia enthusiasts than cactus growers. If you would like to raise a few epiphytic cacti along with your collection of ordinary species, we recommend that the plants should be hung up in the gentle shade of a tree in the summer. It is important to check that the root balls do not dry out. A very effective method of ensuring this is to spray over them frequently with water which is as far as possible lime-free. In autumn the level of humidity should be reduced somewhat to help the new growth mature. In winter epiphytic cacti must be kept warmer than ordinary species, and an adequate level of atmospheric humidity must be maintained; the use of humidifiers, misting with lime-free water and cultivation in a partitioned-off flower window or in a plant showcase are all

suitable methods. In these conditions many epiphytic cacti will produce their flowers in winter, whether it is the well-known flowers of the Christmas cacti or the 'strings of pearls' of small, white or yellow flowers produced by *Rhipsalis*.

The climbing Cerei including the well-known Queen of the Night (*Selenicereus*) and the Hylocerei are not epiphytic cacti in the strict sense of the term, but they share the same tropical forest habitats. There they climb up high on ancient forest trees like lianas. These plants can only really thrive and flower **abundantly in cool temperate areas if they have plenty of space. They require a large flower tub or trough in** the greenhouse for their extensive root system. Their projecting shoots require a large, strong frame, perhaps on the less sunny side of the greenhouse. A nutritious, humus-rich, but permeable soil is recommended, and they appreciate the addition of a general purpose fertilizer to the water in the growth period.

The *Nopalxochia* hybrids, generally known as 'Phyllocacti', also deserve a mention in connection with epiphytic cacti. The parent species of these hybrids include epiphytic cacti as well as ground-based types, and as a result their cultural requirements lie somewhere between those of the epiphytic and ordinary cacti. They like a well-lit and half-shaded location, protected from the brilliant midday sun where possible. The soil should be rich in nutrients, permeable and high in humus. We recommend a standard (John Innes No. 2) soil with the addition of sand and Perlite. Ordinary general-purpose flower fertilizer can be used as a feed. In summer the plants should be kept well ventilated and not too dry. A location in the open air where they will be shaded by a tree around the middle of the day is ideal. In winter many types will tolerate cool, dry conditions. Other species require slight moisture and a somewhat higher temperature. If you like these plants we suggest that you select from the wide range of available types which grow well in your conditions, which are compact, not too expansive, and which readily produce their beautiful flowers.

Winter-hard cacti

Many cactus enthusiasts link the term cacti with the idea of a warm, sunny, frost-free climate, but there are cacti which can be cultivated in the open air all year round under temperate continental conditions. Amongst these winter-hard cacti are several species of *Opuntia*, which are accustomed to hard winters from their North American home. Wild Opuntias have been found in old vineyards in South West Germany where they have flourished for years without any care. We can gain some idea of how to cultivate these plants by studying the conditions at these natural locations.

A site in full sunshine is absolutely essential if you wish to grow winter-hard cacti in the open air; growing them in full or partial shade offers no prospect of success. The site should also be warm. A good position would be a sloping bed facing south, or against a south-facing house wall, bounded by a large stone or drystone wall. The stones store the warmth of the sun and also shelter the plants from the wind. The soil should be very permeable, as stagnant moisture is bad for the plants in summer and winter. The porosity of a heavy soil can be improved by adding a drainage layer of gravel and expanded polystyrene or Styromull chips, and mixing the topsoil with coarse sand. Opuntias are hardy plants, tolerant of minor errors in cultivation, but they still prefer a slightly acid soil, like virtually all cacti.

For planting out in the open you should only consider plants which have always been grown 'hard', i.e. not raised in a greenhouse. Opuntias require great care in handling because of their powerful, malicious spines. Once planted, Opuntias should be left undisturbed for several years, so it is important to arrange them in such a way that vigorous plants will not overwhelm smaller, slower growing specimens.

After planting the soil surface can be covered with lava waste or gravel. These materials store the heat of the sun, prevent the rain washing away the soil and mud spray soiling the plants. Opuntias like to have plenty of moisture in the vegetation period, but the quantity of water they receive in one of our rainy summers can be too much for them despite all our attempts at drainage, and the result can be dangerous fungus infections. For this reason a site sheltered from the worst of the rain is especially favourable for the cultivation of winter-hard Opuntias, such as the south side of a house where a projecting roof provides some degree of shelter from rain. You then need to take care that the plants receive adequate water in dry spells during the vegetation period. Opuntias are generally vigorous plants, and require generous feeding. Because the soil is particularly porous, there is a strong tendency for nutrients to be washed out of the soil, and the plants are then undernourished. Inadequately fed plants flower poorly, and for this reason Opuntias should be given a low-nitrogen (but not nitrogen-free) fertilizer from March to July.

In autumn Opuntias shrivel up markedly, thereby concentrating their cell fluid; in doing so they become able to survive quite severe frosts. Plants which were formerly turgid with fluid and standing erect now become shrivelled and lie prostrate on the ground. At this stage it is advisable to support a sheet of glass over the plants to keep the worst of the late autumn and winter precipitation off them. This reinforces the shrivelling process, and fungus infections are kept at bay. Do not cover Opuntias with foliage or twigs, as they will flower more readily if they are kept in a light location in winter. No damage results if the plants are snowed in during the winter; they will even survive being buried under snow for weeks on end, as this also occurs in their native habitat. By the early spring the Opuntias are a pathetic sight. They lie on the ground, crumpled up, slack of body and grey/green in colour, and it is tempting to believe that they have succumbed to the winter. However, with the onset of warm, sunny weather the plants quickly fill out, regain their usual appearance, and - if you have cared for them correctly - will soon bring forth flowers in profusion.

Amongst the winter-hard Opuntias are *Opuntia fragilis, O. phaeacantha, O. polyacantha,* and *O. hystricina* var. *bensonii (O. rhodantha)*. In some books you will find listed an amazingly large number of species and varieties of winter-hard Opuntias, but you will seek them in vain from colleagues and the trade. In fact these long lists of names were drawn up at a time when the great breadth of variation amongst cacti had not been taken into account in the naming of the species.

The truth behind these names, which appear to have been copied repeatedly from one book to the next, is that most of them are no more than forms within the range of variation of a particular species.

Cacti for cold winter conditions

In addition to the small number of cacti which can survive in the open in cool temperate winters there are others which can survive relatively cold conditions as long as they are protected from moisture, but which cannot be left outside. These plants are of great interest to many growers who have to overwinter their cacti in fairly low temperatures, or who wish to keep temperatures low in order to save on heating costs. It is not an easy matter to provide temperatures which are just high enough for individual genera and species, as the length of the cold spell has to be considered as well as the lowest temperature which is likely to be reached. Towards the end of a fairly long cold spell cacti may suffer harm at temperatures which

Opuntia hystricina var. bensonii growing in the open air.

they survived without difficulty at the start of the period, when they were in a stronger state. Moreover, many cacti can tolerate short nocturnal frosts without damage, and even appear to enjoy the experience, provided that the daytime temperature rises to about +8 to +15° C or more. The plants are then able to keep their metabolism 'ticking over'.

The following list provides an approximate classification of cacti according to their ability to survive frost:

1. Cacti which can survive the winter in the open air in temperate continental conditions, such as central Europe. This group, consisting of a few winter-hard Opuntias, has already been discussed.

2. Cacti which can survive under temperate continental conditions, such as central Europe, in an unheated greenhouse - and thus protected from excess moisture. In addition to the winter-hard Opuntias this group includes *Neobesseya missouriensis, Coryphantha vivipara* and many Echinocerei, especially in the large group based

on *Echinocereus triglochidiatus, E. viridiflorus* and *E. chloranthus*. Marginal cases are a few species of the genus *Pediocactus*, which were previously classified under the independent genera *Coloradoa, Navajoa, Pilocanthus, Toumeya* and *Utahia*. Most of these are endemic to the North American states of Arizona, Colorado and New Mexico. In their native habitat these cacti are subjected to hard winters, and in theory they can survive a cold winter in Europe. In practice these small rarities are very difficult to cultivate, especially in the vegetative period, and even when grafted they generally do not survive very long.

3. Cacti which can tolerate short nocturnal frosts down to -5°C if they are kept dry, especially if the daytime temperature rises to +8 to +15°C. This group includes many species whose home is in the more elevated areas of North America, Mexico or the South American Andes. There these plants are sometimes subjected to quite severe night frosts in the dormant period, i.e. when they are dry and atmospheric humidity is low. For

98

example, the absolute minimum monthly temperature in Sucre (Bolivia) drops to -3°C in June and -4° in July. In Salta (north-west Argentina) the figures are -8° in June, -9.5° in July and -5.5° in August and September. The areas around these cities, which might well experience rather lower temperatures than the cities themselves, are home to numerous species of cacti.

This group of cacti, which can tolerate at least short night frosts during the winter, includes almost all the species of the genera *Rebutia, Lobivia, Sulcorebutia, Weingartia, Trichocereus, Oreocereus, Oroya, Neowerdermannia* and *Ariocarpus*, as well as many species of the genera *Echinocereus* (especially the pectinate sub-group), *Echinopsis* (in particular the sub-group *Pseudolobivia*) and *Opuntia* (especially the sub-group *Tephrocactus*), and even a few species of the genus *Mammillaria* (including *Mammillaria senilis* and the group based around *Gymnocalycium gibbosum*).

4. Cacti which are generally unable to tolerate frost, and which should be overwintered at 5-10°C. Amongst this group are many species of the genera *Astrophytum, Cleistocactus, Coryphantha, Echinofossulocactus, Echinopsis, Gymnocalycium, Mammillaria, Notocactus, Parodia* and many others.

5. Cacti from the hot regions of Mexico, Brazil and the Caribbean, which should not be overwintered below 12-15°C. This group includes most species of the genera *Melocactus, Discocactus, Ferocactus* and *Pilosocereus*.

Groups 1 to 3 include the species which are most suitable for cool winter conditions under glass. The prerequisite here is that the greenhouse should receive full sun even in winter. It is essential to seal the greenhouse as effectively as possible against heat loss by fitting double glazing, stretching plastic film inside the glass, sealing all gaps and fitting expanded polystyrene slabs to all glass surfaces which are not the primary sources of light. Before risking plants which may be irreplaceable, it is worthwhile monitoring the

temperatures in the greenhouse for an entire winter, comparing them with the outdoor temperatures. A maximum/minimum thermometer is ideal for this, and it should be read at least once a week. A garden cold frame is only suitable for this form of overwintering if it is situated in a very sheltered position, because the smaller volume of trapped air cools off quite rapidly.

All plants intended for cold winter conditions must be cultivated hard during the growth period. This means good ventilation, strong sunlight and marked temperature differences between day and night. Cacti raised in a warm, humid greenhouse atmosphere and fed with excessive nitrogen will not survive. The plants should be growing on their own roots; the only grafted plants which can be considered are those grown on robust *Trichocereus* stocks (e.g. *Trichocereus pasacana*). Plants intended for cool overwintering should be hardened off adequately in the autumn and must be kept completely dry in the winter.

Cacti in group 3 require some form of heating in the winter. The heating should be controlled by a thermostat, cutting in when the temperature drops to -4° or - 5°C. The heating will only cut in on occasional nights, because the greenhouse will be heated by the winter sun in the daytime, and should retain the heat well if your insulation measures are effective. Such heating is quite cheap to run, and the initial installation itself can be less costly.

These conditions - bright, cool and with marked temperature differences between day and night - correspond much more closely to the native conditions of the high mountain cacti than the provision of even temperatures. In this respect cacti from the higher elevations are easier to accommodate than might be imagined. They will thrive outstandingly well in such conditions, and will show their gratitude for their harsh treatment during the winter with an abundance of flowers in the spring.

The cold winter treatment described here for certain cacti is based on our experience in Stuttgart. Stuttgart has a wine-growing climate of a relatively

continental nature. Cactus growers in other regions, in particular with high atmospheric humidity in winter, are advised to carry out experiments with selected test plants, to establish whether this method of overwintering is suitable for their own micro-climatic conditions.

Columnar cacti

Many a cactus enthusiast is keen to raise a few columnar cacti to round off his collection of globular species. There is often one or more of these plants even in the small collections kept on an indoor window ledge, and they usually do surprisingly well. There are also specialist growers who devote themselves more or less exclusively to the cultivation of columnar cacti.

There are a number of differences in the cultivation of columnar cacti compared with ordinary globular types. In their native habitat many columnar cacti grow to 3-5 metres or more, which indicates that they grow very strongly. The cultivator has to take this into account when selecting a plant container, otherwise the plants often grow narrow and inelegant. In particular they like to be able to extend their root system laterally, so the pot should be broad and of average depth rather than tall and narrow.

Columnar cacti only grow to their full splendour when planted out freely in the bed of a greenhouse. Most species love warmth, including warm soil, and for this reason a central bed in the greenhouse is ideal, as the side beds of a greenhouse tend to cool down markedly in winter due to their contact with the outside soil. Even if the air temperature is kept adequately high, columnar cacti will then languish or even die. This fate can only be avoided by installing greenhouse foundations which are effectively insulated, and fitting soil heating. Even so the more vigorous columnar cacti will soon reach the roof if grown in a side bed. All things considered, the central bed in the greenhouse is always preferable for columnar cacti.

Standard cactus soil mixtures have proved to be suitable for columnar cacti, although the majority of species prefer a mixture with a somewhat higher humus and nutrient content. The topmost layer of the soil should be very permeable and contain a high proportion of coarse sand and chippings. This top layer should extend from the top of the roots up, a point which should be borne in mind when planting out cuttings taken from the crown of columnar cacti. To avoid these cuttings falling over it is tempting to set them a little deeper in the soil, but as the buried part of the plant has been growing above the ground until then it is prone to rotting. It should thus be embedded in a permeable soil which dries out quickly.

Columnar cacti can only grow rapidly if fed well, so it is advisable to give the plants plenty of nutrients. You do not need to stick to ordinary low-nitrogen cactus fertilizers, and a standard flower fertilizer or general-purpose nutrient salt can be given now and then.

Many columnar cacti come from warm regions, some of them even humid. Hard cultivation and cold conditions in winter will only be tolerated by Oreocerei, Trichocerei and a few Cleistocacti. Ordinary columnar cacti should therefore be kept sunny and warm, and even in winter the temperature should not drop below 10° or 15°C, depending on original habitat. It is advisable to keep many species slightly moist the whole year round, giving small quantities of water regularly. Large greenhouse beds maintain a mild level of moisture at the bottom even in winter; if you are using embedded clay pots the bedding soil should be moistened slightly; plants grown indoors should be given one or two dessertspoonsful of water once a week. The conditions we have described explain why the more robust columnar cacti often flourish well even on an indoor window ledge.

Many columnar cacti are accustomed to mist and dew precipitation in the wild, and they appreciate quite high atmospheric humidity, especially at night. However, the atmospheric humidity in a hot, sunny greenhouse often drops surprisingly low, and for this reason it is often recommended that columnar cacti should be sprayed or misted in the evening during the vegetative period. Unfortunately spraying detracts a lot from the plants' beauty, as the water damages their chalky or waxy coatings, which are the very reason why many species are collected. If calcareous or dirty water is used for spraying the plants, unsightly deposits build up on the long hairs and bristles of some species.

If it is at all possible, it is far better to raise the atmospheric humidity inside the greenhouse in the evening without spraying the plants directly. For example the greenhouse path can be watered (damped down), humidifiers can be set up, or large lumps of lava waste set between the columnar cacti can be sprayed. If you have to spray the plants directly, do at least take care to use clean water, free of dirt and mineral substances.

The white-haired or woolly columnar cacti are also liable to lose much of their beauty if subjected to dust. Such species should be cultivated under glass to avoid this happening.

The flowers of columnar cacti often do not appear until the plants are quite large, and these species can only be brought to flower if you have a tall greenhouse. Other species, including *Trichocereus grandiflorus*, *Cleistocactus smaragdiflorus* and *Eriocereus jusbertii*, flower when quite small. A note is included in the information on genera and species where plants flower at an early age. Otherwise the beauty of columnar cacti lies in the powerful symmetry of their growth, their spine formations which are often finely coloured, their delicate woolly coverings and hair formation, and the chalky or waxy coatings of the plants' bodies. The main point of raising columnar cacti should be to allow these characteristics to develop to the full.

Imported cacti

With the expansion of air travel in the last few decades cacti imported from their homelands sometimes become available commercially. Basically the care of imported cacti is difficult. The plants are used to a different climate and are often accustomed to a different rhythm of growth. If you are a beginner or an enthusiast who lacks ideal cultural facilities, you would be better served with a healthy cultured plant than with an import.

Imported plants rooted by the nurseryman can be brought directly into your collection after checking them for pests or areas of rot. The object should be to provide the plant with conditions as close as possible to those of its natural habitat, in order to encourage the spines of the new growth to be as close as possible in strength and colour to those of the original parts. If your imported plant has not yet rooted but retains at least part of its original root system, then it will be relatively easy to root. Older plants from which the roots have been drastically removed often present difficulties. For this reason the collector of imported plants should always attempt to retain at least a proportion of the root system. Plants which have not yet rooted should be carefully cleaned and checked for pests and areas of rot. Pressure points or areas damaged in transit can easily result in rot, and these areas should be cut back to healthy tissue using a sharp, clean knife which must be disinfected prior to each cut. The cut surfaces must be allowed to dry out thoroughly for at least three or four weeks. No further cultivation of the plant should be attempted until this period is over. The healthy but unrooted plant is then placed in warm water at 35-40°C for a few hours to stimulate root formation. This process

also removes any remaining dirt; layers of corky skin at the base of the root tend to hinder new root formation, but they are loosened by the warm water and the plant absorbs a little moisture via the outer skin and spines. After this the plant is kept in a warm, light, but not sunny situation on dry Perlite or pumice gravel. Soil warmth is very helpful to the formation of underground roots, and this can be achieved with a small, electrically heated propagator.

The imported plants must be shaded from strong light. In brilliant sunshine they could easily sustain ugly scorch marks, as the plants do not yet have the benefit of a working root system. The formation of new roots can take longer than a year if the imported plant is old and large, and during this period the plants should be regularly sprayed over lightly with lime-free water once any cut surfaces have dried out. When the new rooting points are visible the plants can be set in a light, loose and permeable soil - we recommend a high proportion of Perlite - and cultivated with great care from then on.

Of the many imported plants collected from their home sites in recent years a very large proportion has undoubtedly not survived, as a result of incorrect treatment or inadequate cultural facilities. The number of many species of rare, slow-growing cacti in the natural habitat has dropped seriously. In view of this problem the true cactus lover should feel a sense of responsibility towards the conservation of cacti in their natural location, and should do nothing which encourages more plants to be collected. In fact the enthusiast can contribute to the propagation of rare cacti from existing plants, or from seed collected in the natural habitat.

Many countries are signatory to the Washington Species Protection Treaty, which seeks to control the international trade of endangered species of wild animals and plants, and as a result their importation is only possible if an import licence has been granted. Cacti are protected plants, and living material (as opposed to seed) may only be imported under licence.

Raising cactus hybrids

A hybrid cactus is a cross between different species of cacti. The species crossed are usually of the same genus, although crosses between species of different genera have succeeded in certain cases. The hybrid plant shares the genetic material of the two parent plants, and exhibits characteristics of both parents, but these features are combined in a new way.

To the cactus enthusiast hybrids are a problem; more so than for lovers of other plant families. Many cactus enthusiasts specialize in the collection of genetically pure species; theirs are botanical collections of pure-bred, naturally occurring species. As these collections would be devalued by the uncontrolled introduction of hybrids these enthusiasts are fundamentally opposed to any form of hybridization in cacti. This basic attitude to the hybrid problem has also become ingrained in the opinions of the cactus magazines over the decades.

Now, we do not wish to undermine this concentration on pure cactus species. Such collections and observations made from them have widened our knowledge, supplemented the descriptions of cacti and helped to define genera and species. On the other hand we should acknowledge the great efforts which have been made to improve plants by raising hybrids. The production of valuable and beautiful hybrids by cactus growers has also won many new converts to cactus cultivation. In recent years the opinion of many enthusiasts on this subject has changed; more and more nurserymen and amateurs are now involved in the problems of raising new cacti, and the more beautiful hybrids are gaining many friends. Even the cactus magazines are beginning to widen their coverage of the problems and techniques involved in raising hybrids.

Planned and unplanned hybrids

The genetic material of plants includes barriers which are intended to prevent hybridization. In the case of many interesting cactus genera, including Rebutias, Lobivias, Mammillarias and Gymnocalyciums, these genetic barriers are not very effective. In our collections we have cacti growing and flowering next to each other which are separated in their natural locations by vast distances or mountain ranges. As the flowers are often large and conspicuous, they are a prime target for insects, and unwanted hybrids often occur. An additional factor is the desire of many enthusiasts to have a try at hybridizing; it is tempting to cross-pollinate two plants which just happen to be flowering at the same time, without planning or considering the likely outcome. These accidental and unplanned hybrids virtually always produce a watered down version of the parent plants rather than an improvement. If this accidental hybrid or its seed should subsequently be passed on to another enthusiast under a misleadingly precise name, and with no indication that it is a hybrid, the eventual confusion can be a serious nuisance.

Serious hybridizing is aimed at combining in one plant certain characteristics distributed among different species. For example, we might have a species with large, well formed flowers which are white in colour, and another with brilliant red flowers which are rather small. The aim of the hybridization would be to produce a plant with large, well formed, brilliant red flowers.

There are a number of prerequisites to successful hybrid raising. One of them is to establish a clear purpose from the outset, preferably not directed solely at the flower formation. It is far better to consider the plants' spine formation, growth rate, robustness and their tendency to flower early and abundantly as extra factors. The resultant hybrids must also be classified and evaluated, and the many inferior plants discarded. In each work of hybridizing the number of plants grows from generation to succeeding generation. The only way to prevent yourself sinking in a flood of poor quality plants is to reject ruthlessly all inferior descendants. Clear documentation and eventual publication of the final results enable subsequent cactus growers to build on your work. Only in this way can we avoid the situation where the same species are crossed time and time again, and the resultant hybrids brought to the market under different names.

Techniques for raising hybrids

Raising cactus hybrids can be a very interesting occupation. The possibility of crossing plants with differing characteristics to produce a range of descendants varying in shape, spine habit and flower has gripped many a cactus enthusiast completely. Unfortunately it is not always quite so simple to raise hybrids in a purposeful and considered fashion. For many years the subject of hybrids has been ruled by a conspiracy of silence amongst writers on cacti, and for this reason little has been written on the techniques involved. The first task is to establish a careful plan, as has already been emphasized more than once. It will often happen that the stated goal cannot be achieved within one plant generation, and that the sowing, raising and documentation of each stage of hybridization are greedy of space and time, but the successes and occasionally the unexpectedly beautiful surprise results are ample compensation for such trouble.

If your particular pleasure is the broad range of hybrid descendants it is best not to start with pure species. Crossing pure-bred species results in very uniform offspring, at least in the first generation. However, if you acquire two existing hybrids and cross them the result is a broad spread of characteristics amongst the offspring. The 'multi-hybrids' which result from crossing Lobivias or Echinopses, for example, exhibit an astoundingly wide range of different flower colours, while those from *Astrophytum* include a large number of plants differing in rib count, body form and woolly fluff formation.

We have already indicated in the section entitled Cactus seed that the planned pollination of cactus flowers requires that accidental pollination by insects be prevented, by placing a bell of fly gauze over the parent plants in good time. When raising hybrids it is necessary to prevent self-pollination as well as unintentional foreign pollination. Many a cactus grower has imagined he has succeeded in a difficult cross, but has merely allowed the plant to pollinate itself due to carelessness. He then plants the seed, only to produce cacti identical to the mother plant instead of the desired hybrids. Even with cacti which are not normally self-fertile the stimulus of foreign pollination sometimes causes self-fertilization to occur. It is clear then that great care must be taken to ensure that the only pollen which reaches the stigma of the mother plant is that from the father plant. Fastidious growers carefully remove all the anthers from the mother plant right at the outset.

Not all planned crosses succeed. Many plants pollinated from the same plant (self-pollination) produce no seed, so it is inevitable that pollination by very distantly related plants often fails to produce fertile seed. In fact the ease with which two different species produce hybrids is a useful measure of how closely they are related.

The obstacles to fertilization between different species are of two kinds: on the one hand there are physical differences in flower structure, and on the other there are enzyme reactions. Attempts can be made to overcome these problems, and sometimes they are successful. For example if you wish to cross a plant whose flowers have a long tube with a plant with short-tubed flowers, then it would be wise to select the species with the long flower tube as the father plant. At fertilization its pollen grains will form pollen tubes corresponding in length to the flower tube, and they are sure to reach the ovary of the short-tubed plant. In the reverse case the pollen corresponding to the short flower tube might well not reach the ovary, located deep in the elongated flower tube. To overcome this, some enthusiasts have attempted to split the style and place the flower pollen directly in its heart.

With plants other than cacti chemical methods of eliminating barriers to fertilization have been successfully tried. Some enthusiasts have carried out similar experiments with cacti, but it seems that the seed gained by such devious tricks either does not germinate at all, or the young seedlings are chlorotic as a result of genetic incompatibility, i.e. they form no chlorophyll and die shortly after germinating.

What can be done if the two intended parent plants do not flower simultaneously? If flower pollen is stored cool, dry and in the dark, it remains viable for several days. Accordingly if the one parent plant flowers, and its intended partner is not

Echinopsis hybrids

expected to bloom for a few days, you can store the pollen as follows: wrap a little cotton wool round one end of a few wooden matchsticks, and transfer ripe flower pollen from the flowering father plant to the balls of cotton wool. Take a glass jar which has an airtight lid and fill it about one quarter full with ordinary cooking salt.

The bare ends of the sticks with their burden of pollen are then pushed into the salt, and the sealed glass stored in the refrigerator at a temperature of 5-8°C. The atmospheric humidity inside the jar remains constant because of the effect of the cooking salt.

A different procedure which is similar in principle is described by W. Mohring: remove entire filaments from the flowering father plant and store them in a test-tube filled three quarters full with paraffin wax. Cork the test-tube, and keep it in a glass jar with an airtight seal, itself filled about one third full with gravel. Here again the suggested method of storage is at 5-10°C in a refrigerator. Experience has shown that both procedures allow viable pollen to be stored for one to two weeks.

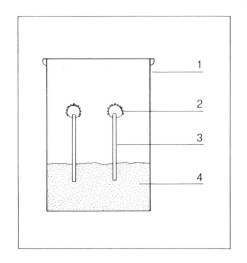

Storing flower pollen in the refrigerator
1 – glass container with airtight lid
2 – small ball of cotton wool with pollen adhering to it
3 – wood stick
4 – cooking salt

'Cleistopsis' hybrid between Cleistocactus strausii and Echinopsis.

103

Suggested species for hybridization

Probably the best known of cactus hybrids are those involving *Epiphyllum*, which are commonly known as 'Phyllocacti'. Cactus growers have been working with various species of the genera *Epiphyllum, Heliocereus, Nopalxochia, Selenicereus* and *Aporocactus* for more than 150 years, and many hybrids have been produced. The first focus of attention was the size, colour and scent of the flowers, but other qualities have been given consideration since then. The plant should be of erect habit, but should not spread excessively. It should be robust and produce flowers reliably when still young. Lack of adequate documentation and non-publication of cultivators' results has unfortunately led to the situation where many species have been crossed again and again by different growers, with widespread confusion as the inevitable result. A vast number of hybrids have been produced with an equally broad spread of names, many of them synonymous. In later years the Anglo-Saxon region has become the centre of work on hybrids, and notable efforts have been made to establish order amongst the names and to clarify the lines of development and origins of the hybrid plants already known.

Astrophytum is a relatively isolated cactus genus which encompasses a reasonably small number of well-defined species, and the plants' distinctive shapes and white flocked coverings make them stand out in any cactus collection. This genus has also been a centre of hybridizing work since the last century. In this case the aim of the cultivators has been to produce particularly interesting plant shapes and flocking formations rather than to improve the flowers. The possibilities and limitations of *Astrophytum* hybrids have been described in detail in various publications (e.g. Haage, Walther & Sadovsky, *Kakteen-Sterne* Radebeul 1957).

Chamaecereus silvestrii is very closely related to the genus *Lobivia* and is included in it by certain recent

authors. Because of this close relationship it is hardly surprising that the species is easily crossed with Lobivias, and it has proved possible to raise a broad range of flower colours from the rare white version via yellow, orange and red to violet, whereas the original flower was red only. The hybrid plants are better in another respect also: the segments of the original species were prone to fall off, but those of the hybrids are stronger. On the other hand many of these hybrids illustrate how unwise it is to concentrate on the flowers alone, as they are temperamental plants, and the spine formation often leaves something to be desired. Moreover some of the plants grow so poorly on their own root that grafting is essential. Once grafted, they are very susceptible to pest attack. Little published material on the results of this work has been made available to date, with the result that there are hardly any named hybrids which have found general acceptance. This situation makes the evaluation and selection of hybrids much more difficult.

Echinopsis hybrids are very popular amongst cactus enthusiasts. These plants were the result of crossing various species of *Echinopsis* with each other and with species of the genera *Lobivia, Trichocereus, Cleistocactus* and perhaps *Aporocactus*. A first generation of hybrid growers was very successful in Germany in the 1930s but their work received scant attention from cactus enthusiasts, and the work was subsequently continued in the United States of America. At a later date German nurserymen and amateurs resumed the work by collecting the earlier hybrids which were still in existence and crossing them with new material from the USA. The result was plants with large and well-formed flowers of widely varying colour. At first many of these plants were rather temperamental, with uninteresting spine formations and a tendency to produce corky tissue at the base, but these points have since been given greater attention.

In recent years hybrids between the high mountain species of *Echinopsis* have become very popular with cactus growers. They were earlier included in

the independent genus *Pseudolobivia*. These cacti are robust plants which grow vigorously. Young plants flower abundantly, producing slender flowers which are large in relation to the plant body. As well as white flowering species this group includes plants with brilliantly coloured flowers, and all of them hybridize readily (results of *Echinopsis* hybridization were published in the cactus magazine *Stachelpost* between 1968 and 1974).

The diagram shows those hybridizations between different cactus genera which have been achieved to date. In spite of the large number of successful hybrids between genera it is by no means true that any two of them can be crossed. It is especially interesting to see that hybrids between different tribes have been successful in a few instances. To some extent the degree of success in crossing reflects the relationships between genera, and in view of this it would be extremely interesting to cross other generic types in a systematic manner. The diagram also shows that there are a number of genus crossings which could well be of general value to cactus raising.

Hybridizations between cactus genera (after G.D. Rowley, *Nat. Cact. & Succ. J.* Vol 37/1,2, 1982, and M.W. Hawkes, *Cactus & Succulent Journal* (U.S.) Vol. 54, 55, 1982)

B	= Browningieae
Ca	= Cacteae
Ce	= Cereae
E	= Echinocereae
H	= Hylocereae
L	= Leptocereae
N	= Notocacteae
P	= Pachycereae
T	= Trichocereae

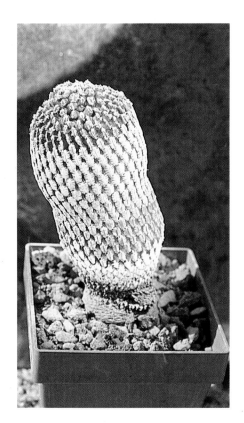

Tissue damage on a cactus caused by a chemical which the plant could not tolerate.

sunshine, warmth and moisture during the application are also significant. For these reasons what little information we already have on cacti's tolerance of these chemicals cannot be relied upon. For example, we have heard that E 605 forte has been found to damage young cactus plants; other enthusiasts, amongst them the author (Gröner), have found this preparation effective and harmless. Many growers believe that the nematode killer Nemafos can eventually damage the plants. However, consequential damage cannot always be clearly attributed to the chemical concerned because of the long period between the application and the appearance of the damage, and the slow growth of the plants themselves. Viewed overall, it seems fair to say that epiphytic cacti are more sensitive to pest-control chemicals, and in their case it would be wise to act with caution.

When applying a chemical in the water supply or as a spray be sure to use water which has been left to stand, i.e. it should not be too cold. Chemical solutions should always be applied on a warm day, but not in full sun. Spraying insecticides in brilliant sunshine has been known to lead to severe damage to the outer skin of cacti. The cacti can be shaded lightly for one or two days if necessary. Chemical solutions should not be applied to completely dry root balls. Before using any chemical on a large scale it would be wise to refer to the appropriate horticultural advice centre and government department for their latest information and advice. Small-scale experiments can also be undertaken using a number of test plants.

If you encounter a particular problem with plant diseases or pests, or require advice on the use, dosage and tolerance of the compounds currently available, we suggest you study the appropriate specialist literature.

The genera and species of cacti

Identifying cacti

Determining the genus and species of an unknown plant is termed identification. Identifying a cactus plant is usually much more difficult than with other flowering plants. Special identification books are available for indigenous flowering plants, by means of which almost any species can be identified right down to the particular species simply and reliably, once you have had a little practice and have learned the basic specialized terms. The matter is not so straightforward with cacti, and there are several reasons for this.

As with other flowering plants, the most important characteristics for recognizing and differentiating cacti lie in the flowers. In fact the majority of cacti can be more or less easily identified with reference to the flowers alone. However, cactus flowers are very short-lived, and are open for only a few days or even a few hours per year. If you miss the right moment you usually have to wait a further twelve months until you can try to define the species again. Many species cannot be identified in the absence of flowers even by experts. In fact in some cases the site of discovery has to be known before identification is possible. Many cacti, especially the columnar species, do not flower for the first time until they are many years old, and many globular cacti are reluctant to flower at all. In many cases these plants cannot be identified until they have flowered for the first time.

A further complication is that very many cactus species are unusually variable, and different species merge into one another more or less without a clear dividing line. Indeed certain genera of cacti are very poorly defined one from another. The root cause of this uncertainty lies in the fact that cacti are a family of plants which is still developing strongly. An added factor is that hybrid plants are very common in culture. Naturally enough, the plants which have suffered most from uncontrolled pollination and massed raising from seed are the highly popular genera such as *Mammillaria, Rebutia, Lobivia* and *Gymnocalycium*. These plants are usually sold under their genus names alone, such as 'Lobivia'. Many of these plants cannot be classified at all, as accidental hybrids cannot all be accommodated in a key. Usually it is not even possible to establish the parent species of an unknown hybrid.

The most likely method of establishing a hybrid's genealogy is to repeat the supposed cross, and compare the resultant plants with the hybrid in question. If more than two species are combined in one hybrid, or a hybrid has been re-crossed with one of the parent species, then it is virtually impossible to establish its origins. If the seed of a hybrid is sown a vast range of characteristics is exhibited by the offspring. Amongst them the characteristics of the original species will be combined in all imaginable permutations plus intermediate types, and the species descriptions used in this book are of no use with such plants.

On the other hand a wide variation in characteristics in the offspring plants is a strong indication — often the only one — that the plant in question is indeed a hybrid. For this test to be meaningful the plant must be fertilized with its own pollen. If no seed is set, pollen from a second, exactly identical plant can be used; but the second plant must not be a cutting of the first. If only one plant is available, re-crossing with one of the supposedly pure original species will also result in wide variation in the offspring. Hybrids within other plant families can often be recognized by the fact that they are unable to produce seed, but this seldom applies to cactus hybrids, even those between different genera. Establishing the nature of a hybrid can be seen to be very complicated, and the effort is only worthwhile if the subject is a single plant of uncommon interest. If you wish to have hybrids with a definite name, it is clearly essential to know precisely the species of the parents when hybridizing, and to propagate hybrids exclusively by grafting or by taking cuttings.

In view of this situation, please do not lose heart if it takes you a long time to identify and classify your plants. Even the experienced connoisseur almost always has a more or less large remainder of plants which he has either not yet identified or has classed as unidentifiable.

There are two basic reasons for wanting to identify a plant:

1. You have acquired the plant under a particular name. First check whether the name matches your plant. As there are many synonyms amongst cacti, first find out under which name that genus or species is listed in this book. Once you have found the corresponding species, compare the description of the genus and species very carefully word for word with the plant. If one characteristic does not fit, that should be enough to raise your

suspicions; check right through again very carefully.

If several characteristics in the description do not match the plant, and the illustration also looks different, you can be fairly certain that the name is not correct. In this case you have to treat the plant as unidentified, and follow the procedure outlined below.

2. You have acquired the plant without a name, or the label has proved to be incorrect. In this case you have several possible courses of action:

a) First you can try to find out the genus by using the genus key on page 114. You then turn to the genus description, and compare your plant with the generic characteristics listed there. If you are doubtful about a particular element in the key, or if that characteristic cannot be established, you have to follow up both possibilities. Usually one of the two routes will lead up a blind alley, i.e. none of the possible choices is correct. This route can then be eliminated.

The second stage is to establish the species. We have to admit that the chances of finding the precise species are not very high, as it proved far from possible to include all cultivated species in this work. The plant you are attempting to identify may well be a similar species which is not included here. You will be able to establish whether this is the case in the vast majority of cases if you compare the brief species description word for word with your plant. If not all the characteristics listed apply to your specimen, it is almost certainly either a species or variety which is not included here. Naturally you should compare your plant carefully with the illustration of the species, as well as with the illustrations of similar species in the same genus.

b) If the plant exhibits any unusual characteristics it is worthwhile referring to the table 'Special identifying features of individual genera and species' on page 122.

This is often a very easy and rapid means of narrowing down the choice of genera or species to a small number.

c) The last method is to simply leaf through the illustrations and refer to the corresponding text when you find the right illustration, or one very similar. If you opt for this method, it is essential to compare your plant with the description of the generic characteristics and the brief description of the species. An illustration can be an effective means of leading you onto the right track, but for a definite identification it is hardly ever sufficient on its own, as one picture cannot show all the characteristics which are essential for recognition and identification. There are very many superficial similarities in the world of cacti. Many species which are extremely similar in appearance in fact belong to different genera, and are easily confused if you are not aware of the precise distinguishing characteristics.

A key cannot possibly provide a comprehensive summary of a cactus system. The key's purpose is identification, and to this end it tends to concentrate on characteristics which are more or less easily recognizable, but which are often less significant in systematic terms; the external shape of the plant is a good example of this. The key groups within the Cactoideae (page 114) are in fact entirely artificial and of purely practical merit, with no systematic value. Unfortunately it is not possible to construct any form of key — not even a very complex one — for the phylogenetic groups of Cactoideae set up by Buxbaum (see page 38).

In some cases an individual genus has been divided up in the key, and thus appears in various places; this has been done deliberately in order to allow the use of the simplest possible characteristics for the purposes of identification.

Using the key

If you have a completely unknown cactus your first task is to establish the genus, referring to the genus key on page 114. Once you have established the genus, you can look it up in the alphabetical listing of genera and species on pages 124 to 316. If the genus includes more than a few species, you will find a species key, which helps to identify a particular species. If and when you establish what the species is, without textual contradictions, you can compare your specimen carefully with the description and if necessary with the illustration.

All the keys in the book are what are known as dichotomous (branching) keys, that is you must always select one of a contrasting pair of possible answers. Each pair of contrasting questions is indented by an equal number of spaces, and where the key is complex the two are prefixed with the same number. When you select one of the pair of answers, you then move to the pair immediately below it, and indented by one further space. If the key is numbered, the subsequent pair does not necessarily bear the next sequential number, but in all cases it will have a higher number. When you have answered the last pair of questions you will find a name on the right-hand side, i.e. a genus or a species, and you have then reached your goal.

This type of key appears complex at first, but you do not need to refer to any other list, you can always see clearly to what extent the choice has already been narrowed down, and you can also follow the key backwards again if it becomes clear that you have taken a wrong turning at some point.

To give you an idea of how the key works we will use *Notocactus ottonis*. In this case we can simply skip the first few pages of the key, as a glance at the drawing on page 115 shows at once that it must belong to the 'globular cacti' group. The genus key for this group is on page 117. In question 1 we are bound to take the second choice, as the plant does not possess a distinctly recessed cephalium. We then move on to question 3 below it, and its counterpart several lines below, also numbered 3. Here again the second possible answer is the correct one, as the flowers of *Notocactus ottonis* are only bristly/hairy. Question 6 follows, and here again the second possibility is the correct one, as the flowers are located close to the crown. In question 11 we have to select the first alternative, thus ending up at question 12, where again the first answer applies. In question 13 we reach the end of the road by selecting the first possibility, and discover that the genus is *Notocactus*.

In the alphabetical section of the book Notocactus is found on page 251, as is the species key for the genus. In this case the questions which belong together are paired by means of equal indentation and by identical first words, rather than by identical numbers. In the first key we arrive at the sub-genus *Notocactus* via the following route:

Central spines not hooked
  Crown straight. Stigma lobes red
    Areoles not distinctly fuzzy when young
      Flowers more or less in a ring round the crown
        Stamens along the entire length of the tube

Group 4 *Notocactus*

In group 4 (*Notocactus*) the following answers apply, which eventually lead to the species *Notocactus ottonis*:

Flowers yellow
  Crown woolly
    Style not brilliant red like the stigma lobes
      Stigma lobes deep red
        Flowers 4 to 7 cm. long
          Ribs 6 —13
            N. ottonis

The plant can now be compared carefully with the brief species description to confirm identification.

Identification key to cactus genera

Main groups of cacti according to external form

Plants with flat leaves   **A Pereskia-type cacti**
Plants with leaves which may be up to circular in cross-section, but which usually soon fall off, or plants without leaves (leaf-like structures bearing areoles are not leaves but flat shoots)
  Plants with circular cross-section leaves initially. Stems often consisting of short, round or flat segments with areoles all over their surface (with the exception of *Maihuenia* always with glochids, and seed with a thick, light-coloured, rock-hard seed coat)   **B Opuntia-type cacti**

  Plants without leaves, at most featuring small support scales for the areoles. If the stems are distinctly jointed, flat segments only bear areoles on the edges (except *Epiphyllanthus*). (No glochids, seed black or brown, with thin aril if at all)
    Cacti with short cylindrical or flat segments   **C segmented cacti**
  Cacti with elongated segments or not segmented
    Stems flattened with two sharp edges, leaf-like   **D leaf cacti**
  Stems with several ribs, round or with tubercles
    Body with very large tubercles similar to leaves   **E leaf tubercle cacti**
  Body ribbed or with simple tubercles
    Cacti with furrowed or unfurrowed tubercles and with flowers growing from the axils (both characteristics must apply)   **F genuine tubercle cacti**

Cacti with ribs; if warty, then tubercles always unfurrowed and flowers never in the axils
  Body spherical to oval, rarely more than 3 times as high as diameter, at most slightly elongated when old   **G globular cacti**
  Body columnar even when young
    Stems climbing or pendant, with aerial roots   **H trailing cacti**
    Stems erect to prostrate, without aerial roots   **J columnar cacti**

A Pereskia-type cacti

Leaves ribbed. Flowers on stalk. Seed black and smooth (no glochids)
  Ovary superior   *Pereskia*
  Ovary central to inferior   *Rhodocactus*
Leaves with midrib only or no ribs. Flowers not on stalk. Seed light-coloured, with rock-hard seed coat
  Branches often whorled. Segments break off easily. No real glochids, instead long bristle-shaped versions. Seed bare   *Quiabentia*
  Branches not whorled. Plants tree or bush-shaped. Genuine glochids present. Seed with felty hair   *Peireskiopsis*

B Opuntia-type cacti

Plants without glochids, seed glossy black   *Maihuenia*
Plants almost always with glochids, seed with thick, light-coloured, rock-hard seed coat
  Segments thin, cylindrical, almost climbing
    Flowers with long tube and with ring of hairs between the flower petals and the stamens, flowering in the evening
    Flower petals rolled back   *Tacinga*

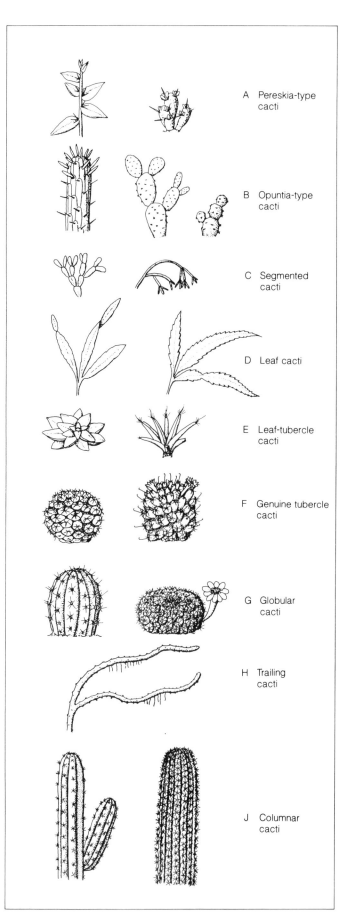

A Pereskia-type cacti

B Opuntia-type cacti

C Segmented cacti

D Leaf cacti

E Leaf-tubercle cacti

F Genuine tubercle cacti

G Globular cacti

H Trailing cacti

J Columnar cacti

Segments thick, cylindrical, flattened or bellied, not climbing. Flowers with short tube or no tube, without ring of hair.
  Flowers terminal, sunken
  Style enclosed. Bursting capsule fruit with winged seed (roots bulbous)   *Pterocactus*
  Flowers lateral or close to the top, very seldom terminal, not sunken. Style projecting. Fruit fleshy or dry with non-winged seed   *Opuntia*

C Segmented cacti

(see also External forms of segmented and leaf cacti, page 116)
Flowers more or less lateral, no more than 2.2 cm. long (segments round, cylindrical)   *Rhipsalis*
Flowers terminal
  Flowers up to 2.5 cm. long
    Segments round, club-shaped   *Hatiora*
    Segments flattened, triangular, club-shaped *Pseudozygocactus*
  Flowers more than 3 cm. long
    Segments round or opuntia-like with areoles on the surface (flowers with short tube, more or less zygomorphic)   *Epiphyllanthus*
    Segments flattened, leaf-like, with areoles only on the edges.
      Flowers radially symmetrical, without tube   *Rhipsalidopsis*
      Flowers radially symmetrical or zygomorphic, with long tube and stamens merged at the base   *Schlumbergera*

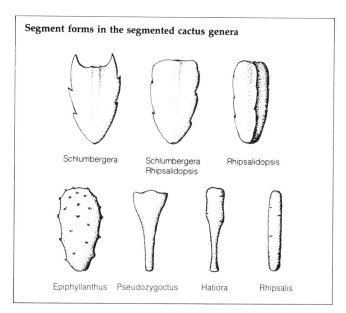

Segment forms in the segmented cactus genera

Schlumbergera

Schlumbergera Rhipsalidopsis

Rhipsalidopsis

Epiphyllanthus   Pseudozygoctus   Hatiora   Rhipsalis

D Leaf cacti

(see also External forms of segmented and leaf cacti on page 116)
1a Flowers with elongated tube, nocturnal (over 8 cm. long)
  Flower externally bristly and hairy (plant climbing)   *Strophocactus*
  Flower externally not both bristly and hairy   *Epiphyllum*

115

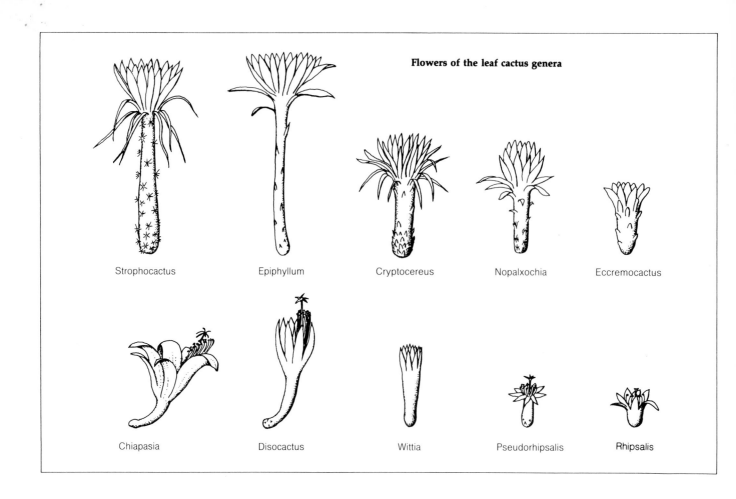

Flowers of the leaf cactus genera

Strophocactus   Epiphyllum   Cryptocereus   Nopalxochia   Eccremocactus

Chiapasia   Disocactus   Wittia   Pseudorhipsalis   Rhipsalis

1b Flowers without markedly elongated tube
  2 Flowers large (5 — 12 cm. long), flower petals more or
    less widely spread
    3 Flowers with many petals, tube almost always scaly with
      bristles or hairs (not always with *Nopalxochia*)
      Tube thorny or bristly, flower petals projecting and
      curved back   *Cryptocereus*
      Tube bristly, felted or bare   *Nopalxochia*
      Tube felted, flower petals not projecting   *Eccremocactus*
    3 Flowers with few petals, tube virtually devoid of scales
      and bare
      Flowers lilac. Stamens many. Ovary
      spherical   *Chiapasia*
      Flowers red to whitish-purple, stamens few. Ovary
      elongated   *Disocactus*

  2 Flowers small (approx. 2.5 cm. long), flower petals erect
    (tube not scaly, fruit angular)   *Wittia*

1c Flowers with very short tube or no tube (flowers no more
    than 3 cm long, with few petals and not scaly. Areoles in
    the axils of small scales)
    Tube very short   *Pseudorhipsalis*
    Tube absent
    Flowers externally spiny or hairy. Shoots
    spiny   *Acanthorhipsalis*
    Flowers bare. Stems no more than bristly
    Ovary not sunken into the stems   *Rhipsalis*
    Ovary sunken into the stems   *Lepismium*

External forms of segmented and leaf cacti

1) ribbed	a) spiny	*Pfeiffera*
	b) bristly	*Erythrorhipsalis, Lepismium marnieranum*
	c) more or less naked	*Rhipsalis: Goniorhipsalis* (in part)
2) 3-edged or 3-winged	a) 3-edged, bristly	*Lepismium cruciforme*
	b) 3-winged, spiny	*Acanthorhipsalis*
	c) 3-winged, spineless, ribs continuous	*Rhipsalis: Goniorhipsalis* (in part), *Lepismium trigonum*
	d) 3-winged, spineless, ribs offset	*Lepismium paradoxum*
3) leaf-type stems (spineless)		*Epiphyllum, Disocactus, Chiapasia, Pseudorhipsalis, Wittia, Nopalxochia, Eccremocactus, Rhipsalis: Phyllorhipsalis*
4) short, flat segments	a) leaf-type, bristly	*Rhipsalidopsis*
	b) leaf-type, not bristly	*Schlumbergera, Rhipsalidopsis, Pseudozygocactus*
	c) Opuntia-type segments or pads	*Epiphyllanthus* (in part)

5) short, club-
shaped,
round
segments | | *Hatiora*

6) round, thin
stems or
segments | a) bristly | *Erythrorhipsalis, Rhipsalis: Ophiorhipsalis, Lepismium* (in part)
| | b) not bristly | *Rhipsalis* s. str, *Lepismium* (in part), *Epiphyllanthus* (in part)

E Leaf tubercle cacti
(all with thick tap root)

Tubercles very long (up to 15 cm.) and thin, 3-edged, with long papery spines   *Leuchtenbergia*

Tubercles leaf-like, flat, spineless or spines soon falling off
  Tubercles not flattened against body (fruit fleshy)
    Tubercles in a flat rosette. Young tubercles spineless or with spines only a few millimetres long   *Ariocarpus*
    Tubercles forming a more or less rounded body. Young tubercles with bristly spines
      Tubercles with four sharp edges, curving back at the tip   *Obregonia*
      Tubercles rounded off, 4-sided, very blunt-tipped when old   *Strombocactus*
  Tubercles flattened against body like fir cone scales (furrowed above, fruit dry)   *Encephalocarpus*

F Genuine tubercle cacti

Tubercles all unfurrowed
  Flowers bare   *Mammillaria*
  Flower ovary with soft hair   *Neolloydia (Ortegocactus)*
Tubercles furrowed, at least the flowering ones
  Spines in comb formation on the areoles   *Pelecyphora*
  Spines not in comb formation
    Seed black, warty. Fruit dry, paper-thin eventually   *Neolloydia*
    (see also *Thelocactus* with long, furrowed areoles)
    Seed dark brown with fine tubercles. Fruit greenish (areoles with long furrows and hooked spines)   *Ancistrocactus*
    Seed black or dark brown, grooved. Fruit fleshy, not scaly. External flower petals usually ciliate (fringed)
      Flowers scaly. Tubercles short, numerous, persisting as woody knobs after the spines have fallen off   *Escobaria*
      Flowers not scaly. Tubercles long, less numerous, not persisting after the spines have fallen off   *Neobesseya*
    Seed light brown, smooth. Fruit watery, reddish, not scaly. External flower petals usually entire   *Coryphantha*

G Globular cacti

1 Flowers in a cephalium which is strongly recessed, cap-shaped to elongated
  2 Flowers nocturnal, 3-8 cm. long, trumpet-shaped with broadly spreading tips, white   *Discocactus*
  2 Flowers diurnal, 0.64 cm. long, funnel-shaped, more or less coloured   *Melocactus*
1 Flowers may be on areoles with different spines and hairs, but not in a cephalium which is distinctly recessed
  3 Ovary and tube spiny (with the exception of a few Lobivias (*Acantholobivia*) in which only the ripening ovary is spiny)
    4 Flowers lateral, rarely close to the end of the shoots, stigma lobes almost always conspicuously green. Body soft-fleshed   *Echinocereus*
    4 Flowers close to the crown or terminal. Stigma lobes not distinctly green

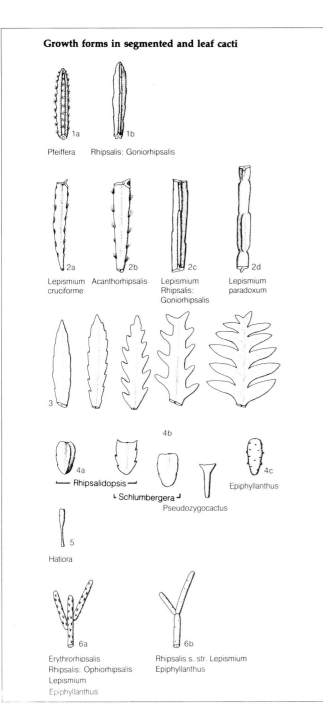

Growth forms in segmented and leaf cacti

1a Pfeiffera
1b Rhipsalis: Goniorhipsalis

2a Lepismium cruciforme
2b Acanthorhipsalis
2c Lepismium Rhipsalis: Goniorhipsalis
2d Lepismium paradoxum

3

4a / 4b — Rhipsalidopsis —
└ Schlumbergera ┘
Pseudozygocactus
4c Epiphyllanthus

5 Hatiora

6a Erythrorhipsalis Rhipsalis: Ophiorhipsalis Lepismium Epiphyllanthus
6b Rhipsalis s. str. Lepismium Epiphyllanthus

5 Body with very coarse spines and 20-80 cm. wide. Fruit a
  typical hollow fruit   *Eriosyce*
5 Body with fine spines, up to about 15 cm. wide. Fruit
  not hollow   *Notocactus* (sub-genus *Brasilicactus*)
3 Ovary and tube not spiny, at most bristly and hairy
 6 Flowers more or less lateral (including also the *Buiningia*
   species, which are mostly columnar, with lateral cephalium
   and bare flowers with sparse scales)
   7 Flower scales more or less papery, the upper ones
     modified into spines. Flowers with a ring of hair at the
     base   *Acanthocalycium*
   7 Flower scales not papery. Flowers without ring of hair at
     the base.
    8 Stamens with a clearly recessed ring of throat stamens.
      Flowers woolly. Style not merged with the tube
     9 Tube elongated and slim. Flowers 9-25 cm. long, mostly
      nocturnal   *Echinopsis*
     9 Tube not greatly elongated and thicker. Flowers up to 9
      cm. long, always diurnal   *Lobivia*
                       and a few day-flowering
                  Echinopsis (*Pseudolobivia*)
    8 Stamens without clearly recessed ring of throat stamens
      OR flowers bare OR style merged into the tube at the
      base
     10 Characteristics combined: root beet-like, spines in comb
       formation, flowers naked with separate
       style   *Sulcorebutia*
     10 Characteristics not all occurring in combination   *Rebutia*

 6 Flowers close to crown or terminal (rarely close to lateral on
   Gymnocalycium, but then with large, bare scales with
   membranous edges)
  11 Flowers bristly to felty in the axils of the scales
   12 Flowers almost always bristly in the axils of the scales
    13 Stigma lobes conspicuously red or purple   *Notocactus*
    13 Stigma lobes not conspicuously red or purple
     14 Hooked spines present   *Parodia*
     14 Hooked spines absent
      15 Body with woolly patches   *Uebelmannia*
      15 Body without woolly patches
       16 Style very thick (stamens in two groups. Seed black)
                       Austrocactus
       16 Style not conspicuously thick
        17 Seed wrinkled or warty
         18 Seed warty, black   *Neoporteria*
         18 Seed wrinkled, brown   *Uebelmannia*
        17 Seed smooth
         19 Seed very fine, pollen-like, with strophiole,
          brown   *Parodia*
         19 Seed not fine, pollen-like, sometimes with
          strophiole, brown to dark brown (black). Flowers
          often cleistogamous   *Frailea*

  12 Flowers hairy, woolly or felty in the axils of the scales
  20 Scales of the flowers prickly. Style very thick   *Echinocactus*

  20 Scales of the flowers not prickly. Style not conspicuously
   thick
   21 Body with woolly patches or with only 4-8 very wide ribs
                      Astrophytum
   21 Body without woolly patches
    22 Flowers cylindrical with narrow opening and without
     spreading tips, but with projecting stamens and
     pistil   *Denmoza*

    22 Flowers of different form
    23 Flowers bi-laterally symmetrical (zygomorphic)
     24 Flowers borne central at the crown. Fruit dry,
      bursting at the base   *Arequipa*
     24 Flowers usually slightly lateral at the crown. Fruit
      fleshy, dehiscent along lengthwise lateral
      grooves   *Matucana*
    23 Flowers radially symmetrical, not zygomorphic
     25 Body dwarf, up to 2 cm. wide, unribbed and
      spineless   *Blossfeldia*
     25 Body larger, clearly ribbed or warty, almost always
      with spines
      26 Tube very short   *Copiapoa*
      26 Tube well formed
       27 Flowers with slim, greatly elongated tube and clearly
        recessed throat stamens   *Echinopsis*
               (see also *Pygmaeocereus* with very short
           filaments and without distinct ring of throat stamens)
       27 Flowers with moderately long tube
        28 Fruit like gooseberry. Plants more or less forming
         a cushion   *Mila*
        28 Fruit self-opening
         29 Fruit splitting laterally   *Matucana*
         29 Fruit opening at the base, more or less hollow
               Neoporteria and *Oroya*

11 Flowers bare, scaly or not scaly
 30 Flowers bi-laterally symmetrical (zygomorphic)   *Matucana*
 30 Flowers radially symmetrical, not zygomorphic
  31 Scales present on the flowers
   32 Scales large, wide, blunt and with membranous
    margins. Body usually has grooves above the areoles
    33 Areoles in the depressions between the
     tubercles   *Neowerdermannia*
    33 Areoles on the ribs or tubercles   *Gymnocalycium*
               and *Weingartia*, the latter
               always with short flower tube
   32 Scales elongated, fairly small, not wide and with
    membranous margins
    34 Ribs very numerous and like thin gills, more or less
     wavy   *Echinofossulocactus*
    34 Ribs not very thin and wavy
     35 Body almost always distinctly waxy grey or brown-
      green, often with woolly crown. Flowers with short
      tube. Fruit has terminal lid   *Copiapoa*
     35 Body and flowers not featuring all these characteristics
      36 Body ribbed. Style thick. Hairs above the stamens
                   Ferocactus
            (and *Echinofossulocactus*
             coptonogus, the latter
           without hairs above the stamens)
      36 Body more or less bumpy to warty. Flowers without
       thick styles and without hairs above the stamens
       37 Flowers produced above the spines at the end of
        a more or less long, furrowed areole.
        38 Hooked spines present. Seed dark brown, with
         fine tubercles   *Ancistrocactus*
        38 Hooked spines absent, seed black, with coarse
         tubercles   *Thelocactus*
       37 Flowers not on long areoles or furrows
        39 Tubercles with four sides, very blunt at the tip.
         Spines only on young areoles   *Strombocactus*
        39 Tubercles not so blunt or body more or less ribbed,
         usually spiny   *Pediocactus*

31 Scales absent on the flowers. Flowers thus completely naked
  40 Body more or less ribbed, spineless except at the crown
    41 Body with sharp ribs and distinct lateral bands   *Aztekium*
    41 Body with blunt ribs, without cross bands   *Lophophora*
  40 Body more or less warty, spiny
    42 Spines very short and numerous, completely covering the body. Tubercles very small, only 1 mm. long   *Epithelantha*
    42 Spines different. Tubercles larger   *Turbinicarpus*

H Trailing cacti

1 Flowers more than 2.5 cm. long, with distinct scaly tube
  2 Tube greatly elongated, slim
    3 Scale axils thorny or bristly
      4 Diurnal flowering
        5 Ribs 7-12. Flowers 7-10 cm. long, red or pink, sometimes bi-laterally symmetrical, produced laterally on the stems   *Aporocactus*
        (see also *Morangaya* with flowers only about 5-6 cm. long, radially symmetrical, borne towards the end of the stems)
        5 Ribs or wings 3-8. Flowers 20-28 cm. long, white or light yellow (fruit very spiny)   *Deamia*
      4 Nocturnal flowering (flowers 12-40 cm. long)
        6 Stems usually 3 (-6) sided or winged   *Mediocactus*
        6 Stems (3-) 4-10 -edged or -ribbed   *Selenicereus*
        6 Stems usually two-sided, leaf-like   *Strophocactus*
    3 Scale axils bare (scales large. Flowers nocturnal)   *Hylocereus*
  2 Tube short to moderately long, thick (nocturnal flowering)
    7 Tube black, thorny. Flowers 8 to more than 10 cm. long   *Werckleocereus*
    7 Tube with stiff bristles to bare. Flowers up to 7 cm. long
      8 Ovary warty, with very small scales   *Weberocereus*
      8 Ovary not warty, with large scales   *Wilmattea*
1 Flowers up to 2.5 cm. long, without tube and without scales   *Rhipsalis*

External forms of trailing cacti

Stems ribbon-like, winding   *Strophocactus*
Stems with wide wings   *Deamia*
Stems ribbed to angular
  Stems less ribbed or angular
    With hooked protruberances   *Selenicereus hamatus*
    Usually thicker than 2 cm.   *Hylocereus, Mediocactus*
    Usually thinner than 2 cm.   *Willmattea, Werckleocereus Weberocereus, Mediocactus*
  Stems many-ribbed
    Climbing   *Selenicereus*
    Pendant   *Aporocactus*
Stems round   *Rhipsalis*

J Columnar cacti

Flowers in a cephalium or pseudo-cephalium
  Flowers bristly or hairy   Group I
  Flowers bare (or slightly woolly)   Group II
Flowers not in a cephalium or pseudo-cephalium, at most from slightly modified areoles
  Flowers spiny   Group III
  Flowers at most bristly, hairy or slightly woolly   Group IV
  Flowers bare   Group V

Group I. Flowers in a cephalium, bristly or hairy

1 Cephalium lateral or a lateral dome cephalium enclosing the crown (flowers scaly)
  2 Flowers bristly and hairy, in a dome cephalium (fruit hairy, flowers light yellow)   *Vatricania*
  2 Flowers hairy, in a lateral cephalium
    3 Areoles with long hairs. Plants bushy or solitary columns
      4 Fruit almost naked, not bursting. Flowers pink   *Espostoa*
      4 Fruit scaly, bursting. Flowers light yellow or purple   *Thrixanthocereus*
    3 Areoles only spiny. Plants tree-shaped, abundantly clustering (flowers pink. Fruit scaly and hairy)   *Facheiroa*
1 Cephalium not lateral
  5 Diurnal flowering with narrow tubular flowers   *Cleistocactus*
  5 Nocturnal flowering
    6 Ribs 4-6 (flowers bristly/woolly or woolly, with very short flower petals)   *Neoabbottia*
    6 Ribs almost always more numerous (see also x *Neobinghamia* with very hairy flowers)
      7 Dome-shaped cephalium. Ribs 5-11 (Flowers bristly/woolly)   *Backebergia*
      7 Cephalium in a ring round the stem. Ribs 11-30 (see also *Lasiocereus* which lacks a real cephalium, but bears flowers on very long-bristled areoles)
        8 Cephalium terminal. Flowers hairy (fruit dry)   *Cephalocereus*
        8 Cephalium a pseudo-cephalium. Flowers bristly/hairy or hairy
          9 Pseudo-cephalium formed from hairs, more or less annular and grown through each year (fruit fleshy)   *Neodawsonia*
          9 Pseudo-cephalium not grown through each year, bristly-hairy   *Mitrocereus*

Group II. Flowers in a cephalium, bare or slightly woolly

(Flowers nocturnal, almost always radially symmetrical and with nectar chamber (except *Buiningia*)
1 Bottom stamens taper sharply below the anthers to thread-like form. Flowers practically devoid of scales (lid fruit)
  2 Flowers in a cephalium. Bottom stamens merged at the base   *Arrojadoa*
  2 Flowers in a pseudo-cephalium. Bottom stamens merged strongly into scale-like base (flowers less than 2 cm. long)   *Micranthocereus*
1 Bottom stamens without broader base and sharp taper below the anthers. Flowers almost always with individual scales
  3 Flowers narrow-tubed, inner flower petals clearly different from the outer petals and erect. Nectar chamber not clearly enclosed   *Buiningia*
  3 Flowers funnel-shaped or broad and cylindrical, without distinctly different inner erect petals. Nectar chamber clearly enclosed
    4 Ovary scaly. Terminal flower zone, densely spined. Several flowers per areole   *Lophocereus*
    4 Ovary not scaly, or only very sparsely. Lateral cephalium or pseudo-cephalium
      5 Cephalium annular, not grown through each year   *Stephanocereus*
      5 Cephalium not annular and grown through each year

    6 Cephalium grooved   *Coleocephalocereus*
    6 Cephalium lateral, not distinctly recessed
        7 Flowers very small, 2.5-4 cm. long. Bottom stamens clearly recessed from the others. Fruit not bursting   *Austrocephalocereus*
        7 Flowers 4 cm. or more long. Bottom stamens not so clearly recessed. Fruit bursting
            8 Fruit hairy, more or less dry   *Haseltonia*
            8 Fruit bare, fleshy
                9 Nectar chamber short, enclosed without fluted zone   *Pilosocereus*
                9 Nectar chamber not enclosed, with fluted zone   *Pseudopilocereus*

Group III. Flowers not in a cephalium, spiny

1 Stigma lobes distinctly green
  2 Stems low, hardly more than 50 cm. tall, columnar cacti with soft flesh   *Echinocereus*
  2 Stems rod-shaped, hardly as thick as a pencil. Root thickened greatly like a beet   *Wilcoxia*
1 Stigma lobes not conspicuously green
  3 Tube very short to almost absent (flowers diurnal, usually brightly coloured, white only in the case of *Pfeiffera*)
    4 Tube absent. Shoots with only 2-3 ribs   *Acanthorhipsalis*
    4 Tube short. Shoots with (3-) 4-25 ribs
      5 Stamens in two groups. Flowers almost terminal (see also *Eulychnia castanea*)   *Corryocactus*
      5 Stamens not in two groups. Flowers lateral (also close to the ends of the stems in the case of *Pfeiffera* only)
        6 Ribs 14-25 (yellow flowers)   *Bergerocactus*
        6 Ribs (3-) 4-9
          7 Stems only up to 0.5 m. long. Flowers funnel-shaped   *Pfeiffera*
          7 Stems long, plant bushy or tree-shaped. Flowers bell-shaped/cylindrical   *Leptocereus*
  3 Tube moderately long to greatly elongated
    8 Flowers bi-laterally symmetrical (zygomorphic)
      9 Stamens and style with tips projecting. Flowers diurnal with tips folded back (ribs 4-8)   *Rathbunia*
              (this might also include a few *Haageocereus* species, although they are nocturnal-flowering)
    8 Flowers radially symmetrical, not zygomorphic
      10 Root thick, beet-like
        11 Flowers diurnal, red. Shoots scarcely as thick as a pencil   *Wilcoxia*
        11 Flowers nocturnal, white, pink or light yellow. Stems usually thicker   *Peniocereus*
              (a few *Nyctocereus* species also have thick roots)
      10 Root not thick, beet-like (flowers nocturnal with the exception of *Machaerocereus*)
        12 Flower tube moderately long. Flowers yellowish or lilac. Nectar chamber short, very obviously enclosed
          13 Stems powerful, with up to about 9 (-10) thick ribs. Flowers with long downward-pointing scales and a few bristly spines   *Neobuxbaumia (Rooksbya)*
              (see also *Stenocereus (Marshallocereus) thurberi* with 6-17 ribs and very spiny ovary)
          13 Stems with (3-) 4 (-5) thin ribs. Flowers with dense, even scales like roof tiles   *Pterocereus*
        12 Flower tube elongated. Flowers white or pink (*Armatocereus rauhii* also carmine red) nectar chamber

open or narrow and elongated
  14 Stems with 3-5 thin, wing-like ribs. Flowers with internal felted ring   *Dendrocereus*
  14 Stems with thick ribs, rounded to very flat. Flowers without felted ring inside
    15 Stems short columnar (30-60 cm. tall), with 13-16 ribs. Flowers with narrow tips   *Brachycereus*
    15 Stems columnar, slender with 2-12 ribs
      16 Flowers thick, funnel-shaped with narrow tips   *Armatocereus*
      16 Flowers with narrow tube and long, spreading or rolled-back petals
        17 Stamens in two distinct groups   *Eriocereus*
        17 Stamens not in two distinct groups
          18 Tube hardly spiny (ribs 8-12)   *Machaerocereus*
          18 Tube spiny
            19 Stems with 5-13 ribs, almost always flat   *Nyctocereus*
            19 Stems with 2-5(-7) tall ribs   *Acanthocereus*

Group IV. Flowers not in a distinct cephalium, externally bristly, hairy or felted

1 Flower tube very short to absent
  2 Ribs only 2-3 or indistinct. Young areoles in the axils of scales
    3 Ribs 2-3. Flowers lateral. Tube absent   *Acanthorhipsalis*
    3 Ribs 8-10, but indistinct. Flowers more or less terminal. Tube very short   *Erythrorhipsalis*
  2 Ribs 5 to about 50
    4 Flowers yellow, orange or red. Low, columnar cacti
      5 Flowers bristly and woolly. Stamens in two groups. Style thick   *Austrocactus*
      5 Flowers slightly woolly. Stamens all rising close to the base of the flowers. Style not markedly thick   *Copiapoa*
    4 Flowers white, pink or greenish. Large, bushy to tree-shaped cacti
      6 Ribs 5-9. Several flowers to an areole. Flowers with petals rolled back and long projecting stamens and style. Fruit similar to bilberry   *Myrtillocactus*
      6 Ribs 9-20. Flowers single on the areoles. Flowers more or less tubular
        7 Flowers with hairs formed of modified stamens   *Zehntnerella*
        7 Flowers without such hairs   *Eulychnia*
1 Flower tube moderately long to greatly elongated
  8 Flowers more or less bi-laterally symmetrical (zygomorphic) or elongated tubular without erect, elongated inner petals (flowers diurnal and almost always brightly coloured, with more or less elongated tube)
    9 Flowers tubular/cylindrical, without layered petals   *Cleistocactus*
    9 Flowers funnel-shaped or with several more or less erect layers of petals
      10 Flowers bristly and woolly, without enclosed nectar chamber   *Aporocactus*
      10 Flowers hairy, with enclosed nectar chamber
        11 Fruit large and hollow. Areoles usually with long hairs   *Oreocereus*
        11 Fruit without hollow cavity

12 Flowers with thick wall between seed cavity and nectar chamber *Weberbauerocereus*

12 Flowers without thickened wall between seed cavity and nectar chamber

13 Inner flower petals short and erect, white *Hildewintera*

13 Inner flower petals projecting and long *Borzicactus* (see also *Matucana* with laterally dehiscent fruits)

8 Flowers radially symmetrical and with erect tips, not purely tubular (see also *Lasiocereus* with nocturnal flowers on long bristly areoles and with bristly ovary)

14 Flowers with distinct recessed ring of throat stamens.

15 Tube more or less elongated. Plants columnar from the start

16 Stems with 3-10 ribs, thin, rising more or less curved *Eriocereus*

16 Stems usually multi-ribbed, erect *Trichocereus* (see also *Weberbauerocereus* with thick wall between seed cavity and nectar chamber)

15 Tube not markedly elongated. Plants usually flower even when still more or less globular *Lobivia*

14 Flowers without distinct ring of throat stamens

17 Flowers with greatly elongated, thin tube, always nocturnal

18 Flowers at best slightly woolly (strong red, tube with few scales) *Jasminocereus*

18 Flowers very hairy or woolly

19 Tube with felted ring above the nectar chamber (few scales. Stems with only 3-5 ribs) *Dendrocereus*

19 Tube without felted ring

20 Enclosed nectar chamber present *Armatocereus*

20 Enclosed nectar chamber absent

21 Plants bushy

22 Fruit bursting. Seed without air cavity *Eriocereus*

22 Fruit not bursting. Seed with air cavity *Harrisia*

21 Plants dwarf. Stems only up to 50 cm. long

23 Filaments much longer than the anthers. Ribs deeply notched *Arthrocereus*

23 Filaments hardly longer than the anthers. Ribs slightly notched or not notched

24 Some flower scales ending in long bristles. Bottom of style merged into the tube *Setiechinopsis*

24 Scales not ending in long bristles. Style free-standing *Pygmaeocereus*

17 Flowers with normal length tube

25 Flower petals break-through a pore when blooming (Stems with 3-5 ribs) *Calymmanthium*

25 Flower petals do not break through a pore

26 Flowers in groups of several on greatly enlarged areoles *Neoraimondia*

26 Flowers not on unusually enlarged areoles, solitary

27 Flowers diurnal

28 Flowers 8-17 cm. long. Stems usually with only 3-4 ribs *Heliocereus*

28 Flowers 4-7 cm. long. Stems with 4-16 ribs

29 Plants small columnar, up to only approx. 30 cm. tall (flowers at the end of the stems) *Mila*

29 Plants bushy or tree-shaped

30 Ribs 12-16. Flowers laterally on the stems, with loose scales *Leocereus*

30 Ribs 3-9. Flowers close to the end of the stems

31 Flowers with loose scales. Fruit spiny *Leptocereus*

31 Flowers scaly like roof-tiles. Fruit at best bristly (nectar chamber enclosed)

32 Flowers with leathery scales *Escontria*

32 Flowers not with leathery scales and with very thick-walled, short tube *Heliabravoa*

27 Flowers nocturnal, some of them persisting until the following morning

33 Flowers with distinct recessed ring of throat stamens *Rauhocereus*

33 Flowers without distinct recessed ring of throat stamens

34 Style merged with the tube at the base (flowers on modified areoles) *Carnegiea*

34 Style not merged with the tube

35 Enclosed nectar chamber absent

36 Flowers with dense scales arranged like roof tiles, on areoles with elongated spines *Castellanosia*

36 Flowers without these characteristics *Samaipaticereus*

35 Sealed nectar chamber more or less distinctly formed (fruit spiny, flowers on ordinary areoles)

37 Ovary and tube with abundant wool, hair and bristly spines *Pachycereus*

37 Ovary and tube felty or slightly woolly

38 Fruit moderately spiny *Neobuxbaumia*

38 Fruit very spiny *Stenocereus*

Group V. Flowers, bare, on normal areoles or areoles with fairly dense spines or hairs

1 Flowers with tube, very small, with few petals. Young areoles with support scale

2 Ovary sunk into the stem *Lepismium*

2 Ovary not sunk into the stem *Rhipsalis*

1 Flowers at least with short tube. Areoles without support scales

3 Flowers diurnal

4 Flowers bi-laterally symmetrical (zygomorphic), with long tube *Matucana* (see also *Rathbunia* with slightly scaly tube and spiny fruits)

4 Flowers radially symmetrical, not zygomorphic. Tube short to almost absent

5 Low columnar cacti. Flowers without leaf-like or papery scales, stamens usually at the base of the flower *Copiapoa*

5 Powerful, more or less tree-shaped columnar cacti. Flowers with large, leaf-like or papery scales, stamens in several rows

6 Scales papery, tube medium-length. Fruit scaly *Escontria*

6 Scales leaf-like. Tube very short. Fruit spiny *Polaskia*

3 Flowers nocturnal

7 Flowers with even, dense scales in roof-tile arrangement *Browningia*

7 Flowers with much larger scales, more or less loose, to almost scale-less

8 Flowers bi-laterally symmetrical (zygomorphic), with two groups of stamens. (Flowers close to the end of the stems and with enclosed nectar chamber) *Brasilicereus*

8 Flowers radially symmetrical, not zygomorphic (if slightly zygomorphic, then flowers on special areoles and without other stated features)

9 Flowers on special areoles (fruit bare, fleshy)

10 Nectar chamber enclosed, short, without fluted
   zone   *Pilosocereus*
10 Nectar chamber not enclosed, but with fluted zone
                                           Pseudopilocereus
 9 Flowers on ordinary areoles
   11 Nectar chamber enclosed, without fluted zone (ribs
      12-50)   *Neobuxbaumia*
   11 Nectar chamber not enclosed, with more or less fluted
      zone
      12 Ribs 15-18. Flowers strong red (tube elongated)
                                           Jasminocereus

12 Ribs 3-14. Flowers white or pale-coloured
13 Scales on ovary and fruit leaf-like, hairs
   inside the tube formed by modified
   stamens   *Stetsonia*
13 Scales different, no hairs in the tube
   14 Flower remains more or less persisting on the
      fruit   *Monvillea*
   14 Flower remains falling off after the flower, the
      style often persisting   *Cereus*
      (see also *Subpilocereus* with flower-bearing areoles
      hairy at least initially)

Special identifying features of individual genera and species

(excluding columnar and trailing cacti)

An experienced amateur can immediately recognize quite a large proportion of cactus genera and many species from particular characteristics which are relatively uncommon. These special features are often a far quicker means of identifying a plant than plodding through the key system, although they do require a degree of prior knowledge: what characteristics might constitute 'special' features, and what are 'normal', i.e. widespread.

The following list includes a fairly large number of these special, reasonably rare characteristics. Neither the characteristics nor the listed genera and species are complete, as we have concentrated on the more commonly cultivated species, mainly the globular and tubercle cacti. Nevertheless you will find that this list often answers your question much more quickly and more easily than the genus key.

Unfortunately a large proportion of genera and species have no such special feature, and are only distinguished by a particular combination of fairly common characteristics. For this 'remainder' the only means of identification is to use the key.

Characteristics of non-flowering plants

External form
(see also genus key, page 114)

Leaves
Flat leaves: *Pereskia, Rhodocactus, Quiabentia, Peireskiopsis*
Subulate (bodkin-like) leaves: *Opuntia, Maihuenia*

Segments
Flat, Opuntia-type pads: *Opuntia, Epiphyllanthus*
Flat segments with two sharp edges: *Schlumbergera, Rhipsalidopsis*
Serrate segments: *Schlumbergera truncata*
Flat stems: (see Leaf cacti, page 115)
Nopalxochia hybrids ('Phyllocacti'), *Nopalxochia, Rhipsalis, Acanthorhipsalis, Chiapasia, Disocactus, Eccremocarpus, Epiphyllum, Pseudorhipsalis, Wittia*
Lobed flat stems: *Cryptocereus, Epiphyllum*
Three-edged, offset segments: *Lepismium paradoxum*
Small, club-shaped segments: *Hatiora*
Coral-like, thin, round segments: *Rhipsalis, Lepismium*
Freely clustering, finger-like segments: *Mammillaria elongata, M. gracilis, M. viperina* and others, *Lobivia silvestrii,*

Rebutia (sub-genus *Digitorebutia*), *Echinocereus*
Branching (dichotomous): *Mammillaria*

Ribs
Body more or less devoid of ribs and tubercles: *Blossfeldia, Astrophytum asterias, Frailea*
5-ribbed globes: *Astrophytum, Echinocereus knippelianus*
Many thin, wavy ribs: *Echinofossulocactus*

Tubercles (warts)
Leaf-like tubercles: (see leaf tubercle cacti, page 117)
Ariocarpus, Leuchtenbergia, Encephalocarpus, Obregonia, Strombocactus
Angular tubercles: *Mammillaria, Coryphantha, Turbinicarpus, Encephalocarpus, Leuchtenbergia*
Furrowed tubercles: *Coryphantha, Escobaria, Neobesseya, Neolloydia, Ariocarpus, Pelecyphora, Ancistrocactus, Thelocactus*
Tubercles with milky sap: *Mammillaria*

Spines
Comb-formation spines: *Pelecyphora aselliformis, Mammillaria pectinifera* and *M. solisioides, Turbinicarpus pseudopectinatus, Echinocereus, Lobivia, Sulcorebutia, Rebutia densipectinata, R. heliosa, Oroya, Gymnocalycium, Discocactus horstii, Epithelantha*

Hooked spines: *Mammillaria, Coryphantha, Neolloydia, Ancistrocactus, Ferocactus, Echinocactus, Pediocactus whipplei, Lobivia, Echinopsis, Neowerdermannia, Gymnocalycium, Parodia*
Transversely ringed spines: *Echinocactus, Echinofossulocactus, Ferocactus, Thelocactus*
Sheathed spines: *Opuntia*
Pinnate spines: *Mammillaria plumosa, M. pennispinosa, M. theresae, M. prolifera*
Glochids: *Opuntia, Peireskiopsis, Pterocactus, Tacinga*
Flattened spines: *Ferocactus, Echinofossulocactus*
Papery spines: *Opuntia articulata f. papyracantha, Pediocactus papyracanthus, Leuchtenbergia*
Distinct rows of areoles: *Uebelmannia, Notocactus magnificus, Ferocactus, Echinocactus, Astrophytum*
Spines in the depressions between the tubercles: *Neowerdermannia*
Virtually spineless: *Astrophytum, Echinocereus knippelianus, Echinopsis, Matucana madisoniorum, Frailea, Blossfeldia, Neoporteria, Turbinicarpus, Lophophora, Aztekium, Strombocactus, Encephalocarpus, Ariocarpus*

Colour and surface quality
Brown or dark brown: *Copiapoa, Gymnocalcium, Neoporteria*
Chalky white: *Copiapoa*
Red: *Gymnocalycium mihanovichii* var. *friedrichii* 'Rubra'
Yellow: *Gymnocalycium mihanovichii* var. *friedrichii* 'Aurea', forms of *Echinopsis eyriesii, Lobivia silvestrii* 'Aurea'

Wool tufts: *Astrophytum, Uebelmannia*
Woolly or bristly axils: *Mammillaria, Coryphantha, Neolloydia, Pelecyphora, Ariocarpus, Encephalocarpus*
Distinctive lateral bands: *Aztekium, Gymnocalycium mihanovichii*
Body covered in dense white wool: *Mammillaria hahniana, Escobaria, Neoporteria, Oreocereus*

Characteristics of flowering plants

Flower position
Cephalium: *Melocactus, Discocactus, Buiningia, Oreocereus*
Lateral flowers: *Echinopsis, Lobivia, Acanthocalycium, Rebutia, Sulcorebutia, Gymnocalycium*
Flowers from the axils, unfurrowed tubercles: *Mammillaria, Neolloydia*

Flower form
Flowers bi-laterally symmetrical (zygomorphic): *Arequipa, Matucana, Oreocereus, Denmoza, Mammillaria (Cochemiea), Zygocactus, Epiphyllanthus*
Flowers almost closed, tubular: *Denmoza*
Cleistogamous flowers: *Frailea*
Inner petals erect: *Neoporteria* (sub-genus *Neoporteria*), *Oroya, Lobivia, Matucana*

Exterior flower features
Spines: *Echinocereus, Eriosyce, Notocactus* (sub-genus *Brasilicactus*)

Thorny scales: *Acanthocalycium, Echinocactus*
Large, membranous, bare scales: *Gymnocalycium, Weingartia*

Inner flower petals
Feather-like: *Echinocactus texensis*
Ciliate: *Coryphantha vivipara*

Flower colour
Greenish to brownish: *Echinocereus chloranthus, E. viridiflorus, Notocactus graessneri, Mammillaria marksiana* and others
Yellow with red centre: *Ferocactus acanthodes, F. setispinus, Astrophytum, Thelocactus, Coryphantha*
Lilac with red throat: *Echinocactus horizontalonius, E. texensis, Echinocereus, Thelocactus, Coryphantha poselgeriana*, and others
With darker throat: *Echinocereus, Lobivia jajoiana* and others, *Ferocactus*

Time of flowering
Nocturnal: *Echinopsis, Discocactus*

Clearly defined ring of throat stamens:
Echinopsis, Lobivia, Acanthocalycium

Special stigma colour
Red: *Notocactus, Echinocactus horizontalonius, Mammillaria albicans, M. fraileana, M. yaquensis* and others
Green: *Echinocereus*

Style merged with the base of the tube:
Rebutia (sub-genera *Aylostera, Digitorebutia, Mediolobivia*), *Mammillaria* (sub-genus *Dolichothele* and *Oehmea*)

The genera and species of cacti in alphabetical sequence

In the following section of the book the genera and species of cacti are listed alphabetically. All the genera are included, even those of which no species are cultivated. Many common genus names are synonymous. These are printed in smaller type and refer back to the genus names which are now considered as correct. Amongst the globular cacti we have mainly used the generic and specific names listed by Donald in *Ashingtonia* (1974). In general terms the genera are narrowly defined. The only ones which we have combined are Backeberg's excessively sub-divided mini-genera, which lack any clear distinguishing features. The more common synonyms for each genus are given in brackets, including at least all the genus names from Backeberg's *Cactus Lexicon* (1977), Endler and Buxbaum's *Pflanzenfamilie der Kakteen* (1974) and Britton and Rose's *The Cactaceae* (1919-23). The cactus systems of Backeberg and Buxbaum are the ones in most widespread use at present, while the work of Britton and Rose remains a very valuable reference work.

A brief explanation of the name is given, followed by a short descriptive text stating in each case a small number of very typical features. Although short, these descriptions are almost always sufficient to define the genus unambiguously. In the majority of cases the following information is provided: the external form, stem cross-section, flower position and external flower features. The number of known species for any genus is always taken from Donald's list (1974), but includes the species recently described by Ritter. Except where a genus embraces only a small number of species, most of these figures should only be considered as a very rough guide, as the results of up-to-date research are only available for a very small number of genera. Under 'Native to' we state the countries in which species of that genus occur

naturally. Brief cultural notes are provided for many genera; we have concentrated on the particular requirements which are at variance with more standard practice.

About 750 cultivated species are listed. It is likely that the total number of cultivated species is double that figure, while the overall figure for known cactus species is around 2700. The selection of the species is bound to be more or less arbitrary. A few genera such as *Mammillaria* and *Parodia* include so many species which are suitable for the amateur enthusiast that it is not possible to describe them all. The most important synonyms of the species names are also stated in brackets, including at least the names used in Backeberg's *Cactus Lexicon* and Britton and Rose's terms.

We have restricted ourselves to very typical features in the species descriptions. The size, rib count and size of flower are stated for all species, in order to allow the amateur to estimate the age and state of health of his plants. A general description of spine formation and flower colour are also provided. Generic characteristics are not repeated under the individual species. In the description of individual species we have almost always concentrated on those features which allow the species to be identified unambiguously amongst the

types listed. However, this approach cannot ensure that there is enough information to identify one plant reliably amongst all the species of the genus, not only those included here. Cultural information is only included exceptionally amongst the individual species, as the notes on cultivation usually apply to an entire genus.

Acanthocalycium Backeb. 1935
(Greek akantha = thorn, kalyx = calyx)

These cacti are short-cylindrical to flattened globular, with 8-15 ribs and flowers 3-7.5 cm. long; they are very similar to Lobivias. The flowers are borne laterally but feature membranous, papery scales, of which the top ones are modified into spines. The scale axils have long woolly hair, as has *Lobivia*, but there is a ring of hair at the base of the flower formed from modified stamens. 12 species. Native to North Argentina (Salta, Catamarca, Cordoba). Cultural conditions similar to·those for *Lobivia*, but winter temperatures around 6-8°C.

Acanthocalycium aurantiacum

A. aurantiacum Rausch
Body 5 cm. tall, 9 cm. wide, grey-green, 10-16 ribs. Radial spines 5 (-7), 3-4 cm. long, central spines usually absent, seldom 1. Spines whitish or yellowish, with black tip. Flowers orange-yellow, 5 cm. long and wide. Inner petals with more reddish margins. Argentina (Catamarca).

A. glaucum Ritter
Up to about 15 cm. high and 7 cm. wide, blue-green, with 8-14 ribs. Radial spines 5-10, black, 0.5-2 cm. long. Central spines usually absent, seldom 1-2. Flowers golden yellow, 6 cm. long and wide. Argentina (Catamarca).

A. klimpelianum (Weidl. & Werderm.) Backeb.
Body up to 10 cm. wide, dark green, with around 19 slightly notched ribs. Radial spines 6-8 (-10). (1-) 2-3 (-4) central spines. Spines initially brown-tipped, later grey. White flowers, 3-4 cm. long. Argentina (Cordoba).

A. peitscherianum Backeb.
Approx. 8 cm. tall, 10 cm. wide, grey-green, with around 17 ribs. Radial spines 7-9, central spines 1. All spines pale to light brown, black-tipped, up to 2 cm. long. Flowers whitish-lilac-pink, 6 cm. long. Argentina (Cordoba).

Acanthocalycium violaceum

Acanthocalycium violaceum

A. violaceum (Werderm.) Backeb.
Up to about 20 cm. tall and 13 cm. wide, dull green, with around 15 ribs or more. 10-12 (-20) spines, yellow-brown, flowers light lilac, up to 7.5 cm. long and 6 cm. wide. Argentina (Cordoba).

Acanthocereus (Berger) Br. & R. 1909
(*Pseudoacanthocereus*)
(Greek akantha = thorn)

Bushy or climbing columnar cacti with 2-5 (-7) ribs. Flowers with elongated tube, scaly and spiny externally, white, nocturnal, 9-15 cm. long.
14 species. Native to USA (Florida) via Mexico, Guatemala, Colombia and Venezuela to Brazil (Bahia).

Acantholobivia Backeb. see *Lobivia*

Acanthorhipsalis (K. Schum.) Br. et R. 1923
(Greek akantha = thorn)

Epiphytic plants with spiny stems, 3-winged or flat and leaf-like. Small, 1.2-2 cm. long tubeless flowers borne laterally, with scaly and spiny or only hairy ovary. The genus *Rhipsalis* is similar, but its stems are not spiny and the ovary is not scaly.
6 species. Native to Peru, Bolivia, ?N.E. Argentina.

A. monacantha (Griseb.) Br. & R.
var. samaipatana (Card.) Backeb.
Stems notched, 2-3 cm. wide. Areoles with spines up to 1 cm. long. Flowers waxy, orange, up to 1.5 cm. long. Bolivia (Santa Cruz).

Akersia Buin. see *Borzicactus*

Acanthorhipsalis monacantha var. samaipatana

Fruiting Acanthorhipsalis monacantha var. samaipatana

Anhalonium Lem. see *Lophophora* and *Ariocarpus*

Anisocereus Backeb. see *Pterocereus* and *Escontria*

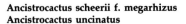

Ancistrocactus scheerii f. megarhizus
Ancistrocactus uncinatus

Ancistrocactus Br. & R. 1923
(*Glandulicactus, Hamatocactus* p.p.)
(Greek ancistron = barb)

Globular cacti with ribs deeply notched or warty, and hooked central spines. The flowering areoles are extended in a furrow. Ovary with few scales, otherwise bare. Seed dark brown with very fine tubercles. Taproot or thick, fleshy roots.
4 species. Native to Mexico, USA (Texas)

A. crassihamatus (Web.) L. Benson
(*Ferocactus c.* (Web.) Br. & R.;
Glandulicactus c. (Web.) Backeb.;
Hamatocactus c. (Web.) Buxb.)
Body 10-15 cm. thick with around 13 more or less deeply notched ribs. Areoles with glands. Radial spines 7-11, up to 3 cm. long. Central spines initially 1, later up to 5, main spine hooked, up to 6 cm. long. Spines more or less red, lighter at the tip. Purple flowers, lighter margins, 2-3 cm. long. Mexico (Querétaro).

A. scheerii (Salm-Dyck) Br. & R.
Up to about 12 cm. tall and 7 cm. wide. Tubercles arranged in about 13 helical rows. Radial spines 15-17, white to straw-coloured, approx. 1 cm.

long. Central spines 3-4, yellow (brown at the base), the bottom one hooked, 1.5-5 cm. long. Yellow-green flowers, up to 3 cm. long. USA (Texas), Mexico (Chihuahua, Nuevo León).

This species has a uniquely beautiful spine formation and flowers, but is temperamental in cultivation. It requires much light and warmth and needs to be watered very carefully.

f. megarhizus (Rose) Krainz
(*A. megarhizus* (Rose) Br. & R.)
Radial spines 20 or more. Flowers 2 cm. long. Mexico (Tamaulipas).

A. uncinatus (Gal.) L. Bens.
(*Hamatocactus u.* (Gal.) Buxb.;
Glandulicactus u. (Gal.) Backeb.)
Short columnar, 10-20 cm. tall and 5-7 cm. wide, with 9-13 straight, deeply notched ribs. Areoles with flat, yellow glands with ring of hair. Radial spines 7-8, the bottom ones hooked, 2.5-5 cm. long. Central spines 1-4, hooked, the bottom one up to 9 cm. long. All spines red at first, later brown or cream-white. Flowers brownish purple, 2-2.5 cm. long. USA (Texas), Mexico (Chihuahua to San Luis Potosí).

Aporocactus Lem. 1860
(Greek aporos = tangled)

Thin-stemmed, usually trailing cacti with 7-12 ribs, with aerial roots. Flowers with elongated, thin, scaly, bristly-woolly tube. The diurnal flowers are red or pink, 7-10 cm. long and more or less bi-laterally symmetrical.
5 species. Native to Mexico (Hidalgo, Oaxaca, ?Chihuahua).

Very rewarding cacti even for the beginner. They love sunshine, but need gentle shade from brilliant midday sun, and rich but well drained soil. During the flowering and growth periods they need much water, and slight moisture even in winter. They are vulnerable to spider mite attack.

Flowers almost radially symmetrical, spines yellowish (radial and central spines) *A. martianus*
Flowers bi-laterally symmetrical
  Spines red when young, radial and central spines different. Flowers dark pink *A. flagriformis*
  Spines red-brown, all the same. Flowers pink *A. flagelliformis*

A. flagelliformis (L.) Lem.
Plants abundantly clustering. Stems 1.5-2 cm. thick and up to 1.5 m. long, trailing, with 10-14 ribs. 15-20 spines, red-brown to brown. Flowers bi-laterally symmetrical, pink, similar to those of Christmas cactus, around 8 cm. long. Mexico.

A. flagriformis (Zucc.) Lem.
Stems similar to the previous species, but with 7-10 thicker ribs. Spines red when young. Radial spines 5-6. Central spines 2 or more. Flowers dark pink, 8-9 cm. long. Mexico (Oaxaca).

A. martianus (Zucc.) Br. & R.
Stems blue-green, with approx. 8 ribs. Yellowish spines. Radial spines about 8. Central spines 3-4. Flowers almost radially symmetrical, deep pink, about 10 cm. long. Mexico (Oaxaca)

A. mallisonii hort. is a hybrid of *A.flagelliformis* x *Heliocereus speciosus* and has luminous red flowers.

Arequipa Br. & R. 1922
(after the town of Arequipa in Southern Peru)

Short columnar to globular, ribbed cacti with red flowers 5-8.5 cm. long. The flowers are borne terminally, are scaly and hairy and more or less bi-laterally symmetrical with a long flower tube which is usually curved. *Arequipa* differs from the very similar genus *Matucana* only in its dry fruit, bursting at the base. The genus is included in *Borzicactus* by many authors, along with other South American cacti with bi-laterally symmetrical flowers.

5 species. Native to S. Peru to Chile. These plants require high levels of sun, mineral soil and need Winter temperatures of 6-8°C.

A. leucotricha (Phil.) Br. & R.
(*Borzicactus l.* (Phil.) Kimn.)
Up to 60 cm. tall and 10 cm. wide, grey-green, with around 20 bumpy ribs and much pale yellow wool at the crown. Radial spines 8-12, pale yellow, up to 3 cm. long. Central spines 3-4, up to 4.5 cm. long. Spines at first deep yellow or orange-red and brown-tipped. Flowers scarlet, up to 7.5 cm. long and 3-3.5 cm. wide. Chile (Tarapacá) on volcanic ashes at altitude of 2000 m. Older plants flower very readily.

A. rettigii (Quehl) Oehme
(*A. erectocylindrica* Rauh & Backeb.; *Borzicactus hempelianus* (Gürke)

Aporocactus flagelliformis

Arequipa weingartiana

Donald var. *rettigii* (Quehl) Donald)
Up to 50 cm. tall with 10-20 ribs. Very
powerful spine formation. Radial
spines 20-30, translucent white, up to
1 cm. long. Central spines up to 10,
up to 3 cm. long. Scarlet flowers, up
to 6 cm. long. S. Peru (around
Arequipa).

A. weingartiana Backeb. (*Borzicactus
hempelianus* (Gürke) Donald var.
weingartianus (Backeb.) Donald)
Up to 40 cm. tall and 10 cm. wide,
grey-green, with 14-16 ribs. Radial
spines about 12 or more, up to 1.5
cm. long. Central spines 4, up to 5
cm. long. Flowers light brick-red, up
to 5.5 cm. long and 2.5 cm. wide. N.
Chile at altitude of 3,500 m. (as far as
S. Peru?). Flowers when only about 6-7
cm. tall. Both species would probably
be better classified as varieties of *A.
hempeliana* (Gürke) Oehme.

Ariocarpus Scheidw. 1838
(*Neogomesia, Roseocactus, Anhalonium* p.p.)
(Greek aria = haw; karpos = fruit)

Ariocarpus is one of the most curious of
cactus genera. The large, flat, tubercles
with an angular keel along the bottom,
look like leaves, and in consequence
the plants look rather like small
agaves. *Leuchtenbergia*, with its long,
thin tubercles and papery spines, is
the only other genus which differs
equally strongly from the usual cactus
forms. *Obregonia* and *Encephalocarpus*
also feature flat, leaf-like tubercles, but
they do not form flat rosettes in the
same way, are more globular in shape
and are closer to other cacti with large
tubercles. *Ariocarpus* species have a
thick taproot. In their native habitat in
Mexico the plants are set very low in
the ground, and look deceptively
similar to the boulders or loamy soil
of their surroundings. Such plants,
which are so effectively camouflaged
that they are almost invisible, are
termed mimicry plants. However,
although devoid of spines *Ariocarpus* is
probably not entirely defenceless. *A.
fissuratus* is said to contain a narcotic
similar to that of the well-known
Peyotl cactus (*Lophophora williamsii*).
6 species. Native to N. Mexico, USA
(SW Texas).

Ariocarpus are very popular with cactus
enthusiasts because of their curious
appearance.

A. kotschoubeyanus achieved what is
probably the highest price ever paid
for a cactus. In 1840 Karwinsky
brought the first three plants to
Europe. One of them was bought by
Prince Kotschoubey, after whom the
species was named, for 1000 francs,
and another sold for 200 dollars. *A.
kotschoubeyanus* grows in an extremely
unusual location for cacti, namely in
loamy terrain which is occasionally
flooded.

Ariocarpus are not easy to maintain in
cultivation, and are not recommended
to beginners. They can only be
cultivated under glass in a sunny
garden frame or a greenhouse. In their
natural habitat the roots are located so
deep in the soil that the plants almost
vanish in the dormant period, but we
recommend that the plants should be
set rather higher when cultured. The
soil should be very permeable and
purely mineral. The upper part of the
root should be bedded in small
pebbles to promote good drainage. In
the vegetative period the plants should
be kept in a warm, sunny location and
watered moderately — less often than
for other cacti. Always water from
underneath, not into the woolly heart
of the plant. In the dormant period
they should be kept completely dry
and cool. A few species will tolerate
temperatures around 0°C. The plants
grow very slowly by nature, and must

Ariocarpus fissuratus

Ariocarpus kotschoubeyanus

Ariocarpus kotschoubeyanus

not be forced by excessive watering and feeding. Raising the plants from seed is an attractive proposition for the experienced cactus grower. The seedlings grow very slowly and do not flower for many years, but they are very pretty. Please bear in mind that these plants are becoming rare in their homeland, so you will do them a favour by propagating them from seed.

The flowers of the different species are borne in very different positions: on the youngest tubercles in the centre of the plant, in a ring, in the axils of the tubercles, or at the base of a furrow. Backeberg distinguished two genera based on this characteristic: *Neogomesia* and *Roseocactus,* but they are only listed as sub-genera now.

Tubercles with woolly furrow above
  Tubercles with wrinkled furrow above
    Tubercles with distinct marginal
    angle, more or less flat
         A. fissuratus var. *fissuratus*
    Tubercles without distinct marginal
    angle, but with central angle
    curving outward
         A. fissuratus var. *lloydii*

Tubercles no more than rough
  above   *A. kotschoubeyanus*

Tubercles not furrowed above
  Tubercles 3-edged, broader than
  long, areoles at the tip, 5 mm. wide
                 A. retusus
  Tubercles 2-6 times as long as wide
   Areoles absent, or not located at the
   tip
    Areoles located 0.5-1.2 cm. from
    the tip   *A. agavoides*
    Areoles absent
     Tubercles yellow-green, sharply
     pointed at the end. Flowers
     yellowish   *A. trigonus*
     Tubercles grey-green, blunt at the
     end. Flowers violet-pink
            A scapharostrus

A. agavoides (Castañeda)
Anderson (*Neogomesia a.* Castañeda)
Plant 4-8 cm. wide. Tubercles up to 4 cm. long and around 0.6 cm. wide, flat at the top, rounded at the bottom. Areoles 0.5-1.2 cm. from the tip of the tubercles, occasionally 1-3 short spines. Pink flowers, 2.5-4.2 cm. wide. Mexico (Tamaulipas).

A. fissuratus (Engelm.) K. Schum.
(*Roseocactus f.* (Engelm.) Berger)
Plant up to 10 (-15) cm. wide. Greyish tubercles, 3-edged, 1.5-2.5 cm. wide at the base, deeply wrinkled at the top

and with a very woolly central furrow. Flowers pink, 2-4.5 cm. wide.

var. fissuratus
Tubercles flat above, as if enclosed by a marginal angle. USA (SW Texas)

var. lloydii (Rose) Marsh.
(*Roseocactus l.* (Rose) Berger)
Plants up to 15 cm. wide. Tubercles without marginal angle, angled outward from the furrow. Mexico (Coahuila, Nuevo León, Zacatecas, San Luis Potosí, Tamaulipas).

A. kotschoubeyanus (Lem.) K. Schum.
(*Roseocactus k.* (Lem.) Berger)
Plant up to 7 cm. wide. Tubercles 3-edged, up to 1 cm. wide and 1.3 cm. long, flat above, dark green, with woolly furrow. Flowers pink or light purple, 1.5-2.5 cm. wide. Mexico (Zacatecas, Nuevo León, San Luis Potosí, Tamaulipas, Querétaro).

A. retusus Scheidw.
(*A. furfuraceus* Thomson).
Plant up to 25 cm. wide. Tubercles blue to olive-green, smooth, not furrowed. Flowers white or pale pink, 4-5 cm. wide. Mexico (Coahuila, Nuevo León, San Luis Potosí, Tamaulipas).

A. scapharostrus Bód.
Plants 3-7 cm. wide. Tubercles grey-green, flat above and unfurrowed, blunt at the end. Flowers violet-pink, 3-4 cm. wide. Mexico (Nuevo León).

A. trigonus (Web.) K. Schum.
Plants 4-30 cm. wide. Tubercles yellow-green, flat above and unfurrowed, sharply pointed at the end. Flowers yellowish, 3-5 cm. wide. Mexico (Nuevo León, Tamaulipas).

Armatocereus Backeb. 1935
(Latin armatus = armed)

Tree- or bush-shaped columnar cacti with 3-11 ribs. Lateral flowers, with long tube, externally scaly with spines and felt or bristles and felt, nocturnal, with long, narrow nectar chamber, up to 10 cm. long. 16 species. Native to Colombia, Ecuador, Peru.

Ariocarpus scapharostrus

Arrojadoa Br. & R. 1920
(after Dr⸱ Miguel Arrojado, Lisboa, Brazil)

Sparsely branching columnar cacti with 10-40 ribs and lateral or terminal flowers in a cephalium. Flowers tubular, up to about 3.5 cm. long,

Arrojadoa penicillata

bare, no scales, reddish or red. The filaments below the anthers are thin, like threads, while the lower stamens form a nectar chamber. 5 species. Native to Brazil (Pernambuco, Piauhy, Bahia, Minas Gerais).

A. aureispina Buin. & Bred.
Clustering from the base. Stems up to 1 m. tall and 5-5.5 cm. thick, with around 14 blunt ribs. Radial spines 12-13, central spines approx. 9. Spines golden yellow, around 1.4 cm. long. Flowers borne in a yellowish-white cephalium which is grown through each year. Flowers luminous dark pink, about 3 cm. long and up to 1 cm. wide. Occasionally flowers are also produced from the cephalium formed three years before. Brazil (Bahia).

A. penicillata (Gürke) Br. & R.
Bushy, clustering. Stems prostrate, up to 2 m. long and slightly thicker than a pencil, with 10-12 very low ribs. Radial spines 8-12, central spines 1-2. Spines very fine, spreading, initially yellowish, later brown and grey, 1-3 cm. long. Flowers in bunches from a fox-red flower tuft, carmine pink, 2 cm. long and wide. Brazil (Bahia). This species flowers very readily.

A. rhodantha (Gürke) Br. & R.
Erect, climbing or decumbent. Stems dark green, 0.4-2 m. long and 2-4 cm. thick, with 9-14 low ribs. Radial spines about 20 and central spines 5-6 and similar. Spines at first yellowish to brownish or dark brown, later grey, 1-

Arrojadoa rhodantha

Arthrocereus campos-portoi

Arthrocereus rondonianus

3 cm. long. Areoles with short wool. Every year the violet-red flowers are produced from a cephalium with 1.5-2 cm. long wool and up to 3 cm. long reddish-brown bristles. They are 3-3.5 cm. long and around 1.2 cm. wide. Brazil (Pernambuco, Piauhy, Bahia, N. Minas Gerais).

Arthrocereus Berger 1929
(Greek arthron = limb, member)

Erect or prostrate columnar cacti, one species comprising short segments. Stems with 7-16 ribs, flowers towards the end of the stems, funnel-shaped with elongated, scaly and hairy tube. Flowers white to lilac-pink, nocturnal, 7-12 cm. long. 5 species. Native to Brazil (Minas Gerais).

A. campos-portoi (Werderm.) Backeb. Decumbent and more or less clustering. Segments cylindrical or club-shaped, up to 15 cm. long and 3 cm. thick, with about 12 low ribs. Radial spines 25-35, white, brownish when young, up to 0.7 cm. long. Central spines 1-2, up to 4 cm. long. White flowers, up to 8.5 cm. long. Brazil (Minas Gerais).

A. microsphaericus (K. Schum.) Berger. Stems decumbent, glossy green, distinctly jointed. Segments up to 6.5 cm. long and 3 cm. thick, with 7-11 low, rounded ribs. Radial spines about 12 and the same number of bristles, central spines 4-12. All the spines are fine, white, brownish or reddish-brown and 2-4 mm. long. Areoles brownish, flowers white, green externally, scented, 7-11 cm. long and 5 cm. wide. Brazil (Minas Gerais). Flowers repeatedly and readily throughout the year.

A. rondonianus Backeb. & Voll. Branching, stems bright green, 20-50 cm. tall and 2-4 cm. thick, with 13-18 low, rounded ribs. Radial spines 40-60, about 0.5 (-2) cm. long. Central spines 1-2, up to 7 cm. long. Spines very fine, golden yellow. Flowers lilac-pink, 8-11 cm. long. Brazil (Minas Gerais).

Astrophytum Lem. 1839
(Greek astron = star, phyton = plant)

This small genus has attractive yellow flowers, 3-9 cm. long, scaly and woolly and close to the crown. The body has relatively few ribs (5-10), exceptionally only 3 or 4. In all these characteristics *Astrophytum* is similar to the genus *Echinocactus* and the latter is probably closely related, but Buxbaum included *Astrophytum* in his Notocacteae. However, this is the only North American genus in an otherwise exclusively South American group.

Echinocacti are usually very large and have many ribs, but the principal difference is that *Astrophytum* has no spiky scales on the flowers. A typical feature of *Astrophytum* is small woolly patches on the skin, a characteristic shared only with *Uebelmannia*. The

131

woolly patches are only absent in a few varieties.

6 species. Native habitat Mexico, USA (Texas).

Rare is the collection which does not include *Astrophytum*. The small number of ribs, the resultant characteristic form and the woolly patches on the body make them very distinctive. They require a soil of mainly mineral content with a fairly high proportion of loam, pumice gravel, lava waste, igneous rock waste and Perlite. All Astrophytums like to be warm in the vegetation period, and the white and densely spined species like as bright a light as possible, while the green forms can be kept in semi-shade. They should only be watered very sparingly. *A. asterias* and *A. coahuilense* in particular are very sensitive to excess moisture. In winter Astrophytums should be kept light and dry, and at moderate temperatures (7-8°C). *A. asterias* demands higher temperatures, as in its homeland, but neither *A. ornatum* nor *A. myriostigma* like to be kept too cool, otherwise they easily form cold spots. Relatively low winter temperatures are tolerated by the group centred on *A. capricorne* (and *A. coahuilense*). They sometimes experience snow in their natural habitat, but ground temperatures apparently never drop below 0°C. Astrophytums have large seed which germinate readily and quickly, and propagation is a real pleasure. Many *Astrophytum* species flower when quite small, as early as 3-4 years after sowing. *A. ornatum* does not flower until it is a fairly large plant, about 6-7 years old. Astrophytums hardly ever produce side shoots.

A number of forms exist with a particularly low number of ribs, with differently coloured spines and without the typical woolly patches (known as the *nuda* forms), and a very wide variety of hybrids has also been produced. Hybrids between *A. capricorne* x *A. asterias* are particularly attractive plants. According to Haage and Sadovsky all *Astrophytum* species, with a few exceptions, can be crossed with each other. The only difficult hybrid is that between *A. asterias* and *A. ornatum,* and it is evidently impossible to cross *A. coahuilense* with *A. myriostigma.*

Ribs completely flat (body only furrowed) with large, white areoles. Flowers 3 cm. long.
                                                                                                                                    A. asterias
Ribs sharp. Flowers 4-9 cm. long
  Plants spineless
    Fruit green, produced laterally. Flowers yellow   *A. myriostigma*
    Fruit purple-red, opening at the bottom. Flowers yellow, red inside
                                                                                                                                    A. coahuilense

  Plants with powerful spine formation
    Spines 5-11, up to 4 cm. long, more or less straight. Woolly patches usually in isolated bands   *A. ornatum*
    Spines up to 10, 3-10 cm. long, more or less curved and twisted, with sharp edges or flattened. Woolly patches evenly distributed.   *A. capricorne*
    Spines 15-20, twisted, thin and soft. Woolly patches absent   *A. senile*

A. asterias (Zucc.) Lem.
Body flattened globular, with (6-) 8 (-10) completely flat ribs, but clear furrows between them and white, rather large areoles without spines. Woolly patches sparse to absent. Flowers yellow, reddish in the centre, 3 cm. long. Fruit green, borne laterally. USA (Texas) to Mexico (Tamaulipas, Nuevo León). A small number of examples of this species, which is almost impossible to see in its homeland but is very conspicuous when cultivated, were sent to Europe by Karwinski in 1843. It was not until 80 years later that the species was rediscovered in its homeland by Frič.

A. capricorne (A. Dietr.) Br. & R.
Body round to oval, with usually 8 sharply defined ribs and brownish to grey-white areoles. Spines more or less numerous, acute, long and tortuous, yellow to black-brown and 3-10 cm. long. Woolly patches moderately dense to completely absent. Flowers soapy yellow with carmine red centre, 6-7 cm. long. N. Mexico.

Astrophytum capricorne

Astrophytum asterias hybrid

Astrophytum myriostigma

A very variable species with the most beautiful flowers of the genus.

A. coahuilense (Möll.) Kayser
Body globular, later elongated, usually with 5 ribs, covered closely with white spots. Spines absent. Fruit purple-red, opening at the bottom. Flowers sulphur yellow, with orange to scarlet centre. Mexico (Coahuila).

Old specimen of Astrophytum ornatum

A. myriostigma Lem.,
Body rounded to slightly oval with (4-) 5 (-8) sharp ribs with brownish, spineless areoles. Woolly patches very dense. Flowers yellow or yellow with reddish centre, 4-6 cm. long. Mexico (central to Northern uplands).

var. columnare (K. Schum.) Tsuda
With elongated body

var. strongylocarpum Backeb.
With few or no woolly patches and pure green body.

A. ornatum (DC.) Web.
Body more columnar with 8 ribs. Isolated plants are said to reach a diameter of 35 cm. and 1 (-3) m. in height. The woolly patches are usually confined to separated bands, in contrast to the other species. 5-11 spines, straight, yellow to brown. Flowers light yellow, 7-9 cm. long. Mexico (Hidalgo, Querétaro).

var. glabrescens (Web.) Backeb.
With few or no woolly patches.

A. senile Frič
Body at first globular, later elongated, with 8 ribs, devoid of woolly patches. 15-20 spines, tortuous, brown-red to brown-black. Flowers same as *A. capricorne*. Mexico.

Austrocactus patagonicus

Aztekium ritteri

Austrocactus Br. & R. 1922
(Lat. australis = southern)

Fairly small columnar cacti with 6-12 ribs, sometimes with aerial roots. Flowers at the end of the stems, with short tube, scaly and with long bristles and wool, diurnal, red 3.5-6 cm. long. Thick style. Distinct ring of throat stamens. 5 species. Native to Argentina, Chile.

A. patagonicus (Web.) Backeb.
Body up to 50 cm. tall and 8 cm. thick, with 9-12 notched ribs. Radial spines 6-16, white with brown tip, 1-2 cm. long. Central spines 1-4, horn-coloured, up to 4 cm. long, thicker at the base and sometimes hooked. Flowers whitish to pink-white, 4 cm. long and 5 cm. wide. Stigma violet. South Argentina (Patagonia), South Chile.

Austrocephalocereus Backeb. 1937
(Espostoopsis)
(Lat. australis = southern, Greek kephale = head)

Bushy columnar cacti with 12-25 ribs.

Flowers lateral in a cephalium, tubular, 2.5-4 cm. long. Tube almost devoid of scales, bare and with distinct nectar chamber. Flowers white or pink, nocturnal. 2 species. Native to Brazil (Bahia).

A. dybowskii (Gosselin) Backeb.
(*Cephalocereus d.* Gosselin; *Espostoopsis d.* (Gosselin) Buxb.)
Erect, branching from the base. Stems 2-4 m. tall and up to 10 cm. thick, with 20-28 narrow, low ribs. Areoles with dense, white wool. Many fine, short, acute spines. Central spines 1-3, yellowish to brownish, 1-3 cm. long. Cephalium up to 60 cm. long, densely matted with woolly hairs. Flowers white, bell-shaped, around 4-6 cm. long. Brazil (Bahia).

A. purpureus (Gürke) Backeb.
(*Cephalocereus p.* Gürke)
Erect, seldom branching. Stems pale green to blue-green, up to 5 m. tall and 12 cm. thick, with up to 25 ribs, 1 cm. high, with blunt bumps. Radial spines 15-20 or more, yellowish to brownish, up to 1.5 cm. long. Central spines 4-6, one of them up to 5 cm. long. Cephalium of grey-white wool

and with brown to black bristles, up to 1 m. long. Flowers pale pink, whitish inside, 3.5 cm. long. Brazil (S. Bahia).

Austrocylindropuntia Backeb.
see *Opuntia*

Aylostera Spegazz. see *Rebutia*

Azureocereus Akers & Johnson see *Browningia*

Aztekium Bód. 1929
(From the unique external form, which is reminiscent of Aztek sculptures)

The single species is easily recognized even without flowers, as the body features distinct lateral ribs and bears no spines except at its tip. The areoles form continuous rows on the ribs. The flowers are only 1 cm. long, grow close to the crown, and have no scales. They have relatively few petals and stamens. The seed possess a strophiole, a membranous attachment point. 1 species. Native habitat Mexico (Nuevo León) on steep slate slopes. Culture is difficult, and only recommended to the experienced

134

Backebergia militaris

Blossfeldia liliputana

grower. The plant has a taproot, requires mineral soil and grows very slowly.

A. ritteri (Bód.) Bód.
Flattened globular, about 5 cm. wide, with 9-11 ribs. 1-4 spines, flattened, papery, white, 0.3-0.4 cm. long. Flowers about 1 cm. long and 0.8 cm. wide, white or pink.

Backebergia Bravo 1954
(after G. Backeberg (1894 — 1966), the well-known German cactus researcher)

Tree-shaped columnar cacti with 5-11 ribs. Flowers in a dome cephalium , externally scaly, bristly and woolly, nocturnal. 1 species. Native to Mexico (Guerrero, Michoacán).

B. militaris (Audot) Bravo
Up to 6 m. tall. Stems about 12 cm. thick and with 5-7, later 9-11 ribs. Radial spines 7-13, central spines 1-4. All spines grey, sharply pointed, 1 cm. long. Flowers orange-reddish, around 5-7 cm. long and 4 cm. wide. One often sees imported top cuttings of this species featuring the typical dome cephalium.

Bartschella Br. & R. see *Mammillaria*

Bergerocactus Br. & R. 1909
(after Alwin Berger (1871-1931), an important researcher into succulents)

Bushy or decumbent columnar cacti with 14-20 (-25) ribs. Flowers lateral, scaly, spiny and felty, yellow, diurnal. This genus also forms natural hybrids with *Myrtillocactus* and *Pachycereus,* which are sold as *Myrtgerocactus* and *Pachgerocereus.* 1 species. Native to USA (SW California), Mexico (lower California).

B. emoryi (Engelm.) Br. & R.
Yellow to yellow-brown spines. Flowers 2 (-5) cm. long.

Blossfeldia Werderm. 1927
(after its discoverer H. Blossfeld jun., Brazil)

This genus embraces miniature cacti which are less than 1.5 cm. wide. Their small bodies are unribbed and spineless. The flowers are 0.6-1.5 cm. long, have a very short, scaly, woolly

tube, and are borne close to the crown. A further characteristic feature is the minute seed, only 0.2 mm. long, with a fine papilla and a strophiole. 4 species. Native to N. Argentina, Bolivia.

According to Rauh the plants are found on steep slopes of stony or loamy soil with many fragments of rock.

This genus includes the smallest known cacti. The plants are difficult to cultivate; the two species listed here grow well if grafted, but then tend to lose their natural appearance.

B. liliputana Werderm.
Body 0.7-1 cm. in diameter. Flowers white, up to 1 cm. wide. N. Argentina (Jujuy), Bolivia (Tarija, Chuquisaca, Potosi).

B. minima Ritter
Body 0.4-0.65 cm. wide and thus the smallest known cactus. Bolivia (Chuquisaca, Potosi).

Bolivicereus Card. See *Borzicactus*

Borzicactella Ritter see *Borzicactus*

Borzicactus Riccob. 1901

(*Akersia, Bolivicereus, Borzicactella, Clistanthocereus, Loxanthocereus, Seticereus*)
(after Antonio Borzi, Palermo botanical gardens)

Mostly fairly small columnar cacti, some of them decumbent, with 6-21 ribs. Flowers diurnal, red, with long tube and more or less zygomorphic. Tube round or laterally compressed, scaly and bristly or hairy, with distinct nectar chamber and often a ring of woolly hairs in the tube. Around 70 species known. Native to Ecuador, Peru, Bolivia.

Kimnach included all the South American day-flowering species with red zygomorphic flowers within *Borzicactus,* but retained many former genera as sub-genera. The names no longer made it possible to recognize the groups of species, and for this reason some of the more narrowly defined genera have been retained here, namely *Arequipa, Hildewintera, Matucana* and *Oreocereus.*

B. aurivillus (K. Schum.) Br. & R.
Bushy and clustering. Stems 2.5 cm. thick, with 16-18 ribs deeply notched. Areoles yellow and woolly. 30 spines or more, translucent apart from the yellow base. Flowering zone with tufts

Borzicactus aurivillus

Flowers narrow and tubular with tips hardly spreading	
Ribs only notched. Flowers zygomorphic	*B. roezlii*
Ribs divided. Flowers radially symmetrical	*B. samnensis*
Flowers with spreading zygomorphic tips	
Flowers lilac pink	*B. roseiflorus*
Flowers strong red	
Tube has tiny woolly hairs externally (spine formation very densely bristly)	*B. aurivillus*
Tube has long hairs externally	
Petals with lighter tips	*B. samaipatanus*
Petals not distinctly lighter at the tips	
Radial spines up to 30	*B. sextonianus*
Radial spines up to 15	
Stems erect	*B. sepium*
Stems more or less trailing	*B. serpens*

of bristles. Flowers slightly zygomorphic, carmine red, with tiny woolly hairs externally, 5-7 cm. long. North Peru (near Huancabamba).

B. roezlii Backeb. (*Seticereus r.* (Haage jr.) Backeb.)
Bushy, with grey-green stems up to 7 cm. thick, with 7-14 ribs, notched above the areoles. Radial spines 9-14, light brown, up to 1 cm. long. Central spines usually 1, light grey later, 1-4 cm. long. Flowering zone with tufts of bristles. Red flowers, 6-7 cm. long. North Peru.

B. roseiflorus (Buin.) Kimnach (*Akersia r.* Buin.)
Bushy, sprawling. Stems bright green, up to 1 m. or more tall, 4-5 cm. thick, with 16-17 very low ribs. 30-40 spines, golden yellow, up to 1 cm. long, up to 3.5 cm. long in the flowering zone. Bristles on outside of flowers, lilac pink, 5 cm. long. ?North Peru.

B. samaipatanus Card.
Branching. Stems up to 1.5 m. long, but usually up to 70 cm. tall, 3-5 cm. thick, with 13-16 low, laterally furrowed ribs. 13-22 spines, thin, of uneven length, 0.4-3 cm. Flowers strongly curved, 4-6 cm. long. Flower petals blood red with lighter margins. Bolivia (Santa Cruz).

This species produces glorious flowers in profusion and is strongly recommended. After reaching a certain height it adopts a pendant habit. First flowers are produced when stems reach 30-40 cm. long. The

plants' full beauty is only achieved if they are grown in pots of adequate size or if planted out in the greenhouse. As the species comes from the warm regions of Bolivia it must not be kept too cool in winter.

B. samnensis Ritter (*Clistanthocereus s.* (Ritter) Backeb.)
Bushy, up to 1.5 m. tall. Stems grass green, 5-7 cm. thick with 6-10 divided ribs. Radial spines 5-10, 0.3-1.2 cm. long. Central spines 1 (-4), 1.5-8 cm. long. Spines coffee brown or brown-black, later turning grey. Flowers radially symmetrical, violet/purple,

Borzicactus roezlii

Borzicactus samaipatanus

V-shaped notches. Radial spines 8-10, up to 1 cm. long. Central spines 1-3, one pointing downward and up to 4 cm. long. Flowers scarlet, 4 cm. long. Ecuador. Flowers readily after reaching a height of 1 m.

var. morleyanus (Br. & R.) Krainz
(*B. m.* Br & R.)
A variation on the type specimen: stems up to 6 cm. thick, with 13-16 ribs. Flowers carmine red, up to 6 cm. long.

B. sextonianus (Backeb.) Kimn.
(*Loxanthocereus s.* (Backeb.) Backeb.)
Stems semi-decumbent, up to 1.5 m. long, 2-3 cm. thick and generally with 13-15 deeply notched ribs. Radial spines up to 30, 0.5 cm. long. Central spines 1-2, up to 3 cm. long. Flowers strongly zygomorphic, red, 5-6 cm. long. Peru (near Mollendo).

B. serpens (H.B.K.) Backeb.
Stems up to 2 m. long, sprawling and producing roots, with 8-11 ribs. Radial spines 10-15, very fine and short. Central spines 1 or 0, light yellow to brown, up to 3 cm. long. Flowers red, 5 cm. long, inner flower petals long and narrow. N. Peru.

with woolly hairs externally, 5-7 cm. long and only 0.7 cm. wide. Peru (Ancash to Cajamarca).

B. sepium (H.B.K.) Br. & R.
Erect or prostrate and curving upward. Stems up to 1.5 m. long and up to 4 cm. thick, with 8-11 or more ribs with

Brachycalycium Backeb.
see *Gymnocalycium*

Borzicactus samnensis

Borzicactus sextonianus

137

Brachycereus Br. & R. 1920
(Greek brachys = short)

Bushy columnar cacti with 13-16 ribs. Flowers scaly, spiny, white, nocturnal. 1 species. Native to Galapagos islands.

Brasilicactus Backeb. see *Notocactus*

Brasilicereus Backeb. 1938
(from Brasilia: Brazil)

Bushy or decumbent columnar cacti with 8-14 ribs. Flowers lateral, a few scales or bare, zygomorphic, nocturnal with nectar chamber, 4-6.5 cm. long. 3 species. Native to Brazil (Bahia, Minas Gerais).

Brasiliparodia Ritter see *Notocactus*

Browningia Br. & R. 1920
(*Azureocereus, Gymnanthocereus, Gymnocereus*)
(after the American botanist H.W. Browning)

Tree-shaped, many-ribbed columnar cacti. Lateral flowers on specially formed areoles. Tube with dense covering of roof-tile-like scales, bare. Flowers pink, yellowish or white, nocturnal, radially symmetrical or slightly zygomorphic. *Browningia* in the narrower sense includes trees with very spiny stem and virtually spineless branches. The branches cannot be used for cuttings or for grafting. 11 species. Native to Peru, N. Chile.

B. hertlingiana (Backeb.) Buxb.
(*Azureocereus h.* (Backeb.) Backeb.)
Stems erect, acquiring light blue glaucous appearance after 10 cm. height, if the plant is in a sunny position. Up to 8 m. tall and 30 cm. thick, with up to 18 or more ribs, which are raised like tubercles around the areoles, and are later sometimes divided up completely. Radial spines about 4, central spines 1-3 when young, up to 8 cm. long, later up to 30 spines. Spines yellow with brown tips. Flowers white, tube slightly curved, 5 cm. wide. Peru (Mantaro valley).

Browningia hertlingiana

This plant with its beautiful blue bloom should never be sprayed with water. Cultivate warm and bright, water sparingly.

Buiningia Buxb. 1971
(after the cactus researcher A. Buining)

Fairly small columnar cacti with 10-18 ribs. Flowers in a cephalium, tubular in form with erect inner petals. Tube sparsely scaly and bare. Flowers narrow tubular, 2.5-3.7 cm. long, nocturnal. 3 species. Native to Brazil (Minas Gerais).

B. brevicylindrica Buin.
Initially globular, later short cylindrical, clustering at the base. Stems fresh green, up to 30 cm. tall and up to 17 cm. thick, with up to 18

Buiningia brevicylindrica

138

ribs which bulge above the areoles. Radial spines about 7, up to 2 cm. long, the lateral ones up to 3 cm. and the upper ones up to 1.5 cm. long. Central spines about 4, yellow, the lower ones up to 6 cm. long, the side ones up to 3 cm. long and the upper ones up to 2.5 cm. long. Cephalium produced when the globe is only 8 cm. in diameter. The cephalium is on one side, consists of white wool and is pierced by strong golden yellow bristly spines. Flowers cream-coloured, tubular, up to 3.2 cm. long and 1.5 cm. wide. Brazil (Minas Gerais). This species flowers readily, and likes mineral soil and temperatures not below 10°C in winter.

B. purpurea Buin. & Bred.
Short to elongated columnar, clustering at the base. Stems green to dark green, up to 90 cm. long and 10 cm. thick, with 13 ribs. Radial spines about 12, 1.2-2.5 cm. long. Central spines about 4, around 7 cm. long. Spines yellow-brown, red-brown to red, later grey. Lateral cephalium, up to 50 cm. long, grey, woolly, pierced by yellow, reddish or grey bristles. Flowers purple-red, 3 cm. long and up to 1.2 cm. wide. Brazil (Minas Gerais).

Calymmanthium Ritter 1962
(Greek kalumma = veil, covering; anthos = flower)

Tree-like or bushy columnar cacti with 3-5 ribs. Flowers lateral, nocturnal, scaly and bristly/felty. The flower buds are like shoots, the flower petals eventually emerge through a pore. 2 species. Native to Peru.

C. substerile Ritter
Tree-shaped, up to 8 m. tall in its homeland. Stems 4-8 cm. thick, with 3-4 tall, narrow ribs. Radial spines 3-8, 0.5-1 cm. long. Central spines 1-6, 1-5 cm. long. White spines. White flowers, externally reddish-brown, 9.5-11 cm. long. N. Peru (Prov. Jaén).

Carnegiea Br. & R. 1908
(after A. Carnegie (1835-1919), American philanthropist and promoter of science)

Tree-shaped columnar cacti. Flowers virtually terminal, on specially formed areoles, funnel-shaped with scaly tube with sparse wool. Base of the style merged with the tube. 1 species. Native to USA (S. Arizona, S.E. California), Mexico (Sonora).

C. gigantea (Engelm.) Br. & R. 'Saguaro'
Erect, slightly branching. Stems dark green, up to 14 m. tall, and up to 65 cm. thick in its natural habitat, with 12-24 blunt ribs. Radial spines about 12 or more, 1-2 cm. long. Central spines 3-6, up to 8 cm. long. Spines brown, later grey, dark-tipped, thicker at the base. White flowers, externally greenish, around 12 cm. long and wide, open from midnight to the following afternoon. Fruit edible. The largest specimens are estimated to be 150-200 years old. The plants grow very slowly and young plants are sometimes kept by enthusiasts.

Castellanosia Card. 1951
(after the Argentinian botanist A. Castellanos)

Bushy columnar cacti up to 6 m. tall with about 9 ribs. Flowers borne towards the end of the stems on specially formed areoles with long spines. Flowers are felty, purple, 3-5 cm. long, and densely covered externally with scales like roof-tiles. 1 species, *C. caineana* Card. Native to E. Bolivia. ?S. Peru.

Cephalocereus Pfeiff. 1838
(Greek kephale = head)

Tall columnar cacti. Flowers in a cephalium. Tube scaly and hairy. Flowers with nectar chamber, nocturnal. Fruit dry and hairy. 1 species. Native to Mexico (Hidalgo, Guanajuato).

C. senilis (Haw.) Pfeiff., 'Old man cactus'
Usually solitary. Stems green at first, later grey, up to 15 m. tall and 40 cm. thick in the wild, with 12-15 ribs on young plants, later 25-30 low, rounded ribs. Radial spines 20-30, white, 6-12 cm. long, central spines 1-5, 1-2 cm. long, up to 5 cm. long on older plants. The entire plant appears to be a mass of hair because of the long, white, hairy radial spines. The cephalium first develops when the plant is about 6 m. tall, and eventually surrounds the entire end of the stem. Flowers pale yellowish-white, up to 9.5 cm. long and 7.5 cm. wide.

Cephalocereus senilis

The Old Man cactus demands very high levels of light and warmth. Even in winter it does not like to be colder than 12-15°C. Water sparingly!

Cephalophorus Lem. see *Pilosocereus*

Cephalocleistocactus Ritter see *Cleistocactus*

Cereus Mill. 1754
(*Piptanthocereus*)
(Latin cereus = wax candle, wax torch)

Originally the genus *Cereus* included all the columnar cacti, and even today columnar cacti are commonly called 'Cerei'. The genus *Cereus* now embraces columnar cacti with (3-) 4-8 (-10) ribs, including some species 15-25 m. in height. The 8-30 cm. long flowers, usually white, grow from normal areoles and flower at night. The ovary and tube bear few or no scales at all and are bare. The flower envelope usually falls down over the ovary quite early, but the style remains attached to the ovary. The fleshy red, purple or white fruits of some species are collected and eaten.

Around 50 species. Native to South America (Venezuela, Tobago, Surinam, Brazil, Uruguay, Paraguay, Argentina, Bolivia, Peru).

Cereus species are very vigorous plants and demand relatively nutritious soil, rich in humus. Young plants are extremely pretty with their blue-green

Cereus peruvianus

colour and very powerful spine formation. In summer they should be kept warm, watered plentifully and fed from time to time. In winter they like very slight moisture and a temperature around 6-10°C. *Cereus* species are unlikely to flower unless planted out in the greenhouse. They can be propagated by taking cuttings, but the seed also germinates well. Cuttings grow very quickly, and sowing is also invariably successful, even with beginners. For this reason ordinary 'cactus seed mixtures' usually include *Cereus* seed.

Ribs 3. Red flowers   *C. trigonodendron*

Ribs 4-10. White flowers
  Ribs blunt   *C. peruvianus*
  Ribs forming S-shaped lines   *C. forbesii*
  Ribs sharp
    Stems not glaucous. Spines
    yellowish   *C. jamacaru*
    Stems glaucous. Spines very dark (at least some)
      Spines all black   *C. chalybaeus*
      Spine formation with white radials
      and dark centrals   *C. azureus*

C. azureus Parm.
Up to 3 m. tall. Stems blue glaucous, 6-7 ribs, 3-3.5 cm. thick. Areoles with brown felt and grey wool. Radial spines 8-12, white, dark-tipped. Central spines 1-3, dark brown to black. Spines 0.5-1 cm. long. Flowers diurnal, white, externally reddish-brown, (10? -) 20-30 cm. long. N. Argentina, S. Brazil.

C. chalybaeus Otto
Sparsely branching, up to 3 m. tall, glaucous blue columns with 5-6 ribs. Black spines, radial spines 7-9, central spines 3-4. Flowers red or pink outside, white inside, 20 cm. long. N. Argentina, Uruguay.

C. chalybaeus is one of the most strongly blue-coloured cacti. It flowers from a height of about 50 cm., and is very strongly recommended.

C. forbesii Otto
(*C. validus* Haw.)
Columns up to 7 m. tall, light blue-green, later grey-green with 6 (4-7) ribs. Radial spines 5-7,

central spines 1-4. White flowers, 6 cm. long. Argentina (Catamarca, Tucuman, Jujuy, Córdoba).

C. jamacaru DC. & Pfeiff.
Cactus trees up to 10 m. tall, succulent green, usually not glaucous, with 4-6 ribs, later up to 10. Up to 20 spines, yellowish. White flowers, 20-30 cm. long. Brazil. The oldest specimen in Europe stands before the casino in Monte Carlo. The species is very vigorous and undemanding and is also well known as a stock for grafting.

C. peruvianus (L.) Mill.
Abundantly clustering, up to 3 m. or more tall. The stems are initially light green, blue-green in the second year and have 5-8 ribs. Radial spines 4-7, central spines 1-2. White flowers, up to 16 cm. long.

The species has been cultivated since 1576 and is not known wild. A monstrous form is very common.

C. trigonodendron K. Schum.
Columnar cacti up to 15 m. tall with 3-ribbed stems. Usually 6 spines, black, 1 central spine. Red flowers, about 10 cm. long. Peru (Loreto).

This species varies substantially from other Cerei and arguably belongs in another genus. It was discovered in N. Peru, but since then has never been rediscovered.

Chamaecereus Br. & R. see *Lobivia*

Chiapasia Br. & R. 1923
(Chiapas: Mexican federal state)

Epiphytic plants with flat, leaf-like stems. Flowers with bare, naked tube, not elongated, only about 8 petals but many stamens. 1 species. Native to Mexico (Chiapas), Honduras.

C. nelsonii (Vaup.) Br. & R.
Stems notched, 3-4 cm. wide. Lateral flowers, scented, 5-8 cm. long.

Chileorebutia Ritter see *Neoporteria*

Chilita Orcutt see *Mammillaria*

Cinnabarina Ritter see *Lobivia*

Cipocereus Ritter see *Pilosocereus*

Cleistocactus Lem. 1851

(Cephalocleistocactus, Seticleistocactus)
(Greek cleistos = closed)

Cleistocacti are slim columnar plants, branching from the base, with many more or less rounded ribs and fine, dense spines. Between the areoles there are usually lateral furrows. The flowering zone is sometimes very bristly, or there may be a pseudo-cephalium. The flowers project laterally or towards the end of the stems, and have a narrow tube with dense scales, bristles or wool, and short inner petals which do not curve back. The tube may be straight, S-shaped, or bent sharply above the ovary. These flowers are ideal for pollination by humming birds, with their brilliant red, yellow or green colouring and unusual shape, although the flowers of a few species hardly open at all; they pollinate themselves and are therefore cleistogamous. The fruit are small, round berries. Around 70 species are known. Native to Peru, Bolivia, Argentina, Paraguay and Uruguay, from 500 m. altitude in Paraguay and Uruguay to over 3000 m. in Bolivia.

Cleistocacti are among the most beautiful and rewarding of columnar cacti. They require rich soil and like to be kept in bright, warm conditions. They like high levels of atmospheric humidity and frequent misting in the

Cleistocactus brookei

evening in the spring and summer. Densely spined species have a summer dormant period from about July to August, and grow most strongly from autumn to December, less in spring (April to May). The upland species from Bolivia can be kept completely dry in winter and will even tolerate mild frosts. The lowland types on the other hand should not be allowed to dry out completely in winter, as shrivelled specimens are difficult to revive. In a few Cleistocacti, e.g. *C. smaragdiflorus,* flowers can be expected from a height of 20 cm., appearing in the spring.

C. baumannii (Lem.) Lem.
Approx. 14-16 ribs. Flowers S-shaped, brilliant red, 6-7 cm. long. The plants flower abundantly after 50 cm. Uruguay, Paraguay, N. Argentina, E. Bolivia.

C. brookei Card.
(C. flavescens (Otto) W. Haage;
C. wendlandiorum Backeb.)
Approx. 22-25 ribs. Flowers bent sharply above the ovary, blood red to light red, 5 cm. long. Bolivia (Santa Cruz).

C. buchtienii Backeb.
Approx. 18 ribs. Flowers wine red, 6-9.5 cm. long. Bolivia.

C. candelilla Card.
11-12 ribs. Flowers straight, brilliant red with yellow tip, 3.5 cm. long. Bolivia (Florida).

C. jujuyensis (Backeb.) Backeb.
17-25 ribs. Flowers straight, light red, 4 cm. long. Plant flowers profusely after reaching 70 cm. Argentina (Jujuy, Salta), Bolivia.

C. ritteri Backeb.
(Cephalocleistocactus r. (Backeb.) Backeb.)
Up to 14 or more ribs. Flowering zone bears straight, white bristles, 3-4 cm.

Cleistocactus candelilla

Flowering zone with long, white bristles	*C. ritteri*
Flowering zone without long white bristles	
Flowers S-shaped or bent sharply above the ovary	
Flowers S-shaped (around 14-16 ribs)	*C. baumannii*
Flowers bent sharply above the ovary	
Plant erect. Spines like needles	
Flowers 6-9.5 cm. long	*C. buchtienii, C. tupizensis*
Plant erect. Spines like hairs	
Flowers 6 cm. long	*C. vulpis-cauda*
Plant pendant. Spines bristly.	
Flowers 5 cm. long	*C. brookei*
Flowers straight	
Flowers with green margin	
Flowers completely green	*C. viridiflorus*
Flowers with red tube	*C. smaragdiflorus*
Flowers red to orange	
Plants with dense spines, snow-white	
Flowers 8-9 cm. long (uniform red. About 25 ribs)	*C. strausii*
Plants not densely covered in snow-white spines. Flowers 3.5 – 4 cm. long	
Flowers red with yellow tips. Around 11-12 ribs.	*C. candelilla*
Flowers light red. Around 20 ribs.	*C. jujuyensis*

Cleistocactus smaragdiflorus

Cleistocactus tupizensis

Cleistocactus strausii var. fricii

long. Flowers green-yellow, slightly curved downward, around 4 cm. long. Bolivia (Yungas).

Grows well and flowers at a height of only 50-60 cm. if it is not kept too dry.

C. smaragdiflorus (Web.) Br. & R. 12-16 ribs. Flowers straight, with red tube and green tip, 3.5 to about 5 cm. long. Flowers after a height of 25 cm. throughout the summer. Paraguay, Argentina (Jujuy, Salta, Catamarca, La Rioja), Bolivia.

C. strausii (Heese) Backeb. Approx. 25 ribs, covered with dense snow-white bristles. Straight flowers, dark carmine red, 8-9 cm. long. Does not flower until 1 m. tall, but is one of the most beautiful of cacti even without flowers. Bolivia (Tarija).

var. fricii (Dörfl.) Backeb. Dense snow-white hairs, 3-5 cm. long, as well as white bristles. The flower tube is also silky white.

C. tupizensis (Vaup.) Backeb. 10-24 ribs with pale reddish to fox-red spines. Flowers wine red, 8 cm. long. Bolivia (Tupiza).

Cleistocactus vulpis-cauda

C. viridiflorus Backeb. 12-17 ribs. Flowers straight, light green all over, 3.5-4 cm. long. Flower-bearing areoles carry fine bristles, more brownish. Bolivia.

C. vulpis-cauda Ritter & Cullm. Naturally hangs down from rocks. 18-22 ribs. Flowers bent down at the ovary, red, 6 cm. long. Plants flower amazingly readily almost the whole year round. Bolivia.

Clistanthocereus Backeb. see
Borzicactus

Cochemiea (K. Brandeg.) Walton
see *Mammillaria*

Coleocephalocereus Backeb.
1938
(Greek koleos = sheath; kephale =
head)

Erect or prostrate columnar cacti, no
more than 2 m. tall with 10-24 ribs.
Flowers in a lateral grooved
cephalium, nocturnal. Tube with few
scales, bare. Red lid-type fruits.
Compared with the related genus
Buiningia the inner flower petals are
spread out in a wheel shape, rather
than standing out erect. 7 species.
Native to Brazil (Bahia, Rio de Janeiro,
Sao Paulo, Minas Gerais).

The genus was discovered in 1923 and
was first described as a *Cereus,* but
remained largely unknown for a long
period. Eventually the research travels
of A. Buining extended our knowledge
of this genus. The plants like to be
kept in the greenhouse all winter at a
daytime temperature of 15-20°C, and
not below 10°C at night.

C. aureispinus Buin. & Bred.
1-2 m. tall. White flowers, light pink to
yellowish-pink outside, 3.4 cm. long.
Fruit blue, bare, just 4 cm. long.
Brazil (Bahia).

C. luetzelburgii (Vaup.) Buxb.
(*Pilosocereus l.* (Vaup.) Byl. & Rowl.)
Solitary, initially globular, then oval
and finally produces a slimmer upper
part, assuming the shape of a Chianti
bottle. Stems up to 1 m. tall with 13-
16 ribs, 15-18 spreading radial spines,
up to 1.5 cm. long. 4-5 or more
central spines, up to 3 cm. long.
Spines honey-coloured, becoming grey
at the tip. Areoles with white wool.
Flowers white, glossy olive green
outside, around 5 cm. long. Brazil
(central Bahia).

C. pluricostatus Buin. & Bred.
Erect, clustering from the base. Stems
up to 3.5 m. tall and up to 9 cm.
thick, with about 20-25 closely spaced
ribs with furrows above the areoles.
Radial spines 5, about 1.1 cm. long. 1

central spine, about 0.6 cm. long.
Cephalium with yellow, brown or
brown-black bristles. Flowers white,
approx. 2.6 cm. long. Brazil (Minas
Gerais).

Coloradoa Boiss. & Davids see
Pediocactus

Consolea Lem. see *Opuntia*

Copiapoa Br. & R. 1922
(*Pilocopiapoa*)
(After the city of Copiapo in Chile)

Copiapoa has yellow, scaly, bare or
sparsely woolly flowers with a very
short tube, but a distinct nectar
chamber. The fruit has an opening lid
above. The genus *Neoporteria* which
also occurs in Chile has a longer tube.
Weingartia has much larger scales. Most
Copiapoa species are distinctive when
not flowering because of their body
colour, which is chalky or more or less
brown. 46 species acording to Ritter,
17 according to N.P. Taylor. Native to
coastal regions of N. Chile
(Antofagasta, Atacama, Coquimbo).

Copiapoa plants are usually not the
easiest of cacti to cultivate. They have
an unusual vegetative rhythm which is
even retained in plants raised from
seed. In Europe their main growth
period occurs in late summer and
autumn. For this reason they should
be kept drier and preferably in half-
shade in the summer. In their habitat
the sky is often overcast at this time of
year. Some of the species have clearly
defined taproots, and therefore
demand a very permeable, gravelly
soil to avoid the roots rotting. The
genus can be divided into two groups.
The one comprises the large, glaucous
species, such as *C. cinerea.* As the
seedlings of these species do not
feature the glaucous body covering,
quite large plants are sometimes
imported, but these grow poorly and
rarely become accustomed to our
conditions. Plants of this group hardly
ever flower in European conditions.
The second group includes the small,
brown-black species such as *C. hypogaea*
and *C. tenuissima.* These flower as
relatively small plants, and they will
thrive really well provided that the
cultivator learns how to treat them; the
usual mistake is to water them at the
wrong time .

Copiapoa cinerea var. albispina

143

C. calderana Ritter
(*C. lembckei* Backeb.)
Body whitish-grey-green, not
glaucous, up to 10 cm. wide, ribbed.
Crown light brown, woolly. Spines
bright yellow on older areoles.
Taproot. Chile (Atacama)

C. cinerea (Phil.) Br.& R.
Body cylindrical when old, up to 20
cm. wide and 1.5 m. tall, the young
part apparently covered in chalk. Ribs
of even width, continuous, or
narrower between the areoles. Crown
white-grey, hairy. Few spines, initially
black. No taproot. Chile (Antofagasta).

C. coquimbana (Karw.) Br. & R.
Body pale green, up to 12 cm. wide,
ribs more or less deeply notched
forming warts. Crown not hairy.
Spines very coarse, initially black.
Taproot. Chile (Coquimbo).

Copiapoa hypogaea

Taproot absent
  Spines long and bristly, more or less enveloping the body   *C. krainziana*
  Spines not enveloping the body
    Body glaucous; chalky-ash grey   *C. cinerea*
    Body not chalky or glaucous   *C. cinerea* var. *haseltoniana*

Taproot present
  Body with continuous ribs
    Areoles almost merged into one another   *C. marginata*
    Areoles clearly separate   *C. calderana*
  Body more or less covered with tubercles arranged in helical rows
    Crown more or less bare. Spines very coarse, initially black, later grey
                              C. coquimbana

    Crown white, woolly. Spines short, falling off later
      Body brown to brown-green, with rough surface   *C. hypogaea*
      Body almost black, not rough   *C. tenuissima*

Copiapoa cinerea

Copiapoa tenuissima

C. hypogaea Ritter
Body up to 6.5 cm. wide, brown-
green, outer skin rough with fine
warts. Ribs divided into tubercles.
Crown white, woolly. Few spines,
brown, falling off later. Thick taproot.
Chile (Antofagasta, Atacama).

C. krainziana Ritter
Body grey-green, up to 12 cm. wide,
ribbed. Crown grey, woolly. The body
is entirely enveloped in dense, white,
bristly spines. No taproot. Chile
(Antofagasta)

C. marginata (Salm-Dyck) Br. & R.
Body dirty grey to light green in
cultivation, up to 10 cm. thick, ribbed.
Crown yellowish, hairy. 6-12 spines, at
first dark brown. Taproot. Chile
(Antofagasta).

C. tenuissima Ritter
Body almost black, up to 5 cm. wide,
warty. Crown fairly white, woolly. 8-15
spines. Taproot. Chile (Antofagasta).

Corryocactus Br. & R. 1920
(*Erdisia*)
(after T.A. Correy, Peruvian engineer,
20th century)

Columnar cacti with 4-12 ribs. Flowers
lateral or towards the end of the
stems, funnel or bell-shaped with a
short tube, externally scaly and spiny/

woolly, diurnal, red to yellow. Style
very thick, bottom stamens borne
close to its base. Many species have a
powerful taproot. 44 species. Native to
Peru, Bolivia, Chile. The listed species
flower readily if grafted.

C. aureus (Meyen) Hutchison (*Erdisia
meyenii* Br. & R.)
Club-shaped or cylindrical plant, erect.
In culture, stems up to 50 cm. long
and 3-5 cm. thick with 5-8 ribs. Radial
spines 9-11, around 2 cm. long. 1 (-2)
central spines, up to 6 cm. long.
Spines brownish to blackish. Flowers
orange-yellow to red, around 4 cm.
long. S. Peru (Arequipa).

C. quadrangularis (Rauh & Backeb.)
Ritter (*Erdisia q.* Rauh & Backeb.)
Bushy, sometimes trailing. Stems up to
1.5 m. long and about 5 cm. thick,
with 4-5 (-6) ribs. Radial spines 4-8, 1-
2 cm. long, central spines 3-4, up to 6
cm. long. Spines yellowish. Flowers
brilliant vermilion, 4-5 cm. long. Peru
(Ayacucho).

C. tenuiculus (Rauh & Backeb.)
Hutchison (*Erdisia t.* Rauh & Backeb.)
Prostrate to semi-erect plants, with
thick, woody taproot. Stems up to 1 m.
long and 1.5-4 cm. thick, with 8-10
notched ribs. 15-25 spines, white, up
to 3 cm. long. Flowers orange to
blood red, about 2.5-3.5 cm. long.
Peru (Ancash).

Corynopuntia F.M. Knuth see *Opuntia*

Coryphantha (Engelm.) Lem.
1868
(*Lepidocoryphantha*)
(Greek coryphe = crown; anthos =
flower)

This genus of tubercle cacti is
characterized by flower-bearing
tubercles which are furrowed above.
The flowers are formed at the base of
the furrow in the axil of the tubercle.
The main differences between
Coryphantha and the very similar genera
Neolloydia, *Neobesseya* and *Escobaria* are
its light brown, smooth seed and
greenish fruit. Coryphanthas also look
similar to Mammillarias, but the latter
never have furrowed tubercles.

Corryocactus aureus

Coryphanthas are generally larger and
have relatively large flowers for
tubercle cacti. There is a nectary
in the axil of the tubercle in many
species of *Coryphantha*. 78 species.
Native to Mexico and S. USA, *C.
vivipara* to S. Canada.

The genus *Coryphantha* includes many
very beautiful plants, some of them
with wildly curving spines. Many offer
attractive colour contrasts, with their
white crown wool, white radial spines
and a coarse, curving, black central
spine. They also bear large, beautiful
flowers. Enthusiasts with suitable
facilities are very warmly
recommended to these plants.

Coryphanthas require a very sunny
position under glass. Cultivation by an
indoor window is difficult. If a garden
frame or a bright greenhouse is
available, they can be strongly
recommended. Coryphanthas thrive
very well if they are kept in bright and
warm conditions and — except when

they are flowering — not too moist.
The only species which like slightly
more moisture are those with thick
tubercles, less spines, and of a brighter
green overall appearance. They also
appreciate slightly more humus in the
soil and relatively large pots. The
strongly spined species should be
provided with a higher proportion of
mineral material and loam in a very
permeable soil, and the neck of the
root should be embedded in pebbles
or pumice rubble. In winter all species
should be kept completely dry. In this
state many species will tolerate
nocturnal frosts without difficulty. In
the spring they are relatively late to
produce new growth, and should not
be watered too early. The best method
of propagation is from seed. The
plants do not flower until they are 5-8
years old. The strongly spined species
grow rather more slowly when young.
Species which form clusters can also
be propagated by offsets, which
usually root easily.

Flowers more or less hairy. Tubercle furrow not extending to the base
  lilac flowers with ciliate petals   *C. macromeris* var. *runyonii*
Flowers bare. Furrow usually extending to the base
  Glands in the furrow absent
    Flowers lilac to violet-pink (central spines absent)
      Flower petals linear, ciliate. Flowers about 5 cm. wide   *C. vivipara*
      Flower petals wider, not ciliate. Flowers up to about 1.5 cm. wide.   *C. minima*

Flowers pink to salmon-pink or white
  Hooked spines present. Tubercles elongated   *C. robustispina*
  Hooked spines absent. Tubercles up to 6 cm. wide   *C. elephantidens*
Flowers yellow to pale yellow
  Tubercles very large, around 2 cm. long or more
    Central spines absent (Flowers with red throat)   *C. bumamma*
    Central spines present
      Central spine very strong, hooked   *C. robustispina*
      Central spines not hooked
        Body grey-green to olive green. Flowers with red filaments. 1 central
        spine   *C. calipensis*
        Body glossy green. Flowers with yellow filaments. 5-7 central spines
           C. andreae
  Tubercles smaller
    Central spines absent
      Spines 6-7   *C. maiz-tablasensis*
      Spines 7-12   *C. cornifera*
      Spines 12-20 or more, comb-formation   *C. radians*
    Central spines present
      Central spine with hooked tip   *C. palmeri*
      Central spine not hooked, possibly curved
        Radial spines 7-12. 1 central spine   *C. cornifera*
        Radial spines more than 14. 1-3 central spines or more
        Central spine up to 1.5 cm. long. Axils woolly   *C. pallida*
        Central spine around 2.5 cm. long. Only young axils slightly woolly.
        Tubercles with keel below.   *C. reduncuspina*
Glands present in the furrow
  Flowers violet-pink. 18-25 radial spines   *C. pseudoechinus*
  Flowers pink-white with red throat. 5-7 radial spines   *C. poselgeriana*
  Flowers yellow
    Central spines 2-4, amber (flowers 5.5-6 cm. long)   *C. erecta*
    Central spines absent or 1
      Central spines 1, almost black   *C. pseudonickelsae*
      Central spines absent or 1, horn-coloured   *C. schwartziana*

Coryphantha elephantidens

C. andreae (J. A. Purp. & Böd.) Böd.
Glossy, deep green body up to 9 cm. wide, with tubercles up to 2.5 cm. wide and 2 cm. long. Axils white, woolly. Radial spines up to about 10, up to 1.2 cm. long. Central spines 5-7, 2.5 cm. long. Flowers light yellow, 5-6 cm. wide. Mexico (Veracruz).

C. bumamma (Ehrenb.) Br. & R.
Bluish to dark green globes up to 10 cm. in diameter, with very large, round tubercles. Axils white, woolly. Radial spines 5-8, grey-brown, about 2 cm. long. Central spines absent. Flowers yellow with red throat, 5-6 cm. wide. Mexico (Morelos, Guerrero).

C. calipensis Bravo
Body 9 cm. tall and 5-8 cm. wide, clustering, grey-green to olive-green. Tubercles 3 cm. long and wide. Radial spines 10-16, 1-1.5 cm. long. 1 central spine, 1.5 cm. long. Flowers yellow, 5.5-6 cm. wide with red filaments. Mexico (Puebla).

C. cornifera (DC.) Lem.
Green to grey-green globes up to 10 cm. in diameter with tubercles almost rhomboid at the base. Radial spines 7-12, up to 0.9 cm. long. Central spine curved downward, up to 1.5 cm. long, less often absent. Flowers lemon yellow, 5-7 cm. wide, with pink filaments. Mexico (Hidalgo).

C. elephantidens (Lem.) Lem.
Body glossy dark green, up to 14 cm. tall and 20 cm. wide, with conspicuously large tubercles, up to 4 cm. long and 6 cm. wide at the base. Axils white, woolly. Radial spines 5-8, brownish, up to 2 cm. long. Central spines absent. Flowers pink to carmine with brownish sheen and red throat, up to 10 cm. wide. Mexico (Michoacán).

C. erecta (Lem.) Lem.
Body cylindrical, 6-8 cm. wide and 30 cm. tall, yellow-green. Crown white, woolly. Radial spines 8-14 (-18), up to 1.2 cm. long. Central spines 2-4, up to 2 cm. long. Spines all amber, darker later. Flowers light yellow, 5.5-6 cm. long. Mexico (Hidalgo).

Coryphantha calipensis

Coryphantha macromeris var. runyonii

C. macromeris Engelm. **var. runyonii**
(Br. & R.) L. Bens.
(*C.r.* Br. & R.; *Lepidocoryphantha r.*
(Br. & R.) Backeb.)
Freely clustering, forming clumps.
Body bears cylindrical, round or
flattened tubercles, 1-2 cm. long. In
contrast with other species listed
here the furrow only extends about
half-way along the tubercle, and the
plants have a taproot. Radial spines
about 6, up to 3 cm. long. 1 (-3)
central spines. Flowers light purple,
externally slightly hairy, up to 5 cm.
wide. Flower petals narrow, linear,
with ciliate margins. USA (E. Texas).

C. maiz-tablasensis Backeb.
Clustering bluish-green globes up to
5.5 cm. wide. Radial spines 6-7, grey-
white, up to 1.2 cm. long. Flowers
pale yellow. Mexico (San Luis, Potosí).

C. minima Baird (*Escobaria nellieae*
(Croiz.) Backeb.)
Body elongated with tubercles only 2
mm. long. Radial spines 13 to around
18, radiant honey yellow or slightly
darker, up to 1 cm. long. Central
spines absent. Flowers pink-violet, up
to 1.5 cm. long and wide. USA (Texas).

This pretty species is quite often to be
found in collections, and is usually
grafted.

C. pallida Br. & R.
Body globular, bluish-green, up to 12
cm. wide. Radial spines 20 or more,
white. Central spines 1-3 or more, the
bottom one projecting, black or black-
tipped. Flowers light yellow, 5-7 cm.
wide. Mexico (Puebla).

C. palmeri Br. & R.
Pale green globes 6-8 cm. in diameter.
Radial spines 11-14, whitish and — in

Coryphantha poselgeriana

contrast to the other species listed here
— with one hooked, brownish central
spine, curving downward. Flowers
yellow, 3-4 cm. long. Mexico
(Durango, Zacatecas, Coahuila).

C. poselgeriana (A. Dietr.) Br. & R.
Body hemi-spherical, more or less
blue-grey-green, up to 20 cm. tall.
Tubercles up to 2.5 cm. wide at the
bottom. Radial spines 5-7, dagger-like,
red-brown, up to 2 (-5) cm. long. 1
central spine, red-brown at the base,
whitish at the tip, up to 5 cm. long.
Flowers often yellowish with red throat
at first, later pink, 4-6 cm. long.
Mexico (Coahuila).

C. pseudoechinus Böd.
Body up to 9 cm. tall and 5 cm. wide,
leaf green to grey-green. Tubercles
about 1 cm. long. Axils woolly. Radial
spines 18-25, 1.2-1.5 cm. long. 1
central spine, 2-2.5 cm. long. All
spines grey-white to brown or almost
black. Flowers violet-pink with lighter
margins, 2 cm. long. Mexico
(Coahuila).

C. pseudonickelsae Backeb.
Clustering globes, 5-6 cm. wide.
Radial spines 15-18, whitish, up to 1.6
cm. long and 1 almost black central
spine. Flowers light yellow, 3.5 cm.
long. Mexico (Durango).

Coryphantha sp.

Coryphantha vivipara

C. radians (DC.) Br. & R.
Body globular to oval, green, 5-7 cm. wide. Crown felty. Radial spines 12-20 or more, comb-formation, white to yellowish, up to 3 cm. long. Central spines usually absent. Flowers lemon yellow, up to 7 cm. or more wide. Mexico (including Hidalgo)

C. reduncuspina Böd.
Light green globes up to 10 cm. in diameter, with keeled tubercles. Radial spines 15-20, short. Central spines 2-3 or more, approx. 2.5 cm. long. Flowers pure yellow, 4-5 cm. long. Mexico (Tamaulipas to ?Coahuila).

C. robustispina (Schott) Br. & R.
(*C. scheeri* (O. Kuntze) L. Benson var. *r.* (Schott) L. Benson)
Body round or elongated, up to 15 cm. long, pale grey-green. Tubercles up to 2.8 cm. long. Radial spines 10-15, the bottom 3 very powerful, brownish, the top ones soft and pale. Central spines 1 (-2), very strong, more or less curved to hooked, yellow, up to 3.5 cm. long. Flowers yellow, salmon pink or white, 4-5 cm. long. USA (S. Arizona), Mexico (N. Sonora).

C. schwartziana Böd.
Elongated egg-shaped body about 8 cm. in height. Radial spines up to 20, almost white, up to 0.9 cm. long. Central spine, if present, darker, straight. Flowers yellow. Mexico (Guanajuato).

C. vivipara (Nutt.) Engelm.
(*Escobaria v.* (Nutt.) Buxb.)
Very freely clustering, squat globular to short cylindrical body. Radial spines 12-40, white or brown. Central spines 1-6, brownish, up to 2 cm. long. Flowers deep pink-red with long, narrow petals, ciliate margins. Flowers 3.5 cm. long and around 5 cm. wide. Canada (Manitoba, Alberta), USA (Kansas to Colorado and N. Texas).

A species with many different varieties. If kept dry it can survive the winter in an unheated greenhouse.

Cryptocereus Alex. 1950
(Greek kryptos = hidden)

Epiphytic plants with leaf-shaped flat stems. The attractive flowers have narrow outer petals which are curved back. The ovary is scaly and spiny or bristly. The flowers are borne laterally on the stems. 3 species. Native to Mexico, Costa Rica, Ecuador.

C. anthonyanus Alex.
Stems 7-15 cm. wide, the edges deeply indented. Areoles wth short spines. Flowers nocturnal, creamy-white, externally red, around 12 cm. long. Mexico (Chiapas). Cultivate as *Epiphyllum*.

Cumarinia Buxb. see *Neolloydia*

Cylindropuntia (Engelm.) F.M. Knuth emend. Backeb. see *Opuntia*

Cylindrorebutia Frič & Kreuzgr. see *Rebutia*

Cullmannia Distef. see *Wilcoxia*

Deamia testudo

Deamia Br. & R. 1920
(after C. C. Deam, American botanist, 20th century).

Climbing 3-8-ribbed or winged cacti with aerial roots. Flowers with elongated, narrow, scaly tube, bristly and hairy or hairy and felty in the axils of the scales. The nocturnal flowers are white or light yellow and very large (20-28 cm. long). The fruit is very spiny. 2 species. Native to Mexico to Colombia.

D. testudo (Karw.) Br. & R.
Stems 3-5-8-winged, about 8 cm. wide, up to 20 cm. wide in its native habitat. Areoles bear 3-4 spines initially, later up to 10 or more, first yellowish then grey, up to 2 cm. long. Flowers white to creamy-white, up to 28 cm. long and 20 cm. wide. S. Mexico to Colombia.

Delaetia Backeb. see *Neoporteria*

Dendrocereus Br. & R. 1920
(Greek dendron = tree)

Tree-shaped columnar cacti, up to 10 m. high, with 3-5 ribs. Flowers borne towards the end of the stems, with elongated; slightly scaly tube, spiny-woolly or only woolly, nocturnal, white, 10-21 cm. long, with a ring of felt internally above the nectar chamber. Fruit with woody rind. 1 species. Native to Cuba.

Denmoza Br. & R. 1922
(Anagram of Mendoza, a province of Argentina)

The characteristic feature of this small cactus genus is the cylindrical, almost closed flowers. They are bi-laterally symmetrical and are borne on specially formed hairy areoles. There are hairs inside the base of the flower formed from modified stamens. The fertile stamens project out of the flowers. As with the related genus *Matucana* the flowers are borne close to the crown, are scaly and hairy and possess a nectar chamber. The body is globular to elongated and has 15-30 ribs. 2 species. Native to Argentina (Mendoza, La Rioja, San Juan, Tucuman, ?Salta).

The particular attraction of these plants is their red spines. In summer

Denmoza rhodacantha

they should be kept warm and sunny, in winter cool and bright. They only grow to their full beauty if they have plenty of space.

D. erythrocephala (K. Schum.) Berger
Body 15-30 cm. wide and up to 1.5 m. tall, with 20-30 ribs. Spines up to 30 or more, fox red, up to 6 cm. long. Numerous white hairy bristles and woolly hairs on the areoles of flowering plants. Flowers red, up to 7.5 cm. long. Argentina (Mendoza, La Rioja, San Juan, ?Salta).

D. rhodacantha (Salm-Dyck) Br. & R.
Body 9-16 cm. wide and tall, with about 15 sharp ribs, between them deep furrows. Radial spines 8-10. Central spines absent or 1. Spines at first yellowish-red or red-brown, later grey, up to 3 cm. long. Red flowers, 7 cm. long. Argentina (Tucuman, ?Mendoza).

Digitorebutia Frič & Kreuzgr. see *Rebutia*

Discocactus Lindl. 1835
(Greek discos = disc)

Discocactus is the only globular cactus genus with the exception of *Melocactus* which features a recessed cephalium, although the two genera are not closely related. *Discocactus* has attractive, 3-8 cm. long nocturnal flowers, compared with *Melocactus'* small diurnal blooms, although they are also bare and devoid of scales or only slightly scaly. The body is globular to compressed globular, and has around 10-20 ribs.

11 species. Native to Brazil (Bahia, Paraná, Mato Grosso, Minas Gerais), Paraguay, Bolivia (Santa Cruz). Discocacti are very beautiful plants, but are extremely difficult to cultivate. Imports are very sensitive and hardly ever survive, while seed has only been available for a short while. The winter temperature should be relatively high at around 15°C or more.

D. boliviensis Backeb.
Body up to 7 cm. tall and more than 15 cm. wide, with approx. 13 ribs.

Discocactus boomianus

D. boomianus Buin. & Bred.
Body up to 6 cm. tall and 10 cm.
wide, with 16-20 bumpy ribs. Radial
spines 10, more or less arranged in
comb-formation, yellow to light
brown, darker tipped, 3 cm. long.
Central spines absent, occasionally 1,
up to 3.5 cm. long. Flowers white, 9
cm. wide. Brazil (Bahia).

D hartmannii (K. Schum.) Br. & R.
Body up to 6 cm. tall and 15 cm.
wide, with 12-16 bumpy ribs. Radial
spines 6-12, curving back or appressed,
up to 2 cm. long. 1 central spine, up
to 1 cm. long. Flowers white, up to
10 cm. Paraguay.

D. horstii Buin. & Bred.
Body up to 6 cm. wide with up to 22
ribs. 8-10 spines, brownish to grey-
white, as if powdered with flour,
arranged in comb-formation.
Cephalium up to 2 cm. wide, white,
woolly with individual brown bristles,

Discocactus horstii

Discocactus magnimammus

Radial spines 5, dirty horn-brown, up
to 3 cm. long. Cephalium up to 4 cm.
wide, hairy, without bristles and
spines. Flowers white, 5 cm. long,
external petals pale pink. Bolivia (high
plains of La Cruz).

Discocactus hartmannii

enclosed by thick, grey, brown-tipped spines. Flowers white, up to 6 cm. long. Brazil (Minas Gerais).

Cultivate in acid soil with much sharp sand, bright and warm in summer, 12-15°C in winter.

D. magnimammus Buin. & Bred. Body 6-7 cm. tall and 17 cm. wide, with 16 ribs, subdivided into plump tubercles. Numerous spines, light horn-colour. Brazil (Mato Grosso).

Disocactus Lindl. 1837
(Greek dis = double)

Epiphytic plants with flat, leaf-type stems. Flowers lateral with bare, naked tube, not elongated, and few petals and stamens. 3 species. Native to Guatemala, Honduras.

D. eichlamii (Weingt.) Br. & R. Stems dentate to notched, 3-5 cm. wide. Flowers carmine red, 6-7 cm. long. Stamens and style projecting. Guatemala.

Dolichothele (K. Schum.) Br. & R. emend. Backeb. see *Mammillaria*

Eccremocactus Br. & R. 1923
(Greek ekkremao = to hang on)

Epiphytic plants with flat leaf-type stems. The laterally borne flowers lack a distinctly elongated tube; the petals are only slightly expanded and the tube is scaly and felty. 1 species. Native to Costa Rica.

Echinocactus grusonii

Echinocactus Link & Otto 1827
(*Homalocephala*) (Greek echinos = hedgehog)

This genus includes giant ribbed cacti, globular and barrel-shaped, up to 3 m. and more in height and 1 m. in diameter, with very powerful spines. Echinocacti bear their flowers close to the crown; they are only 2-6 cm. long, usually yellow, with sharp, woolly scales and a very thick style. Ferocacti, many of which are also very large, have hooked spines and nectar glands on the areoles.

Prior to the work of Britton and Rose

the genus *Echinocactus* embraced the majority of globular cacti apart from *Mammillaria*. Schumann distinguished 138 species around the turn of the century, and more than 1000 names were coined for the plants. Many catalogues and older collections include a vast variety of globular cacti of many genera under the name *Echinocactus*. These synonyms are not listed here.

9 species. Native to Mexico, USA (California, Arizona, New Mexico, Texas, Nevada, Utah).

These giant cacti are among the most

decorative of globular cacti for the larger greenhouse. They demand much sun and warmth and a light, dry situation in the greenhouse in winter. They have to be propagated from seed, as they rarely provide offsets.

E. grusonii Hildm.
'Mother in law's chair'
Up to 1.3 m. tall and 40-80 cm. thick with 20-30 or more tall, sharp ribs. Radial spines 8-10, yellow, up to 3 cm. long. Central spines 3-5, initially golden-yellow or reddish, up to 5 cm. long. Flowers 4-6 cm. long, whitish-

151

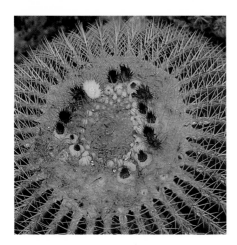

Echinocactus grusonii

yellow to golden-yellow. Mexico (San Luis Potosí to Hidalgo).

Large specimens of this species are often seen in botanical gardens. It grows very well in permeable soil, but likes high temperatures and will not tolerate stagnant moisture. In winter the temperature must not fall below 10-12°C, otherwise very ugly cold spots develop. The soil should not be allowed to dry out completely in winter.

E. horizonthalonius Lem.

Up to 40 cm. wide and 25 cm. tall, with 8 (-13) white-grey frosted ribs. Radial spines 6-9, flattened, transversely ringed, often curved like a claw, 2-4 cm. long. 1 central spine or none. Spines red to yellow. Flowers pink, around 3 cm. long. Stigma pink to yellow-red. Mexico, USA (W. Texas, S. New Mexico). The species demands very high levels of sunshine and warmth and is fairly difficult to cultivate.

E. ingens Zucc.

Up to 1.5 m. tall and 1.25 m. wide, with up to 50 or more ribs. Areoles with yellowish wool. Radial spines about 8. 1 central spine. Spines all transversely ringed, brown, 2-3 cm.

Echincocactus ingens

long. Flowers yellow, 2-3 cm. long. Mexico (Hidalgo).

var. grandis (Rose) Krainz
(*E. grandis* Rose)
Flowers 4–5 cm. long.

E. texensis Hopff. (*Homalocephala t.* (Hopff.) Br. & R.)

In its native habitat up to 30 cm. wide and 15 cm. tall, in Europe up to 20 cm. wide and 10 cm. tall, with 13-27 ribs. Radial spines about 6 (-7), reddish, somewhat flattened, transversely ringed, 1-4 cm. long. 1 central spine, up to 6.5 cm. long and 0.8 cm. wide at the base. Flowers pink outside, orange and scarlet inside, 5-6 cm. long and wide. The flower petals are long and curiously frayed. Central to N. Mexico, USA (Texas, S.E. New Mexico).

The flowers are so uniquely beautiful, their individual petals narrow and feather-like, that the plant is recommended to all cactus enthusiasts who can find a bright, hot site right by the glass. The species requires mineral soil with plenty of loam, high levels of moisture at the beginning of the growth period in spring, and dry conditions in high summer and winter. The flowers can be expected once the plants have reached 10 cm. diameter.

Echinocactus horizonthalonius

Echinocereus Engelm. 1848
(Greek echinos = hedgehog)

One of the first cactus genera to be established. These very soft-fleshed small columnar cacti are usually bushy and branched, and seldom more than 40 cm. tall; as such they do not fit neatly into the large columnar cacti nor into the globular cacti. The flowers have strong external spine formations and almost all species feature distinctly green stigmas. The fruit are also very spiny, at least when young. The flowers are usually large (up to 12 cm. wide), often stay open for a week or more, and emerge through the outer skin above the areoles, as do the side shoots. 65 species. Native to Mexico, USA (from about Mexico City northwards to California, Utah, Wyoming and S. Dakota).

To date only the species from the USA described by L. Benson have been properly examined and sifted down to a few species. If the Mexican species were examined in the same way it is likely that only about 30 *Echinocereus* species would remain.

Echinocerei are very popular amongst cactus growers. The plants often possess beautiful, brightly-coloured spines, while the flowers are large, brilliantly coloured and persist for several days. New interest in this genus has been promoted by the discovery of new species, to add to those already known and loved.

All Echinocerei like to be in a sunny, hot situation in the growth period. The only species which need to be accustomed carefully to the full sun in the spring are those with sparse spines, such as *E. knippelianus* or *E. subinermis*. The soil for Echinocerei can contain plenty of loam and sand; it should be nutritious and yet highly permeable. Stagnant moisture is not appreciated by Echinocerei. Flowering specimens should not be watered in the spring until the flower buds have clearly emerged, otherwise the flowers tend to disappear again. In the early summer the plants like plenty of water, but less in high summer and early autumn. From late autumn to the following spring they should be kept entirely dry. All the soft-fleshed Echinocerei

are vulnerable to attack by red spider mite, and should be examined for pest attack regularly, using a good magnifying glass if necessary.

As the region which includes the various species' natural habitats is so large, the cultural conditions for Echinocerei are not identical in all respects. For example, there are considerable differences in winter temperatures. Species from lower California like to be kept relatively warm, and many species from Mexico like to be kept at moderate temperatures. Other species, including *Echinocereus chloranthus, E. engelmannii, E. pectinatus, E. reichenbachii* and *E. viridiflorus*, will survive short night frosts if they are dry. *E. triglochidiatus* will even survive temperatures below -10°C for short periods.

The plants' performance when grown on their own root is variable. Species such as *E. blanckii, E. engelmannii, E. pentalophus, E. salm-dyckianus, E. scheerii* or *E. triglochidiatus* grow very well on their own root. If they are planted in large, flat pots, or even planted out in the central bed of a greenhouse, they eventually form extensive groups. At the other extreme are species such as *E. davisii* or *E. knippelianus*. They do not grow very well on their own root and are usually grafted. The group of Echinocerei based around *E. pectinatus* tend to form an unsatisfactory and

vulnerable root system, and these plants should either be set in a purely mineral, humus-free, very permeable soil, and watered with care, or they should be grafted onto a robust stock. The rootstock should have a similar level of sensitivity to low temperatures as the scion, and should also not grow too strongly, otherwise the *Echinocereus* will grow elongated, with no really beautiful spines except at the top. Suitable stocks are certain *Trichocereus* species which grow relatively thick, such as *Trichocereus chilensis, T. pasacana* and *T. terscheckii*.

Different Echinocerei also vary in their willingness to flower. Many species, such as *E. delaetii* rarely produce flowers at all. The group based around *E. triglochidiatus* evidently includes forms or clones which flower seldom or sporadically and others which flower very profusely. Naturally nurserymen and amateurs alike should propagate the richly flowering forms. Other *Echinocereus* species flower readily and abundantly. A large group of Echinocerei overloaded with flowers makes a splendid sight. In general terms the formation of flowers is promoted by a bright winter location, as sunny as possible, and cool, dry conditions.

Only a few Echinocerei are suitable for cultivation indoors. As well as species such as *E. pentalophus* and *E. salm-*

Echinocereus brandegeei

Echinocereus chloranthus var. davisii

Echinocereus chloranthus

dyckianus, which form clusters which remain fairly small, it might be worth while experimenting with grafted species with pectinate (comb-formation) spines if you have a sunny window site available. Many of the less densely spined, 'green', clustering species can be kept in a sunny position in the open from spring to late autumn if they are sheltered from heavy rain. They only need to be shifted into their winter quarters when fairly severe frosts threaten. The plants react to such harsh treatment by producing flowers in profusion. The hairy species such as *E. delaetii* and the species with dense, comb-formation spines, such as the group based around *E. pectinatus*, are more sensitive. They will only exhibit their full beauty in a sunny garden frame or in the greenhouse. Echinocerei can easily be propagated from seed. Care should be taken to provide a very permeable soil and to preclude attack by vegetative fungi. With the clustering species it is also possible to propagate by rooting the shoots.

1 Spines 1-3, soon falling off. Body globular to oval, with 5-7 very flat ribs.
  E. knippelianus
1 Spines more numerous, persisting. Body strongly ribbed
  2a Flowers greenish to brownish (2.5-3 cm. long)
    3 Flowers yellowish or brownish, without darker central stripe   *E. chloranthus*
    3 Flowers green with darker central stripe   *E. viridiflorus*
  2b Flowers carrot-coloured (10-12 cm. long)   *E. salm-dyckianus*
  2c Flowers scarlet
    4 Ribs 5-8 (-10). Spines acute. Radial spines 3-6 (-8)   *E. triglochidiatus*
    4 Ribs 8-11. Spines round. Radial spines 5-12   *E. triglochidiatus* var. *melanacanthus*
  2d Flowers yellow or lilac
    5 Body more or less enveloped by hairs   *E. delaetii*
    5 Body not enveloped by hairs
      6 Radial spines 35-45. Central spines 8-12   *E. albatus*
      6 Radial spines up to 30. Central spines up to 8
        7 Spines arranged in comb-formation
          8a Flowers canary-yellow   *E. pectinatus* var. *neomexicanus*
          8b Flowers lilac with lighter centre
            9 Radial spines 25-30. Central spines 2-6   *E. pectinatus*
            9 Radial spines 16-22. Central spines absent   *E. pectinatus* var. *rigidissimus*
          8c Flowers uniformly lilac or lilac with carmine-red centre
            10a Radial spines 20-32. Central spines absent (or 1-2)
              E. reichenbachii var. *reichenbachii*
            10b Radial spines 12-14. Central spines 1-3, more or less the same colour as the radial spines.   *E. reichenbachii* var. *albispinus*
            10c Radial spines 18-22. Central spines 4-7, different colour from radial spines. Flowers with carmine-red centre   *E. reichenbachii* var. *fitchii*
        7 Spines not arranged in comb-formation. Areoles more or less roundish
          11 Flowers yellow
            12 Spines at most 5 mm. long. Stems 5-7 cm. thick. Flowers yellow.
              E. subinermis
            12 Spines more than 5 mm. long. Stems 2.5-4 cm. thick. Flowers yellow with red centre   *E. blanckii* var. *angusticeps*
          11 Flowers lilac
            13 Stems 3-7 cm. thick (Ribs 7-17)
              14 Central spines up to 1.5 cm. long. Radial spines multi-coloured
                E. sciurus
              14 Central spines more than 1.5 cm. long. Radial spines not multi-coloured
                15 Tubercles very pronounced. Flowers with lighter centre   *E. brandegeei*
                15 Tubercles moderately pronounced. Flowers without lighter centre

16 Flowers 3-4 cm. long. Radial spines 16-20   *E. radians*
16 Flowers 4.5-8 cm. long. Radial spines 7-13
  17 Radial spines swollen at the base like an onion. Central spines 1(-3).
    Ribs 7-10   *E. enneacanthus*
  17 Radial spines not swollen at the base like an onion. Central spines
    2-6. Ribs 10-14   *E. engelmannii*
13 Stems up to 3 cm. thick (ribs 4-10)
 18 Flowers with white throat (4-6 ribs)   *E. pentalophus*
 18 Flowers without white throat
  19 Flowers 6-8 cm. long. 5-7 ribs
   20 Spines all about 1-2 mm. long   *E. gentryi*
   20 Spines more than 5 mm. long
    21 Radial spines up to 2 cm. long. Central spines about 3 cm. long
                                                 E. blanckii
    21 Radial spines up to 1 cm. long. Central spines up to 2 cm. long
                              E. blanckii var. *berlandieri*
 19 Flowers about 12 cm. long. 8-10 ribs.   *E. scheerii*

Echinocereus knippelianus

E. albatus Backeb.
Stems up to 4 cm. thick with about 12 bumpy ribs. Radial spines around 40, central spines approx. 10. Spines white and brittle. Flowers pinkish-red, about 10 cm. wide. Petals with darker central stripe. Mexico.

E. baileyi see *E. reichenbachii* var. *albispinus*

E. blanckii (Poselg.) Palmer **var. blanckii**
Stems usually densely clustering, 2.5-3 cm. thick and with 5-6 (-7) very bumpy ribs. Radial spines 8-9, white, one usually red initially, up to 2 cm. long. Central spines 1 (-2), brown or black, about 3 cm. or more long. Flowers violet-red, 6.5 to about 9 cm. long and up to 7 cm. wide. Mexico (Tamaulipas).

E. blanckii (Poselg.) Palmer **var. berlandieri** (Poselg.) Backeb.
Stems 1-2.5 cm. thick. Radial spines 6-8, yellow-white, later whitish, 0.8-1 cm. long. 1 central spine, yellow-brown, up to 2 cm. long. USA (Texas), North-East Mexico (near Aguas Calientes).

E. blanckii (Poselg.) Palmer **var. angusticeps** (Clov.) L. Bens. (*E. papillosus* Linke)
Stems 2.5-4 cm. thick with 6-10 ribs. Radial spines approx. 7-10, white to brownish, up to 1.5 cm. long. Central spines 1 (-3), yellow, up to 2.5 cm. long. Flowers yellow with red centre. USA (Texas).

E. brandegeei (Coult). K. Schum.
Stems slightly clustering, 3-5 cm. thick, with 7-8 very bumpy ribs. Radial spines 12-16, reddish-yellow to grey, 0.5-1.5 cm. long. Central spines 1-4, flattened, up to 8 cm. long. Flowers pink-carmine, up to 5 cm. long and 4-5 cm. wide. Flower petals with olive central stripe. Mexico (lower California).

E. caespitosus see *E. reichenbachii* var. *reichenbachii*

E. chloranthus (Engelm.) Rumpl. (*E. viridiflorus* Engelm. var. *c.* (Engelm.) Backeb.)
Stems solitary, 4-7 cm. thick with 13-

18 ribs. Radial spines 12-20, variable in colour. Central spines (2-) 3-5, usually purple, up to 3 cm. long. Flowers yellowish to brownish, 2.5-3 cm. long. USA (Texas, New Mexico to Colorado), N. Mexico.

var. davisii (A.D. Houghton) Marsh. (*E. d.* A.D. Houghton).
Stems no more than 2.5 cm. tall, single or clustering, with 6-9 ribs. 9-14 spines, up to 1.7 cm. long. Flowers dirty greenish-yellow, 2.5 cm. long and 2 cm. wide. USA (Texas).

This variety remains small and flowers as a very small plant; it is popular and widespread. It does not grow well on its own root and is usually grafted.

E. coccineus see *E. triglochidiatus* var. *melanacanthus*

E. dasyacanthus see *E. pectinatus* var. *neomexicanus*

E. davisii see *E. chloranthus* var. *davisii*

E. delaetii Gürke
Stems clustering and sometimes prostrate, 5-7 cm. thick and with 20-24 ribs. Radial spines 18-36, white to grey-white, up to 1 cm. long. Central spines 4-5, yellowish, red-tipped, 2-3 cm. long. The entire body is enveloped in irregularly curved, white hairy spines. Flowers light purple-pink, 6-7 cm. long and up to 6.5 cm. wide. Mexico (Coahuila).

The species is very eye-catching with its white hair. Rather temperamental under cultivation, only thrives under glass and demands much warmth. Rarely flowers.

E. engelmannii (Parry) Rümpl.
Stems clustering, 4-6 cm. thick, with 10-14 ribs, slightly bumpy. Radial spines 10-12 (-13), 1-1.5 cm. long. Central spines 2-6, up to 7 cm. long. All spines very variable in colour, from light yellow to brown and more or less acute. Flowers purplish-red, 5-8 cm. long and up to 7.5 cm. wide. USA (South-west states), N. Mexico.

E. enneacanthus Engelm.
Stems clustering, more or less prostrate, 3.5-5 (-7) cm. thick, with 8-10 bumpy ribs. Radial spines 7-9 (-12), white to yellowish, up to 1.5 cm. long. Central spines 1 (-3), whitish to

Echinocereus pectinatus var. pectinatus

Echinocereus pentalophus

156

brownish, up to 6.5 cm. long. Flowers light purple, 4.5-6 cm. long and up to 7.5 cm. wide. USA (New Mexico, S. Texas), Mexico (Chihuahua, Coahuila).

E. fitchii see *E. reichenbachii* var. *fitchii*

E. gentryi Clov.
Stems clustering, 2.5 cm. thick, with perhaps 5 ribs. Radial spines 8-12, brownish, 1-2 mm. long. 1 central spine, similar to the radials. Flowers pink, up to 8 cm. long and 5-6 cm. wide. Mexico (Sonora).

E. knippelianus Liebn.
Stems globular to oval, not clustering, almost black-green, 5 cm. thick and with about 5 rounded ribs. 1-3 spines, about 1.5 cm. long, yellowish or white, bristly and soon falling off. Flowers pink, around 4 cm. long. Mexico (Coahuila).

Grown on its own root the plant is not robust and is therefore usually grafted. The flowers appear very early in the spring.

E. papillosus see *E. blanckii* var. *angusticeps*

E. pectinatus (Scheidw.) Engelm. **var. neomexicanus** (Coult.) L. Bens. (*E. dasyacanthus* Engelm.)
Stems 5-10 cm. thick with 15-21 ribs. Radial spines 16-24, up to 1.2 cm. long. Central spines 3-8, up to 0.8 cm. long. Spines pink, later greying and forming zones of differing colour. Flowers canary yellow, up to 10 cm. long and 7.5-12.5 cm. wide. External flower petals have orange-coloured central stripe. Fruit purple. Flowers are only open around midday. USA (W. Texas, S. New Mexico, E. Arizona), Mexico (Chihuahua).

E. pectinatus (Scheidw.) Engelm. **var. pectinatus**
Stems rarely clustering, 4-7 cm. thick and with 20-23 ribs. Areoles elongated and radial spines arranged in comb formation. Radial spines 25-30, up to 1 cm. long. Central spines 2-6, up to 0.3 cm. long. Spines white, yellow, red or dark brown. Flowers purple with lighter greenish centre, 6-8 cm. long and wide. Mexico (Coahuila to Guanajuato), USA (Arizona, Texas).

E. pectinatus (Scheidw.) Engelm. **var. rigidissimus** (Engelm.) Engelm. (*E. rigidissimus* (Engelm.) Rose)
As *E.p.* var. *pectinatus,* but has only 18-22 radial spines and no central spines. USA (Arizona, New Mexico), Mexico (Sonora).

E. pentalophus (DC.) Lem.
Stems clustering, 2 cm. thick with approx. 5 ribs. Radial spines 3-5 (-6), white or yellowish, later grey, up to 0.7 cm. long. Central spines absent or rarely 1, darker, up to 1.5 cm. long. Flowers pink or lilac with white throat, 7-12 cm. long and wide. USA (S. Texas) to N. Mexico .

E. radians Engelm.
Stems cylindrical, with 13-15 ribs. Radial spines 16-20, 0.2-1 cm. long. 1 central spine, brown to black, 2.5 cm. long. Flowers light purple, 3-4 cm. long and around 5 cm. wide. Mexico (Chihuahua). A generally popular species.

E. reichenbachii (Terschek) Haage **var. albispinus** (Lahmann) L. Bens. (*E. baileyi* Rose)
Stems clustering, 4-5 cm. thick with about 15 ribs. Areoles elongated in plan form, and spines almost in comb formation as a result. Radial spines 12-16, initially white, then reddish, up to 2.5 cm. long. Central spines usually absent (sometimes 1-3). Flowers purple-pink with carmine red centre, 6-7 cm. long and around 9 cm. wide. USA (Texas, Oklahoma), N. Mexico.

E. reichenbachii (Terschek) Haage **var. fitchii** (Br. & R.) L. Bens. (*E. fitchii* Br. & R.)
Stems rarely clustering, egg-shaped, 4-8 cm. thick and with 10-14 ribs. Radial spines in comb formation, around 20, white or straw-coloured, up to 0.7 cm. long. Central spines 4-6, mostly brownish, up to 0.6 cm. long. Flowers purple- pink with carmine red centre, 6-7 cm long and about 9 cm. wide. USA (Texas).

Echinocereus reichenbachii var. albispinus

157

Echinocereus reichenbachii var. fitchii

Echinocereus salm-dyckianus, short-tubed form

E. reichenbachii (Terschek) Haage **var. reichenbachii** (*E. caespitosus* Engelm.)
Stems clustering, 6 cm. thick, with 12-18 ribs. Radial spines 20-30, straw-coloured to grey, comb formation. Central spines absent or 1-2, short. Flowers pink, with dark throat, 6-8 cm. long and up to 8 cm. wide. USA to N. Mexico (Saltillo).

E. salm-dyckianus Scheer
Stems clustering, 2-3 cm. thick and with 7-9 slightly bumpy ribs. Radial spines 8-9, yellowish with red tip, up to 1 cm. long. 1 central spine, light horn- coloured to red, up to 1.5 cm. long. Flowers carrot-coloured, 10-12 cm. long and 5-8 cm. wide. The flowers persist for 8-10 days. Mexico (Chihuahua, Durango). Popular and generally widespread species.

E. scheerii (Salm-Dyck) Rümpl.
Stems decumbent, clustering, 2.5-3 cm. thick with 8-10 slightly bumpy ribs. Radial spines 7-12, white, yellow at the base, up to 0.3 cm. long. 1-3 central spines, red-tipped, more than 1 cm. long. Flowers pure pink, about 12 cm. long. Mexico (Chihuahua).

E. sciurus (K. Brand.) Br. & R.
Stems abundantly clustering, 3.5-5 cm. thick with 12-17 bumpy ribs. Radial spines 15-18, up to 1.5 cm. long. Approx. 4 central spines, shorter. All spines pale yellow, brown-tipped. Flowers pink-purple, 7-9 cm. long and about 9-12 cm. wide. Mexico (Lower California).

E. subinermis Salm-Dyck
Stems initially globular, later elongated, seldom clustering, 7-9 cm. thick, with 5-9 ribs. Initially 3-8 radial spines and one yellowish central spine, up to 5 mm. long, later only 3-4 spines, hardly more than 1 mm. long, or none at all. Flowers yellow, 7-8.5 cm. long and 7-9 cm. wide. Mexico (Chihuahua, Sonora, Coahuila, Durango, Sinaloa). One of the few Echinocerei with splendid yellow flowers.

E. triglochidiatus Engelm. **var. triglochidiatus**
Stems cylindrical, freely clustering, around 6-7.5 cm. thick, with (6-) 7 (-10) ribs. Radial spines 3-5 (-8), ash-grey, up to 2.5 cm. long. 1-5 central spines, or none, grey. All spines acute. Flowers scarlet, 5-7.5 cm. long and 5 cm. wide. Flower petals blunt. USA (W. Texas to S. Colorado and Arizona).

E. triglochidiatus Engelm. **var. melanacanthus** L. Bens. (*E. coccineus* Engelm.)
Stems globular to egg-shaped, later cylindrical and clustering, 3-7 cm. thick and with 8-11 bumpy ribs. Radial spines 8-12, mostly white, up to 2 cm. long. 2-4 central spines, yellowish, reddish to blackish, up to 3 cm. long. Flowers scarlet, yellowish in the throat, 3.5-7 cm. long and 2.5-3.7 cm. wide. Flower petals blunt. Fruit red. USA (Arizona to Utah and Colorado).

Echinocereus triglochidiatus var. melanacanthus

Echinocereus viridiflorus

E. viridiflorus Engelm.
Stems more or less globular, rarely
clustering, 2-5 cm. thick and with 13-
15 ribs. Areoles elongated. Radial
spines 13-15, 0.5 cm. long. 2-3 or no
central spines, short. All spines patchy
white or brown. Flowers green with
darker central stripe, 2.5-3 cm. long
and 3 cm. wide. USA (from New
Mexico and Texas to S. Dakota and
Wyoming).

Echinofossulocactus Lawr.
1841
(Latin echinus = hedgehog, fossula =
small furrow, trench)

The genus *Echinofossulocactus* was
established by Lawrence in 1841. K.
Schumann attempted to introduce the
shorter and more easily pronounced
name *Stenocactus* for this group of
plants, but according to the rules of
botanical nomenclature the older
name remains valid. Almost all
Echinofossulocacti (with the exception
of *E. coptonogonus*) are characterized by
their very numerous, 30-60 (-120),
thin, gill-like and often wavy ribs. The
seedlings initially look like small
Mammillarias, as the thin ribs are not

formed until about one year later.
Often the upper central spine is more
or less flattened and papery. *E.
coptonogonus* with only 10-15 thicker
ribs, only qualifies as an
Echinofossulocactus by its flowers. The
flowers in this genus are borne close
to the apex, have a short to very short
tube, and large, membranous but bare
scales. The related genus *Ferocactus*,
with similar flowers, has a ring of hairs
above the stamens, and nectar glands
on the areoles. The South American
genus *Gymnocalycium* also produces
flowers with a short tube and large,
bare scales, but its round, laterally
furrowed ribs give it a quite different
external form.

All Echinofossulocacti are globular

Various Echinofossulocacti

are less than 10 genuine species; the work is not yet finished.

The Echinofossulocacti come from Mexico, more precisely from the central and northern parts of the country, where they tend to grow on dry grassland. The plants are not generally difficult in cultivation. They like bright conditions, but not full sunshine, as they are slightly shaded in their homeland by other vegetation. They appreciate gentle shading from the brilliance of the midday sun even in European conditions. They are grown in ordinary cactus soil, perhaps with a slight addition of humus. In the vegetative period they should be provided with plenty of water, while in the winter they should be kept cool and dry. A bright winter location is advisable, as many species set their flowers very early in the spring. The flowers persist for up to a week, are sometimes yellowish or greenish-white, but often striped with deep violet-red. It is interesting to observe how the flowers push through the dense spines. Raising Echinofossulocacti from seed is easy.

Echinofossulocactus crispatus

cacti about 10 cm. wide, with flowers about 2.5-3.5 cm. long. Probably less than 10 species, but very variable. Native to Mexico.

The naming of Echinofossulocacti is unusually confused, but these easily cultivated cacti are very popular amongst cactus enthusiasts for their interesting, gill-like ribs, their fine, exaggerated spine formations and their pretty flowers.

It is relatively easy to define the genus *Echinofossulocactus,* but it is very much more difficult to define the individual species. Reference to more than 30 species will be found in cactus literature, but many of them only qualify as varieties or forms now, considering the broad range of variation within many species, and especially in the group centred on *E. crispatus.* Other former species can no longer be identified because of their inadequate descriptions. More recent work on this genus, including that by N. Taylor in England, has produced the provisional conclusion that there

Echinofossulocactus multicostatus

Echinofossulocactus phyllacanthus

Ribs 10-15, 0.5 cm. or more wide
E. coptonogonus
Ribs more than 25, 1-3 cm. wide and more or less wavy
  Ribs 50-120   *E. multicostatus*
  Ribs 25-40
    Flowers with more or less wide violet central stripe, perhaps 4 cm. long
E. crispatus
    Flowers white, yellowish to light pink, sometimes with reddish centre, about 2 cm. long
      Radial spines around 10-25. Central spine very long   *E. vaupelianus*
      Radial spines 2-7. Central spines inconspicuous   *E. phyllacanthus*

E. coptonogonus (Lem.) Lawr.
Only 10-15 ribs, not wavy. Spines horn-coloured, up to 3 cm. long and transversely ringed. Flowers whitish to purple with carmine-red centre. Central Mexico (Hidalgo, Guanajuato, San Luis Potosí, Zacatecas).

E. crispatus (DC.) Lawr. (*E. violaciflorus* (Quehl) Br. & R.)
26-35 ribs. Radial spines up to 8, up to 3.5 cm. long, the topmost spine flattened. Central spines 3-4. Flowers violet with more or less wide darker central stripe, about 4 cm. long. Mexico (Hidalgo to Oaxaca).

Practically indistinguishable from *E. lamellosus* (A. Dietr.) Br. & R. and *E. hastatus* (Hopff.) Br. & R.

E. multicostatus (Hildm.) Br. & R.
80-120 thin, cardboard-like ribs. Central spines 3. Spines varying widely in length, one of them more or less acute. Flowers white with purple-violet centre, according to other information yellowish. Eastern Mexico (Coahuila, Durango).

E. phyllacanthus (Mart.) Lawr.
Ribs 30-35, radial spines 2-7, upper spines 3, all flat, with a keel and sometimes transversely ringed, initially pink to ruby red, then brownish, 4-8 cm. long. Flowers yellowish-whitish with reddish centre, 1.5-2 cm. long. Mexico (Hidalgo).

E. vaupelianus (Werderm.) Tiegel & Oehme (*E. albatus* (A. Dietr.) Br. & R.; *E. ochoterenaus* (Tiegel) Oehme)
Ribs 30-40. Radial spines needle-shaped, around 10-25. Central spines

161

1-4, very strong, the topmost more or less flattened, yellow to brown-black, up to 7 cm. long. Flowers white, yellowish or white-pink, around 2 cm. long. Mexico.

Echinomastus see *Neolloydia*

Echinopsis Zucc. 1837
(*Pseudolobivia*)
(Greek echinos = sea-urchin, opsis = appearance)

About 70 species are distinguished today, although the true number is probably far smaller. Native to Brazil, Uruguay, Paraguay, Argentina, Bolivia. The genus *Echinopsis* was established in 1837, and is therefore one of the oldest cactus genera. Echinopses are large, green, globular cacti with 8-30 ribs, usually sharp and continuous. They have more or less uniform spines, i.e. the radial and central spines are not clearly differentiated, and never have a woolly crown. When old they tend to become slightly elongated columns. The real distinguishing feature of Echinopses is the flowers. They are usually borne laterally, are long and trumpet-shaped and are very hairy and scaly. There is always a distinct ring of throat stamens separate from the other stamens. Initially only white or pale lilac flowers were known; they appeared in the evening, were usually strongly scented and remained open for 1, 2 or 3 days. In the past few decades certain day-flowering species have been discovered with yellow or red blooms which are otherwise identical. These diurnal species come from altitudes between 1700 and 3500 m., while the nocturnal species are lowland plants. It appears that the nocturnal insects required for pollination are absent in the uplands. The diurnal species with brightly-coloured flowers are mostly compressed globular in form and have notched ribs like *Lobivia*. The similarity between the genera *Echinopsis* and *Lobivia* has made it difficult to distinguish between them, and for this reason Backeberg established the genus *Pseudolobivia* for the diurnal, long-tubed species, in order to indicate the plants' position midway between the two genera.

None of the proposed definitions of the inter-related genera based around *Echinopsis* has found general acceptance. There is no doubt that *Trichocereus*, *Echinopsis* and *Lobivia* are closely related, as are the genera *Helianthocereus*, *Pseudolobivia* and *Soehrensia* which have been split off from them. All of them possess scaly and very woolly radially symmetrical flowers with a recessed ring of throat stamens. There are five characteristic features which are most widely used as generic criteria here, and the number of separate genera which is differentiated depends on which of these features is taken to be critical and given first priority. The genera thus defined include very different groups of plants (see table under *Lobivia*). At one extreme the only separation is between *Lobivia* and *Echinopsis* (with *Trichocereus* as a sub-genus), while at the other Backeberg distinguished six genera. One result of such confusion is that there is a very wide variety of names in use for these plants, but this does not greatly affect the systematic groupings; provided that the same species remain linked together within the genera or sub-genera, it is only their rank in the systematic hierarchy which alters.

Echinopsis hybrid

The basic problem is that any species which exhibits few of the major distinguishing features is difficult to place in the former genera or sub-genera, e.g. the *Soehrensia* species or *Echinopsis arachnacantha*.

In this book we have adhered to the simple classification according to external form: *Trichocereus* (columnar) and *Echinopsis / Lobivia* (more globular) and according to tube length: *Trichocereus / Echinopsis* (long) and *Lobivia* (short).

In terms of culture the Echinopses are generally robust and tolerant plants, and they provide an abundance of beautiful flowers. Differences do arise between the ideal conditions for Echinopses in the narrower sense, which come predominantly from Uruguay, Paraguay, north Argentina and south Brazil, and the upland Echinopses of the former genus *Pseudolobivia*, most of which come from north-west Argentina and Bolivia. Plants of the genus *Echinopsis* (in the narrower sense) have been cultivated in Europe for more than a century, and are widely known and loved. The most popular plants are hybrids from within the highly variable group based on *E. eyriesii*, *E. oxygona*, *E. multiplex* and *E. tubiflora*. In summer the plants are prized for their large, funnel-shaped, pale pink flowers which open in the evening and close at midday of the following day. For this reason Echinopses are often wrongly called Queen of the Night, even though they have nothing in common with the genuine Queen of the Night (*Selenicereus*). In some quarters these Echinopses are known as farmer cacti, probably because splendid Echinopses are often found in farmhouses.

Echinopsis species require permeable soil, fairly rich in humus. They should not be kept too cold in winter (not below 6°C) and not completely dry. Echinopses kept too cold and too dry in the winter are difficult to persuade into growth in the following spring, and then flower late or only sparsely. In the vegetation period they should be kept in bright conditions, but sheltered from the brilliance of the midday sun. They also like a generous supply of water and fertilizer. They do not appreciate excessively dry air, as can occur in a situation in full sun. Many of these plants — including the more recent hybrids raised from them — suffer from delayed flower formation or flower buds which fail to develop if the conditions in the vegetative period are incorrect: dry soil, dry air, or excessively hot or cool weather. In general terms these Echinopses can be regarded as excellent plants for moderate, well-balanced cultural conditions. In the growth period the Echinopses can also be cultivated on an outside window ledge, if it is sheltered from penetrating rain.

Echinopses can be raised from seed. The seedlings initially grow slowly, but are capable of flowering after the fourth year. Those species which tend to form pups are particularly easy to propagate, as the shoots often form roots while still attached to the mother plant. It is advisable to propagate only from those plants which flower richly and easily, rather than those which produce many shoots but few flowers. Plants which are healthy in themselves tend to produce too many pups if they are fed with excessive nitrogen, and if allowance is not made for the requisite rest period, i.e. if they are kept too warm and too moist in the winter.

The upland Echinopses from the former genus *Pseudolobivia* are becoming increasingly popular among cactus enthusiasts. They often feature robust spines and sometimes characteristic central spines curved into a hook. The plants reliably produce flowers which are very large (relative to body size), and are only open in the daytime. They may be very slender and of elongated funnel-shape, but are sometimes shorter. The flowers may be yellow, red or violet in colour as well as white and pink. It is evident that these upland Echinopses in certain respects represent an intermediate stage between the Echinopses in the narrower sense and the Lobivias; for instance, they can be crossed with many plants from these two groups. Their readiness to hybridize, their beautiful flowers and their often powerful spine formations have ensured that present-day cactus hybridizing is based more and more on the upland Echinopses.

High mountain Echinopses of the sub-group Pseudolobivia and their hybrids

The cultural conditions for upland Echinopses are closely matched to those for Lobivias: standard, highly permeable cactus soil; a bright but not too hot situation, good ventilation; adequate watering and feeding with low-nitrogen fertilizer in the vegetative period; completely dry and cool in winter; plants cultivated hard and kept dry will tolerate short night frosts. The upland Echinopses can be cultivated in a greenhouse with an appropriately controlled climate, and also do very well during the growth period in a cold frame or on an outside window ledge protected from rain. Propagation is mainly from seed, as many species hardly ever or never produce shoots.

Flowers white

Flowers 12-20 cm. long

Spines more or less straight (nocturnal flowering)
Spines no more than 0.5 cm. long (body dark green)   *E. eyriesii*
Spines 0.5-1.5 cm. long
Body bright grass green. Radial spines 11-18   *E. calochlora*
Body dark green. Radial spines 5-9   *E. tubiflora*
Spines curved or hooked
Spines 5-10 cm. long, curving upward. Nocturnal flowering   *E. leucantha*
Spines up to 5 cm. long. (diurnal flowering)
Spines almost all slightly curved, 1-5 cm. long   *E. obrepanda*
Central spine hooked, up to 2 cm. long
Flowers around 20 cm. long. Radial spines 8-15. Central spines 1-4
    E. hamatacantha
Flowers 12-16 cm. long. Radial spines 3-9. Central spines 1   *E. ancistrophora*

Flowers about 10 cm. long (diurnal)

Spines often curved or hooked, up to 1 cm. long. Flowers with thin tube
    E. polyancistra
Spines a few centimetres long. Flowers with thick tube   *E. ferox*
Flowers up to 5 cm. long (central spine curved or slightly hooked) *E. kratochviliana*

163

Flowers not white

  Flowers nocturnal, strongly scented, pale red to pink
    Flowers pink, 15-20 cm. long   *E. multiplex*
    Flowers pale red, about 22-25 cm. long. Body slightly frosted   *E. oxygona*

  Flowers diurnal, yellow to carmine red or brilliant flesh-coloured
    Spines projecting
      Flowers yellow   *E. aurea*
      Flowers carmine red   *E. mammillosa var. kermesina*
      Flowers pink, white or yellow   *E. ferox*
    Spines more or less curved
      Flowers orange-red   *E. calorubra*
      Flowers bluish-red   *E. toralapana*
    Spines appressed
      Flowers brilliant flesh-coloured with greenish-white throat, 8-10 cm. long
                                             E. cardenasiana

    Flowers yellow to carmine red, no more than about 5 cm. long   *E. arachnacantha*

Echinopsis arachnacantha

E. ancistrophora Spegazz. (*Pseudolobivia a.* (Spegazz.) Backeb.) .
Diameter 5-8 cm. Radial spines 3-9, whitish. Central spine 1, hooked, light brownish. Flowers white, 12-16 cm. long, diurnal. Argentina (Tucuman to Salta).

E. arachnacantha (Buin. & Ritter) H. Friedr. (*Lobivia a.* Buin. & Ritter)
Diameter up to 4 cm. Radial spines up to 15, initially pale brown, later whitish, appressed. Central spine usually 1, black. Flowers golden yellow to orange, about 5 cm. long, diurnal. Bolivia (Samaipata).

var. torrecillasensis (*E. t.* Card.) H. Friedr.
Has more or less carmine red flowers.

E. aurea Br. & R. (*Pseudolobivia a.* (Br. & R.) Backeb; *Lobivia a.* (Br. & R.) Backeb.)
Diameter up to 7 cm. Radial spines 8-10, light brown. Central spines 1-5, darker brown to black. Flowers light yellow to golden yellow, 9 cm. long, diurnal. Argentina (Cordoba).

var. leucomalla (Wessn.) Rausch (*Lobivia l.* Wessn.) (*Lobivia famatimensis* (Spegazz.) Br. & R. var. *leucomalla* (Wessn.) Backeb.).
Covered with very dense white bristly spines.

E. calochlora K. Schum.
Diameter 6-9 cm. Body light grass green. Radial spines 11-18, yellow to brownish. Central spines 3-4, darker. Flowers white, around 16 cm. long, nocturnal. Brazil (Corumba).

E. calorubra Card. (*Pseudolobivia c.* (Card.) Backeb.; *E. obrepanda* (Salm-Dyck) K. Schum. var. *caloruba* (Card.) Rausch)
Up to 14 cm. wide. Radial spines 9-13, one curving upwards gently, yellowish. Central spine 1, up to 2.5 cm. long. Spines becoming grey with brown tips. The flowers are orange-red, bluish-pink towards the base, 15 cm. long. Bolivia (Santa Cruz).

E. cardenasiana (Rausch) H. Friedr. (*Lobivia c.* Rausch)
Diameter up to 10 cm. Radial spines 12, appressed. Central spines 1-3. Spines white to yellowish with brown to black tip. Flowers brilliant bluish-

Echinopsis aurea

Echinopsis cardenasiana

red with greenish-white throat, 8-10 cm. long, diurnal. Bolivia (Eastern Tarija).

E. eyriesii (Turpin) Zucc.
Diameter 12-15 cm. Radial spines up to 10. Central spines 4-8. Spines no more than 0.5 cm. long, dark brown. Flowers white, 17-25 cm. long, nocturnal, opening by late afternoon. South Brazil to Argentina (Entre Rios, Buenos Aires) and Uruguay. Of this species there are many forms and hybrids, usually with pale pink flowers.

E. ferox (Br. & R.) Backeb. (*Lobivia ferox* Br. & R.; *Pseudolobivia f.* (Br. & R.) Backeb.)
Diameter up to 20 cm. Radial spines 10-12, up to 6 cm. long. Central spines 3-4, up to 15 cm. long. The flowers are white, more rarely pink or yellow, 10 cm. long, diurnal. Bolivia (East of Oruro).

E. hamatacantha Backeb. (*Pseudolobivia h.* (Backeb.) Backeb.; *E. ancistrophora* Spegazz. var. *hamatacantha* (Backeb.) Rausch)
10-15 cm. wide. Radial spines 8-15. Central spines 1-4. Spines sometimes hooked, yellowish-white to horn-coloured or reddish, 0.4-1.2 cm. long. Flowers white, scented, up to 20 cm. long. Argentina (Salta).

E. kratochviliana Backeb. (*Pseudolobivia k.* (Backeb.) Backeb.; *E. ancistrophora*

Spegazz. var. *kratochviliana* (Backeb.) Rausch)
Diameter up to 6 cm. Radial spines 10-12, whitish. Central spines 1-4, darker, curved or slightly hooked. Flowers white, no more than 5 cm. long, diurnal. Argentina (Salta).

E. leucantha (Gill.) Walp.
Diameter up to 15 cm. Radial spines 9-10, yellowish-brown. Central spine 1, brown, curving upward, 5-10 cm.

long. Flowers white, up to 20 cm. long, nocturnal, scented. N.W. Argentina.

E. mammillosa Gürke **var. kermesina** (Krainz) Friedr. (*Pseudolobivia k.* Krainz; *E. k.* (Krainz) Krainz)
Diameter up to 15 cm. or more. Radial spines 11-16, reddish-yellow. Central spines 4-6, rather darker. Flowers carmine red, 15-18 cm. long, diurnal. ?Argentina.

Echinopsis ferox

Echinopsis polyancistra

E. multiplex (Pfeiff.) Zucc.
Diameter 15 cm. Radial spines 5-15, brownish-yellow. Central spines 2-5, darker. Flowers flesh-coloured, pink at the tip, 15-20 cm. long, nocturnal, strongly scented. S. Brazil.

E. obrepanda (Salm-Dyck) K. Schum. (*Pseudolobivia o.* (Salm-Dyck) Backeb.)
Diameter up to 10 cm. Radial spines 7-11, white to brownish. Central spines absent or 1-3. Spines almost all slightly curved. Flowers white, 18-20 cm. long, diurnal. Bolivia (Cochabamba).

E. oxygona (Link) Zucc.
Diameter up to 25 cm. Radial spines 5-16. Central spines 2-7. All spines horn-coloured, black above. Flowers pale red, about 22-25 cm. long, nocturnal. S. Brazil, Uruguay, N.E. Argentina.

E. polyancistra Backeb. (*Pseudolobivia p.* (Backeb.) Backeb.; *E. ancistrophora* Spegazz. var. *polyancistra* (Backeb.) Rausch)
Up to 6 cm. wide. Spines numerous, fine, often curved to hooked. Central spines 1-4, up to 1.2 cm. long. Flowers white, scented, with long thin tube, up to 10 cm. long. Argentina (Salta).

E. silvestrii Spegazz.
Diameter up to 15 cm. Radial spines 5-9. Central spine 1. Spines first yellow, later dirty grey, up to 1 cm. long. The flowers are white, 20 cm. long, unscented. Argentina (Tucuman-Salta border).

E. toralapana Card. (*Pseudolobivia t.* (Card.) Backeb.; *E. obrepanda* (Salm-Dyck) K. Schum. var. *purpurea* Salm-Dyck)
Up to 16 cm. wide. Spines 6-10, curved, grey-white, up to 5 cm. long. Flowers bluish-red, up to 14 cm. long. Bolivia (Arani province).

E. tubiflora (Pfeiff.) Zucc.
Diameter up to 12 cm. Radial spines 7-9. Central spines 1-3. Spines yellow, black-tipped. Flowers white, 20 cm. long, nocturnal. Argentina (Tucuman, Catamarca, Salta).

Echinopsis hybrids

Encephalocarpus strobiliformis

Epiphyllum hybrid 'Frau H.M. Wegener'.
Epiphyllum hybrids are also known as
Phyllocacti

Epiphyllum hybrid 'Mae Marsh'

Epiphyllum hybrid 'Pfersdorffii'

Epiphyllanthus obovatus

Encephalocarpus Berger 1929
(Greek en = in, kephale = head,
karpos = fruit)

Leaf-like tubercles with keel below,
closely appressed like fir-cone scales.
Spines frail. The flowers are produced
from the areoles of the youngest
tubercles which are furrowed above.
Fruit dry. 1 species. Native to Mexico
(Tamaulipas).

E. strobiliformis (Werderm.) Berger
(*Pelecyphora s.* (Werderm.) Frič &
Schelle)
Plant 4-6 cm. wide. Spines very small.
Flowers violet-red, 3-4 cm. wide.
Difficult to cultivate. Mainly mineral,
permeable soil with loam, hot position
in summer and complete dryness in
winter.

Eomatucana Ritter see *Matucana*

168

Epiphyllanthus Berger 1905
(Greek epi = on, phyllon = leaf, anthos = flower)

These plants consist of elongated segments or pads like Opuntias, round or flattened in cross-section, bearing areoles on the surface. The bi-laterally symmetrical flowers have a very short tube, are located at the end of the segments and feature bare scales. The stamens project out of the flower and form a distinct nectar chamber at their base. The fruit is round in cross-section. 3 species. Native to Brazil (Rio de Janeiro, Sao Paulo, Minas Gerais).

E. obovatus (Engelm.) Br. & R.
(*Schlumbergera opuntioides* (Loefgr. & Dusén) Hunt)
Segments up to 3 cm. thick and 2-6 cm. long. Areoles white, felty and with very fine spines. Flowers purple, about 4.5 cm. long. Brazil (Rio de Janeiro, Sao Paulo, Minas Gerais).

Epiphyllopsis Berger see *Schlumbergera*

Epithelantha micromeris

Epiphyllum Haw. 1812
(*Marniera*) leaf cactus
(Greek epi = on, phyllon = leaf)

Epiphytic plants with flat, leaf-like, spineless stems and nocturnal flowers with elongated tube. The small flowers are borne laterally and feature scales with bare or bristly axils. The fleshy berries eventually dehisce. The seedling is strongly curved and has flat, fleshy cotyledons. 17 species. Native from Mexico via Central America to Argentina.

Cultivation in a moist, heated greenhouse. Soil mixture as for *Nopalxochia*.

E. chrysocardium Alex. (*Marniera c.* (Alex.) Backeb.)
Stems serrate forming broad lobes, indented as far as the midrib, up to 30 cm. wide. Lobes 4 cm. wide. Areoles sometimes with 2-3 bristles. Outer flower petals dirty purple-pink, inner ones white. Flowers 32 cm. long. Mexico (Chiapas).

E. oxypetalum (DC.) Haw.
Stems deeply notched, up to 12 cm. wide. Outer flower petals reddish, inner ones white. Flowers 25-30 cm. long and up to 12 cm. wide, with unpleasant smell. Mexico, Guatemala, Venezuela to Brazil.

Epiphyllum hybrids see page 249

Epithelantha (Web.) Br. & R. 1922
(Greek epi = on, thele = nipple, anthos = flower)

Small tubercle cacti with very dense, short spines, similar to many Mammillarias. The flowers are close to the crown and grow from the tips of the tubercles, not from the axils. The fruit is a red berry with black seed. According to Glass and Foster there is only 1 species with 6 varieties. Native to USA (S. Texas), Mexico (Coahuila, Nuevo León).

E. micromeris (Engelm.) Web.
Globular, flattened at the crown, up to 6 cm. thick, with tubercles 1-3 mm. long. Spines numerous, mostly white and less than 3 mm. long, but densely covering the body. In mature plants the upper spines are up to 8 mm. long and have a gland at the tip, later falling off. Flowers white to pink, up to 1 cm. wide, with few petals and stamens.

Erdisia Br. & R. see *Corryocactus*

Eriocactus Backeb. see *Notocactus*

Eriocereus (Berger) Riccob. 1909
(*Roseocereus*)
(Greek erion = wool)

Slender-stemmed, usually climbing columnar cacti with 3-10 ribs. Flowers borne towards the end of the stems, with elongated tube, 12-25 cm. long, externally scaly and spiny/woolly or just woolly, nocturnal. In contrast to the similar genus *Harrisia*, *Eriocereus* features a distinctly recessed ring of throat stamens. The red berries eventually dehisce; the seed contains no air cavity. 11 species. Native to N.E. Brazil, Uruguay, Paraguay, N. Argentina, S.E. Bolivia.

169

Eriocereus bonplandii

E. bonplandii (Parment.) Riccob. (*Harrisia b.* (Parment.) Br. & R.)
Decumbent to climbing. Stems blue-green, later grey, up to about 3 m. long and 3-8 cm. thick, with (3-) 4-7 low ribs. Spines 3-8 (-10), initially red, later grey, up to 4 cm. long. Flowers white, externally brownish-green, up to 25 cm. long and 20 cm. wide. Brazil, Paraguay, Argentina.

The flowers are self-fertile and the brilliant red fruits, up to 6 cm. in diameter, provide a dash of colour for months on end. The species is completely undemanding, flowers from a height of only 1 m., and is recommended to anybody who has the space for it.

E. jusbertii (Rebut) Riccob.
Mainly solitary. Stems dark green, 4-6 cm. thick, with 5 (-6) low ribs. Radial spines about 7 and 1-4 similar central spines. Spines dark grey to almost black, thick and conical, up to 0.5 cm. long and very distinctive. Flowers white, externally greenish, about 15 cm. long. Said to come from Argentina or Paraguay, but no natural location is known, therefore widely considered to be a hybrid.

This species is generally known as a rootstock for grafting, and flowers from a height of only 20 cm. The plant is self-fertile and *E. jusbertii* plants grown from seed always come true to type. Even if pollen from another species is placed on the stigma no hybrids result. The plants like temperatures above 10°C in winter.

E. martinii (Lab.) Riccob. (*Harrisia m.* (Lab.) Br. & R.)
Stems sprawling, green to grey-green, up to 2 m. long and 2-5 cm. thick with 4-5 wide ribs. Radial spines usually 5-7, very short. 1 central spine, light brown, darker top and bottom, 2-3 cm. long. Flowers white, externally light green, about 20 cm. long. Argentina (Chaco).

E. tortuosus (Forb.) Riccob (*Harrisia t.* (Forb.) Br. & R.)
Bushy, decumbent. Stems up to 1 m. long, 2-4 cm. thick, dark purple-green with 5-7 rounded ribs with sharp furrows. Radial spines 5-10, up to 2 cm. long. Central spines 1-3, initially reddish-brown, 3-4 cm. long. Flowers white, 16 cm. long. Argentina (Buenos Aires).

This plant flowers abundantly, and can be grown on a trellis in the greenhouse. It is also a useful grafting stock if you can provide warm cultural conditions for it.

Eriosyce Phil. 1872
(*Rodentiophila* n. n. Ritter)
(Greek erion = wool, sykon = fig)

These large globular cacti produce flowers with a spiny and hairy tube. The flowers tend to grow laterally on specially formed areoles. The fruit is a very typical hollow type. 7 species. Native to Chile, Argentina.

Culture similar to *Neoporteria*. The seed are reluctant to germinate.

E. ceratistes (Otto) Br. & R.
Up to 50 cm. thick and 1 m. tall, with 20 to about 35 ribs, white, woolly at the crown. Up to 20 spines, strong, often curved like a claw, variously coloured, often yellow, later brownish, 2.5-3.5 cm. long. Flowers yellow to

carmine red, 4 cm. long and up to 3.5 cm. wide. Chile (North of Santiago de Chile, Argentina.

E. ihotzkyana Ritter
Up to 40 cm. tall and thick, with up to 37 ribs. Radial spines around 8-12, usually 2-4 cm. long. Central spines usually 2-7. Spines very sturdy, grey-black to honey yellow. Flowers purple with whitish or pale yellow margins. 3-4 cm. long. Chile (Coquimbo).

E. rodentiophila Ritter (*Rodentiophila atacamensis* n.n. Ritter)
Body up to 32 cm. wide and 70 cm. tall, with 19-35 ribs. Radial spines 12-15. Central spines 5-12. All spines often very brightly coloured when young, whitish/light red or brownish. Flowers light purple with wide, pale yellowish-green margins, 3.5-4 cm. long. Chile (Antofagasta).

Erythrorhipsalis Berger 1920
(Greek erythros = red)

Stems cylindrical, with 8-10 indistinct ribs. Flowers usually terminal, with very short tube, externally slightly scaly and bristly/woolly. 1 species. Native to Brazil (Sao Paulo, Rio de Janeiro).

Erythrorhipsalis pilocarpa

E. pilocarpa (Loefgr.) Berger
Usually whorled, bushy and pendant.
Stems dirty grey-green, 3-12 cm. long
and 0.3-0.6 cm. thick. Spines 3-10,
bristle-like, greyish. Flowers white to
pale yellow, up to 2.5 cm. wide.

The scented flowers usually appear
around Christmas.

Escobaria Br. & R. 1923
(After Romulo and Numa Escobar,
Mexico 19/20th century)

Cacti with furrowed tubercles and
flowers borne in the axils. The flowers
are scaly and the seed have a smaller
aril than *Neobesseya,* whose seed is also
grooved black or dark brown. The
fruit bear many small tubercles at all
stages, eventually becoming woody. 12
species. Native to Mexico, USA (W.
Texas, Arizona, New Mexico).

As the genus can only be distinguished
by its seed and fruit, several species
are also known under the name of
Coryphantha. The plants are relatively
small and like a mineral soil and
plenty of sun.

E. bella Br. & R.
Stems cylindrical, clustering when old,
up to 8 cm. long. Brownish gland in
the areole furrow. Radial spines up to

Escobaria roseana

Escobaria tuberculosa

15, whitish, up to 1 cm. long. Central
spines 3-5, brown, 1-2.5 cm. long.
Flowers white or pink, almost 2 cm.
wide. USA (Texas).

E. chaffeyi Br. & R.
Up to 12 cm. tall and 5-6 cm. wide.
Radial spines numerous, bristly, white.
Central spines one to several, brown-
or black-tipped, shorter. Flowers
yellowish-white with brownish central
stripe, 1.5 cm. long and 1 cm. wide.
Mexico (Zacatecas).

E. nellieae see *Coryphantha minima*

E. roseana (Bód.) Backeb.
Egg-shaped, up to 4 cm. tall and 3
cm. wide. Radial spines 15, up to 1.5
cm. long. Central spines 4-6, tending
to curve upward. All spines yellowish.
Flowers small, reddish-white. Mexico
(Coahuila).

E. tuberculosa (Engelm.) Br. & R.
Cylindrical, up to 18 cm. tall and 6
cm. wide. Radial spines 20-30, white,
0.5-1.5 cm. long. Central spines 5-9,
white with black tip, longer and
stronger. Flowers pink, externally

violet-pink, 2.5 cm. wide. USA (W.
Texas, S. New Mexico) to N. Mexico.

Escontria Rose 1906 emend. Bravo
(*Anisocereus* p. p.)
(after the Mexican Don Blas Excontria)

Tree-form columnar cacti with 7-9
ribs. Flowers produced towards the
end of the stems, with dense external
covering of leathery or papery scales
like roof-tiles, bristly/felty or bare,
diurnal, yellow, 3-7 cm. long, with
nectar chamber. 2 species. Native to
Mexico (Puebla to Oaxaca),
Guatemala.

Espostoa Br. & R. 1920 emend.
Werderm. (*Pseudoespostoa*)
(after N. E. Esposto, botanist at Lima,
Peru, 20th century)

Bushy or tree-shaped columnar cacti
with 18-30 ribs, white, woolly and as if
enclosed in spun wool. Flowers lateral
in a ring cephalium, funnel-shaped,
externally scaly and hairy, with
internal nectar chamber. Flowers
white, nocturnal, 4-8 cm. long. 13
species. Native to Ecuador, N. Peru.

Espostoa plants, usually completely
enveloped in hair, should only ever be
sprayed over with completely lime-free
water, otherwise ugly lime deposits will
build up on the hairs. They must also
be protected from dust and soiling.
Cultivation under glass, not below
10°C in Winter.

E. lanata (H. B. K.) Br. & R.
Candelabra- to tree-shaped. Stems
green, up to about 4 m. tall and up to
15 cm. thick in habitat, with 20-30 low
ribs. Radial spines about 12,
translucent yellow, yellowish-white or
reddish, short. Central spines (1)-2,
red-tipped, up to 8 cm. long. Areoles
with many white or pale yellow hairs,
1-2 cm. long, covering the body.
Flowers white, about 5-6 cm. long,
nocturnal. N. Peru.

There are many varieties and forms of
this species. All of them are very
beautiful even as seedlings and grow
very well. They like nutritious soil and

Espostoa lanata

Eulychnia ritteri

Eulychnia breviflora

constant slight moisture, except for in winter. Unfortunately there is little hope of the plants flowering.

E. mirabilis Ritter
Bushy to tree-shaped. Stems up to several metres tall and 9 cm. thick. Spines white or reddish, inter-woven and projecting, individual spines like hairs. Flowers 5.5 cm. long. N. Peru. Seedlings initially form a ring of bristles at the base, like *Thrixanthocereus blossfeldianus*.

Espostoopsis Buxb.
see *Austrocephalocereus*

Eulychnia Phil. 1860
(Philippicereus)
(Greek eu = well; lychnos = torch)

Tree-like or bushy columnar cacti. Flowers borne at the stem ends, with very short or virtually absent tube,

with dense scales, bristly/spiny, woolly or felty externally, 2-7.5 cm. long 27 species. Native to S. Peru, N. Chile.

Eulychnias make no special cultural demands. Even young plants are very beautiful, with their white felty areoles and long woolly hairs.

E. breviflora Phil. (*E. spinibarbis* Br. & R.)
Bushy. Stems up to 3 m. tall and 6-10 cm. thick, with 10-13 ribs. Radial spines 10-22, up to 3 cm. long. Central spines 3-6, up to 15 cm. long. Spines dark brown, soon turning grey. Flowers light pink to white, 7-8 cm. long. Chile (Coquimbo).

E. ritteri Cullm.
Tree-like or bushy, densely branched. Stems up to 4 m. tall and 6-8 cm. thick with 13-20 ribs. Radial spines around 12, brownish, 0.5-2 cm. long. Central spines 1-4, black, 3-8 cm.

172

long. Areoles almost touching, with long grey-white woolly felt. Flowers pink, hardly opening, about 2 cm. long and 1.5 cm. wide. Peru (Arequipa).

E. saint-pieana Ritter
Bushy or tree-shaped, 2-4 m. tall, stems 7-10 cm. thick with 10-15 ribs. Radial spines about 8-12. 1 central spine, 2.5-10 cm. long. Spines dark brown, soon turning grey. Areoles with long, projecting, snow-white woolly hairs and pale grey felt. Flowers white, sometimes with pink central lines, 6-7.5 cm. long and 5-7.5 cm. wide. N. Chile (Atacama).

Facheiroa Br. & R. 1920
(facheiro = Brazilian name for certain cacti)

Tree-shaped columnar cacti with 15-32 ribs. Flowers borne in a lateral grooved cephalium, externally scaly and densely hairly, nocturnal, white or pink, 3-4.5 cm. long. 2 species. Native to Brazil (Bahia, Minas Gerais).

Ferocactus Br. & R. 1922
(*Hamatocactus*)
(lat. ferox = strongly armed, wild)

This genus has very characteristic flowers. They have a very short tube and are covered in broad, bare scales. Between the stamens and the innermost flower petals there is often a ring of hairs, and the style is very thick. The flowers are 2-7 cm. long, red, yellow or violet, and are produced close to the crown. Although the flowers are unique, this is not the feature for which Ferocacti are noted; the obvious characteristic of the genus is that it embraces giant, barrel-shaped globular cacti, as does the related genus *Echinocactus*. When old they are often elongated into columnar forms, 3-4 m. in height. The spines are strong and very variable in form. There are usually 4, rarely 1 or 8 central spines which are subulate, flattened, smooth or transversely ringed, twisted or hooked and sometimes very brightly coloured. Often there are spine-like glands on the areoles which secrete nectar.

39 species. Native to S. USA (California, Utah, Nevada, Arizona, New Mexico, Texas), Mexico, Guatemala.

In the plants' homeland small pieces of the stem are cut off, candied and eaten. Because of their bright, very distinctive spines, and especially the powerful, hooked central spines, Ferocacti are extremely popular. Although they do grow very large they are suitable for cultivation as they grow very slowly. Large plants may well be 200 years old, so there is no need to worry that your plants will grow too large in a short time.

Ferocacti require plenty of loam in the soil. Strong sunshine is essential if they are to produce the typical brightly-coloured spine formation. In the vegetative period they should only be watered moderately. In winter they should be kept dry and the temperature not allowed to fall below 8°C. A few species from lower California such as *F. latispinus* are sensitive and must be kept warm in winter. Others, including *F. setispinus*, are extremely tolerant. Raising the plants from seed is possible. The young plants look splendid with their relatively outsized spines.

F. acanthodes (Lem.) Br. & R.
Thick columns, up to 3 m. tall when old, with 13 to about 27 ribs. Radial spines 9-13. Central spines 1-4, flattened, often curved, up to 12 cm. long. All spines red with white and yellow or only yellow. Flowers yellow to orange, 4-6 cm. long. Bears flowers even when young. Mexico (lower California).

F. chrysacanthus (Orcutt) Br. & R.
Body globular to cylindrical, up to about 1 m. tall and 30-40 cm. wide, with 13-22 ribs. Radial spines 4-6, bristly, white. Central spines 4-10, curved, yellow or red, up to 7 cm. long. Areoles with nectar glands. Flowers yellow, about 3 cm. long and 5 cm. wide. Mexico (lower California).

F. emoryi (Engelm.) Backeb. (*F. covillei* Br. & R.)

Flowers with long, thin tube and widely spread margin (nectar glands on young areoles, central spines hooked)
    Radial spines thin, rather weak. Central spines 1 (-3), up to 4 cm. long   *F. setispinus*
    Radial spines more or less like needles. Central spines 4, one up to 12 cm. long
                                                    F. hamatacanthus
Flowers broad, bell-shaped
  Spines very variable; radial spines fine, hairy or bristly, central spines powerful
    Central spines: one half-round, flattened and exceptionally strong   *F. peninsulae*
    Central spines: lacking a half-round, flattened, exceptionally strong one
      Flowers greenish-yellow. Spines more or less straight (body grey-green)
                                         F. viridescens
      Flowers yellow to orange-carmine. Spines more or less hooked
        Radial spines 15-20. Central spines about 4, distinctly transversely ringed
                                      F. wislizenii
        Radial spines 4-14
          Radial spines 4-6. Central spines 4-10   *F. chrysacanthus*
          Radial spines 9-14
             Central spines 1-4. Flowers yellow to orange   *F. acanthodes*
             Central spines 9 (-11). Flowers yellow with red central stripe   *F. gracilis*
  Spines lacking hairy or bristly radial spines, radial and central spines all like needles
    Flowers yellow
      Central spines more or less identical to the radial spines or absent (body blue-green)
                                        F. glaucescens
      Central spines very noticeably thicker than radial spines
        Ribs about 8. Forming colonies   *F. robustus*
        Ribs about 24. Individual globes   *F. histrix*
    Flowers white, pink, red-orange or red
      Areoles with one central spine, up to 8 mm wide, flat   *F. latispinus*
      Areoles lacking a wide, flat central spine
        Central spine 1, straight to hooked. Ribs initially bumpy   *F. emoryi*
        Central spines 4, at most curved. Ribs slightly notched, sharp-edged
         Body soon cylindrical, clustering   *F. stainesii*
         Body compressed globular   *F. macrodiscus*

Ferocactus glaucescens

Ferocactus setispinus

Body globular-cylindrical, up to 2.5 m. tall, with 22-32 ribs. Radial spines 5-8, central spines 1, transversely ringed, straight to hooked. All spines red. Flowers yellow-red, 6 cm. long. USA (S. Arizona), Mexico (Sonora).

F. glaucescens (DC.) Br. & R.
Globes 30-50 cm. in diameter, blue-green, with 11-15 ribs. Radial spines 6-7, transversely ringed, yellow. Central spines 1 or absent, straight. All spines yellow and about 3 cm. long. Flowers yellow, 3-3.5 cm. long. E. Mexico.

F. gracilis Gates
Body cylindrical, up to 1 m. tall and 30 cm. thick, with 13-20 ribs. Radial spines 10-14, thin, yellowish-white. Central spines 9 (-11), red and transversely ringed, one occasionally curved to hooked at the end, 6-7 cm. long. Flowers straw-yellow with red central stripe, about 4 cm. long. Mexico (lower California).

var. coloratus (Gates) Linds. (*F.c.* Gates) Central spine not curved.

F. hamatacanthus (Mühlpf.) Br. & R. (*Hamatocactus h.* (Mühlpf.) Br. & R.) Globular, somewhat elongated when old, up to 60 cm. tall and 30 cm.

thick, with about 13-17 ribs. Radial spines 8-12, brown to grey. Central spines 4, semi-cylindrical, partially ringed, the lower one acute and hooked, up to 12 cm. long. There are nectar glands on the young areoles, 2-4 mm. long, which later turn into thorns. Flowers light yellow, occasionally with red throat, up to 7 cm. long. USA (Texas, Arizona, New Mexico), Mexico (Chihuahua to Puebla).

F. histrix (DC.) Linds.
Large globes, up to 70 cm. tall and with about 24 ribs. Radial spines 7-12. Central spines 3-4, up to 6 cm. long. All spines thin, amber to brown. Flowers light yellow, up to 3.5 cm. long. E. Mexico.

F. latispinus (Haw.) Br. & R.
Broad globular, up to 40 cm. in diameter, with 15-23 ribs. Radial spines 6-12. Central spines 4, the bottom one up to 8 mm. wide and hooked. All spines pale reddish to light brown, up to 3.5 cm. long. Flowers whitish to pink or purple, 3.5 cm. long. Mexico.

F. macrodiscus (Mart.) Br. & R.
Flattened globular, up to almost 50

174

cm. in diameter, with 16-21 ribs. Radial spines 6-8. Central spines 4, curved. Spines yellow to red, up to 3.5 cm. long. Flowers dark red to purple or carmine red, with dark central stripe. 5 cm. long. Mexico (San Luis Potosí to Oaxaca).

F. peninsulae (Web.) Br. & R. (*F. horridus* Br. & R.)
Body initially globular, later columnar, up to 2.5 m. tall and 50 cm. thick, with 13-21 ribs. Radial spines about 11, up to 3 cm. long, the upper ones

thin, white and straight, the lower ones acute, slightly ringed, red, later grey. Central spines 5-8, the bottom one hooked and acute, 6-7 cm. long. Flowers yellow or purple with carmine red central stripe, about 4.5-6 cm. long. Mexico (Lower California).

F. robustus (Link & Otto) Br. & R.
Forming colonies, individual heads up to 20 cm. wide, with 8 ribs. Radial spines 10 to about 14, upper ones bristly, yellowish, lower ones like needles. Central spines 4 (-6), often

flattened, initially brown or red, up to 6 cm. long. Flowers yellow, about 4 cm. long. Mexico (Puebla).

F. setispinus (Engelm.) L. Bens. (*Hamatocactus s.* (Engelm.) Br. & R.)
Globular, more elongated when old, up to 15 cm. tall and 10 cm. wide, with 13, often more or less wavy, very bumpy ribs. Radial spines 6-16, fine, white or brown. Central spines 1 (-3), hooked, up to 4 cm. long. Nectar glands on young areoles. Flowers yellow with red centre, up to 7 cm. long. USA (Texas), N. Mexico.

This species is very popular among cactus growers. It flowers when young and likes nutritious soil and plenty of sunshine.

F. stainesii (Hook.) Br. & R.
Body soon cylindrical and clustering, up to 3 m. tall and 60 cm. wide, with 15- 20 ribs. Radial spines 4-6. Central spines 4, transversely ringed, flattened, curved but not hooked. Spines reddish to pure carmine, up to 4 cm. long. In addition to the spines the areoles bear many white bristly hairs and a short gland thorn. Flowers orange-red, 4 cm. long. Flowers easily from a height of only 20 cm. Mexico (San Luis Potosí).

var. haematacanthus (Salm-Dyck) Backeb.
Has purple-red or flame-red flowers, 6 cm. long.

var. pilosus (Gal.) Backeb.
Has copious white hairs on the areoles.

F. viridescens (Torrey & A. Gray) Br. & R.
Body more or less globular, up to 45 cm. tall and 35 cm. thick, with 13-21 ribs. Radial spines 9-20, about 2 cm. long. Central spines 4, flattened underneath, some of them slightly curved, up to 3.5 cm. long. Flowers yellowish-green, 3-4 cm. long. USA (S. California), Mexico (N. lower California).

F. wislizenii (Engelm.) Br. & R.
Thick columns up to 2 m. tall and with 15-25 ribs. Radial spines 15-20, bristly. Central spines about 4, flattened and ringed, one hooked, up to 5 cm. long. Spines brownish to

Ferocactus latispinus

Ferocactus stainesii

175

Frailea sp.

reddish. Flowers yellow to orange, 5-6 cm. long. USA (Texas to Arizona), N. Mexico (Chihuahua, Sonora to ?lower California).

Floribunda Ritter see *Pilosocereus*

Frailea Br. & R. 1922
(after Manuel Fraile, born in 1850, an American cactus grower from Washington)

The genus *Frailea* consists of dwarf cacti which usually grow to a diameter of up to 3 cm. and a height of 5-8 cm. The bodies are elongated to compressed globular, with 10-33 warty ribs. The flowers are borne close to the crown, 1.8-4 cm. long, yellow, scaly and bristly/woolly. The genus is difficult to distinguish from *Parodia* and *Notocactus*. 35 species. Native to Brazil, Uruguay, Paraguay, Argentina, Bolivia, Colombia.

Fraileas are small, pretty plants which make no special cultural demands, and can be recommended to amateurs. They can also form the basis for a specialized collection if space is limited. Interesting new finds have increased interest in the genus in recent years. The plants like a slightly acid soil, even levels of moisture and a warm location not in full sun, as they usually stand amongst grass and scrub in their natural habitat. Full sunshine is only required at flowering time, otherwise the flowers do not open fully. Even so, plenty of fertile seed are formed if the flowers do not open. The flowers are cleistogamous, i.e. they pollinate themselves as buds. Many Fraileas do not flower until late summer or autumn. Raising them from seed is easy, but the seed must be fresh, as they soon lose their power to germinate.

Body almost spineless (ribbed)
                   F. asteroides
Body spiny
  Spines approx. 5, very short, up to 2 mm. long   *F. cataphracta*
  Spines 6 or more
    Spines tortuous (radial spines about 14, central spine 1)   *F. curvispina*
    Spines partially projecting (Radial spines 15-20, central spines 3-6)
                  F. horstii
  Spines more or less appressed
    Ribs 13-21 (spines white, 6-14)
                 F. pygmaea
  Ribs modified into 10-13 rows of fairly low tubercles
    Radial spines initially yellow, 9-11   *F. grahliana*
    Radial spines blackish, (10-) 12-14. Central spine 1 *F. schilinzkyana*

F. asteroides Werderm. (*F. castanea* Backeb.)
About 3 cm. wide with 10-15 ribs. Body red-brown, similar to a small sea-urchin. Spines scarcely visible. Flowers pale yellow, about 4 cm. wide. N. Uruguay, Brazil (Rio Grande do Sul).

F. cataphracta (Dams) Br. & R.
Up to 4 cm. wide with about 15 rows of bumps. Body usually dirty dark red, with red, brown or violet spots under the areoles. Radial spines 5, golden yellow, later greyish, up to 0.2 cm. long. Central spine absent. Flowers light yellow, about 4 cm. wide. Paraguay.

F. curvispina Buin. & Bred.
Up to 5 cm. tall and 3 cm. wide, with about 32 warty ribs. Body slightly grey-green. Spines tortuous, dense whitish to yellowish, translucent. Radial spines about 14, 0.4-0.6 cm. long. Central spine 1. Flowers yellow, up to 3 cm. in size. Brazil (Rio Grande do Sul).

F. grahliana (Haage jr.) Br. & R.
Body bluish-green, 3-4 cm. wide, with low tubercles in about 13 rows. Spines 9-11, curved, initially yellow, less than 0.5 cm. long. Flowers yellow, about 4 cm. wide and long. Paraguay, Argentina (Misiones).

F. horstii Ritter
Body 2-2.5 cm. thick and up to 18 cm. long, with 20-33 ribs. Radial spines 15-20. Central spines 3-6, brown. Flowers about 4 cm. long and 5 cm. wide. Brazil (Rio Grande do Sul).

Frailea asteroides

Frailea sp.

F. pygmaea (Spegazz.) Br. & R.
Body up to about 3 cm. in diameter, 13-31 ribs, dirty to slightly grey-green. Spines 6-14, usually all appressed, white, 1-4 mm. long. Flowers yellow, 2-5 cm. long. Highly variable species. Uruguay, Brazil (Rio Grande do Sul), Argentina (Entre Rios).

F. schilinzkyana (Haage jr.) Br. & R.
Body light green, 2-4 cm. wide, with 10-13 rows of low tubercles. Radial spines (10-) 12-14, blackish, curving back and appressed, 2-3 mm. long. Central spine 1. Flowers sulphur yellow, up to 3.5 cm. long, seldom opening. Paraguay, Argentina (Misiones).

Glandulicactus Backeb. see *Ancistrocactus*

Grusonia F. Reichenb. see *Opuntia*

Gymnanthocereus Backeb. see *Browningia*

Gymnocactus Backeb. see *Neolloydia* and *Thelocactus*

Gymnocalycium Pfeiff. 1845
(*Brachycalycium*)
(Greek gymnos = naked, kalyx = calyx)

The genus *Gymnocalycium* is easily recognized by its flowers, whose ovary and tube bear very large, blunt, membranous scales with completely bare axils. The only other genera in which similar scales occur are *Weingartia* and *Neowerdermannia*. The flowers of *Weingartia* are a deep yellow or violet in colour and very short-tubed, while the spines of *Neowerdermannia* are located in the depressions between the tubercles. Gymnocalyciums usually have pink or white flowers, but sometimes they are yellow. The very scaly flowers and distinctive external form were soon noticed by early researchers, and *Gymnocalycium* was one of the first globular cactus genera to be established in 1845. Even without flowers Gymnocalyciums are usually easy to distinguish. The body is generally squat globular to compressed disc-shaped, and almost always has rounded ribs. Virtually all species feature lateral furrows between the areoles.

Approx. 90 species. The genus *Gymnocalycium* occurs in Bolivia, Paraguay, Uruguay, and far South into Brazil towards Argentina. This is a gigantic area, and it no surprise to find that the genus is very wide-ranging in form. At one extreme we have the large examples based around *G. saglionis*, at the other the small plants based around *G. mihanovichii*. The Gymnocalyciums are among the most rewarding of cacti. With their large, beautiful flowers and their defiantly wild spine formations they are very popular among cactus growers. They only fail if you make very basic errors in cultivation. Once they have reached a certain minimum size they flower profusely and reliably.

Since the conditions which prevail in the widespread habitat are bound to be highly variable, the cultural requirements of Gymnocalyciums are not completely uniform. In general terms they thrive well in soil containing some loam and humus. Many species are sensitive to stagnant moisture, hence the soil should be permeable. Care should also be taken that the soil is acid, i.e. that it has an acid pH value. In alkaline soil the plants often turn yellowish and appear chlorotic. If this should happen, stand the pot for one hour in water acidified to a value of pH 4-5.

Gymnocalyciums usually grow in grassland, and as a result they are usually content with a half-shaded position. Those species with less dense spines should be sheltered from excessively hot sun, especially in the spring, otherwise they may sustain ugly scorch marks. The species from central and N.W. Argentina such as the robust *G. gibbosum* will tolerate fairly low winter temperatures, but those from Uruguay, Paraguay and South Brazil must be kept warmer. Most Gymnocalyciums thrive well on their own roots. The group based around the dwarf *G. mihanovichii* is more difficult. These plants are better grafted, preferably on a slow-growing stock in accordance with their own slow rate of growth.

The clustering species are very easy to propagate by means of offsets, but Gymnocalyciums are also ideal for raising from seed. The seed take about 3-4 weeks to germinate; many species, such as the permanently small *G. andreae*, *G. baldianum* and *G. bruchii*, flower when only 2-3 years old. Most species are self-sterile, but develop fruit and seed reliably and rapidly after artificial fertilization with the pollen of another plant. Hybrids between many species are easily

Small species of Gymnocalycium in flower: G. andreae, G. baldianum, G. bruchii and hybrids.

achieved, but the resultant plants are rarely more beautiful or easier to cultivate than the wild species.

A very wide variety of different flowers is produced within the genus. The ovary may be rounded to narrow and elongated. The majority of species have a distinct nectar chamber, which is enclosed by the bottom stamens. In a number of cases the stamens are divided into two groups. The stigma lobes also take very different forms; recessed or not recessed, erect or more rarely pointing down. Buxbaum and Frank sub-divided the genus almost exclusively according to the various seed types. The resultant 12 groups are indicated by numbers in the individual species descriptions, in order to distinguish between closely related species. Another division into 5

sub-genera, also almost entirely based on the seed, was set up by Schütz:

Sub-genus *Gymnocalycium* (G)
Seed black, 1-3 mm. in diameter, more or less round. Fruit green or greenish when ripe. Species from Uruguay and Paraguay.

Sub-genus *Ovatisemineum* (Ov)
Seed black, about 1 mm. in diameter, semi-circular, thicker at the hilum end. Fruit mostly greyish or bluish when ripe

Sub-genus *Microsemineum* (Mic)
Seed black or brown, usually only 0.1-0.5 mm. in diameter. Fruit green, grey or blue when ripe

Sub-genus *Trichosemineum* (Tr)
Seed glossy brown, up to 1 mm. in length, mussel-shaped. Fruit blue-grey when ripe

Gymnocalycium andreae

Gymnocalycium cardenasianum

Gymnocalycium baldianum

Gymnocalycium bruchii

Sub-genus *Muscosemineum* (Mus)
Seed light brown, up to 1 mm. in diameter, semi-circular. Fruit usually red when ripe. Outer skin red or red-brown, especially when young

(Ov; 3) **G. andreae** (Bód.) Backeb.
Dark blue-green, often with a bronze-coloured sheen, clustering, 4.5-5 cm. wide. Ribs only about 8. Radial spines (5-) 7, short. Central spines 1-3. Flowers sulphur-yellow, 3 cm. long. Argentina (Córdoba).

A popular and robust species which flowers profusely and readily even as a young plant.

(Mus) **G. anisitsii** (K. Schum.) Br. & R.
Body glossy green to leaf green, seldom clustering, 7-10 cm. wide. Spines 5-7 (- 9), acute, variously curved, the top one up to 6 cm. long. Flowers white, 4-5 cm. long and wide. Paraguay.

(Ov; 3) **G. baldianum** (Spegazz.) Spegazz.
Dark grey to blue-green, up to 7 cm. wide. Radial spines 5-7. Flowers light red to dark red, 3-5 cm. long. Argentina (Catamarca).

One of the most beautiful and rewarding species.

(Mic; 4) **G. bicolor** Schütz
Dark green, up to 15 cm. wide. Radial spines around 11, 2-3 of them

pointing downward, of similar size and colour to the central spine, others thinner and whitish. Central spine 1, blue-grey. The flowers are white (or pink), 4 cm. long. Argentina (Córdoba).

(8; Tr) **G. bodenbenderianum** (Hoss.) Berger
Brownish to grey-green, up to 8 cm. wide. Radial spines 3-5, appressed, short and thin. Flowers pink or white with pink throat, 3.5 cm. long. Argentina (Córdoba and La Rioja).

(Ov; 2) **G. bruchii** (Spegazz.) Hoss. (*G. lafaldense* Vaupel)
Dark green, clustering, 3 (-6) cm. wide. Radial spines 10-12. Central spines 0-3. Spines short and appressed to long and projecting. Flowers pale pink, 3 cm. long. Argentina (Córdoba).

The delicate pink flowers appear in the early spring, even on small plants. Several forms have been defined according to the spine formation, which is very variable. The species is easily propagated from offsets.

(Mic; 3) **G. calochlorum** (Bód.) Y. Ito
Glossy light green, slightly clustering, up to 6 cm. wide. Radial spines up to 9, appressed. Flowers pale pink or white with pink throat, up to 6 cm. long. Argentina (Córdoba).

(Mic; 3) **G. capillaense** (Schick) Backeb.
Bluish-green, clustering, 8-9 cm. wide. Radial spines about 5, thin and

Gymnocalycium denudatum hybrid

Gymnocalycium denudatum

Gymnocalycium gibbosum

Gymnocalycium horridispinum

appressed. Flowers delicate pink-white, up to 7 cm. long. Fruit light blue when ripe. Argentina (Córdoba).

(Mic; 10) **G. cardenasianum** Ritter
Grey-green, up to 28 cm. wide. Radial spines 3-6. Central spines absent or 1-2. Spines usually curved and interwoven and about 4 cm. long. Flowers pink to white, 5 cm. long. Bolivia (Tarija).

(Mus; 12B) **G. damsii** (K. Schum.) Br. & R.
Green to copper-brown, depending on time of year, with fairly sharp ribs. Spines 2-6, projecting. Flowers white to pink and wine-red in the throat, up to 6.5 cm. long. N. Paraguay.

(G; 1B) **G. denudatum** (Link & Otto) Pfeiff.
Usually glossy dark green, up to 15 cm. wide, with only 5-8 ribs. Radial spines 5 (-8), thin and more or less appressed. Flowers glossy pure white (seldom pink), external green central stripe, 5-7 cm. long. N.E. Argentina (Misiones), S.E. Brazil (Rio Grande do sul) and N. Uruguay.

A popular plant with distinctive spines appressed to the body, looking like a mass of spiders.

(G; 1) **G. fleischerianum** Backeb.
Body glossy light green, sometimes clustering, up to 10 cm. wide. Tubercles lack lateral furrow. Radial spines about 20, radiating, like flexible bristles. Flowers white with pink throat, 4 cm. long. Paraguay.

(Ov; 1) **G. gibbosum** (Haw.) Pfeiff.
Generally dark blue-green, up to 15 cm. wide and up to 60 cm. tall. Radial spines 7-10 (-14). Central spines (0-) 1-3 (-5). Spines standing out like needles, flowers whitish, occasionally reddish, up to 6.5 cm. long. Fruit almost black when young. S. Argentina (La Plata, Mendoza, San Luis).

A very robust, tolerant species.

(Mic; 9) **G. horridispinum** G. Frank
Dark green, up to 8 cm. wide and more or less columnar. Radial spines 10-12. Central spines 4. Spines rigid and projecting, metallic grey with brownish tips, flowers white with pink

margins or entirely purple-pink, 6 cm. long. Argentina (Córdoba).

(Mic) **G. horstii** Buin.
Fresh glossy green, up to 11 cm. wide. Ribs only 5-6, sometimes slightly bumpy. Radial spines 5, projecting at an angle, up to 3 cm. long. Central spines absent. Flowers lilac-pink to cream-white, up to 11 cm. long and wide. Brazil (Rio Grande do Sul).

var. bueneckeri Buin.
With larger spines. Body dark green. Flowers dark pink.

(Mic) **G. hypobleurum** (K. Schum.) Backeb.
Body dull green or grey-green. Radial spines usually 9, curved back and inter-woven. Central spines absent. Flowers white to greenish-white with greenish-pink throat, up to about 4 cm. long. Argentina (Córdoba).

(G; 3) **G. hyptiacanthum** (Lem.) Br. & R.
Body dark green, up to 10 cm. wide. Radial spines 5-9, slightly curved back,

up to 1 cm. long. Central spines absent to 1. Flowers white to yellowish-white, 4.5-5 cm. long. Probably Argentina.

(G; 1A) **G. leeanum** (Hook.) Br. & R.
Bluish-green, about 7.5 cm. wide with more or less 6-sided tubercles, radial spines 5-10, appressed. Central spines 0 (-1). Flowers pale yellow, 4.5-5 cm. long. Uruguay and neighbouring Argentina.

(Mic; 3) **G. leptanthum** (Spegazz.) Spegazz.
Dark grey-green, 7 cm. wide. Radial spines 7 (-9), short and thin, appressed. Flowers white with reddish throat and narrow tube, 5 cm. long. Argentina (Córdoba).

(G; 1B) **G. megalothelos** (Sencke) Br. & R.
Bright light green to dark green, up to about 16 cm. wide. Radial spines 7-8, curved and appressed. Central spine 1. Flowers pink white or whitish, about 5 cm. long. Paraguay.

Gymnocalycium mihanovichii var. friedrichii 'Rubra'

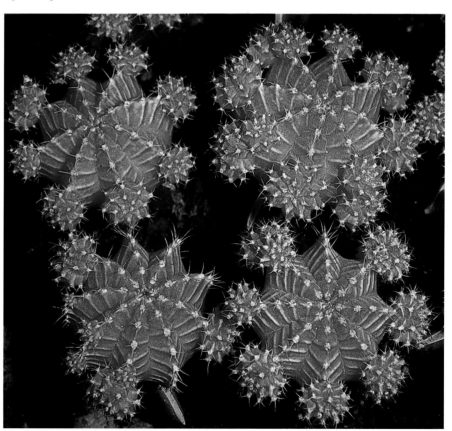

Gymnocalycium mihanovichii var. friedrichii 'Rubra'   Gymnocalycium mihanovichii var. friedrichii 'Aurea'

(Mus; 12B) **G. mihanovichii** (Frič & Gürke) Br. & R.
Grey-green or reddish green, usually 8 ribs, more or less cross-banded and sharp, up to 6 cm. wide. Radial spines usually 5 (-6). Flowers greenish outside, whitish, yellowish or pink inside, 4-5 cm. long. Paraguay.

A red mutation, 'Rubra', of the variety *friedrichii* Werderm. is available, and its existence is due to the attentiveness of the Japanese E. Watanabe. In 1941 two examples of this mutation appeared when 10,000 seeds were sown. They were brilliant light red, completely devoid of chlorophyll. Watanabe recognized the significance of these seedlings at once, and grafted them when they were tiny miniature globes. This was the only way they could be kept alive, as without chlorophyll photosynthesis is not possible. For this reason these plants must always be grown on a robust rootstock; they then produce shoots in profusion. They are easy to propagate, and are widespread and popular throughout the world. In 1970 a brilliant golden-yellow mutation cv. 'Aurea' of *G. mihanovichii* var. *friedrichii* appeared on the market, and in the meantime other coloured varieties have appeared.

(Mic) **G. monvillei** (Lem.) Br. & R.
Body glossy light green, solitary, up to about 30 cm. wide. Radial spines 7-13, curving upward and turning inward.

Central spines absent. Flowers white, flushed pink-red, up to 8 cm. long. Paraguay.

(Mic; 4) **G. mostii** (Gürke) Br. & R.
Dark (blue-) green, up to 13 cm. wide. Radial spines about 7, curved, 0.6-2.2 cm. long. Central spines 1 (-2). Flowers light salmon-pink to pink-red, up to 7.5 cm. long. Argentina (Córdoba).

var. kurzianum (Gürke) Backeb. (*G. kurzianum* Gürke) Br. & R.)

Gymnocalycium multiflorum

Spines curving strongly upward, 2.5-4 cm. long, white flowers with red throat, 7-8 cm. long. Argentina (Córdoba).

(Mic) **G. multiflorum** (Hook.) Br. & R.
Blue-green, up to 12 cm. wide. Radial spines 7-10, yellow, reddish (seldom white) at the base, more or less in comb-formation. Flowers (pink to) almost white, externally brownish-green, up to 4 cm. long. Argentina (Córdoba and San Luis).

A generally popular species, producing many large flowers.

(Mic) **G. nidulans** Backeb.
Body matt brown-green, solitary, up to 10 cm. wide. Radial spines about 6, one of them curving upward and projecting. Central spines absent or occasionally 1. Flowers pink-white with darker throat. N. Argentina.

(Mic; 4) **G. oenanthemum** Backeb.
Matt grey to blue-green, up to 10 cm. wide. Spines mostly 5-6, pink-grey. Flowers wine red to salmon pink, 4-5 cm. long. The fruit is almost blue, and formed by self-pollination. Argentina (Mendoza).

Gymnocalycium schickendantzii

Gymnocalycium guehlianum

(Mic; 11) **G. pflanzii** (Vaup.) Werderm.
Silky matt green to yellowish-green, up to 50 cm. wide in its habitat. Radial spines 6-9, curved. Central spine 1. Flowers white to salmon pink, slightly violet in the throat, 5 cm. long. Bolivia (Pilcomayo valley) to N. Argentina.

Very robust species, but does not flower until quite old.

var. zegarrae (Card.) Donald (*G. zegarrae* Card.)
Grey-green, 11-18 cm. wide. Flowers white to salmon-pink, 4-5 cm. long. S. Bolivia (Cochabamba).

(3) **G. platense** (Spegazz.) Br. & R.
Green to dark bluish-green, up to 10 cm. wide. Radial spines (5-) 7. Central spines absent. Flowers white with reddish throat, 5 cm. long. Argentina (Buenos Aires).

(Tr; 8) **G. quehlianum** (Haage jr.) Berger
Matt grey-green, usually tinged with reddish-brown, up to 7 cm. wide. Radial spines about 5, only 0.5-1 cm. long. Flowers white, often with reddish eye, 5-7 cm. long. Argentina (Córdoba).

(Tr; 8) **G. ragonesii** Castell.
Smoke-grey, 3-4 cm. wide. Ribs very flat and only slightly notched. Radial spines usually 6, bristle-fine, appressed, up to 3 mm. long. Central spines absent. Flowers white, 4.5-6 cm. long. Argentina (Catamarca).

(Mic; 10) **G. saglionis** (Cels) Br. & R.
Blue-green, up to 30 cm. wide, with 10-32 ribs. Radial spines 7-15. Central spines (1-) 3 (- more). Spines curved, up to 4 cm. long. Flowers white or slightly pink, only 3.5 cm. long. Fruit red. N. Argentina (Salta, Tucuman, Catamarca, San Juan, La Rioja, San Luis).

A robust, easily maintained species, but does not flower until old.

(Mus; 12A) **G. schickendantzii** (Web.) Br. & R.
Distinctive dark olive green, up to 10 cm. wide. Radial spines 5-7, more or less flattened, often grooved above. Flowers white to reddish, externally olive green, up to 5 cm. long. Argentina (S. Córdoba to Catamarca, Tucuman, Salta).

Flowers late in the year, even from old areoles.

(Mic; 10) **G. spegazzinii** Br. & R.
Body blue- or grey-green to brownish, solitary, up to 18 cm. wide. Radial spines 5-7, more or less curved, up to 5.5 cm. long. Central spines usually absent, sometimes 1. Flowers whitish to slightly pink with rose-red throat, 6-7 cm. long. Argentina (Salta).

(Tr; 8) **G. stellatum** Spegazz.
(*G. asterium* Y. Ito)
Grey-brown-green, up to 10 cm. wide. Radial spines 3-5, appressed. Flowers white with pink centre, 6-6.5 cm. long. Argentina (Córdoba, La Rioja, Catamarca).

(Mic) **G. tillianum** Rausch
Up to 15 cm. wide, blue-grey-green. Radial spines 7, curved towards the body. Central spines 0-1. Spines black to brown, later turning grey, up to 3 cm. long. Flowers dark red with carmine-pink throat, 3 cm. long. Argentina (Sierra Ambato).

(G; 1A) **G. uruguayense** (Arech.) Br. & R.
Dark green. Radial spines usually 3, seldom more. Central spines absent.

Flowers pale green-yellow outside, yellow or pale lilac to white inside, around 4 cm. long. Uruguay.

(Mic; 4) **G. valnicekianum** Jajo
Dark grass green, up to 18 cm. wide. Radial spines 7-15 or more. Central spines 1-6. Flowers white with reddish throat, 5 cm. long. Argentina (Córdoba).

(Tr; 8) **G. vatteri** Buin.
Matt olive green, up to 9 cm. wide. Spines 1-3 (-5), appressed. Flowers white or white with reddish throat, 5 cm. long. Argentina (Córdoba).

Gymnocereus Backeb. see *Browningia*

Haageocereus Backeb. 1934
(Binghamia, Peruvocereus)
(after W. Haage, Erfurt, owner of the well-known cactus firm)

This genus contains columnar cacti which branch from the base, bearing nocturnal, radially symmetrical flowers. The tube is slim and scaly, but has few hairs. The fleshy fruit are spherical and carry the dried remains of the flower.

30-40 species. Native to Peru on the west side of the Andes and N. Chile, from the coast to 2400 m. altitude.

Haageocerei are among the relatively few columnar cacti which can be recommended to amateur enthusiasts. They feature dense coverings of very brightly coloured spines. Most of them grow no taller than about 1-1.5 m., and will flower in the greenhouse or in a cactus frame in the garden. The flowers of many species are open by 3-4 p.m. and remain open until about 10 a.m. the following morning. Haageocerei require good, permeable soil with plenty of loam and a sunny position. When they are growing they should be provided with plenty of moisture and low-nitrogen feeds. In summer they have a dry rest period, and they resume growth in the autumn. It is only after about December that the winter dormant period begins. Then too they need to be kept warm, at around 10-15°C ideally, with a low level of soil heating.

The different species are very difficult

to distinguish, as the spine formations alter under cultural conditions.

Stems prostrate   *H. chalaensis*
                  H. decumbens

Stems erect or curving upward, with hair bristles between the spines
                  H. albispinus
                  H. chosicensis
                  H. multangularis

Without hair bristles between the spines   *H. limensis*
                  H. pacalaensis
                  H. versicolor

H. albispinus (Akers) Backeb.
Very similar to *H. multangularis,* but has yellow spines and white bristle spines. Central Peru (Eulalia valley).

H. chalaensis Ritter
Up to 1 m. long, decumbent. Stems 4-5 cm. thick and with 12-19 ribs. Radial spines around 30 and more, 0.5-0.7 cm. long. Central spines about 15. Spines brown, turning grey, 0.5-1 cm. long. Flowers white. Peru (Arequipa).

H. chosicensis (Werderm. & Backeb.) Backeb.
Up to 1.5 m. tall. Stems 6-10 cm. thick with 18-26 ribs. Spines white, yellow or fox-red, with white bristles. Central spines 1-4, up to 2 cm. long. Flowers (white to) lilac red, 6-7.5 cm. long.

Haageocereus chosicensis

Haageocereus albispinus

Central Peru (Chosica and Eulalia valley).

var. rubrospinus (Akers) Backeb. (*H. r.* (Akers) Backeb.)
Up to 1.5 m. tall. Stems up to 6 cm. thick. Spines yellowish or reddish with fine white bristles. Flowers carmine pink, up to 6 cm. wide. Peru.

H. decumbens (Vaup.) Backeb.
Up to 1 m. long, decumbent. Stems 4-6 cm. thick and with about 15-20 ribs. Spines white to red, turning grey, up to 0.5 cm. long. Central spines 1-5, up to 5 cm. long. Flowers white, externally chocolate brown, 6-8 cm. long. S. Peru (Chala region and near Mollendo).

Many specimens flower when only 20 cm. in length.

var. brevispinus Ritter
Stems about 3 cm. thick, usually with 13-14 ribs. Radial spines 0.3-0.5 cm. long. Central spines the same, except for 1-2 of them which are 1-2 cm. long. Flowers white.

var. multicolorispinus Buin. & Cullm.
Red, white and brown spines. Peru (between Nazca and the sea). More beautiful and more willing to flower than the species proper.

H. limensis (Salm-Dyck) Ritter (*H. olowinskianus* Backeb.)
Up to 1 m. tall. Stems up to 7.5 cm. wide, about 13 ribs. Spines brown,

turning grey. Radial spines more than 30, up to 1 cm. long. Central spines 10-12, 1 (-3) of them very powerful and up to 6 cm. long. Flowers white, about 8 cm. long. Central Peru (near Lima).

H. multangularis (Willd.) Ritter
Up to 1.5 m. tall. Stems 4-9 cm. wide with 14-18 ribs. Spines 40-60, brown to yellowish. Flowers white to red to greenish, 6-8 cm. long.

var. pseudomelanostele (Backeb.) Ritter (*H. p.* (Werderm. & Backeb.) Backeb. var. *chrysanthus* (Akers) Ritter; *H. chrysanthus* (Akers) Backeb.). Approx. 1 m. tall. Stems up to 10 cm. thick, with 22 or more ribs. Spines together with fine hairy bristles.

Haageocereus pacalaensis

Haageocereus decumbens

Flowers greenish-white or red, 4-5 cm. long. Central Peru (Cajamarquilla).

var. turbidus (Rauh & Backeb.) Ritter (*H. t.* Rauh & Backeb.)
Up to about 1.2 m. tall. Stems 5-8 cm. thick. Radial spines about 19, initially yellow to fox-red with very thin curly supplementary spines. Main spines 1-2, up to 8 (-10) cm. long with yellow base, yellowish to reddish above. Flowers 5 (-6) cm. long, white, wine-red and green outside. Peru (Nazca valley).

H. pacalaensis Backeb.
Up to 2 m. tall. Stems 5-6 cm. thick, with 17-20 ribs. Spines powerful, about 40-50, yellow. Central spines up to 7 cm. long. Flowers white,

externally green, about 10 cm. long. N. Peru (close to the coast in the department of Libertad).

An extremely vigorous species.

H. versicolor (Werderm. & Backeb.) Backeb.
1-2 m. tall. Stems up to 5 cm. thick with 16-22 ribs. Spines yellowish, reddish or brown, forming variously coloured zones. Central spines 1-2, up to 4 cm. long. Flowers white, green outside, up to 10 cm. long. N. Peru (Eastern desert region).

Haageocereus chosicensis var. rubrospinus

Hamatocactus Br. & R. see *Ferocactus* and *Ancistrocactus*

Harrisia Britt. 1908
(after the botanist James Harris of Jamaica)

Tree-shaped, bushy or climbing columnar cacti with (5-) 8-12 ribs. Flowers borne towards the end of the stems, with elongated tube, scaly and woolly, nocturnal, pink or white, 12-22 cm. long. Seed has large hollow cavity.

Harrisia is related to the genus

Eriocereus, from which it can be distinguished by a recessed ring of throat stamens, and fruit which are not bumpy and are not dehiscent. 10 species. Native to USA (Florida), Bahamas, Greater Antilles.

Haseltonia Backeb. 1949
(after the North American cactus expert Scott Haselton, 20th century)

Tree-shaped columnar cacti with up to 16 or more ribs. Flowers borne laterally in a cephalium, externally scaly and bare, nocturnal, with nectar chamber, 4-5 cm. long. Fruit dry, hairy. 1 species. Native to Mexico (Puebla to Oaxaca).

Hatiora Br. & R. 1923
(Anagram of Thomas Hariot, a 16th century English botanist, as the original name *Hariota* had already been adopted for a different plant genus).

Club-shaped segments, thickening towards the top, with round cross-section. The small flowers, no more than 2.2 cm. long, grow at the end of the segments and have no tube. The yellow flowers feature bare scales. Only two rows of stamens are present, produced from the base of the flower petals. It is very similar to *Pseudozygocactus* and is probably not closely related to *Rhipsalis,* although it was formerly included in that genus. 4 species. Native to Brazil (Rio de Janeiro, Sao Paulo, Minas Gerais).

H. herminiae (Campos-Porto & Castell.) Backeb.
Segments dichotomous or whorled, cylindrical, only slightly thickened higher up. Areoles with 1-2 small bristles. Flowers dark pink, 2 cm. long. Fruit olive green. Brazil (Campos do Jordao).

H. salicornioides (Haw.) Br. & R.
Segments usually whorled in groups of 3-5, 1-3 cm. long and 0.4-0.7 cm. thick. Areoles with short white bristles. Flowers yellow, up to 1.3 cm. long. Fruit white, reddish at the tip. Brazil (Rio de Janeiro, Minas Gerais).

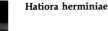

Hatiora herminiae

Hatiora salicornioides

Hatiora salicornioides

This species grows very slowly, but is tolerant and flowers readily. Half-shady location.

Heliabravoa Backeb. 1956
(after the female Mexican botanist Helia Bravoa, 20th century)

Tree-shaped columnar cacti. Flowers borne towards the end of the stems, with dense scales and bristly-hairy outside, diurnal. 1 species. Native to Mexico (Puebla to Oaxaca).

H. chende (Gosselin) Backeb. (*Lemaireocereus c.* (Gosselin) Br. & R.) Up to 7 m. tall and 6-10 cm. thick, with 7-9 fairly sharp ribs. Radial spines 1-6, 1-2 cm. long. Central spines 1 (or absent). Spines yellow to brown. Flowers white, externally pink with darker centrelines, 4-5 cm. long. Mexico (Puebla, Oaxaca). Of no interest for cultivation because of its size, but a very impressive species in its habitat.

Helianthocereus Backeb. see *Trichocereus*

Heliocereus (Berger) Br. & R. 1909
(Greek helios = sun)

Columnar cacti with only 3-4 (-7) ribs and aerial roots. Flowers lateral, externally scaly and bristly-felty, white or red, diurnal, 8-17 cm. long. 6 species. Native to Mexico, Guatemala.

H. speciosus (Cav.) Br. & R. Mostly erect and sprawling, but also pendant and epiphytic. Stems initially reddish-green, later dark green, up to 1 m. or more long and 2-3 cm. thick, with (3-) 4 (-5) ribs. Spines 5-8, later also more numerous, yellowish to brownish, 1-1.5 cm. long. Flowers brilliant violet-carmine, 12-15 cm. long. Central Mexico (often around Mexico City).

The flowers of this species are among the most beautiful of all cacti. The plant prefers nutritious soil with a fairly high proportion of humus. The species is included in many Phyllocacti. It likes a half-shady location in summer, and constant mild levels of soil moisture.

Heliocereus speciosus

var. amecamensis (Heese) Weingt. (*H.a.* (Heese) Br. & R.) with white flowers.

Hertrichocereus Backeb. see *Stenocereus*

Hickenia Br. & R. see *Parodia*

Hildewintera Ritter 1966
(*Winteria, Winterocereus*)
(after Hilde Winter, the sister of the cactus collector F. Ritter)

Columnar cacti with 16-17 ribs.

Heliocereus speciosus var. amecamensis

Flowers lateral, externally scaly and slightly woolly, radially symmetrical, inner petals short and erect, distinctly different from the inner petals, diurnal. 1 species. Native to Bolivia (Prov. Florida).

H. aureispina (Ritter) Ritter (*Winteria a.* Ritter; *Winterocereus a.* (Ritter) Backeb.; *Loxanthocereus a.* (Ritter) Buxb.) Branching and pendant. Stems green, up to 1.5 m. long and up to 2.5 cm. thick, with 16-17 ribs, slightly undulating between the areoles. Spines about 50, delicate, flexible and golden yellow, 0.4-1 cm. long, slightly longer on flowering stems. Flowers 4-6 cm. long and 5 cm. wide. External flower petals orange-yellow with vermilion to blood-red central stripe, inner petals shorter, white to pale pink.

This fine species was discovered by Ritter in 1958.

Homalocephala Br. & R. see *Echinocactus*

Horridocactus Backeb. see *Neoporteria*

Hylocereus (Berger) Br. & R. 1909
(Greek hylos = forest)

Climbing, 3 (-5) ribbed or angled cacti with aerial roots. The nocturnal flowers have a greatly elongated tube and are white or occasionally red. The ovary and tube bear large scales overlapping like roof-tiles. In contrast to other trailing cacti the axils of the scales are bare.

24 species. Native to Mexico, Central America, West Indies, Venezuela, Guyana, Columbia, Peru.

Hylocerei require similar cultural conditions to *Selenicereus*. The plants are usually too large for the amateur enthusiast. However, certain *Hylocereus* species (*H. undatus* and *H. trigonus*), which are not usually specifically named, are finding increasing favour as grafting rootstocks. They are only suitable as host to warmth-loving, very vigorous species. They like an even, humid, warm climate. Excessively low temperatures, dryness and in particular the provision of water which is too cold result in the plants languishing and rotting, even on cool days in summer.

187

Hildewintera aureispina

Jasminocereus Br. & R. 1920
(Jasminum = Persian or Arabian plant name)

Tree-shaped columnar cacti with 15-18 ribs. Flowers with elongated tube, externally scaly and slightly woolly or bare, nocturnal, red, 5-10 cm. long. 2 species. Native to Galapagos islands.

Krainzia Backeb. see *Mammillaria*

Lasiocereus Ritter 1966
(Greek lasios = rough)

Columnar cacti with 10-21 ribs. Flowers terminal, on specially formed areoles with long bristles, tubular, externally scaly and bristly/woolly, nocturnal. 2 species. Native to Peru.

L. rupicola Ritter
Tree-shaped, 3-4 m. tall. Stems 4.5-7 cm. thick, with 18-21 very bumpy ribs. Radial spines about 20, pale yellow, 0.5-1 cm. long. Central spines about 12, often 1 or 2 thicker, up to 3 cm. long. Flowers white, outer petals with long black tips, 5 cm. long. Peru (Cajamarca).

Lemaireocereus Br. & R. see *Pachycereus* and *Stenocereus*

H. trigonus (Haw.) Safford
Climbing, up to 10 m. tall. Stems 3-edged and very wavy, 2-3 cm. thick. Edges not horny. Spines around 8, dark brown, 0.5-1 cm. long. Flowers white, very large. Antilles.

H. undatus (Haw.) Br. & R.
Stems generally 3-angled, with diameter of 5-12 cm. Edges horny when old. Areoles with 1-3 spines, 2-4 mm. long, brown or black initially. External flower petals greenish-yellow, inner petals white. Flowers up to 30 cm. long. Native habitat unknown.

Hymenorebutia Frič & Buin. see *Lobivia*

Islaya Backeb. see *Neoporteria*

Isolatocereus (Backeb.) Backeb. see *Stenocereus*

Leocereus Br. & R. 1920
(after L. Pacheco Leao, former director of the Botanical Gardens of Rio de Janeiro)

Bushy or climbing columnar cacti with 12-17 ribs. Flowers lateral, scaly and woolly, nocturnal, with nectar chamber, white or violet, 4-7 cm. long. 5 species. Native to Brazil (Bahia, Minas Gerais).

Lepidocoryphantha Backeb. see *Coryphantha*

Lepismium Pfeiff. 1835
(Greek lepis = scale; on account of the areole scales)

The genus *Lepismium* is identical to *Rhipsalis,* except that the ovary is sunken into the stems during the flowering period. However, as this modification probably occurred many

Hylocereus undatus

times in the history of the race, the plants could also be classified into the various sections of *Rhipsalis*. 17 species. Native to Venezuela, E. Brazil, Paraguay, Argentina, ?Bolivia.

Except for a few species, amongst them *L. cruciforme* and *L. paradoxum*, all have stems of circular cross-section, and cannot be distinguished from *Rhipsalis* species without examining the flowers.

L. cruciforme (Vellozo) Miquel (*Rhipsalis c.* (Vellozo) Castell.).

Segments 3 (-5) angled, about 2 cm. wide and up to 30 cm. long, bristly. Flowers whitish, externally reddish, 1.2-1.5 cm. long. Fruit violet. Brazil, Argentina, Paraguay.

L. paradoxum Salm-Dyck (*Rhipsalis p.* Salm-Dyck)
Stems pendant. Segments 3 (-4) angled, 2.5-5 cm. long. The edges of each segment are offset from those of

189

its neighbour. Areoles slightly woolly, 1-2 bristles when young. Flowers white, about 2 cm. long, flower petals with green stripe. Fruit reddish. Brazil (Sao Paulo).

L. saxatile Friedr. & Redecker
Segments with about 6 very poorly defined angles, 1.5 cm. thick. Areoles with up to 15 bristles. Flowers canary yellow, up to 1.5 cm. wide. Fruit flesh red. Brazil.

Leptocereus (Berger) Br. & R. 1909
(Greek leptos = thin, slender)

Tree-shaped, climbing or decumbent columnar cacti with between 4 and 9 ribs. Flowers lateral, externally scaly and thorny or bristly, diurnal. 10 species. Native to Cuba, Hispaniola, Puerto Rico.

Leptocladodia Buxb. see *Mammillaria*

Leuchtenbergia Hook. 1848
(after the Duke of Leuchtenberg, Eugene de Beauharnais 1781-1824, French statesman; he was the son of Josephine, the first of Napoleon's consorts)

The single species, with its long, thin tubercles bearing papery spines at the ends, is quite different from all other cacti. The yellow flowers are up to 8 cm. long, have a silky sheen and are produced at the end of young tubercles. They are scaly, but otherwise bare. Silky hairs grow above the stamens. 1 species. Native to Central and N. Mexico (Coahuila, Zacatecas, Guanajuato, San Luis Potosí, Hidalgo).

This genus represents one of the most extreme forms of cactus. Nevertheless, crossings with *Ferocactus* and *Thelocactus* have been successful in Japan.

L. principis Hook.
A plant similar to the agave, up to 70 cm. tall, woody when old. Tubercles blue-green, slender, 10-12 cm. long, with three angles. Radial spines 8-14, whitish to yellowish-brown, flattened like paper, irregularly twisted, up to 10 (-15) cm. long, 1-2 similar central spines. Flowers yellow, with a silky sheen, scented, up to 8 cm. long and 5-6 cm. wide.

Leuchtenbergia principis

The plant requires plenty of sunshine, a loose, purely mineral soil and little moisture generally; complete dryness in winter.

Leucostele Backeb. see *Trichocereus*

Lobeira Alex. see *Nopalxochia*

Lobivia Br. & R. 1922
(*Acantholobivia, Chamaecereus, Cinnabarina, Hymenorebutia, Neolobivia, Pygmaeolobivia*)

Drawing the dividing line between the genus *Lobivia* and the closely related genera *Echinopsis* and *Trichocereus* is very difficult, and the distinctions are still disputed today. Many species have already been shunted to and fro

	Form*	flowering time	tube length	flower colour white or translucent	brightly coloured
Trichocereus	0	night	long	×	
'Helianthocereus'	0	day	long	×	×
Echinopsis in the narrower sense	◯	night	long	×	
Pseudolobivia	◯	day	long	×	×
Lobivia	◯	day	short	(×)	×
Characteristics of	——— typical Trichocerei				
	— — — typical Echinopses				
	· · · · · · typical Lobivias				

Several species do not fit into this simple scheme.

* Typical Trichocerei only exhibit the globular form as seedlings and do not flower until they have become columnar.

Typical Echinopses and Lobivias retain their globular form for a long time or permanently, and always flower in their globular form.

Lobivia pentlandii with clearly visible ring of
throat stamens.

between these genera several times.
The principle of including the 3
genera under the name *Echinopsis*
cannot be rejected out of hand, but
this does not solve the problem of
dividing the group into natural sub-
sections. All 3 genera have
characteristic flowers which are
externally scaly and woolly, with a very
prominent ring of stamens in the
throat.

The simple scheme shown in the table
appeared initially to be an adequate
means of classification: all diurnally
flowering species with short flower
tubes were designated Lobivias. Every
other criterion which has been
suggested as the definitive
characteristic of *Lobivia* has been found

wanting. Not all short-tubed, day-
flowering species have a globular or
elongated body. There are a few with
an extended cylindrical or columnar
body, which have often been listed
under their own genus *Soehrensia* or
included in the genus *Trichocereus,* not
to mention all the less clearly defined
forms. The ribs of many Lobivias are
deeply notched, forming spirally
disposed tubercles, but there are also
several species with continuous ribs
which are otherwise indubitably
Lobivias. Thus this characteristic on its
own cannot serve to differentiate
Lobivia from *Echinopsis*. Seeds featuring
a slanting hilum are also not
characteristic of all Lobivias.

To get round these difficulties

'intermediate genera' have been
established: *Helianthocereus, Pseudolobivia*
and *Soehrensia.* Yet whichever
characteristics are selected to define
the whole group, there are always a
few species left over . Nonetheless,
most species can still be classified by
the simple scheme shown in the table
here, and for this reason the method
has again been adopted .
According to recent research a total of
perhaps 35 species of *Lobivia* might be
omitted from the main body of those
described; these species are also to
some extent separated geographically
from the majority.

The genus *Lobivia* was established by
Britton and Rose in 1922, although a
few Lobivias had been described soon

191

Lobivia densispina group

the Lobivias are now divided into fairly large groups according to body form; many former specific names have been withdrawn in the process. In this area Rausch's work has been the chief influence, although his geographically clearly separated sub-species have been left as species.

The Lobivias are among the most popular of all cacti. They grow well, and flower readily and copiously, even though the flowers usually remain open for just a single day, or as little as a few hours in warm weather. However, they often open early in the morning, so that the early riser can admire the flowers before he sets off to work.

The Lobivias are native to the South American Andean uplands of Argentina through Bolivia to Southern

after 1840; at that time they were classified as *Echinocactus* or *Echinopsis*. The generic name *Lobivia* invented by Britton and Rose is an anagram of the region in which the plants are most widespread: Bolivia. *Lobivia* species vary widely in their appearance, in their spine formation, and in their flowers. Even in a single species the spine habit may be more or less prominent, and the spines themselves may be gleaming yellow, brown or almost black when young. Similarly

the flowers may vary in colour from white through yellow to red with many intermediate shades — sometimes in a single locality. This variable nature has caused considerable confusion in terms of species identification.

The definition of the genus and its subdivision into species have been revised several times in recent years. The contributions of Donald, Friedrich and Rausch are of particular note here. The outcome of this work is that

Lobivia densispina group

Lobivia densispina group

Peru. In their native habitat they are often subject to arduous conditions, and one result of this is that they are reasonably tolerant of variations in cultural conditions. As they are endemic to mountainous regions they should be provided with bright light but only moderate temperatures. Good ventilation is essential, and they appreciate marked temperature differences between day and night and between summer and winter. Lobivias suffer in constant heat and without nocturnal cooling. Plants kept in excessively shady conditions produce only a desultory spine formation, and tend to aetiolate. However, even when grown in sunshine the spines are often

192

Lobivia densispina group

not as long and dense as in their high, mountainous home locations. As a result cultivated plants often do not entirely match the description of the original.

Lobivias thrive well in standard, slightly acid cactus soil, but particular care should be taken with those species which produce a tap root; be sure to provide a soil which drains really well. In the growing season they will tolerate somewhat more moisture than other cacti, but the tap-rooted species should again be watered rather more sparingly. Plants should be kept in cool (not more than 6-8°C), dry and bright conditions in winter. Plants cultivated hard will tolerate short nocturnal frosts without problem provided that they are kept dry.

Lobivias grow well on their own root; grafting is not necessary. They can easily be propagated from cuttings or from seed; unfortunately unwanted hybrids sometimes develop from the seed. They thrive in a suitable garden frame, or in a well-ventilated greenhouse which is adjusted to the demands of these high-altitude plants. In summer an open-air situation protected from heavy rain will suit them admirably. Lobivias will give much pleasure to the cactus enthusiast even in regions with an inclement climate.

The following key for *Lobivia* and diurnal-flowering *Echinopsis* and smaller *Trichocereus* species, based mainly on Rausch's information, is no more than an attempt to gather together distinguishing features in this very difficult group.

1 Body with thin, cylindrical segments, abundantly clustering — *L. silvestrii*
1 Body with different external form
  2 Flowers with darker throat
    3 Throat red to red-brown. Seed rough and matt
      4 Flowers 6-7.5 cm. long — *L. rubescens*
      4 Flowers about 5 cm. long
        Tubercles in straight rows — *L. chrysantha*
        Tubercles offset diagonally — *L. marsoneri*
        see also *L. saltensis* var. *schreiteri*
    3 Throat and bottom stamens brown-red to black-violet. Seed glossy (tubercles offset diagonally) — *L. jajoiana*
  2 Flowers not with darker throat
    5 Flowers more or less terminal (tubercles in straight rows or with continuous ribs)
      6 Body rounded. Flowers about 17-20 cm. long. Seed with bulging hilum ring — *E. mamillosa*
      6 Body elongated to cylindrical. Flowers shorter. Seed without aril bulge
        7 Plant clustering. Flowers about 13 cm. long — *T. huascha*
        7 Plant not clustering. Flowers about 6-8 cm. long
          8 Fruit large, about 4 cm. long. Seed with slanting hilum, glossy black
            9 Flowers light yellow to golden. Body more or less columnar — *T. formosa*
            9 Flowers light red to dark red or creamy-white. Body columnar — *T. tarijensis*
            9 Flowers yellow or red. Body elongated
              10 Flowers red. Plants large — *T. bruchii*
              10 Flowers yellow or red. Plants small — *T. grandis*
          8 Fruit small, about 1 cm. in diameter. Seed with straight hilum
            11 Ribs about 20 — *L. lateritia*
            11 Ribs up to 9 — *L. caineana*
  5 Flowers lateral
    12 Tubercles in straight rows
      13 Body flattened — globular. Flowers 8-20 cm. long
        14 Flowers 12-20 cm. long, white — *E. ancistrophora*
          see also *E. obrepanda*
        14 Flowers 5-10 cm. long, not white
          15 Flowers yellow-orange — *E. arachnacantha*
          15 Flowers violet to pink — *E. cardenasiana*
          15 Flowers red — *E. pojensis*
      13 Body elongated or rounded, if flattened globular then with taproot. Flowers shorter
      16 Taproot absent (usually clustering)
        17 Flowers about 5-7 cm. long. Fruit small, about 1 cm. long (flowers red) — *L. rauschii*
          see also *L. hertrichiana,* flowers usually lighter inside
        17 Flowers about 8-9 cm. long. Fruit medium-sized, about 1.5-2.5 cm. long
          18 Seed with slanting hilum. Flowers yellow-red — *L. caespitosa*
          18 Seed with straight hilum. Flowers yellow (red) — *E. aurea*
      16 Taproot pronounced

193

19 Flowers broad funnel-shaped (Spines more or less appressed. Flowers yellow) *L. famatimensis*
19 Flowers not broad funnel-shaped
  20 Fruit very small, about 1 cm. long. Seed with slanting hilum *L. saltensis*
  20 Fruit medium-sized, about 1.5-2.5 cm. long. Seed with straight hilum
    21 Flowers without white throat
      22 Spines fine and bristly, partially appressed
        23 External flower petals usually narrow and curved back *L. tiegeliana*
        23 Outer flower petals similar to the inner petals *L. densispina*
      22 Spines not fine and bristly *L. haematantha*
      L. chorillosensis, flowers only 4-5 cm. long
    21 Flowers with white throat *L. kuehnrichii*
12 Tubercles offset diagonally (body rounded to flattened)
24 Flowers usually 10-20 cm.long *E. obrepanda*
24 Flowers shorter
  25 Spines generally more or less flattened like a dagger. Seed acute (taproot) *L. pugionacantha*
  25 Spines not dagger-like. Seed not acute
    26 Spines very sturdy. Fruit very large, about 3 cm. long *E. ferox*
    26 Spines less sturdy. Fruit smaller
      27 Spines more or less curved and appressed *L. tiegeliana*
      27 Spines more or less projecting
        28 Body usually solitary
          29 Flowers with lighter throat
            30 Taproot pronounced
              31 Throat white
                32 Fruit medium-sized, about 2 cm. long (spines thin) see also *L. kuehnrichii* *L. chrysochete*
                32 Fruit small, around 1 cm. long
                  33 Flowers lilac-red (about 3 cm. long) *L. zecheri*
                  33 Flowers orange to red
                    34 Spines thin *L. saltensis* var. *schreiteri*
                    34 Spines usually curved and hooked. Seed glossy *L. sanguiniflora*
              31 Throat orange (skin blue — blue/green) *L. pampana*
            30 Taproot not pronounced
              35 Flower petals short. Ovary and fruit partially spiny. Seed with slanting hilum *L. tegeleriana*
              35 Flower petals not short. Flowers broad funnel-shaped. Seed with straight hilum *L. acanthoplegma*
          29 Flowers without lighter throat
            36 Anthers red (flowers dark blue-red) *L. prestoana*
            36 Anthers yellow
              37 Flowers carmine, broad funnel-shaped. Seed with straight hilum *L. cinnabarina*
              see also *L. hertrichiana* var. *simplex* and *E. obrepanda* var. *mizquensis*
              37 Flowers lilac or ruby red. Seed with slanting hilum
                38 Flowers delicate lilac, about 4-4.5 cm. long. Spines white *L. wrightiana*
                38 Flowers ruby red, 6-9 cm. long *L. winteriana*
        28 Body forming shoots
          39 Flowers small, about 3-6 cm. long. Fruit about 1 cm. long see also *L. hertrichiana*
            40 Flowers carmine with white throat, about 4.5 cm. long *L. backebergii*
            40 Flowers yellow to carmine, without lighter throat, about 3 cm. long (spines very dense) *L. schieliana*
          39 Flowers larger, 6-8 cm. long. Fruit about 2 cm. long
            41 Inner stamens resting against the style (flowers red, yellowish inside)
              42 Inner flower petals much shorter and erect *L. maximiliana*
              42 Inner flower petals different *L. caespitosa*
            41 Inner stamens not resting on the style
              43 Flowers yellowish or honey-coloured *L. westii*
              43 Flowers red *L. quiabayensis*
              43 Flowers from lemon yellow to vermilion and violet-red *L. pentlandii*

L. acanthoplegma (Backeb.) Backeb. (*L. cinnabarina* (Hook.) Br. & R. ssp. *a.* (Backeb.) Rausch)
Not clustering, no taproot. Body flattened globular with about 18 spiral ribs, notched to form tubercles. Radial spines about 15, up to 1.5 cm. long. Central spines absent. Flowers lateral, light red with light throat, 3 cm. long. Bolivia (Cochabamba).

L. arachnacantha see *Echinopsis a.*

L. backebergii (Werderm.) Backeb.
Solitary or only slightly clustering, no taproot. Body globular to oval, with approx. 15 spirally notched ribs. Radial spines (3-) 5-7, yellowish to brown and 0.5-5 cm. long. Central spines absent. Flowers lateral, light carmine red with light throat, 4.5-5.5 cm. long. Bolivia (La Paz, Oruro).

L. binghamiana see *L. hertrichiana*

L. breviflora see *L. sanguiniflora* var. *breviflora*

L. bruchii see *Trichocereus b.*

L. caespitosa (J.A. Purp.) Br. & R. (*L. maximiliana* (Heyder) Backeb. ssp. *c.* (Purp.) Rausch ex G.D. Rowl.)
Clustering, no taproot. Body with 9-16 straight or spiral warty ribs. Spines strong, yellow or brown. Flowers lateral, yellow-red, 4.5-9 cm. long. Bolivia (La Paz, Cochabamba).

The plant rapidly becomes etiolated if kept too dark.

L. caineana Card.
Solitary, no taproot. Body globular to oval with up to 9 straight ribs. Spines strong, up to 7 cm. long. Flowers close to the crown, deep pink-red or white, up to 7 cm. long. This species' straight ribs and flower position make it substantially different from the rest of the Lobivias. Bolivia (upper valley of the Rio Caine).

L. chrysantha (Werderm.) Backeb.
Solitary. With taproot. Body matt greyish-green, globular and later elongated, with about 13 straight ribs. Radial spines 3-8, up to 2 cm. long. Central spines absent. Flowers lateral, golden to orange-yellow, with greenish throat, purple-red at the base, about 5 cm. long, scented. Seed rough and matt. Argentina (Salta).

Rather temperamental species in cultivation. Water carefully and avoid stagnant moisture because of the taproot.

L. cinnabarina (Hook.) Br. & R. Usually solitary. With slender taproot. Body glossy dark green, flattened globular to globular, with 18-21 spiral warty ribs. Radial spines 8-10, up to 1.5 cm. long. Central spines 1-3, pale brown. Spines all more or less curved. Flowers lateral, broad funnel-shaped, carmine red, 5.5-7 cm. long and about 8 cm. wide. Bolivia.

L. densispina (Werderm.) Backeb. (*L. haematantha* (Spegazz.) Br. & R. ssp. *d.* (Werderm.) Rausch ex G.D. Rowl.) *L. densispina* is the '*L. famatimensis*' claimed by Backeberg, but it was an error, and the genuine *L. famatimensis* was not found again until 1955 by Ritter.

Clustering. Root beet-like. Body green to brown-violet, cylindrical with straight ribs. Radial spines numerous. Central spines 4-7. Spines short and fine, yellowish to brownish, arranged in comb-formation or somewhat shaggy. Flowers lateral, pale yellow to red and almost violet with more or less dark throat. Argentina (Jujuy).

var. densispina (*L. densispina* Werderm.) Body green. Spines projecting. Flowers yellow, also red.

Lobivia densispina var. rebutioides

var. rebutioides (Backeb.) Buin. (*L.r.* Backeb.; *L. haematantha* (Speg.) Br. & R. ssp. *densispina* (Werderm.) Rausch ex G.D. Rowl. var. *r.* (Backeb.) Rausch ex G. D. Rowl.) Body green. Spines few, translucent and bristly. Radial spines 5-9 or more. Central spines 1 (-2). Flowers pale yellow to red.

L. pectinifera Wessn. (*L. haematantha* (Speg.) Br. & R. ssp. *densispina* (Werderm.) Rausch ex G.D. Rowl. var. *pectinifera* (Wessn.) Rausch ex G.D. Rowl.) Body grey-green. Spines short, appressed. Flowers yellow.

L. sublimiflora Backeb. (*L. rebutiodes* Backeb. var. *s.* (Backeb.) Backeb.; *L. haematantha* (Speg.) Br. & R. ssp. *densispina* (Werderm.) Rausch ex G.D. Rowl. var. *s.* (Backeb.) Rausch ex G.D. Rowl) Body dark green to violet. Spines appressed. Flowers pale yellow, yellow, orange, red, pink to almost violet.

L. drijveriana see *L. kuehnrichii*

L. famatimensis (Speg.) Br. & R. Solitary. Root beet-like. Body cylindrical with 18-24 more or less straight ribs. Radial spines 8-14, about 0.6 cm. long, appressed. Central spines 1-3. Flowers lateral, pale to dark yellow, up to 5 cm. long. Argentina (La Rioja, San Juan).

Lobivia famatimensis

Lobivia hertrichiana

For a long time this species was confused with *L. densispina.* The real *L. famatimensis* is still a rarity in collections.

L. fricii see *L. tiegeliana* var. *f.*

L. haageana see *L. rubescens*

L. hertrichiana Backeb. (*L. backebergii* (Werderm.) Backeb. ssp. *h.* (Backeb.) Rausch ex G.D. Rowl.; *L. binghamiana* Backeb.; *L. incaica* Backeb.; *L. planiceps* Backeb.)
Solitary or clustering. Body globular or oval, with 11-22 straight or spiral notched ribs. Radial spines 5 to about 14, around 2 cm. long. Central spines 1-7, up to 2.5 cm. long. Flowers lateral, yellow, orange, carmine or pink, sometimes with lighter throat, about 5-7.5 cm. long. Peru (Cuzco).

L. incaica see *L. hertrichiana*

L. jajoiana Backeb. (*L. chrysantha* (Werderm.) Backeb. ssp. *j.* (Backeb.) Rausch ex G.D. Rowl.)
Usually solitary. Taproot. Body oval to cylindrical, with 10-18 spiral notched ribs. Radial spines 8-11, 1-3 cm. long. Central spines 1-3, 1.5-6 cm. long, one of them pointing upwards and hooked. Flowers lateral, yellow, orange, wine-red or dark tomato red with blackish throat and ring of varnished appearance, from which the dark, glossy stamens emerge. Flowers about 6 cm. long, scented. Seed glossy. Argentina (Jujuy). One of the most beautiful of all cactus flowers.

L. kuehnrichii Frič (*L. haematantha* (Speg.) Br. & R. ssp. *k.* (Frič) Rausch ex G.D. Rowl.; *L. drijveriana* Backeb.)
Solitary, rarely clustering. Taproot. Body globular to oval, with about 12-

Various flower colours within Lobivia jajoiana

197

Lobivia kuehnrichii group

Lobivia maximiliana

15 ribs. Radial spines 10-12. Central spines 1-4, darker to black, 1.5 (-6) cm. long. Flowers lateral, pale yellow to reddish-yellow. Argentina (Salta).

L. lateritia (Gürke) Br. & R.
Solitary. Root not beet-like. Body oval to cylindrical, about 20 straight ribs. Radial spines 10 or more, about 2.5 cm. long. Central spines 1-2, up to 4 cm. long. The flowers are terminal, white, pink, yellow to red, 4.5-8 cm. long. Bolivia (Potosí, Chuquisaca).

L. leucomalla see under *Echinopsis aurea* var. *leucomalla*

L. marsoneri (Werderm.) Backeb. (*L. chrysantha* (Werderm.) Backeb. ssp. *m.* (Werderm.) Rausch ex G.D. Rowl.)
Solitary, with taproot. Body globular, with about 20 spiral notched ribs. Radial spines 8-12, up to 3 cm. long. Central spines 2-5, more or less hooked. Flowers lateral, yellow to red, with orange-red to purple throat, about 5 cm. long and 6 cm. wide, scented. Seed rough and matt. N. Argentina.

L. maximiliana (Heyder) Backeb. (*L. pentlandii* (Hook.) Br. & R. var. *m.* (Heyder) Backeb.)
Clustering. Root not beet-like. Body flattened globular, with spirally offset tubercles. Flowers lateral, red outside, yellowish-red or yellowish inside, 6-8

cm. long. Inner flower petals much shorter than the outside ones and usually erect. Peru (Cuzco, Puno), Bolivia (La Paz), up to 4500 m. altitude.

L. mistiensis see *L. pampana*

L. pampana Br. & R. (*L. mistiensis* (Werderm. & Backeb.) Backeb.)
Solitary, rarely clustering. Root beet-like. Body blue- to grey-green,

Lobivia pampana

globular to oval, with 25-30 spiral notched ribs. Radial spines 5-9, yellowish, up to 5 cm. long. Central spines 1-3, hooked, usually brown, up to 5 cm. long. Flowers lateral, yellow flushed with red, 6-8 cm. long. The very beautiful flower is of an elongated funnel-shape, and only opens fully in brilliant sunshine in the morning. Peru (Arequipa, Moquegua).

L. peclardiana see *L. tiegeliana*

Lobivia pugionacantha var. rossii

Lobivia silvestrii hybrid

Lobivia rubescens

L. pectinifera see under *L. densispina*

L. pentlandii (Hook.) Br. & R. (*L. boliviensis* Br. & R.; *L. higginsiana* Backeb. *L. raphidacantha* Backeb.; *L. schneideriana* Backeb.; *L. titicacensis* Card.)
Solitary or clustering. Root not beet-like. Body globular to oval, with 10-20 spiral notched ribs. Spine formation extremely variable. Radial spines 6-15, 0.4-4.5 cm. long. Central spines 0-1 (or more), 3-9 cm. long. Flowers lateral, yellow, orange to carmine, tinged with light red to pink or yellowish-white and pink-violet, often with lighter throat, 3-8 cm. long. Peru (Puno), N. Bolivia.

A very variable species in spine formation and flower colour.

L. planiceps see *L. hertrichiana*

L. pugionacantha (Rose & Bód.) Backeb.
Solitary or clustering, with taproot. Body globular, with about 17 spiral notched ribs. Spines 4-7, pale yellow, usually dagger-like, up to 2.5 cm. or more long. Flowers lateral, yellow to dark red, or pink, about 4.5 cm. long and wide. Bolivia.

var rossii (Bód.) Rausch (*L.r.* (Bód.) Bód. ex Backeb.).
Radial spines 4-16, yellowish. Central spines often absent when young, later

1-4 (-6). Flowers lemon yellow to orange-yellow, 4-7 cm. long. Bolivia (Potosi), up to 4500 m. altitude

L. rebutioides see *L. densispina* var. *rebutioides*

L. rossii see *L. pugionacantha* var. *rossii*

L. rubescens Backeb. (*L. haageana* Rausch; *L. chrysantha* (Werderm.) Backeb. ssp. *marsoneri* (Werderm.) Rausch ex G.D. Rowl. var. *rubescens* (Backeb.) Rausch ex. G.D. Rowl.)
Solitary or clustering. Root beet-like. Body elongated with more or less straight ribs. Radial spines about 7-10, up to 3 cm. long. Central spines 1-4, often black, up to 7 cm. long, sometimes hooked. Flowers lateral, golden yellow to reddish-yellow or red, with black-red throat, 6-7.5 cm. long and wide. Argentina (Jujuy).

A species with particularly beautiful spines and flowers. The plant is often tinged slightly with red in the spring. This is normal and healthy. The plant should be cultivated hard, otherwise the spines suffer and the plant becomes too elongated.

L. sanguiniflora Backeb.
Usually not clustering. Root beet-like. Body globular or flattened globular, with about 18 spiral notched ribs. Radial spines about 10, 0.8-1.5 cm. long. Central spines 1-3, 2 (-8) cm. long, usually hooked. Flowers lateral,

pale red, blood-red or carmine violet with white throat, 4.5-5 cm. long. Argentina (Salta)

var. breviflora (Backeb.) Rausch (*L.b.* Backeb.)
Crown of the plant depressed. Spines arranged in comb formation. Flowers with very short tube, 3 cm. long, usually pale blood-red.

L. schieliana Backeb. (*L. backebergii* (Werderm.) Backeb. ssp. *s.* (Backeb.) Rausch ex G.D. Rowl.)
Clustering. Body more or less oval, with spiral notched ribs. Radial spines about 14. Central spines 0-1, 0.5-0.6

199

Lobivia tiegeliana

cm. long. Flowers lateral, light carmine to yellow, 3 cm. long. Bolivia (La Paz).

L. silvestrii (Speg.) Rowley (*Chamaecereus s.* (Speg.) Br. & R.) Abundantly clustering. Root not beet-like. Body with stems about as long and thick as a finger, soft-fleshed, with 6-10 straight, continuous ribs. Radial

Lobivia winteriana

spines 10-15, bristly, 0.2 cm. long. Central spines absent. Flowers lateral, vermilion, about 4-5.5 cm. long. Argentina (Tucumán in fairly elevated locations).

This species, still generally known by the name *C. silvestrii,* is widespread and flowers readily and profusely when cultivated correctly. The plant should

be kept in permeable soil containing some humus, and not in brilliant sun. Keep cool in winter; night temperatures can drop below freezing point if conditions are light and dry. The plants shrink and may become reddish in colour, but will then flower all the more profusely. Grafted and 'soft' plants are very susceptible to attack by red spider mite. Many hybrids of this species have been produced, especially with Lobivias, and the resultant plants feature flower colours from yellow via orange and red to violet.

L. sublimiflora see under *L. densispina*

L. tiegeliana Wessn.
Solitary or clustering. Root beet-like. Body globular to flattened globular, with 16-20 notched ribs. Radial spines 8-14, curved, up to 1.2 cm. long. Central spines 0-1, dark brown, 0.5-1 cm. long, curving upwards. Flowers lateral, external flower petals very narrow and curving backward, violet-pink with paler throat, more rarely flowers yellow or red, 2.5-4.5 cm. long. Bolivia (Tarija), Argentina (N. Jujuy and Salta).

These plants produce beautiful spines, flower profusely, and remain small. There is also a yellow-flowering variety (var. *flaviflora* (Ritter) Rausch) and a red-flowering variety (var. *ruberrima* Rausch)

var. distefanoiana Cullm.
With elongated areoles and comb-formation spines

var. fricii (Rausch) Rausch (*L. fricii* Rausch)
All flower petals very narrow

L. peclardiana Krainz (*L. tiegeliana* var. *p.* (Krainz) Krainz)
Presumably a hybrid between *L. tiegeliana* and *Echinopsis,* with white, pink or carmine red flowers, profusely flowering.

L. westii Hutch. (*L. maximiliana* (Heyder) Backeb. ssp. *w.* (Hutch.) Rausch ex G.D. Rowl.)
Clustering. Root not beet-like. Body flattened globular, with 16-18 spiral notched ribs. Radial spines around 8, up to 0.9 cm. long. Central spines 1,

up to 2.5 (-4) cm. long. Spines straw-yellow to brown. Flowers lateral, narrow funnel-shaped, brilliant orange/golden-orange, up to 7 cm. long. Peru (Apurímac).

L. winteriana Ritter (*L. backebergii* (Werderm.) Backeb. ssp. *wrightiana* (Backeb.) Rausch ex G.D. Rowl. var. *winteriana* (Ritter) Rausch)
Solitary. Root slightly beet-like. Body grey-green, later slightly elongated, with 13-19 spiral notched ribs. Radial spines 6-14, curving towards the body, about 0.4-0.7 cm. long. Central spines 0-1 (-3), partially hooked, 1-3 (-6) cm. long. Flowers lateral, ruby red, 6-9 cm. long and 7-9 cm. wide, very large in relation to the plant. Peru (Huancavelica).

L. wrightiana Backeb. (*L. backebergii* (Werderm.) Backeb. ssp. *w.* (Backeb.) Rausch ex G.D. Rowl.)
Usually solitary. Root beet-like. Body oval, with 12-17 spiral notched ribs. Radial spines 6-10, 0.5-3 cm. long. Central spine usually 1, 1-4 (-7) cm. long, rather soft, irregularly curved and twisted, usually hooked at the tip. Flowers lateral, delicately lilac-coloured, 4-4.5 cm. long, appearing early in the year. Central Peru (Mantaro valley).

A well-known and popular species. The long central spine only appears in its full beauty on rather old plants which have been cultivated hard. It is likely that this is the only *Lobivia* found in Chile (in its *chilensis* 'form')

L. zecheri Rausch (*L. backebergii* (Werderm.) Backeb. ssp. *z.* (Rausch) Rausch ex G.D. Rowl.)
Usually solitary. Body light blue-grey, globular, with 12-18 spiral notched ribs. Radial spines 7-11, 3-5 cm. long. Central spines 0-1, 6 cm. long. Spines hard and piercing. Flowers lateral, dark red to violet red with white throat, about 3 cm. long. Peru (Ayacucho).

Lobivia wrightiana

Lophocereus (Berger) Br. & R. 1901
(Greek lophos = crest, plume)

Tree-shaped or bushy columnar cacti with 4-15 ribs. Flowers terminal in a pseudo-cephalium, one or several on one areole, externally scaly and bare, nocturnal, 2.5-4 cm. long. 4 species. Native to USA (Arizona), Mexico (Baja California, Sonora, Sinaloa).

Lophocereus schottii

Lophophora Coult. 1894
(*Anhalonium* p.p.) peyotl, peyote
(Greek lophos = crest, plume; phorein = to carry)

Globular cacti with flattened, blunt-ribbed body, spineless when mature. Powerful taproot. Flowers pink-white or yellowish, not scaly, bare.

3 species. Native to USA (New Mexico, S. Texas) to Mexico (Querétaro).

Lophophora contains a narcotic and plays a major role in the magical rites and customs of the Indians of S.W. USA and Mexico.

The plants should be cultivated in almost purely mineral soil with moderate moisture and complete dryness in winter. They will then flower reliably.

L. williamsii (Lem. ex Salm-Dyck) Coult.
Body solitary, blue-green, up to 7.5 cm. wide, with about 7-10 ribs and low, indistinct tubercles. Areoles with yellowish-white felt spots. Flowers pink (or whitish), about 1.2 cm. wide. USA (New Mexico, S. Texas), Mexico (Northern states as far as Querétaro).

Loxanthocereus Backeb. see *Borzicactus*

Lophophora williamsii

Small cacti, up to about 30 cm. tall. The flowers are located more or less at the end of the segments, and have erect or slightly spreading petals. There is no flower tube, and stamens and style do not project beyond the petals. 5 species. Native to Southern Andean region of Argentina and Chile.

M. poeppigii (Otto) Web.
Stems up to 6 cm. long with a diameter of 1 cm. Usually 3 spines, 0.5-2 cm. long. Flowers pale yellow, up to 3 cm. long. Chile (Chillan). Very slow growing. Winter-hard in Europe, but the plant must stand on a well drained base.

Maihueniopsis Spegazz. see *Opuntia*

Malaccocarpus Salm-Dyck see *Notocactus*

Mamillopsis (E. Morr.) Weber see *Mammillaria*

Mammillaria Haw. 1812
(*Bartschella, Chilita, Cochemiea, Dolichothele, Krainzia, Leptocladodia, Mamillopsis, Mammilloydia, Neomammillaria, Oehmea, Phellosperma, Porfiria, Pseudomammillaria, Solisia*)

Mammillaria is the cactus genus with the greatest number of species next to *Opuntia*. Hundreds of species have been described, although only about 170 of them represent 'good' species. The number of new discoveries and the number of species which have been re-introduced into the genus is

Machaerocereus Br. & R. 1920
(Greek machaira = dagger)

Bushy or decumbent columnar cacti with 8-12 ribs. Flowers lateral with elongated tube, externally scaly and thorny/woolly. Central spines laterally flattened or with keel. 2 species. Native to Mexico (lower California, ?Sonora).

These plants require rich, primarily mineral soil and a hot, sunny location.

M. eruca (T.S. Brandeg.) Br. & R.
Prostrate, only rising at the tips, rooting over its entire length. Stems 1-3 m. long, 4-8 cm. thick, with about 12 ribs. Radial spines about 20, red and white, later grey. Central spine 1, milk-white, almost dagger-like, up to 3.5 cm. long. Flowers white, 10-14 cm. long, nocturnal. Mexico (Lower California)

M. gummosus (Engelm.) Br. & R.
Bushy. Stems up to 1 m. long and 4-6 cm. thick, with 8 (-9) ribs. Radial spines 8-12, up to 1 cm. long. Central spines 3-6, slightly flattened, up to 4 cm. long. Flowers white to pink inside, externally purple, 10-14 cm. long. Mexico (Lower California).

Maihuenia Phil. 1883
(maihuen = Chilean folk name)

Maihuenia, with its globular, short-cylindrical segments, looks similar to an *Opuntia.* However, it has no glochids and is in fact related to *Pereskia,* although more highly specialized. The small leaves, of rounded cross-section, are permanent.

Maihuenia peoppigii

now approximately equal.

The name *Mammillaria* comes from the Latin mammilla = nipple. Mammillarias have no ribs, and the body is completely covered with tubercles. However, the tubercles are not arranged in an irregular pattern, but form angled, spiralling rows, crossing over each other. By far the most common numbers of rows are 5 and 8, 8 and 13, and 13 and 21. Cacti of very similar appearance occur in the South American genera such as *Rebutia* and *Parodia,* but these are not related at all. Without flowers, the only Mammillarias which are easy to distinguish from any other cacti are those which produce superficial milky sap which is released spontaneously at the slightest injury. In a proportion of *Mammillaria* species a central spine is curved into a very conspicuous hook at the end, but this feature also occurs in Parodias. In a fairly large number of *Mammillaria* species the axils are more or less woolly or bristly. This feature is typical of *Coryphantha,* but not of the South American cacti such as *Parodia* and *Rebutia.*

The crucial feature of the *Mammillaria* genus is the position of the flowers. They do not grow from the areoles at the end of the tubercles, as is normal for other cacti, but from the axils. There is a small number of related genera in which the flowers are also borne in the axils, such as *Coryphantha,* but in these cases the tubercles of flowering plants are to some extent furrowed; thus the areole and axil merge into each other. Flowers borne in the axils together with unfurrowed tubercles is a combination of features which is exclusive to *Mammillaria,* except for a few species of the genus *Neolloydia.*

Mammillarias are fairly small cacti, usually globular, but may become elongated when old. Not many species grow to more than 12 cm. wide or more than 20 cm. tall, although *M. guerronis* grows very elongated and columnar when old, reaching heights of up to 70 cm. Of the other exceptions, the species of the sub-genus *Cochemiea* in particular are extended columnar in form. *M. poselgeri* is said to reach a length of as much as 2 m. with a thickness of only 4 cm. The

Mammillaria elegans

smallest Mammillarias belong to the Longiflorae, such as *M. saboea* and *M. louisae*. These only grow to a height of 1-3 cm., but they possess the largest flowers of all the Mammillarias. *M. gracilis, M. prolifera* var. *texana* and *M. Viperina* produce particularly thin, elongated segments, only 1.5-2 cm. thick.

Mammillarias may be of solitary or clustering habit. Especially interesting are the dichotomous species, i.e. those which repeatedly branch into two forks. An example of this is *M. parkinsonii.* The flowers of Mammillarias are usually arranged in a ring around the crown, most species bearing very small flowers, no more than 2 cm. long with more or less erect petals, although those of a few species are up to about 5 cm. long with a fairly long tube. Externally the flowers are completely bare and devoid of scales. *M. senilis* of the sub-genus *Mamillopsis* is the only species whose flower tube is scaly. The outer flower petals often have frayed or serrate margins. The flowers usually open in the morning and close again in the afternoon, but often last for 2 or 3 days. The fruit are smooth, juicy, club-shaped berries. Often they are brilliant red and more distinctive than

the flowers.

The many species of the genus *Mammillaria* are extremely widely dispersed, although the vast majority of species occurs in Mexico. Only about 10 species grow in the south of the USA or extend as far north as Canada. A few types reach south of Mexico to Central America, the Greater and Lesser Antilles and even the coast of Venezuela. One species even occurs in Peru.

The long list of generic synonyms is evidence of the repeated attempts that have been made to sub-divide and thus clarify this giant genus, by removing species which differ strongly in particular features. For example, *Dolichothele* possesses especially large tubercles, *Solisia* features axe-shaped warts with spines arranged in comb-formation, Cochemiea has bi-laterally symmetrical flowers, *Krainzia* produces particularly large flowers and seed with a small white seed-coat, *Mamillopsis* has a scaly flower tube, *Phellosperma* and *Porfiria* produce more or less corky seed. The remaining groups are usually divided up according to particular characteristics. In the summary we have included as sub-genera some of the suggested generic names, but these do not include a very large proportion of the main mass of the Mammillarias.

A simple, effective summary of the large genus was offered by Schumann around the turn of the century. It was altered and improved by Berger, Borg and more recently by Hunt. The division by Buxbaum is based almost exclusively on seed characteristics, and only includes a proportion of the species. In practice this deficiency renders it virtually useless. It is very difficult to find a natural system for *Mammillaria,* as the critical distinguishing features, of which there are only about 15, are present in all possible permutations in the different species. There are hardly any major gulfs between the various species. Natural groupings in this very problematical genus only become evident when geographical dispersal is taken into account.

The most accurate and detailed descriptions are found in Craig's book: *The Mammillaria Handbook.* However, since 1945 a whole series of new species have been discovered which are of particular interest to the amateur enthusiast. The book lists around 120 species, but there are many further types under cultivation. The species within each group are prefixed by letters or Roman numbers corresponding to Hunt's classification. The very brief descriptions are limited to a few important characteristics.

Mammillaria bombycina

Classification of the genus Mammillaria according to Hunt, 1981
(*The Cactus and Succulent Journal of Great Britain.* Vol. 43(2/3):41-8)

Abbreviation used for the species descriptions: ( )	No. of species
Sub-genus *Mammilloydia* (My)	1
Sub-genus *Oehmea* (Oe)	1
Sub-genus *Dolichothele* (Do)	7
Sub-genus *Cochemiea* (Co)	3
Sub-genus *Mamillopsis* (Ms)	1
Sub-genus *Mammillaria*	155
Section *Hydrochylus*	
1. *Longiflorae*	5
2. *Ancisracanthae*	29
3. *Stylothelae*	23
4. *Proliferae*	7
5. *Lasiacanthae*	12
6. *Sphacelatae*	3
7. *Leptocladodae*	4
8. *Decipientes*	1
Section *Subhydrochylus*	
9. *Heterochlorae*	4
10. *Polyacanthae*	11
11. *Supertextae*	7
Section *Mammillaria*	
12. *Leucocephalae*	9
13. *Macrothelae*	32
14. *Polyedrae*	8
	168 species

Important aspects of Mammillaria for the cactus grower

The genus *Mammillaria* offers the enthusiast a large number of beautiful and rewarding cacti. Many Mammillarias feature an absolutely precise, almost mathematical spine arrangement, and the spines are often strongly coloured, ranging from brilliant white via yellow and red to dark brown. In fact a well tended *Mammillaria* collection always makes a splendid sight, not just at flowering time. The flowers are generally small, it is true, but they are often attractively arranged in regular rings around the crown of the plant. They are sometimes followed several months later by decorative rings of brilliant red seed berries.

The broad range of species and their wide variety of spine formations are an obvious attraction to the collector. As many of the plants remain small, quite a large collection can be accommodated even in a restricted space. Many cactus growers have concentrated on Mammillarias, and have built up splendid specialized collections. The vast majority of species make no special cultural demands. However, as the genus covers a vast area in terms of natural habitat, and embraces many different species, it is difficult to provide cultural notes which are generally applicable. Most species have shallow, spreading roots, and thrive particularly well in flat pots or dishes. Young plants or species which remain small grow better in groups of several in a flat pan than individually in deep pots. Species of clustering habit, such as *M. parkinsonii* or *M. bombycina* eventually form large cushions, which can be kept in a large, flat tray, or planted out in the bed of the greenhouse. Mammillarias tend to prefer a mineral, permeable, but nutritious soil. It is advisable to include about one third of coarse sand in the soil, and Perlite, lava or pumice waste are also recommended.

The species which are so densely covered in spines or hairs that they appear white, yellow or brown overall appreciate a particularly sunny, warm

Mammillaria group

position. The more sparsely spined types — those which look green overall — are happy with half-shade. The same applies to the sub-genus *Dolichothele*.

In the vegetative period Mammillarias should be watered normally, although plants with dense spines, dense white spines in particular, and those with taproots, should be watered rather more sparingly. None of the Mammillarias like stagnant moisture. In winter they are kept virtually completely dry at standard winter temperatures of 5-10°C. The species from the coast of Mexico and lower

California like to be kept warmer in the winter. Plants which produce their flowers in late autumn or winter, such as *M. plumosa* or *M. schiedeana* should be kept warmer and slightly moist. The large-flowered types, including members of the sub-genera *Mamillopsis* and *Dolichothele* and the *Longiflorae* group, are usually slightly more difficult to cultivate, and call for special care.

In the vegetative period Mammillarias should be fed with standard low-nitrogen cactus fertilizers. Strongly spined plants appreciate occasional doses of manuring lime or super-

phosphate. Clustering Mammillarias are easy to propagate by rooting the offsets. Cuttings of plants which produce milky sap should only be taken during the period of growth. The cuttings are allowed to dry out for two weeks, and the cut surface treated with charcoal powder to prevent rotting. Mammillarias are also readily raised from seed. The seed are usually small, but the plants grow vigorously and often flower when quite young. In fact Mammillarias, together with Rebutias and Gymnocalyciums, are some of the best cacti for raising from seed, as they produce flowering plants quite rapidly.

Key to flowering plants

Group key

Milky sap in the tubercles absent
  Flowers at least 3 cm. long or wide   **Group A**
  Flowers less than 3 cm. long and wide
    Hooked spines present   **Group B**
    Hooked spines absent   **Group C**
Milky sap in the tubercles present   **Group D**

Group A (large flowers)

1 Tube scaly (with hooked spines)   *M. senilis*
1 Tube not scaly
  2 Flowers zygomorphic (body cylindrical with hooked
    spines, flowers red)   *M. poselgeri*
  2 Flowers radially symmetrical
    3 Flowers yellow or yellowish-green. Style merged with the
      tube. Tubercles usually conspicuously long
      4 Hooked spines absent
        5 Central spines 5-6. Radial spines 30-35   *M. baumii*
        5 Central spines 0-1 (-3). Radial spines 9-15
          6 Tubercles 2.5-7 cm. long   *M. longimamma*
          6 Tubercles 0.8-1.6 cm. long   *M. sphaerica*
      4 Hooked spines present
        7 Radial spines 12-15. Central spines 2-6. Flowers
          milky marigold yellow   *M. beneckei*
        7 Radial spines 16-24. Central spines 1 (-2).
          Flowers yellowish-green   *M. heidiae*
    3 Flowers white, yellowish or red. Style not merged
      with the tube. Tubercles not elongated
      8 Hooked spines absent
        9 Spines all pinnate   *M. theresae*
        9 Spines not pinnate
          10 Radial spines 10-15
            11 Radial spines 10-12, taproot. Flowers with
              lighter eye   *M. napina*
            11 Radial spines 13-15   *M. mazatlanensis*
          10 Radial spines 17-45
            12 Central spines absent
              13 Radial spines 17-25   *M. saboae*
              13 Radial spines 33-45   *M. saboae* var. *goldii*
            12 Central spines (0-) 1-6
              14 Radial spines 20-21, translucent white
                M. deherdtiana var. *dodsonii*
              14 Radial spines 33-36, initially pale yellow
                M. deherdtiana
      8 Hooked spines present
        15 Flowers white to yellowish with reddish central
          stripe (tubercles long)   *M. zephyranthoides*
        15 Flowers pink or purple
          16 Radial spines more than 30
            17 Flowers with central stripe. Radial spines
              30-60. Seed corky   *M. tetrancistra*
            17 Flowers without central stripe. Radial spines
              60-80. Seed with white aril   *M. guelzowiana*
          16 Radial spines up to 30
           18 Radial spines 20-30
            19 Flowers 4-5 cm. long, with long tube
                M. longiflora
            19 Flowers shorter
              20 Central spines 4-7   *M. mercadensis*

20 Central spines 1-3 (-4)   *M. microcarpa*
18 Radial spines 10-20
  21 Axils bristly. Tubercles in 5 and 8 rows
    (flowers with darker eye. Body cylindrical)
    22 Tubercles in 5 and 8 rows   *M. fraileana*
    22 Tubercles in 8 and 13 rows   *M. swinglei*
  21 Axils not bristly
    23 Body cylindrical
      24 Flowers without darker eye
        25 Axils sparsely woolly. Central spines 3-4
            M. mazatlanensis
        25 Axils bare. Central spine 1
            M. patonii var. *sinalensis*
      24 Flowers with darker eye and central stripe
        (axils bare. Central spines 1-4)
        26 Tubercles with a keel   *M. sheldonii*
        26 Tubercles rounded   *M. swinglei*
    23 Body rounded
      27 Radial spines 15-20   *M. blossfeldiana*
      27 Radial spines 9-15
        28 Flowers olive- to bluish-green with pink
          margins. Central spines 4   *M. louisae*
        28 Flowers light purple. Central spines
          1-2 (-4)   *M. schumannii*

Group B (Hooked spines)

1 Flowers yellow
  2 Style merged with the tube. Central spines 1-2. Radial
    spines up to 15 *M. surculosa*
  2 Style not merged with the tube. Central spines 3 or more.
    Radial spines 20 or more
    3 Central spines 3-4. Radial spines 20 or more
              M. boedeckeriana
    3 Central spines 8-10. Radial spines 35-40 *M. moelleriana*
1 Flowers whitish to red
  4 Spines distinctly pinnate and hairy   *M. pennispinosa*
  4 Spines not distinctly pinnate and hairy
    5 Axils (at least initially) hairy and bristly together
      6 Radial spines 30-40   *M. bombycina*
      6 Radial spines 11-30
        7 Flowers white, at least inside
          8 Central spines 3.5-5.5 cm. long   *M. magnifica*
          8 Central spine up to 1.5 cm. long
            9 Tubercles with keel   *M. verhaertiana*
            9 Tubercles more or less round   *M. dioica*
        7 Flowers red
          10 Central spines (2-) 4-6
            11 Body cylindrical, clustering. Axils with 15-20
              bristles   *M. guerreronis*
            11 Body more or less globular, solitary. Axils with
              up to 8 bristles   *M. rekoi*
          10 Central spines 7-15   *M. spinosissima*
    5 Axils not hairy and bristly together
      12 Radial spines more than 30
        13 Radial spines 50-70. Central spines 1   *M. glassii*
        13 Radial spines 30-40. Central spines 2-9
          14 Central spines 2-4. Axils profusely woolly
              M. bombycina
          14 Central spines 8-9. Axils bristly   *M. schwarzii*
      12 Radial spines up to 30
        15 Radial spines like hairs, 20-30
        16 Axils bare

    17 Central spines 1 (-3) *M. bocasana*
    17 Central spines 4-7 *M. mercadensis*
   16 Axils with long wool/hair or bristly (central spines 3-4) *M. longicoma* and *M. kunzeana*
  15 Radial spines not like hairs
   18 Axils bristly *M. erythrosperma*
   18 Axils not bristly
    19 Central spines 1-2 (-3)
     20 Central spines 20-30 *M. insularis*
     20 Radial spines 10-20
      21 Body cylindrical, with 5 and 8 rows of tubercles
       22 Axils hairy when young. Stigma purple-red *M. yaquensis*
       22 Axils bare *M. thornberi*
      21 Body rounded, with 8 and 13 or 13 and 21 rows of tubercles
       23 Axils with few bristles. Radial spines 15-18. Flowers 1-1.5 cm. long *M. trichacantha*
       23 Axils bare. Radial spines 10-15. Flowers 2-2.5 cm. long
        24 Inner flower petals with ciliate margin. Stigma lobes dark red. Seed black *M. mainae*
        24 Inner flower petals entire. Stigma lobes greenish. Seed brown *M. carettii*
    19 Central spines 3-5
     25 Axils with few hairy bristles. Body globular to elongated *M. wildii*
     25 Axils bare, if with bristles then body slender columnar
      26 Tubercle rows 13 and 21
       27 Radial spines 20 - 24 *M. zacatecasensis*
       27 Radial spines 15 - 18 *M. zeilmanniana*
      26 Tubercle rows 8 and 13 or 5 and 8
       28 Roots more or less beet-like *M. blossfeldiana* var. *shurliana*
       28 Root not beet-like
        29 Body more or less globular with 8 and 13 rows of tubercles. Radial spines 18-20 *M. rettigiana*
        29 Body slender columnar with 5 and 8 rows of tubercles. Radial spines 12-18 *M. occidentalis*

Group C (small flowers without milky sap in the tubercles and without hooked spines)

1 Body consisting of profusely clustering, thin, cylindrical, small segments
 2 Central spines 0 (-1). Radial spines around 20. Seed brown *M. elongata*
 2 Central spines 0-5. Radial spines 12-14. Seed black *M. gracilis*
1 Body not consisting of thin, cylindrical, small segments
 3 Central spines absent
  4 Radial spines 4-8, hair-like. Tubercles very long *M. camptotricha*
  4 Radial spines 12-100. Tubercles not elongated
   5 Spines hairy *M. plumosa*
   5 Spines no more than rough under a magnifier
    6 Radial spines rough under a magnifier (up to 75, hair-like) *M. schiedeana*
    6 Radial spines smooth
     7 Radial spines around 70-100
      8 Axils bare or slightly woolly
       9 Axils bare. Flowers 2-2.5 cm. long *M. herrerae*
       9 Axils slightly woolly. Flowers 1 cm. long *M. magallanii*
      8 Axils hairy and bristly *M. humboldtii*
     7 Radial spines 12-50
      10 Flowers with central stripe. Body more or less rounded
       11 Flowers red. Axils hairy. Radial spines 12-20 *M. supertexta*
       11 Flowers white to pink. Axils bare. Radial spines 25-30
        12 Spines not in comb-formation *M. aureilanata*
        12 Spines in comb formation (flowers yellowish-white) *M. solisioides*
      10 Flowers without central stripe
       13 Body globular to elongated (flowers whitish). See also *M. albicoma* (usually has central spines) *M. lenta*
       13 Body cylindrical
        14 Flowers red. Axils more or less bristly, hairy. Radial spines 25-30 *M. viperina*
        14 Flowers whitish to pink. Axils not bristly, initially hairy. Radial spines 30-50 *M. microhelia*
3 Central spines present
 15 Body cylindrical
  16 Radial spines 30-50. Flowers yellowish-green *M. microhelia* and *microheliopsis*
  16 Radial spines 10-35. Flowers white to red
   17 Flowers pale reddish *M. albicans* see also *M. verhaertiana* (flowers white with greenish or reddish central stripe, central spine hooked when old)
   17 Flowers red
    18 Flowers red, without central stripe
     19 Radial spines 10-15 *M. sphacelata*
     19 Radial spines 20-30 *M. guerreronis*
    18 Flowers reddish, with central stripe
     20 Central spines 1 *M. matudae*
     20 Central spines 4-8
      21 Radial spines 12-18. Central spines 4-5 *M. occidentalis*
      21 Radial spines up to 35. Central spines 7-8 *M. pottsii*
 15 Body more or less rounded
  22 Flowers sulphur yellow or whitish
   23 Flowers sulphur yellow, externally reddish, inner flower petals without central stripe (radial spines 20-25) *M. densispina*
   23 Flowers whitish, with central stripe
    24 Central spines rough under a magnifier *M. prolifera*
    24 Central spines smooth
     25 Radial spines about 50-75
      26 Radial spines 70-75. Central spines 1. Axils slightly woolly *M. magallanii*
      26 Radial spines about 50. Central spines 8-12. Axils bristly *M. candida*
     25 Radial spines up to 40
      27 Central spines 1-4
       28 Radial spines 7-8. Central spines 1 *M. decipiens*

28 Radial spines 30-40, enveloping the body.
    Central spines 1-4   *M. albicoma*
27 Central spines 6-11
  29 Axils bristly
    30 Radial spines 34-40   *M. schwarzii*
    30 Radial spines 6-10   *M. viereckii*
  29 Axils without bristles. Radial spines 16-20
                           M. discolor
22 Flowers pink to dark red, seldom whitish
  (*M. vaupelii*), if so then without central stripe
  30 Central spines 7-15   *M. spinosissima*
  30 Central spines 1-7
    31 Radial spines absent to a few *M. obconella*
    31 Radial spines 8-34
      32 Axils bare
        33 Central spines 1. Tubercles with keel
                         M. erectacantha
        33 Central spines 2. Tubercles rounded *M. elegans*
      32 Axils hairy or bristly, at least at first
        34 Axils bristly
          35 Axils only bristly. Radial spines 25-30
                         M. nunezii
          35 Axils hairy and bristly. Radial spines 12-22
            36 Flowers virtually white. Flower petals entire.
               Tubercles acute. Central spines 2 (-4)
                          M. aupelii
            36 Flowers red. Flower petals with ciliate or
               serrate margins. Tubercles not acute. Central
               spines 4-6 (-7)
              37 Flowers with white eye. Central spines
                 7-8 mm. long. Stigma lobes green *M. ruestii*
              37 Flowers without white eye. Central spines
                 10-25 mm. long
                38 Flowers 20 mm. long (Stigma pink to
                   straw-coloured)   *M. rhodantha*
                38 Flowers 8-10 mm. long   *M. pringlei*
      34 Axils hairy, but not bristly
        39 Radial spines 15-35. Central spines 2-6
          40 Central spines 2-5 mm. long
            41 Flowers about 7 mm. long. Body usually
               solitary   *M. albilanata*
               See also *M. supertexta* with larger flowers
               and no wool at the crown
            41 Flowers 5-15 mm. long. Body branching
               dichotomously later
              42 Central spines 4-6   *M. crucigera*
              42 Central spines 2   *M. perbella*
           40 Central spines 6-30 mm. long
            43 Central spines 1-2
             44 Central spines not conspicuously long
              45 Stigma lobes reddish   *M. perbella*
              45 Stigma lobes greenish   *M. haageana*
            44 Central spines: one much longer
                       M. dixanthocentron
           43 Central spines 2-7
            46 Central spines more than 1 cm. long
             47 Radial spines 15-20. Central spines 6 (-7)
                       M. pringlei
             47 Radial spines 24-30. Central spines 4-6
                   M. dixanthocentron
           46 Central spines 6-8 mm. long *M. columbiana*

Group D (small flowers with milky sap in the tubercles)

1 Tubercles axe-shaped. Spines in comb-formation
                           M. pectinifera
1 Tubercles roundish or acute. Spines not in comb-formation
  2 Hooked spines present   *M. uncinata*
  2 Hooked spines absent
    3 Radial spines 15-35
      4 Flowers red (Radial spines like hairs)
        5 Axils hairy or hairy and bristly
          6 Axils hairy and bristly. Stigma lobes greenish
            7 Body completely enveloped in hairs *M. hahniana*
            7 Body not enveloped in hairs *M. mendeliana*
          6 Axils only hairy. Stigma lobes reddish *M. brauneana*
        5 Axils bristly (tubercles acute)   *M. woodsii*
      4 Flowers whitish to light pink
        8 Radial spines 30-35
          9 Tubercles with fine points. Body clustering,
            dichotomous   *M. parkinsonii*
          9 Tubercles lacking fine points. *M. klissingiana*
        8 Radial spines 15-25
          10 Tubercles with 3-4 edges
            11 Radial spines not like hairs. Central spines 2 (-6)
              (tubercles with fine points) *M. chionocephala*
            11 Radial spines like hairs. Central spines 0-1.
              (Root beet-like)   *M. coahuilensis*
          10 Tubercles more or less rounded
            12 Axils bristly and hairy (central spines 2-4 (-6)
             13 Body abundantly clustering *M. geminispina*
             13 Body solitary   *M. canelensis*
            12 Axils at most woolly
             14 Central spines 2-6. Flowers 15 mm. long
                       M. formosa
             14 Central spines 1. Flowers 20-25 mm. long
                       M. heyderi
    3 Radial spines 0-12
      15 Flowers yellow
        16 Axils white, woolly with up to 10 bristles. Flowers
          with brownish central stripe *M. voburnensis*
        16 Axils white, woolly, later bare. Flowers with greenish
          sheen   *M. marksiana*
      15 Flowers red, pink, white or whitish
        17 Axils bare
          18 Central spines 4. Radial spines white *M. zeyeriana*
          18 Central spines 0-1 (-2). Radial spines more or less
            horn-coloured, dark-tipped *M. meiacantha*
        17 Axils not bare
          19 Axils hairy
            20 Radial spines absent or soon falling off (central
             spines 4 (-5)   *M. carnea*
            20 Radial spines 3-10
             21 Central spines 4-6. Radial spines 8-12
              22 Flowers with carmine red centre *M. gigantea*
              22 Flowers without carmine red centre *M. nivosa*
            21 Central spines 0-4. Radial spines 3-8
             23 Flowers deep pink with dark eye (central
               spine 1)   *M. melanocentra*
               See also *M. centricirrha* with deep carmine red
               flowers and *M. sempervivi* with reddish central
               stripe
             23 Flowers yellowish
              24 Central spines 2 (-3 -4) *M. sempervivi*
              24 Central spines absent or 1

25 Central spine 1. Radial spines 6-8   *M. bocensis*
25 Central spines 0 (-1). Radial spines 3-5
                                    M. magnimamma
      See also *M. winterae,* not clustering
19 Axils hairy and bristly
  26 Central spines 3-4. Radial spines 5-6 (-10)
     (flowers purple-pink with light eye)   *M. mystax*
  26 Central spines 0-1
    27 Central spines 0 (-1). Radial spines 3-6
      28 Spines 2-7 cm. long. Flowers deep purple/red
                                  M. compressa
      28 Spines no more than 3 cm. long. Flowers
         whitish to pale red   *M. karwinskiana*
         See also *M. praelii*
    27 Central spines 1. Radial spines 7   *M. collinsii*

Key to non-flowering plants

Group key

The group is found by answering the following questions
in sequence:
1. Body elongated cylindrical   **Group A**
  2. Milky sap in the tubercles   **Group B**
    3. Pinnate spines present   **Group C**
      4. Hooked spines present   **Group D**
        5. Central spines absent   **Group E**
          6. Central spine(s) present   **Group F**

Group A (elongated cylindrical)

1 Hooked spines absent
 2 Axils no more than slightly woolly
  3 Radial spines 30-50   *M. microhelia*
  3 Radial spines up to 35
   4 Central spines 7-8   *M. pottsii*
   4 Central spines up to 5
    5 Central spines 0 (-1). Radial spines about 20-30
     6 Axils bare. Radial spines about 20   *M. elongata*
     6 Axils slightly woolly and occasionally with bristles
       Radial spines 25-30   *M. viperina*
       See also *M. gracilis* var. *pulchella* with 12-14 radial
       spines
    5 Central spines 1-5. Radial spines 12-20
     7 Tubercles with four indistinct edges, in 13 and 21
       rows (Axils bare. Central spines 1. Radial spines 18-20)
                                  M. matudae
     7 Tubercles round, in 3 and 5 or 5 and 8 rows (axils
       slightly woolly)   *M. gracilis*
       See also *M. mazatlanensis* and *M. occidentalis* (key
       No. 17) with bare or slightly bristly axils
 2 Axils woolly and bristly
  8 Radial spines 10-20
   9 Radial spines 10-15. Central spines 1-4. Tubercles in 5
    and 8 rows.   *M. sphacelata*
   9 Radial spines 15-20. Central spines 3-8. Tubercles in
    more rows.   *M. albicans*

  8 Radial spines 20-30 (Central spines 2-4 (-5). Tubercles
    in 8 and 13 rows)   *M. guerreronis*
    See also *M. magnifica* with tubercles in 13 and 21 rows
1 Hooked spines present
 10 Radial spines 30-60   *M. tetrancistra*
 10 Radial spines 7-25
  11 Radial spines 7-9, all spines dark-tipped (central spine
    1. Axils woolly)   *M. poselgeri*
  11 Radial spines 10-25, not dark-tipped (except *M. thornberi*
    with bare axils, and *M. swinglei* with bare or bristly axils)
   12 Axils woolly and bristly (radial spines white)
    13 Central spines 1-4 (-5)
     14 Radial spines 20-30   *M. guerreronis*
     14 Radial spines 11-22   *M. dioica*
    13 Central spines 4-6

Mammillaria elongata (group A)

15 Central spines up to 1.2 cm. long. Tubercles in 8
  and 13 rows (tubercles with keel)   *M. verhaertiana*
15 Central spines 3.5-5.5 cm. long. Tubercles in 13
  and 21 rows   *M. magnifica*
12 Axils bare, slightly woolly or with few bristles
  16 Central spines 3-5
    17 Tubercles about 10 mm. wide at the base. (Body
      3-4 cm. thick)   *M. mazatlanensis*
    17 Tubercles 3-4 mm. wide at the base
      18 Radial spines 12-18, 3-8 mm. long. Central spines
        4-5 (body 2-3 cm. thick)   *M. occidentalis*
      18 Radial spines 11-12, 8-10 mm. long. Central
        spines 3-4   *M. fraileana*
  16 Central spines 1-4
    19 Tubercles in 8 and 13 rows
      20 Radial spines 10-15, upper ones reddish-brown.
        Tubercles with keel below   *M. sheldonii*
      20 Radial spines 11-18, white, dark-tipped, tubercles
        rounded   *M. swinglei*
    19 Tubercles in 5 and 8 rows
      21 Radial spines 10-12, grey, brown-tipped
                                       M. patonii var. *sinalensis*
      21 Radial spines 12-20
        22 Radial spines cream-coloured   *M. yaquensis*
        22 Radial spines white, dark-tipped   *M. thornberi*

Mammillaria gigantea (group B)

Group B (with milky sap in the tubercles)

1 Radial spines 40-50, comb-formation (Central spines
  absent. Axils bare)   *M. pectinifera*
1 Radial spines 0-35, not in comb-formation
  2 Radial spines 15-35 (axils not completely bare)
    3 Tubercles 3-edged. Only about 16 radial spines and 0-1
      central spines   *M. coahuilensis*
    3 Tubercles not 3-edged. Spine numbers different
      4 Central spine 1-0. Axils woolly initially only *M. heyderi*
      4 Central spines 2-6, if only 1, then axils woolly and
        bristly (radial spines more or less hair-like. Central
        spines almost always dark-tipped)   *M. sempervivi*
      5 Axils woolly
        6 Tubercle rows 13 and 21. Tubercles with fine white
          points
          7 Body light green
            8 Central spines 4-6   *M. formosa*
            8 Central spines 2   *M. microthele*
          7 Body blue-green (central spines 2-4 (-6)
                                       M. chionocephala
        6 Tubercle rows 21 and 34. Tubercles devoid of fine
          white points (Body grey-green, central spines 2-4)
                                       M. brauneana
      5 Axils woolly and bristly
        9 Radial spines like hairs. Central spines not
          conspicuously long
          10 Radial spines up to 30, white
            11 Radial spines not very bristly   *M. mendeliana*
            11 Radial spines like hairs
              12 Radial spines 4-8 mm. long, not enveloping
                the body
              12 Radial spines 5-15 mm. long, matted,
                enveloping the body   *M. hahniana*

          10 Radial spines 30-35, white with yellowish base
                                       M. klissingiana
          9 Radial spines fine needle-like. Central spines more
            than 25 mm. long
            13 Central spines more or less equally thick. Radial
              spines 16-25
              14 Radial spines 22-25. Central spines orange-yellow
                                       M. canelensis
              14 Radial spines 16-20. Central spines not orange-
                yellow   *M. geminispina*
            13 Central spines: central one much longer and
              thicker than the others. Radial spines 30-35
                                       M. parkinsonii
  2 Radial spines 0-12
    15 Central spines hooked   *M. uncinata*
    15 Central spines not hooked
      16 Axils bristly
        17 Central spines 1.5-2 cm. long, one of them up to
          7 cm. long (central spines 3-4)   *M. mystax*
        17 Central spines not as long or at most radial spines
          very long
          18 Central spines 1-3. Radial spines 7-9
            19 Tubercles more or less rounded   *M. collinsii*
            19 Tubercles acute   *M. voburnensis*
          18 Central spines 0 (-1). Radial spines 4-6
            20 Radial spines initially red   *M. karwinskiana*
            20 Radial spines white to brownish
              21 Radial spines 2-7 cm. long, very uneven
                                       M. compressa
              21 Radial spines 0.2-0.8 cm. long   *M. praelii*
      16 Axils not bristly
        22 Radial and central spines initially brilliant yellow,
          central spines very long   *M. nivosa*
        22 Radial and central spines not yellow
          23 Spines very short, only about 3-4 mm. long (central
            spines 2 (-4)
          23 Spines, at least central spines, powerful
            24 Central spines 4-6
              25 Radial spines absent or 1-2. Axils yellow, woolly.
                Central spines flesh-coloured   *M. carnea*

210

25 Radial spines 6-12. Axils white, woolly or bare.
  Central spines not flesh-coloured
  26 Axils bare (central spines initially ruby red to
    nut brown)   *M. zeyeriana*
  26 Axils white, woolly, at least initially
    27 Central spines black initially. Radial spines
      like hairs (axils becoming bare)   *M. orcuttii*
    27 Central spines yellow to purple. Radial spines
      not like hairs   *M. gigantea*
24 Central spines absent or 1 (-2)
  28 Radial spines 3-6. Central spines 0 (-1). Axils
    woolly
    29 Tubercles 10-12 mm. wide   *M. magnimamma*
    29 Tubercles 15-25 mm. wide   *M. winteriae*
  28 Radial spines 6-10. Central spines 1 (-2). Axils
    becoming bare
    30 Root beet-like   *M. meiacantha*
    30 Root fibrous
      31 Central spine golden yellow   *M. marksiana*
      31 Central spine reddish brown to black
        32 Central spine 8-12 mm. long   *M. bocensis*
        32 Central spine 20-25 mm. long   *M. melanocentra*
16 Axils bristly
  33 Central spines 1.5-2 cm. long, one of them up to
    7 cm. long (central spines 3-4)   *M. mystax*
  33 Central spines not as long or at most radial spines
    very long
    34 Central spines 1-3. Radial spines 7-9
      35 Tubercles acute   *M. voburnensis*
      35 Tubercles more or less rounded   *M. collinsii*
    34 Central spines 0 (-1). Radial spines 4-6
      36 Radial spines red, later dark-tipped *M. karwinskiana*
      36 Radial spines white to brownish
        37 Radial spines 2-8 mm. long   *M. praelii*
        37 Radial spines 2-7 cm. long, very uneven
                                             M. compressa

Group C (feathery spines)

1 Hooked central spine present   *M. pennispinosa*
1 Hooked central spine absent
  2 Central spines 5-12
    3 Central spines appressed, white. Axils woolly *M. theresae*
    3 Central spines projecting, pale yellow. Axils bristly
                                                 M. prolifera
  2 Central spines absent (around 40 tufty radial spines)
                                                 M. plumosa

Group D (hooked spines)

(not including *M. rekoi* and *M. heidiae*)
1 Radial spines up to 20 (mostly yellowish or dark-tipped
  and not like hairs)
  2 Axils bare, at most slightly woolly
    3 Radial spines white, black-tipped. Axils woolly, at least
      initially
      4 Tubercles tubular, light to yellow green. Central spines
        (2-) 4 (-6), radial spines smooth   *M. beneckei*
      4 Tubercles short, 4-sided at the base, grey-green. Central
        spines 1 (-4). Radial spines with fine hairs *M. schumannii*

Mammillaria pennispinosa (group C)

  3 Radial spines differently coloured, or axils bare
    5 Radial spines brown, dark-tipped. Axils initially white,
      woolly (Central spines 4)   *M. louisae*
    5 Radial spines white to yellowish, usually dark-tipped
      (Central spines 1-4)
      6 Axils slightly woolly   *M. blossfeldiana*
      6 Axils bare
        7 Radial spines 1-2 (-3)
          8 Radial spines not dark-tipped
            9 Tubercles 7-9 mm. long
              10 Tubercles in 5 and 8 rows   *M. surculosa*
              10 Tubercles in 8 and 13 rows   *M. carettii*
            9 Tubercles 20-25 mm. long (tubercles in 5 and 8
              rows)   *M. zephyranthoides*
          8 Radial spines dark-tipped
            11 Tubercles 5 mm. long   *M. thornberi*
            11 Tubercles 8-10 mm. long   *M. mainae*
        7 Radial spines 3-4 (without darker tips)
          12 Tubercles in 8 and 13 rows. Radial spines 18-20,
            smooth   *M. rettigiana*
          12 Tubercles in 13 and 21 rows. Radial spines 15-18,
            with fine hairs   *M. zeilmanniana*
  2 Axils bristly
    13 Axils woolly and with 15-20 bristles. Tubercles with
      keel. Central spines 4-6   *M. verhaertiana*
    13 Axils with more or less hair-like bristles only. Tubercles
      rounded. Central spines 1-4
      14 Tubercles in 8 and 13 rows, white spots
                                                  M. erythrosperma
      14 Tubercles in 13 and 21 rows
        15 Central spines 2 (-3), chestnut brown. Radial spines
          15-20   *M. trichacantha*
        15 Central spines 3-4, yellowish to brownish. Radial
          spines 8-20   *M. wildii*
1 Radial spines 20 and more, more or less hair-like
  16 Axils more or less bare
    17 Radial spines about 80 (Central spines 1)
                                                  M. guelzowiana
  17 Radial spines 20-40
    18 Central spines 1 (-3)

Mammillaria moelleriana (group D)

4 Spines not in comb-formation
  5 Spines not covering the body
    6 Radial spines 10-12, whitish to pale yellow   *M. napina*
    6 Radial spines 17-45, translucent white (spines initially
       yellow, later white, see *M. deherdtiana*)
      7 Radial spines 17-25   *M. saboae*
      7 Radial spines 35-45   *M. saboae* var. *goldii*
  5 Spines covering the body
    8 Radial spines 12-20   *M. supertexta*
    8 Radial spines 25-40
      9 Radial spines 25-30. Axils bare   *M. aureilanata*
      9 Radial spines about 30-40. Axils woolly (and bristly)
        10 Radial spines bristly, more or less appressed
                                      M. lenta
        10 Radial spines fine hair-like, more or less
           projecting   *M. albicoma*
3 Spines more than 50
  11 Axils bare (radial spines appressed)   *M. herrerae*
  11 Axils white, woolly, at least slightly
    12 Radial spines with fine hairs or rough under a
       magnifier (Axils with long white wool)   *M. schiedeana*
    12 Radial spines smooth
      13 Axils white, woolly and with 7-8 bristles *M. humboldtii*
      13 Axils slightly hairy   *M. magallanii*

19 Radial spines very fine and long   *M. bocasana*
19 Radial spines needle-like. Root beet-like. *M. insularis*
    See also *M. microcarpa* with more elongated body
18 Central spines several
  20 Central spines 3-4, radial spines 20-30
    21 Spines rough under a magnifier   *M. longiflora*
    21 Spines smooth
      22 Radial spines pale yellowish-green, central spines
         not dark-tipped   *M. zacatecasensis*
      22 Radial spines white, central spines dark-tipped
                                M. boedeckeriana
  20 Central spines 4-10, radial spines 25-40
    23 Radial spines 4-7, radial spines 25-30 *M. mercadensis*
    23 Central spines 8-9 (-10). Radial spines 35-40
                                M. moelleriana
16 Axils woolly and/or bristly
  24 Central spine 1. Radial spines 50-60   *M. glassii*
  24 Central spines 2-15
    25 Radial spines 40-60 (central spines 3-4) *M. tetrancistra*
    25 Radial spines 20-40
      26 Central spines 2-4
        27 Radial spines 30-40   *M. bombycina*
        27 Radial spines 20-30   *M. longicoma* and *M. kunzeana*
      26 Central spines 5-15
        28 Central spines 5-6. Radial spines 30-40   *M. sensilis*
        28 Central spines 7-15. Radial spines 20-30
                                M. spinosissima
    See also *M. schwarzii* with 30-40 radial spines

Group E (species without central spines)

1 Radial spines 4-10. Tubercles very long
  2 Spines 4-7 (-8), bristly, matted. Axils with 2-5 bristles
                                M. camptotricha
  2 Spines 9-10, dark-tipped. Axils only felty or bare
                                M. longimamma
1 Radial spines 10 to about 100. Tubercles not unusually long
  3 Spines up to 45
    4 Spines in comb-formation   *M. solisioides*

Mammillaria saboae f. haudeana (group E)

Group F (with central spines, no special features)

1 Radial spines up to 14
  2 Tubercles about 1-7 cm. long
    3 Tubercles 2.5-7 cm. long (Radial spines about 9-10)
      M. longimamma
    3 Tubercles 1-1.6 cm. long
      4 Radial spines 7-8. Central spines 1.2-1.8 cm. long
        M. decipiens
      4 Radial spines 12-15. Central spines 0.3-0.4 cm. long
        M. sphaerica
  2 Tubercles not particularly elongated
    5 Central spines 1-2
      6 Axils bare. Central spine 1 · *M. erectacantha*
      6 Axils slightly woolly at first. Central spines 1-2
        M. backebergiana
    5 Central spines 3-11
      7 Central spines 3-6. Axils more or less woolly
        8 Radial spines absent or a few thin ones *M. obconella*
        8 Radial spines 12-14 (body abundantly clustering)
          M. gracilis
      7 Central spines 9-11. Axils woolly and bristly *M. vierckii*
1 Radial spines 14 or more
  9 Radial spines about 70-75
    (central spines up to 3 mm. long) *M. magallanii*
  9 Radial spines up to about 50
    10 Radial spines about 50. Central spines 8-12. All spines
      white *M. candida*
    10 Radial spines up to 50 and central spines fewer; if as
      many, then not all spines white
      11 Axils bare and spines white (central spines 2,
        dark-tipped) *M. elegans*
      11 Axils at least more or less felty or woolly initially.
        Spines not all white, except *M. albilanata*
        12 Radial spines like hairs
          13 Axils only woolly at first (central spines 5-6)
            M. baumii
          13 Axils bristly
            14 Axils white, woolly and with hair-like bristles.
              Central spines 0-4 *M. albicoma*
            14 Axils with up to 6 bristles. Central spines 8-9
              M. schwarzii
        12 Radial spines not like hairs
          15 Axils bristly (some woolly)
            16 Axils with hairy bristles. Radial spines 30-50
              M. prolifera var. *texana*
            16 Axils woolly and bristly or only bristly. Radial
              spines up to 30
              17 Radial spines 20-30
                18 Axils only bristly. Central spines 2-4 (-6)
                  M. nunezii
                18 Axils woolly and bristly. Central spines 7-15
                  M. spinosissima
              17 Radial spines 16-22
                19 Tubercles with fine white spots, 4-sided at the
                  base. Body blue-green *M. vaupelii*
                19 Tubercles without fine white spots. Body not
                  blue-green
                  20 Body dark matt green *M. rhodantha*
                  20 Body grass green *M. ruestii*
          15 Axils not bristly
            21 Axils woolly
              22 Central spines 6 (-7), yellow. Radial spines 15-20,

Mammillaria geminispina (group F)

yellowish *M. pringlei*
              22 Central spines 2-4 (-6)
                23 Central spines golden brown, red-brown to black
                  24 Central spines 3-6, golden brown *M. columbiana*
                  24 Central spines 2, red-brown to black
                    M. haageana
                23 Central spines white to yellow
                  25 Central spines about 25 mm. long
                    M. dixanthocentron
                  25 Central spines only 2-3 cm. long
                    26 Radial spines 15-20. Central spines white
                      M. albilanata
                    26 Radial spines 25 or more. Central spines
                      yellowish *M. crucigera*
            21 Axils only initially or slightly woolly
              27 Central spines with one up to 3 cm. long, yellow,
                particularly strong central spine *M. dixanthocentron*
              27 Central spines different
                28 Radial spines 33-36 (central spines (0-) 1 (-6)
                  M. deherdtiana
                28 Radial spines up to 30
                  29 Central spines 1-2 *M. perbella*
                  29 Central spines 3-6 (-8)
                    30 Radial spines 16-20 *M. discolor*
                    30 Radial spines 20-25
                      31 Radial spines translucent white. Tubercles in
                        5 and 8 rows. Body up to 4 cm. wide and
                        3 cm. tall. *M. deherdtiana* var. *dodsonii*
                      31 Radial spines darker later. Tubercles in 8
                        and 13 rows. Body up to 10 cm. wide
                        and tall. *M. densispina*

Mammillaria aureilanata

Mammillaria baumii

(2) **M. albicans** (Br. & R.) Berger
Later elongated and clustering, without milky sap. Axils at first woolly and bristly. Radial spines 15-20, white. Central spines 3-8, often dark-tipped. Flowers reddish, about 1.8 cm. wide. Seed black. Mexico (lower California).

(4) **M. albicoma** Bód.
Globular, clustering, without milky sap. Axils white, woolly and with hair-like bristles. Radial spines about 30-40, white, hair-like, enveloping the body. Central spines 0-4, white, tipped red-brown. Flowers pale greenish-yellow to white, 1-1.5 cm. long. Seed dark grey. Mexico (Tamaulipas).

(11) **M. albilanata** Backeb. (*M. fuauxiana* Backeb.)
Short cylindrical, usually solitary, without milky sap. Axils white, hairy. Radial spines 15-20, chalk white, somewhat brownish at the base. Central spines 2 to (seldom) 4, only 2-3 mm. long, white. Flowers dark pink to deep carmine, only 7 mm. long. Seed light brown. Mexico (Guerrero).

(5) **M. aureilanata** Backeb.
Solitary globes without milky sap, with bare axils. Radial spines 25-30, hair-like, golden yellow-white. Central spines absent. Flowers whitish to pale pink with pale pink central stripe, about 3 cm. long and 1.8 cm. wide. Seed black. Mexico (San Luis Potosí).

Water fairly sparingly.

(10) **M. backebergiana** Buchenau
Globular to elongated, soon clustering, with milky sap inside. Axils initially slightly white, woolly. Radial spines 8-10. Central spines 1-2, usually brown and dark-tipped. Flowers carmine red, 1.8 cm. long. Seed brown. ?Mexico.

(Do) **M. baumii** Bód. (*Dolichothele b.* (Bód.) Werderm. & Buxb.)
Elongated, clustering, without milky sap. Axils woolly, but only at first. Radial spines 30-35, hair-like, white. Central spines 5-6, pale yellow. Flowers yellow, 3 cm. long and wide, strongly scented. Seed black. Style merged with the tube. Mexico (Tamaulipas).

Likes gentle shade from brilliant sun and is sensitive to stagnant moisture.

(Oe) **M. beneckei** Ehrenb. (*Dolichothele b.* (Ehrenb.) Backeb.; *Oehmea nelsonii* (Br. & R.) Buxb.).
Elongated, clustering stems without milky sap. Axils slightly woolly. Radial spines 12-15, white, dark-tipped. Central spines 2-6, usually dark, one hooked. Flowers milky marigold yellow, 3-4 cm. wide. Seed black. Style merged with the tube. Mexico (Guerrero).

(2) **M. blossfeldiana** Bód.
Rounded, solitary, without milky sap. Axils slightly woolly. Radial spines 15-20, at first yellowish at the bottom, dark brown to blackish at the top.

Central spines (3-) 4, one hooked, dark brown to black. Flowers pink carmine with darker central stripe, up to about 3.5 cm. long and about 2 cm. wide. Seed black. Mexico (Lower California).

var. shurliana (H.E. Gates) Wiggins (*M.s.* H.E. Gates)
Has a thicker main root, 3 central spines and 2 cm. long flowers.

(3) **M. bocasana** Poselg.
Globular, forming groups, without milky sap. Axils naked. Radial spines 25-30, hair-like, white. Central spines 1 (-3), yellowish-brownish, one hooked. Flowers yellowish-white with pink or brownish central stripe 1.6 cm. long and up to 1.2 cm. wide. Seed glossy dark brown. Mexico (San Luis Potosí).

A widespread and very popular species. The brilliant red fruit, 3-4 cm. long, are more distinctive than the flowers. Do not keep the plant too moist.

(13) **M. bocensis** Craig (*M. rubida* Backeb.)
Solitary, globular, with milky sap. Axils slightly woolly and sometimes with 1-2 bristles. Radial spines 6-8, reddish-brown to reddish-black. Central spine 1, same colour. Flowers greenish-white, margins sometimes slightly pink, 2 cm. long. Seed light brown. Mexico (Sonora).

214

(3) **M. boedeckeriana** Quehl
This species may belong to *M. moelleriana*. Globular to elongated, not clustering, without milky sap. Tubercles finely spotted, axils bare. Radial spines 20 or more, white. Central spines 3-4, light brown, dark-tipped. Flowers brownish-yellow with brownish-pink central stripe, up to 3 cm. long. Seed black. Mexico (San Luis Potosí).

(3) **M. bombycina** Quehl
Elongated, solitary or clustering, without milky sap. Axils profusely woolly. Radial spines 30-40, white. Central spines 2-4, white to yellow, one hooked. Flowers light carmine to pink, 1.5 cm. long and wide. Seed black. Mexico (San Luis Potosí, Coahuila).

A popular, very beautifully spined species. Some plants have almost yellow central spines, others are deep red-brown. Bright conditions in winter are required for good flower setting. Do not keep too moist. (See illustration page 204)

(12) **M. brauneana** Bód. (*M. saetigera* Bód. & Tiegel)
Hunt includes this species under *M. hahniana*. Usually solitary, slightly elongated, with milky sap. Axils white, woolly, with thin bristles. Radial spines 25-30, hair-like, white. Central spines 2-4, reddish, black-tipped. Flowers violet-red, with central stripe, 1.3 cm. long. Seed dark-brown. Mexico (Tamaulipas).

M. bucareliensis Craig see *M. magnimamma*

(8) **M. camptotricha** Dams (*Dolichothele c.* (Dams) Tiegel; *Dolichothele albescens* (Tiegel) Backeb.; *Pseudo-mammillaria c.* (Dams) Buxb.)
Profusely clustering, globular, without milky sap, with long tubercles. Axils slightly woolly, with 2-5 yellow bristles. Radial spines 4-7 (-8), hair-like, yellow. Central spines absent. Flowers white with greenish central stripe, 1.3-2 cm. long and 1 cm. wide. Seed brown. Mexico (Querétaro).

A popular, robust species. It is also known in some areas as the 'bird's nest cactus' because of its matted spines.

(13) **M. canelensis** Craig
Solitary, globular, with milky sap. Axils white, woolly and with white bristles. Radial spines 22-25, white. Central spines 2-4, orange-yellow. Flowers light greenish-yellow, 1.8 cm. long and 1.5 cm. wide, seed brown. Mexico (Sonora/Chihuahua border area).

(My) **M. candida** Scheidw. (*M. ortizrubiona* (Bravo) Werderm.)
Solitary, also clustering, globular to very elongated, without milky sap. Axils with up to 7 bristles. Radial spines about 50, white. Central spines 8-12, white, tinged with pink. Flowers dirty pink with whitish margins, 2 cm. long. Seed black. Mexico (San Luis Potosí).

A very attractive plant with its dense spines. The pink-spined forms are very beautiful and especially prized. The species grows slowly, requires permeable, sandy soil and does not like to be kept too moist.

(14) **M. carnea** Zucc.
Solitary, also clustering, globular to elongated, with milky sap. Tubercles angular. Axils yellow, woolly. Radial spines absent or 1-2. Central spines 4 (- 5), flesh-coloured, black-tipped. Flowers pink, with darker central stripe and pale green throat, 1.5-2 cm. long and 1.2-1.5 cm. wide. Seed light brown. Mexico (Hidalgo, Guerrero, Puebla, Oaxaca).

Mammillaria carnea

Mammillaria camptotricha

M. orcuttii Bód. is included in *M. carnea* by Hunt. However, it has very white, woolly axils initially, and 6-8 white, hair-like radial spines which soon fall off.

(Do) M. carrettii Rebut
Usually solitary, round to slightly elongated, without milky sap. Axils bare. Radial spines 14-15, yellow, the upper ones brown. Central spines 1, brown, hooked. Flowers whitish with pink central stripe, 2.5 cm. long, scented. Seed brown. Mexico (probably Nuevo León).

M. celsiana Lem. see *M. dixanthocentron*

M. centricirrha Lem. see *M. magnimamma*

(12) M. chionocephala J.A. Purpus
Globular, seldom clustering, with milky sap. Tubercles 4-edged, spotted white. Axils white, woolly, with many hairs. Radial spines 22-24, white. Central spines 2 (-6), dirty white to brownish, blackish-tipped. Flowers white to flesh-coloured, with red central stripe, 1.8-2.2 cm. long. Seed light brown. Mexico (Coahuila, Durango).

(13) M. coahuilensis (Bód.) Moran (*M. schwartzii* (Bód.) Backeb.; *Porfiria*

Mammillaria crucigera

schwartzii (Frič) Bód.)
Solitary, globular, with milky sap. Tubercles triangular at the base. Axils slightly woolly. Radial spines about 16, white-grey. Central spines absent or 1, brownish. Spines slightly scaly. Flowers whitish with centre tinged light pink and darker central stripe, up to 3 cm. wide. Seed light brown or almost black. Root beet-shaped. Mexico (Coahuila).

(14) M. collinsii (Br. & R.) Orcutt
At first solitary, later forming groups, globular, with milky sap. Axils very white, woolly and bristly. Radial spines 7, light-coloured, dark-tipped. Central spines 1, yellowish. Flowers yellowish with pink central stripe about 1.5 cm. long. Seed light brown. Mexico (Oaxaca).

(9) M. columbiana Salm-Dyck
Globular to elongated, without milky sap. Axil densely woolly. Radial spines 18-30, white. Central spines 3-6, golden brown. Flowers deep pink with darker central stripe, greenish-yellow in the throat, 0.8-1 cm. long. Seed light brown. Colombia, Venezuela.

(13) M. compressa DC. (*M. seitziana* Mart.)
Forming cushions, round or oval body with milky sap. Axils with white wool and bristles. Radial spines (2-) 4-6,

usually white, but also brownish, 2-7 mm. long. Central spines absent. Flowers deep purple-red, up to 1.5 cm. long. Seed light brown. Mexico (Querétaro, Hidalgo, San Luis Potosí).

This is one of the 'green' Mammillaria species, and is recommended to the beginner. It grows strongly and forms large cushions with increasing age. With its green body, white wool and red fruit the plant looks very pretty. The species is very variable, and a number of forms are available.

M. cowperae Shurley see
M. moelleriana

(11) M. crucigera Mart.
Elongated body with milky sap, divides by branching. Axils woolly. Radial spines 24 or more, white. Central spines 4 (-6), yellowish. Flowers purple-red, very small. Seed brown. Mexico (Oaxaca, Pueblo Hidalgo, San Luis Potosí).

This species grows slowly and requires permeable soil and little water.

M. dealbata Dietr. see *M. elegans* hort.

(8) M. decipiens Scheidw. (*Dolichothele d.* (Scheidw.) Tiegel)
Clustering, globular, without milky sap. Axils slightly woolly, up to 4 bristles. Radial spines 7-8, yellowish-white. Central spines 1 (-2), yellowish at the bottom, reddish-brown above. Flowers white with pink central stripe. 1.5-2 cm. long. Seed brown. Mexico (San Luis Potosí).

(1) M. deherdtiana Farwig
Compressed globular, solitary, without milky sap. Axils slightly woolly, sometimes bare. Radial spines 33-36, at first light yellow, later white. Central spines (0-) 1-6, light to dark red-brown. Flowers light pink-violet with darker central stripe, up to 5 cm. wide. Seed dark brown-black. Mexico (Oaxaca).

var. dodsonii (Bravo) Glass & Foster (*M.d.* Bravo)
Dwarf variety from an altitude of 3000 m.; only 20-21 radial spines and 3-5 central spines.

Mammillaria deherdtiana var. dodsonii

Mammillaria dixanthocentron

(7) **M. densispina** (Coult.) Vaup.
Solitary, globular or slightly elongated, without milky sap. Axils only woolly at first. Radial spines 20-25, yellowish. Central spines 5-6, yellow to fox red. Flowers reddish outside, pale yellow inside, up to 2 cm. long and about 1 cm. wide. Seed reddish-brown. Mexico (San Luis Potosí, Querétaro, Guanajuato).

(2) **M. dioica** K. Brandeg.
Cylindrical, clustering, without milky sap. Axils slightly woolly and with 5-15 bristles. Radial spines 11-22, white to pink, dark-tipped. Central spines 1-4, one hooked, brownish to brown-black. Flowers cream-coloured with purple-pink central stripe, 1.2-3 cm. long, not completely dioecious. Seed black. USA (S. California), Mexico (Lower California).

(9) **M. discolor** Haw.
Globular to oval, usually clustering, without milky sap. Axils slightly woolly or bare. Radial spines 16-20, white. Central spines 4-6 (-8), light-coloured. Flowers white with pink central stripe, 2 cm. long and 1.6 cm. wide, exceptionally up to 2.5 cm. Seed brown. Mexico (Puebla).

(11) **M. dixanthocentron** Backeb. (*M. celsianas* Lem.)
Solitary body, slightly elongated when old, with watery or semi-milky sap, depending on time of year. Axils woolly. Radial spines 19-30, white. Central spines 2-4 (-6), yellowish-white, one of them about 2.5 cm. long. Flowers light red, about 1.5 cm. long. Seed brown. Mexico (San Luis Potosí to Oaxaca).

A very beautiful species with its distinctive spine formation. It likes a bright, warm summer location and not too much water.

M. dodsonii Bravo see *M. deherdtiana* var. *dodsonii*

M. dumetorum J. A. Purpus see *M. schiedeana*

M. echinaria DC. see *M. gracilis* (11)

M. elegans hort. (*M. dealbata* Dietr.)
These plants are included in *M. haageana* by Hunt. Solitary, globular, with milky sap. Axils bare. Radial spines 25-30, according to the original description by DC.; only 16-23 in cultivated *M. elegans* specimens. Central spines (1-) 2, white, brown-tipped. Flowers carmine red, about 1.5 cm.

long. Seed brown. Mexico (Puebla, Oaxaca, Hidalgo, Morelos) see illustration page 203.

(7) **M. elongata** DC.
Abundantly clustering, thin elongated segments without milky sap. Axils bare. Radial spines about 20, whitish to yellow or fox red to brown. Central spines 0 (-1). Flowers whitish to pale yellow, 1-1.5 cm. long. Seed light brown. Mexico (Hidalgo).

This popular and widely cultivated species forms beautiful groups when old. It likes sandy, permeable soil and not too much water. A sunny location ensures a dense, well-coloured spine formation (see illustration page 209).

var. rufocrocea (Salm-Dyck) K. Schum. Spines red-yellow. Central spine usually absent.

var. stella-aurata (Mart.) K. Schum. Spines golden yellow, brown-tipped. Central spine present.

(9) **M. erectacantha** Först.
Solitary, globular, with milky sap. Tubercles with keel. Axils bare. Radial spines 10-11, white, brown-tipped. Central spine 1, brownish, darker-tipped. Seed brown. Mexico (Hidalgo, Mexico).

217

Mammillaria guelzowiana

(3) **M. erythrosperma** Bód.
Clustering, globular or slightly
elongated, without milky sap. Axils
bristly only. Radial spines 15-20, white
with yellowish base. Central spines 1-3
(-4), hooked, yellow with reddish tips.
Flowers carmine with light margins,
1.5 cm. long. Seed black-red. Mexico
(San Luis Potosí).

M. fasciculata Engelm. see *M. thornberi*

M. flavescens (DC.) Haw. see *M. nivosa*

(12) **M. formosa** Gal.
Solitary, later clustering, globular to
elongated, with milky sap. Axils
woolly. Radial spines 20-25, white.
Central spines 4-6, flesh-coloured, with

black tips. Flowers purple-pink with
lighter margins, up to 1.5 cm. long
and wide. Seed light brown. Mexico
(?Guanajuato, San Luis Potosí,
Hidalgo).

Hunt includes *M. microthele* Mühlpf. in
M. formosa, but it only has 2 central
spines and white flowers with red
central stripes. Mexico (Tamaulipas,
Coahuila).

M. fragilis Salm-Dyck see *M. gracilis*
var. *fragilis*

(2) **M. fraileana** (Br. & R.) Bód.
Cylindrical body without milky sap,
later clustering. Axils bare, bristles few.
Radial spines 11-12, brownish to

218

white. Central spines 3 (-4), hooked. Flowers white, tinged with pink, with darker throat, up to about 3 cm. wide. Seed black. Mexico (Lower California).

A fine, large-flowered, but slightly temperamental species, which should be kept warm and watered with care.

M. fuauxiana Backeb. see *M. albilanata*

(12) **M. geminispina** Haw.
Profusely clustering globes with milky sap. Axils white, woolly and bristly. Radial spines 16-20, white. Central spines 2-4 (-6), more or less brown-tipped, very long. Flowers yellowish with red centre and central stripe, 1.9 cm. long. Seed light brown. Mexico (Hidalgo, San Luis Potosí, Veracruz).

With their long central spines, almost pure white in many forms, this species is very ornamental. It requires a sunny location, permeable soil and a little manuring lime now and then (see page 213 for illustration).

(13) **M. gigantea** Hildm.
Solitary globes with milky sap. Axils woolly. Radial spines 12, almost white. Central spines 4-6, yellow to purple. Flowers greenish cream-coloured with carmine red centre, about 1.5 cm. long and wide. Seed light brown. Mexico (Guanajuato, Querétaro) (See page 210 for illustration).

(3) **M. glassii** Foster
Clustering, globular, without milky sap. Axils with hair-like bristles. Radial spines 50-60 external and 6-8 internal, white. Central spine 1, hooked, amber. Flowers light pink, up to 1.4 cm. long. Seed black. Mexico (Nuevo León).

M. glochidiata Mart. see *M. wildii*

M. goldii Glass & Foster see *M. saboae* var. *goldii*

(4) **M. gracilis** Pfeiff. (*M. echinaria* DC.)
Abundantly clustering, elongated, without milky sap. Axils slightly woolly. Radial spines 12-14, more or less whitish. Central spines 3-5, light to dark brown. Flowers yellowish-white, 1.7 cm. long and 1.3 cm. wide. Seed black. Mexico (Hidalgo, Querétaro).

A very popular, well-known and variable species. The side shoots fall off easily and root very readily. The species needs permeable soil, not too much water and a sunny location. The plant becomes etiolated if kept too dark.

var. fragilis (Salm-Dyck) Berger (*M. fragilis* Salm-Dyck)
With 1-2 central spines.

var. pulchella Salm-Dyck
No central spines and weaker, brownish radial spines.

(2) **M. guelzowiana** Werderm. (*Krainzia g.* (Werderm.) Backeb.)
Solitary, later clustering, globular, without milky sap. Axils bare. Radial spines about 80, hair-like. Central spines 1, hooked, yellow, red or brown. Flowers brilliant carmine pink, 5 cm. long and up to 6 cm. wide. Seed almost black, with small white aril. Mexico (Durango).

Mammillaria haageana

These hair-covered globes with their large, brilliant flowers are amazingly beautiful, but they do require a warm, sunny location, permeable soil, and sparse watering, and are very sensitive to stagnant moisture.

(10) **M. guerreronis** (Bravo) Backeb. Cylindrical, clustering, with milky sap inside. Axils white, woolly, with 15-20 bristles. Radial spines 20-30, white. Central spines 2-4 (-5), initially or occasionally hooked, white or pink. Flowers red. Seed brown. Mexico (Guerrero).

(11) **M. haageana** Pfeiff.
Globular to elongated, solitary, seldom clustering, without milky sap. Axils flocked with wool. Radial spines 18-20 (-25), white. Central spines 2, red-brown to black. Flowers purple-pink with darker central stripe, 1.2 cm. long. Seed light olive brown. Mexico (Veracruz).

Mammillaria hahniana   **Mammillaria heidiae**

(11) **M. hahniana** Werderm.
Group-forming, globular with milky
sap. Axils with short white wool and
up to 20 bristles. Radial spines 20-30,
white hair-like. Central spines 1 (-2 -5),
whitish, dark-tipped. Flowers carmine
to purple-red, 1.5-2 cm. wide. Seed
dirty brown. Mexico (Querétaro,
Guanajuato).

This plant's body, enveloped in fine
white hairs, is very beautiful. The
species likes a sunny, warm location
and sparse watering. It will only flower
profusely in full sunshine.

M. haudeana Lau & Wagner see *M.
saboae* var. *haudeana*

(Do) **M. heidiae** Krainz
Globular, solitary, without milky sap.
Axils bristly. Radial spines 16-24,
translucent white. Central spines 1 (-2),
hooked, yellowish brown, red-brown
towards the tip. Flowers yellowish-
green, 3 cm. long and 2.5 cm. wide.
Seed black. Mexico (Puebla).

(5) **M. herrerae** Werderm.
Solitary or slightly clustering, globular,
without milky sap. Axils bare. Radial
spines about 100, white to ash-grey,
very fine. Central spines absent.
Flowers pale pink to violet with darker
central stripe, 2-2.5 cm. long and 2-3
cm. wide. Seed matt black. Mexico
(Querétaro).

The fine white spines completely
envelop the plant. Plants grown on
their own root only grow to a size of
3-3.5 cm., but the flowers are
comparatively very large. The species
is rather temperamental and often
needs to be grafted onto a slow-
growing rootstock. It requires a warm,
sunny position, a permeable, rather
mineral soil and a sparing supply of
water.

(13) **M. heyderi** Mühlpf.
Solitary, globular to compressed, with
milky sap. Axils initially woolly. Radial
spines 20-22, almost white. Central
spines 1, seldom absent, brownish-
white. Flowers bluish-pink with cream-
coloured margins, 2-2.5 cm. long.
Seed reddish-brown. USA (Texas,
New Mexico, S.E. Arizona) as far as
Mexico (Sonora, Chihuahua, Zacatecas
to Tamaulipas and Nuevo León).

M. hidalgensis J.A. Purpus
see *M. obconella*

(5) **M. humboldtii** Ehrenb.
Solitary, occasionally slightly clustering,
globular to elongated, without milky
sap. Axils white, woolly and with 7-8
bristles. Radial spines up to 80 or
more, brilliant white. Central spines
absent. Flowers light carmine, 1.5 cm.
wide. Seed black. Mexico (Hidalgo).

A very beautiful species, with snow-

220

Mammillaria longiflora

Mammillaria longimamma

white spines. It requires permeable, rather mineral soil and should only be watered sparingly.

(2) **M. insularis** Gates
Globular, clustering, without milky sap, with taproot. Axils bare or with sparse white wool. Radial spines 20-30, white. Central spines 1, hooked, light-coloured below, golden-brown to black above. Flowers white with light pink central stripe. 1.5-2.5 cm. long. Seed black. Mexico (lower California).

(11) **M. karwinskiana** Mart. (*M. nejapensis* Craig & Dawson)
Solitary or dichotomously branching, globular to elongated, with milky sap. Tubercles angular below. Axils woolly and bristly. Radial spines 3-6, initially red, later only dark-tipped. Central spines absent or seldom 1. Flowers whitish wth red central stripe, 2 cm. long and 1.5 cm. wide. Seed light brown. Mexico (Pueblo, Oaxaca). *M. neomystax* Backeb. is very similar to *M. karwinskiana* but has light red flowers, only 0.7 cm. long and 1.3 cm. wide.

(12) **M. klissingiana** Böd.
Solitary or clustering, globular or elongated, with milky sap. Axils woolly and bristly. Radial spines 30-35, white with yellowish base. Central spines 2-4, white, dark-tipped. Flowers delicate pink with almost white margins and

greenish throat, 1 cm. long and 0.8 cm. wide. Seed dark reddish-brown. Mexico (Tamaulipas).

(3) **M. kunzeana** Böd & Quehl
Globular to elongated, later clustering, without milky sap. Axils with numerous bristles. Radial spines 20-25, snow-white, central spines 3-4, like fine hairs, one hooked, usually with differently coloured zones. Flowers pink outside, white inside, 2 cm. long and 1.5 cm. wide. Seed dark brown to black. Mexico (Zacatecas, Querétaro).

M. lanata (Br. & R.) Orcutt
see *M. supertexta*

(5) **M. lenta** K. Brandeg.
Globular to elongated, single or clustering, stems divide by forking, without milky sap. Axils with short wool and sometimes one bristle. Radial spines 30-40, yellowish to transparent white. Central spines absent. Flowers whitish, 2 cm. long and 2.5 cm. wide. Seed black. Mexico (Coahuila).

(3) **M. longicoma** (Br. & R.) Berger.
This species is very similar to *M. bocasana*. Globular to elongated, single or clustering, without milky sap. Axils with long woolly hairs. Radial spines 25 or more, hair-like, white. Central spines 4, hairy, 1 or 2 of them

hooked, brown with lighter base. Flowers almost white to cream-pink with pale green central stripe, 1.7 cm.long. Seed black. Mexico (San Luis Potosí).

Cultivate in warm but half-shaded conditions, not below 10°C in winter.

(1) **M. longiflora** (Br. & R.) Berger (*Krainzia l.* (Br. & R.) Backeb.)
Solitary, sometimes clustering, globular, without milky sap. Axils bare or slightly felty. Radial spines 25-30, white. Central spines 4, one of them hooked, light yellow to red-brown. Flowers pink, often with darker central stripe, up to 4.5 cm. long, about 4 cm. wide. Seed almost black, with small white aril. Mexico (Durango).
A popular, large-flowered species, which should only be watered with care as it is sensitive to stagnant moisture.

(Do) **M. longimamma** DC. (*Dolichothele l.* (DC.) Br. & R.)
Solitary or clustering, globular, without milky sap. Axils felty or bare. Tubercles very long, 2.5-7 cm. Radial spines 9-10, white to pale yellow, dark-tipped. Central spines absent or 1 (-3), light brown. Flowers pale yellow, about 6 cm. long and 6 cm. wide. Style merged with the tube. Seed black. Mexico (Hidalgo).

221

Mammillaria magallanii, flowers

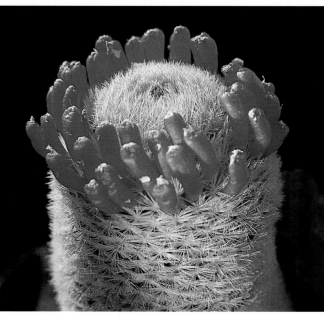

Mammillaria magallanii, fruit

(2) **M. louisae** Linds.
Solitary, rarely clustering, globular, without milky sap. Axils initially with white felt. Radial spines about 11, light brown, dark-tipped. Central spines 4, one of them hooked, brown and dark-tipped. Flowers lavender-coloured pink inside, with light red or white margins, 3.5 cm. long and up to 4 cm. wide. Seed black. Mexico (Lower California).

Like all large-flowering lower Californian Mammillarias this species needs to be kept warm — even in winter — and watered sparingly.

(5) **M. magallanii** Schmoll
Globular, solitary, without milky sap, with taproot. Axils slightly woolly. Radial spines 70-75, brownish-orange below, brown-tipped above, soon turning chalky white. Central spines 0-1, occasionally hooked. Flowers cream-coloured with brownish-pink central stripe, 1 cm. long and 0.6 cm. wide. Seed black. Mexico (Coahuila).

This beautiful and popular species remains relatively small and grows slowly. It flowers very early in spring with inconspicuous flowers, but the red berries which appear later are very decorative.

(10) **M. magnifica** Buchenau
Group-forming, elongated, with milky sap. Axils white, woolly and bristly.

Radial spines 18-24, translucent white. Central spines 4-6, one of them almost always hooked. Flowers pink, flesh-coloured, white inside, with brownish margins, 2 cm. long and about 1.2 cm. wide. Seed dark brown. Mexico (Puebla).

(13) **M. magnimamma** Haw. (*M. bucareliensis* Lem.)
Clustering, compressed globular, with

milky sap. Axils white, woolly. Tubercles with four edges. Radial spines 3-6, horn-coloured, black-tipped. Central spines absent, seldom 1 (-2). Flowers dirty cream with reddish central stripe (Flowers deep carmine red: *M. centricirrha* Lem.), 2-2.5 cm. long and wide. Seed dark brown. Mexico (Hidalgo, Mexico, San Luis Potosí).

Mammillaria magnimamma

(2) **M. mainae** K. Brandeg.
Solitary, also clustering, elongated, without milky sap. Axils bare. Radial spines 10-15, yellowish, dark-tipped. Central spines 1-2 (-3), darker, one of them hooked. Flowers white with red central stripe, up to 2 cm. long and 2.5 cm. wide. Seed black. Mexico (Sonora, Sinaloa), USA (Arizona).

(Co) **M. maritima** (Linds.) Hunt (*Cochemiea* m. Linds.)
Clustering, cylindrical, without milky sap. Radial spines 10-15, central spines 4, the bottom one hooked. All spines reddish-brown. Flowers scarlet-red, bilaterally symmetrical, 3 cm. long. Seed black. Mexico (lower California). Included in *M. pondii* Greene by Hunt.

(13) **M. marksiana** Krainz
Solitary, globular to compressed globular with milky sap. Axils white, woolly, later bare. Tubercles with four indistinct edges. Radial spines 8-10, yellow. Central spines 1, golden yellow. Flowers yellow with greenish sheen, about 1.5 cm. wide. Seed light to dark brown. Mexico (Sinaloa).

Distinctive yellow flowers, which are rare in the *Mammillaria* family in the more narrow sense.

M. martinezii Backeb. see *M. supertexta*

Mammillaria maritima

(10) **M. matudae** Bravo
Cylindrical, clustering, with milky sap. Tubercles with four indistinct edges. Axils bare. Radial spines 18-20, white with yellowish base. Central spines 1, initially pink or pink-tipped, later white. Flowers light purple, 1.2 cm. long. Seed light brown. Mexico (Mexico, Guerrero).

(2) **M. mazatlanensis** (Rebut) K. Schum. & Gürke
Abundantly clustering, cylindrical, without milky sap. Axils slightly woolly. Radial spines 13-15, white. Central spines 3-4, light reddish-brown, one of them often hooked. Flowers carmine to purple-pink, 4 cm. long and up to 3 cm. wide. Seed black. Mexico (Sinaloa).

The species likes permeable, sandy soil, a warm situation and sparing supplies of water.

(13) **M. meiacantha** Engelm. (*M. heyderi* Mühlpf. var. *m.* (Engelm.) L. Benson)
Rounded, usually not clustering, with taproot and milky sap. Tubercles with 4 edges. Axils bare. Radial spines 5-9. Central spines absent or 1 (-2). Spines all more or less horn-coloured, dark-tipped. Flowers white with pale red central stripe, 2.5-3.2 cm. long and 2 cm. wide. Seed yellow-brown. USA (Texas, New Mexico, Arizona), Mexico (South as far as Zacatecas).

(13) **M. melanocentra** Poselg.
Solitary, compressed globular to globular, with milky sap. Axils initially white, woolly. Tubercles with four sharp edges. Radial spines 7-9, at first black, then grey. Central spines 1, black, soon brownish. Flowers deep pink with darker centre, 1.8 cm. long and 2.5 cm. wide. Seed reddish-brown. Mexico (Nuevo León, Coahuila), USA (Texas, New Mexico).

(12) **M. mendeliana** (Bravo) Werderm.
Globular to elongated, solitary, with milky sap. Tubercles with four edges at the base. Axils strongly white, woolly and bristly. Radial spines numerous,

Mammillaria mercadensis

taking the form of short, white, bristly hairs. Central spines 2-4, brown-red with black tip. Flowers pink with deep red central stripe, 1 cm. long. Seed light brown. Mexico (Guanajuato, Querétaro).

(3) **M. mercadensis** Pat.
Solitary or slightly clustering, globular to slightly elongated, without milky sap. Axils bare. Radial spines 25-30, initially hair-like, white. Central spines 4-7, brown, reddish or yellowish, one of them hooked. Flowers yellowish-white to pale pink, 3 cm. wide. Seed black. Mexico (Durango).

This species has beautiful spines. Water sparingly.

(2) **M. microcarpa** Engelm.
Globular to cylindrical, solitary or

223

clustering, without milky sap. Axils naked. Radial spines 15-30, white to dark yellow, brown-tipped. Central spines 1-3 (- 4), one hooked, light brownish to black. Flowers pink with darker central stripe, 2-2.5 cm. long and 4 cm. wide. Seed black. Mexico (Sonora, Chihuahua), USA (Texas, Arizona).

(7) M. microhelia Werderm.
(*Leptocladodia m.* (Werderm.) Buxb.)
Usually solitary, cylindrical, without milky sap. Axils initially slightly woolly. Radial spines almost 50. Central spines absent to 4, red to dark brown. Flowers white to yellowish-green or pink, 1.6 cm. long and wide. Seed golden brown. Mexico (Querétaro).

This species is very popular and widespread, and flowers readily in the spring. The name *microhelia* means 'small sun', and refers to the attractive patterns of the radial spines.

var. microheliopsis (Werderm.) Backeb. (*M.m.* Werderm).
Radial spines 30-40. Central spines 6-8. Flowers light purple.

M. microheliopsis Werderm. see *M. microhelia* var. *microheliopsis*

Mammillaria microhelia

M. microthele Mühlpf see *M. formosa*

(3) M. moelleriana Böd.
Solitary, globular to oval, without milky sap. Axils bare. Radial spines 35-40, white. Central spines 8-9 (-10), hooked, light honey-coloured. Flowers yellowish-cream with pink central stripe, 1.5 cm. long and wide. Seed glossy black. Mexico (Durango, Zacatecas), see illustration page 212.

This species flowers in the early spring. It is sensitive to stagnant moisture and therefore requires a permeable soil.

M. multiceps Salm-Dyck see *M. prolifera* var. *texana*

(14) M. mystax Mart.
Solitary or clustering, globular to slightly elongated, with milky sap. Axils white, woolly and bristly. Tubercles 4-edged. Radial spines 5-6 (-10), white, brown-tipped. Central spines 3-4, often purple when young, later grey, 1.5-2 cm. long, one up to 7 cm. long. Flowers purple-pink, lighter inside, up to 2.5 cm. long and 2 cm. wide. Seed dark brown. Mexico (Hidalgo to Oaxaca).

(1) M. napina J.A. Purp.
Solitary or clustering, flattened globular, without milky sap. Root beet-like. Axils slightly woolly or bare. Radial spines 10-12, whitish to pale yellow. Central spines absent. Flowers dark pink to light carmine, lighter inside, about 4 cm. wide. Seed black. Mexico (Puebla).

As with all taprooted species, water sparingly.

M. nejapensis Craig & Dawson see *M. karwinskiana*

M. neomystax Backeb. see *M. karwinskiana*

(13) M. nivosa Link (*M. flavescens* (DC.) Haw.; *M. flavescens* (DC.) Haw. var. *nivosa* (Link) Backeb.)
Usually solitary, but may be clustering or profusely clustering, globular to slightly elongated, with milky sap. Axils densely white, woolly. Radial spines 8-10, yellow. Central spines 1-5, yellow. Flowers pale sulphur yellow, up to 1.5 cm. wide. Seed brown. Bahamas, Puerto Rico, Lesser Antilles.

(10) M. nunezii (Br. & R.) Orcutt
Slightly clustering, later elongated, without milky sap. Axils with 8-10 bristles. Radial spines 25-30, white. Central spines (2-) 4 (-6), dark-tipped. Flowers deep to purple-pink, 1.5 cm. long. Seed brown. Mexico (Guerrero).

(9) M. obconella Scheidw. (*M. hidalgensis* J.A. Purpus; *M. tetracantha* (Salm-Dyck) Br. & R.)
Later clustering and columnar, without milky sap. Tubercles 4-sided or rounded. Axils densely white, woolly initially. Radial spines absent or a few thin ones. Central spines 2-4 (-6), brownish-yellow. Flowers carmine with pink margins, around 2 cm. long and 1.5 cm. wide. Seed yellow-brown. Mexico (Jalapa, Vera Cruz, Hidalgo, Querétaro).

(2) M. occidentalis (Br. & R.) Böd.
Clustering, cylindrical, without milky sap. Some axils have a few bristles. Radial spines 12-18, white to yellowish, brown-tipped. Central spines 4-5, hooked or straight, reddish-brown. Flowers pink to deep pink, with darker central stripe, 1 cm.

Mammillaria moelleriana

long. Seed black. Mexico (Colima, Nayarit, Sinaloa).

M. occidentalis (Br. & R.) Böd. var. *sinalensis* Craig see *M. patonii* var. *sinalensis*

M. orcutti Böd. see *M. carnea*

M. ortiz-rubiona (Bravo) Werderm. see *M. candida*

(12) **M. parkinsonii** Ehrenb.
Forming forked branches, globular to elongated, with milky sap. Tubercles finely spotted. Axils white, woolly and bristly. Radial spines 30-35, white. Central spines 2-4 (-5), often reddish or red-brown tipped, the bottom one

up to 3.5 cm. long. Flowers cream-coloured to dirty pink with brownish-pink central stripe, 1.5 cm. long. Seed light brown. Mexico (Hidalgo to Querétaro).

This very decorative species eventually forms large groups which should then be grown in a pan. Full sun and occasional small doses of manuring lime help to promote the beautiful spine formation.

(2) **M. patonii** (Bravo) Werderm. **var. sinalensis** (Craig) Backeb. (*M. occidentalis* (Br. & R.) Böd. var. *sinalensis* Craig)
Columnar, clustering, without milky sap. Axils bare. Radial spines 10-12, grey, brown-tipped. Central spines 1,

hooked, black-red. Flowers purple-pink, 2.5 cm. long and 4 cm. wide. Seed black. Mexico (Sinaloa).

(5) **M. pectinifera** Web. (*Solisia pectinata* (Stein) Br. & R.)
Solitary, globular, with milky sap. Axils naked. The tubercles are axe-shaped, radial spines about 40-50, pure white, comb-formation. Central spines absent. Flowers pink to almost white, 2 cm. long and up to 2.5 cm. wide. Seed black, boat-shaped, with large hilum. Root beet-like. Mexico (Puebla, ?Oaxaca).

This species grows slowly and is rather sensitive to moisture. It therefore requires a mineral, permeable soil and

225

Mammillaria parkinsonii

Mammillaria pennispinosa

sparse watering (see illustration on page 227).

(3) **M. pennispinosa** Krainz
Solitary, oval to elongated, without milky sap. Axils with short felt, but only initially. Radial spines 16-20, pinnate, grey-white. Central spine 1 (-3), red-brown, hooked. Flowers pale yellowish to pink, with carmine pink central stripe and pink throat, 1.5 cm. long and 1.2 cm. wide. Seed black with large seed mantle. Root beet-like. Mexico (Coahuila).

This species is very distinctive with its feathery spines. The flowers appear early in the spring. However, the species is rather temperamental and demands a permeable soil and sparse watering (see illustration on page 211).

(12) **M. perbella** Hildm.
Globular or elongated, solitary or branching, without superficial milky sap. Axils slightly woolly. Radial spines 14-30, white. Central spines 1-2. Flowers pink or carmine red with darker central stripe, 1-1.5 cm. long. Seed brown. Mexico (Querétaro, Hidalgo, Mexico, Oaxaca).

(5) **M. plumosa** Web.
Abundantly clustering, globular, without milky sap. Axils white, woolly. Radial spines up to 40, tufted, soft, feathery, white to yellowish. Central spines absent. Flowers yellowish to greenish-white, with darker central stripe and greenish throat, 1.5 cm. long and 1-1.5 cm. wide. Seed black. Mexico (Coahuila).

Easy to recognize with its tufts of feathery spines enveloping the entire body. It flowers in late autumn or winter. It is sensitive to excess moisture, and should therefore only be watered sparingly.

(Co) **M. poselgeri** Hildm. (*Cochemiea p.* (Hildm.) Br. & R.)
Clustering, more or less cylindrical, without milky sap. Axils white, woolly, some bristly. Radial spines 7-9, central spine 1, hooked. All spines brown. Flowers glossy scarlet, bi-laterally symmetrical, 3 cm. long. Seed matt black. Mexico (Lower California). Like many other cactus species from lower California it is somewhat difficult in

Mammillaria pectinifera

cultivation. It demands much warmth and even in winter does not like temperatures below 12°C.

(7) **M. pottsii** Scheer (*M. leona* Poselg.) Abundantly clustering, cylindrical, without milky sap. Axils slightly woolly. Radial spines up to 35, white. Central spines 7-8, white to yellowish or reddish. Flowers pink, margins orange-pink, 1 cm. long. Seed dark brown. Mexico (Durango to Zacatecas), USA (Texas).

(14) **M. praelii** Mühlpf. Globular, later clustering, with milky sap. Tubercles with 4-6 edges. Axils densely white to brownish, woolly with 15-18 long bristles. Radial spines 4 (-6), initially yellowish-cream to brown, later white, brown-tipped. Central spines absent. Flowers greenish yellow-white with reddish central stripe, 1.5-2 cm. long and 1 cm. wide. Seed brown. Mexico (Oaxaca, ?Guatemala).

(9) **M. pringlei** (Coult.) Brand. Solitary, globular to oval, with milky sap. Axils white, woolly, occasionally

Mammillaria pringlei

with short bristles. Radial spines 15-20, yellowish. Central spines 6 (-7), yellow. Flowers brilliant carmine red, about 1 cm. long. Seed brown. Mexico (San Luis Potosí, Mexico).

This robust species has very decorative spines which are encouraged by a sunny location. The species does not flower until late summer. The main difference between this species and the similar *M. rhodantha* is its curved central spines.

(4) **M. prolifera** (Mill.) Haw. Abundantly clustering, globular to oval, without milky sap. Axils slightly woolly, bristly. Radial spines 25-40, hair-like, white. Central spines 5-9 (-12), hairy, pale yellow to red-brown. Flowers cream-yellow with reddish or brownish central stripe, 1.4 cm. long. Seed black. West Indies, Texas.

A well-known species. The profusion of red berry fruit is more distinctive than the relatively inconspicuous flowers.

var. haitiensis (K. Schum.) Krainz Central spines snow-white, yellow

227

when young and on young plants. Cuba, Hispaniola.

var. texana Borg (*M. multiceps* Salm-Dyck; *M.p.* (Mill.) Haw. var. *multiceps* (Salm-Dyck) Berger)
Central spines reddish to brownish. Mexico (Tamaulipas, Nuevo León).

M. pullihamata Backeb. see *M. rekoi*

(10) **M. rekoi** (Br. & R.) Vaup. (*M. pullihamata* Backeb.)
Solitary, globular to elongated, with milky sap. Axils white, woolly and with up to 8 bristles. Radial spines about 20, whitish. Central spines 4-6, reddish-brown, one hooked. Flowers deep purple, 1.5 cm. long. Seed brown. Mexico (Oaxaca).

(3) **M. rettigiana** Böd.
Usually solitary, oval, without milky sap. Axils bare or slightly woolly. Radial spines 18-20, white to yellowish. Central spines 3-4, red to dark brown, one of them hooked. Flowers yellowish, with pink central stripe, 1.5 cm. wide. Seed brownish-black. Mexico (Hidalgo, Guanajuato).

(9) **M. rhodantha** Link & Otto
Usually solitary, globular to oval, without milky sap. Axils white, woolly and bristly. Radial spines 16-20. Central spines mostly 4 (-7). Spines whitish to yellowish to dark brown (var. *rubens* Pfeiff.). Flowers deep purple-pink, 2 cm. long and about 1.5 cm. wide. Seed light brown. Mexico (Hidalgo, Mexico, Querétaro).

M. rubida Backeb. see *M. bocensis*

(11) **M. ruestii** Quehl
Solitary, later also clustering, globular to oval, without milky sap. Axils white, woolly and bristly. Radial spines 16-22, white. Central spines 4 (-5), light to dark red-brown. Flowers carmine with white throat, 2 cm. long and 1.5-2 cm. wide. Seed brown. Honduras, Guatemala.

(1) **M. saboae** Glass var. **saboae**
Solitary or clustering, globular, without milky sap. Axils bare. Radial spines 17-25, translucent white, yellow at the base. Central spines absent. Flowers pink with dark central stripe, 4 cm. long and wide. Seed glossy black.

Mammillaria rhodantha

Mexico (S.W. Chihuahua at 2300 m. altitude)

f. haudeana (Lau & Wagner) Hunt (*M. haudeana* Lau & Wagner)
Flowers dark lilac-pink, about 6.5 cm. wide (see illustration, page 212).

var. goldii (Glass & Foster) Glass & Foster (*M.g.* Glass & Foster)
Radial spines 35-45. Flowers lavender pink, 3.3 cm. wide. Mexico (Sonora).

M. saetigera Böd. & Tiegel see *M. brauneana*

(5) **M. schiedeana** Ehrenb.
Solitary or clustering, flattened globular, without milky sap. Axils with long, white wool. Radial spines up to 75, hair-like, with fine hairs under a magnifier, golden yellow to whitish. Central spines absent. Flowers yellowish-white, 2 cm. long. Seed black. Mexico (Hidalgo).

It is sensitive to moisture and should be watered sparingly. The flowers do not appear until autumn or late autumn.

(2) **M. schumannii** Hildm. (*Bartschella s.* (Hildm.) Br. & R.)
Clustering, globular, without milky

sap. Tubercles 4-sided at the base. Axils woolly, but only initially. Radial spines (9-) 12 (-15). Central spines 1 (-4), one of them hooked. All spines white, black-tipped. Flowers light purple, 4 cm. wide. Seed matt black. Mexico (lower California).

Very pretty but rather temperamental, like many lower Californian species. It likes a warm position, not below 10°C in winter, and sparse water.

M. schwartzii (Böd.) Backeb. see *M. coahuilensis*

(4) **M. schwarzii** Shurley
Globular, clustering, without milky sap. Axils with up to 6 bristles. Radial spines 34-40, hair-like, white. Central spines 8-9, one of them sometimes hooked, glossy white, mostly light above, brown-red. Flowers white with slightly green or red central stripe, 1.5 cm. long and 1.2 cm. wide. The seed is black. Mexico (N. Guanajuato).

M. seitziana Mart. see *M. compressa*

(12) **M. sempervivi** DC.
Occasionally clustering, globular to oval, with milky sap. Axils woolly.

Tubercles 4-edged. Radial spines 3-7, white. Central spines 2 (-4), reddish to yellowish. Flowers dirty white, sometimes yellowish-pink, with reddish central stripe, 1 cm. long. Seed light brown. Mexico (Hidalgo to Veracruz).

The plant's appearance is somewhat reminiscent of many *Sempervivum* species (house-leek).

(Ms) **M. senilis** Lodd. (*Mamillopsis s.* (Lodd.) Web.)
Clustering when old, globular to oval, without milky sap. Axils white, woolly and bristly. Radial spines 30-40, yellowish-white to snow-white, central spines 5-6, one of them hooked, tip more or less yellow-brown. Flowers orange-red to violet, with darker central stripe, up to 7 cm. long and 6 cm. wide. Seed black. Ovary and tube scaly, in contrast to other *Mammillaria* species. Mexico (Chihuahua, S. Durango, Nayarit, Oaxaca).

The species occurs at an altitude of 2500-3000 m., and is accustomed to frost and snow. In Europe it is sometimes reluctant to flower. Evidently it only produces its large flowers if the winter conditions are

correct: cool, but as bright and sunny as possible. A permeable soil and a sparse water supply are recommended.

(2) **M. sheldonii** (Br. & R.) Böd.
Solitary or clustering, later cylindrical, without milky sap. Axils bare. Radial spines 10-15, reddish-brown. Central spines 1-3, dark reddish-brown, one of them hooked. Flowers light pink with darker eye and wide white margins, 2 cm. long and 3 cm. wide. Seed black. Mexico (Sonora).

M. shurliana H.E. Gates see *M. blossfeldiana* var. *shurliana*

(5) **M. solisioides** Backeb.
Rounded, solitary, with beet-like root, without milky sap. Axils bare. Radial spines about 25, comb-formation, white. Central spines absent. Flowers yellowish-white, around 1.4-2.2 cm. long and 1.5-2.6 cm. wide. Seed black. Mexico (Puebla).

(6) **M. sphacelata** Mart.
Plant consisting of a group of stems as thick as a finger, up to 20 cm. long, without milky sap. Axils woolly and bristly. Radial spines 10-15, white or red. Central spines 1-4, white with brownish tip. Flowers dark red, 1.5 cm. long and 0.8 cm. wide. Seed black. Mexico (Puebla, Oaxaca).

Mammillaria spinosissima

(Do) **M. sphaerica** A. Dietr. (*Dolichothele s.* (A. Dietr.) Br. & R.)
Globular, clustering, without milky sap. Tubercles 0.8-1.6 cm. long. Axils bare or slightly woolly. Radial spines 9-15, white to pale yellow with darker base. Central spines 1, chalky-yellowish. Flowers pale yellow, 6-7 cm. wide. Seed black. USA (Texas) to N. Mexico (Tamaulipas, Nuevo León).

(10) **M. spinosissima** Lem.
Solitary, oval, without milky sap. Axils woolly and bristly. Radial spines 20-30, usually white, but also yellow, light brown or red. Central spines 7-15, sometimes one of them hooked. Flowers light carmine to purple, up to 2 cm. long and 1.5 cm. wide. Seed reddish-brown. Mexico (Morelos, Hidalgo, Puebla, Michoácan, Guerrero).

Mammillaria senilis

Mammillaria surculosa

Mammillaria theresae

A very variable species, popular and widespread, which grows well and flowers profusely.

(11) **M. supertexta** Mart. (*M. lanata* (Br. & R.) Orcutt; *M. martinezii* Backeb.) Solitary or clustering, globular to elongated, without superficial milky sap. Axils at first woolly. Radial spines 12-20, white. Central spines absent or up to 2. Flowers light red to carmine, about 1 cm. long. Seed brown. Mexico (Hidalgo, Puebla, Oaxaca).

(Do) **M. surculosa** Böd. (*Dolichothele s.* (Böd.) Buxb.) Clustering, globular, without milky sap. Axils bare. Radial spines up to 15, yellowish-white. Central spines 1-2, one of them hooked, yellow to brown. Flowers sulphur yellow, with orange central stripe and red tips, up to 2 cm. wide, strongly and pleasantly scented, but mainly at night. Seed brown. Style merged with the tube. Root beet-like. Mexico (Tamaulipas).

The species requires shelter from brilliant sun and should be watered with particular care because of its taproot.

(2) **M. swinglei** (Br. & R.) Böd. Columnar, clustering, without milky sap. Axils bare or bristly. Radial spines 11-18, matt white with dark tip. Central spines 1-4, one of them hooked (in exceptional cases straight), dark brown to black. Flowers white to cream-coloured, with pink or greenish central stripe, 3 cm. wide. Seed black. Mexico (Sonora).

M. tetracantha (Salm-Dyck) Br. & R. see *M. obconella*

(2) **M. tetrancistra** Engelm. (*Phellosperma t.* (Engelm.) Br. & R.) Solitary or clustering, elongated, without milky sap. Axils bare or bristly. Radial spines 30-60, white. Central spines (1-) 3-4, hooked, brown or black-tipped. Flowers purple with lighter margins, up to 4.5 cm. long and 3.5 cm. wide. Seed matt black with large corky aril. USA (California, Arizona, Nevada, S. Utah), Mexico (Sonora, Lower California).

(1) **M. theresae** Cutak Usually solitary, oval, without milky sap. Axils woolly. Radial spines 20-30, pure white. Central spines 9. All

spines feathery. Flowers violet-purple, 3.5-4.5 cm. long and up to 3.5 cm. wide. Seed black. Mexico (Durango at 2200 m. altitude; discovered in 1967)

(2) **M. thornberi** Orcutt (*M. fasciculata* Engelm.)
Densely clustering, oval to cylindrical, without milky sap. Axils bare. Radial spines 13-20, white with dark tip. Central spines 1 (-3), dark, one of them hooked. Flowers white with red central stripe, 3 cm. long and 2 cm. wide. Seed black. USA (S. Arizona), Mexico (N. Sonora).

(3) **M. trichacantha** K. Schum.
Globular to elongated, solitary, seldom clustering, without milky sap. Axils with few hair-like bristles. Radial

Mammillaria uncinata

spines 15-18, white below, yellowish above. Central spines 2 (-3), one of them hooked, chestnut brown. Spines all with fine hairs. Flowers 1-1.5 cm. long and wide, greenish-cream with light green central stripe. Seed black. Mexico (San Luis Potosí, Querétaro).

(13) **M. uncinata** Zucc.
Solitary, seldom clustering. Body bluish-green, globular, with milky sap. Axils initially white, woolly. Radial spines 4-7, the upper ones flesh-coloured, the lower ones white, black-tipped. Central spines 1 (-2-3), 1 or occasionally 2 of them hooked, flesh-coloured, dark-tipped. Flowers reddish-white with brownish central stripe and pink tips, 1.5-2 cm. long,

1.8 cm. wide. Seed light brown. Exceptionally this species features milky sap and hooked spines together. Mexico (Hidalgo, Guanajuato, San Luis Potosí).

Grows well and flowers readily. Shade from brilliant sun is recommended.

(10) **M. vaupelii** Tiegel
Solitary, more or less globular, with milky sap. Tubercles with 4-sided base and fine white spots. Axils hairy and bristly. Radial spines 16-21, glossy white. Central spines 2 (-4), orange-brown. Flowers light purple-pink, throat white, 1.7 cm. long and 1 cm. wide. Seed yellow-brown. Mexico (Oaxaca).

M. verhaertiana Böd.
Later elongated and clustering, without milky sap. Tubercles with keel. Axils woolly and with 15-20 bristles. Radial spines 15 to more than 20, yellowish. Central spines 4-6, hooked when old, yellowish-white below, yellowish-brown above, later white. Flowers white with greenish or reddish central stripe, 2 cm. long. Seed black. Mexico (Lower California).

(4) **M. viereckii** Böd.
Usually solitary, elongated when old, without milky sap. Axils white, woolly and bristly. Radial spines 6-7 (-10), white to yellowish. Central spines 9-11, yellowish. Flowers cream-coloured with pale green central stripe, up to 1.2 cm. long. Seed black. Mexico (Tamaulipas).

(6) **M. viperina** J.A. Purp.
This species is considered by Hunt to be a variety of *M. sphacelata*. Stems prostrate, as thick as a finger, 15-20 cm. long, clustering, without milky sap. Axils somewhat woolly and sometimes bristly. Radial spines 25 – 30, yellowish-white to reddish and dark brown. Central spines absent. Flowers light carmine to carmine-violet, about 1 cm. long. Seed light brown. Mexico (Puebla).

These plants demand a permeable sandy soil.

(14) **M. voburnensis** Scheer (*M. woburnensis* Scheer)
Globular to elongated, clustering, with milky sap. Axils white, woolly, with up

to 10 bristles. Radial spines 8-9, cream-coloured with red brown tips. Central spines 1-3, at first dark brown, later more yellowish and with red-brown tips. Flowers yellow with brownish-red central stripe, 2 cm. long. Seed yellowish-brown. Guatemala.

(3) **M. wildii** A. Dietr. (*M. glochidiata* Mart.)
Densely clustering, globular to oval, without milky sap. Axils with few hair-like bristles. Radial spines 8-20, white. Central spines 3-4, yellowish to brownish, one of them hooked. Flowers whitish or pink, 1.2-1.5 cm. long and wide. Seed black. Mexico (Hidalgo, Querétaro).

A popular species, recommended to the beginner. All it requires is slight protection from brilliant sunshine.

(13) **M. winteriae** Böd. (with *M. zahniana* Böd. & Ritter)
Rounded, not clustering, with milky sap. Axils woolly. Tubercles slightly 4-edged. Radial spines 4, yellowish-grey to slightly reddish at the top, with brownish tip. Central spines absent. Flowers yellowish-white with yellowish (or pink) central stripe, 3 cm. long and 2.5 cm. wide. Seed light reddish-brown. Mexico (Nuevo León).

M. woburnensis Scheer see *M. voburnensis*

(12) **M. woodsii** Craig
This species is considered by Hunt to belong to *M. hahniana*. Solitary, later more or less elongated, with milky sap. Axils densely white, woolly and with bristles up to 2.5 cm. long. Tubercles angular. Radial spines 25-30, hair-like, translucent white. Central spines 2 (-4), purple-pink, black-tipped. Flowers dark pink with darker central stripe, 1-1.2 cm. long, around 1.5 cm. wide. Seed matt brownish. Mexico (Guanajuato).

A very beautiful, vigorous species which flowers readily. The density of the wool and the spines is somewhat variable.

(2) **M. yaquensis** Craig
Densely clustering, cylindrical, without milky sap, axils with traces of felt. Radial spines 18, cream-coloured.

Central spines 1, red-brown to almost black, hooked. Flowers pink with darker central stripe, up to 2 cm. long and wide. Seed black. Mexico (Sonora).

These tiny plants have relatively large flowers, but they are sometimes reluctant to produce them. The species likes plenty of sunshine, a mineral, permeable soil and sparse watering. Be very careful when handling the plants, as the hooked spines immediately stick when they make contact, and the shoots are then easily torn off.

(3) **M. zacatecasensis** Shurley
Solitary, globular, without milky sap. Axils bare. Radial spines 20-24, pale yellowish-green. Central spines 3-4, yellowish to reddish-brown, one of them hooked. Flowers white or delicate pink with darker centre and pink central stripe, 1.7-1.8 cm. long and 1.4-1.5 cm. wide. Seed black. Mexico (Zacatecas).

M. zahniana Böd. & Ritter see *M. winteriae*

(3) **M. zeilmanniana** Böd.
Solitary to slightly clustering, globular to oval, without milky sap. Axils bare. Radial spines 15-18, often hair-like, white. Central spines 4, reddish-brown, one of them hooked. Flowers carmine violet to purple-pink, seldom white, up to 2 cm. long. Seed black. Mexico (Guanajuato).

A popular and widespread species.

(2) **M. zephyranthoides** Scheidw.
(*Dolichothele z.* (Scheidw.) Backeb.)
Solitary, compressed globular, without milky sap. Axils bare. Tubercles up to 2.5 cm. long. Radial spines 12-18, almost hair-like, whitish, central spines 1 (-2), yellowish to brown, one of them hooked. Flowers whitish to yellowish with red central stripe, up to 4 cm. long and wide. Seed black. Mexico (Oaxaca, Puebla, Hidalgo, Querétaro).

(13) **M. zeyeriana** Haage jr.
Solitary, globular, with milky sap. Axils bare. Radial spines around 10, white. Central spines 4, ruby red to nut-brown, later grey. Flowers reddish-orange with yellowish margins. Seed brown. Mexico (Coahuila, Durango).

Mammillaria zeilmanniana

Mammillaria zeilmanniana, form with white flowers

Mammilloydia Buxb. see *Mammillaria*

Marenopuntia Backeb. see *Opuntia*

Marginatocereus (Backeb.) Backeb. see *Stenocereus*

Marniera Backeb. see *Epiphyllum*

Marshallocereus Backeb. see *Stenocereus*

Matucana Br. & R. 1922
(*Eomatucana, Submatucana*)
(after a location near Lima in Peru)

This genus includes flattened globular to cylindrical cacti with 7-30 ribs. A

Mammillaria zephyranthoides

characteristic feature is its flowers, which are always more or less bi-laterally symmetrical. They are borne close to the crown of the plant, and are either scaly and woolly or bare. The lowest stamens are merged together to form a sealed nectar chamber. The fleshy fruit splits open at the side.

Bi-laterally symmetrical flowers are a feature which *Matucana* shares with *Borzicactus,* with which it has already been amalgamated once, but the typical *Borzicactus* is a columnar plant. *Matucana* is even more similar to the genus *Arequipa.* The only distinguishing feature of the latter genus is its dry fruit, which burst open at the base. About 16 species. Native to Peru.

The various species of *Matucana* originate in areas of widely different character. *M. madisoniorum* grows in warm river valleys at an altitude of 400-500 m. and thus likes similar levels of warmth. This species flowers relatively easily. *M. haynei* and related species grow at altitudes of 2500-3000 m. and so do not require such warmth, but they flower poorly in our conditions. The other species, *M. aurantiaca, M. intertexta* and *M. ritteri,* lie somewhere between these two species in terms of culture.

Flowers virtually bare

Ribs 7-12. Flowers slim, tubular, radially symmetrical, golden yellow inside   *M. oreodoxa*
Ribs 25-30. Flowers zygomorphic, carmine to scarlet   *M. haynei*

Flowers hairy

Flowers radial, pure golden yellow, 3-4.5 cm. long   *M. aureiflora*
Flowers more or less zygomorphic, orange, red to lilac, not pure golden yellow, more than 5 cm. long
  Spines 25-40
    Spines up to 2.5 cm. long
                M. myriacantha
    Spines 3-6 cm. long   *M. weberbaueri*
  Spines up to about 25
    Flowers orange, dark red towards the centre   *M. aurantiaca*
    Flowers red to lilac
      Ribs 11-25. Spines 9-20
        Flowers vermilion to carmine or blood red   *M. intertexta,*
                M. ritteri
      Flowers lilac   *M. krahnii*
      Ribs 7-12. Spines 0-9
        Spines 4-9, persisting. Flowers about 5.5 cm. long   *M. paucicostata*
        Spines 1-5, easily falling off. Flowers 8-10 cm. long
                M. madisoniorum

M. aurantiaca (Vaup.) Buxb. (*Submatucana a.*(Vaup.) Backeb.; *Borzicactus a.* (Vaup.) Kimn. & Hutchison)
Globular, about 16 ribs. Spines 10-25 (-30), yellow to reddish-brown, 2-4.5 cm. long. Flowers orange, dark red towards the centre, up to 9 cm. long. N. Peru (Cajamarca, La Libertad).

M. aureiflora Ritter (*Submatucana a.* Backeb.; *Borzicactus a.* (Ritter) Donald)
Body flattened globular, 11-27 ribs, glossy dark grey-green, with taproot.

Matucana aureiflora

Matucana crinifera

Radial spines 8-13, slightly comb-formation, 0.7-1.8 cm. long. Central spines 1-4, only on older plants, 1.2-2.5 cm. long. Spines black to red-brown below, usually yellow to yellow-brown above. Flowers golden yellow, radially symmetrical, widely spreading, 3-4.5 cm. long. According to Ritter a species adapted to pollination by bees. Peru. (Cajamarca).

M. haynei (Otto) Br. & R. (*Borzicactus h.* (Otto) Kimn. & Hutchison).
Globular to elongated, with 25-30 ribs. Spines about 30 or more, central spines longer, white to brownish with dark tip, up to 3.5 cm. long. Flowers bare, carmine to scarlet, 6-8 cm. long. Central Peru.

Also **M. hystrix** Rauh & Backeb. **M. pallarensis** Ritter is also similar.

var. atrispina
Has more or less comb-formation spines, up to 5 cm. long. Central spine dark brown. And **H. herzogiana** Backeb.

var. perplexa Backeb.
Has white to cream-yellow spines, enveloping the body, and flowers not more than 5.5 cm. long.

M. crinifera Ritter is similar, but has orange flowers.

M. intertexta Ritter (*Submatucana i.* (Ritter) Backeb.; *Borzicactus i.* (Ritter) Donald)
Globular to columnar, with 15-25 ribs, without taproot. When old radial spines 8-12, brown, 0.7-2 cm. long. Central spines 1-4, brown with black tip, 2-3.5 cm. long. Flowers blood red, 7.5-10.5 cm. long. Peru (Cajamarca).

Borzicactus krahnii Donald (not yet reclassified as *Matucana krahnii*)
Body flattened globular to globular, clustering, grey-green, with about 18 ribs. Radial spines 8. Central spines 1-4. Spines black, brown-tipped, 0.5-1 cm. long, later up to 8 cm. long. Flowers slightly zygomorphic, lilac, 7-8 cm. long and 5.5-7 cm. wide. Peru (Amazonas).

M. madisoniorum (Hutchison) G. D. Rowl. (*Submatucana m.* (Hutchison) Backeb.; *Borzicactus m.* Hutchison; *Eomatucana m.* (Hutchison) Ritter)
Globular to elongated, 7-12 ribs, with blue-green, rough outer skin. The spines fall off easily, number 0 to 5, initially brown, then black and up to 3 (-6) cm. long. Flowers vermilion, 6-10 cm. long. Peru (Amazonas).

M. myriacantha (Vaup.) Buxb. (*Submatucana m.* (Vaup.) Backeb.; *Borzicactus m.* (Vaup.) Donald)
Flattened globular with about 26 ribs, transversely notched. Radial spines 20-

Matucana pallarensis

Matucana myriacantha

Matucana paucicostata

30, 0.6-1.8 cm. long. Central spines about 10, up to 2.5 cm. long. All spines like stiff bristles, initially yellow to red-brown, later grey-black or grey. Flowers golden yellow to orange-red, with slightly or more strongly carmine to purple margins, 6-8 cm. long. Peru (Amazonas).

Eomatucana oreodoxa Ritter (*Borzicactus o.* (Ritter) Donald; not yet reclassified as *Matucana o.*)
Flat-globular to hemi-spherical, rarely clustering, with taproot and 7-12 bumpy ribs. Spines 4-12, brownish, turning grey, 0.75-4 cm. long. Flowers radially symmetrical, with slender tube, practically bare, golden yellow to orange-red inside, orange to deep red outside, 4-6 cm. long. Peru (Ancash).

M. paucicostata Ritter (*Submatucana p.* (Ritter) Backeb.; *Borzicactus p.* (Ritter) Donald)
Later elongated, producing side shoots, 7-12 ribs with transverse notches. Taproot. Radial spines 4-8, yellow to chestnut brown, turning grey, 0.5-4 cm. long. Central spine absent or 1, similar to the radials.

Flowers dark vermilion with violet margins, roughly 6 cm. long. Peru (Ancash).

M. ritteri Buin. (*Submatucana r.* (Buin.) Backeb.; *Borzicactus r.* (Buin.) Donald). Flattened globular with 12-22 ribs. Radial spines 7-10 (-14), 1-3 cm. long. Central spines 1-2 (-5), 2-4 cm. long. Spines all slightly curved, brown-black. Flowers vermilion to carmine, 7-9 cm. long. Peru (La Libertad).

M. weberbaueri (Vaup.) Backeb. Body flattened globular, with 18-25 bumpy ribs. Spines 25-30, 3-5 cm. long, golden yellow to orange-red to black-brown. Flowers orange-yellow, 5.5 cm. long. Peru (Chachapoyas). See illustration, page 34.

Mediocactus Br. & R. 1920
(Latin medius = middle)
Climbing cacti with aerial roots. Flowers nocturnal, very large (12-40 cm. long) with elongated tube, the latter scaly and spiny to bristly and hairy. The genus is very closely related

to *Selenicereus* and only differs in its stems, which are usually 3-edged or -winged, compared with the normal 4-10 edges or ribs of *Selenicereus*. Its area of distribution overlaps with that of *Selenicereus* to the South.

6 species. Native to ?Colombia, Peru, Bolivia, Argentina, Paraguay, Brazil.

Mediolobivia Backeb. see *Rebutia*

Melocactus Link & Otto 1827
(Lat. melo = melon/apple)

This genus includes globular cacti with tall, clearly defined ribs and usually a powerful spine formation. When the plants reach flowering maturity after about 7-10 years, they cease growing and form a cephalium at the crown composed of woolly hairs and bristles, from which are produced small flowers, mostly pink in colour, and similar to those of *Mammillaria*. The club-shaped, brilliant red fruit, about 2 cm. long, are also reminiscent of many *Mammillaria* fruit.

The flowers are pushed outward by

235

the pressure of the cephalium wool. The cephalium increases in height every year, and in many species may be several times taller than the body of the plant. The only other globular genus in which a comparable cephalium occurs is *Discocactus,* the flowers of which are quite different and large in size. The genus is not closely related to *Melocactus*.

Species of this genus, originally designated simply *Cactus*, were the first cacti to be discovered by Europeans,

Melocactus sp.

as they grow on the coasts of the West Indian islands first discovered by Columbus. It seems that self-pollination is widespread in *Melocactus,* with the result that many species have evolved which are very similar to each other.

Around 60 species, some of them scarcely distinguishable from each other. Native to Mexico, Central America, West Indies, Venezuela, N.E. Brazil, Colombia, Peru.

Melocacti like mineral soil, roughly one half coarse sand, the other half loam and broken crocks. In summer they should be kept in a very bright and warm position in the greenhouse or cold frame, and given plenty of water. As they come from a humid climate they like to be sprayed quite

frequently. In winter they should be kept in bright, relatively warm conditions (around 15°C) and watered sparingly. Imported plants are especially sensitive. Many enthusiasts overwinter Melocacti indoors by a window, where it is usually too warm for ordinary cacti. Imported plants which have already developed a cephalium do not grow any further. In general terms young imported plants which are not yet accustomed to our conditions are very sensitive and demanding in terms of warmth, and are not suitable for beginners. Plants raised from seed and grown on their own roots are slightly more robust, but they do grow slowly. All things considered Melocacti can only be recommended to experienced growers with suitable cultural facilities.

Ribs more or less round-edged
(cephalium narrow, brown-bristled)
M. maxonii
Ribs sharp-edged
  Cephalium with numerous sharp, fox red bristles, projecting about 5 cm.
M. peruvianus
  Cephalium without long, sharp, projecting bristles
    Body with deep blue frosted appearance *M. azureus*
    Body not frosted
      Cephalium with many brown bristles. Flowers pink *M. bahiensis*
      Cephalium white with red bristles. Flowers carmine *M. concinnus*
      Cephalium distinctly orange-red. Flowers pink *M. matanzanus*
      Cephalium with dense white wool, red bristles below only. Flowers up to 2.3 cm. long *M. albicephalus*

All the species listed have about 7-11 radial spines and (0-) 1 (-4) reddish or brown central spines.

M. albicephalus Buin. & Bred. Body green, 12-15 cm. wide with 9-10 ribs, bumpy between the areoles. Cephalium densely white, woolly, with red bristles below. Flowers carmine red, up to 2.3 cm. long and thus fairly large for the genus. Brazil (Central Bahia).

M. azureus Buin. & Bred. Body with deep blue frosted appearance, about 14 cm. wide and with 9-10 sharp ribs. Cephalium white, hairy, pierced through by fine red bristles. Flowers carmine red to

Melocactus azureus

Top: Melocactus matanzanus
Centre: Melocactus onychacanthus
Bottom: Melocactus concinnus

Melocactus maxonii

violet-carmine, up to 1.4 cm. long.
Brazil (Bahia).

M. bahiensis (Br. & R.) Werderm.
(*Discocactus b.* Br. & R.)
Body dull green, about 15 cm. wide,
with around 10-12 ribs. Cephalium
with many brown bristles. Central
spines 1 (-4). Flowers pink, about
2 cm. long. Brazil (Bahia).

M. concinnus Buin. & Bred.
Body green, about 9-11 cm. wide and
with 10-13 sharp ribs. Cephalium
white, hairy with red bristles. Flowers
carmine, about 1.8 cm. long. This
species flowers particularly readily.
Brazil (Bahia).

M. matanzanus Leon
Body pale green, up to 9 cm. wide,
with 8 or 9 sharp-edged ribs.
Cephalium distinctly orange-red.
Flowers pink, about 1.7 cm. long.
Cuba (Matanzas).

M. maxonii (Rose) Gürke (*Cactus m.*
Rose)
Body dark green to grass green,
around 10 cm. wide with 11-15 more
or less round-edged ribs. Cephalium
narrow, brown, bristly. Flowers pink,
4 cm. long. Guatemala.

M. onychacanthus Ritter is similar.

M. peruvianus Vaup. (*Cactus townsendii*
Br. & R.)
Body grass green, occasionally
clustering, up to 15 cm. wide, with 12-
14 sharp ribs. Cephalium with
numerous fox red bristles. Flowers
pink, 2.5 cm. long. Peru.

Micranthocereus Backeb. 1938
(Greek mikros = small, anthos
= flower)

Bushy columnar cacti with 15-20 ribs.
Flowers borne laterally in a pseudo-
cephalium, externally bare, not scaly,
nocturnal, pink, less than 2 cm. long.
The bottom stamens have a scale-like
base, and form a nectar chamber.
Fruit with lid.

3 species. Native to Brazil (Bahia,
Minas Gerais).

Little was known of this genus until
Buining's research expeditions.

M. violaciflorus Buin.
Stems up to 1 m. tall and to 4 cm.
thick, with 14 sharp ribs. Radial spines

237

Mila caespitosa

up to 25 or more, white to light brown. Central spines 1, red, 2.5 cm. long. Areoles with whitish to brownish hairs. Pseudo-cephalium consisting of dense white to brownish wool located in annual zones of annular form. Flowers violet outside, bluish-violet inside, about 2.3 cm. long. Brazil (Minas Gerais).

Micropuntia Daston see *Opuntia*

Mila Br. & R. 1922
(An anagram of Lima, the capital of Peru)

Squat cylindrical plants with 9-15 ribs. Flowers small, towards the end of the stems, with yellow scales and slightly woolly. 13 species. Native to Peru.

M. caespitosa Br. & R.
Forming groups. Body 10-15 cm. tall and 2-3 cm. thick, with about 10 ribs. Radial spines 20 or more; white, yellowish to brownish-tipped, up to 1 cm. long. Central spines 1-3, up to 3 cm. long. Flowers yellowish to reddish-yellow when fading, about 1.5 cm. long and 3 cm. wide. Peru.

Mirabella Ritter see *Monvillea*

Mitrocereus (Backeb.) Backeb.
1951 (*Pseudomitrocereus*).
(Latin mitra = Bishop's mitre)

Large columnar cacti with 11-14 ribs. Flowers close to the crown in a pseudo-cephalium, externally scaly

and bristly/hairy, with nectar chamber, nocturnal. 1 species. Native to Mexico (Puebla, Oaxaca).

M. fulviceps (Web.) Backeb.
(*Pseudomitrocereus f.* (Web.) Bravo & Buxb.; *Pachycereus chrysomallus* Br. & R.) Bushy. Stems grey-green, 12 (-18) m. tall and up to 1 m. thick in the natural habitat, when cultivated stems about 6-12 cm. thick with 11-15 ribs. Radial spines 8-12, up to 2 cm. long. Central spines (1-) 3 (-more), about 3 (-13) cm. long. Spines brownish, later greyish. Flowers borne in a helmet-shaped cephalium, creamy-white, about 8 cm. long.

Monvillea Br. & R. 1920
(*Praecereus*)
(After M. Monville, owner of a famous cactus collection in France around 1800)

Bushy, climbing or sprawling columnar cacti with (4-) 5-12 ribs. Flowers borne towards the end of the stems, with elongated tube, externally slightly scaly and bare, nocturnal, 7-19 cm. long. Fruit bears remains of flower. 26 species. Native to Ecuador, Peru, Bolivia, N. Argentina, Paraguay, E. Brazil.

Ritter has recently established a new

Monvillea spegazzinii

genus *Mirabella*. It is diurnal flowering and all stamens are very short, but it is otherwise extremely similar to *Monvillea*.

Monvillea species are rewarding to cultivate. All species grow strongly and flower when only 1 m. tall. They like abundant moisture in summer, and will also tolerate half-shade. They are less suited to cultivation by a window, as they take up too much space.

M. haageana Backeb.
Branching. Stems light blue-green, 3-4 m. long, 2-4 cm. thick, tapered at the end, with 5 (-6) ribs. Radial spines about 7, almost white, dark-tipped. Central spines 1, black-brown, up to 0.4 cm. long. Flowers white, nocturnal. Paraguay.

M. spegazzinii (Web.) Br. & R.
Bushy, creeping or climbing. Stems dark blue-green, marbled, 1.5-3 m. long and about 1.5-2 cm. thick with 3-4 (-5) ribs. Radial spines 3 (-5) blackish, much thicker at the base, up to 0.4 cm. long. Central spines absent or rarely 1, up to 1.5 cm. long. Flowers cream-white, externally pale pink or reddish, about 13 cm. long. Paraguay.

Morangaya Rowley 1974
(after R.V. Moran, North American botanist)

Cacti with thin, long stems, aerial roots and spiny, orange-red, radially symmetrical flowers borne towards the end of the stems. The genus is the same as *Echinocereus* in its flowers, and like *Aporocactus* in external form. 1 species, *M. pensilis* (K. Brandeg.) Rowley (*Echinocereus p.* (K. Brandeg.) Purpus). Native to Mexico (lower California).

Morawetzia Backeb. see *Oreocereus*

Myrtillocactus Console 1897
(after *Vaccinium myrtillus* = bilberry because of the similarity of the fruit)

Tree-shaped or bushy columnar cacti with 5-9 ribs. Flowers lateral, up to 10 per areole, with very short tube, scaly and slightly woolly, diurnal, 2.5-

Myrtillocactus geometrizans

3.5 cm. long. 4 species. Native to Mexico (Baja California, San Luis Potosí to Oaxaca and Puebla), Guatemala.

M. geometrizans (Mart.) Console Tree-shaped, with thick crown and short trunk. Stems initially of deep bluish frosted appearance, up to 4 m. tall and 6-10 cm. thick, with 5-6 slender ribs. Radial spines 5 (-9), 0.7-1 cm. long. Central spines 1, acute, 1-7 cm. long. Spines brown to almost black. Flowers up to 5-9 per areole, greenish-white, 2.5-3.5 cm. wide. Fruit bluish-purple berries. Mexico, Guatemala.

Requires abundant moisture and much warmth, even in winter.

Neoabottia Br. & R. 1921
(Greek neos = new; W.L. Abott, America, 20th century)

Tree-shaped columnar cacti with 4-6 ribs. Flowers borne towards the end of the stems or terminal in a pseudo-cephalium. Flowers externally scaly and bristly/woolly, with short tips, nocturnal, up to 5 cm. long. 2 species. Native to Hispaniola.

Neobesseya Br. & R. 1923
(*Ortegocactus*)
(Greek neos = new)
after C.E. Bessey (1845-1915), an outstanding American botanist, who was the first to establish a phylogenetic plant system.)

Cacti with furrowed tubercles; flowers borne in the axils, not scaly, bare. The genus is very similar to *Escobaria,* and develops similar fleshy red fruit. The seed are also pitted like *Escobaria,* but feature a much larger aril. 4 species. Native to Mexico (Coahuila), USA, Canada (Manitoba, British Columbia).

Neobesseya is an interesting genus with distinctive flowers. It demands particularly permeable cactus soil with a high mineral content. In the vegetative period the plants like to be watered plentifully, but they are sensitive to stagnant moisture. In winter they should be kept cool and completely dry, with the result that they shrivel up considerably. Kept in these conditions *N. missouriensis* will even survive night frosts, and can be overwintered in an unheated greenhouse in a favourable position.

N. macdougalii (Alex.) Kladiwa (*Ortegocactus m.* Alex.) Only 3-4 cm. in size with fairly large pale grey-green tubercles. Radial spines 7-8, 0.5-1 cm. long. Central spines 1, about 0.5 cm. long. All spines black or whitish with black tip. Flowers pure yellow, 2-3 cm. long. Fruit dark red, slightly hairy. Mexico (Oaxaca). Winter temperatures of 12-15°C required, otherwise the plants easily develop ugly spots.

N. missouriensis (Sweet) Br. & R. Solitary or forming small cushions, up to 6 cm. tall and 6 cm. wide. Tubercles 1-1.5 cm. long. Radial spines 9-20. Central spines absent or 1. Spines like fine hairs, grey, brown-tipped. Flowers greenish-yellow, about 2 cm. long and 2.5-5 cm. wide. Outer flower petals with ciliate margins. Canada (Manitoba), USA (N. Dakota and Montana to Colorado and N. Texas).

N. wissmannii (Hildm.) Br. & R. Solitary or group-forming, bluish-green, up to 10 cm. tall. Tubercles up to 2.5 cm. long. Axils white, woolly. Radial spines 7-20. Central spines absent to 3. Flowers glossy, light yellow to dark yellow 4-5 cm. wide. Outer flower petals with entire margins in contrast to *N. missouriensis.* USA (Central Texas).

Neobesseya missouriensis

Neobinghamia Backeb. emend. Backeb. 1950
(Espostoa x Haageocereus)
(Greek neos = new)

Bushy, columnar cacti with 19-27 ribs, more or less covered with white wool. Flowers borne laterally in a pseudo-cephalium, externally scaly and hairy, nocturnal.

According to Ritter these plants occur exclusively in the region where *Espostoa* and *Haageocereus* overlap. Its appearance also leads to the assumption that it is a natural hybrid between the two genera. When Ritter sowed seed which had been harvested from *Espostoa* plants, the seedlings included a few which were the same as *Neobinghamia*. All this evidence indicates that *Neobinghamia* is a hybrid genus. 4 'species'. Native to Peru.

Neobuxbaumia Backeb. 1938
(Rooksbya)
(after Professor Franz Buxbaum, Austrian botanist and cactus researcher)

Tree-shaped or bushy columnar cacti with 10-50 ribs. Flowers lateral or at the tips of the stems, externally scaly and spiny, bristly, felty or bare, nocturnal. 6 species. Native to Mexico (Guerrero, Hidalgo, Puebla, Oaxaca, Tamaulipas, Veracruz).

N. euphorbioides (Haw.) Buxb.
(Cephalocereus e. (Haw.) Br. & R.; *Rooksbya e.* (Haw.) Backeb.)
Stems pale grey-blue-green, several metres tall, 6-9 cm. wide with 8-9 (-10) narrow, sharp ribs. Spines 1-2 (-5), initially blackish, up to 3 cm. long. Flowers lateral, pink-red, 8-10 cm. long. Mexico (Tamaulipas).

N. polylopha (DC.) Backeb.
(Cephalocereus p. (DC.) Br. & R.)
Solitary columns, light green, later turning grey, up to 13 m. tall in their habitat and up to 35 cm. thick at the base, with up to about 50 slightly rounded ribs. Radial spines 7-9, 1-2 cm. long. Central spines 1. On flowering stems central spines up to 7 cm. long and yellow bristles. Flowers light to dark red, 4-5 cm. long. Mexico (Hidalgo).

Neobuxbaumia polylopha

N. tetetzo (Web.) Backeb.
Tree-form, up to 15 m. tall and 30 cm. thick. Stems grey, 11-15 cm. thick with 13-17 (-20) rounded ribs. Radial spines 8-13, 1-1.5 cm. long. Central spines 1-5 cm. long or longer. All spines blackish. The flowers are close to the crown, whitish and about 6 cm. long. Mexico (Puebla to Oaxaca).

Neocardenasia Backeb. see *Neoraimondia*

Neochilenia Backeb. see *Neoporteria*

Neodawsonia Backeb. 1941
(Greek neos = new, Yale Dawson, North America)

Tree-form or bushy columnar cacti with 22-28 ribs. Flowers lateral or terminal in a pseudo-cephalium which is later grown through, externally scaly and bristly/hairy or only hairy, nocturnal, 3.5-6 cm. long. Fruits fleshy, hairy. 3 species. Native to Mexico (Oaxaca).

Neoevansia W.T. Marsh. see *Peniocereus*

Neogomesia Castaneda see *Ariocarpus*

Neolloydia Br. & R. 1922
(Cumarinia, Echinomastus, Gymnocactus p.p., Rapicactus)
(after F.E. Lloyd, an American botanist of the 19th/20th century)

In this genus the tubercles of older plants are furrowed on the top, as in *Coryphantha*. The flowers are formed at the base of the furrow in the axil of the tubercle. In a few species the furrows between areole and flower are barely visible. The flowers bear scales, but are otherwise bare. The genus differs little from *Escobaria* and *Coryphantha*, but the fruit are dry and turn thin and papery, the seed black and warty. The genus has sometimes been defined slightly differently in the past.

About 18 species. Native to Mexico, USA (Texas, New Mexico), Cuba.

Neolloydia embraces very decoratively spined plants with beautiful flowers, and in consequence they are highly prized by cactus growers. However, cultivation is not usually very easy and they are only recommended to the experienced grower with appropriate cultural facilities.

They only thrive well under glass, preferably in a greenhouse in permeable, predominantly mineral soil (up to one half perlag or gravel). The summer location should be sunny and warm, and they should be kept dry in winter. Care is needed with watering in summer. With many species it is advisable to graft onto a stock which does not grow too strongly.

Radial spines 6-8. Flowers ivory white or yellow
  Central spines absent. Flowers ivory white   *N. gielsdorfiana*
  Central spines 1. Flowers pure yellow   *N. macdougalii*

Radial spines more than 8. Flowers pink to violet
  Spines supplemented by bristles more than 3 cm. long   *N. subterranea*
  Spines not supplemented by long bristles
    Flowers spreading. Central spines projecting
      Areoles yellow, felty (spines more or less enveloping the body)   *N. macdowellii*
      Areoles dense white, woolly. Radial spines appressed, up to 0.6 cm. long   *N. conoidea*

Radial spines round, longer, translucent white   *N. viereckii*

  Flowers more or less funnel-shaped with erect petals. Areoles not dense white, woolly. Central spine angled upwards

(flowers pink with dark centre)
N. erectocentra

N. conoidea (DC.) Br. & R. **var. grandiflora** (Otto) Kladiwa & Fittkau (*N.g.* (Otto) Berger)
Plants 8-10 cm. tall and 4 cm. wide, rarely clustering. Axils white, woolly. Radial spines about 16-25, white, completely appressed, 0.4-0.6 cm. long. Central spines absent, 1 or 2, black, 3 cm. long. Flowers dark purple-pink or white, widely spreading, 2.2-3.8 cm. long. Mexico (Tamaulipas, Nuevo León, San Luis Potosí, Coahuila).

Globular, seldom clustering, tubercles arranged helically, up to 7.5 cm. tall and 5 cm. wide. Areoles white, woolly. Radial spines 6-8, black or brown, lighter at the base, up to 2 cm. long. Central spines absent. Flowers ivory white, up to about 2.5 cm. long. Mexico (Tamaulipas).

N. macdowellii (Rebut) H.E. Moore (*Echinomastus m.* Rebut) Br. & R.; *Thelocactus m.* (Rebut) Kladiwa & Fittkau)
Globular, up to 12.5 cm. wide. Crown yellow, felty. Radial spines 15-27, white, almost enveloping the body,

Neolloydia conoidea var. grandiflora

Neolloydia macdowellii (Thelocactus)

N. erectocentra (Coult.) L. Bens. (*Echinomastus e.* (Coult.) Br. & R.)
Squat cylindrical, up to 20 cm. tall and 10 cm. wide with 15-21 bumpy ribs. Radial spines about 13-18, whitish, about 1.25 cm. long. Central spines 1-2, reddish, often purple, up to 2.5 cm. long. Flowers pink with dark centre, 3 (-5) cm. long and 2 cm. wide. Better grafted. USA (S.E. Arizona).

N. gielsdorfiana (Werderm.) F.M. Knuth (*Gymnocactus g.* (Werderm.) Backeb.; *Thelocactus g.* (Werderm.) Bravo)

1.5-3 cm. long. Central spines 3-4, flattened, dark below, translucent straw-coloured above, 2.5-6 cm. long. Flowers pink, up to 5 cm. long. N. Mexico.

N. subterranea (Backeb.) H.E. Moore (*Gymnocactus s.* (Backeb.) Backeb.; *Rapicactus s.* (Backeb.) Buxb. & Oehme)
Up to 10 cm. tall and 3-4 cm. wide. Radial spines about 16, white, 0.2-0.6 cm. long. Central spines 2, blackish, up to 2 cm. long. Additionally a few white bristles, more than 3 cm. long. A connecting piece about 10 cm. long but only 2-4 cm.

Neolloydia subterranea

Neolloydia viereckii

thick forms between the shoot and the root. Mexico (Tamaulipas).

Particularly difficult on its own root, but does well when grafted.

N. viereckii (Werderm.) F.M. Knuth (*Gymnocactus v.* (Werderm.) Backeb.; *Thelocactus v.* (Werderm.) Bravo) Globular to short cylindrical, 5-7 cm. wide, solitary or slightly clustering. Tubercles in 15-18 rows. Crown dense white, woolly. Radial spines about 20, translucent white, up to 1 cm. long. Central spines 4, white below, dark above, black-tipped, up to 3 cm. long. Flowers lilac-pink, spreading, about 2 cm. long. Mexico (Tamaulipas).

Neomammillaria Br. & R. see *Mammillaria*

Neoporteria Br. & R. 1922
(*Chileorebutia, Delaetia, Horridocactus, Islaya, Neochilenia, Pyrrhocactus, Reicheocactus, Thelocephala*) (Greek neos = new; C.E. Porter, Chilean entomologist, 20th century)

This genus of globular to elongated cacti, often brownish or grey in colour, has radially symmetrical flowers borne close to the crown. The flowers are externally scaly and hairy/felty, seldom also bristly. The fruit are also distinctive, being hollow when ripe, with an opening pore at the base.

The genus *Neoporteria,* established by Britton and Rose, was later split up into several genera but subsequently reunited by Donald and Rowley, as no very clear differences exist. Almost all species occur in Northern and Central Chile. About 90 species (probably much fewer if considered critically). Native to Chile, a few S. Peru, Argentina.

The two main groups of the genus, *Neoporteria* in the narrower sense, and the earlier genus *Neochilenia,* require different cultural conditions. The inner flower petals of *Neochilenia* are erect when fully unfolded and are coloured white, yellow or reddish. In Europe these plants usually flower in the spring and early summer. The species of this group make no special cultural demands and are recommended. Even in half-shade they still grow well and

Neoporteria islayensis var. grandis

flower readily. Older plants often produce whole clusters of flowers at the crown. In winter they need a temperature of 8-10°C.

The flower petals of *Neoporteria* in the narrower sense are inclined and straighter, and carmine pink in colour. These plants originate in the rocky coastal deserts of Central and Northern Chile. In Europe the flowers often appear in autumn or early winter or in the early spring. Neoporterias often feature an attractive spine formation. They thrive well but require careful cultivation, and are thus only recommended to experienced cactus growers. They require mineral soil and a bright location. In summer they have a rest period during which they should not be watered or sprayed. Their main growth period is in the autumn. Plants which set flowers in late autumn should then be kept moderately moist, light and warm, so that the flowers are able to develop. Non-flowering Neoporterias in the narrower sense should be kept in dry, bright conditions, but not too warm.

Special attention is required for the dwarf Neoporterias with a pronounced taproot, such as *N. occulta* or *N. reichei*. They are accustomed to extreme locations, often just cracks in rocks, where they have to be very economical with water. They demand a particularly permeable, mineral soil and must be watered sparingly. If these plants are grafted, do not use a vigorous stock.

Neoporteria
(Group key according to Donald and Rowley)

Flower petals narrow, like bristles   (*Delaetia*)
Flower petals not narrow like bristles
  Flowers small, bell-shaped, lilac pink with purple stigmas; fruit initially fleshy
    Sub-genus I Neoporteria
  Flowers usually large and spreading, yellow to lilac with yellowish to pink stigmas;
    Fruit dry   **Sub-genus II Pyrrhocactus**
    Flowers pale yellow to lilac with pink stigmas   **Group A**
      (*Neochilenia, Horridocactus*)
    Flowers yellow (seldom lilac) with yellowish stigmas
      Plants with naked crown; flower tube urn-shaped; fruit round   **Group B**
        (*Pyrrhocactus*)
      Crown more or less woolly; flower tube conical; fruit longer than wide
        Flowers large about 3.5 cm. in diameter, with long, woolly tube   **Group C**
          (*Reicheocactus*)
        Flowers usually small, 2.5 cm. in diameter, with short, woolly, bristly tube
          Group D (*Islaya*)

(Delaetia)
Flower petals almost like bristles. Spines transversely ringed, only 3-4   *N. woutersiana*

I Neoporteria
Distinct radial and central spines
Spines hair-like and tortuous   *N. laniceps*
Spines curved, enveloping the entire body   *N. nidus*
Spines more or less straight, not enveloping the body
  Flowers 3-4 cm. long   *N. subgibbosa*
  Flowers 2-2.5 cm. long
    Radial spines 12-20   *N. villosa*
    Radial spines 10-14   *N. wagenknechtii*

II Pyrrhocactus

II A (*Neochilenia, Horridocactus*)
Spines more or less similar

Spines strong, 1-3 cm. long. Areoles not conspicuously white, woolly
  Spines straight, white when young   *N. tuberisulcata*
  Spines curved
    Spines yellowish   *N. curvispina*
    Spines almost black   *N. choapensis*
Spines strong to very short. Areoles white, woolly
  Spines very strong, more or less enveloping the body. Radial spines about 18- 20
    N. taltalensis
  Spines strong. Radial spines up to about 10
    Ribs 12-17. Body dark green to almost black   *N. jussieui*
    Ribs 12-13. Body leaf-green   *N. hankeana*
    Ribs 8-12. Body green to blue-green   *N. paucicostata*
  Spines short. Radial spines 0.2-0.5 cm. long   *N. napina, N. odieri, N. dimorpha*
  Spines minute. Radial spines 0.2-0.3 cm. long   *N. esmeraldana*
Spines reduced or absent
  Body up to 10 cm. tall and 5 cm. wide   *N. napina* var. *mitis*
  Body only up to 2.5 cm. wide   *N. occulta*

II B (*Pyrrhocactus*)
Spines very long
Spines 9-20   *N. straussianus*
Spines 30-55, curved upwards and enveloping the body   *N. umadeave*

II C (*Reicheocactus*)
Spines very short to almost absent   *N. reichei*

II D (*Islaya*)
Spines more or less identical. Areoles white, woolly. Ribs hardly bumpy
Central spines and radial spines similar   *N. islayensis*
Central spines 4-8. Flowers 3.25 cm. long   *N. krainziana*
Central spines 1-4. Flowers 2 cm. long   *N. mollendensis, N. bicolor*

N. aerocarpa see *N. reichei*

(IID) **N. bicolor** (Akers & Buin.) Donald & G.D. Rowl. (*Islaya b.* Akers & Buin.)
Up to 10 cm. wide and 20 cm. tall, sometimes tinged with purple, 12-26 ribs. Radial spines 6-14, 0.3-1 cm. long. Central spines 1-4, up to 1.25 cm. long. Spines grey, brown-tipped. Flowers yellow with reddish tips, about 2 cm. long and wide. S. Peru.

N. castaneoides see *N. subgibbosa*

(IIA) **N. choapensis** (Ritter) Donald & G.D. Rowl. (*Horridocactus c.* (Ritter) Backeb.)
Up to 10 cm. diameter, dark bluish-green with 14-22 ribs. Radial spines 8-10, 1-2 cm. long. Central spines 4-7 (-9). All spines almost black. Flowers light greenish-yellow, up to 4.5 cm. long and 5 cm. wide. Central Chile (Illapel).

(IIA) **N. curvispina** (Bert.) Donald & G.D. Rowl. (*Horridocactus c.* (Bert.) Backeb.; *Malacocarpus c.* (Bert.) Br. & R.)

16 cm. diameter, grey-green to grass green with about 16 ribs, divided into large tubercles. Radial spines 6-10. Central spines 2-4. All spines curving upwards strongly, yellowish, up to 3 cm. long. Flowers pale yellow, externally greenish, 3.5 cm. long. Chile (Santiago region).

(IIA) **N. dimorpha** (Ritter) Donald & G.D. Rowl. (*Neochilenia d.* (Ritter) Backeb.)
Diameter 2-6 cm., almost black, with 13-16 ribs. Radial spines 6-10 when young, black to almost white, 2-5 mm. long, later 8-12 radial spines and 1-3 central spines. Flowers light yellow to brownish-yellow, up to 3.5 cm. long. Root beet-like. Chile (Coquimbo).

(IIA) **N. esmeraldana** (Ritter) Donald & G.D. Rowl. (*Neochilenia e.* (Ritter) Backeb.)
Diameter 5-7 cm., strongly clustering, black to reddish, ribs divided up into tubercles. Radial spines 4-12. Central spines 1. All spines blackish, 2-3 mm. long. Flowers silky white, slightly yellowish or reddish, up to 5 cm. long and 4.5 cm. wide. N. Chile (Esmeraldas).

Neoporteria carrizalensis

Neoporteria esmeraldana

Neoporteria napina

Neoporteria nidus var. gerocephala

N. gerocephala see *N. nidus* var. *gerocephala*

(IIA) **N. hankeana** (Först.) Donald & G.D. Rowl. (*Neochilenia h.* (Först.) Dolz; *Neoporteria fusca* (Mühlpf.) Br. & R.; *Neochilenia ebenacantha* hort. non Monv.) Leaf-green with 12-13 ribs. Radial spines about 10. Central spines 1-4, curving upwards, initially black, up to 3 cm. long. Flowers cream-white, 3-4 cm. long and wide. Chile.

(IID) **N. islayensis** (Först.) Donald & G.D. Rowl. **var. grandis** (Rauh & Backeb.) Donald & G.D. Rowl.) (*Islaya g.* Rauh & Backeb.) Globular, up to 30 (50) cm. tall and 20 cm. wide, grey-blue-green with up to 17 ribs. Radial and central spines fairly similar, 9-20, initially frosted, horn-coloured and dark-tipped, 1-3 cm. long. Flowers yellow, 1.5 cm. long. Peru (Arequipa).

(IIA) **N. jussieui** (Monv.) Br. & R. (*Neochilenia j.* (Monv.) Backeb.) About 12 cm. tall and 7 cm. wide, dark green to almost black with 12-17 ribs. Radial spines 7-14, brownish, 1 cm. long. Central spines 1-2, brownish to black, 2-2.5 cm. long. Flowers dirty pink with darker central stripe, up to 4 cm. long. Chile.

(IID) **N. krainziana** (Ritter) Donald & G.D. Rowl. (*Islaya k.* Ritter) Cylindrical, later prostrate, up to

75 cm. long and 12 cm. thick, grey-green, with 16-23 ribs. Areoles white, woolly, especially at the crown. Radial spines around 8-10, 0.5-1 cm. long. Central spines 4-8, yellowish-brownish, up to 1.5 cm. long. Flowers yellow, pleasantly scented, up to 3.25 cm. long. N. Chile, extreme desert areas.

(I) **N. laniceps** Ritter (*N. planiceps* Ritter) Up to 40 cm. in diameter and 20 cm. tall and thus the largest known species, bright green to brownish, with 13-17 ribs. Spines 25-40, hair-like and tortuous, white or brownish. Central spines several, brown or darker, 2-4 cm. long. Flowers carmine, about 3 cm. long. N. Chile (Totoral Bajo).

N. litoralis see *N. subgibbosa*

N. malleolata see *N. reichei*

N. mitis see *N. napina*

(IID) **Islaya mollendensis** (Vaup.) Backeb. (not yet reclassified as *Neoporteria m.*) Elongated globular, 10-20 cm. tall and 10 cm. wide, dark green with about 16-19 slightly indented ribs. Radial spines up to about 10, 1 cm. long. Central spines 3-4. Spines at first dark brown-red, later almost black. Flowers dull yellow, 2 cm. long. Fruit very large, air-filled and with few seeds. S. Peru (Mollendo).

(IIA) **N. napina** *(Phil.) Backeb.* (*Neochilenia n.* (Phil.) Backeb.; *Malacocarpus n.* (Phil. Br. & R.) Up to 10 cm. tall and 5 cm. thick, dark grey to blackish-green, with about 14 ribs, divided up into tubercles. Radial spines about 10, blackish, appressed, up to 3 mm. long. Central spines 4. Flowers cream-yellow, 2.5 cm. long. Long taproot. Chile (near Huasca).

var. mitis (Phil.) Donald & G.D. Rowl. (*Neochilenia m.* (Phil.) Backeb.) Globular, around 3.5 cm. wide, brownish to grey-green. Spines 6-8, about 0.1 cm. long. Chile (Copiapo dept.)

(I) **N. nidus** (Söhr.) Br. & R. Globular, some specimens elongated later, up to 10 cm. wide. Spines 25-30, densely matted and enveloping the body. Flowers light red, 3-6 cm. long. N. Chile (Ovalle region).

var. nidus Devoid or almost devoid of taproot. Spines grey or grey-brown, up to 3 cm. long. Radial spines 12-15. Flowers 3-5 cm. long.

var. gerocephala (Y. Ito) Ritter (*N.g.* Y. Ito, *N. senilis* Backeb.) With yellowish taproot. Spines white, some of them often black, up to 5 cm. long. Radial spines around 20. Flowers 4-6 cm. long.

N. nigrihorrida see *N. subgibbosa*

(IIA) **N. occulta** (Phil.) Br. & R. (*Neochilenia o.* (Phil.) Backeb.) Globular, 1.3-2.5 cm. diameter, yellow-brownish to blackish with 8-10 ribs. Radial spines 6-10, up to 0.8 cm. long. Central spine 1, 1.5 cm. long. Older plants virtually spineless. Flowers pale golden yellow, 2.5 cm. long. Root beet-like. Chile (Copiapo to Cobre).

(IIA) **N. odieri** (Lem.) Berger (*Neochilenia o.* (Lem.) Backeb.) Up to 6 cm. wide, grey-brown to reddish-brown with about 13 ribs. Radial spines 6-10, more or less reddish grey-brown, up to 0.5 cm. long. Central spines absent. Flowers white (to pink), up to 5 cm. long and about 5 cm. wide. Chile (Copiapo, Huasco).

(IIA) **N. paucicostata** (Ritter) Donald & G.D. Rowl. (*Neochilenia p.* (Ritter) Backeb.) Approx. 6-8 cm. thick. blue-grey-green, with a whitish or green tinge, 8-12 ribs. Radial spines 5-8. Central spines often absent at first, later 1-4, up to 4 cm. long. Spines grey-black, later lighter. Flowers reddish-white, about 3-5 cm. long and up to 5 cm. wide. N. Chile.

These blue-grey plants are particularly beautiful, but grow relatively slowly.

N. planiceps see *N. laniceps*

(IIC) **N. reichei** (K. Schum.) Backeb. (*Neochilenia r.* (K. Schum.) Backeb.; *Malacocarpus r.* (K. Schum.) Br. & R.) Up to 7.5 cm. wide, grey-green to brownish green, ribs deeply notched, forming tubercles. Radial spines 4-10, central spines absent or 1-2. Spines very variable in colour, 0.2-0.6 (-1) cm. long. Flowers yellow, 2.5-4 cm. long.

var. reichei
Body more or less grey-green. Spines 7-9, translucent or white, 3 mm. long. Flowers glossy yellow, 2.5-3.5 cm. long. Chile.

f. aerocarpa (Ritter) Donald & G.D. Rowl. (*Neochilenia a.* (Ritter) Backeb.; *Thelocephala a.* Ritter) Body brownish. Radial spines 8-10, reddish-brown to dark. Central spine absent or 1-2, blackish. All spines 4-6 (-10) cm. long. Flowers silky cream-pink with darker central stripe, 3 (-5) cm. long and 5 cm. wide. Chile (Dept. Freiriana).

Neoporteria taltalensis var. flaviflora

Neoporteria occulta

Neoporteria paucicostata

Neoporteria reichei var. reichei

Neoporteria reichei f. aerocarpa

f. pseudoreichei (Lemb. & Backeb.)
Donald & G.D. Rowl. (*Reicheocactus pseudoreicheanus* Backeb.)
Body olive green. Radial spines 10, tiny, up to 0.2 cm. long. Central spine 1, up to 0.35 cm. long. All spines initially pale yellow, later translucent grey. Flowers reddish outside, yellowish inside, up to 3.5 cm. in size. Chile.

var. malleolata (Ritter) Donald & G.D. Rowl. (*Neochilenia m.* (Ritter) Backeb.)
Body grey-green, clustering. Areoles white, felted. Radial spines 4-8, brownish to yellowish, 0.2-0.4 cm. long. Central spines absent. Flowers brownish to reddish-yellow, about 4 cm. long. Chile (North of Chanaral).

(IIB) **N. straussiana** (K. Schum.)
Donald & G.D. Rowl. (*Pyrrhocactus s.* (K. Schum). Berger; *Malacocarpus s.* (K. Schum.) Br. & R.)
Globular to short columnar, up to 16 cm. tall and 9 cm. thick, blackish, grey-green with up to 13 bumpy ribs. Spines 9-20, black, later grey or brownish, up to 3 cm. long. Flowers salmon pink, 1.5 cm. long. S. Argentina (North of the central course of the Rio Colorado).

(I) **N. subgibbosa** (Haw.) Br. & R.
Globular to moderately elongated and up to 10 cm. diameter, grass green to dark grey-green, with 14-21 ribs. Radial spines about 16-30, up to 2 cm. long. Central spines 4-8, up to 3 cm.

long. Spines amber to black. Flowers carmine pink, up to 4 cm. long.

var. subgibbosa
Spines yellowish to blackish.

f. subgibbosa
Radial spines about 24. Central spines 4. All spines light amber, later darker with light base. Flowers about 4 cm. long. Chile (near Valparaiso).

Neoporteria bulbocalyx

f. litoralis (Ritter) Donald & G.D. Rowl. (*N.l.* Ritter)
The body is grass-green. Radial spines about 30. Central spines 8-12. All spines as fine as hairs, yellow-white to yellow brown, or brown to blackish. The flowers are up to 2.75 cm. long. Chile (along the shore).

f. castaneoides (Ritter) Donald & G.D. Rowl. (*N. c.* (Cels) Werderm.)

Body grey-green. Radial spines up to 20, central spines up to 6. All spines pure light golden yellow to golden brown. Flowers white inside. Chile (Region of Copiapo).

var. nigrihorrida (Backeb.) Donald & G.D. Rowl. (*N.n.* (Backeb.) Backeb.) Spines black. Body matt dark grey-green. Radial spines about 16, 1.5 cm. long. Central spines 6-7, up to 3 cm. long. Flowers white inside, 4 cm. long. Chile (South of Coquimbo).

(IIA) N. taltalensis (Hutchison) Backeb. (*Neochilenia t.* (Hutchison) Backeb.) Globular, about 5-8 cm. diameter, with 12-14 bumpy ribs. Radial spines about 18-20, brownish, straight or curved, 0.8-2 cm. long. Central spines 4 (-6), blackish, 3-5 cm. long, straight. Spines covering the body. Flowers around 3-4 cm. long. Chile (Taltal).

var. flaviflora (Ritter) Backeb. Has pale yellow flowers.

(IIA) N. tuberisulcata (Jacobi) Donald & G.D. Rowl. (*Horridocactus t.* (Jacobi) Y. Ito; *Malacocarpus t.* (Jacobi) Br. & R.; *Horridocactus horridus* (Colla) Backeb.) Globular, up to 20 cm. wide, blackish blue-green, with 14-20 warty ribs. Radial spines 10-12, brown, turning grey. Central spines 4-5. Spines up to 2.5 cm. long, all of them very strong. Flowers brownish-yellow, with reddish central stripes, up to 4.5 cm. long. Chile.

(IIB) N. umadeave (Frič) Donald & G.D. Rowl. (*Pyrrhocactus u.* (Frič) Backeb.) Globular, up to 11 cm. diameter, up to 25 cm. in its natural habitat, matt green, with 18 (-27) bumpy ribs. Spines 30-35, whitish to black, 3-4 cm. long. Spines rigid, sharp, curving upward and enveloping the body. Flowers pale yellow, 3-3.5 cm. in size. N. Argentina (Puerto Tastil; Jujuy).

(I) N..villosa (Monv.) Berger (*Echinocactus v.* (Monv.) Lab.) About 15 cm. tall and 8 cm. wide, grey-green, violet, turning blackish, with 13-15 ribs. Areoles white, woolly.

Radial spines 12-20, light yellow, light brown or grey, 1-2 cm. long. Central spines about 4, darker, up to 3 cm. long. Flowers pale pink to white, 2-2.5 cm. long. Chile (region of Huasco).

(I) N. wagenknechtii Ritter Globular, elongated when old, up to 30 cm. tall and 11 cm. wide, blackish grey-green, with 11-17 ribs. Radial spines 10-14, white to dark grey, up to 2.5 cm. long. Central spines 3-6, dark brown to grey-brown, 2-3 cm. long. Flowers light purple, up to 2.2 cm. long. Chile (North of La Serena, Juan Soldado).

N. woutersiana (Backeb.) Donald & G.D. Rowl. (*Delaetia w.* Backeb.) Globular, grey-green, with 13 ribs. Spines usually 4, with black to grey-black transverse rings, 1-2.5 cm. long. Flowers brownish-orange 2 cm. long. Flower petals almost as narrow as bristles. ?Chile.

According to Ritter a cultivated form of *N. taltalensis* with stunted flowers.

Neoraimondia Br. & R. 1920
(Neocardenasia)
(after Antonio Raimondi (1825-1890), Peruvian geographer)

Tree-like or bushy columnar cacti with 4-8 ribs. Flower-bearing areoles are specially formed, thickened, elongated, up to 5 cm. long. Flowers are externally scaly and bristly/felty or only felty, diurnal. 3 species. Native to Bolivia, Peru, Chile.

Neowerdermannia Frič 1930
(after Erich Werdermann 1892 — 1959, German botanist and cactus researcher)

Globular cacti with ribs divided up into tubercles, bearing flowers almost laterally. Flowers scaly but bare with distinct nectar chamber. The genera *Gymnocalycium* and *Weingartia* are very similar, but the areoles of *Neowerdermannia* are located in the depressions between the tubercles and the tiny fruit contain very few seed. Thick taproot. 3 species. Native to Peru, Bolivia, Chile, Argentina. Up to 4000 m. altitude in the Andes.

Because of their taproot the plants require permeable, mineral soil and

Neowerdermannia vorwerkii

will not tolerate stagnant moisture. In the winter months the plants are kept completely dry; in their habitat they then shrink almost into the ground, and in this way are able to survive nocturnal frosts.

N. vorwerkii Frič (*Weingartia v.* (Frič) Backeb.)
6-8 cm. wide with about 16 or more ribs, divided up into tubercles. Spines up to about 10, up to 1.5 cm. long. Central spine 1, 1-1.5 cm. long, often hooked. Flowers white or light lilac, 2-2.5 cm. long and wide. A curious feature is the flower buds which are completely black. N. Argentina to N. Bolivia.

Nopalea Salm-Dyck see *Opuntia*

Nopalxochia Br. & R. 1923
(*Lobeira, Pseudonopalxochia*)
(after the Aztek name nopal for *Opuntia* species; xochitl = flower)

Epiphytic plants with flat leaf-like stems. The diurnal flowers lack a distinct, elongated tube. The flowers are bristly (*Pseudonopalxochia*), felty (*Lobeira*) or bare (*Nopalxochia* in the narrower sense). 4 species. Native to Mexico.

Epiphyllum hybrid (Phyllocactus)

N. ackermannii (Haw.) F.M. Knuth
(*Heliocereus speciosus* x *Nopalxochia phyllanthoides*)
Stems notched, wavy, dark green. Flowers brilliant red, 12 cm. long. Mexico (Chiapas, Oaxaca).

N. phyllanthoides (DC.) Br. & R.
Stems slightly dentate, light green to yellowish-green, central and lateral ribs visible. Flowers pink or pale red, 7-10 cm. long. Mexico (Puebla).

Under the name *Epiphyllum* hybrids or Phyllocacti a great number of cultivated hybrids are available. Link established '*Phyllocactus*' in 1831, but the genus was later equated with *Epiphyllum*. The most important base species of these cacti are now included in their own genus *Nopalxochia*. They are diurnal flowering plants, as opposed to the nocturnal *Epiphyllum* species. *Nopalxochia phyllanthoides* with its light red to pink flowers and *Nopalxochia ackermannii* with its brilliant deep red flowers were the basis for the hybridizing work which began early in the last century, although *N. ackermannii* itself was a hybrid of *Heliocereus speciosus* and *Nopalxochia phyllanthoides*. In 1840 *N. crenata* was added, with white flowers. As

Epiphyllum hybrid (Phyllocactus)

Epiphyllum hybrid (Phyllocactus)

Epiphyllum hybrids (Phyllocacti). See also illustrations on page 168.

epiphytes the plants were initially rather sensitive, and had sprawling, rather flabby stems.

Heliocereus speciosus is erect, not epiphytic and has multi-ribbed stems, but its flowers are extremely similar to those of *Nopalxochia*. This species proved ideal for hybridizing, and the admixture improved the hybrids considerably. In time the *Epiphyllum* hybrids grew to be some of the most popular of indoor plants.

In order to obtain even larger flowers species of *Selenicereus* were then added, including the 'Queen of the Night'. These plants possess the largest of all

cactus flowers but are nocturnal, and individual hybrids retained this characteristic. The best known *Phyllocactus* hybridizer after 1900 was C. Knebel of Saxony, and his work was continued by Haage. Today there are several thousand named sorts. Recently the genera *Aporocactus* and *Disocactus* have been increasingly added to the mixture. Provided that the parent names of the hybrids are known, proper names can also be used for the hybrid genera, e.g:

x *Heliochia* (= *Heliocereus* x *Nopalxochia*)
x *Epixochia* (= *Epiphyllum* x *Nopalxochia*)
x *Heliphyllum* (= *Heliocereus* x *Epiphyllum*)

x *Seleniphyllum* (= *Selenicereus* x *Epiphyllum*) and others.

Nearly all the flowers range from white, cream, yellow, orange, salmon and red to carmine violet in colour. Many flowers are also bi-coloured, usually with lighter inner petals. The flowers are up to 20 cm. wide and are among the most beautiful of cactus flowers. They certainly bear comparison with orchid flowers, and in fact 'Phyllocacti' are commonly called 'orchid cacti'.

As epiphytes play a role in their lineage, these plants require an acid soil containing humus. However, the individual sorts are not all equally demanding. Many thrive well in standard soil although an addition of sand and Perlite is an improvement. Half-shade is ideal, but the position should be bright. In shady conditions they flower poorly; in brilliant sun they flower well, but soon look scorched. The roots require constant slight moisture; frequent misting suits the plants well. The individual sorts vary widely in their tolerance of low winter temperatures. Many will survive temperatures of just above 0°C.; others, such as *N. phyllanthoides* and its hybrids, look quite exhausted even at 5°C. The main flowering period lasts from April to June and the individual flowers last for several days. In summer the plants can even be set in a half-shady place in the open. Propagation of genetically identical plants can only be achieved by taking cuttings in spring or August. In sandy soil the cuttings root readily after a few weeks once they have been dried off thoroughly. Plants raised from seed do not develop their first flowers until they are 4 to 8 years old. Even if you select the parent plants with great care, you can only expect one plant out of many hundred to show any possible improvement on the original sorts, owing to the intensity of the hybridizing work which has gone before. If you are aiming at producing worthwhile new hybrids it is probably easier to start with other cactus genera.

Normanbokea Kladiwa & Buxb. See *Turbinicarpus*

Notocactus (K. Schum.) 1898
Berger emend. Buxb.
(*Brasilicactus, Brasiliparodia, Eriocactus, Malacocarpus, Wigginsia*)
(Greek noton = back / spine)

Notocacti are cacti of elongated to squat globular form with 6-60 ribs. The flowers are borne close to the crown, and are scaly, while the ovary and tube feature dense wool mixed in with bristles or spines. The obvious distinguishing feature is the red or purple stigmas, which stand out very conspicuously from the flowers and stamens, which are usually yellow. Only a few species have yellowish stigmas. The fruit is dry and carries the remains of the flower.

Notocactus seeds have a light-coloured strophiole at the point where they are attached, as has the related genus *Parodia*. Buxbaum divides the two genera by means of a fine distinction in seed structure. The seed cord of *Notocactus* is dry and easily breaks off, while that of *Parodia* is merged with the spongey tissue of the strophiole. This definition divides the plants into the genus *Notocactus* (including the lowland Pampas species) and *Parodia*, including the upland Andean species. Using this criterion certain species with hooked spines and yellow stigmas, which are externally like Parodias, e.g. *Parodia brevihamata*, have to be included in *Notocactus*.

The genus *Frailea*, which is less similar to *Notocactus*, includes small cacti, only up to 5 cm. wide, with tiny spines and funnel-shaped flowers which are usually cleistogamous.

Brasilicactus and *Eriocactus* lack the characteristic red stigmas, and were earlier considered to be separate genera, but are now usually considered to be sub-genera of *Notocactus*. The species of the former genus *Malacocarpus* have a distinctive woolly crown, which can look almost like a small *Melocactus* cephalium. As the name *Malacocarpus* had already been used for another plant genus, the name had to be altered later, and *Wigginsia* was selected. However, apart from their more or less woolly crown the *Wigginsia* species are typical Notocacti. For this reason they are almost invariably included in the genus *Notocactus* today. Roughly 80 species. Native to Argentina, Uruguay, S. Brazil, Paraguay.

Notocacti include a large number of vigorous cacti which flower readily, and are thus ideal for the beginner. All the species are attractive even without flowers.

They like nutritious soil containing humus, and a constant but low level of moisture in the vegetative period. In summer they appreciate a bright, warm situation, although those species without dense spines should be protected from brilliant sun. As grassland plants they will even tolerate half-shade, and can be left in the open in summer. Notocacti like balanced cultural conditions rather than extremes. Certain popular species such as *N. ottonis* grow and flower well even on a window ledge. In winter they must not be kept too cold nor too dry. If they are left in a bright situation in winter, they set flowers in the middle of that season. Seedlings flower profusely after the second year, when they are about 3 cm. in diameter. The large and beautiful flowers are usually yellow, have a silky sheen, and persist for several days.

Central spine hooked (stigma lobes yellow) — *Gr. 3 Brasiliparodia*
Central spines not hooked
  Crown angled. Stigma lobes yellow
    Body more or less columnar, with distinct ribs. Flowers 4 cm. or more long, yellow — *Gr. 1 Eriocactus*
    Body more or less rounded. Flowers up to 2 cm. long, greenish-yellow or red — *Gr. 2 Brasilicactus*
  Crown straight. Stigma lobes red
    Areoles with 1-2 cm. long felt when young, forming a pseudo-cephalium.
      Flowers borne centrally on the crown — *Gr. 6 Wigginsia (Malacocarpus)*
    Areoles not so felty when young. Flowers more or less in a ring at the crown
      Stamens borne over the whole length of the tube — *Gr. 4 Notocactus*
      Stamens only borne at the bottom of the tube — *Gr. 5 Neonotocactus*

251

Group 1 Eriocactus

Ribs about 30. Areoles separated
  Spines more than 10. Body columnar   *N. leninghausii*
  Spines 4-7 (-10). Body more globular   *N. schumannianus*
Ribs 11-15, areoles felted over when old   *N. magnificus*

Group 2 Brasilicactus

Crown (almost always) with yellow spines only. Flowers light green   *N. graessneri*
Crown woolly, with white spines. Flowers yellow-red to blood red   *N. haselbergii*

Group 3 Brasiliparodia   *N. brevihamatus*

Group 4 Notocactus in the narrowest sense

Flowers red or lilac
  Central spines absent, radial spines about 6, but of unequal length
                                           N. uebelmannianus
  Central spines 4 (-6)   *N. herteri*
Flowers yellow
  Crown woolly
    Style brilliant red like the stigma lobes
      Ribs 30-35. Central spines 3-4   *N. scopa*
      Ribs 18-24. Central spines 8-12   *N. sucineus*
    Style not brilliant red like the stigma lobes
      Stigma lobes orange-yellow to pink   *N. horstii*
      Stigma lobes deep red
        Flowers 3-4 cm. long
          Crown very densely woolly. Flowers golden yellow   *N. arechavaletai*
          Crown woolly. Flowers light sulphur yellow   *N. fuscus*
        Flowers 4-7 cm. long
          Ribs 6-13   *N. ottonis*
          Ribs 16-20   *N. concinnus*
Crown more or less bare but usually spiny
  Central spine 1. Radial spines 7-10   *N. crassigibbus*
  Central spines 4
    Radial spines few, weak   *N. buiningii*
    Radial spines 16-20
      Stamens: upper ones yellow, lower ones red. Style red. Body light green
                                       N. apricus
      Stamens all yellow. Style yellow. Body blue-green   *N. tabularis*

Group 5 Neonotocactus

Flowers carmine pink with yellow throat   *N. rutilans*
flowers yellow
  Crown woolly
    Central spines flattened   *N. submammulosus*
    Central spine not flattened   *N. mammulosus*
  Crown woolly and spiny
    Stigma lobes pale carmine. Flowers about 3 cm. long   *N. mueller-melchersii*
    Stigma lobes red. Flowers up to 6 cm. long   *N. floricomus*

Group 6 Wigginsia (*Malacocarpus*)

Central spines initially black   *N. arechavaletai*
Central spines white or dark-tipped
  Spines around 6-13. Flowers up to 5 cm. long
    Radial spines 7-12   *N. corynodes*
    Radial spines 5-7   *N. tephracanthus*
  Spines up to 8. Flowers about 3 cm. long
    Radial spines 6-7   *N. fricii*
    Radial spines 4   *N. sessiliflora*

N. apricus (Arech.) Berger (*Malacocarpus a.* (Arech. Br. & R.)
Body clustering, 5 cm. thick with 15-20 ribs. Crown (almost) spiny only. Radial spines bristly, 18-20, red-yellow when young. Central spines 4, reddish and curved, up to 3 cm. long. Flowers yellow, 6-8 cm. long. Upper stamens yellow, lower ones red. Uruguay.

N. arechavaletai (Spegazz.) Herter (*Malacocarpus a.* (Spegazz.) Berger; *Wigginsia a.* (Spegazz.) D.M. Porter)
Body around 10 cm. wide with 13-21 ribs. Crown very woolly and spiny. Radial spines up to 9 or more, reddish or yellowish. Central spines 1 (-4), black, later grey. Spines up to 2 cm. long. Flowers golden yellow, 3-4 cm. long. Uruguay.

N. brevihamatus (W. Haage) Buxb. (*Parodia b.* W. Haage)
Body 3-6 (-9.5) cm. wide with 20-26 ribs. Crown spiny. Radial spines about 16, yellowish-white. Central spines (1-) 4-6, yellow, brown-red towards the tip, hooked. Spines up to 6 (-10) mm. long. Flowers golden yellow, around 4 cm. long. Stigmas yellow. Brazil (Rio Grande do Sul).

N. buiningii Buxb.
Body up to 12 cm. wide with about 16 ribs. Crown not woolly. Central spines 4, very strong, dark brown at the base, translucent yellowish at the tip, with a few weak supplementary spines. Flowers yellow, 7 cm. long. Uruguay.

N. concinnus (Monv.) Berger (*Malacocarpus c.* (Monv.) Br. & R.)
Body 6-10 cm. wide and half as high, with 16-20 ribs. Crown woolly. Radial spines bristly, 10-12, yellow, up to 0.7 cm. long. Central spines 4 forming a cross, dark yellow to brownish, the bottom one up to 2 cm. or more long, curving downward. Flowers light yellow, 7 cm. long. S. Brazil, Uruguay.

N. corynodes (Otto ex Pfeiff.) Krainz (*Malacocarpus c.* (Otto ex Pfeiff.) Salm-Dyck; *Wigginsia c.* (Otto ex Pfeiff.) D.M. Porter)
Body 10 cm. wide and up to 20 cm. tall, with 13-16 ribs. Crown densely woolly. Radial spines 7-12, dark yellow, up to 2 cm. long. Central spines 0-1, slightly longer. Flowers canary yellow, up to 5 cm. long and wide. Uruguay, Argentina.

Notocactus arechavaletai

N. crassigibbus Ritter
Body 5-16 cm. wide with 10-15 ribs.
Crown bare, not spiny. Radial spines
7-10. Central spines usually 1. Spines
light brown, turning grey, up to 3 cm.
long. Flowers sulphur yellow, 5-6 cm.
long. Brazil (Rio Grande do Sul).

N. floricomus (Arech.) Berger
Body columnar when old, up to 30 cm.
tall and 13 cm. wide with around 20
ribs. Radial spines about 20, whitish to
reddish, 0.5-1 cm. long. Central spines
4-5, yellowish to reddish, up to
2.5 cm. long. Flowers yellow, up to
6 cm. long. Uruguay.

var. velenovskii (Frič ex Backeb.)
Krainz
Has more numerous glossy
white radial spines.

N. fricii (Arech.) Krainz (*Wigginsia f.*
(Arech.) D.M. Porter)
Body 10 cm. wide with 15-20 ribs.
Crown woolly. Radial spines 6-7,
yellowish. Central spines absent or
tiny. Areoles dense yellowish-white,
woolly, very large. Flowers yellowish,
around 3 cm. long. Uruguay.

N. fuscus Ritter
Body up to 7 cm. wide with 19-26
ribs. Crown white, woolly. Radial
spines 12-16, pale yellowish-brownish,
0.5-1.2 cm. long. Central spines 2 or
4, violet-grey with red base, 1-2.5 cm.
long. Flowers light sulphur yellow,
around 3 cm. long. Brazil (Rio Grande
do Sul).

N. graessneri (K. Schum.) Berger
(*Brasilicactus g.* (K. Schum.) Backeb.;
Malacocarpus g. (K. Schum.) Br. & R.)
Body 10 cm. or more wide with 50-60
ribs, completely divided up into
tubercles. Crown angled, almost spiny
only. Radial spines around 50, pale
yellow or golden yellow. Central
spines 5-6, up to 2 cm. long. Flowers
light yellow-green, 1.8 cm. long.
Stigma lobes yellow. Brazil (Rio
Grande do Sul).

var. albiseta Cullm.
Numerous bristly hairs, up to 3 cm.
long, in addition to the spines; the
plant looks almost white as a result.

N. haselbergii (Haage jr.) Berger
(*Brasilicactus h.* (Haage jr.) Backeb.;
Malacocarpus h. (Haage jr.) Br. & R.)
Body about 10 cm. wide with 30 or
more ribs. Crown angled, woolly and
spiny. Radial spines 20 or more,
white, up to 1 cm. long. Central spines
(3-) 4 (-5), yellowish. Flowers yellow-
red to blood-red, 1.5 cm. long, often
in a dense cluster. Stigmas dark
yellow. Brazil (Rio Grande do Sul).

N. herteri Werderm.
Body up to 15 cm. wide with about 22
ribs. Crown with woolly spots,
spineless. Radial spines 8-11, white or
brown-tipped, up to 2 cm. long.
Central spines 4 (-6), brown-red.
Flowers purple-red, about 4 cm. long.
Brazil (Rio Grande do Sul).

N. horstii Ritter
Body up to 14 cm. wide with 12-16
ribs. Crown spiny and white, woolly.
Radial spines 10-15, pale brown to
almost white, 1-3 cm. long. Central
spines 1-4, brown, slightly longer than
the radial spines. Flowers orange-red
to vermilion, orange-yellow inside, 3-
3.5 cm. long. Stigma lobes orange-
yellow to pink. Brazil (Rio Grande do
Sul).

N. leninghausii (Haage jr.) Berger
(*Eriocactus l.* (Haage jr.) Backeb.;
Malacocarpus l. (Haage jr.) Br. & R.)
Body columnar with angled crown, up
to 1 m. tall and 10 cm. wide with
about 30 ribs. Radial spines thin,
about 15, light yellow. Central spines
3-4, bristly, golden yellow, up to 4 cm.
long. Flowers pure yellow, 4 cm. long.
Stigmas yellow. Brazil (Rio Grande do
Sul).

N. magnificus (Ritter) Krainz
(*Eriocactus m.* Ritter)
Body globular, later elongated, bluish-
green, 7-15 cm. wide, with slightly
sloping, depressed crown and 11-15
narrow ribs, whose areoles are later

long. Central spines 2-3 (-4), yellow
with brown tip. Flowers canary yellow,
about 4 cm. long. Uruguay, Argentina.

N. mueller-melchersii Frič & Backeb.
Body about 8 cm. tall and 6 cm. wide
with around 22 ribs. Crown woolly
and spiny. Radial spines 15-18,
yellowish-white, up to 0.8 cm. long.
Central spines 1, light horn-coloured
with darker base, up to 2 cm. long.
Flowers pale golden yellow, around
3 cm. long. Uruguay.

N. ottonis (Lehm.) Berger (*Malacocarpus
o.* (Lehm.) Br. & R.)
Body 5-6 (-11) cm. wide with 6-13 ribs.

Notocactus leninghausii

Notocactus herteri

felted over. Radial spines numerous,
white, about 0.8 cm. long. Central
spines 8-12, brown, 0.8-2 cm. long.
Later 12-15 similar golden-yellow
spines. Flowers sulphur yellow, 4.5-
5.5 cm. long and wide. Stigmas light
yellow. Brazil (Rio Grande do Sul).

N. mammulosus (Lem.) Backeb.
(*Malacocarpus m.* (Lem.) Br. & R.)
Body 6 cm. wide with 18-20 ribs,
crown woolly. Radial spines 10-13
(-15), yellowish-white, hardly 0.5 cm.

Crown woolly. Radial spines 8-15,
yellow. Central spines 3-4, seldom
absent, brown, 1-2.5 cm. long. Flowers
dark yellow, 4-6 cm. long. S. Brazil,
Uruguay, Paraguay, Argentina.

N. rutilans Dan. & Krainz
Body about 5 cm. wide with 18 (-24)
ribs. Crown sunken, white, woolly.
Radial spines 14-16, white, brown-
tipped, up to 0.5 cm. long. Central
spines 2, brilliant brown-red, up to
0.7 cm. long. Flowers carmine pink,

throat lighter to yellow-white, 3-4 cm.
long and up to 6 cm. wide. Uruguay.

N. schumannianus (Nicolai) Berger
(*Malacocarpus s.* (Nicolai) Br. & R.;
Eriocactus s. (Nicolai) Backeb.)
Body more or less club-shaped later,
up to 1 m. tall with angled crown and
up to 30 or more ribs. Spines 4-7
(-10), later yellowish to brownish or
darker. Central spines absent. Flowers
lemon yellow to golden yellow, around
3.5 cm. long. Stigmas yellow. Paraguay.

N. scopa (Spreng.) Berger (*Malacocarpus
s.* (Spreng.) Br. & R.)
Body up to 25 cm. tall and 10 cm.
wide with 30-35 ribs. Crown woolly
and spiny. Radial spines up to 40,
white, up to 0.7 cm. long. Central
spines 3-4, brownish-red, up to 1 cm.
long. Flowers light yellow, around
4 cm. long. Style red, like stigma lobes.
Uruguay, Brazil (Espíritu Santo).

var. ruberrima hort.
Has pale red to deep ruby red central
spines and snow-white radial spines.

N. sessiliflorus (Hook.) Krainz
(*Malacocarpus s.* (Mackie) Backeb.;
Wigginsia s. (Mackie) D.M. Porter)
Body up to 20 cm. wide with 15-30
tall, sharp ribs. Crown very densely
woolly. Radial spines 4, forming a
cross, whitish, the upper one about
0.5 cm. long, the others up to 2 cm.

Notocactus rutilans

Notocactus submammulosus var. pampeanus

long. Central spines absent, seldom 1. Flowers canary yellow, around 3.5 cm. long. Uruguay, Argentina.

N. submammulosus (Lem.) Backeb. Body about 6-9 cm. wide with around 13-16 ribs, divided up into tubercles. Crown woolly. Radial spines around 6, about 1 cm. long. Central spines 2 or 1, flattened, up to 2 cm. long. Spines

Notocactus uebelmannianus

all yellowish-white. Flowers pale yellow, about 4 cm. long. Uruguay, Argentina.

var. pampeanus (Spegazz.) Backeb. Body glossy, darker green. Radial spines 5-10. Central spines 2-3. Argentina, Uruguay.

N. sucineus Ritter
Body 3-7 cm. wide with 18-24 ribs. Crown spiny. Radial spines 15-30, amber-coloured, 0.3-0.6 cm. long.

Central spines 8-12, golden yellow to brown-yellow, 0.7-2 cm. long. Flowers sulphur yellow, 3.5 cm. long. Style purple, like the stigma lobes. Brazil (Rio Grande do Sul).

N. tabularis (Cels ex K. Schum.) Berger
Body up to about 8 cm. wide with 16-23 ribs. Crown spiny. Radial spines 16-18, translucent, up to 1 cm. long. Central spines 4 in cross-form, white with brown tip, up to 1.2 cm. long. Flowers yellow, 6 cm. long. Uruguay.

N. tephracanthus (Link & Otto) Krainz. (*Malacocarpus t.* (Link & Otto) K. Schum.; *Wigginsia t.* (Link & Otto) D.M. Porter)
Body up to 15 cm. wide, with 16-22 ribs. Crown with abundant woolly felt. Radial spines 5-7, the lower ones up to 2.5 cm. long. Central spines 1, often only formed later, up to 2 cm. long. Spines all horn-coloured. Flowers canary yellow, up to 5 cm. long. S. Brazil, Uruguay, N. Argentina.

N. uebelmannianus Buin.
Body up to 17 cm. wide with 12-16 thick, rounded ribs. Crown woolly, without spines. Radial spines around 6, white to whitish-grey, matted 1-3 cm. long, of uneven length. Flowers glossy wine-red or blood red, up to 4.5 cm. long. Brazil (Rio Grande do Sul).

Nyctocereus (Berger) Br. & R. 1909
(Greek nyctos = naked)

Erect or sprawling, slender-stemmed columnar cacti with 5-13 ribs. Flowers lateral or terminal, externally scaly and thorny/woolly, nocturnal, white to pink, 4-20 cm. long. 6 species. Native to Mexico, Guatemala, Nicaragua.

Demands high levels of warmth and thus only flowers well in the greenhouse. Tolerates half-shade.

N. serpentinus (Lag. & Rodr.) Br. & R. Erect with overhanging end, pendant or creeping. Stems up to 6 m. long, 2-5 cm. thick, with 10-13 low, rounded ribs. Spines approx. 12, thin, light-coloured, sometimes dark-tipped, 1-3 cm. long. Flowers white inside, pink towards the outside and reddish-green, 15-20 cm. long, nocturnal. Mexico (never rediscovered in the wild, probably from the East coast).

Obregonia Frič 1925
(After the then Mexican state president Obregon)

Plants with flat, leaf-like tubercles (a feature only shared with *Ariocarpus*) which are flat above, with a sharp keel below. Spines are only found on the youngest tubercles if at all, and soon fall off. The flowers are produced at the end of young tubercles, and bear the remains of scales above, but are otherwise naked. 1 species. Native to Mexico (Tamaulipas).

Because of the similarity of its flowers the species has been included under *Strombocactus,* but it has a distinctly different exterior form. As such a major difference is just as valid a genetic characteristic as differences in the flower or seed, it has been considered as a generic feature here.

O. denegrei Frič (*Strombocactus d.* (Frič) G.D. Rowl.)
Plant 8-12 cm. in diameter. Tubercles 2-2.5 cm. wide at the base, 1-1.5 cm. long. Initially 2-4 bristly spines, up to 1.5 cm. long, the older areoles not spiny. Flowers white or light pink, 2-4 cm. wide. Fruit a white berry. Unfortunately this curious plant is very temperamental. It requires a purely mineral soil and half-shade. In full sun it dries out.

Obregonia denegrei

Oehmea Buxb. see *Mammillaria*

Opuntia Mill. 1754 'fig cactus'
(*Brasiliopuntia, Consolea, Corynopuntia, Cumulopuntia, Grusonia, Maihueniopsis, Marenopuntia, Micropuntia, Nopalea, Platyopuntia, Tephrocactus*)
(In ancient times the name for a type of thistle in the region of the Opuntiani, a Greek tribe)

The genus *Opuntia* embraces the largest number of cactus species next to *Mammillaria.* In recent times this giant genus has been sub-divided into several smaller genera, but the whole genus is extremely uniform, and for this reason the smaller genera are listed here as sub-genera. The characteristic feature of Opuntias is the glochids: fine spines covered with barbs. The subulate or scale-like leaves, round in cross-section, usually fall off quite early. The flowers are borne laterally, close to the end of the segments, and very occasionally terminally. They have a very short tube, and the ovary carries leaf-like scales. On most species the stamens fold in towards the style when touched, and then curve back again after a few minutes.

Around 470 species. Native to Canada (British Columbia) via USA and Mexico to S. Chile; Opuntias have also become wild more than any other cactus genus, making their home in many other parts of the world, especially Australia, the Mediterranean region and South Africa.

Amongst the very large number of species from all climatic regions there are several which remain reasonably small, and which can be recommended to the amateur for their distinctive body colour, their spine formation and their beautiful flowers. Please bear in mind that all *Opuntia* species must be handled with the greatest of care, because the tiny glochids are highly malicious and penetrate the skin with the greatest of ease. They are almost invisible and are difficult to remove. For this reason Opuntias should never be touched with the bare hand.

The plants are very rewarding in cultivation, as they are attractive and some of them flower readily. The only drawback is that they easily become too large, their broad, flat segments tending to shade the other species in the collection. For this reason they are best grown in pots, rather than being planted out in the greenhouse bed, as they will then stay smaller. They need a mineral soil with plenty of loam and a hot, sunny location. There are even winter-hard Opuntias suitable for open-air cultivation (see winter-hard cacti in the first part of the book).

The genus is subdivided into a number of sub-genera (or genera)

Stems round in cross-section

Stems cylindrical, round. Flowers not properly terminal
    Sheath spines absent. Leaves long, subulate   *Austrocylindropuntia*
    Sheath spines present (sometimes only on young areoles). Leaves short, scale-like
                                                  Cylindropuntia
Stems cylindrical, ribbed. Flowers borne at the crown   *Grusonia*
                 (and *Marenopuntia* with sunken flowers and fruit)
Stems globular, club-shaped or short cylindrical. Stems consisting of one to a few segments
    Stems club-shaped to slightly elongated   *Corynopuntia* (with *Micropuntia*)
    Stems globular to short cylindrical   *Tephrocactus* (with *Maihueniopsis*)

Stems flattened

    Round main stem, with more or less whorled slab-like branches. Flowers with hair-like staminodes (ovary laterally compressed. Fruit usually with only one seed)
                                                Brasilopuntia

    All stems flattened. Flowers without staminodes
        Flowers open. Stamens shorter than the flower petals   *Opuntia* (*Platyopuntia*)
                   (with *Consolea* with more or less cruciform branches)
        Flowers virtually closed. Stamens exserted   *Nopalea*

according to the form of the segments:

Sub-genera of Opuntia
Geographical distribution and number of species (not including Ritter's newly described species)

	species
Austrocylindropuntia	
South America	15
Cylindropuntia	
S. USA, Mexico, Hispaniola	36
Grusonia	
Mexico (Coahuila, lower California)	2
Marenopuntia	
Mexico (Sonora)	1
Corynopuntia	
USA (Nevada, Arizona, New Mexico, Texas), N. Mexico	13
Micropuntia	
USA (Utah, Nevada, Arizona, California)	6
Tephrocactus	
Peru, Bolivia, Argentina, Chile	79
Maihueniopsis	
Argentina (Jujuy)	1
Brasiliopuntia	
South America (Brazil, Paraguay, Argentina, Bolivia, Peru)	4
Opuntia (*Platyopuntia*)	
Canada (British Columbia) to Argentina	259
Consolea	
USA (Florida), West Indies	8
Nopalea	
Mexico and Central America (Guatemala, Honduras, Nicaragua)	9

Summary of the Opuntia species included in this book

Sub-genus Austrocylindropuntia
Body covered with long white hairs   *O. vestita*
Body with normal spine formation
    Stems smooth, not sub-divided, up to 1.5 cm. thick   *O. salmiana*
    Stems with clearly defined segments, 3-10 cm. thick
        Spines 2-3 (-6), about 1 cm. long. Leaves 1-1.5 cm. long   *O. cylindrica*
        Spines 12, up to 8 cm. long and more. Leaves up to 10 (-15) cm. long   *O. subulata*

Sub-genus Cylindropuntia
                                          O. bigelowii
                                          O. tunicata

Sub-genus Corynopuntia
Segments up to 2.5 cm. long, blue-green. Central spine thicker at the base
                                          O. bulbispina
Segments 6-10 cm. long   *O. invicta*

Sub-genus Tephrocactus
Segments spineless
    Glochids brown, short. Body grey-green   *O. articulata*
    Glochids red-brown, in dense clusters. Body dark green   *O. molinensis*
Segments hairy or spiny
    Body more or less enveloped in hairs   *O. floccosa*
    Body with normal, needle-like or shaving-like spines
        Spines more than 10. Radial and central spines different   *O. sphaerica*
        Spines up to 10, all more or less the same
            Spines papery or like wood shavings   *O. articulata* f. *papyracantha*
            Spines normal, needle-like
                Segments purple-black when young. Spines initially purple-black, up to 4 cm. long. Flowers purple   *O. nigrispina*
                Segments all green. Spines light, up to 8.5 cm. long. Flowers yellow or reddish-yellow   *O. pentlandii*

Sub-genus Opuntia (Platyopuntia)
1 Segments covered with short velvety hairs over their entire surface.
    Areoles closely spaced, with many glochids
        Areoles very spiny
            Glochids yellow. Spines 1-5   *O. leucotricha*
            Glochids red. Spines up to 10   *O. pycnantha* var. *margaritana*

257

Areoles with glochids and hairs only, no more than 1 spine
   Flowers purple-pink (to white). Usually 1 spine. Segments bluish-grey
                                                               O. basilaris
   Flowers pale or reddish-yellow. Usually devoid of spines. Segments grass
   green to grey-green
      Flowers reddish-yellow. Segments grey-green   *O. rufida*
      Flowers pale yellow. Segments grass green   *O. microdasys*
1 Segments bare on the surface
  2a Numerous white, matted hairs in addition to the spines   *O. scheerii*
  2b Spines 5 — many (fruit dry, except for *O. robusta*)
    Spines long, bristly   *O. hystricina* var. *ursina*
    Spines flattened   *O. hystricina* var. *bensonii*
    Spines not flattened, more or less appressed   *O. polyacantha*
    Spines not flattened, projecting
      Segments not of frosted appearance, 2-8 cm. long, easily breaking off. *O. fragilis*
      Segments of frosted appearance, up to 30 cm. wide, not easily breaking off
                             O. robusta
  2c Spines few (up to 4) or absent
    Segments frosted
      Spines 2-12, white or yellow   *O. robusta*
      Spines 1-3, usually on the upper part of the segments only, almost black
                             O. azurea
    Segments not of frosted appearance
      Spines curved and twisted (inner flower petals narrow and erect) *O. marnierana*
    Spines straight or absent
      Spine formation powerful. Spines usually 2-4. Flowers red or salmon
      coloured (in *O. phaeacantha* also yellow)
        Spines round in cross-section (flowers up to 2.5 cm. in size)   *O. macbridgei*
        Spines flattened to compressed
          Segments rounded   *O. phaeacantha*
          Segments narrow oval   *O. bergeriana*
      Spine formation weak. Flowers yellow or flushed yellow and red
        Segments only spiny on the topmost areoles. Flowers flushed yellow and red
                             O. violacea
      Segments uniformly spiny or spineless. Flowers yellow
        Areoles hairy. Segments 7.5-30 cm. long
          Growth erect. Glochids yellow   *O. vulgaris*
          Growth decumbent. Glochids brown   *O. humifusa*
        Areoles of bare appearance. Segments very large, 30-50 cm. long
                             O. ficus-indica

Opuntia subulata

Sub-genus Austrocylindropuntia

O. cylindrica (Lam.) DC.
(*Austrocylindropuntia c.* Lam.) Backeb.)
1-2 m. tall. Stems with lozenge
markings, 4-5 cm. thick. Leaves 1-1.5
cm. long. Spines 2-3 (-6), whitish,
about 1 cm. long. Flowers pink to red.

A cristate form **f. cristata** of this
species is frequently cultivated. S.
Ecuador (as far as N. Peru?)

O. salmiana Parment. (*Austrocylindropuntia s.* (Parment.) Backeb.)
Segments elongated cylindrical, not
warty, deep blue-green, often with a
reddish tinge, up to 25 cm. long and
1-1.5 cm. thick. Spines 3-5 or absent,
yellowish or whitish, up to 1.5 cm.

long. Flowers yellowish to reddish, up
to 3.5 cm. long. S. Brazil, Paraguay, E.
Argentina, Bolivia.

O. subulata (Mühlpf.) Engelm.
(*Austrocylindropuntia s.* (Mühlpf.)
Backeb.)
2-4 m. tall. Stems round, tubercles
oblong, flat with darker border, 6-10
cm. thick. Leaves up to 12 (-15) cm.
long. Spines 1-2 to more, pale yellow,
up to 8 cm. long. Flowers red, about 7
cm. long. Probably N. Argentina and
Bolivia, cultivated in Peru.

O. vestita Salm-Dyck (*Austrocylindropuntia v.* (Salm Dyck) Backeb.)
Forming flat clusters like a lawn,

almost hemi-spherical in its habitat.
Stems pale green, 20-40 cm. long, 2-3
cm. thick. Leaves up to 1 cm. long.
Spines 4-8, usually up to 4 mm. long,
exceptionally up to 2 cm. long.
Areoles covered with beautiful white
hairs. Flowers violet, 3-4 cm. wide.
Fruit woolly. Flowers exceptionally
rarely. Bolivia (La Paz).

Sub-genus Cylindropuntia

O. bigelowii Engelm. (*Cylindropuntia b.*
(Engelm.) Knuth)
Tree-like, up to 1 m. tall. Segments 5-
15 cm. long. Tubercles not very
prominent.

Radial spines 6-10, 1-1.5 cm. long.
Central spines 6-10, slightly longer.
Spines all with pale yellow,
membranous sheath. Flowers purple,
4 cm. wide and long. USA (California,
S. Nevada, Arizona), Mexico (N. lower
California).

O. tunicata (Lehm.) Link & Otto
(*Cylindropuntia t.* (Lehm.) F.M. Knuth)
Small trees, around 50 cm. tall.
Segments very warty, blue-green, 6-15
cm. long. Spines 6-10, in papery white
sleeves, about 5 cm. long. Flowers
yellow (pink in var. rosea), 3-5 cm. in
size. Mexico. A very beautiful species.

Opuntia phaeacantha

O. violacea Engelm. **var. macrocentra** (Engelm.) L. Bens. (*O. macrocentra* Engelm.)

Segments blue-green and often with a lilac or reddish tinge, rounded to oval, 8-20 cm. wide. Central spines (0-) 1-2 (-3), only on the topmost areoles at the ends of the stems, black, tinged with violet or red-brown, often white-tipped, up to 8 cm. long. Flowers yellow or yellow flushed with red, 5 cm. long and 6-7.5 cm. wide. Plants develop the splendid flowers even when they consist only of three segments. USA (W. Texas, E. Arizona), Mexico (Chihuahua).

O. vulgaris Mill.
Up to 6 m. tall. Segments 10-30 cm. long and 5-15 cm. wide. Spines absent or 1-2, greyish, up to 2 cm. long. Glochids yellow. Flowers pale yellow, up to 9 cm. long, *c.* 5 cm. wide. Fruit deep red. Canada (Ontario), E. USA (Massachusetts to Virginia).

O. xanthosoma see *O. hystricina* var. *bensonii*

Opuntia pycnantha

O. pycnantha Engelm. **var. margaritana** Coult.
Segments 10-20 cm. long and up to 15 cm. wide. Spines up to 10, white to reddish, most of them angled obliquely downward, 5-11 mm. long. Areoles with red glochids. Flowers pale yellow, around 4 cm. wide. The species flowers readily, and its blooms are very beautiful. Mexico (lower California).

O. rafinesquei see *O. humifusa*

O. rhodantha see *O. hystricina* var. *bensonii*

O. robusta Wendl.
Segments of grey-green frosted appearance, up to 30 cm. wide. Spines 2-12, white or yellow, brown at the base, up to 5 cm. long. Flowers yellow, 5-7 cm. wide. Central Mexico.

O. rufida Engelm.
Segments grey-green, circular, with velvety hairs, 6-25 cm. wide. Spines absent. Areoles large, with reddish-brown glochids. Flowers reddish-yellow, 5 cm. long and 4 cm. wide. Seldom flowers. USA (Texas), Mexico (Durango).

O. scheeri Web.
Segments blue-green, oval, up to 30 cm. long. Spines 8-12, yellow, about 1 cm. long. Numerous matted bristly hairs in addition to the spines. Areoles with brownish felt and glochids. Flowers sulphur yellow to reddish, up to 10 cm. wide. This very beautiful species is usually too large for amateur cactus growers. Mexico (Querétaro).

263

Oreocereus (Berger) Riccob. 1909
(*Morawetzia*)
(Greek oros = mountain)

Mostly very hairy columnar cacti with 10-25 ribs. Flowers borne towards the end of the stems on ordinary areoles, or in a pseudo-cephalium. Flowers have long tube, are zygomorphic, scaly and hairy outside, diurnal, pink to purple, 4-11 cm. long.

About 7 species. Native to Peru, Bolivia, N. Chile, N. Argentina, even at altitudes above 4000 m.

The Oreocerei are among the most beautiful of columnar cacti. Unfortunately they are not ideal as indoor plants, but they grow excellently on their own roots in a *Cereus* frame in the garden or in the greenhouse. They like strong sunshine and a difference in temperature between day and night in summer and in winter, as befits the altitude of their habitat. The night temperature may safely be allowed to drop to 0°C, but in the afternoon it should rise again to about 12-15°C. The soil should not include too much humus, otherwise the plants become flabby. Good ventilation is absolutely essential; stagnant heat and low aerial humidity do not suit the plants.

O. celsianus (Lem.) Riccob.
Usually branching from the base.

Oreocereus celsianus var. celsianus

Oreocereus doelzianus

Stems up to 2 m. long and 8-12 cm. thick, with 10-25 ribs. Radial spines about 7-9, central spines 1-4 together with long woolly hairs.

var. celsianus
Spines yellowish to reddish-brown. Woolly hairs, usually white, but sometimes even brownish. Flowers dirty pink, 7-9 cm. long. S. Bolivia to N. Argentina.

var. fossulatus (Backeb.) Krainz (*O.f.* Backeb.)
Spines translucent honey yellow. Flowers red. Peru to Bolivia.

var. ritteri (Cullm.) Krainz (*O.r.* Cullm.)
Spines stiff, projecting, brilliant yellow, up to 10 cm. long, usually with dense snow-white hairs. Flowers carmine to carmine-violet, 7-9 (-11) cm. long. S. Peru. The most beautiful form of the genus. The species *O. hendriksenianus* Backeb. var. *densilanatus* Rauh & Backeb. is listed as synonymous, but has spines only 1-1.5 cm. long.

O. doelzianus (Backeb.) Borg
(*Morawetzia d.* Backeb.)
The only way of distinguishing *Morawetzia* from *Oreocereus* with its lateral flowers is the former's terminal cephalium. Densely branching from the base. Stems up to about 1 m. long, 4-8 cm. thick and with about 9-11 ribs. Radial spines 10-16, up to 1.5 cm. long. Central spines 4, up to 4 cm. long. Spines yellowish to dark brown. Cephalium at the end of the stems, woolly and bristly. Flowers blue-carmine, up to about 10 cm. in length. Central Peru. A vigorous species, but requires much space.

O. hendriksenianus Backeb. (*O. celsianus* (Lem.) Riccob. var. *h.* (Backeb.) Krainz)
Branching from the base, up to 1 m. tall. Stems almost 10 cm. thick with about 10 ribs. Radial spines around 8 – 9. Central spines (1-) 4, horn-coloured to dark brown. Profuse woolly hairs from the crown, white,

Oreocereus hendriksenianus

yellowish, red-brown to black, but soon bleaching. Flowers carmine red, around 7 cm. long. S. Peru to N. Chile.

O. trollii (Kupper) Backeb. (*O. celsianus* (Lem.) Riccob. var. *t.* (Kupper) Krainz) Stems usually less than 0.5 m. long, with 15-25 ribs. Radial spines 10-15. Central spines 1 to several, yellow, reddish or brown. Densely white, woolly, completely enveloped in hairs. Flowers pink to carmine, around 4 cm. long. S. Bolivia, N. Argentina.

Oreocereus celsianus var. ritteri

Oroya Br. & R. 1922
(Oroya is a place name in central Peru)

Squat globular cacti with around 20-35 ribs and flowers borne close to the crown, only 1.5-2.5 cm. long, yellow to orange to red. The flowers are scaly and no more than slightly woolly and have inner petals which are inclined inwards, two groups of stamens and a nectar chamber. The seeds are pitted. 3 species. Native to Peru, at altitudes of 3500–4000m.

According to Rauh these species grow in typical black, slightly acid Puna soil, containing humus, in their native

Oroya borchersii

habitat, and should therefore be cultivated in nutritious, permeable, slightly acid soil. In summer they like warm, bright conditions with marked differences in temperature between day and night, as in their homeland. A light and cool location in winter. Better grafted if required as indoor plants.

O. borchersii (Böd.) Backeb. Up to 20 cm. or more wide and 30 cm. tall, with 25-30 ribs. Body completely enveloped in dense spines, yellow to fox-red. Spines about 30-40, in comb-formation, 2-3 cm. long. Flowers lemon yellow to yellowish-green, 2 cm. long. N. Peru (Ancash). Does not flower as willingly as *O. peruviana*.

O. neoperuviana Backeb. Up to about 40 cm. tall and 25 cm. wide, with 24-40 ribs. Radial spines about 20-30, matted, up to about 1.5 cm. long. Central spines up to 5, honey yellow with brown base. Flowers carmine red to pale red, yellowish inside, around 2.5 cm. long. Central Peru (Oroya).

O. peruviana (K. Schum.) Br. & R. Up to about 15 cm. wide and 10 cm. tall, with 12-23 ribs. Spines white via yellow and reddish to black-brown. Radial spines about 15-20, comb-formation. Central spines absent to 6, 1-3 cm. long. Flowers light carmine to vermilion, whitish to lemon yellow at the base, around 2.5 cm. long. Central Peru.

Some specimens of this species flower very profusely.

Ortegocactus Alex. see *Neobesseya*

265

Oroya peruviana

Pachycereus (Berger) Br. & R.
1909
(some *Lemaireocereus*)
(Greek pachys = thick)

Giant tree-shaped or bushy columnar cacti. Flowers lateral or close to the crown, scaly and bristly/hairy, bristly/woolly or only woolly outside, nocturnal, 4-10 cm. long. Fruit dry and very spiny. 7 species. Native to Mexico. One of the dominant features in the landscape in its natural habitat. Young plants are occasionally cultivated in Europe. Keep them warm!

P. pringlei (S. Wats.) Br. & R.
Usually tree-shaped, up to 12 m. or more tall, up to 1 m. and more thick at the base in their habitat. Stems with 10-16 ribs. Spines approx. 20, at first reddish to dark brown, later black or ash grey, up to 2 (-12) cm. long. Mexico (lower California, Sonora to Nayarit close to the coast).

P. weberi (Coult.) Backeb.
(*Lemaireocereus w.* (Coult.) Br. & R.)
Tree-shaped, up to 10 m. or more tall in their habitat. Stems dark blue-green, with white frosting. Radial spines 6-12, up to 2 cm. long. Central spines 1, flattened, dark red-brown to blackish, up to about 10 cm. long. Flowers yellow-white, up to 10 cm. long. Mexico (Puebla, Oaxaca).

Parodia Spegazz. 1923 (*Hickenia*)
(after Dr. L.R. Parodi (1895 — 1966), an Argentinian botanist)

The genus *Parodia* embraces ribbed or warty globular cacti. The flowers are borne close to the crown, and are usually brilliant yellow, orange or red. The short tube bears small scales, is woolly or hairy and almost always features supplementary bristles. This type of flower also occurs in the genera *Notocactus, Frailea* and *Neoporteria*.

Parodia is quite closely related to *Notocactus* and *Frailea,* some of which share the characteristic of a seed with a strophiole. However, *Notocactus* species have either typical red stigmas or thorny/woolly flowers. Nevertheless it is very difficult to distinguish the two genera clearly, as is explained in greater detail under *Notocactus*. *Frailea* species are small dwarf cacti with tiny spines. At least some Parodias have hooked spines, whereas the other genera mentioned here have none, and in many Parodias the ribs are completely sub-divided into helical rows of tubercles. The young areoles are often densely covered in white wool.

Since 1965 a very large number of new Parodias has been discovered. Brandt in particular described many for the first time around 1975, although their classification is widely disputed.

110 species. Native to Highlands of N. Argentina, Bolivia.

It is likely that only 35-40 species would remain if the genus were revised. Buxbaum claims that all the Parodias from Paraguay, Central and South Brazil should belong to *Notocactus*.

Even the non-flowering Parodias are amongst the most beautiful of cacti, with their dense, brightly coloured spines. They do not grow excessively large and flower readily. Even quite young plants develop their relatively large flowers from the crown. Older plants usually produce whole clusters of flowers, of which the individual blooms often survive for several days.

In general terms culture of Parodias is not difficult. The plants can be cultivated in ordinary cactus soil. The fibrous-rooted species from Brazil and Paraguay require a soil which is rather richer in humus, while a more mineral mixture suits the species with stronger root systems. Parodias must receive plenty of light if they are to develop their fine spine formations, but excessive heat should be avoided by means of effective ventilation. Avoid protracted dry periods as well as high levels of moisture. Most Parodias will not tolerate excessively low temperatures and should be kept at around 5-10°C in the winter. A few species, especially *P. mutabilis, P. sanguiniflora* and *P. nivosa* and their close relations, are sometimes slightly difficult on their own root, and many enthusiasts consider grafting these slightly temperamental species. If you do this it is important to select a rootstock which does not grow too strongly, otherwise the plants lose their naturally attractive appearance and their characteristic spine formation. The seed of many Parodias is as fine as dust, and the seedlings' initial rate of growth is very slow. Nevertheless, in spite of the difficulties of raising them from seed the results are worthwhile.

Spines all straight
  Flowers red or orange
    Radial spines 10-14. Central spines 4, initially pink — *P. ritteri*
    Radial spines 15-20. Central spines 1-4, white (crown with dense white wool) — *P. nivosa*
    Radial spines around 40. Central spines 15-20 — *P. penicillata*
  Flowers yellow to orange
    Body ribbed
      Central spines 1, radial spines 8-9 — *P. ocampoi*
      Central spines 4, radial spines 10-11 — *P. ayopayana*
      (see also *P. procera* with usually 1 hooked central spine)
    Body warty
      Crown woolly
        Spines around 17, short — *P. saint-pieana*
        Spines 30-40 — *P. chrysacanthion*
      Crown not woolly
        Radial spines 8-14. Central spines 3-5, white with chestnut brown tip — *P. cardenasii*
        Radial spines 20-30. Central spines 6-12, fox red — *P. formosa*
Spines: at least one of them strongly curved or hooked
  Radial spines around 40-50
    Central spines around 6. Hooked spine golden yellow — *P. aureispina*
    Central spines 4. Hooked spine red to light orange — *P. mutabilis*
  Radial spines up to 25
    Central spines 6, up to 10 cm. long. Radial spines around 25 — *P. rauschii*
    Central spines 1-4, up to 4 cm. long. Radial spines up to about 20
      Flowers yellow or yellow-red
        Central spines 1 (-3). Radial spines light brown (helical ribs) (flowers yellow-red) — *P. mairanana*
        Central spines (3-) 4. Radial spines not light brown
          Spines all grey, frosted white (flowers yellow red) — *P. tuberculata*
          Spines including white radials
      Flowers pale yellow
        Radial spines hair-fine, 0.7-1.5 cm. long — *P. procera*
        Radial spines bristle-like, up to 0.5 cm. long — *P. catamarcensis*
      Flowers golden yellow to orange
        Central spines 1.5-2.5 cm. long, whitish-brownish — *P. taratensis*
        Central spines up to 0.9 cm., red to brown — *P. microsperma*
        Central spines up to 5 cm. long — *P. microsperma* var. *macrancistra*
    Flowers red
      Areoles permanently distinctly white, woolly
        Body almost black. Radial spines initially solid black — *P. culpinensis*
        Body lighter. Radial spines whitish to brownish — *P. schwebsiana*
      Areoles only distinctly white, woolly when fairly young
        Flowers funnel-shaped, 1.5 cm. wide. Radial spines like needles — *P. maassii*
        Flowers widely spreading, up to 4 cm. wide. Radial spines like fine bristles — *P. sanguiniflora*

P. aureispina Backeb.
Body up to about 6.5 cm. wide. Ribs divided up into tubercles. Radial spines around 40, fine, white, up to 0.6 cm. long. Central spines about 6, golden yellow, the bottom one hooked, up to 2 cm. long. Flowers golden yellow, around 3 cm. wide and 2.5-4 cm. long. Argentina (Salta).

P. ayopayana Card.
Body up to about 9 cm. wide with 11 ribs. Crown white, felty. Radial spines 10-11, white, 1.2-2 cm. long. Central spines 4, straight, light brown or whitish, up to 3.5 cm. long. Flowers golden yellow, 3 cm. long. Bolivia (Cochabamba).

P. cardenasii Ritter
Similar to *P. formosa,* but radial spines 8-14, whitish. Central spines 3-5, white with chestnut brown tip. Flowers sulphur yellow, 3 cm. long. Bolivia (Tarija).

P. catamarcensis Backeb.
Body up to about 8 cm. tall and 4 cm. wide. Ribs divided up into tubercles. Crown white, woolly. Radial spines about 9, white, up to 0.5 cm. long. Central spines 4, the bottom one hooked, dark red. Flowers whitish-yellow, 3-4 cm. wide. Argentina (?Catamarca).

P. chrysacanthion (K. Schum.) Backeb.
(*Echinocactus c.* K. Schum.)
Approx. 10 cm. wide. Ribs divided up into tubercles. Crown covered in thick yellowish wool. Spines 30-40, hair-fine, straight, golden yellow, 1-2.5 cm. long. Flowers yellow, up to 2 cm. long and wide. Argentina (Jujuy, Salta).

P. culpinensis Brandt
Body almost black. Ribs helical. Radial spines approx. 10. Central spines 1-4, hooked, 3 cm. long, initially solid black. Flowers carmine to blood red, around 5 cm. wide. Bolivia (Chuquisaca).

P. formosa Ritter
Body up to 8 cm. wide, bright green. Crown not woolly. Ribs divided up into tubercles. Radial spines 20-30, 0.3-0.8 cm. long. Central spines about 6-12, 0.3-1.2 cm. long, fox red. Flowers sulphur yellow, 3-4 cm. long. Bolivia (Tarija).

P. maassii (Hesse) Berger
Body up to 20 cm. tall and 15 cm. wide. Ribs helical. Radial spines 7-15,

Parodia chrysacanthion

Parodia maassii var. subterranea

up to 1 cm. long. Central spines 4, hooked, up to 4 cm.long. Flowers brick red to purple or salmon-coloured, 2-4 cm. long. S. Bolivia, N. Argentina.

var. commutata (Ritter) Krainz

f. maxima (Ritter) Krainz (*P. maxima* Ritter)
Spines up to 11 cm. long, white to pale brownish. Flowers red.

var. rubida (Ritter) Krainz (*P.r.* Ritter)
Radial spines 12-16, whitish. Central spines 3-6, curved, brown-black. Flowers carmine red. Bolivia.

var. subterranea (Ritter) Krainz (*P.s.* Ritter)
Body no more than 6 cm. wide. Crown white, woolly. Radial spines around 10, whitish horn-coloured or the upper ones black-grey. Central spines 1 (-4), black, hooked on young plants. Flowers ruby red to purple, 2-3 cm. long. Bolivia (Prov. Cinti).

var. suprema (Ritter) Krainz (*P.s.* Ritter)
Body blue-black-green. Spines yellow-brown to almost black. Flowers scarlet. Bolivia (Tarija).

P. mairanana Card.
Body up to 5 cm. wide, olive grey-green. Helical ribs. Radial spines 9-14, 0.3-1.2 cm. long. Central spines 1-3, curved to hooked, 1-2 cm. long. All spines light brown. Flowers golden yellow to orange-yellow, 3-3.5 cm. long and 2 cm. wide. Bolivia (Florida).

P. microsperma (Web.) Spegazz.
Body up to 20 cm. tall and 10 cm. wide, warty. Radial spines 10-25, white, up to 0.6 cm. long. Central spines 3-4, red to brown, up to 2 cm. long, the bottom one hooked. Flowers yellow-orange, 3-5 cm. long. N. Argentina (Tucumán, Catamarca, Salta).

var. macrancistra (K. Schum.) Borg
Central spines up to 5 cm. long, flower petals brown-tipped. Argentina (Tucumán).

P. mutabilis Backeb.
Body up to 8 cm. wide. Ribs divided up into tubercles. Radial spines around 50, hair-fine, white, up to 1 cm. long. Central spines 4, hooked, light orange or red-brown, up to 1.2 cm. long. Flowers yellow or with red throat, up to 4 cm. wide. Argentina (Salta).

P. nivosa Frič ex Backeb.
Body up to 15 cm. tall and 8 cm. wide. Ribs divided up into tubercles. Crown densely white, woolly. Radial spines 15-20, white, 1.2 cm. long. Central spines 4, straight, white, up to 2 cm. long. Flowers light blood red, 4-5 cm. wide and 3 cm. long. Argentina (Salta).

P. ocampoi Card.
Body up to 6 cm. thick, ribs 13-20. Radial spines 8-9, 1 cm. long. Central spines 1, straight, 0.5 cm. long. Spines initially reddish to light brown. Flowers golden yellow, around 3 cm. long. Bolivia (Cochabamba).

Parodia mutabilis

Parodia schwebsiana

Parodia mairanana var. atra

P. penicillata Fechs. & Steeg
Body up to about 30 cm. tall and
12 cm. thick. Ribs divided up into
tubercles. Radial spines around 40.
Central spine 1, straight, up to 5 cm.
long. Spines white to yellow, dense
and appressed. Flowers orange to
vermilion, up to 5 cm. long and 4 cm.
wide. Argentina (Salta).

P. procera Ritter
Body 30-50 cm. tall and 3-5 cm. wide.
Ribs (10-) 13. Radial spines around 8-
11, white, hair-fine, 0.7-1.5 cm. long.
Central spines 4, hooked or not,
chestnut brown and 1.5-2 cm. long.
The flowers are lemon yellow and up
to 3 cm. long. Bolivia (Chuquisaca).

P. rauschii Backeb.
Body up to 25 cm. tall, 15 cm. wide.
Ribs slightly helical. Radial spines up
to 25, whitish or yellowish, 1-
1.2 cm.long. Central spines 6, yellow
to brown, up to 10 cm. long, one of
them hooked. Flowers orange to red.
Argentina (Salta).

P. ritteri Buin.
Body up to 10 cm. thick, cylindrical
when old. Ribs 15-21, straight to
helical. Radial spines 10-14, initially
one of them hooked, later slightly
curved. Spines very dense, at first pink
with white base, later whitish and red-
tipped, 1.5-4 cm. long. Flowers blood
red to bluish-red, around 3 cm. long.
Bolivia (Tarija).

P. saint-pieana Backeb.
Body 4-6 cm. thick, abundantly
clustering. Ribs divided up into
tubercles. Spines around 17, straight,
yellowish to brownish, very short.
Flowers pure yellow, 2-2.5 cm. in size.
Argentina (Jujuy).

P. sanguiniflora Frič ex Backeb.
Up to 8 cm. in size. Ribs divided up
into tubercles. Radial spines around
15, white, 0.6-0.8 cm. long. Central
spines 4, the bottom one hooked, red
to brownish, up to 2 cm. long. Flowers
yellowish-red to blood red or carmine,
3-4 cm. wide. Argentina (Salta).

269

P. schwebsiana (Werderm.) Backeb.
Up to 14 cm. tall and 11 cm. wide.
Ribs slightly helical. Crown densely
white, woolly. Radial spines around
10, up to 1 cm. long. Central spines
up to 4, the bottom one hooked, up
to 2 cm. long. All spines white to
yellowish or brownish. Flowers
brilliant blood red or salmon-
coloured. Bolivia (Cochabamba,
Chuquisaca).

P. taratensis Card.
Body 3 cm. tall and 4-5 cm. wide.
Radial spines around 17, white, 0.3-
1.5 cm. long. Central spines 4,
hooked, whitish-brownish, 1.5-2.5 cm.
long. Flowers golden yellow, 3 cm.
long. Bolivia (Cochabamba).

P. tuberculata Card.
Body 5 cm. tall and up to 7 cm. wide,
grey-green tarnished appearance. Ribs
divided up into tubercles. Radial
spines 10-11, up to 1 cm. long.
Central spines 4, hooked, up to
1.8 cm. long. All spines grey, frosted
white. Flowers yellow-red, 1.8 cm.
long. Bolivia.

Pediocactus Br. & R. 1913
(*Coloradoa, Navajoa, Pilocanthus,
Sclerocactus, Toumeya* p.p. *Utahia*)
(Greek pede = ankle iron)

The genus *Pediocactus* is very difficult to
define in general terms. The flowers
are borne more or less at the crown,
are 1-8 cm. long, and either bear small
scales (bare or slightly felted), or the
scales are absent and the flowers are
completely naked. The remains of the
flower persist on the dry, dehiscent
fruit. These characteristics would not
be sufficient to differentiate the genus
from other Echinocactanae genera, if
the latter did not also exhibit
particular features which are absent in
Pediocactus.

Pediocactus species vary widely in body
form, with 8-17 ribs, or ribs which are
completely sub-divided into tubercles.
The spines are particularly variable,
ranging from flat and papery (*Toumeya*),
corky and transversely grooved
(*Navajoa*), hair-like (*Pilocanthus*) or more
or less normal. The former genus
Utahia has frayed-edged scales on the
flowers but in other respects the
different species are extremely similar,

Pediocactus knowltonii

and the work of L. Benson and Arp in
recombining them to form one or two
genera is probably justified.

The natural habitat of almost all the
species is very small in area, and each
species tends to grow on a particular
type of rock soil. Some of them are
under close protection, and a few are
directly threatened with extinction.
Fortunately they are hard to find, as
they withdraw into the soil during the
dry period.

13 species. Native to California,
Arizona, New Mexico, Colorado,
Nevada, Utah, Idaho, Kansas,
Montana, Oregon, Washington.

The species listed here are very rare,
temperamental cacti which grow best
when grafted, in particular on slow
growing stocks such as *Trichocereus
pasacana*. Other growers use *Echinopsis*
pups as rootstock. Nevertheless, the
plants are still difficult to cultivate even
when grafted. In accordance with their
native mountain conditions they
appear to need sharp temperature
differences between day and night and
like to be kept cool over the winter. In
their homeland they also have a short
vegetative period, which they retain in
Europe. If they are watered outside
this short period of growth they tend
to rot.

Seed is hardly ever obtainable, and
raising the plants from it is equally
difficult. Overall, therefore, *Pediocactus*
species should really only be
considered by very experienced cactus
growers with appropriate cultural
facilities.

Spines papery, flat	*P. papyracanthus*
Spines corky, transversely furrowed or grooved	*P. peeblesianus*
Spines hair-like, up to 7 cm. long (taproot up to 15 cm. long)	*P. paradinei*
Spines like hairs, up to 1.4 mm. long	*P. knowltonii*

Spines like needles or flattened
  Central spine hooked   *P. whipplei*
                                 P. wrightiae

  Central spine not hooked
    Central spine initially black. Scales on
    the flowers with frayed edges *P. sileri*
    Central spine red brown. Scales not
    frayed   *P. simpsonii*

P. knowltonii L. Bens. (*P. bradyi* L.
Bens. var. *k.* (L. Bens.) Backeb.)
Up to 3.8 cm. tall and 2 cm. wide.
Radial spines 18-23, white to pink,
with fine hairs, up to 1.4 mm. long.
Central spines absent. Flowers pink,
about 1-1.5 cm. long. USA (Colorado,
New Mexico).

P. papyracanthus (Engelm.) L. Bens.
(*Toumeya p.* (Engelm.) Br. & R.)
Up to 10 cm. tall and 3.5 cm. wide.
Radial spines 5-9, white, 3-4 mm.
long. Central spines 3-4, white to
brown, flat, papery, 1-5 cm. long.
Flowers white, up to 2.25 cm. long.
USA (New Mexico, N. Arizona).

P. paradinei B.W. Bens. (*Pilocanthus p.*
(B.W. Bens.) B.W. Bens. & Backeb.)
3-5 cm. tall and 6-8 cm. wide. Radial
spines around 20, central spines 4-6,
all thin, hair-like, white, individual
spines up to 4 or 7 cm. long. Flowers
cream, inner petals with pink central
stripe, up to 2.5 cm. wide. USA
(Arizona).

P. peeblesianus (Croizat) L. Bens.
(*Navajoa p.* Croizat)
2.5-7 cm. long and up to 2.5 cm. wide.
Radial spines 3-7. Central spine 1,
horn-coloured, corky, slightly
transversely furrowed and grooved,
0.5-3 cm. long. Flowers yellow to
yellow-green or whitish with pink
central bands, up to 1.7 cm. long.
USA (Arizona).

var. fickeisenii (Backeb.) L. Benson
(*Navajoa f.* Backeb.)
With body up to 5 cm. wide and
yellowish to yellow flowers.

Pediocactus papyracanthus

Pediocactus peeblesianus var. fickeisenii

Pediocactus simpsonii

Pediocactus wrightiae

P. sileri (Engelm.) L. Bens. (*Utahia s.* (Engelm.) Br. & R.)
Up to 15 cm. tall and 12 cm. wide. Radial spines 11-15, white 1.3-2 cm. long. Central spines 3-7, black, up to 3 cm. long, also much white wool. Flowers yellowish, 2.5-2.8 cm. long. USA (N. Arizona near the border with Utah).

P. simpsonii (Engelm.) Br. & R.
Up to 22 cm. tall and 15 cm. wide. Radial spines 15-25 (-30), white or cream, 1-2 cm. long. Central spines 5-8 (-11), brown, occasionally white at the base, up to 2.5 cm. long. Flowers very variable, yellowish, pink or white, up to 2.5 cm. long. USA (Washington and Montana to Arizona, New Mexico and W. Kansas). Mountain locations of 2000-3000 m. altitude.

P. wrightiae (L. Benson) Arp (*Sclerocactus w.* L. Benson)
Radial spines 8-10, white, 0.6-1.2 cm. long. Central spines 4, light below, dark brown above, 1.2-1.5 cm. long, one lower one hooked. Flowers lavender coloured, 1.9 cm. long and wide. Flower petals have lighter margins. USA (Utah).

P. whipplei (Engelm.) Arp (*Sclerocactus w.* (Engelm. & Bigel.) Br. & R.)
Body up to 20 cm. tall and 9 cm. wide, with white wool in the crown. Radial spines 7-11, slightly flattened, white or black, up to 2 cm. long. Central spines initially absent, later (2-)4 (-5), a few or all of them hooked, the top one flattened, the lower ones brown or black, up to 3.5 cm. long. Flowers white, pink to purple, up to 5 cm. long. USA (Utah, Colorado, New Mexico, Arizona).

Peireskia Steud. see *Pereskia*

Peireskiopsis Br. & R. 1907
(opsis = face)

Peireskiopsis is highly reminiscent of *Pereskia*, with its flat leaves. However, the plants possess glochids and seed with a hard, white seed coat, and therefore belong to the sub-family of the Opuntioideae. They form trees, bushes or climbing plants with round stems. The flowers are usually borne laterally, have spreading petals and no tube. The few seed are covered with felty hairs. 12 species. Native to Mexico, Guatemala.

P. velutina Rose
Bushes, about 1.2 m. tall. Stems about 1 cm. thick. Leaves dark green and velvety, 2-6 cm. long, 1.5-2.5 cm. wide. Areoles with white hair and tiny glochids. A few white spines, a few millimetres to 1 cm. long. Flowers yellow, 1-2 cm. in size. Mexico (Querétaro).

Pelecyphora Ehrenb. 1843
(Greek pelekys = axe, phoros = bearing)

Tubercle cacti with axe-shaped tubercles much taller than they are wide, and distinctive comb-formation spines. The flowers are formed in the axils of the tubercles and are naked. The root is thick like a beet. Very similar axe-shaped tubercles and comb-formation spines are also exhibited by the species *Turbinicarpus pseudopectinatus* (*Normanbokea p.*) and *Mammillaria pectinifera* (*Solisia pectinata*), but they are not closely related.

Peireskiopsis velutina

1 species. Native to Mexico (San Luis Potosí, Nuevo León).

P. asseliformis Ehrenb.
Body 5-10 cm. tall and 2-5.5 cm. thick, grey-green, with flat, laterally compressed tubercles. Axils woolly. Areoles of elongated form like a woodlouse, with 8-60 spines in comb-formation, up to 0.5 cm. long, touching at the base. Flowers violet-red, 2.5-4 cm. wide.

Pelecyphora asseliformis

This species is very distinctive and hence well known and popular. It is not temperamental in cultivation; it prefers a mineral, permeable soil and likes to be kept warm and bright in the vegetative period, but should not be left in brilliant sun. Not much water is required, and the plant should be watered less frequently than other cacti. The species is slow-growing, but must not be forced, otherwise it loses its characteristic appearance. Raising plants from seed is quite feasible, using a predominantly mineral soil, but you will need patience, as the seedlings grow slowly.

Peniocereus (Berger) Br. & R.
1909 (*Neoevansia*)
(Latin penis = tail)

Upright or climbing columnar cacti with very thin stems, round or 3-10-ribbed, and few spines. Thick taproot. Flowers lateral with elongated tube, externally scaly and spiny/woolly, nocturnal, 5.2-20 cm. long.

9 species. Native to USA (Arizona, New Mexico, Texas), Mexico.

P. greggii (Engelm.) Br. & R.
Loosely bushy. Stems dark green, almost black, initially downy, up to 3 m. long and 2-2.5 cm. thick, with 3-6

angles. Radial spines 6-9. Central spines 0 (-1-2). Spines blackish, small, only 2 mm. long. Flowers white, slender-tubed, 15-20 cm. long. USA (W. Texas, New Mexico, Arizona), Mexico (Sonora, Chihuahua, Zacatecas). The distinctive feature of this species is the giant taproot which can be up to 60 cm. thick and weigh more than 60 kg.

Pereskia Mill. 1754 (*Peireskia* Steud.)
(after N.F.C. de Peiresc (1580 — 1673), a French academic)

The genus *Pereskia,* together with its close relative *Rhodocactus,* does not fit into the standard cactus mould at all. Pereskias are only slightly succulent, forming trees, bushes or climbing shrubs, with flat, ribbed leaves. The flowers are borne on a stalk, have no tube and the ovary is superior.

10 species. Native to Florida and the West Indies via Mexico and tropical South America to N. Argentina.

Pereskias are tolerant plants, and grow well in any nutritious soil. For this reason they are very frequently used as a rootstock for grafted Christmas and Easter cacti. *Pereskia* and the genus *Peireskiopsis* are among the few cacti which can tolerate a mildly alkaline soil reaction, up to about pH 8. Both are only slightly succulent, the thin stems storing little water. Nevertheless they cannot tolerate moist conditions in the long-term. They must be watered moderately but regularly, as they do not like protracted dry periods.

P. aculeata Mill. (*P. pereskia* (L.) Karsten)
Stems climbing and trailing, up to 10 m. long. Leaves up to 9 cm. long and 4 cm. wide. Areoles usually bear two strong, curved climbing spines, up to 2 cm. long. Flowers in clusters, white, pale yellow, pale pink, up to 4.5 cm. wide. Florida and W. Indies as far as Paraguay and S. Brazil (Rio Grande do Sul).

var. godseffiana (Sand.) F.M. Knuth
Underside of leaves purple-red. A cultivated variant produced in Australia.

Pereskia bahiensis

Pereskia aculeata

Rhodocactus sacharosus

P. bahiensis Gürke
Tree-shaped or bushy, up to 8 m. tall. Leaves up to 9 cm. long. Areoles initially spineless, later with up to 40 spines, up to 9 cm. long. Flowers in clusters, pink, up to 4 cm. long. N.E. Brazil.

Peruvocereus Akers see *Haageocereus*

Pfeiffera Salm-Dyck 1845
(after Ludwig Pfeiffer (died 1877), doctor and botanist from Kassel)

Fairly small, columnar cacti, some of them epiphytic, with (3-) 4-7 (-8) ribs. Flowers lateral or terminal, with short tube, externally scaly and spiny/woolly, diurnal, white or yellowish, 1.5-2.2 cm. long. Ovary relatively large and angular. 4 species. Native to Bolivia, Argentina.

P. erecta Ritter
Erect, little tendency to branch. Stems up to 30 cm. long and 0.6-1.2 cm. thick, with 5-7 ribs. Spines around 6-12, white to yellow-brown, 0.4-1 cm. long. Flowers white, 1.5 cm. long. Bolivia (Santa Cruz).

P. gracilis Ritter
Prostrate, creeping, covering considerable distances. Stems up to 60 cm. long, 0.5-0.8 cm. thick, with 5-7 ribs. Spines 5-10, needle-shaped, yellow-brown, 0.2-0.6 cm. long. Fruit globular, light red to brownish-red, 0.8-1.2 cm. thick. Bolivia.

P. ianthothele (Monv.) Web.
Bushy. Stems pale green, often tinged with violet on the areoles, 15-20 cm. long, 1.5-2 cm. thick, with (3-) 4 sharp-edged wavy ribs. Spines 6-7, bristly, yellowish, 4-5 mm. long. Flowers cream-white, pink outside, 2-2.5 cm. long. Bolivia, Argentina.

Phellosperma Br. & R. see *Mammillaria*

Philippicereus Backeb. see *Eulychnia*

Phyllocactus Link see *Chiapasia, Epiphyllum,* but mainly *Nopalxochia*

Pilocanthus B.W. Benson & Backeb. see *Pediocactus*

Pilocereus K. Schum. see *Pilosocereus*

Pilocopiapoa Ritter see *Copiapoa*

Pilosocereus Byl. & Rowl. 1957
(Cephalophorus, Pilocereus)
(Latin pilosus = hairy)

Tree-like or bushy columnar cacti with 4-30 ribs. Flowers on specially-formed areoles or in a pseudo-cephalium, externally scaly and slightly woolly or bare, nocturnal, 4-10 cm. long.

54 species. Native to USA (Florida), Greater and Lesser Antilles, Mexico, Guatemala, Colombia, Ecuador, Venezuela, Brazil.

Pilosocereus chrysacanthus

Pilosocereus palmeri

Ritter has recently established two new genera *Cipocereus* and *Floribunda*. Both have non-dehiscent fruit, in contrast to *Pilosocereus*. The flowers of *Floribunda* are only 1.6 cm. long.

P. chrysacanthus (Web.) Byl. & Rowl. *(Cephalocereus c.* (Web.) Br. & R.) Branching from the base, up to 5 m. tall. Stems glossy green, frosted at the ends, 6-8 cm. thick, with 9-12 sharp ribs. Areoles closely spaced, with short golden yellow hairs. Spines around 12-15, golden yellow or golden brown, 1-4 cm. long. Flowering stems densely covered with golden yellow hairs. Flowers more or less pink, 7-8 cm. long and 5 cm. wide, externally hairy. Mexico (Puebla, Oaxaca).

P. palmeri (Rose) Byl. & Rowl. *(Cephalocereus p.* Rose) Tree-shaped, up to 6 m. tall. Stems

274

dark green, glaucous above, 8 cm. thick and with 7-9 rounded ribs. Areoles with long, grey-white, 2-4 cm. long clusters of wool. Radial spines 7-12, 1-3 cm. long. Central spines 1, up to 3 cm. long. All spines brown to grey. Flowers purple to brownish, 8 cm. long, nocturnal. Mexico (Tamaulipas). Require a winter temperature of 15-20°C.

Piptanthocereus Riccob. see *Cereus*

Polaskia Backeb. 1949
(after the North American cactus expert, C. Polaski, 20th century).

Tree-form columnar cacti with 7-12 ribs. Flowers borne towards the end of the stems or terminally, with very short tube, externally bearing large, leaf-like scales, bare, diurnal, cream-white. 1 species. Native to Mexico (Puebla, Oaxaca).

Porfiria Böd. see *Mammillaria*

Praecereus Buxb. see *Monvillea*

Pseudoacanthocereus Ritter see *Acanthocereus*

Pseudoespostoa Backeb. see *Espostoa*

Pseudolobivia (Backeb.) Backeb. see *Echinopsis*

Pseudomammillaria Buxb. see *Mammillaria*

Pseudomitrocereus Bravo & Buxb. see *Mitrocereus*

Pseudonopalxochia Backeb. see *Nopalxochia*

Pseudopilocereus Buxb. 1968
(Greek pseudo = false, pilos = cap, hat)

Tree-form or bushy columnar cacti with 4-12 ribs. Flowers lateral or close to the crown, borne on specially formed areoles or in a pseudo-cephalium, externally slightly scaly or not scaly, bare, radially symmetrical to zygomorphic, nocturnal. 23 species. Native to Brazil (Minas Gerais, Bahia).

Requires warm conditions, even in winter, as in its habitat.

P. fulvilanatus Buin. & Bred. Tree-form. Stems blue, glaucous when young, up to 3 m. tall and 10-11 cm. thick, with 5 (-6) ribs. Radial spines around 11, 1-2.5 cm. long. Central spine 1, pointing upward, up to 4.5 cm. long. Spines initially brown, later grey. The areoles form a golden brown woolly band. Flowers white, green outside, nocturnal, 5.2 cm. long. Brazil (Minas Gerais).

A beautiful columnar cactus even without flowers.

P. glaucescens (Lab.) Buxb. (*Pilocereus g.* Lab.; *Pilosocereus g.* (Lab.) Byl. & Rowl.)
Tree-shaped. Stems light blue, glaucous, up to 6 m. tall and up to 10 cm. thick, with 8-10 ribs. Radial spines 13-18, yellowish-white, 0.5-1.5 cm. long. Central spines 5-7, yellowish-grey, thicker at the base, up to 1.5 cm. long. Areoles with up to 2 cm. long white hairs. Flowers white, 6-7 cm. long. Brazil (Bahia to Minas Gerais).

P. glaucochrous (Werderm.) Buxb. (*Pilocereus g.* (Werderm.) Byl. & Rowl.)
Usually solitary, erect. Stems with beautiful light blue glaucous surface, up to 4 m. tall and 5-7 cm. thick, with 5-9 bumpy ribs with sharp transverse furrows. Radial spines 9-12, 1.5 cm.

Pseudopilocereus sp.

long. Central spines around 3-4, up to 5 cm. long. Spines yellowish. Flower-bearing areoles white, woolly and with up to 4 cm. long white hairs. Flowers pink or whitish, 5-5.6 cm. long. Brazil (Bahia).

Pseudorhipsalis Br. & R. 1923
(Greek pseudos = false)

Epiphytic plants with flat leaf-like stems. Small, lateral flowers with very short, naked tube and few petals. Stems always devoid of spines. Differs from *Rhipsalis* in its short flower tube, which is entirely absent in that genus. 3 species. Native to Mexico (Oaxaca), Costa Rica, Jamaica.

P. macrantha Alex. (*Disocactus m.* (Alex.) Kimnach & P.C. Hutch.)
Stems pendant, up to 90 cm. long and 4.5 cm. wide, notched. Flowers solitary or in pairs, pale lemon yellow, 5 cm. long and 3 cm. wide. Globular berry fruit, red, 7-8 mm. thick. Mexico (Oaxaca).

Pseudozygocactus Backeb.
1938 (Greek pseudos = false)

This genus is very similar to *Hatiora*. The segments are wider towards the top, as in *Hatiora*, but are flat. The small flowers are also produced at the end of the segments, are radially symmetrical and without tube. The yellow flowers carry bare scales outside and only two rows of stamens at the base of the flower. The ovary has four sharp angles. 1 species. Native to Brazil (Sao Paulo, Rio de Janeiro).

P. epiphylloides (Campos-Porto & Werderm.) Backeb.
Segments 1 cm. wide and up to 2.5 cm. long. Areoles tiny, bare. Flowers about 1 cm. long.

Pterocactus K. Schum. 1897
'Winged cactus'
(Greek pteron = wing)

This genus is similar to *Opuntia*, has glochids and small leaves of round cross-section which, like those of *Opuntia*, soon fall off. However, the root is thickened and tuberous, the flowers are more or less sunken into the stems and the fruit are dry, dehiscent capsules. The most characteristic feature is the wide-winged seeds, which do not occur in any other cactus genus. The decumbent, branching plants have globular or cylindrical segments. The flowers are produced at the end of the stems and have erect or slightly spreading petals and no tube. Stamens and stigmas are not projecting. 7 species. Native to Argentina.

P. tuberosus (Pfeiff.) Br. & R. Stems brownish-reddish, up to 40 cm. long and 1 cm. thick, thickened towards the end. Taproot up to 12 cm. long and 8 cm. thick. Spines hair-like, numerous, short and appressed. Flowers yellow, 3 cm. long. Argentina (Mendoza).

Pterocereus MacDougal & Miranda 1954 (*Anisocereus* p.p.) (Greek pteron = wing)

Tree-like columnar cacti with 3-4 thin to wing-like ribs. Flowers lateral, externally scaly and spiny/felty, 5-9.5 cm. long. 2 species. Native to Mexico (Chiapas, Yucatán).

Pygmaeocereus H. Johnson & Backeb. 1957 (Greek pygmaios = dwarf)

Very squat columnar to globular cacti with taproots. Flowers long, funnel-shaped, nocturnal, with very short stamens, externally scaly and hairy. Fruit fleshy. 4 species. Native to S. Peru

Pygmaeolobivia Backeb. see *Lobivia*

Pyrrhocactus Berger emend. Backeb. see *Neoporteria*

Quiabentia Br. & R. 1919 (after a Brazilian place name)

This is one of the few cactus genera with flat and more or less permanent

Pterocactus tuberosus

leaves, like *Pereskia*. The plants possess a glochid-like formation and the typical seed of the Opuntioideae subfamily, with a hard, white seed coat. Compared with the related genus *Peireskiopsis* the segments of *Quiabentia* easily break off, and are often whorled. The flowers are located more or less at the end of the stems. Trees or bushes with round stems. Flowers red, spreading, and without tube. 5 species. Native to N. Argentina and Bolivia, separately also in Brazil (Bahia).

Rapicactus Buxb. & Oehme see *Neolloydia*

Rathbunia Br. & R. 1901 (after the American nature researcher R. Rathbun, 1852-1918)

Tree-form or bushy columnar cacti with 4-8 ribs. Flowers lateral, with elongated tube, externally scaly and spiny/felty, zygomorphic, diurnal, red, 4-12 cm. long. Stamens strongly projecting. 4 species. Native to Mexico (States on the W. coast).

Rauhocereus Backeb. 1957 (after the German botanist W. Rauh)

Tree-form or bushy columnar cacti with 5-6 ribs, divided into tubercles by furrows. Flowers towards the end of the stems, externally scaly and woolly, nocturnal, with nectar chamber, white, 8-10 cm. long. 1 species, *R. riosaniensis* Backeb. Native to Peru.

Rebutia K. Schum. 1895 emend. Buin. & Donald (*Aylostera, Cylindrorebutia, Digitorebutia, Mediolobivia*) (after P. Rebut, 19th Century French cactus expert and dealer)

Rebutias are exclusively very small globular cacti, many of which form large clusters. Within the genus it is possible to see the development of elongated cacti with straight but slightly bumpy ribs into species with angled, then helical and very bumpy ribs, and eventually to the squat globular tubercle or wart cacti, sometimes even sunken in at the top; the latter looking very similar to

Rebutia muscula

Mammillarias. In the warty species the number of ribs is only indicated by the helical rows of tubercles. Compared with Mammillarias these plants usually have thinner spines, more bristle-like and never hooked. The crown is usually devoid of spines and wool. The tubercles never contain milky sap.

The flowers of Rebutias are borne quite low down on the sides. They are very large in relation to body size, usually brilliant red, orange or yellow, and survive for a few days. They close towards evening but open again on the following morning. The trumpet-shaped flowers with their thin, scaly tube are slightly reminiscent of Lobivias. In many species the throat stamens are clearly separate, as also in

Lobivia. However, the tube has relatively few hairs or bristles, or is completely bare. The fruit is a small, spherical, scaly berry.

Around 50-60 species. Native to uplands of N. Argentina (Tucumán) to Bolivia (Cochabamba and Oruro), at altitudes of 1500 to 4000 m.

Rebutia is a particularly rewarding cactus genus, and is recommended to the collector.

Like Mammillarias, Rebutias are very small, and an entire collection takes up relatively little space. Rebutias do not offer such a rich variation in their spine formation as the Mammillarias, but their flowers are much more distinctive in compensation. Rebutias are also counted among the most

willing and reliable of flowering cacti. Usually they flower in the spring, but they often flower a second time in the autumn. They are very undemanding in terms of culture, and under experimental conditions they have flowered in sand, gravel and pure humus, and even in half-shade. Ideally they like a nutritious, permeable standard cactus soil.

Rebutias are mountain plants. Marked temperature differences between day and night and summer and winter are beneficial to them. If they are cultivated under glass effective ventilation is absolutely essential. The plants often thrive surprisingly well in hard cold-frame conditions or on an outside window ledge, provided that they are sheltered from full sun and

277

Rebutia Table of sections
(based mainly on Donald's data)

Abbreviation in the species descriptions	Section or sub-section	Body form	Body surface	Body firmness	Style merged with tube	Flower covering	Fruit	Fertility
C	**Cylindrorebutia** Buin. & Donald		ribs weak	soft	unattached	hairy (hairy/ bristly)	naked	self-steri
S	**Setirebutia** Buin. & Donald		ribs weak	soft	unattached	hairy (hairy/ bristly)	virtually naked	self-steri
R	**Rebutia*** K. Schum.		warty	soft	unattached	naked	naked	usually self-steri
M	**Mediorebutia***		warty	soft	1-2 mm. merged	naked (felty)	naked	self.steril
D	**Digitorebutia** Frič & Kreuz. & Buin.) Buin. & Donald		ribbed, straight or spiral	soft or hard	part merged (30% or less	hairy	naked slightly hairy	self-steril
A	**Aylostera** (Spegazz.) Buin. & Donald		(ribbed) warty	hard	fully merged	hairy/bristly	bristly	mostly self-sterile

* The sub-sections Rebutia and Mediorebutia together form the section Rebutia

Flower structure in Rebutia

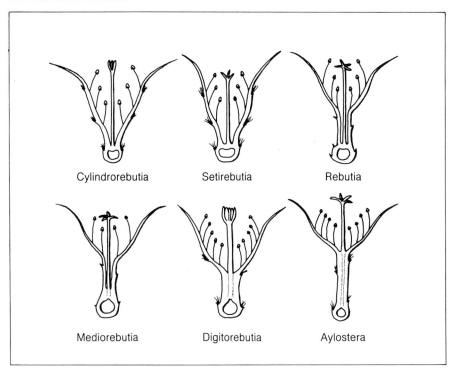

Cylindrorebutia   Setirebutia   Rebutia

Mediorebutia   Digitorebutia   Aylostera

prolonged rain.

Rebutias need bright light, but gentle shade from the brilliance of the midday sun in the spring and summer. This applies in particular to the bright green species with less dense spines. They like adequate moisture in the vegetative period and fairly high atmospheric humidity. They do poorly if kept dry in the summer and if the air is very dry. Do not water in the spring until the buds are clearly formed. In winter the plants should be kept dry, in which state they will even tolerate slight night frosts.

Rebutias are well suited to propagation from seed. In fact they often propagate themselves in this way, and you will often find a number of small seedlings around a plant. *Rebutia* seeds do not remain viable for long, and should be sown during the year following the harvest. In a bright location and in temperatures between 15 and 25°C they germinate very well. Often the

Other features	Distribution
...owers yellow, short ...pines, thicker at ...e base. Body mostly ...iolet-tinged	N.W. Arg. (Salta)
...ody often lilac or ...rown	N.W. Arg. (Salta)
	N.W. Arg.
	N.W. Arg. (Jujuy, Salta) to Bolivia
...igma lobes short and ...ick, less than 10 mm. ...ng and more than 3 mm. ...ick. Spines thickened like ...tuber at the base	N.W. Arg. to Bol. (Oruro)
...igma lobes long and thin, ...be more than 10 mm. ...ng and less than 3 mm. thick	N.W. Arg. to S. Bol.

plants will produce flowers when only one year old, when they are no more than 1 cm. in size; the flowers may be 2-3 times as large as the plant's body.

Grafting is not necessary with Rebutias, as they grow well on their own roots. Plants grown 'soft' are very vulnerable to spider mite attack.

Rebutia species hybridize very easily under cultivation, and many of the plants owned by growers are hybrids which cannot be classified as particular species. In fact the nomenclature of the genus *Rebutia* is more confused than virtually every other cactus genus. Many former species have later been reclassified as varieties or forms, and vice versa. The division of the genus into 6 sections or sub-sections is now reasonably well established. Of these *Aylostera* and *Digitorebutia* include the greatest variety of species, but they are also the most problematic in systematic terms.

Aylostera section

Flowers white to deep lilac pink
  Flowers white to light pink, body grey-green, inner flower petals pointed
    Flowers 25 mm. wide, white — *R. albiflora*
    Flowers 40 mm. wide, white to light pink — *R. narvaecensis*
  Flowers deep lilac pink. Body grass-green. Inner flower petals blunt — *R. perplexa*
Flowers orange to carmine
  Spines pectinate, appressed
    Radial spines 11-18, 2-4 mm. long — *R. albopectinata*
    Radial spines 24-26, 1 mm. long. Taproot. Areoles brown, felty — *R. heliosa*
  Spines not pectinate
    Flowers carmine red, buds almost black. Body cylindrical — *R. pseudodeminuta*
    Flowers orange to vermilion, buds lighter. Body no more than oval
      Flowers 35-40 mm. wide
        Body short columnar to barrel-shaped. Crown covered in spines and wool. Radial spines up to 5 mm. long, seldom longer. Central spines up to 4 mm. long. Tube around 2.5 cm. long — *R. spegazziniana*
        Body compressed globular. Crown naked. Radial spines 5-8 mm., central spines up to 12 mm. long. Tube around 1.5 cm. long — *R. kupperiana*
      Flowers 15-30 mm. wide
        Flowers 15-18 mm. wide — *R. pulvinosa*
        Flowers 25-30 mm. wide
          Radial spines around 50, central spines not clearly differentiated — *R. muscula*
          Radial spines numerous, central spines 2-6
            Body round. Central spines 5-6 — *R. spinosissima*
            Body elongated. Central spines 2-5
              Radial spines 25-40 — *R. fiebrigii*
              Radial spines up to 12. Central spines absent — *R. deminuta*

Cylindrorebutia section

R. einsteinii

Digitorebutia section

(Body more or less cylindrical, with 8 to 15 straight or slightly helical ribs. Radial spines 7-12, central spines absent.)

Spines up to 3 mm. long (taproot)
  Spines 1 (-2) mm. long with areoles almost touching — *R. torquata*
  Spines more than 3 mm. long — *R. haagei, R. pygmaea*
Spines about 5-12 mm. long
  Flowers pure white to pink-white — *R. eos*
  Flowers golden yellow or golden bronze with white stamens — *R. auranitida*
  Flowers orange to flame-red or purple-red
    Throat darker
      Body light green. Flowers brilliant light red, throat madder red — *R. eucaliptana*
      Body grey-green or brown-green. Flowers flame-red, orange-red or purple-red, throat violet-red. Spines dark-tipped — *R. ritteri*

Diagrammatic table of sections

Style		unattached to the tube	partially merged with the tube	merged with the tube
Body form	◻-◻	Cylindrorebutia	Digitorebutia	Aylostera
	◯-◯	Setirebutia (flowers woolly) Rebutia (flowers naked)	Mediorebutia	

Throat same colour
  Ribs 8-9. Flowers orange-red. Buds black-green   R. costata
  Ribs 12. Flowers light scarlet   R. brachyantha
Also: Stamens carmine-violet. Flowers carmine red to bluish-carmine, usually with
  differently coloured throat   R. euanthema

Mediorebutia section
Flowers yellow

Flowers red   R. marsoneri
  Spines up to 2 mm. long   R. krainziana
  Spines more than 2 mm. long   R. wessneriana

Rebutia section

Spines 15-20. Flowers up to 2 cm. wide. Fruit yellow, more globular than flattened
                                                          R. xanthocarpa

Spines 20-30. Flowers 2-4 cm. wide. Fruit orange-red to red, flattened
  Spines up to 1 cm. long. Tube 1-1.5 cm. long   R. minuscula
  Spines up to 3 cm. long, flexible, more or less matted. Tube 1.5-2 cm. long
                                                          R. senilis

Setirebutia section   R. aureiflora

A = *Aylostera*   M = *Mediorebutia*
C = *Cylindrorebutia* R = *Rebutia*
D = *Digitorebutia*   S = *Setirebutia*

(A) **R. albiflora** Ritter & Buin. (*Aylostera a.* (Ritter & Buin.) Backeb.)
Abundantly clustering. Body globular, with 14-16 helical ribs. Radial spines up to 15. Central spines around 5. Spines 2-5 mm. long. Flowers white with pink central stripe, only 2.5 cm. wide. Tube bristly, merged with the style. Bolivia (Tarija).

(A) **R. albopectinata** Rausch (*R. densipectinata* n.n. Ritter)
Solitary or slightly clustering. Taproot. Body pale green or purple-brown, elongated, with 10-18 bumpy ribs. Radial spines 11-18, in comb-formation, white with dark brown, thicker base, 2-4 mm. long, sometimes 1-3 central spines. Flowers 3-4 cm. long and 3.5 cm. wide, orange-red to vermilion. Tube merged with the style. Bolivia (South-Cinti province).

(D) **R. auranitida** (Wessn.) Buin. & Donald (*Mediolobivia a.* (Wessn.) Krainz)
Clustering. Body matt dark green, bronze-coloured or touched with bronze, elongated, with 11-14 spiral ribs. Radial spines around 9, up to 7 mm. long. Flowers golden yellow, 3 cm. wide. ?Bolivia.

(S) **R. aureiflora** Backeb. (*Mediolobivia a.* (Backeb.) Backeb.)
Profusely clustering. Body green with hint of black-violet, squat globular, warty. Radial spines 10-16, up to 6 mm. long. Central spines 1-4, 3-25 mm. long. Flowers lemon yellow or blood red to lilac with white or delicate lilac throat, about 4 cm. wide. Argentina (Jujuy-Salta).

ssp. aureiflora Body flat. Spines short, appressed.

f. aureiflora
Flowers yellow to orange-yellow.

f. kesselringiana (Cullm.) Köhler (*Mediolobiva a.* var. *rubriflora* (Backeb.) Backeb.; *R.a.f.* rubriflora (Backeb.) Buin. & Donald)
Flowers lilac

ssp. elegans (Backeb.) Donald
Body larger, globular, spines longer, more projecting.

var. elegans (Backeb.) Donald
Flowers yellow-orange

var. sarothroides (Werderm.) Donald (*R.a.f.s.* (Werderm.) Buin. & Donald; *Mediolobivia a.* var. *s.* (Werderm.) Backeb.).
Flowers full red

(D) **R. brachyantha** (Wessn.) Buin. & Donald (*Mediolobivia b.* (Wessn.) Krainz)
Body elongated, with about 12 ribs.

Radial spines 7-9 (-10), around 5 mm. long. Flowers light scarlet. Style short, merged with the tube.

(D) **R. costata** Werderm. (*Mediolobivia c.* (Werderm.) Krainz)
Abundantly clustering. Body elongated with 8-9 ribs. Radial spines up to 12, about 7 mm. long. Flowers orange-red. Style short, merged with the tube. N. Argentina.

(A) **R. deminuta** (Web.) Br. & R. (*Aylostera d.* (Web.) Backeb.)
Profusely clustering. Body globular, with 11-13 rows of tubercles. Radial spines up to 12, 6 mm. long. Flowers dark orange-red, 3 cm. wide. Tube hairy and bristly, merged with the style. Argentina (Tucumán).

(C) **R. einsteinii** Frič (*Mediolobivia schmiedcheniana* (Köhler) Krainz var. *e.* (Frič) Backeb.)
Strongly clustering. Distinct taproot. Body pure green, tinged strongly with red, or dark brown-green, elongated, only about 2 cm. thick on the type specimen. 13-16 straight or spiral ribs. Radial spines up to 12, 3-7 mm. long. Flowers deep golden yellow with pale yellow throat, around 2.5 cm. wide. Argentina (Salta).

The plant requires a permeable soil and does not like to be too damp. It should not be forced otherwise it will grow long and narrow and flower poorly.

f. rubroviridis (Backeb.) Buin. & Donald (*Mediolobivia schmiedcheniana* (Köhler) Krainz var. *r.* (Frič) Backeb.)
Body matt dark green to violet, about 3 cm. thick. Radial spines densely pectinate, brown to red-brown.

f. schmiedcheniana (Köhler) Buin. & Donald (*Mediolobivia s.* (Köhler) Krainz)
Body about 1.5-2 cm. thick. Spines yellow to red-brown.

(D) **R. eos** Rausch (*Mediolobivia e.* Rausch)
Body short cylindrical, blue-green. Taproot. Ribs 12-13, divided up into tubercles. Radial spines 8-10, up to 6 mm. long, brown-grey with brown base. Central spine 1, up to 5 mm. long, brown to black. Flowers 4 cm. long and 3.5 cm. wide, pure white to white-pink. Argentina (Jujuy).

Rebutia albopectinata

Rebutia einsteinii group

Rebutia eos

(D) **R. euanthema** (Backeb.) Buin. & Donald (*Mediolobivia e.* (Backeb.) Krainz)
Strongly clustering. Body grey to olive-green, elongated, with about 10-14 ribs. Radial spines about 12. Flowers carmine red to bluish-carmine, 3 cm. wide. Border area of S. Bolivia / N. Argentina.

Rebutia euanthema f. oculata

f. euanthema
Flowers reddish inside, then yellow-red, carmine outside.

f. fricii (Backeb.) Buin. & Donald
(*Mediolobivia e*.f. *fricii* (hort.) Backeb.)
Throat glossy blood red.

f. oculata (Werderm.) Buin. & Donald
(*Mediolobivia e.f.o.* (Werderm.) Krainz)
Tube semi-matt, whitish. Flowers only two-coloured, yellowish to golden bronze towards the inside.

(D) **R. eucaliptana** (Backeb.) Donald
(*Mediolobivia e.* (Backeb.) Krainz; *R. costata* Werderm. *f.eucaliptana* (Backeb.) Buin. & Donald)
Profusely clustering. Body elongated, with 7-10 ribs. Radial spines 9-12, 0.5-1.2 cm. long. Flowers brilliant light red with madder red throat. Style short, merged with the tube. Bolivia (La Paz).

(A) **R. fiebrigii** (Gürke) Br. & R. **var. densiseta** Cullm.
Clustering. Body globular to oval, with around 17 rows of tubercles. Radial spines 25-40. Central spines 2-5. Spines 2-20 mm. long. Flowers brilliant yellow-red, 2.5-3.5 cm. long. Style merged with the tube. Bolivia (Tarija).

(D) **R. haagei** Frič & Schelle
Solitary to strongly clustering. Body light bluish-green, elongated, with 10-11 ribs. Radial spines 10-12, around 3 mm. long. Flowers light salmon-coloured to flame-red, up to 4 cm. wide. N. Argentina.

(A) **R. heliosa** Rausch (*Aylostera h.* Rausch)
Solitary to abundantly clustering. Body with up to 38 rows of tubercles. Radial spines in comb-formation, 24-26, only 1 mm. long. Flowers orange, orange-yellow inside with whitish throat, 5 cm. long and 4 cm. wide. Style merged with the tube. Bolivia (Tarija).

This species, with its outstanding spine formation, was first described by Rausch in 1970. Already several varieties have been listed, varying in spine formation and flowers. The species demands a permeable soil because of its taproot, and should be watered sparingly. Grafted plants become flabby if forced, hence plants on their own root are preferable.

(M) **R. krainziana** Kesselr. (*R. wessneriana* Bewerunge var. *k.* (Kesselr.) Buin. & Donald)

Rebutia minuscula ssp. violaciflora f. kariusiana

Rebutia heliosa

Rebutia krainziana

Rebutia kupperiana

Rebutia marsoneri 'Brevispina'

Rebutia minuscula

Clustering. Body matt light green, squat globular, warty. Areoles white, relatively large. Spines 8-12, only 1-2 mm. long. Flowers bright red with yellowish throat, 4 cm. wide. Argentina (Jujuy?).

A distinctive plant whose origins are unclear. Kesselring described it in 1948 from material which he believed had been collected by F. Ritter, but Ritter disputes this. In spite of great efforts by experienced researchers the plant has not been rediscovered in its homeland.

A popular species, which should be sheltered from brilliant sun. White-flowering forms ('Stirnadel's masterpiece') are a result of hybridization.

(A) **R. kupperiana** Böd. (*Aylostera k.* (Böd.) Backeb.)
Clustering. Body globular with around 15 rows of tubercles. Radial spines 13-15, 5-8 mm. long. Central spines dark brown, 1-3 (-4), to 1.2 (-2) cm. long. Flowers vermilion to brilliant orange-red with pale green throat, 2.7-5 cm. long. Style merged with the tube. Bolivia (Tarija).

(M) **R. marsoneri** Werderm.
Solitary or clustering, squat globular, warty. Radial spines around 30-35, 3-15 mm. long. Flowers pale yellow to deep yellow, 3-3.5 cm. wide. Buds crimson. Argentina (Jujuy).

'Brevispina' with spines only 3-4 mm. long, similar in form to *R. krainziana*

f. sieperdaiana (Buin.) Buin. & Donald (*R. senilis* Backeb. var. *s.* (Buin.) Backeb.)
Snow-white spines.

(R) **R. minuscula** K. Schum.
Usually richly clustering. Body flattened globular, warty. Spines 20-30, more or less the same, usually no more than 1 cm. long. Tube 10-15

Rebutia minuscula ssp. violaciflora

mm. long, with few scales, bare. Style free-standing. Argentina (Salta, Tucumán).

ssp. minuscula
Body glossy green. Spines whitish. Flowers flesh-red with yellowish throat, 3 cm. wide.

ssp. grandiflora (Backeb.) Donald (*R.g.* Backeb.)
Flowers roughly twice the size, brilliant carmine red.

ssp. violaciflora (Backeb.) Donald (*R. m.* var. *minuscula* f. *violaciflora* (Backeb.) Buin. & Donald; *R. violaciflora* Backeb.)
Body usually solitary, yellow green. Spines golden brown. Flowers light violet, 2.5-3 cm. wide. Radial spines 0.3-2.5 cm. long.

f. kariusiana (Wessn) Buin. & Donald (*R.k.* Wessn.)
Flowers flamingo pink. Fruit yellowish-green.

f. knuthiana (Backeb.) Buin. & Donald (*R. violaciflora* Backeb. var. *k.* (Backeb.) Donald)
Body matt pale green. Flowers dull to brilliant carmine red. Radial spines about 30 or more.

(A) **R. muscula** Ritter & Thiele (*Aylostera m.* (Ritter & Thiele) Backeb.)
Slightly clustering. Body elongated later, green, warty. Spines around 50, all about the same, 2-4 mm. long, white, enveloping the body. Flowers orange, 3.5 cm. long and 3 cm. wide. Tube merged with the style. Bolivia (Tarija).

284

Rebutia narvaecensis

Rebutia perplexa

(A) **R. narvaecensis** (Card.) Donald (*Aylostera n.* Card.; *R. espinosae* Knize n.n.)
Clustering. Body grey-green, squat globular, with 18-22 spiral ribs. Spines 20-30, 2-5 mm. long. Flowers white to pale pink, 4 cm. wide. Ovary hairy and bristly. Style merged with the tube. Bolivia (Cochabamba, ?Tarija).

(A) **R. perplexa** Donald (formerly generally listed under the name *R. narvaecensis* (Card.) Donald)
Clustering. Body grey-green, more or less globular to short cylindrical, with 16-18 slightly spiral ribs. Radial spines 10-16, 1-2 mm. long. Flowers deep lilac pink, 2.5-3 cm. wide. Ovary hairy and bristly. Style merged with the tube. Bolivia (Tarija / Chuquisaca).

(A) **R. pseudodeminuta** Backeb. (*Aylostera p.* (Backeb.) Backeb.)
Solitary. Body elongated, warty. Radial spines more than 10, 2-7 mm. long. Central spines 2-3, 12-15 mm. long. Flowers carmine red, 3-4 cm. wide. Buds almost black-red. Style merged with the tube. Argentina (Salta).

(A) **R. pulvinosa** Ritter & Buin. (*Aylostera p.* (Ritter & Buin.) Backeb.)
Clustering. Body globular to elongated, with 16-20 ribs. Radial spines 15-22, up to 3 mm. long. Flowers orange-yellow, about 1.8 cm. wide. Style merged with the tube. Bolivia (Tarija).

(D) **R. pygmaea** (R.E. Fries) Br. & R. (*Mediolobivia p.* (R.E. Fries) Backeb.)
Solitary to clustering. Body grey to light bluish-green, with taproot. Spines 8-12, 2-3 mm. long, in comb-formation on the crown. Flowers pink to salmon-coloured, sometimes streaked. Argentina (Jujuy) and the border area with Bolivia.

f. atrovirens (Backeb.) Buin. & Donald (*Mediolobivia pectinata* (Backeb.) Backeb. var. *a.* (Backeb.) Backeb.)
Flowers flame-red to red.

f. haefneriana (Cullm.) Buin. & Donald (*Mediolobiva h.* Cullm.)
Flowers cherry-red to blood red, near the crown.

(D) **R. ritteri** (Wessn.) Buin. & Donald (*Mediolobivia r.* (Wessn.) Krainz)
Body grey-green, globular to elongated, with 10-15 rows of tubercles. Spines 8-12, 0.3-1 cm. long. Flowers fiery vermilion with red-violet throat, 3-4 cm. long and 4.5 cm. wide. Bolivia (Tarija).

var. nigricans (Wessn.) Buin. & Donald (*Mediolobivia n.* (Wessn.) Krainz)
Body brown-green, about 11 ribs. Flowers flame-red, 2.5-3.5 cm. wide.

(R) **R. senilis** Backeb.
Profusely clustering. Body flattened globular, warty. Spines around 25, flexible, more or less matted, up to 3 cm. long. Flowers with 15-20 mm.

long tube. Fruits orange-red to red, flattened. Argentina (Salta).

ssp. senilis
Spines white. Tube 2 mm. thick at the base, 4 mm. at the tip.

f. senilis
Flowers carmine red with white throat, around 3.5-4 cm. wide.

f. lilacinorosea (Backeb.) Buin. & Donald (*R.s.* var. *l.* Backeb.)
Flowers lilac to carmine red with pink tube.

ssp. chrysacantha (Backeb.) Donald (*R.c.* Backeb.)
Spines usually yellowish. Tube about 2.5 mm. thick, constant thickness. Flowers smaller.

f. iseliniana (Krainz) Buin. & Donald (*R.s.* var. *i.* Krainz)
Flowers orange, brown outside, 2-3 cm. wide.

f. kesselringiana (Bewerunge) Buin. & Donald (*R.s.* var. *k.* Bewerunge)
The flowers are lemon yellow, green outside.

(A) **R. spegazziniana** Backeb. (*Aylostera s.* (Backeb.) Backeb.)
Strongly clustering. Body globular. Central spines 5-6, bristly, brown-tipped. The flowers are light vermilion, 2.5-3 cm. wide. Style merged with the tube. Argentina (Salta).

285

Rebutia pygmaea

Rebutia torquata

Rhipsaphyllopsis graeseri

(A) **R. spinosissima** Backeb. (*Aylostera s.* (Backeb.) Backeb.)
Abundantly clustering. Body globular, light green. Spines dense, bristly. Central spines 5-6. Flowers light vermilion, 2.5-3 cm. wide. Style merged with the tube. Argentina (Salta), Bolivia (Tarija).

(S?) **R. spiralisepala** Jajo (*Mediolobivia s.* Jajo)
According to Donald possibly a sub-species of *R. aureiflora.*

Body elongated. Radial spines up to about 16, up to 8 mm. long. Central spines 4, around 2 cm. or more long. Flowers orange-red with reddish central stripe, 3.2 cm. wide.

(D) **R. torquata** Ritter & Buin.
Body columnar. Taproot. With 8-10 twisted, bumpy ribs. Radial spines 6-10, 1 (-2) mm. long with thicker, red-brown base. Central spines absent. Areoles almost touching. Flowers orange, pale yellow inside, 3 cm. long. Style merged with the tube. Bolivia (Prov. South-Chichas).

(M) **R. wessneriana** Bewerunge (*R. krainziana* Kesselr. var. *hyalacantha* (Backeb.) Buchheim)
Clustering. Body green with slight violet hue, squat globular, warty. Spines around 25, approx. 2 cm. long. Flowers red. Argentina (Jujuy).

f. wessneriana
Crown bare. Flowers brilliant blood

red, up to 5.5 cm. wide. Spines around 25, about 2 cm. long. Richly clustering.

f. calliantha (Bewerunge) Buin. & Donald (*R.c.* Bewerunge)
Slightly clustering. Crown covered with spines. Flowers vermilion to carmine with pale orange throat. Spines 15-21, 6-10 mm. long.

(R) **R. xanthocarpa** Backeb.
Abundantly clustering. Body globular, warty. Spines 15-20, 0.5-0.7 cm. long. Flowers no more than 2 cm. wide and short-tubed. Fruits yellow, more globular than flattened. Argentina (Salta).

Flowers carmine red with slightly lighter throat, up to 2 cm. wide, in the normal form.

f. salmonea (Backeb.) Buin. & Donald (*R.x.* var. *s.* Frič & Backeb.)
Flowers more or less salmon pink,.

f. violaciflora (Backeb.) Buin. & Donald (*R.x.* var. *v.* (Backeb.) Backeb.)
Flowers brilliant violet.

Reicheocactus Backeb. see *Neoporteria*

Rhipsalidopsis Br. & R. 1923
(*Epiphyllopsis, Rhipsaphyllopsis*)
(Greek rhips = reed, basketwork; opsis = face)

These plants consist of flat segments. The radially symmetrical flowers have

Rhipsalidopsis gaertneri

Rhipsalidopsis rosea

a very short tube and are borne at the end of the segments. They are completely naked externally and the ovary is slightly angular. The stigma lobes spread outwards. 2 species. Native to Brazil (Parana).

Culture: as for *Schlumbergera*

R. gaertneri (Regel) Moran
(*Schlumbergera g.* (Regel) Br. & R.;
Epiphyllopsis g. (Regel) Berger)
'Easter cactus'
Segments with 3-5 tubercles on each side, 2-2.5 cm. wide and 4 (-7) cm. long. Areoles with 1-2 bristles. Flowers scarlet, 4-5 cm. long. Flower petals long, tapered. Brazil (Parana, Minas Gerais, Santa Catarina).

R. x graeseri (Werderm.) Moran (x.
Rhipsaphyllopsis g. Werderm.;
Rhipsalidopsis gaertneri x *R. rosea*)
Very similar to *R. gaertneri,* but has somewhat smaller flowers, whose petals are not so long and tapering.

R. rosea (Lagerh.) Br. & R.
Segments 2-, 3-or 5-edged, usually slightly reddish, up to about 1 cm. wide and 2-4 cm. long, with bristly hairs. Flowers pink or pink-white, 3-4 cm. wide. Brazil (Parana).

Rhipsalis Gaertn. 1788
(Greek rhips = reed, basketwork)

Of all the cactus genera *Rhipsalis* embraces the widest range of external forms. However, the flowers are very uniform over the entire genus, and for this reason the different growth forms are only listed as sub-genera.

Together with a few other genera *Rhipsalis* has completely tube-less flowers with few petals and stamens. The small flowers are borne more or less laterally and develop into berries. Those species whose ovary is sunken into the stem are usually considered as their own genus *Lepismium.* 65 species. Native to Central and S. America. Tropical W. and E. Africa, Madagascar, Ceylon.

Most species of *Rhipsalis* - those of the sub-genus *Rhipsalis* - do not fit in with our usual conception of cacti. They are tropical epiphytes with trailing, reed-like stems, or the shoots are divided

287

Rhipsalis sp.

stems, but these species are hardly ever cultivated.

Rhipsalis is the only cactus genus which is not confined to the New World, i.e. America, although the species found in the Old World are identical or at least very similar to those in the New World. The mistletoe-like berries have very sticky seeds, which are undoubtedly very widely dispersed by birds.

The cultural conditions for *Rhipsalis* species must be designed to match their natural mode of life as tropical epiphytes. For this reason the plants are usually grown by orchid or bromeliad specialists, or gardeners with a heated greenhouse for tropical plants; they are rarely grown by cactus enthusiasts. *Rhipsalis* species are best kept as hanging plants in orchid baskets. A thick drainage layer of clay crocks constitutes the bottom layer in the basket, while the soil mixture should include much sand, peat and — where possible — moss peat. They are sensitive to lime, and will not do well even in neutral soil; thus it is essential to use rainwater or acidified water for watering. The root system should never be allowed to dry out completely. The parts of the plant above the ground are not very sensitive to dry air but they appreciate fairly frequent misting. Most species grow almost constantly and consequently need a high level of nutrition. The best method of

Fruiting Rhipsalis species

into long, thin stems and short, profusely branching, coral-like segments. Even the flowers do not look like those of a cactus, for they are usually small, only about one centimetre long, and very numerous. They are white, yellowish or greenish in colour, and they often remain open for a week. The nectar is freely accessible and available to all possible pollinators. The plants are especially pretty when they are densely covered with their pea-sized berries, which may be white, red or almost black.

The second large group of *Rhipsalis* species (sub-genus *Phyllorhipsalis*) is so

similar to 'Phyllocacti' that the two are often confused unless flowers or fruit are present. Like the latter they possess leaf-like, flattened stems, which are only round or angular at the base. Both *Rhipsalis* groups contain a fairly large number of species, many of which are difficult to distinguish. In many cases there is a wide difference between the typical external form of old and young tissue, the two forms even existing on the same plant. Initially the stems are often bristly, but later stems are usually virtually bare.

The remaining *Rhipsalis* species have a closer resemblance to ordinary cacti, as they have bristly or multi-ribbed

288

Rhipsalis clavata

Rhipsalis crispimarginata

providing this is to water fairly often with a solution of a normal flower fertilizer. As epiphytic plants they like to have plenty of light, but they will not tolerate direct sun. They do not require high levels of warmth. In summer they can even be left in half-shade, hung up under trees in the garden. In Europe most species flower in the middle of winter after a short dormant period, so they should not be sprayed for 6 to 8 weeks around September / October, and generally kept rather drier.

Stems flattened, like leaves, or angled or ribbed in cross-section
  Stems flattened, like leaves (at least at the end)
                    Sub-genus *Phyllorhipsalis* (P)
  Stems with 3-7 angles or ribs
                    Sub-genus *Goniorhipsalis* (G)
Stems more or less circular in cross-section
  Stems with bristles
                    Sub-genus *Ophiorhipsalis* (O)
  Stems hairy or bare
                    Sub-genus *Rhipsalis* (R)

The species listed here are only examples. The two sub-genera *Phyllorhipsalis* and *Rhipsalis* include a very large number of species which are very difficult to distinguish.

(R) R. capilliformis Web.
Long stems 10-15 cm. long and 2-3 mm. thick, short stems 3-7 cm. long and thinner. Areoles slightly woolly. Flowers greenish-white, around 0.7 cm. long. Fruit white. E. Brazil.

(R) R. cassutha Gaertn.
Stems 10-20 (-50) cm. long and 2-4 mm. thick. Areoles with 1-2 very short bristles at first. Flowers greenish to yellowish-white, around 0.5 cm. long. Fruit white or reddish. The species is very widespread in the tropics of the New and Old World. However, there are very many similar species which are difficult to differentiate.

(R) R. cereuscula Haw.
Long stems 10-30 cm. long and 3-4 cm. thick, short stems about 1.5 cm. long and 1-3 cm. thick. Areoles with short wool and with 2-4 very short bristles. Flowers white, about 1.5 cm. long. Flower petals with yellowish external stripes. Fruit white. Brazil

(Sao Paulo), Argentina (Entre Rios), Paraguay, Uruguay.

(R) R. clavata Web.
Stems slightly club-shaped, i.e. thicker towards the tip, 3-5 cm. long and 2-3 mm. thick. Areoles occasionally with 1-5 white hairs. Flowers white, yellow in the bud, 1.5 cm. long and 1 cm. wide. Fruit white or greenish-white. Brazil (Rio de Janeiro).

(P) R. crispimarginata Loefgr.
Stems flat, 4-6 cm. long, margins

Rhipsalis fasciculata

Rhipsalis mesembryanthemoides

Rhipsalis pentaptera

Rhipsalis purpusii

irregularly notched and wavy, with strong central nerve. Flowers white, around 1.2 cm. wide. Fruit white or pink. Brazil (Rio de Janeiro).

(O) **R. fasciculata** (Willd.) Haw.
Stems whorled, branching, 4-5 cm. thick, round, no more than 6-10 very indistinct ribs. Areoles with fragile bristles. Flowers greenish-white, 6-8 mm. long and 5 mm. wide. Fruit white to pale greenish, with distinct areoles. Brazil (Bahia).

(P) **R. houlletiana** Lem.
Stems 10-20 cm. long and 2.5-3.5 cm. wide, dentate. Teeth 2-3 mm. long. Flowers white to yellowish-white, up to 2 cm. long. Fruit carmine red. Brazil (Rio de Janeiro, Sao Paulo, Minas Gerais).

(R) **R. mesembryanthemoides** Haw.
Long stems 10-20 cm. long and 1.5-2 mm. thick with many tubercles, short stems 0.7-1.5 cm. long and 2-4 mm. thick. The overall impression is of a leafed plant. Areoles woolly, the terminal ones having 3-4 short bristles. Flowers white to light pink, with yellowish central stripes, roughly 0.8 cm. long and 1-1.5 cm. wide. Fruit white or reddish. Brazil (Rio de Janeiro).

(G) **R. pentaptera** Pfeiff.
Stems up to 40 cm. tall, dichotomous, occasionally also whorled, branching. Segments 7-12 cm. long and 6-15 mm. thick, with 5 (-6) notched angles. Areoles with few small bristles. Flowers distributed over the stems, whitish, around 8 mm. long. Fruit white or pale pink. S. Brazil, Uruguay.

(P) **R. purpusii** Weingt.
Segments flat, 8-20 cm. long and 1-3 cm. wide, with notched margins and depressed central rib. Flowers greenish-white, 11 mm. long. Fruit white. Mexico (Chiapas), Guatemala.

Rhipsaphyllopsis Werderm. see *Rhipsalidopsis*

Rhodocactus (Berger) F.M. Knuth 1935
(Greek rhodon = rose)

This genus is closely related to *Pereskia* and is often united with it, but there is one difference: the ovary is central to inferior. This fundamental difference in the flower probably justifies a separate genus. 16 species. Native to West Indies and Mexico to N. Argentina.

R. bleo (H.B.K.) F.M. Knuth (*Pereskia b.* (H.B.K.) DC.)
Bushy, up to 7 m. tall. Leaves up to 20 cm. long and 4-5 cm. wide, 2-3 cm. long, borne on a stalk. Spines (1-) 5-6 (-more), black. Flowers in groups of 2-4, with short stalks, rose-red, with 12-15 petals, 3.5 cm. long. Colombia (near Badillas).

Ritterocereus Backeb. see *Stenocereus*

Rodentiophila Ritter see *Eriosyce*

Rooksbya Backeb. see *Neobuxbaumia*

Roseocactus Berger see *Ariocarpus*

Roseocereus (Backeb.) Backeb. see *Eriocereus*

Samaipaticereus Card. 1952
(*Yungasocereus*)
(after the Bolivian place-name Samaipata)

Tree-form columnar cacti with 4-9 ribs. Flowers lateral, externally scaly and bristly/woolly or only woolly, nocturnal, white, up to 5 cm. long. 2 species. Native to Bolivia.

Schlumbergera Lem. 1858
(*Zygocactus*)
(after Friedrich Schlumberger, 19th century cactus expert)

The plants of this genus are composed of short, leaf-like segments with notched or dentate margins. The radially symmetrical or zygomorphic flowers are borne at the end of the stems and have a long tube and a round to angular ovary. The bottom stamens are merged into a tube around the style. Both project out of the flowers. The stigma lobes are erect and not spreading. 3 species. Native to Brazil (Rio de Janeiro, Sao Paulo)

Schlumbergera (with *Zygocactus*) are epiphytes of the humid tropical rain forests, and must be cultivated in corresponding conditions. If they are to be grown on their own root they must be provided with virtually pure humus soil, ideally with an addition of peat. They are sensitive to any build-up of lime, i.e. soil alkalinity, and for this reason it is advisable to use rainwater or acidified water for watering. They like warm, humid air and constantly moist soil. For this reason some of the finest examples are to be found in farmhouse kitchens. Even in winter they like to be kept warm. In the case of the 'Christmas cactus' the plants should be kept slightly cooler and given almost no water after August; this helps the young segments mature, and promotes the formation of buds. After September the nocturnal temperature should be around 20°C. If buds develop after a few weeks the plants should be watered again slightly more generously, starting very slowly and building up. You can reckon on a period of about 3 months from the appearance of the first buds to the formation of the flowers, thus the date of flowering can be influenced within certain limits by varying the time at which they are kept dry and cool. See illustrations on pages 315-16.

S. gaertneri (Regel) Br. & R. (*Epiphyllopsis g.* (Regel) Berger; *Rhipsalidopsis g.* (Regel) Lindgr.) 'Easter cactus'
Segments with 3-5 tubercles on each side, 2-2.5 cm. wide and 4 (-7) cm. long. Areoles with 1-2 bristles. Flowers scarlet, 4-5 cm. long. Flower petals long, pointed. Brazil (Parana, Minas Gerais, Santa Catarina). See illustration on page 287.

S. bridgesii (Lem.) Loefgr. (*Epiphyllum b.* Lem.) 'Christmas cactus'
Segments with 2-3 notches on each side, 1.5-2.5 cm. wide and 2-5 cm. long. Flowers virtually radially symmetrical, cherry red, up to 7.5 cm. long. Ovary 4-5 angled. Presumably a hybrid.

S. truncata (Haw.) Moran (*Zygocactus truncactus* (Haw.) K. Schum.) Segments with 2-4 teeth on each side, 1.5-2.5 cm. wide and 4.5-5.5 cm. long. Areoles slightly felty, with 1-3 short, fine bristles. Flowers zygomorphic, pink to deep violet-red, up to 8 cm. long. Ovary round. Brazil (Rio de Janeiro).

Sclerocactus Br. & R. see *Pediocactus*

Selenicereus (Berger) Br. & R. 1909 (Greek selene = moon)

Climbing, thin-stemmed cacti up to 5 cm. thick, with aerial roots. Flowers nocturnal, very large (12-40 cm. long) with elongated, scaly tube, the latter thorny or bristly/hairy. Stems usually with 4-10 angles or ribs. In the very similar genus *Mediocactus* the stems usually feature 3 angles or wings. 25 species. Native to USA (Texas), Mexico, Central America, West Indies, Colombia, probably run wild in Uruguay and Argentina.

Selenicereus flowers grow up to 40 cm. long and 25 cm. wide, and are amongst the largest in the plant kingdom. Unfortunately these marvellous flowers are only open for a few hours in the night; by the following morning they are usually hanging down, slack and withered. Once the buds have grown fat, it is worthwhile staying up at night and keeping watch, as it is quite an experience to observe the flowers unfolding almost as you watch.

Selenicerei are not very demanding and grow and flower well provided that they are kept sufficiently warm, and grown in soil with a slight humus content. They should be cultivated in fairly large pots, or — better — flower troughs, and given plenty of water containing an all-purpose fertilizer, as

Selenicereus grandiflorus

Selenicereus grandiflorus

Setiechinopsis mirabilis

their rapid growth requires a plentiful supply of nitrogen. They need a support consisting of a rod or bamboo framework around which the stems can wind. They should be provided with half-shade if their window faces south or west. Even indoors the plants will flower reliably after a few years. In a greenhouse the plant will rapidly creep over a trellis on the greenhouse wall and form stems several metres long.

Stems with claw-like tubercles   S. hamatus
Stems with distinct tubercles, up to 1.5 cm. thick   S. macdonaldiae
Stems only with angles or ribs, stems usually more than 2 cm. thick.
  Spines like needles   S. grandiflorus
  Spines short, conical   S. pteranthus

S. grandiflorus (L.) Br. & R.
'Queen of the Night'
Stems with 5-7 (-8) ribs, 2-3 cm. thick. Areoles with whitish or yellowish wool, initially with 7-11 yellowish, needly spines, 0.4-1 cm. long. Outer flower petals salmon-coloured, the inner ones white. Flowers 18-30 cm. long and up to 20 cm. wide, strong vanilla scent. Mexico, Cuba, Haiti, Jamaica, Lesser Antilles

The pure species is still rare in cultivation.

S. hamatus (Scheidw.) Br. & R.
Stems with (3-) 4 (-5) ribs, with strong claw-like tubercles for climbing, up to 2.2 cm. thick. Areoles with 5-9 whitish or brownish spines, 4-6 mm. long. Outer flower petals yellow, the inner ones white. Flowers 25-40 cm. long and 20-30 cm. wide. Mexico (Veracruz, Jalapa).

S. macdonaldiae (Hook.) Br. & R.
Stems with 5 (-7) ribs, up to 1.5 cm.

Selenicereus pteranthus

thick, with raised tubercles. Areoles brownish, with a few short brown spines. Outer flower petals reddish or reddish-orange, the inner ones white or cream-coloured. Flowers 30-35 cm. long and up to 25 cm. wide, seldom flowering. ?Honduras.

S. pteranthus (Link & Otto) Br. & R.
(*S. nycticalus* Link)
'Princess of the night'
Stems with 4-5 (-6) ribs, bluish-green, (1.3-) 2-3 (-5) cm. thick. Areoles with short white wool, 6-12 spines, initially yellow, later grey, short conical, up to 6 mm. long. Flowers 25-30 cm. long. Outer flower petals reddish-yellow, the inner ones white or cream. Mexico (Tamaulipas, Veracruz).

Seticereus Backeb. see *Borzicactus*

Seticleistocactus Backeb. see *Cleistocactus*

Setiechinopsis (Backeb.) De Haas 1940
(Latin seta = bristle)

Small columnar cacti with fleshy root. Flowers long, funnel-shaped, nocturnal and with very short stamens; bristly scales and bristly/woolly outside. Style and tube are merged at the bottom to form a column. Fruit dry, bursting. 1

species. Native to Argentina (Santiago del Estero).

S. mirabilis (Spegazz.) Backeb. (*Arthrocereus m.* (Spegazz.) W.T. Marsh.). Usually not branching. Stems dark bluish-green, 10-15 cm. tall and 2-2.5 cm. thick, with 11-12 ribs. Radial spines 9-14, whitish, short. Central spines 1, brownish, 1-1.5 cm. long. Flowers borne at the crown, white and with very narrow inner flower petals, up to about 12 cm. long and 3-4 cm. wide, finely scented. The plant flowers indefatigably and is highly recommended. It regularly develops fruit and vast numbers of seed even when no outside pollination has taken place.

Soehrensia Backeb. see *Trichocereus*

Solisia Br. & R. see *Mammillaria*

Stenocereus (Berger) Riccob. 1929
(*Hertrichocereus, Isolatocereus, Lemaireocereus* p.p., *Marginatocereus, Marshallocereus, Ritterocereus*)
(Greek stenos = narrow)

Tree-form or bushy columnar cacti with (3-) 4-20 ribs. Flowers lateral or towards the end of the stems, externally scaly and felty, seldom bare, sometimes with supplementary bristles or spines, white or pink, 3-10 cm. long, usually nocturnal. Fruit very spiny when young. 23 species. Native to Mexico, Guatemala, Honduras, Costa Rica, Greater Antilles, Curacao, Venezuela.

Body covered with white, floury coating of wax   *S. beneckei*
Body with bluish-white frosted appearance at the ends of the stems
                                                         S. pruinosus
Body not conspicuously frosted
  Areoles very closely spaced, almost merging. Ribs very narrow
    Areoles very closely spaced. Radial spines 9-20. Central spines 1-4
                                                        S. dumortieri
  Areoles almost merged into each other. Spines up to 9.   *S. marginatus*
  Areoles not closely spaced
    Areoles white, woolly, no glands. Ribs 7-12 (-15), 6-9 cm. thick.
    V-shaped furrows above the areoles
                                                           S. stellatus

Areoles with black or dark brown hairs, glands. Ribs 12-19, up to 20 cm. thick.   *S. thurberi*

S. beneckei (Ehrenb.) Backeb. (*Lemaireocereus b.* (Ehrenb.) Br. & R.; *Hertrichocereus b.* (Ehrenb.) Backeb.) Initially solitary columns, not branching until old, 2-3 m. tall. Stems covered with pure white powder consisting of floury white wax, with 7-9 ribs, 5-9 cm. thick. Radial spines about 5, up to 4 cm. long. Central spines 1, up to 5 cm. long. Spines brilliant red when young, later black. Flowers ivory-coloured, brownish outside, 6-7.5 cm. long. Mexico (Guerrero, ?Puebla).

The flowers appear in winter close to the crown. This splendid plant is highly recommended, but grows best when grafted. When watering or misting take the greatest care never to allow a single drop of water on the plant, because water destroys the white powdery covering. Cultivation only under glass, not below 15°C in winter.

S. dumortieri (Scheidw.) Buxb. (*Lemaireocereus d.* (Scheidw.) Br. & R.; *Isolatocereus d.* (Scheidw.) Backeb.) Tree-form, up to 15 m. tall and 30 cm. thick. Stems 5-7.5 cm. thick, light green to bluish-green, with 5-9 sharp-edged ribs. Areoles very densely packed. Radial spines 9-20, up to 1.2 cm. long. Central spines 1 - 4, up to 3 cm. long. All spines yellowish-white. Flowers lateral, running down from the crown like a chain, white, red-brown outside, 5 cm. long and 2.5 cm. wide. Mexico (Hidalgo to Oaxaca).

Young plants of this species are usually readily available, as seed is cheap.

S. marginatus (DC.) Buxb. (*Marginatocereus m.* (DC.) Backeb.; *Pachycereus m.* (DC.) Br. & R.) Old specimens often tree-form and branching. Stems dark grey-green, 3-7 m. tall and up to 30 cm. thick in habitat, with 5-6 (-7), narrow-edged ribs. Spines all similar, up to 9, but soon falling off, reddish, later brown, up to 1.5 cm. long. Areoles almost merging into each other. Flowers individual or in groups of 2 (-3) on the areoles, white, reddish outside, 4-5 cm.

long. Mexico (Hidalgo, Querétaro, Guanajuato, Oaxaca).

A popular species which grows well. The short-spined, snow-white to brown areoles run along the sharp edges of the ribs like chains of pearls. In its homeland this species is often planted out as a hedge.

S. pruinosus (Otto) Buxb. (*Lemaireocereus p.* (Otto) Br. & R.; *Ritterocereus p.* (Otto) Backeb.) Tree-form. Stems matt green, bluish-white frosted appearance at the tip, up to 7 m. long and 10-12 cm. thick, with 5-6 bumpy ribs with sharp lengthwise furrows between them. Radial spines 5-9, 1-2 cm. long. Central spines 1 (-4), up to 4 cm. long. All spines reddish at first, then black and finally grey. Flowers white, bluish-green outside, 6-9 cm. long. Central and S. Mexico. The species grows well from seed and is very beautiful even as a young plant. Keep it warm!

S. stellatus (Pfeiff.) Riccob. (*Lemaireocereus s.* (Pfeiff.) Br. & R.) Stems matt dark green, often reddish, 1-4 m. tall and 6-9 cm. thick, with 7-12 (-15) low, slightly bumpy ribs. Areoles in the depressions. Radial spines 8-12, up to 2.5 cm. long. Central spines 1-6, up to 2.5 cm. long. Spines at first dark brown to black, later grey, the strongest thicker at the base. Flowers terminal, white, pale pink outside, 4-6 cm. long. Fruit edible. Mexico (Puebla, Oaxaca).

S. thurberi Buxb. (*Marshallocereus t.* (Engelm.) Backeb.) Branching from the base. Stems dark green, tinged with purple, later bluish-green, 3-7 m. tall and up to 20 cm. thick, with 12-19 ribs. Radial spines 7-10, about 1 cm. long. Central spines 1-3, 2-5 cm. long. Spines brownish to glossy black. Flowers terminal, pink with whitish margins, with nectar chamber, around 7 cm. long. Fruit edible. USA (S. Arizona), Mexico.

Stephanocereus Berger 1926
(Greek stephanos = corona, crown)

Bushy columnar cacti with 12-18 ribs. Flowers borne in a cephalium at the crown which is subsequently grown through and persists as a ring. Flowers slightly scaly outside, bare, white and nocturnal. 1 species. Native to Brazil (Bahia).

S. leucostele (Gürke) Berger
(*Cephalocereus l.* (Gürke) Br. & R.)
Usually solitary, stems blue-green, about 3 m. tall and up to 10 cm. thick, with 12-18 ribs. Radial spines up to about 20, 0.5-1.5 cm. long. Central spines 1 to several, up to 4 cm. long. Spines at first whitish to golden yellow, later greyish to brownish. Areoles with hairs up to 1.5 cm. long. White, woolly annular cephalium with long, projecting yellow bristles. Flowers white with yellowish tube, up to 7 cm. long.

Stetsonia Br. & R. 1920
(after F.L. Stetson, New York, 20th century)

Tree-form columnar cacti with 8-9 ribs. Flowers with elongated tube, with scales like rooftiles, bare, white, nocturnal, with an internal ring of hairs formed by modified stamens. 1 species. Native to Bolivia, Argentina.

S. coryne (Salm-Dyck) Br. & R.
Tree-form, 5-8 cm. tall and up to 40 cm. thick at the bottom. Stems bluish-green, 9-10 cm. thick, with 8-9 ribs with V-shaped furrows above the areoles. Radial spines 7-9, up to 3 cm. long. Central spines 1, up to 8 cm. long. Spines yellowish-brown or white, later glossy black. Flowers white, glossy green outside, up to 15 cm. long. The young plants take the form of club-shaped columns with long, black spines. Keep them warm and not too moist.

Strombocactus Br. & R. 1922
(Greek strombos = whipping top)

The single species has flat, rhomboid tubercles and spines which soon fall off. The bare, scaly flowers are very similar to those of *Turbinicarpus*. For this reason the two genera were formerly united under the name of *Strombocactus*. However, *Strombocactus* has dry thin-walled fruit with tiny seed, only about 0.3 mm. in size, which *Turbinicarpus* does not.

Strombocactus disciformis

1 species. Native to Mexico (Hidalgo), in the fissures of slate rock formations.

S. disciformis (DC.) Br. & R.
Body solitary, compressed globular, grey-green, 5-7 (-15) cm. wide with 12-18 rows of flat, closely spaced tubercles. Spines 1-5, like bristles, whitish, up to 1.5 cm. long, soon falling off. Flowers white to yellowish, up to 4 cm. wide and 2.5-3.5 cm. long. The species is sensitive in cultivation. Grown on its own root it demands mineral soil, full sun and careful watering. In winter it likes to be kept completely dry. Grafted plants are easier to cultivate, but the rootstock must not grow too strongly, otherwise the plants lose their characteristic appearance.

Strophocactus Br. & R. 1913
(Greek strophos = turned)

Epiphytic climbing plants with leaf-like, flat stems and nocturnal flowers with elongated tube. The flowers, borne laterally on the stems, are covered with scales whose axils are bristly and hairy. 1 species. Native to Brazil (Amazonas).

Submatucana Backeb. see *Matucana*

Subpilocereus Backeb. 1938
(Latin sub = under, Greek pilos = felt)

Tree-form or bushy columnar cacti with 4-12 ribs. Flowers lateral, on specially formed areoles, scaly and bare outside, nocturnal, 6-11 cm. long. 7 species. Native to N. Colombia, Venezuela, Curacao, Margarita, Grenada.

Sulcorebutia Backeb. 1951
(Latin sulcus = furrow)

When Backeberg established this genus in 1951 only a single species, *Sulcorebutia steinbachii,* was known. Since then the number of species described has risen to more than 40, as a result of numerous new discoveries, and the reclassification of species originally described as Rebutias. Further newly discovered species have not yet been described. The information available up to 1976 has been very carefully correlated by Brinkmann.

Sulcorebutias are small, upland cacti of elongated to compressed-globular form. The flowers are 2.3-4 cm. long, are borne more or less laterally and are scaly but bare. In fact they are very similar to those of the *Rebutia* section of the genus *Rebutia*. The main differences are Sulcorebutia's elongated areoles with strong, comb-formation spines and a thick taproot. The flower buds of *Sulcorebutia* feature broad scales and are similar to those of *Weingartia* and *Gymnocalycium*. *Sulcorebutia* is probably more closely related to these genera and *Lobivia* than to the genus *Rebutia,* but a distinct dividing line has not been found to date.

44 species up to 1976. Native to Bolivia (Cochabamba, Chuquísaca, Oruro, Santa Cruz).

All Sulcorebutias known to date come from Bolivia. There they occur at altitudes between 2000 and 3000 m. in the foothills of the Andes or on hills of the high plateau between the Andean ridges. The culture of Sulcorebutias is similar in many respects to that of Lobivias, which also come from Bolivia.

Sulcorebutias are fundamentally mountain plants, and as such like plenty of light and fresh air. The central spines of many species (familiar to us from imported plants) only appear here in Europe if the plants are provided with a very bright location. In the mountainous regions of their homeland they are exposed to a great deal of ultra-violet light. For this reason the lid of the cold frame should be opened wide whenever the weather is suitable. Sulcorebutias suffer in oppressive heat, and effective ventilation is very important. The plants will grow strongly if the temperature is allowed to drop markedly during the night. Many Sulcorebutias have a taproot, and in such cases the soil should be very permeable. In winter the plants should be kept in bright, cool, dry conditions. Short nocturnal frosts are tolerated by the majority of species. In the spring the plants should only be sprayed over at first. However, once the buds are clearly visible the plants should be watered to prevent the buds drying out. After flowering — roughly from mid-July to mid-August — the quantity of water given is slightly reduced for the plants' summer dormant period. From mid-August to mid-September the plants resume growth. At this time of year it is particularly important to provide plenty of light and good ventilation, so that the plants harden off well, form strong spine formations and set a profusion of flowers.

Because of their high light requirements Sulcorebutias are generally unsuitable for indoor cultivation. However, they do very well on an outside window ledge — provided that they are given adequate protection from rainfall — or in a well-lit, very well ventilated garden frame or greenhouse. As the plants grow excellently on their own root, grafting is only recommended where you wish to propagate genetically true offspring of a rare species.

Many Sulcorebutias are richly clustering plants, and can very easily be propagated by taking cuttings. The side shoots often form roots when still attached to the mother plant. Propagation from seed is also easy, but good *Sulcorebutia* seed is unfortunately not often available and relatively expensive, as the seed capsules only contain a few seed each. They are located very low down on the plants and are very difficult to harvest. There is also a high risk of of unwanted hybrids with Sulcorebutias.

The genus has quickly made many friends among cactus growers. The spine formation of the plants is often splendid, and the flowers, usually brightly coloured and luminous, are formed profusely and readily. The small size of the plants allows the enthusiast to assemble a specialized collection even when space is limited.

Sulcorebutia arenacea

Flowers yellow or orange
  Spines up to 2 mm. long. Flowers orange with yellow throat, up to 4 cm. long
                                                  S. canigueralii
  Spines more than 2 mm. long. Flowers other colours, up to 3 cm. long
    Radial spines 2-7 mm. long
      Spines of sandy appearance   *S. arenacea*
      Spines not of sandy appearance
        Spines up to 3 mm. long   *S. krugerii*
        Spines 3-7 mm. long   *S. candiae*
    Radial spines more than 8 mm. long
      Ribs up to 32. Spines 8-12 mm. long. Flowers with white throat   *S. krahnii*
      Ribs around 20. Spines 20-30 mm. long. Flowers without white throat
                                                S. glomeriseta
Flowers carmine red to lilac or purple Spines up to 2 mm. long (flowers with white throat)   *S. rauschii*
  Spines 2-7 mm. long
    Spines whitish to yellowish
      Spines with fine ciliate hairs   *S. alba*
      Spines without ciliate hairs
        Flowers with yellow throat. Ribs around 10. Radial spines 10-12 *S. tunariensis*
        Flower throat either white or same colour. Ribs around 16. Radial spines 13-20
          Flowers 4 cm. long. Spines transparent white with dark base *S. taratensis*
          Flowers 3 cm. long. Spines with white tip, pink in the centre, base black
                                               S. mizquensis
    Spines darker
      Central spines present
        Radial spines 14-18. Throat of same colour   *S. mentosa*
        Radial spines 11 or more. Throat yellow   *S. hoffmanniana*
      Central spines absent
        Radial spines 12-14. Throat yellow   *S. verticillacantha*
        Radial spines around 14-20. Throat of same colour   *S. lepida*
  Spines more than 12 mm. long
    Radial spines 6-8   *S. steinbachii*
    Radial spines more than 8
      Spines light. Flowers 2.8 cm. long   *S. glomerispina*
      Spines brilliant yellow (some). Flowers up to 3.5 cm. long   *S. flavissima*
      Spines darker. Flowers 3.5 cm. long
        Ribs 19-21   *S. totorensis*
        Ribs 13-16   *S. tiraquensis*

S. alba Rausch
Body up to 2 cm. tall and 3.5 cm. wide, not clustering, up to 23 ribs, grey-green, often with violet frosted appearance. Radial spines 20-24, 3-4 mm. long. Central spines absent to 6, 2-3 mm. long. Spines all white, reddish to black at the base, with ciliate hairs. Flowers violet-red, throat pink, white underneath, 3 cm. long and wide. Bolivia (Chuquisaca).

S. arenacea (Card.) Ritter
Body 2-3.5 cm. tall and 2.5-5 cm. wide, yellowish-greenish with about 30 ribs. Spines 14-16, whitish-yellowish, sandy effect, 5 mm. long. Flowers golden yellow, 3 cm. long. Bolivia (Cochabamba).

S. candiae (Card.) Buin. & Donald
Body 3 cm. tall and up to 5 cm. wide, dark green with 15-20 ribs. Radial spines yellowish, 3-7 mm. long. Central spines absent. Flowers yellow, up to 3 cm. long. Bolivia (Cochabamba).

S. canigueralii (Card.) Buin. & Donald
2 cm. wide and 1 cm. tall, greyish, with about 13 ribs. Radial spines 11-14, whitish with brown base, 1.5-2 mm. long. Central spines absent (or 1-2). Flowers orange with yellow throat, up to 4 cm. long and wide. Bolivia (Chuquisaca).

S. flavissima Rausch
Body 2.5 cm. tall and 6 cm. wide, fresh green, with up to 18 ribs. Spines up to 24, some of them brilliant yellow, up to 20 mm. long. Flowers magenta, up to 3.5 cm. long. Bolivia (between Aiquile and Mizque).

S. glomeriseta (Card.) Ritter
Body up to about 6 cm. wide, with around 20 ribs. Spines numerous, white, 2-3 cm. long. Flowers golden yellow, 2.5 cm. long. Bolivia (Cochabamba).

S. glomerispina (Card.) Buin. & Donald
5 cm. tall and wide, blue-green, with about 20 ribs. Radial spines 10-14, white to orange, 5-20 mm. long. Flowers purple, up to 3 cm. long. Bolivia (Cochabamba).

S. hoffmanniana (Backeb.) Backeb.
2.5-3 cm. tall and up to 4.5 cm. wide, solitary or clustering in culture, with around 24 ribs. Radial spines 11, later more, brownish, eventually with red-brown base, more than 3 mm. long. Central spines later up to 2, some of them with frosted appearance, up to 8 mm. long. Flowers red with golden yellow throat. Bolivia (Oruro).

S. krahnii Rausch
Body 5 cm. tall and up to 8 cm. wide, with up to 32 ribs. Radial spines about 24, white to grey, 1 cm. long. Central spines 3-7, brown to black, 1.2 cm. long. Flowers yellow with white throat, 2.5-3 cm. long. Bolivia (Santa Cruz).

S. krugerii (Card.) Ritter
Body about 5 cm. wide, light to dark green. Radial spines up to about 20, whitish to yellowish, up to 3 mm. long. Central spines absent (or 1-2), brownish. Flowers golden yellow to orange, up to 2.5 cm.long. Bolivia (Cochabamba).

S. lepida Ritter
Body 1-3 cm. wide, dark green, with about 16 ribs. Spines around 14-20, black, red-brown, brown or golden yellow, 3-7 mm. long. Flowers vermilion to carmine, 2-3 cm. long. Bolivia (Cochabamba).

S. mentosa Ritter
Body 3-6 cm. wide, glossy dark green with about 20 ribs. Radial spines 14-

Sulcorebutia

Sulcorebutia canigueralii

Sulcorebutia flavissima

Sulcorebutia glomeriseta

Sulcorebutia hoffmanniana

Sulcorebutia krahnii

297

Sulcorebutia krugerii

Sulcorebutia mentosa

Sulcorebutia mizquensis

Sulcorebutia rauschii

Sulcorebutia taratensis

Sulcorebutia 'calle-calle', from Sulcorebutia verticillacantha

Sulcorebutia steinbachii, variable in flower and spine formation

18, around 5 mm. long. All spines black or dark red. Flowers purple, 3 cm. long. Bolivia (Cochabamba).

S. mizquensis Rausch
Body about 2.5 cm. tall and 3 cm. wide, with up to 17 ribs. Radial spines up to 20, white-tipped, pink in the centre and black at the base, up to 4 mm. long. Central spines absent. Flowers light to dark magenta, often with white throat, 3 cm. long. Bolivia (Cochabamba).

S. rauschii G. Frank
Body 1.5 cm. tall and up to 3 cm.

thick, black-green to violet with up to 16 ribs. Radial spines up to 11, black, 1-1.5 mm. long. Central spines absent. Flowers magenta-pink with white throat, 3 cm. long. Bolivia (Chuquisaca).

S. steinbachii (Werderm.) Backeb.
Body up to 6 cm. tall and 4 cm. thick, with up to about 13 ribs. Radial spines 6-8, yellowish, brownish to almost black, up to 2.5 cm. long. Central spines 1-3, black or brown, up to 2.5 cm. long. Flowers light red, blood red or carmine-violet, around 3.5 cm. long. Bolivia (Cochabamba).

S. taratensis (Card.) Buin. & Donald
2-5 cm. tall and up to 3.5 cm. wide, dark green to purple, with around 16 ribs. Radial spines 13-16, transparent white with dark base, 3-4 mm. long. Central spines absent, seldom 1. Flowers magenta, 4 cm. long. Bolivia (Cochabamba).

S. tiraquensis (Card.) Ritter
Body up to 5 cm. tall and 12 cm. wide, with 13-26 ribs. Radial spines 12-13 when young, central spines 1-2, yellowish-brownish. Later up to 30 spines or more, dark brown, 0.5-3 cm. long. Flowers purple, 3.5 cm. long. Bolivia (Cochabamba).

S. totorensis (Card.) Ritter
Body up to 2 cm. tall and 6 cm. wide, dark green, with 19-21 ribs. Spines dark brown, 0.3-2 cm. long. Flowers dark purple, 3.5 cm. long. Bolivia (Cochabamba).

S. verticillacantha Ritter
Body up to 3 cm. wide, clustering, with 13-21 ribs divided up into tubercles. Spines 12-14, at first brown with black base, then grey, 2-4 mm. long. The flowers are light, violet-purple to vermilion, orange towards the throat. One variety has yellow flowers. Bolivia.

Tacinga Br. & R. 1919
(derived from Caatinga, the name of the dry North Brazilian bushland)

This genus is a member of the Opuntioideae sub-family, but it does not fit comfortably in that company. It does have glochids and a hard white seed coat, but in other respects has little similarity to Opuntias, for they are climbing plants with leaves of round cross-section and hairy stems. The flowers of *Tacinga* are usually borne at the end of the stems and have a fairly long tube, but relatively few petals which are rolled back. They do not open until the evening. The stamens and style are long and projecting. 2 species. Native to Brazil (Bahia).

T. funalis Br. & R.
Up to 12 m. tall. Stems 1-1.5 cm. thick and round like a shaft. No spines, only very short, fine glochids. Flowers pale green, 7-8 cm. long. Brazil (N. Bahia).

Tephrocactus Lem. emend. Backeb.
see *Opuntia*

Thelocactus (K. Schum.) Br. & R. 1922
(Greek thele = nipple)

The genus *Thelocactus* stands between the North American ribbed globular cacti, such as *Echinocactus* or *Ferocactus,* and the typical tubercled cacti such as *Coryphantha* and *Mammillaria. Thelocactus* includes ribbed species as well as plants whose ribs are divided up into tubercles. This variability also occurs in other genera. More important is the fact that the flower-bearing areoles of *Thelocactus* are elongated in a short furrow, at the end of which the flower develops. In *Coryphantha* the furrow is extended as far as the base of the tubercle, while *Mammillaria* has no hint of a furrow; the flowers are formed in the axils. The very broad, funnel-shaped flowers of *Thelocactus* are borne close to the crown and are scaly but otherwise bare. The coarse, black, warty seeds are typical of the most common type of cactus seed, and are not smooth, pitted or brown, as is characteristic of the North American tubercled cactus genera. 28 species. Native to Mexico, USA (Texas).

Thelocacti are among the most beautiful of cacti and are highly recommended to the amateur, as they often feature powerful, brightly-coloured spine formations and bear large flowers. They thrive very well on their own root in a soil of mainly mineral content, and demand plenty of warmth and sunshine in the vegetative period. Cultivation is not difficult, and even the seedlings grow well.

The majority of species (especially the *T. bicolor* group) should be watered moderately, while a few species need rather less moisture. In winter most of the species like to be kept at around 6-10°C and dry. A few species from warmer native regions (e.g. *T. hexaedrophorus*) should be overwintered slightly warmer at about 12°C and should not be kept completely dry.

T. bicolor (Gal.) Br. & R.
Body up to 10 cm. wide with 8-13 straight or slightly spiral ribs. Radial spines 9-18, up to 3 cm. long. Central spines usually 4, one 3-5 cm. long, the upper one slightly flattened. Flowers 4-6 cm. long, dark purple-pink, lighter at the base. USA (S. Texas) to central Mexico.

This species is one of the most widespread in collections, its great popularity resting on its beautiful spine formation, often brightly coloured, and its large red flowers. It makes no special cultural demands.

var. bolansis (Runge) F.M. Knuth

Spines all strong, not clearly divided into radial and central spines
  Ribs with broad, angular tubercles
    Spines round
      Spines all with fine transverse rings. Flowers white to reddish   *T. hexaedrophorus*
      Spines not ringed. Flowers deep pink   *T. bueckii*
    Spines partially flattened. Flowers light violet   *T. heterochromus*
  Ribs with narrow, tall tubercles
    Spines later falling off   *T. phymatothelos*
    Spines persisting
      Spines around 15, later becoming fibrous   *T. nidulans*
      Spines 3-6   *T. lophothele*
Spines different: radial spines finer, central spines clearly different or absent
  Central spines absent
    Flowers white, 4 cm. wide   *T. rinconensis*
    Flowers lilac, carmine inside, up to 8.5 cm. wide   *T. schwarzii*
  Central spines absent or present. Flowers 2.5-3 cm. long. Root beet-like
       T. knuthianus
  Central spines present
    Flowers spreading, inner flower petals slightly spatula-shaped
      Flowers 2 cm. wide   *T. saueri*
      Flowers 3.5 cm. wide   *T. conothelos*
      Flowers 5-6 cm. wide and long   *T. bicolor*
    Flowers more funnel-shaped, 4 cm. wide and long, with lanceolate inner petals
       T. saussieri

Above and right: members of Thelocactus bicolor group

Thelocactus bicolor var. bolansis

Thelocactus conothelos

Thelocactus hexaedrophorus

Thelocactus knuthianus

White spines and up to 25 radial spines

var. tricolor (K. Schum.) F.M. Knuth
Very powerful, dense spines, tending to red or whitish. N.E. Mexico.

var. wagnerianus (Berger) Krainz (*T.w.* Berger)
Central spines all round with thicker base, 1.5-2 cm. long. E. Mexico.

T. bueckii (Klein) Br. & R.
Body with wide, angular tubercles. Spines around (4-) 7, flexible, reddish. Flowers glossy deep pink. Mexico (Tamaulipas).

T. conothelos (Regel & Klein) F.M. Knuth
Body up to 10 cm. tall and 7.5 cm. wide, with around 12 ribs divided up into tubercles. Radial spines 14-16, white, up to 1.8 cm. long. Central spines (1-) 2-4, light in colour, 1.5 cm. to more than 3.5 cm. long. Flowers purple violet, 3.5 cm. wide. Mexico (Tamaulipas).

var. aurantiacus Glass & Foster
Radial spines around 23. Flowers pale yellow. Mexico (Nuevo León).

T. heterochromus (Web.) van Oosten
Body up to 15 cm. wide with around 8-9 ribs divided into tubercles. Radial spines 7-10, the upper radial spine more or less flattened and wider, up to 3 cm. long. Central spines 1, sometimes furrowed, up to 4 cm. long. All spines reddish to brownish or with bands of very different colours. Flowers pale violet, often darker inside, up to 6 cm. long. Mexico (Chihuahua to Coahuila).

T. hexaedrophorus (Lem.) Br. & R.
Body up to 15 cm. wide, with 12-13 ribs divided up into 6-sided tubercles. Radial spines 6-9, up to 1.8 cm.long. Central spines 0-2, 2-3 m. long. All spines with fine transverse rings, yellowish to reddish or brownish. Flowers white to reddish, 6 cm. long. Mexico (Tamaulipas, San Luis Potosí).

var. decipiens Berger
Small dark green form with appressed spines.

T. knuthianus (Böd.) Bravo (*Neolloydia k.* (Böd.) F.M. Knuth; *Gymnocactus k.* (Böd.) Backeb.).
Body up to 9 cm. tall and wide, with around 13 ribs divided up into

tubercles. Root beet-like. Radial spines 9-20, up to 1.5 cm. long. Central spines absent or 1, slightly longer. Spines initially yellowish-white, reddish-brown above, later white, dark-tipped. Flowers lilac pink, 2.5-3.5 cm. long. Mexico (San Luis Potosí).

T. lophothele (Salm-Dyck) Br. & R. Body up to 25 cm. tall, with 15-20 ribs divided up to form tubercles. Radial spines 3-5, initially black to light brown or yellowish, the upper ones ruby red, up to 4 cm. long. Central spines absent or 1. Flowers yellowish-white to sulphur yellow, peach-coloured and rose red when fading, 4-6 cm. long. Mexico (Chihuahua).

T. nidulans (Quehl) Br. & R. Body up to 20 cm. wide and 10 cm. tall, with 20 or more ribs divided up into tubercles. Spines around 15, projecting at all angles, central and radial spines virtually indistinguishable, the longest ones 4-6 (-10) cm. long, at first brownish, later grey-white and fibrous. Flowers pale yellowish-white, 4 cm. long. Mexico.

T. phymatothelos (Poselg.) Br. & R. Body up to 5 cm. wide, with about 13 spiral ribs, very bumpy. Spines absent or 1-4, at first blackish, later turning grey, 1-2 cm. long. Flowers pink to purple, about 5 cm. long and wide. Mexico.

T. rinconensis (Poselg.) Br. & R. (*T. rinconadensis* (Poselg.) Br. & R.) Body grey-green or blue-green, 6-8 cm. tall and up to 12 cm. thick, usually with 13 ribs, which are divided up into laterally compressed tubercles. Radial spines absent or up to 4, straight, 1.5 cm. long. Central spines absent. Flowers white, 4 cm. long and wide. Mexico (Nuevo León).

T. saueri (Böd.) Berger (*Gymnocactus s.* (Böd.) Backeb.) Body up to 4 cm. tall and 6 cm. wide, dull grey-green, with 13 ribs which are divided up into 6-sided tubercles. Areoles white, woolly. Radial spines 12-14, white, brown-tipped, up to 1.5 cm. long. Central spines 1-2, dark-tipped, up to 2 cm. long. Flowers white with pink throat, up to 2.5 cm. long and 2 cm. wide. Mexico (Tamaulipas).

Thelocactus lophothele

Thelocactus rinconensis

Thelocactus saueri

T. saussieri (Web.) Berger (*Echinocactus s.* Web.)
Body up to 20 cm. wide, with around 20 ribs divided up into tubercles. Radial spines 9-15, white, up to 1.5 cm. long. Central spines 4, brownish, 3-4 cm. long. Flowers purple-red, 4 cm. long. Mexico (San Luis Potosí).

T. schwarzii Backeb.
Body about 6 cm. tall with around 13 ribs. Radial spines 13-14, tending to comb-formation and more or less flattened, whitish or yellowish, red below, 1.5-2 cm. long. Central spines absent. Flowers lilac, carmine inside, up to 8.5 cm. wide. Mexico (Tamaulipas).

Thelocephala Y. Ito see *Neoporteria*

Thrixanthocereus Backeb. 1937
(Greek thrix = hair, anthos = flower)

Bushy, columnar cacti with 14-25 ribs. Flowers produced from a lateral cephalium which is slightly recessed. They are scaly and hairy outside, have a nectar chamber, are nocturnal and evil-smelling. 4 species. Native N. Peru, Ecuador.

According to observations by Cullmann *T. senilis* has black seed similar to *Espostoa,* while the two other species have tiny brown seed with a very greatly enlarged hilum and are of hat- or cap-shaped form. All species grow well on their own root, but do not like to be kept too cold in winter.

Thrixanthocereus blossfeldiorum, cristate form

They are beautiful plants, and if grown in a greenhouse or a *Cereus* frame will eventually produce a cephalium. Only with *T. senilis* does one need rather more patience.

T. blossfeldiorum (Werderm.) Backeb. (*Espostoa b.* (Werderm.) Buxb.)
Usually solitary. Stems up to 4 m. long and 10 cm. thick, with 18-25 ribs. Radial spines around 20-25, translucent, up to 0.8 cm. long. Central spines up to about 7, brownish to black, about 3 cm. long. Areoles initially white, flocked and woolly. Recessed cephalium formed when plants are about 0.8-1 m. tall, covering about 4-7 ribs. The cephalium faces the brighter, warmer side, and consists of dense, yellowish-white wool and numerous white, brownish or black bristles, closely spaced, of which the longest grow to 4-5 cm. Flowers cream-white, up to 6 cm. long. Fruit a dry capsule which splits laterally. N. Peru (Huancabamba- and Olmos valley).

T. cullmannianus Ritter
Usually solitary. Stems grey-green, up to 2 m. or more long and 3-6 cm. thick, with 18-24 ribs. Spines 90-120, most of them very fine, white, odd ones red-tipped or yellowish or brownish, 0.5-3 cm. long. Areoles whitish. Cephalium produced when plants are about 50 cm. tall, divided up into separate flowering zones. Each areole in the cephalium has up to 150 or more fine white or brown spines, 1-3 cm. long. According to Cullmann this is a pseudo-cephalium. Flowers white, 4.5-6 cm. long. N. Peru (Cajamarca).

T. senilis Ritter (*Espostoa s.* (Ritter) Buxb.)
Branching bushes. Stems 2-4 m. long and 4-6 cm. thick, with (14-) 18 slightly bumpy ribs. Radial spines 40-50, central spines 20-30, very similar. 1-3 central spines, stronger, standing in a vertical line, yellow to brownish-red and 3-4 cm. long. Remaining spines white and up to 1 cm. long, plus a further 30 fine white woolly hairs, 1 cm. long, which completely envelop the body. Cephalium produced when plants reach 2 m. tall, yellow,

Thrixanthocereus senilis

brownish or fox red. Unlike the previous species the crown is straight rather than curving over towards the cephalium. The cephalium is grown through each year, leaving annular cephalium zones. Flowers deep purple-red, 4.5-6 cm. long. Fruit a fleshy berry. N. Peru.

Opuntias are a good rootstock for this species. The grafted piece of shoot will cluster, forming an ornamental miniature tree. Grafting is also the best method of propagation, as cuttings root poorly and slowly.

Toumeya Br. & R. see *Pediocactus* and *Turbinicarpus*

Trichocereus (Berger) Riccob.
1909 (*Helianthocereus, Leucostele*)
(Greek thrix = hair)

The genus *Trichocereus* includes more or less strongly branching columnar cacti which are usually multi-ribbed and are very spiny. The large funnel-shaped flowers have a long, slender, scaly tube with dense hair, but devoid of spines and bristles. A clearly separate ring of throat stamens is a feature of the flowers. Most Trichocerei have nocturnal white flowers, more rarely diurnal coloured ones (*Helianthocereus*). This characteristic makes it difficult to distinguish between the genus and *Lobivia* and *Echinopsis*; the problem is explained in greater detail under *Echinopsis*.

Trichocereus hybrid 'Theleflora'

Flowers nocturnal, always white
  Flowers 15-25 cm. long
    Radial and central spines almost indistinguishable. Tree-form
     Spines up to 10 cm. long, yellowish, persisting
      Ribs 8-14. Spines 8-15   *T. terscheckii, T. werdermannianus*
      Ribs 4-8. Spines 2-6   *T. bridgesii*
     Spines up to 2 cm. long, brown, more or less temporary   *T. pachanoi*
    Radial and central spines different. Bush-form
     Central spines more than 1 cm.long (stems usually more than 6 cm. thick)
      Ribs 10-17. Flowers 14-15 cm.long   *T. chilensis*
      Ribs 6-11. Flowers 18-25 cm. long
       Ribs 9-11. Flowers 20-25 cm. long   *T. candicans*
       Ribs 6-9. Flowers 18 cm. long   *T. macrogonus*
     Central spines up to about 1 cm. long (stems glossy green, up to 6 cm. thick)
     Central spines usually 4 (-5). Radial spines around 20, all red at the base
                                       T. purpureopilosus

     Central spines 1 (-4). Radial spines around 10.
      Light green, more or less branching, up to 2 m. tall   *T. spachianus*
      Dark green, usually solitary, up to 30 cm. tall   *T. schickendantzii*
  Flowers 9-12 cm. long (Ribs deeply notched)   *T. fulvilanus*
Flowers diurnal (7-12 cm. long, white, yellow or red)
  Flowers white. Bushy to tree-form   *T. pasacana*
  Flowers yellow or red, more or less terminal. Up to 1 m. tall.
   Body columnar with 12 to about 25 ribs.
    Central spines 6-9, up to 7 cm. long. Radial spines 12-18, up to 4 cm. long
                                        T. poco
    Central spines 1-6, up to 6 cm. long. Radial spines 9-11 or more, around
    1.5 cm. long   *T. huascha*
    Central spines usually 1, about 1 cm. long. Radial spines usually 8-9 (-12)
                                  T. grandiflorus
   Body globular to elongated with very many ribs   *T. bruchii*

Trichocereus candicans hybrid

Trichocereus hybrid

About 75 species. Native to Andes of Ecuador to Chile and Argentina.

The genus *Trichocereus* includes species with very decorative spine formations as well as some which produce very beautiful flowers; those species which remain smaller flower when still young. Many species (e.g. *T. pachanoi, T. spachianus, T. macrogonus, T. bridgesii, T. pasacana* and *T. chilensis* and others) are also widely used as vigorous, sturdy grafting rootstocks. Trichocerei are very robust, tolerant plants, and grow well in ordinary cactus soil provided that it is not too impoverished. Moisture levels should be constant during the growth period and plenty of fertilizer should be supplied. In winter they should be kept cool and dry, in which conditions many species will tolerate night frosts. The larger species will only grow to their full beauty in large pots or — even better — when planted out. They require plenty of sunshine if they are to produce a good spine formation and flower well. The beautiful hybrids between *Trichocereus* and *Echinopsis* are also worthy of mention here. Propagation from seed is possible, but propagation by cuttings is usual with clustering species.

Trichocereus candicans

Trichocereus grandiflorus

Trichocereus fulvilanus

Trichocereus huascha

T. bridgesii (Salm-Dyck) Br. & R. (*Echinopsis lagenaeformis* (Salm-Dyck) H. Friedr. & G.D. Rowl.)
Up to 5 m. tall and 15 cm. thick, light bluish-green with 4-8 ribs. Spines 2-6, up to 10 cm. long. Flowers white, nocturnal, about 18 cm. long, jasmine scent. Good grafting stock. Bolivia (La Paz).

T. bruchii (Br. & R.) Ritter (*Lobivia b.* Br. & R.; *Soehrensia b.* (Br. & R.) Backeb.; *Lobivia formosa* (Pfeiff.) Dodds ssp. *b.* (Br. & R.) Rausch)
Usually solitary. Body globular to

elongated with 50 or more straight ribs. Radial spines 9-14. Central spines up to about 4. Flowers terminal, deep red, diurnal, about 5 cm. wide. Argentina (Jujuy to Catamarca).

T. candicans (Gill.) Br. & R.
Erect to prostrate, up to 1 m. long and 16 cm. thick, grass green to bluish-green with 9-11 ribs. Radial spines 10-14, up to 4 cm. long. Central spines (1-) 4, up to 10 cm. long. Flowers white, nocturnal, 18-25 cm. long. Argentina (Mendoza, Córdoba).

T. chilensis (Colla) Br. & R. (*T. chiloensis* (Colla) Br. & R.; *Echinopsis c.* (Colla) H. Friedr.)
Up to 3 m. tall and 6-12 cm. thick, with 10-17 ribs. Radial spines 8-12, up to 4 cm. long. Central spines 1 (-4), 5-6 (-12) cm. long. Flowers white, nocturnal, about 14 cm. long. Chile (Atacama to Curico).

T. fulvilanus Ritter
Considered by Backeberg to be a form of *T. deserticolus* (Werderm.) Loos. 1-1.5 m. tall and 4-7 cm. thick, grass green to grey-green with 8-12 (-13) deeply notched ribs. Radial spines 9-12, 1.5-3 cm. long. Central spines 2-4 (-6), 3-10 (-18) cm. long. Spines at first dark brown, turning grey. Flowers white, nocturnal, 9-12 cm. long, scented. Chile (Taltal).

T. grandiflorus (Br. & R.) Backeb. (*Helianthocereus g.* (Br. & R.) Backeb.)
Up to 35 cm. tall and 6 cm. thick, with around 14 ribs. Radial spines usually 8-9 (-12). Central spines usually 1, around 1 cm. long. Flowers blood red, diurnal, about 8-10 cm. long. The species flowers easily, from a height of about 10 cm. Argentina (Catamarca).

T. huascha (Web.) Br. & R. (*Helianthocereus h.* (Web.) Backeb.; *Echinopsis h.* (Web.) H. Friedr. & G.D. Rowl.)
Up to 90 cm. tall and 5-8 cm. thick,

with 12-18 ribs. Radial spines 9-11 or more, about 1.5 cm. long. Central spines 1-2, up to 6 cm. long. Flowers golden yellow or red, diurnal, 7-10 cm. long. Argentina (Catamarca).

T. macrogonus (Salm-Dyck) Riccob. (*Echinopsis m.* (Salm-Dyck) H. Friedr. & G.D. Rowl.)
Up to 3 m. tall and 9 cm. thick, green to blue-green, with 6-9 ribs. Radial spines 6-9, up to 2 cm. long. Central spines 1-3, up to 5 cm. long. Flowers white, nocturnal, 18 cm. long. Very good grafting stock. Argentina, Bolivia.

Trichocereus poco

T. pachanoi Br. & R.
Tree-form, up to 6 m. tall and up to 12 cm. thick, bluish-green with 6-8 ribs. Spines 3-7, up to 2 cm. long or almost spineless. The flowers are white, nocturnal, up to 23 cm. long and scented. *T. pachanoi* is a very good grafting stock. Ecuador.

T. pasacana (Web.) Br. & R. (*Helianthocereus p.* (Web.) Backeb.; *Echinopsis p.* (Web.) H. Friedr. & G.D. Rowl.)
Up to 10 m. tall and 30-50 cm. thick, matt pale green, with 15-35 ribs. Spines 4-14 cm. long. Areoles red-brown. Flowers white, diurnal, up to 12 cm. long. Argentina (Catamarca). S. Bolivia. The fruit is edible and is known as 'pasacana'.

T. poco Backeb. (*Helianthocereus p.* (Backeb.) Backeb.)
With about 25 or more ribs. Radial spines 12-18, up to 4 cm. long. Central spines 6-9, up to 7 cm. long. Flowers dark red, diurnal, up to 12 m. long. N. Argentina, Bolivia.

T. purpureopilosus Weingt. (*Echinopsis p.* (Weingt.) H. Friedr. & G.D. Rowl.)
Usually only 20 (-32) cm. tall, 6 cm. thick, glossy dark green with about 12 ribs. Radial spines up to 20, up to 0.7 cm. long. Central spines usually 4 (-5), up to 0.8 cm. long. Flowers white, nocturnal, up to 21 cm. long and 14 cm. wide. Flowers when only 10-15 cm. tall. Argentina.

T. schickendantzii (Web.) Br. & R. (*Echinopsis s.* (Web.) H. Friedr. & G.D. Rowl.)
Up to 30 (-75) cm. tall and 5-6 cm. thick, glossy dark green, with 14-18 ribs. Radial spines about 10. Central spines 1-8, all spines 0.5-1 cm. long. Flowers white, nocturnal, up to 22 cm. long and 15 cm. wide, scented. N.W. Argentina.

T. spachianus (Lem.) Riccob. (*Echinopsis s.* (Lem.) H. Friedr. & G.D. Rowl.)
Up to 2 m. tall and up to 6 cm. thick,

glossy green, with 10-15 ribs. Radial spines 8-10, up to 1 cm. long. Central spines 1 (-3), 1 cm. or longer. Flowers white, nocturnal, 20 cm. long and up to 15 cm. wide. W. Argentina.

T. terscheckii Br. & R.
Up to 12 m. tall and 45 cm. thick with 8-14 ribs. Spines 8-15, up to 10 cm. long. Flowers white, nocturnal, 15-20 cm. long. Argentina (Catamarca, La Rioja, Tucumán, Salta, Jujuy).

T. werdermannianus Backeb. (*Echinopsis w.* (Backeb.) H. Friedr. & G.D. Rowl.)
Trunk up to 5 m. tall and 60 cm. thick. Stems pale green to greyish with 6-14 or more ribs, up to 16 cm. thick. Radial spines around 8, central spine 1. Spines yellowish, horn-coloured or brownish, up to 7 cm. long. Flowers white, up to 20 cm. long. S. Bolivia.

Turbinicarpus (Backeb.) Buxb. & Backeb. 1937 (*Normanbokea, Toumeya* p.p.)
(Latin turbineus = whipping-top shape, Greek karpos = fruit)

Greyish to blue-green or brown cacti, usually small, with spines which are usually papery, hairy or feathery. The flowers are naked, the fruit a laterally

Turbinicarpus group

bursting berry the shape of a whipping-top. The similar genus *Strombocactus* has a dry, thin-walled fruit with tiny seed only about 0.3 mm. in size. *T. pseudopectinatus* and *T. valdezianus* were classified in the genus *Pelecyphora* for a long time. In fact *T. pseudopectinatus* has the same axe-shaped tubercles and comb-formation spines as *Pelecyphora asseliformis*. However, these curious characteristics occur a third time in *Mammillaria pectinifera* (*Solisia pectinata*), but none of the 3 species is closely related. *T. valdezianus* also has a characteristic feature, in this case pinnate, or feathery, spines, but this also occurs in non-related species, e.g. *Mammillaria plumosa*. In the end a separate genus *Normanbokea* was established for the two exceptional species. However, Glass and Forster have pointed out that the curious spine formation also occurs in other *Turbinicarpus* species, but only in young plants, whereas in this case the formation is permanent. The exact definition of the genus is still widely disputed.

6 species. Native to N. and Central Mexico, usually in the Chihuahua desert, all of them discovered in the last 50 years.

Turbinicarpus plants remain small, are very variable in spine formation, and flower very beautifully. They are enjoying increasing popularity amongst cactus growers.

In their native habitat some species evidently grow in rock fissures. In

Turbinicarpus schmiedickeanus var. schwarzii

Turbinicarpus pseudomacrochele

Spines in comb-formation	*T. pseudopectinatus*
Spines not in comb-formation	
Spines with feathery hairs	*T. valdezianus*
Spines devoid of feathery hairs	
Spines thin, bristly, curved (up to 2 cm. long)	*T. pseudomacrochele*
Spines like needles	
Spines no more than 1 cm. long, straight, not flattened, more or less persisting	
	T. lophophoroides
Spines thick, 1-4, curving upward, more or less flattened, later falling off	
	T. schmiedickeanus
Tubercles longer than wide. Spines up to 2.5 cm. long. Flowers pink with darker central stripe	var. *schmiedickeanus*
Tubercles usually wider than long	
Spines up to 1 cm. long. Flowers white to cream-coloured	var. *klinkerianus*
Spines up to 4 cm. long and more. Flowers white to pink	var. *macrochele*
Tubercles completely flat, covered with fine spots. Body reminiscent of *Lophophora*	var. *schwarzii*

cultivation they require a permeable, mineral soil and a warm, bright summer location, but not in brilliant sunshine. Because of their taproot they should be watered fairly infrequently. Some of them flower very early in the spring, and should therefore be kept in a bright but cool (5-8°C) location in the winter. The plants grow slowly and should not be forced, otherwise they soon look unnatural and flabby, and may even split. If you can provide appropriate cultural conditions grafting is not necessary, but in any case a slow growing rootstock should be selected. Propagation from seed is not difficult, but the seedlings grow slowly.

Turbinicarpus pseudopectinatus

Left: Turbinicarpus valdezianus, red and white;
right: Turbinicarpus pseudopectinatus

T. lophophoroides (Werderm.) Buxb. & Backeb. (*Strombocactus l.* F.M. Knuth & Buxb.; *Toumeya l.* (Werderm.) Bravo & W.T. Marsh.)
Up to 4.5 cm. wide. Spines 2-6, light brown to blackish, no more than 1 cm. long. Crown densely woolly. Flowers pink to whitish, 3.5 cm. wide. Mexico (San Luis Potosí).

T. pseudomacrochele (Backeb.) Buxb. & Backeb. (*Strombocactus p.* Backeb.; *Toumeya p.* (Backeb.) Bravo & W.T. Marsh.)
3-4 cm. wide. Spines 6-10, thin bristle-like and curved, up to 2 cm. long. Flowers white with pink central stripe, about 3.5 cm. wide. Mexico (San Luis Potosí).

T. pseudopectinatus (Backeb.) Glass & Foster (*Pelecyphora p.* Backeb.; *Normanbokea p.* Kladiwa & Buxb.)
2.5-4.5 (-6) cm. wide. Tubercles axe-shaped, with around 44-56 comb-formation spines, white, about 1.5 mm. long. Flowers around 3 cm. wide, white, with pink central stripe or reddish-violet. Mexico (Tamaulipas, Nuevo León).

T. schmiedickeanus (Böd.) Buxb. & Backeb.
About 4 cm. wide and up to 5 cm. tall. Spines 1-5, strong, long, curving upward, projecting high above the crown, soon falling off, brownish to blackish. Flowers white or pink, 2.5 cm. wide.

var. schmiedickeanus (*Strombocactus s.* (Böd.) Berger; *Toumeya s.* (Böd.) Bravo & W.T. Marsh.)
Tubercles longer than wide. Spines up to 2.5 cm. long. Flowers pink with darker central stripe. Mexico (Tamaulipas).

var. klinkerianus (Backeb. & Jacobsen) Glass & Foster (*Strombocactus schmiedickeanus* (Böd.) Berger var. *k.* (Backeb. & Jacobsen) G.D. Rowley; *Toumeya k.* (Backeb. & Jacobsen) Bravo & W.T. Marsh.)
Tubercles wider than long. Spines up to 1 cm. long. Flowers white to cream-coloured. Mexico (Tamaulipas).

var. macrochele (Werderm.) Glass & Foster (*T.m.* (Werderm.) Buxb. & Backeb.; *Strombocactus m.* Backeb.; *Toumeya m.* (Werderm.) Bravo & W.T. Marsh.)

Tubercles wider than long. Spines up to 4 cm. long and more. Flowers white to pink-tinged. Mexico (San Luis Potosí).

var. schwarzii (Shurley) Glass & Foster (*T.s.* (Shurley) Backeb.; *Strombocactus s.* Shurley; *Toumeya s.* (Shurley) Bravo & W.T. Marsh.; *T. polaskii* Backeb.; *Strombocactus polaskii* (Backeb.) Hew.)
Tubercles completely flat, with fine spots. Body like *Lophophora.* Spines up to 2 cm. long. Flowers white to lavender-coloured. Mexico (San Luis Potosí).

T. valdezianus (Möller) Glass & Foster (*Pelecyphora v.* Möller; *Normanbokea v.* Kladiwa & Buxb.)
Up to about 2.5 cm. wide. Radial spines around 30, hair-like and feathery, white, 1-2 mm. long. Central spines absent. Flowers pale violet or white, around 2 cm. wide. Thick taproot. Mexico (Coahuila).

Uebelmannia Buin. 1967
(after the cactus importer Uebelmann)

Elongated to globular cacti with 15-40 ribs and small flowers borne close to the crown, only 1.6-2.7 cm. long, greenish to yellow. The flowers are bristly/hairy, bristly or only hairy outside. 6 species. Native to Brazil (Minas Gerais).

In their natural habitat these plants root in the dead remains of lichen, the rotting foliage of bromeliads, bushes and trees, and amongst quartz rocks. These materials are strongly acid. The lower part of the plants is often covered with lichen, a result of the fairly high atmospheric humidity due to plentiful summer rain. To match these conditions we have to keep these beautiful plants in a highly permeable, acid soil with a generous proportion of leaf mould, and mist frequently. They then grow well, although very slowly. The plants like to stay warm, not below 15°C even in winter.

U. buiningii Donald
Body greenish or reddish-brown, covered in tiny, wax-like scales, giving it a rough appearance, up to 8 cm. wide and with about 18 ribs. 4 fairly long spines and 2-4 shorter ones, red-brown. Flowers yellow, up to 2.7 cm. long and 2 cm. wide.

U. gummifera (Backeb. & Voll) Buin.
(*Parodia g.* Backeb. & Voll)
Body grey-green, up to 10 cm. tall and 6 cm. wide, with about 32 bumpy ribs. Radial spines 2 lateral and one longer

one pointing downward, up to 0.5 cm. long. Central spines 1, at first light grey then darker grey with brownish tip. Flowers sulphur yellow, 2 cm. long and 1.5 cm. wide.

U. meninensis Buin.
Body green, up to 50 cm. tall and 10 cm. wide with up to 40 ribs. Spines 2, pointing up and down, seldom more, brown-black, later dark grey, up to 2 cm. long. Flowers yellow, 2.2-3.5 cm. long and 2-3 cm. wide.

U. pectinifera Buin.
Body initially globular, later elongated, up to 50 cm. tall and 10-15 cm. wide, with 15-18 sharp-edged ribs. The outer skin is initially blackish-brown, tinged with dark purple, later white-grey because of the tiny, white, wax-like, minute scales. The areoles are closely spaced and bear black to dark brownish central spines, 0.5-1.5 cm. long, forming distinctive vertical combs. Radial spines absent. Flowers green-yellow, about 1.5 cm. long and 1 cm. wide. Fruit berry-like, cylindrical, up to 2.5 cm. long and 0.8 cm. wide, brilliant wine red. This is the most beautiful and most distinctive species. It was discovered by Horst and Baumhardt in 1966.

Because of the white-grey outer skin and the sharp ribs the plant was first

thought to be related to *Astrophytum*, then to *Copiapoa*. However, *Astrophytum* occurs in Mexico, and *Copiapoa* just as far distant in Chile. When it was possible to examine the flowers it turned out that *Uebelmannia* was a new genus.

var. pseudopectinifera Buin.
Body green and not very spotty. Spines not in comb-formation, radiating laterally.

Utahia Br. & R. see *Pediocactus*

Vatricania Backeb. 1950

Bushy columnar cacti with up to about 27 ribs. Flowers initially borne in a cephalium running down from the crown on one side, later in a superficial dome cephalium. They are scaly and bristly-hairy outside, nocturnal, with nectar chamber. 1 species. Native to Bolivia (Chuquisaca).

V. guentheri (Kupper) Backeb.
(*Espostoa g.* (Kupper) Buxb.)
Branching from the base. Stems light green, up to 2 m. or more tall and up to 10 cm. thick, with about 27 slightly bumpy ribs with indistinct transverse furrows. Spines about 15, around 25 in the flowering zone, yellowish to reddish, 0.5-1.5 cm. long. Central spines up to 2.2 cm. long. Cephalium

Uebelmannia buiningii

Uebelmannia pectinifera

Vatricania guentheri

Weingartia lanata

reddish to strong fox red, with dense masses of yellowish wool and bristles up to 6 cm. long. Flowers yellowish-white, only open at night, 8 cm. long.

Weberbauerocereus Backeb.
(after August Weberbauer 1871-1948)

Tree-form or bushy columnar cacti with 15-35 ribs. Flowers on normal or specially formed areoles, scaly and woolly outside, radially symmetrical or zygomorphic, 6-12 cm. long. 11 species. Native to Peru.

W. rauhii Backeb.
Tree-like, branching on a short trunk, 4-6 m. tall. Stems grey-green, up to 15 cm. thick and with about 20-23 ribs. 50-80 fine whitish-grey bristly spines up to 1 cm. long, and often up to 6 yellow to brown central spines, 2-8 cm. long. Areoles long and grey, felty. Flowers reddish-white, 8-10 cm. long. S. Peru (Nazca and Pisco valleys).

The most beautiful species of the genus, with some similarity to *Cleistocactus strausii*.

W. cephalomacrostibas (Werderm. & Backeb.) Ritter (*Trichocereus c.* Backeb.; *Haageocereus ferox* Ritter n.n.)
Bushy, 2-3 m. tall. Stems 6-7 cm. thick, with 8-12 ribs. Spines 15-30, brownish, brown-black when young,

yellowish-white at the base, the outer ones up to 2 cm. long, the inner ones 3-10 cm. long. Flowers white to pale pink, 7-10 cm. long. Peru (Arequipa).

Weberocereus Br. & R. 1909
(after the French doctor and cactus expert Frederic A.C. Weber 1830-1903)

Climbing, 3-ribbed cacti with aerial roots. The nocturnal flowers have a short bristly/hairy or woolly tube. The ovary is distinctive, bearing tubercles and very small scales. 5 species. Native to Costa Rica, Panama.

W. biolleyi (Web.) Br. & R.
Stems round or irregularly acute, only 4-6 mm. thick, up to 80 cm. long. Areoles occasionally bear 1-3 very short, yellow spines. Outer flower petals dark pink, the inner ones pale pink. Flowers 3-5 cm. long. Costa Rica.

An extremely unusual cactus which is highly recommended. The large flowers are borne on thin stems, only as thick as a pencil. Grown in a hanging basket, the plant grows well and flowers readily.

Weingartia Werderm. 1939
(after Wilhelm Weingart (died 1936), a cactus expert from Thüringen)

These solitary cacti are of elongated to squat globular form and have 12-26 ribs. The 2-6 cm. long flowers are borne close to the crown, have a short tube and large but bare scales. *Weingartia* is difficult to differentiate from related genera.

The scales of *Gymnocalycium* are much larger and more membranous. The ribs of *Neowerdermannia* are more or less divided up into tubercles, like *Gymnocalycium,* and the plants also bear tiny fruit with extremely few seed. The deep yellow flowers were once considered to be the distinguishing feature of *Weingartia* from these other genera, but *Weingartia* species with violet flowers have now been found. The most similar genus is *Sulcorebutia*. Neither the latter's elongated areoles, its taproot nor its flower tube (usually slightly longer than *Weingartia*) are clear distinguishing characteristics. It may be that these two genera will have to be united in the future, or perhaps *Weingartia* will be split up between *Gymnocalycium* and *Sulcorebutia*. 23 species. Native to Bolivian and Argentinian Andes.

Cultivation as for *Sulcorebutia*.

Donald recognizes two groups within *Weingartia*:

Group 1: Areoles round, raised. Spines strong, projecting, piercing. Flowers from the crown, one per areole, long and narrow-tubed.

Group 2: Areoles oval, slightly compressed, with a fan-shaped woollen cushion below the straight, projecting spines. Flowers lateral, up to 4 per areole, short-tubed and of broad funnel-shape.

(1) **W. fidaiana** (Backeb.) Werderm. Body up to 30 cm. tall and 15 cm. wide, warty. Root beet-like with thin neck. Radial spines around 9, up to 3 cm. long. Central spines 3-4, up to 5 cm. long. All spines straw-coloured to violet-black. Flowers yellow, up to 3 cm. long and wide. S. Bolivia (Potosí).

(2) **W. hediniana** Backeb. Body up to 6 cm. thick. Areoles more or less round. Radial spines 12-14, up to 2.5 cm. long. Central spines 4. Spines whitish, turning grey, initially brown above. Flowers yellow, up to 3 cm. long. Stigma branches cream-coloured. Root fibrous. Bolivia.

(2) **W. lanata** Ritter Body up to 17 cm. thick. Areoles elongated. Radial spines about 12-16, 1-4 cm. long. Central spines about 10-15, around 1.5-5 cm. long. All spines yellowish to yellow-brown. Flowers golden yellow to pale yellow, 2.7-3.3 cm. long. Stigma branches white.

Weingartia neocumingii

Wilcoxia albiflora

Root fibrous. Bolivia (Chuquisaca).

(2) **W. longigibba** Ritter Body up to 9 cm. thick. Radial spines about 7-12, one of them up to 2.5 cm. long. Central spines 3-8, 1.5-3.5 cm. long. All spines grey-brown. Flowers golden yellow, 2-3.5 cm. long. Root fibrous. Bolivia.

(2) **W. neocumingii** Backeb. Body up to 10 cm. thick. Radial spines up to 20 or more, white to yellowish, up to 1 cm. long. Central spines 2-10, more brownish, a few longer. Flowers golden yellow to orange-yellow, often very numerous at the crown. Root fibrous. Bolivia (Florida).

Grows and flowers very well on its own root and also when grafted. Plants on their own root grow best in nutritious soil with a humus content, with constant moisture level in the summer.

(1) **W. neumanniana** (Backeb.) Werderm. Body about 5 cm. wide. Radial spines about 6, up to 2 cm. long. Central spines usually 1, up to 2.2 cm. long. All spines reddish to dark brown. Flowers brownish-yellow to orange-red, 2.5 cm. long. Long taproot. Argentina (Jujuy).

(2) **W. riograndensis** Ritter Body 5-10 cm. wide. Radial spines about 5-10, up to 2 cm. long. Central

spines 3-6, 1-2.5 cm. long. Spines initially yellow-grey to grey-brown. Flowers golden yellow, 2-3 cm. long. Root fibrous. Bolivia.

(2) **W. sucrensis** Ritter Body up to 15 cm. thick. Radial spines 10-15, light brown or grey-brown, 0.7-2 cm. long. Central spines 6-12, 1-2 cm. long, dark-tipped. Flowers golden yellow, 2-3.3 cm. long. Short taproot. Bolivia.

Werckleocereus Br. & R. 1909
(after C. Werckle, 20th century)

Climbing cacti with aerial roots. The nocturnal flowers have a moderately long tube and are black with felt and thorns outside. Stems with 3 (-4) ribs. 2 species. Native to Guatemala and Costa Rica.

Of no interest to enthusiasts.

Wigginsia D.M. Porter see *Notocactus*

Wilcoxia Br. & R. 1909 (after Timothy E. Wilcox, US General, 19/20th century)

Bushy columnar cacti with soft stems which are hardly as thick as a pencil, with 3-20 ribs. Taproot. Flowers close to the crown or terminal, scaly and thorny/woolly outside. Stamens

Wilcoxia poselgeri

reaching almost to the base of the tube. Flowers diurnal or nocturnal. 5 species. Native to USA (Texas), Mexico.

The Wilcoxias are beautiful and rewarding flowering plants, which can be recommended to the cactus enthusiast. The plants usually form large root tubers, and in consequence they are best grafted. In this form they grow really well and flower all the more profusely in full sun as well as in half-shade. They are grafted by taking a piece of a shoot about 4 cm. long and halving it along its length; the cut face is then set horizontally on the stock. This is also the best method of propagation, as the plants root poorly and slowly.

W. albiflora Backeb.
Profusely branching. Stems light green, up to 20 cm. long and about 0.6 cm. thick, almost as round as a shaft. Spines 9-12, fine, appressed, 1 mm. long. Flowers usually terminal, white or delicate pink with greenish-brownish eye, around 2 cm. long. Native habitat unknown, probably Mexico.

W. nerispina n.n.
Stems 1-2 cm. thick. Spines blackish. Flowers for the most part lateral, lilac pink.

W. poselgeri (Lem.) Br. & R.
Stiff, erect bushes. Stems dark green, up to 50 cm. long, 0.6-1.5 cm. thick and with 8-10 indistinct ribs. Radial spines 9-12, whitish or greyish, around 2 mm. long. Central spines 1-2, white, grey or black, up to 1 cm. long. Flowers usually at the end of the stems, light purple with darker centre, around 4-5 cm. long, persisting for 4-5 days. Mexico (Coahuila), USA (S. Texas).

Wilcoxia viperina

W. schmollii (Weingt.) Backeb.
Bushy, with taproot about 7 cm. long. Stems up to 25 cm. long and up to 1 cm. thick, up to 2 cm. thick when grafted, with 8-10 ribs more or less divided up into tubercles. Spines up to 35, fine, hair-like, white, grey or blackish, up to 7 mm. long. Flowers light purple, about 3.5 cm. long. Mexico (Querétaro).

This beautiful golden yellow plant can be grown in the greenhouse in a hanging basket, or hanging from a suspended shelf. The species grows fast and is undemanding, especially when grafted. It has proved to be an indefatigable flowering plant in many collections, and is one of the most beautiful and most highly recommended cacti for the amateur.

W. striata (K. Brandeg.) Br. & R.
(*Neoevansia s.* (K. Brandeg.) Sanchez-Mejorada)
Stems up to 1 m. tall, ash grey to grey-green, only about 5 (-8) mm. thick, with 8-9 very low ribs and straight, narrow furrows between them. Spines 9-10, brown or black, 1.5-3 mm. long. Flowers purple, around 10-12 cm.long. Mexico (lower California).

W. viperina (Web.) Br. & R.
(*Cullmannia v.* (Web.) Distef.)
Bushy. Stems grey-green, up to 3 m. long and 2 cm. thick, with 8-10 ribs,

Wilcoxia viperina

velvety. Radial spines 8-9, black, 3-5 mm. long. Central spines 3-4, thicker at the base, mostly pointing downward, blackish, later falling off. Flowers red, up to 8 cm. long and 4 cm. wide, with long, woody tube. Mexico (Puebla).

Wilmattea Br. & R. 1920
(after the 19/20th century American collector Wilmatte P. Cockerell)

Climbing 3-ribbed cacti with aerial roots. The tube of the nocturnal flowers bears very short bristles, or is felty or slightly woolly. The ovary features large scales like rooftiles. 2 species. Native to Guatemala, Honduras.

Winteria Ritter see *Hildewintera*

Winterocereus Backeb. see *Hildewintera*

Wittia K. Schum. 1903
(after W.H. Witt, of Manaos, Brazil, 19th Century)

Epiphytic plants with flat, leaf-like stems with pronounced central rib. Flowers small, about 2.5 cm. long, with naked, bare tube and erect petals. The flowers are borne laterally and

contain two groups of stamens. The fruit is angular and has a deep hilum. 2 species. Native to Panama, Colombia, Peru, ?Venezuela.

Yungasocereus Ritter see *Samaipaticereus*

Zehntnerella Br. & R. 1920 (after the Brazilian nature researcher Leo Zehntner)

Tree-form or bushy columnar cacti with 13-24 ribs. Flowers lateral, with very short tube, densely scaly and woolly outside, white, 3-4.5 cm. long. Nectar chamber usually sealed off by hairs formed by modified stamens. 3 species. Native to Brazil (Piauhy, Joazeiro, Bahia).

Zygocactus K. Schum. see *Schlumbergera*

Schlumbergera hybrid

Schlumbergera hybrid

Schlumbergera hybrid 'Le Vesuv'

Schlumbergera truncata var. delicata

Appendices

Glossary of common specialized terms

In this book we have attempted to use specialized terms as rarely as possible. The following glossary explains a few expressions which are not used in the book, but which occur frequently in cactus literature.

Aerial roots: Roots which are produced on the shoots above the ground, especially on epiphytic and climbing cacti.
Anatomical features: Internal characteristics, only visible when the plant is dissected.
Anatomy: The study of the internal structure.
Areole: The cushion of spines, almost always with fine hairs, which is characteristic of cacti. They represent modified short shoots.
Author: Referring to scientific names, the first person to describe a species, or a different person who has changed the original name.
Axils: The regions at the base of and between the tubercles (warts). Hairs, bristles, side shoots or flowers may be produced in the axils.
Basionym: The first name given to a species; it often needs to be amended later, for instance, if the systematic rank is changed. For example, *Echinocactus ornatus* DC., the narrower genus term, was later amended to *Astrophytum ornatum* (DC.) Web.
Central spines: The spines growing from the centre of the areole, if distinctly different from the radial spines.
Cephalium: A distinctly separate region of certain cactus species, usually with densely bristly or woolly areoles, from which the flowers are produced.
Cerei: All cacti growing in a columnar form.
Collection number (e.g. 'Rausch No. 50'): The temporary designation used to define plants or seed of a species from a particular site of discovery, collected by a particular individual. If the definition of the material is not known, this number

serves as a temporary name. It is better than allotting a temporary name, which may be invalid and confusing. In any case these numbers are always valuable as a means of establishing the precise location of the find.
Comb-formation (or pectinate) spines: Spines projecting strictly horizontally on two sides from elongated areoles.
Cristate form: A variant on the normal growth form, of broad cockscomb shape, in which the usual vegetative point is widened to form a vegetative crown. Cristate forms can be propagated by means of grafting (see page 69).
Cultivar: A minor genetic variation in a cultured species, roughly the same as 'sort'. It may be a form taken from nature, or one which has only been produced in culture by means of selection and breeding. Names of cultivars are given the abbreviation cv. after the specific name, or placed in single quotation marks.
Cuticle: The microscopically thin membrane, almost impermeable to water, covering the cells of the epidermis.
cv. see Cultivar
Distribution area: The geographical region in which a species is found.
Divided distribution area: The distribution area of a group which consists of at least two regions separated from each other, the space between which cannot be bridged by natural means of dispersal such as seed or pollen.
Enclosed distribution area: A region of distribution which is undivided.
Epidermis, or outer skin: The outside layer of cells which covers that part of all plants which is above the soil surface.
Epiphytic: Growing on other plants, but not parasitic on them.
f. see Form
Form: A minor genetic variation which is more or less randomly distributed in the region of a species. The difference between a form and a variety is often vague.
Genus: A group including one or several related species which are clearly separate from other similar groups of species. Generic names consist of one word written with a capital, and usually in italic type, e.g. *Lobivia*.

Glochids: Very fine spines covered with microscopically small barbs, and typical of the Opuntioideae sub-family.
Group: Any systematic group, such as a species, a variety or a genus.
Habit: The external general appearance.
Habitat: The term for the external conditions which obtain where the plant naturally grows, e.g. soil, climate and accompanying vegetation. A habitat might be defined as: the southern slope of a dune. The term should not be confused with the location at which the plant was found, which is the site of discovery.
Hybrid: A cross between two different groups, usually species.
Leaf succulent: Leaves are thick, fleshy, and store water.
Monstrous form: An irregular abnormal growth form, in which the usual arrangement of ribs and areoles is absent.
Morphological characteristics: External, visible features.
Morphology: The study of a plant's external structure and its variations.
Mutation: A genetic variation which arises suddenly.
n.n. see nomen nudum
Nectar chamber: A clearly defined cavity at the base of the tube, closed off by a membrane, scales, hairs or the bottom stamens, in which nectar (a fluid containing sugar which attracts pollinating insects) is secreted.
nomen nudum: A name lacking a valid description or diagnosis. Such temporary names are not recognized according to the rules of nomenclature, but nevertheless they are often very long-lasting.
Ovary: The bottom part of the cactus flower with an internal cavity containing the ovules.
Pectinate spines: See Comb-formation spines
Population: The smallest systematic unit. A group of individuals which exchange genetic material mutually, and are usually located close together geographically, e.g. the plants of one species enclosed in a small valley basin.
Pseudo-cephalium: Similar to a cephalium, bearing areoles with clearly different spines, but not a distinctly separate region from which the flowers are produced.

Radial spines: The spines located round the edge of the areoles, if they are distinctly different in form or colour from the central spines.

Radially symmetrical flowers: Flowers with three or more planes of symmetry, as opposed to zygomorphic flowers.

Receptacle: see Tube

Relic distribution area: The distribution region of a group which is a relic of an earlier, once larger area.

Ribs: Parts of the body of a cactus forming raised ridges running more or less vertically.

Scales: External structures, often formed on the ovary and the tube of cactus flowers.

Site of discovery: The exact geographical location of a plant, e.g. 15 km. East of Veracruz in Mexico.

sp. n. (species nova): A newly discovered and newly described species.

Species: The basic unit of systematics. Nowadays a species is usually defined as a group of individuals or populations which can exchange genetic material amongst each other under natural conditions. Species have two names, the generic name (with a capital initial letter) and the specific name (with a lower-case initial), e.g. *Mammillaria bocasana.* (In older books many species names were written with a capital if they were derived from proper names.)

Spines: In the botanical sense superficial growths on the stems or leaves, as opposed to thorns, which are modified leaves or stems. The spines of cacti should really be termed thorns, as they are modified leaves.

ssp. (sub-species): see Sub-species.

Stamens: The thin, thread-like structures inside the flowers which form the pollen.

Stem succulent: A plant with thick stems which store water.

Sub-species: A systematic unit below the species. Sub-species usually colonize different regions, but merge into each other in the border territories, as they are capable of hybridizing. Sub-species are given the abbreviation ssp. (= sub-species) in addition to the specific name, and a third name written with a lower-case initial.

Succulent: Thick-fleshed and capable of storing large quantities of water.

Synonym: A term which means the same as another name. Many synonyms are invalid according to the rules of nomenclature, e.g. those applying to a single species which has been described several times.

Systematic categories or ranks: The designation of the various systematic groups. They may be higher than the species, e.g. genus, tribe, sub-family and family, or sub-units within a species, such as sub-species, variety or form.

Taxon (plural: Taxa): see Group.

Thorns: In the botanical sense modified leaves. The structures we term the spines of cacti are — botanically speaking — thorns.

Tribe: A group of related genera.

Tube: The tubular part of the cactus flower above the ovary, bearing the flower petals at its tip.

Tubercles: The humps, or warts, which occur on the stems of many cacti, and which bear areoles. In some cacti, e.g. *Rebutia* and *Mammillaria*, the tubercles are all that remain of ribs which have become deeply notched.

Type specimen: A particular example of a group, from which the first description was made. According to the rules of nomenclature the type specimen must be deposited in a public collection.

var. see Variety.

Variety: A systematic unit below the species. Varieties feature minor genetic variations in one or more features, occurring together in a particular region.

Vascular bundle: A bundle of tissues consisting of elongated cells which serve to transport water, nutritional salts and the substances manufactured by the plant. In a section through a cactus shoot the bundles can be seen as an annular arrangement of fine threads.

Wart: see Tubercle

Zygomorphic flowers: Bi-laterally symmetrical flowers, or flowers with only one plane of symmetry, i.e. mirror-image right and left-hand halves, but with different top and bottom halves (assuming the flower lies horizontally).

The authors of cactus names

The name of the author is included in the scientific name of all species in the interests of greater clarity, rather than to satisfy the individual's vanity, as a particular scientific name is sometimes used in different contexts by different authors. However, a more important use of authors' names is to discover which plant names are synonymous (see the section on Cactus Names, page 48). This is of great importance when dealing with cacti, as so many names have been altered subsequently.

Unfortunately authors' names are often abbreviated in a non-standard way, or too severely, even though rules exist. Short monosyllabic names are not shortened. Longer, multi-syllabic names are usually abbreviated by taking the first syllable and its following consonant, e.g. Hildmann becomes Hildm. Where there might be confusion a further one or two letters are added, or the initial letter of the Christian name e.g. K. Schum. for Karl Schumann. Very short abbreviations are in general use for certain early authors who described a particularly large number of plant species, e.g. L. for Carl von Linné (Linnaeus), DC. for P. de Candolle and Br. & R. for Britton and Rose.

Akers = North American botanist, contemporary.
Alex. = E.J. Alexander, born 1901, North American botanist.
Anderson = E.F. Anderson, born 1932, North American botanist.
Arp
Audot
Arech. = J. Arechavaleta y Balpardo 1838-1912, Uruguayan botanist.
Backeb. = Curt Backeberg 1894-1966, travelled extensively in Central and South America. His main works are: *Kaktus ABC* (in conjunction with F.M. Knuth) 1935, also *Die Cactaceae, Handbuch der Kakteenkunde* 1958-62, *Cactus Lexicon* 1966.
Baird = R.O. Baird, wrote in 1931.
B.W. Benson
L. Benson = Lyman D. Benson, born 1909, North American botanist, wrote *The Cacti of Arizona*, 3rd edition 1969 and

The Native Cacti of California 1969.
Berge = E. Berge, owner of a German plant import business around the turn of the century.
Berger = Alwin Berger 1871-1931, German gardener, botanist and succulent researcher. Berger was director of the famous Hanbury garden, La Mortola, in Ventimiglia on the Cote d'Azur from 1897-1914. From 1915 to 1926 he was director of the state gardens of Württemberg. His two main books on cacti are *Die Entwicklungslinien der Kakteen* 1926 and *Die Kakteen* 1929.
Bert. = C.G. Bertero 1789-1831, Italian doctor and botanist.
Bewerunge = contemporary cactus expert.
Bigel. = J. Bigelow 1787- 1879, North American medic and botanist.
Böd. = Bödecker 1867-1937, German painter and cactus expert.
Borg = John Borg 1873-1945, English botanist living in Malta. Borg's life work is the book *Cacti*.
Boiss. & Davids. = Boissevain & Davidson.
Br. & R. = Nathaniel L. Britton and Joseph N. Rose. Britton 1859-1934 was a North American geologist and botanist, director of the Botanical Garden of New York. Wrote the now standard *Illustrated Flora of the United States* in conjunction with J. Brown. Author in conjunction with Rose of the four-volume work *The Cactaceae* 1919-23, one of the standard works on cacti. Joseph N. Rose 1862-1928 was a botanist at the United National Herbarium.
K. Brandeg. = M.K. Brandegee 1844-1920, North American botanist at San Diego, California, wife of T.S. Brandegee.
T.S. Brandegee 1843-1925, North American plant collector and botanist.
Brandt = F.H. Brandt.
Bravo = Helia Bravo-Hollis, born 1903, Mexican botanist and cactus researcher.
Britt. *see* Br. & R. Bred. = J.A. Brederoo, co-author of many new descriptions in conjunction with Buining.
Buchenau = F.G. Buchenau, died 1969.
Buin. = A.F.H. Buining 1901-76, Dutch botanist.
Buxb. = Franz Buxbaum 1900-79,

Austrian botanist, wrote many articles on cacti for various magazines and established a phylogenetic system. His detailed generic descriptions and precise illustrations of flowers and seed published in *Die Kakteen* (Krainz) are of particular value.
Byl. & Rowl. = R.S. Byles and G.D. Rowley, contemporary English botanists.
Campos-Porto = Director of the Botanical Gardens of Rio de Janeiro.
Card. = Cardenas, Bolivian botanist.
Castañeda
Castell. = A. Castellanos 1896-1968, Argentinian botanist.
Cav. = A.J. Cavanilles 1745-1804, Spanish botanist.
Cels = French gardener and cactus dealer, died 1869.
Clov. = E.U. Clover, born 1897.
Colla = Colla 1766-1848, Italian lawyer and botanist.
Console = M. Console 1812-97, Italian botanist.
Coult. = Th. Coulter 1793-1843, Irish doctor, resident in Geneva. Collected plants in Mexico and California.
J.M. Coult. = John M. Coulter 1851-1928, North American botanist, lived in Chicago.
Craig = Robert T. Craig, North American botanist and cactus expert. Craig's *The Mammillaria handbook* 1945 is still the standard work on the large genus Mammillaria.
Croiz. = L.C.M. Croizat, born 1894, North American botanist
Cullm. = Dr Willy Cullmann, German cactus expert and author.
Cutak = L. Cutak, born 1908, North American gardener.
Dams = E. Dams, scientific librarian of Berlin, 19/20th century.
Dan. = A.U. Daniker 1894-1957, Swiss botanist.
Daston
Dawson = E.Y. Dawson 1918-66, North American botanist. DC. = Augustin Pyramus de Candolle 1778-1841, Swiss botanist. De Candolle was one of the most important botanists of all time. Of his many works *Plantarum succulentarum*

historia . . . 1798-1837 is very important in terms of cactus science.

A. Dietr. = A.G. Dietrich 1795-1856, German botanist.

Distef. = Prof. C. Distefano of Catania, Sicily.

Dodds = L. Dodds, wrote in 1937.

Dölz = B. Dölz died 1945, German lawyer and cactus expert.

Donald = John D. Donald, born 1923, English chemist and cactus researcher.

Dörfl. = J. Dörfler 1866-1950, Austrian botanist.

Ehrenb. = Carl Ehrenberg 1801-49, German collector of cacti from Mexico and the Antilles.

Engelm. = Dr Georg Engelmann 1809-84, doctor, lived in St Louis, Missouri, was one of the first to research Texas and the South East of the USA, describing the majority of cacti in the USA.

Farwig

Fechs. = H. Fechser, born 1918, Argentinian cactus collector.

Fittkau = Hans W. Fittkau, Mexican priest.

Fobe = F. Fobe died 1941, cactus expert and director of the Hempelsch. Gutsgartnerei in Ohorn in Saxony.

Forb. = J. Forbes died 1861, gardener to the Duke of Bedford at Woburn Abbey in England.

Foster = R.A. Foster.

Först = C.F. Förster, German 19th century botanist in Leipzig, wrote a manual on cacti in 1846.

G. Frank = Dipl. Ing. G. Frank, Vienna.

Frič = Alberto V. Frič 1882-1944, Czech cactus expert and collector. Frič travelled through Mexico around 1920.

Friedr. = H-C. Friedrich, born 1925, German botanist.

H. Friedr. = Dr Heimo Friedrich, Natters, Austria.

R.E. Fries = K.R.E. Fries 1876-1966, Swedish botanist.

Gaertn. = J. Gärtner 1732-91, German doctor and botanist from Calw.

Ga. = H.G. Galeotti 1814-58, director of the Brussels botanical garden.

Gat. = H.E. Gates.

Gill. = J. Gillies 1792-1834, Scottish doctor and collector of South American plants.

Glass = Charles Glass.

Goss. = R. Roland Gosselin 1854-1925, French succulent researcher.

A. Gray = Asa Gray 1810-88, one of the most important North American botanists.

Greene = E.L. Greene 1843-1915, North American theologian and botanist.

Gürke = M. Gürke 1854-1911, German botanist in Berlin.

W. Haage = Walther Haage, born 1899, well-known writer on cacti and other succulents.

Haage jr. = F.A Haage jr. 1796-1866, founder of a well-known plant business

in Erfurt. Haage possessed one of the largest cactus collections of his time.

De Haas

Haw. = Adrian H. Haworth 1768-1833, English succulent collector and one of the first writers on them.

H.B.K. = F.A. von Humboldt, 1769-1859, German nature researcher and traveller; A.A. Bonpland 1773-1858, French nature researcher, doctor and voyager of discovery; and C.S. Knuth 1788-1850, German botanist.

Hensl. = J.S. Henslow 1796-1861, English botanist.

Heese = E. Heese 1862-1914, German cactus collector.

Herrera = F.L. Herrera y Garmendia 1875-1945, Peruvian botanist.

Herter = W.G.F. Herter 1884-1958, Uruguayan botanist of German extraction, wrote a Flora of Uruguay.

Heyder = E. Heyder 1808-84, German cactus expert.

Hew. = T. Hewitt.

Hildm. = H. Hildmann died 1895, German cactus expert at Birkenwerder near Berlin.

Hook = Sir W.J. Hooker 1785-1865, one of the most important English botanists.

Hopff. = C. Hopffer, 1811-?, German zoologist and owner of a large cactus collection.

Hoss. = C.C. Hosseus 1878-1950, German botanist living in Córdoba, Argentina.

A.D. Houghton 1870-1938.

Hutchison = P.C. Hutchison, born 1924, North American botanist.

Y. Ito, born 1907, Japanese botanist at the Tokyo botanical gardens, published books on cactus cultivation

Jacobi = G.A. von Jacobi 1805-74, German botanist in Berlin.

Jajó

Johnson = H. Johnson, North American cactus gardener.

Karw. = W. Karwinsky von Karwin 1780-1855, German botanist, travelled to Mexico twice.

Karsten = G.K.W.H. Karsten 1817-1908, German botanist.

Kayser = K. Kayser, wrote in 1932.

Kesselr. = W. Kesselring, garden inspector of the Darmstadt Botanical garden.

Kimn. = M.W. Kimnach, born 1922, North American botanist.

Klein, author, writing around 1859.

F.M. Knuth = Frederic M. Knuth of Knuthenborg, born 1904, Danish botanist, wrote *Kaktus ABC* in 1935, in conjunction with C. Backeberg.

Köhler = E. Köhler, contemporary German botanist.

Krainz = Hans Krainz, born 1906, Swiss cactus researcher, founder and long-time director of the Zürich city

succulent collection, publisher of *Die Kakteen* 1956-75 (not completed) and writer on cacti in *Pareys Blumengärtnerei*, (2nd edition, 1961).

Kreuzgr. = K.G. Kreuzinger, contemporary Czech engineer and cactus expert.

O. Kuntze = C.E.O Kuntze 1843-1907, German botanist.

Kupper = W. Kupper 1874-1953, German botanist in Munich.

L. = Carl von Linné (Carolus Linnaeus) 1707-78, Swedish nature researcher, doctor and botanist. Linné founded the binary nomenclature, and his works are the basis of all systematic botany.

Lab. = J. Labouret died 1853, possessed an extensive cactus collection in France and wrote a monograph on cacti.

Lag. = M. Lagasca y Seguro 1776-1839, Spanish botanist.

Lagerh. = N.G. von Lagerheim, 1860-1926, Swedish botanist.

Lahman = B.M. Lahman 1872-?, North American author.

Lam. = J.B.P.A. de Monet de Lamarck 1744-1829, one of the most significant French zoologists and botanists.

Lawr. = G. Lawrence, English gardener and cactus expert, writing in 1841.

Lehm. = J.G.C. Lehmann 1792-1860, German botanist.

Lem. = Charles A. Lemaire 1801-71, French gardener, botanist and cactus expert; lived in Belgium for a long time as editor of *Flore des serres* and wrote very widely on cacti.

Lemb. = H. Lembcke, 1918, cactus collector in Chile.

León = A.P. León, Cuba.

Liebn. = Liebner, wrote in 1895.

Lind. = J.H. Linden 1817-98, Belgian gardener.

Lindl. = J. Lindley 1799-1865, English botanist.

Lindgr. = S.J. Lindgren 1810-49, Swedish botanist.

Linds. = G. Lindsay, born 1916, American botanist.

Linds. = R. Lindsay 1846-1913, Scottish botanist.

Link & Otto = Heinrich Friedrich Link 1767-1851, Professor of Botany at Berlin and director of the Botanical Garden, co-founder of the German gardening association, wrote books on botany which were highly regarded in his time. Christoph F. Otto,1783- 1856, inspector at the Berlin botanical garden from 1805-43.

Linke = A. Linke, German master carpenter, owner of a large cactus collection, mid-19th century.

Lodd. = Loddiges, English gardener and botanist of the 19th century.

Loefgr. = A. Loefgren 1854-1918, Swedish botanist.

Loos. = G. Looser, 1898, Chilean botanist.
Lowry
MacDougall = T.B. MacDougall 1895-1973, Scottish-Mexican botanist.
Mackie
J. Marn.-Lap. = J. Marnier-Lapostolle died 1976, French plant lover.
W.T. Marsh. = William Taylor Marshall 1886-1957, North American cactus researcher, wrote *Cactaceae* (in conjunction with T.M. Bock) in 1941, as a supplement to *Cactaceae* by Britton and Rose, also *Arizona's Cactuses*, 2nd edition, 1953.
Mart. = Karl Friedrich Phillip von Martius 1794-1868, Professor of Botany at Munich, travelled through Brazil in 1817-20, and was the founder and publisher of *Flora Brasiliensis* 1840-1906, the largest Flora work of its time.
I.R. Mey.
Mill. = P. Miller 1691-1771, English gardener and botanist.
Miquel = F.A.W. Miquel, 1811-71, Dutch botanist.
Miranda
Möll. = L. Möller 1847-1910, German gardening writer.
Monv. = M. de Monville, a factory owner in Normandy, owned a large plant collection. Lost his fortune as a result of a hurricane, his plant collection being broken up in 1845. The collection had been used by Lemaire in particular. Monville wrote mainly about palms and cryptogams.
H.E. Moore 1917-80, North American botanist.
Moran = R.V. Moran, born 1916, North American botanist.
E. Morr. = C.J.E. Morren 1833 - 1886, Belgian botanist.
Mühlpf. = F. Mühlenpfordt, 19th century German medic and cactus researcher.
Neumayer = H. Neumayer 1887-1945, Austrian botanist.
Nicolai = E.A. Nicolai 1800-74, German botanist.
Nutt. = Th. Nuttal 1786-1859, English-North American botanist.
Oehme = Hans Oehme died 1944, German painter and cactus expert.
Orcutt = C.R. Orcutt 1864-1929, North American botanist.
van Osten, wrote in 1940
Otto *see* Link & Otto.
Palm. = E. Palmer, 1831-1902.
Parm. = A.A. Chevalier de Parmentier 1737-1813, French pharmacist and agriculturalist.
Pat. = Mrs S.L. Pattison, collected in New Mexico in 1906.
Pfeiff. = Ludwig G.K. Pfeiffer died 1877, practising doctor in Kassel, travelled through Cuba in 1838-39, owned a fairly large cactus collection. He wrote

the first major book on cacti *Enumeratio diagnostica Cactearum* in 1837. Later he devoted his time to the study of snails and mussels.
Phil. = R.A. Philippi 1808-1904, German-Chilean botanist and zoologist.
D.M. Port. = D.M. Porter 1937, American botanist.
Poselg. = H. Poselger died 1883, German doctor and cactus researcher.
J.A. Purp. = J.A. Purpus 1860-1932, German plant collector in Mexico.
Quehl = L. Quehl died 1922, German cactus researcher, owned a large collection in Halle.
Raf. = C.S. Rafinesque-Schmaltz 1783-1840, Italian-North American botanist.
Rauh = Werner Rauh, born 1913, German botanist, director of the Heidelberg Botanical garden, travelled through many South American countries, South Africa and Madagascar and wrote very many treatises, especially on succulents.
Rausch = Walter Rausch, 1928, travelled widely in his research work, especially in the Andean region of South America. Author of the three-volume work *Lobivia*.
Rebut = P. Rebut, died 1898, French cactus expert and dealer.
Redecker
Regel = E.A. von Regel 1815-92, German gardener and botanist, director of the Botanical Garden of St Petersburg, founder of the *Gartenflora*.
F. Reichenb, = F. Reichenbach, German engineer and cactus expert, 19th/20th.
Riccob. = V. Riccobono, Italian gardener and botanist in Palermo around 1900.
Ritter = Fr. Ritter, contemporary German cactus collector and researcher.
Rodr. = J.D. Rodriguez 1780-1846, Spanish botanist.
Rose *see* Br. & R.
G.D. Rowl. = G.D. Rowley, born 1921, English botanist and succulent expert.
Rümpl. = Th. Rümpler 1817-91, German gardener resident in Erfurt. Author of the 2nd edition of Förster's *Handbuch der Kakteenkunde*.
Runge = C. Runge, Texan cactus dealer around 1890.
Safford = W.E. Safford 1859-1926, North American botanist.
Salm-Dyck = Joseph Fürst Salm-Reifferscheid-Dyck 1773-1861, maintained his own very large succulent collection and published several works, some of them illustrated and very extensive, including *Hortus Dyckensis*, 1850.
Sanches-Mejorada
Sand. = H.F.C. Sander 1847-1920, German-English gardener.
Scheidw. = J. Scheidweiler 1799-1861, German-Belgian gardener.
Scheer = F. Scheer 1792-1868, English

cactus expert from Rügen, worked in association with Kew.
Schelle = E. Schelle 1864-1929, German gardener.
Schick = C. Schick 1881-1953, German schoolmaster and succulent expert from Freiburg.
Schmoll = F. Schmoll died 1950, artist and cactus collector in Mexico.
Schott = H.W. Schott 1794-1865, Austrian botanist.
K. Schum. = Karl M. Schumann 1851-1904, German botanist at the Botanical Museum of Berlin. Schumann wrote the *Gesamtbeschreibung der Kakteen*, 2nd edition 1903, one of the standard works on cacti. He also revised many families in Engler and Prantl's *Die natürlichen Pflanzenfamilien*, 1st edition and in *Flora Brasiliens* by Martius.
Schütz = B. Schütz, Czech writer on cacti, especially *Astrophytum*.
Sencke = F. Sencke, cactus gardener at Leipzig, 19th century.
Shurley = E.W. Shurley 1888-1963, English businessman and cactus researcher.
Söhr. = J. Söhrens died 1934, Chilean worker on plant systematics.
Spegazz. = Carlos Spegazzini 1858-1926, Italian-Argentinian botanist.
Spreng. = K.P.J. Sprengel 1766-1833, German botanist and doctor.
Steeg = van der Steeg.
Stein = B. Stein 1847-99, German botanical gardener.
Sweet = R. Sweet 1783-1835, English gardener and botanist.
Terschek = court gardener in Dresden, 19th century.
Thiele = P. Thiele, gardener and cactus enthusiast.
Tiegel = E. Tiegel died 1936, German cactus expert in Duisburg.
Thompson = H.J. Thompson, born 1921, North American botanist.
Torrey = J. Torrey 1796-1873, important North American botanist.
Turpin = P.J.F. Turpin 1775-1840, French plant collector, artist and botanist.
Vaup. = Fr. Vaupel 1876-1927, German botanist.
Vellozo = J.M. da Conceicão Vellozo 1742-1811, Brazilian botanist.
Voll = O. Voll, died 1958, German-Brazilian gardener.
Walp. = W.G. Walpers 1816-53, German botanist.
Walton, wrote in 1899.
S. Wats. = S. Watson 1826-92, North American botanist.
Web. = Frederic A.C. Weber 1830-1903, doctor in the French army, travelled through Mexico in 1865-66 during the French occupation, collecting very large numbers of cacti there.
Weidl. = Weidlich, German cactus

researcher, 19th/20th century.

Weingt. = W. Weingart 1856-1936,
German cactus expert and collector.

Wendl. = J.C. Wendland 1755-1828,
German gardener and writer on botany.

Werderm. = E. Werdermann 1892-1959,
German botanist and cactus expert in
Berlin.

Wesk. = W. Weskamp.

Wessn. = W. Wessner 1904-83, cactus
gardener and expert, wrote about
Lobivias and Rebutias.

Willd. = K.L. Willdenow 1765-1812,
German botanist resident in Berlin.

Zucc. = Joseph Gerhard Zuccarini 1797-
1848, Professor of Botany at Munich,
became well known through his
cooperation with Siebold in the production of *Flora Japonica* 1835-70.

Bibliography

Andersohn, G. *Cacti and Succulents.*
Wakefield 1983

Backeberg, C. *Stachelige Wildnis.* Berlin
1951 (record of cactus-collecting
expeditions)
— *Die Cactaceae*, 6 vols. Jena 1958-62.
— *Cactus Lexicon.* Poole 1976, Stuttgart
1977

Benson, L. *The Native Cacti of California.*
Stanford 1969
— *The Cacti of Arizona* Tucson 1969..
— *The Cacti of the United States and Canada.*
Stanford 1982.

Berger, A. *Die Kakteen.* Stuttgart 1929.

Borg, J. *Cacti: A gardener's handbook for their
identification and cultivation.* Poole 1976.

Bravenboer, S.K. *200 Kakteen in Farbe.*
Munich 1979.

Bravo-Hollis, H. *Las Cactaceas de Mexico.*
Vol 1, Mexico 1978.

Brinkmann, K-H. *Die Gattung Sulcorebutia.*
Titisee-Neustadt 1976.

Britton, N.L. and J.N. Rose. *The Cactaceae*,
4 vols. New York 1963

Buining, A.F.H. *Die Gattung Discocactus
Preiffer.* Venlo, o.J. 1980.

Buxbaum, F. *Kakteenpflege biologisch richtig.*
Stuttgart 1962.

Craig, R.T. *The Mammillaria Handbook.* New
York 1977.

Dawson, E.Y. *How to know the Cacti. Pictured
keys for determining the native cacti of the
United States and many of the introduced
species.* Dubuque, Iowa 1963.
— *Cacti of California.* Stanford 1967.

Earle, W.H. *Cacti of the Southwest.*
Scottsdale, Arizona 1980

Encke, F. *Pareys Blumengartnerei.* Berlin,
Hamburg 1960. (Die Familie
Cactaceae, pages 98-156)
—, G. Buchheim and S. Seybold. *Zander,
Handworterbuch der Pflanzennamen.*
Stuttgart 1980.

Endler, J. and F. Buxbaum. *Die
Pflanzenfamilie der Kakteen.* Minden
1974.

Graf, A.B. Exotica. *Pictorial Cyclopedia of
Exotic Plants from Tropical and Near-tropic
Regions.* Rutherford 1973.
— Tropica. *Color Cyclopedia of Exotic Plants
and Trees from the Tropics and Subtropics.*
Rutherford 1979.

Grunert, C., G. Viedt and H-G

Kaufmann. *Kakteen und andere schone
Sukkulenten.* Berlin 1977.

Haage, W. *Freude mit Kakteen.* Radebeul
1961.
— *Kakteen von A bis Z.* Leipzig, Radebeul
1981.
— *Das praktische Kakteenbuch in Farben.*
Radebeul 1961.
— and O. Sadovsky. *Kakteen-Sterne;
Entwicklung, Entdeckung und Zuchtung der
Kakteen-Gattung Astrophytum.* Radebeul
1957.

Haustein, E. *Der Kosmos-Kakteen-fuhrer.*
Stuttgart 1983.

Hecht, H. *Fortschritte der Kakteen und
Sukkulentenkultur '76.* Published by the
German Cactus Society.
— *BLV Handbuch der Kakteen.* Munich,
Vienna, Zurich 1982.

Hiroshi Hirao. *Colour Encyclopedia of Cacti.*
Japan 1979 (Japanese language and
script, but plant names in Latin).

Krainz, H. (publisher) *Die Kakteen.*
Stuttgart 1956-75 (not completed).
Loose-leaf collection.

Lamb, E. and B. *Cacti and other Succulents
of the Desert.* Poole 1969.
— *The Illustrated Reference on Cacti and other
Succulents.* 5 vols. Poole 1955-78.

Leighton-Boyce, G. and J. Iliff. *The
Subgenus Tephrocactus.* The Succulent
Plant Trust, 1973.

Marshall, W.T. and T.M. Bock. *Cactaceae.*
Pasadena 1941.

Pilbeam, J. *Mammillaria.* London 1981.
— *Sulcorebutia and Weingartia – a collector's
guide.* London 1985.

Putnam, E.W. *Gymnocalyciums.* National
Cactus and Succulent Society, 1978.

Rauh, W. *Schone Kakteen und andere
Sukkulenten.* Heidelberg 1967.
— *Kakteen an ihren Standorten.* Berlin,
Hamburg 1979.

Rausch, W. *Lobivia: die tagblutigen
Echinopsidinae aus arealgeographischer Sicht.*
3 vols. Vienna 1975-6.

Riha, F. and R. Subik. *Illustrated
Encyclopedia of Cacti and other
Succulents.* London 1981.

Ritter, F. *Kakteen in Sudamerika.* 4 vols.
Spangenberg 1979-81.

Rowley, G. *Name that Succulent. Keys to the
families and genera of succulent plants in
cultivation.* Cheltenham 1980.

Sadovsky, O. and B. Schutz. *Die Gattung
Astrophytum.* Titisee-Neustadt 1979.

Schumann, K. *Gesamtbeschreibung der
Kakteen.* Neudamm 1903.

Taylor, N.P. *The Genus Echinocereus.* Feltham
1985.

Weniger, D. *Cacti of the Southwest: Texas,
New Mexico, Oklahoma, Arkansas and
Louisiana.* Austin and London.

Associations and Publications

Britain

British Cactus and Succulent Society, (K. Harrow, 23 Linden Leas, West Wickham, Kent BR4 0SE). Quarterly journal: *British Cactus and Succulent Journal* and yearbook: *Bradleya*.

The Chileans, (Mrs G. Craig, 32 Forest Lane, Kirklevington, Yarm, TS18 5LY). Publication: *Chileans Journal*.

The Epiphytic Plants Study Group, (C.S. Dawson, 1 Belvedere Park, Great Crosby, Merseyside L23 0SP). Quarterly journal: *Epiphytes*.

The Mammillaria Society, (E.C. Double, Bramble Cottage, Milton Street, Polegate, E. Sussex BS26 5RN). Bi-monthly journal: *Mammillaria Society Journal*.

United States of America

The Cactus and Succulent Society of America, (c/o Virginia Martin, 2631 Fairgreen Avenue, Arcadia, CA 91006). Bi-monthly journal: *Cactus & Succulent Journal*, Box 3010, Santa Barbara, CA 93130.

South Africa

South African Aloe and Succulent Society, (P.O. Box 1193, Pretoria 0001, Transvaal) Quarterly newsletter: *Kambroo*. Has a Cactus Club, and the following branches:

Cape Town: Mr R.D. Kratz (Chairman), 20 Van Riebeeck Laan, Kenridge, Durbanville 7550.

Kimberley: Mr W. du Toit (Secretary), P.O. Box 19, Kimberley 8300.

Van Derbylpark: Mr I.J. Jordaan (Chairman), P.O. Box 3556, Drie Riviere 1935.

Johannesburg: Mr F.J.W. Van Den Bergh (Chairman), 63 Anreith Street, Roosevelt Park, Johannesburg 2195.

Australia

NSW

Cactus and Succulent Society of NSW — several branches. (Ian Harvey, 116 Purchase Road, Cherry Brook, NSW 2120). Quarterly journal.

Cactus and Succulent Society of Wagga Wagga, (Ron McNeil, 56 Crawford Street, Wagga Wagga, NSW 2650).

Queensland

Queensland Succulent Society, (Mrs P. Harrison, P.O. Box 65, Fortitude Valley, Queensland 4006). Duplicated journal.

Central Queensland Succulent Society, (Ted McIllwraith, 25 Peterson Street, Rockhampton, Queensland 4700).

Gold Coast Succulent and Bromeliad Society, (Mrs Kay Fleming, Lot 29, Westminster Boulevard, Paradise High Estate, Elanora, Queensland 4221).

Darling Downs Succulent Society, (Mrs M. Utschink, 16 Partridge Street, Toowoomba, Queensland 4350).

South Australia

Cactus and Succulent Society of SA Inc., (Secretary, P.O. Box 37, Rundle Street, Adelaide, SA 5000). Duplicated annual journal.

Adelaide and Country Cactus Club, (J. Bywater, 37 Melville Street, South Plympton, SA 5038).

Succulent Publications of SA Inc, (G. Gilchrist, P.O. Box 572, Gawler, SA 5118). Quarterly journal: *Anacampseros*; also *Calandrinia* vols 1 & 2.

Tasmania

North West Tasmania Cactus and Succulent Society, (G. Polden, 40 Morrison Street, Railton, Tas. 7305).

Southern Tasmanian Cactus and Succulent Club, Colin Drake, 1 Willow Walk, Austins Ferry, Tas. 7011).

Victoria

Cactus and Succulent Society of Australia Inc, (Secretary, 3 Bruce Street, Frankston, Victoria 3200). Quarterly journal.

Ballarat Cactus and Succulent Society, (Noel Main, 8 Margaret Street, Wendouree, Victoria 3355).

Geelong Cactus and Succulent Club, (Noel Charles, 282 Autumn Street, Geelong West, Victoria).

Sunraysia Cactus and Succulent Society, (Mrs Joan O'Connor, P.O. Box 1475, Mildura, Victoria 3500).

Western Australia

The Cactus and other Succulent Study Group of Western Australia, (H. Bake, 32 Barbican Street, Shelley, WA 6155).

Bunbury Cactus and Succulent Study Group, (H.G. Baker, 23 Sweeny Street, Bunbury, WA 6230)

ACT

Cactus and Succulent Society of the ACT, (Lyn West, 6 Pasley Place, Wanniassa, ACT 2903). Duplicated journal.

New Zealand

The Cacti and Succulent Society of New Zealand Inc, (Secretary, 164 Massey Street, Franklin, New Zealand).

Plant suppliers

Britain

Abbey Brook Cactus Nursery, Old Hackney Lane, Matlock, Derbyshire.

Holly Gate Cactus Nursery, Billingshurst Lane, Ashington, W. Sussex RH20 3BA.

Jumanery Cacti, St Catherine's Lodge, Cranesgate Road, Whaplode St Catherine, Spalding, Lincolnshire PE12 6SR.

Oak Dene Nurseries, 10 Back Lane West, Royston, Barnsley, W. Yorkshire S71 4SB.

Southfield Nurseries, Louth Road, Holton-le-Clay, Grimsby, S. Humberside DN36 5HL.

Southwest Seeds, 200 Spring Road, Kempston, Bedford MK42 8ND.

Westfield Cacti, Kennford, Exeter, Devon EX6 7XD.

Whitestone Gardens, Sutton-under-Whitestonecliffe, Thirsk, N. Yorkshire YO7 2PZ.

United States of America

Details of suppliers available through Cactus and Succulent Association of America Inc., 2631 Fairgreen Avenue, Arcadia, CA 91006.

South Africa

National Botanical Gardens, Kirstenbosch, Cape Town, Cape Province.

Pretoria Cactus, Aloe and Succulent Nursery, 376 Kings Highway, Lynwood, Pretoria 0081, Transvaal.

Australia

NSW

Buena Vista Nursery, 31 Wynyard Ave, Rossmore, NSW 2171.

Hamiltons World of Cacti, cnr Taylor Road and Winston Close, Badgerys Creek, NSW 2171.

Mrs J. Burnett, Andoran, Darkes Forest, NSW 2508.

L. Cady, Princes Highway, Kiama, NSW
2533.

Mrs N. Carr, Lot 57, Findley Road,
Bringelly, NSW 2171.

W. Harland, Booalbyn, Blackburn Road,
Wedderburn, NSW 2560.

L.B. Meyers, 57 Wambain Street,
Gilgandra, NSW 2827.

M. Williamson, 20 Ravenhill Road,
Turramurra, NSW 2074.

Queensland

B. Barker, 5 Daniel Street, Nambour,
Queensland 4560.

South Australia

The Aloe, Cactus and Succulent Nursery,
542 Grand Junction Road, Northfield,
SA 5085

Aridaria Gardens, Lot 13, Alexander
Avenue, Evanston Heights, SA 5116.

Cactus Desert Nursery, Mypolonga,
SA 5254.

Victoria

Devon Meadows Cactus Nursery, cnr
Browns and Smith Lane, Five Ways,
Victoria 3077.

Garden World Nurseries, Springvale Road,
Keysborough, Victoria.

Western Australia

Western Australia Cactus Research, Lot 72,
Fraser Road, Canningvale, WA 6155.

New Zealand

New Zealand Cactus Company, Kumeu,
Auckland.

Sources of illustrations

Photographs

Position on the page: l = left, r = right,
c = centre, t = top, b = bottom

Helmut Bechtel: p. 21 tl, 144 tc, 152 tr,
258, 263 b, 290 l.
Dr Jürgen Bosch: p. 17 tl, 129 l, 137 t, 176
t, 182 tr, 186 c, 271 bl, 273 b, 286 b.
Dr Willy Cullmann: p. 17 tc, tr, cr, 21 tr,
b, 69 tr, b, 128 t, 130 bl, 131 r, 136 (2),
137 bl, 140, 141 (2), 142 bl, br, 145, 149 b,
153, 158 tc, 162, 170 t, 172 tr, b, 175 b,
184 (2), 185 (3), 187 t, 236 l, 240, 249 t,
254 b, 264 b, 265 tl, bl, 275, 304 b, 305 t,
306 t, 307 tl, tr, br, 312 l.
Dr Helga Dietrich: p. 32 tr, 237 tl.
Holger Dopp: p. 93 tl, 133 tl, tr, 134 r,
135 r, 138 b, 144 tr, 148 l, 168 tl, 236 r,
256, 291, 294, 314 b.
Jürgen Frantz: p. 149 t, 289 bl.
Dr Reza Geranmayeh: p. 20, 22 (4), 23 (6).
Dr Gerhard Gröner: dust jacket (5), p. 14
r, 47, 69 tl, 85, 92, 93 tr, 103 (2), 111, 127,
128 b, 129 r, 130 t, 132, 137 br, 142 tl, tr,
146, 154 (2), 155, 156 (2), 157, 158 tl, b,
159, 160 (2), 161 (2), 163, 164, 165 (3),
166, 167 (6), 169, 174 r, 178, 179 (4), 180
tl, tr, bl, 182 b, 183 (2), 191, 192 (3), 193,
195 (2), 196, 197 (6), 198 (3), 199 (3), 200
(2), 201 t, 202 t, 203, 204, 205, 209, 210,
211, 212 (2), 213, 214 l, 215 t, 216, 217 (2),
218, 219, 220 l, 221 l, 222 (3), 223 t, 224,
225, 226 (2), 227 (2), 228, 229 (2), 230 b,
231, 232 (2), 234 tl, 239 b, 241 r, 245 (2),
246 cl, bl, 247 tl, tr, 248, 249 bl, br, 250,
253, 254 t, 255 (3), 259 (2), 264 t, 268 (2),
269 (3), 272 b, 277, 281 (4), 282 (2), 283
(4), 284, 285 (2), 286 tl, tr, 287 b, 292 tr,
295, 297 (6), 298 (6), 299, 301 tl, 305 b,
306 b, 307 bl, 308 b, 309 (2), 310 (2),
312 r.
Martin Haberer: p. 24, 68, 181, 182 tl.
Erich Haugg: p. 11, 34 tl, 88, 124, 125 t,
126 tl, cr, br, 130 br, 131 l, 134 l, 135 l,
147 (3), 150 tl, br, 152 b, 171 b, 172 tl,
174 l, 177, 180 br, 187 b, 190, 201 b, 214
r, 221 r, 223 b, 234 b, 237 tr, 241 l, 242
(2), 243, 247 b, 266, 270, 271 tl, tr, br, 274
(2), 276, 288 t, 301 bl, br, 302 r, 303 b,
304 t, 311 l, 315 tl.
Ewald Kleiner: p. 148 r, 215 b, 230 t, 237
bl, 260, 262, 263 t, 301 tr, 302 l, 308 t, 311
r, 315 b.

Fritz Köhlein: p. 98, 261 t.
Wolfgang Krahn: p. 34 tr, 35, 143, 144 b,
188, 202 b, 220 r, 233, 234 tr, 235 (2), 237
cl, 244 (2), 246 tr, cr, 314 t.
Eberhard Morell: p. 138 t, 186 b, 239 t,
287 t, 289 br, 303 t.
Dieter Opitz: p. 17 br, 32 tl.
Kurt Petersen: p. 168 tr, cr, br.
Dr Hans-Georg Preissel: p. 7, 32 bl, br.
Prof. Dr Werner Rauh: p. 14 l, 17 cl, 125
b, 126 tc, 150 tc, bl, 152 tl, 168 bc, 170 b,
171 t, 175 t, 176 b, 186 t, 238 (2), 261 b,
265 r, 272 t, 273 t, c, 288 b, 289 tl, tr, 313
(2), 315 tr.
Karlheinz Rücker: p. 56, 76, 93 b, 133 b.
Hans Seibold: p. 17 bl, 139, 151, 189, 290
r, 292 tl, b, 316 (2).
Michael Walke: p. 2.

Drawings

Kornelia Erlewein: p. 30 and 31 (after
Klimadiagramm-Weltatlas, H. Walter and H.
Lieth, Jena 1967), 50 (design: Dr Götz), 53
(from *Die Pflanzen im Haus*, K. Rücker,
Stuttgart 1982), 67 (design: Dr Gröner), 71
(from *Die Pflanzen im Haus*, K. Rücker,
Stuttgart 1982), 73 (from *Die Pflanzen im
Haus*, K. Rücker, Stuttgart 1982), 74
(design: Dr Cullmann), 79 (design: Dr.
Gröner), 82 t (a = design: Dr Cullmann,
b = design: Dr Gröner, c = after *200
Kakteen in Farbe*, Bravenboer, Munich 1979),
82 b (design: Dr Gröner), 95 (design: Dr
Gröner), 103 (design: Dr Gröner).
Gartenpraxis 9, 79: p. 108, 109.
Dr Erich Götz: p. 10, 12, 14 (2), 15, 16 (2),
18, 19, 20, 22, 24 (2), 25 (3), 26 (2), 27, 28,
29 (2), 70, 115 (2), 116, 117, 278. Armin
Schwarz: p. 66 (design: Dr Gröner).

General index

Asterisks * refer to illustrations

325

Index of Latin cactus names

This index lists all the scientific generic and specific names found in the book, but not the designations of varieties and forms. In this way it is possible to work back from the specific name — which is often the more permanent — to the generic name which is now valid.

The index can also be used to find the name which is now in force from the many synonyms which exist among cacti. *All synonyms are printed in italics,* whilst those now valid are in normal script. Asterisks (*) indicate illustrations. In the case of *Mammillaria* the numbers in brackets indicate the page number within the species key. With all other genera, which have less extensive keys, the species key is not included in the index.

Key to Index

s. = see f. = form
ssp. = subspecies
var. = variety
cv. = cultivar

Wherever a single letter other than 's' or 'f' appears in an entry in this index, the letter refers back to the name at the beginning of that entry. Example:

castaneoides. Neoporteria s. Neoporteria subgibbosa var. subgibbosa f.c. 248

means:

castaneoides, Neoporteria see Neoporteria subgibbosa variety subgibbosa form castaneoides page 248

332

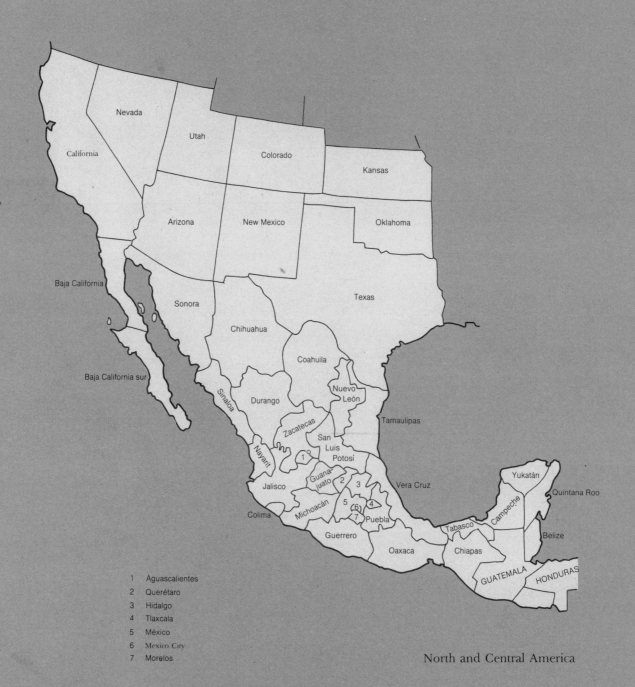

Nevada

Utah

California

Colorado

Kansas

Baja California

Arizona

New Mexico

Oklahoma

Sonora

Texas

Chihuahua

Baja California sur

Coahuila

Sinaloa

Nuevo
León

Durango

Tamaulipas

Zacatecas

San
Luis
Potosí

Navarit

Guana-
juato

Jalisco

2

3

Vera Cruz

Yukatán

Quintana Roo

Michoacán

5

(6)

4

Campeche

Colima

7

Puebla

Belize

Guerrero

Tabasco

Oaxaca

Chiapas

GUATEMALA

HONDURAS

1   Aguascalientes
2   Querétaro
3   Hidalgo
4   Tlaxcala
5   México
6   Mexico City
7   Morelos

North and Central America